REGULATION:
A CASE
APPROACH

REGULATION: A CASE APPROACH

SECOND EDITION

Leonard W. Weiss
University of Wisconsin, Madison

Allyn D. Strickland
National Economic Research Associates, Inc.

McGraw-Hill Book Company

New York   St. Louis   San Francisco   Auckland   Bogotá
Hamburg   Johannesburg   London   Madrid   Mexico   Montreal   New Delhi
Panama   Paris   São Paulo   Singapore   Sydney   Tokyo   Toronto

This book was set in Times Roman by Rocappi, Inc.
The editors were Bonnie E. Lieberman and Scott Amerman;
the production supervisor was Charles Hess.
New drawings were done by Danmark & Michaels, Inc.
The cover was designed by Janice Noto;
the cover photograph was taken by Joe Ruskin.
R. R. Donnelley & Sons Company was printer and binder.

REGULATION: A CASE APPROACH

1234567890 DODO 898765432

ISBN 0-07-069098-7

Library of Congress Cataloging in Publication Data
Main entry under title:

Regulation, a case approach.

Includes index.
1. Public utilities—Law and legislation—United States—Cases. I. Weiss, Leonard W. II. Strickland, Allyn D.

| KF2093.R44 | 1982 | 343.73′09 | 81-13744 |
| ISBN 0-07-069098-7 | | 347.3039 | AACR2 |

CONTENTS

PREFACE

This book provides illustrative cases for an undergraduate course on public control of business. Our first edition focused on traditional economic regulation of the transportation, communications, and energy sectors of the economy as well as the interfaces between regulation, antitrust enforcement, and environmental protection. Our second edition updates this material and adds major sections on antitrust enforcement and social regulation (environmental regulation and consumer and worker protection). The new sections are integrated into the existing text through an introductory chapter that provides the student with background information about the particular policy at hand. Each part is self-contained, and the instructor can present the material in whatever order is deemed desirable. We do, however, believe that the material as ordered here facilitates students' understanding of the different types of government regulation.

A major advantage of this new edition is that an instructor can now use a single casebook to cover all the government's major regulatory policies. This will minimize the cost of books and maintain continuity across subject matter. At the same time, an instructor can also use the regulation section for more detailed courses on this subject.

This book introduces the reader to the major issues in the antitrust and regulation fields, using actual decisions as vehicles. It is divided into four parts, an introduction (Part One) and three substantive case sections. Part Two covers antitrust. The majority of antitrust cases are landmark decisions, primarily by the Supreme Court, that established the meaning of the antitrust laws.

Part Three deals with traditional price and rate-of-return regulation as provided by state public-utility commissions and by such federal regulatory agencies as the Interstate Commerce Commission, the Federal Communications Commission, the Civil Aeronautics Board, and the Federal Energy Regulatory Commission. Since World War II the various states have been free to set their own standards, provided that they observe correct procedures. As a result, decisions in one state do not provide precedents for other states. There are Supreme Court decisions in *federal* regulatory areas, but in most cases the court was interpreting legislation specific to a particular agency. A decision concerning the Interstate Commerce Commission thus had little, if any, precedent value for the Federal Communications Commission. With a few exceptions, therefore, the cases in Part

Three show what particular commissions are doing or, at least, were doing recently.

Part Four deals with the "new regulation"—health, safety, and environmental regulation. Many of the agencies involved were established in the 1970s. Their powers and jurisdictions are still being established, partly by judicial decisions and partly by new legislation. The rules that are appearing do not usually carry over from one agency to another. As a result, the cases will provide a flavor rather than a definitive statement of the law.

Overall, we hope that the book will convey an impression of how American public policy toward business works. If the reader is inclined to go further, there is a large, though aging, literature on antitrust. There is a larger and younger literature on conventional regulation, and a smaller, but growing, literature on safety, health, and environmental regulation.

Leonard W. Weiss
Allyn D. Strickland

REGULATION: A CASE APPROACH

PART ONE

INTRODUCTION

1

ANTITRUST AND REGULATION IN THE COURTS AND THE COMMISSIONS

The United States has had a long, ambivalent relationship with private enterprise. On one hand, a larger proportion of Americans than citizens of most countries believes that competition among private firms will yield the goods that consumers want at low costs, while also providing new and better products and production techniques. At the same time, many Americans are clearly suspicious of business, especially big business. They fear monopolistic restraints on competition. They expect business generally to display callous attitudes toward employees, customers, and the environment. The United States was the first country in the world to adopt antitrust laws (though there were some precedents in English common law), and it still carries antitrust policy much farther than other nations do. The United States is also the world's leader in regulation, though in many other nations the government operates the industries that are regulated here. This is commonly true of railroad, airline, electric power, gas, and telephone services in the noncommunist industrial nations.

Because the first substantive section of this book deals with antitrust, the procedures and practices discussed in this chapter will focus on the antitrust agencies. The Federal Trade Commission is similar in organization and practices to other regulatory commissions and will be used to illustrate their organization and procedures.

Antitrust cases originating in the Justice Department go through the federal courts. Those that start at the Federal Trade Commission are initially tried at the Commission, but they can then be appealed through the federal courts. The same is true of other federal regulatory commissions. A state commission's decision only reaches the federal courts if it raises constitutional questions. These questions were fairly common before World War II but are rare now. However, most state public-utility commissions resemble federal regulatory agencies in both organization and procedure.

THE ANTITRUST AND REGULATORY AGENCIES

The main actors in antitrust cases are the Antitrust Division of the Justice Department, which employs about 280 attorneys and about 50 economists, and the Federal Trade Commission (FTC), whose Bureau of Competition has about 80 attorneys. The FTC also has a Bureau of Consumer Protection that is concerned with deceptive advertising and labeling and a Bureau of Economics that deals with both types of issues.

The federal and state regulatory commissions generally resemble the FTC. Most of the commissions consist of several commissioners appointed for long and overlapping terms; they decide cases brought before them. The chairperson of each commission appoints and supervises the commission's staff. The staff prepares and argues the cases that the commission decides. Although it may appear that commissioners have a conflict of interest because they initiate and try cases, participants in the regulatory process seldom complain about that aspect of the process.

A large part of the Antitrust Division and FTC staffs are young lawyers, just out of law school, who are learning the antitrust trade. After a few years of "apprenticeship," many of them leave for private practice in the antitrust area. This employment pattern is a mixed blessing. The antitrust agencies get some of the best new graduates in the field; corporations that subsequently consult these lawyers when they are in private practice are apt to receive advice in line with antitrust agency policies. On the other hand, much of the agency staff wants to try short-term cases that they are likely to win and will shy away from big cases that require large staffs and long timetables.

WHERE CASES COME FROM

Antitrust cases can originate from public complaints (many of which will come from businesspeople objecting to rivals who compete too hard). Or they may result from careful studies of industries that are both important to the economy and likely to commit antitrust violations. Both the Antitrust Division and the FTC have specialists whose main jobs are to monitor particular industries such as oil, steel, and automobiles. In the regulatory area, rate cases typically originated from the industries in the inflationary 1970s, because most regulated firms found their costs rising while their rates were fixed. When some utility costs were falling in the 1950s and 1960s (electricity and long-line telephone), cases were usually initiated by the commissions' staffs. This approach often led to negotiated settlements without formal hearings.

A crucial point in an antitrust case is the issuance of a complaint. It generally follows a careful examination of the case by the staff, often using data supplied by the firm(s) involved. The complaint must be signed by the Assistant Attorney

General for Antitrust as well as by the Attorney General. A fair number of proposed complaints are turned down by the Assistant Attorney General on economic or legal grounds. The Attorney General's signature is almost automatic, but there have been a few cases quashed in most administrations. At the FTC and other regulatory agencies, the staff prepares a case, though the commission must endorse it before the complaint becomes valid.

NEGOTIATED SETTLEMENTS

A majority of complaints never reach trial. For example, many proposed mergers fold after a complaint is issued. In many other cases, consent decrees (Justice Department) or consent orders (FTC) are negotiated. The defendants agree to abide by the order negotiated but do not acknowledge that they violated the law. In criminal cases the defendant often pleads "nolo contendere," which means that the firm will pay any fines and observe any orders negotiated but does not acknowledge any guilt. A major reason for pleading "nolo" is that if a firm loses in a trial, that decision will be accepted by the courts as evidence to support subsequent suits for triple damages by private plaintiffs. A nolo plea provides no such evidence. However, the court does not have to accept a consent decree or a nolo plea.

TRIALS

If a case is not settled, the two parties enter into a process of "discovery" in which relevant documents are subpoenaed and examined. This may be a limited undertaking in a merger or collusion case, but in major monopolistic cases, such as *U.S. v. IBM,* the documents may number in the millions. An outsider can only guess where the crucial documents are located, so the subpoenas are bound to be very broad in scope. The respondent can be counted on to complain publicly and to cite enormous duplicating bills.

District courts are the trial courts for Justice Department cases. Most Justice Department cases are heard and decided by a judge, but occasionally a defendant in a collusion case will ask for a jury. Quite a number of private triple-damage suits are tried before juries because the plaintiff, who is frequently smaller than the defendant, expects to fare better before a jury. Most regulatory cases are argued before trial examiners (administrative law judges at the federal level).

The major function of a trial is to find facts. The judge and/or jury hears testimony and reads documents to determine exactly what happened. It is the judge's function to apply the law to the facts presented or to instruct the jury as to the relevant law.

District Court cases end in a decision that is cited in the following format: 271 F. Supp. 128. The number 271 is the volume number, while 128 is the number of the first page of the decision. F. Supp. refers to the *Federal Supplement* (available in virtually all law libraries), in which District Court decisions are published. In an FTC or other regulatory agency case, the trial examiner (administrative law judge) writes a proposed decision and transmits it with the trial record to the full commission. The commission may then accept it or may substitute an entirely different decision.

APPEALS

Appeals from the District Court or from a federal commission go to a Court of Appeals, of which there are ten in the United States. Appeals from federal regulatory agencies most often go to the District of Columbia Court of Appeals. Decisions of the Courts of Appeals are published in the *Federal Reporter, Second Series* and are cited in a fashion similar to district court decisions. For example, a decision may be cited as 107 F.2nd 221, where 107 is the volume and 221 the page number. F.2d means *Federal Reporter, Second Series.* Again, this publication is available in most law libraries.

Appeals from the Courts of Appeals are heard by the Supreme Court. The Court's decisions are published in several places, but all the citations to Supreme Court opinions in this book will be of the form 629 U.S. 118. This citation refers to the *United States Reports,* the official publication of Supreme Court decisions. The Courts of Appeals and the Supreme Court do not have to hear an appeal. If they refuse, the lower-court decision holds.

In theory the trial court (or commission) determines the facts, so appeals are limited to questions of law or procedure. That is, the questions that go forward on appeal are supposed to concern what the law means or whether the trial was fair. Some decisions on appeal may seem strange because the appeals court was limited by some very strange findings of fact. It is often difficult to separate questions of law from questions of fact. For instance, most merger cases include findings with respect to how the relevant market is to be defined. Appeals on that issue clearly call for a reconsideration of the market definition based on all the evidence developed in the case.

An overwhelming majority of the antitrust cases presented in this book are Supreme Court decisions, because the Supreme Court provides the definitive interpretations of laws. District Courts do not generally make new law. Their function is to enforce the law as it stands. If they do come to a conclusion that seems far removed from the existing precedents, their decisions are likely to be appealed.

Occasionally the courts are called upon to rule on constitutional issues. These rulings have rarely been important in antitrust, but they played a major role in regulation before World War II. The main constitutional issue concerned the due process guarantees in the Fifth Amendment for federal actions and the Fourteenth Amendment for state cases. Both amendments provide that "No person shall . . . be deprived of life, liberty, or property without due process of law."[1] These constitutional provisions have always been interpreted to require appropriate judicial procedures. The court or commission must permit affected persons to present evidence in hearings of which they are given sufficient notice. These per-

[1] U.S. Constitution, Fifth Amendment.

sons must also have the right to cross-examine witnesses. The *judge,* or commission, must be unbiased (that is, must have no personal, financial, or other interest in the outcome) and must base decisions on substantial evidence revealed in the hearings or documents in the case.

Between the 1870s and the 1940s the courts also required "substantive due process." This means that they examined the substance of decisions to see if they deprived the person involved (usually a corporation) of property without due process. In the extreme, the courts were certainly right. If an order required a firm to sell at a price that yielded it a return of, say, 1 percent, the property of the firm would become practically worthless. The regulatory agency would, in effect, be confiscating the firm's property. In fact, the courts often second-guessed the regulators on rate levels and, in some cases, on the right to regulate at all. This long interlude of judicial intervention ended with the Hope Natural Gas case in 1944 (see pages 228 to 231). Since that decision, regulators have generally been exempt from constitutional limitations if they followed the proper procedures. State regulatory decisions can be appealed in the state courts, but they almost never reach the federal courts any more. And appeals from federal commission decisions almost always involve interpretations of federal regulatory legislation rather than of the constitution. The due process clause is used extensively in civil rights cases today, though it seldom affects antitrust and regulatory cases any more.

PENALTIES AND RELIEF

Once the appeals process has been exhausted, the court must often determine the appropriate punishment (in criminal cases) or relief (in civil cases). This is done by the District Court in Justice Department cases or by the relevant commission in regulatory cases.

In a criminal antitrust case, fines can be as great as $1,000,000 for each corporate offender and $50,000 for each individual. In most cases, the fines are far below these maximums. In a very few cases there have also been short prison sentences. The most important deterrent in these cases, however, is the threat of private triple-damage suits that depend on the preceding cases. These private suits can result in awards in the hundreds of millions of dollars.

In government civil cases the relief may be an order prohibiting some acts or requiring dissolution. Quite a number of merger cases have ended in dissolutions, though in many cases the courts or the FTC have found it extremely difficult to unscramble the scrambled eggs involved. Often the acquiring firm merely sells off some of its least profitable properties. Because of such experiences the Antitrust Division and, since 1975, the FTC usually seek preliminary injunctions preventing the merger until the case is decided. The big monopolization cases against dominant firms are often aimed at dissolution, but that result has, in fact, been quite rare. Less than a dozen such dissolutions have occurred over the entire 90-year history of the antitrust laws.

Many antitrust cases and practically all regulatory cases are oriented toward conduct. Their natural outcomes have been orders prohibiting or requiring particular practices. This has meant court injunctions in Justice Department cases or orders in commission cases. The latter commonly require particular rates or permit or prohibit entry into a market. Injunctive relief in big monopolization cases often misses the mark. The basic problem in those cases is the dominant position of the defendant in its market. Moderate changes in conduct seldom cure that condition.

The courts will not make a decision on a hypothetical question. They require specific defendants and real acts or conditions on which to decide. The commissions, on the other hand, sometimes hold "rule-making proceedings." A proposed rule that will affect many firms will be announced, and all persons with an interest in the proposals are invited to participate in the hearings. An order with a general application may then be adopted.

The antitrust and regulatory processes are often very time-consuming. Regulatory rate hearings, which are the most urgent cases, often take more than a year. Collusion and merger cases that go to trial take two or three years. Big monopolization cases often take more than a decade. The IBM complaint was issued in 1969; trial began in 1975; and the case was still unresolved in 1981.

If any of these cases are appealed, the final decisions are put off at least another year. In many instances the economic setting on which a big case is based has changed greatly by the time relief is finally awarded. For instance, when the Alcoa case began in 1937, Alcoa was the only United States producer of aluminum. When the relief was decided in 1950, Alcoa had two major rivals. The British Restrictive Practices Court, which enforces Britain's collusion law, was able to reach decisions in six to thirty-five hearing days on its first thirty-two contested cases. This was *in spite of the fact* that the law permitted agreements if they could be shown to be in the public interest, an arrangement that is not possible in the United States. The experiences of one of the authors in one regulatory case and one monopolization case left him with the impression that concern for due process has made the adjudicative process on economic issues excessively time-consuming.

PART TWO

ANTITRUST ENFORCEMENT

THE MONOPOLY PROBLEM AND ANTITRUST

The underlying logic of a private enterprise system is that consumers, acting in their own self-interest, will buy that combination of goods and services that yield them the greatest satisfaction, while producers will maximize their profits by producing those goods and services using minimum cost methods.

COMPETITIVE EQUILIBRIUM

Figure 2-1 illustrates the situation more precisely. Assume that the long-run supply in an industry is perfectly elastic, as depicted in Figure 2-1. The underlying assumption in this case is that in the long run (when any number of new plants can be built, old plants can be abandoned, and all firms can build plants of the most efficient type), any amount of output can be produced at the same minimum cost (C). In the short run, however, price may be above cost C if industry capacity is inadequate (price P_1 when short-run supply is S_1). Or price may be below cost if there is excess capacity in the industry (price P_2 when short-run supply is S_2). In the long run, however, the high profits when capacity is inadequate will induce new producers to enter and existing producers to expand until price equals long-run average and marginal cost. All exceptional profits will have then disappeared. Similarly, if the industry is plagued by excess capacity, the resulting losses will induce producers to leave the industry. If your factory burns down you won't build a new one in this industry. Ultimately short-run supply will shift to S_3, and the losses will disappear.

Altogether, the following conditions will hold in a competitive industry in long-run equilibrium: (1) all excess profits and losses will disapppear; (2) all producers will be forced to use minimum cost processes; and (3) the last unit will cost just as

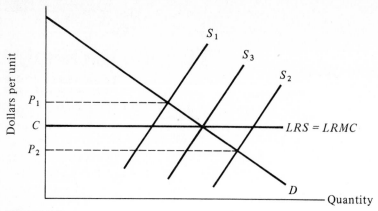

FIGURE 2-1

much as consumers pay for it. In practice, real-life competitive industries seldom reach long-run equilibrium because demand and costs are constantly changing, but competitive industries are normally moving toward long-run equilibrium.

There are several advantages to long-run equilibrium. The LRMC long-run supply curve in Figure 2-1 reflects opportunity costs. This is clearly true of the capital and labor committed to the industry by entrepreneurs. The cost of labor for the owner-manager of a grocery store is what he or she could earn in the best alternative job, perhaps managing a laundry. If the owner could earn more in the laundry, he or she is losing money and will be likely to switch jobs in the long run. Similarly, if the owner is earning 10 percent on the money he has invested in the store and could earn 15 percent on an apartment building, he has an incentive to invest the money in urban real estate when he gets a chance. Of course if our grocer is earning more in the store than he could earn elsewhere, he will stay in the business and may even build another store. And even if he doesn't stay, someone else will because of the high return available in groceries. Alternatively, if he sticks with the store in spite of low earnings, other people will pull out, and his earnings will rise as a result. The tendency for competitive industries to move toward equilibrium does not require that every producer be mobile, just some of them.

The cost of the inputs that our grocer purchases also reflects opportunity costs. When he employs a checkout clerk, he must pay a wage at least as high as the clerk could earn elsewhere. When he buys a case of canned peas, he must pay a high enough price to bid them away from other grocers.

All this implies that the average cost, C, in Figure 2-1 reflects the value of other goods and services that the resources involved could produce in their best alternative employments. At the same time, demand reflects what consumers will give up, in terms of other goods, to get the good being purchased. So, in competitive equilibrium, the last unit purchased induces a sacrifice of alternative products equal to what consumers are willing to give up for this unit in terms of other goods and services. We couldn't gain anything for society by shifting resources out of groceries and into laundries or apartment houses or vice versa.

THE MONOPOLY PROBLEM

The preceding analysis probably does give an accurate picture of the apartment house, laundry, and grocery businesses in many cities, but it certainly isn't accurate for many other industries. For example, many public utilities are monopolies. This is so partly because of regulatory prohibitions to entry and, in such cases as local electric, gas, and telephone service, because costs decrease as a firm's size increases. In addition, our economy contains a number of unregulated monopolists or at least dominant firms (very large sellers with much smaller rivals). This is true of newspapers in many cities and manufacturing firms such as Xerox (copiers), IBM (general-purpose computer systems), Kodak (photographic film), Boeing (commercial aircraft), Gerber (baby foods), Campbell Soup (canned soup), AMAX (molybdenum), and General Motors (buses and locomotives).

An unregulated monopoly is analyzed in Figure 2-2. It is the same as Figure 2-1 except that in this case there is only one seller. The most profitable price for the monopolist is P_1, well above minimum average cost C. At this price, consumers will buy Q_1 units. Another unit of output (say, a can of soup) would be worth P_1 to consumers and would involve a sacrifice of only C in terms of other products given up. Yet another can of soup would be worth only slightly less than P_1 to buyers and would again involve an opportunity cost of C. It would be in society's best interest if output were expanded and prices reduced until $P = C$. But a profit-maximizing soup monopolist would not operate in this way.

In addition, the profits earned by the monopolist cannot be competed away. It isn't inevitable that monopolists are highly profitable. The transit companies in

FIGURE 2-2

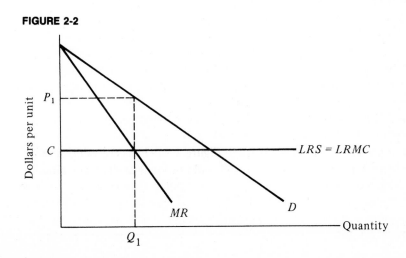

many cities lost a lot of money in spite of the fact that they were usually monopolies. Most cities have taken over their bus companies because the companies were too unprofitable to survive as private enterprises. But most of the unregulated monopolies have, in fact, been very profitable. Many of the great fortunes in society were won in monopolistic enterprise. Don't rush out and buy Xerox stock, however. The market values that stock at a price that reflects the expected future profits of the firm, including any anticipated monopoly profits. The people who received the monopoly profits were those who owned Xerox when its monopoly was first recognized. They experienced some very large capital gains and many have sold out to you and me. We will only earn normal returns on our investments in Xerox stock unless it finds another unanticipated source of yet more profits.

The dominant firm story is not very different from the case of the pure monopolist. The firm is free to set price, but it must take the response of its small rivals into account. Figure 2-3 shows total demand for soup, D_T. It also shows the amounts that the small firms will supply at various prices. This is the ordinary supply curve labeled S. Figure 2-4 shows the demand curve D_M that the dominant firm faces. It is the amount the public will buy (D_T) minus the amounts the small rivals will sell (S). The dominant firm will set price on a monopolistic basis in spite of its smaller rivals.

There is a twist to the dominant firm story, however. If the leading firm has no long-run advantage over other firms in the industry, its small rivals can expand and new firms can enter at prices in excess of average costs. As a result, the dominant firm's large-market share will decline over time. Something like this did happen in several industries where dominant firms were created by huge mergers at the turn of the century. This was true of U.S. Steel, International Harvester, American Can, and AMSTAR (Domino Sugar). In each case, the company's market shares declined for many decades after the original merger. U.S. Steel started off with 66 percent of American steel capacity (mostly between the Appalachians and the Mississippi). Its share has declined continuously down to 20 percent in 1980. This experience might suggest that if one is patient, monopoly will go away, but of course there have been eighty years of inefficiency in between!

Quite a few of the dominant firms of today have been in powerful positions for decades. This is possible if the dominant firm has some systematic advantage over its smaller rivals or potential entrants. This advantage may be due to lower costs (possibly GM in buses and Boeing in commercial aircraft), more favorable access to inputs (for example, ore reserves for AMAX and patents for Xerox), or strong consumer preferences (perhaps Kodak, Gerber, and Campbell Soup). These advantages are commonly referred to as barriers to entry. They may apply to pure monopolists as well as dominant firms. Unless the barriers are overwhelming, the monopolist or dominant firm may find that its best policy is to keep prices below their most profitable levels from a short-run point of view in order to discourage new entry and the expansion of small firms. In general, the lower the barriers to entry, the lower the price.

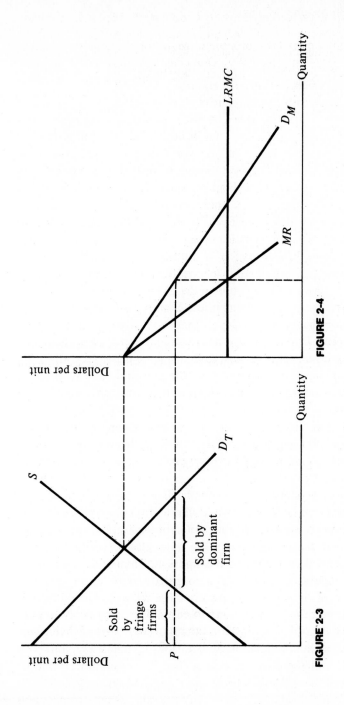

Dollars per unit

S

D_T

Sold by
fringe
firms

Sold by
dominant
firm

P

Quantity

FIGURE 2-3

Dollars per unit

LRMC

D_M

MR

Quantity

FIGURE 2-4

OLIGOPOLY

The case where there are a few leading firms in an industry is much more common than pure monopoly or dominant firm. Such an industry is known as an oligopoly. It typifies American "big business" and characterizes such industries as automobiles, steel, cigarettes, soap, aluminum, glass, copper, tires, tin cans, synthetic fibers, synthetic rubber, cereals, soft drinks, and beer.

In an oligopoly, a single firm cannot control prices unilaterally. It must take into account the reactions of its close rivals. A price cut aimed at taking business away from those rivals will almost certainly fail because the rivals can usually be counted on to meet the price cut. It may still be worthwhile to reduce price if the price cutter believes that sales will respond enough to make a lower price more profitable even if its market share stays about the same. But a monopolist would cut price under the same circumstances. A price increase would only be profitable if the rivals *did* follow. They would be likely to do so if the price rise would increase their profits as well. A monopolist would raise prices under the same circumstances. Some people believe that it is difficult for oligopolists to raise prices because of uncertainty about rivals' reactions. But they seemed to have little difficulty doing so in the accelerating inflation of the 1970s. Almost every week the *Wall Street Journal* carries news about rising prices in one oligopolistic industry or another. The typical story begins with a report that, say, Alcoa is raising aluminum prices by 5.5 percent. In the next few days there are reports on what other firms in the industry do in response. In most cases the price increases go through, but occasionally one of the other major oligopolists does not raise its price or raises it by less than the first firm did. In such cases it is reasonably easy for the first firm to back down.

This story suggests that oligopolists will tend to charge monopolistic prices even though there are several oligopolists. They can act collusively even without actually meeting and discussing price. Of course, explicit collusion may be used too, but it is illegal in the United States.

In real-life oligopolies the story is more complicated. If the oligopolists have different costs their most profitable prices will differ, and the price chosen by the low-cost firm will tend to prevail. If they have different ideas about the elasticity of demand, the firm that expects demand to be more elastic will prefer lower prices than its rivals and will probably win the argument. In neither case will the oligopoly price be as high as that which a monopolist would set in the same situation. In addition, many oligopolies, especially those selling industrial materials or equipment, often make secret price concessions to big customers even when an across-the-board price cut would not be profitable. They hope to divert customers from their rivals without retaliation. It is obvious to almost everyone with a television set that many oligopolists engage in a great deal of nonprice competition even if they succeed in avoiding outright price competition. In general, oligopoly isn't the same as pure monopoly, but it isn't the same as pure competition either. The tendency for oligopolists to price collusively is probably greater the fewer the significant sellers.

The conditions of entry are also important in oligopoly. A few sellers faced with many firms that could readily enter the market or small rivals that could easily expand will tend to set lower prices than would a few firms protected by very high barriers to entry. A particularly potent set of new entrants are well-established foreign firms that ship into the country. Such entry has been a very significant source of new competition in such oligopolies as steel and automobiles in the 1960s and 1970s. But the government has often intervened to protect the domestic industries.

The lines drawn in this chapter are spuriously precise. In the real world, monopoly shades into oligopoly which, in turn, shades into competition. Oligopoly is a particularly broad class. Gas stations are oligopolies in the sense that each firm pays a lot of attention to its closest rivals and sets prices on the expectation that the rivals will react. Yet they are closer in performance to the competitive rental housing industry than to flat glass or cigarettes, which are also oligopolies.

ANTITRUST

Our response to the monopoly problem has been mixed. For the largest part of the economy we attempt to maintain or restore competition by means of antitrust, the subject of this section. For a much smaller but still significant part of the economy we permit or even require monopoly, but we attempt to control it by means of regulation.

Both antitrust and regulation began in the late nineteenth century. The first federal regulatory agency was the Interstate Commerce Commission, established in 1887 to regulate the railroads. The first federal antitrust law was the Sherman Antitrust Act, which was passed three years later, in 1890. Both policies really began to have significant effects in the first two decades of this century.

Both antitrust and regulation have been carried much farther in the United States than in the rest of the world. Before World War II, Japan and much of Western Europe took a completely different approach to monopoly. They permitted and even encouraged collusion through official cartels. Since World War II, quite a few countries have adopted antitrust laws, but none has carried that policy nearly as far as we have.

Many of the industries that we regulate are owned and operated by government agencies abroad. Most of the rest of the world has not chosen to copy our regulation policies.

THE SHERMAN ACT

The Sherman Antitrust Act was named after John Sherman, senator from Ohio and Civil War General Sherman's brother. A trust is an arrangement where one person manages the property of another person, presumably in the owner's interest. There are many thousands of trusts in the United States today, often managed by banks for children or other heirs of the wealthy, and they have nothing to do with monopoly. At the time the Sherman Act was passed, however, some trusts had been vehicles for the creation of monopoly. Until then it was illegal for corporations to hold the stock of other corporations. John D. Rockefeller used the trust device as a way around this restriction. He arranged for all the oil refiners of the Cleveland area, then the center of the industry, to put their stock into a common trust that was managed as a single, monopolistic firm. Today we would describe it as a merger. The trust involved became Standard Oil. It was copied in the sugar and distilling industries in the 1880s. It became obsolete in 1889 when New Jersey eliminated the prohibition of intercorporate stock holdings for corporations registered in the state.

The Sherman Act was a response to the populist movement in the Middle West and the South, where many farmers and residents of small towns were convinced that they were being cheated by the trusts, the railroads, and "Wall Street." Both the Democrats and the Republicans promised some sort of antitrust laws in the 1888 presidential election. The Sherman Act was passed almost unanimously in both houses of Congress.

Restraint of Trade

The Sherman Act has two main parts. Section I provides that:

> Every contract, combination in the form of trust or otherwise, or conspiracy in restraint of trade or commerce among the several states, or with foreign nations, is hereby declared to be illegal. . . .

The "contract in restraint of trade" language came from the common law and had a definite meaning. It covered any agreement on prices or the allocation of territories or customers. By the turn of the century the application of this provision was well established. The prohibition of explicit collusion has been applied quite consistently over the entire century. It is commonly described as a per se prohibition. That is, the mere act of colluding is illegal, regardless of its effect. Since this part of the law is so well established, it is commonly enforced in criminal proceedings.

On the fringe there is the issue of what constitutes collusion. Is the exchange of price information among sellers illegal? What about the tacit collusion described in connection with the discussion of oligopoly covered earlier in this chapter? What if all the members of an industry follow a uniform and complex pricing system even if they do not formally agree on it? What if a manufacturer prohibits its distributors from cutting price below a specified level? Or what if the manufacturer specifies the districts in which it distributors can sell, thus preventing competition among its distributors?

(The basic Section I prohibition of collusion and the questions that it raises will be the subject of Chapter 3.)

One would think that the prohibition of "any . . . combination in restraint of trade in the form of trust or otherwise" would have prevented anticompetitive mergers. In fact it had little effect in the first decades of the new law because of a ridiculous early decision. The merger that formed the "sugar trust" by combining all the sugar refineries in the country was found to be exempt from the law because "manufacturing is not interstate commerce."[1] Later the law was found to be relevant to railroad mergers.[2] But the law on mergers was not clearly applicable to manufacturing until 1914.

Monopolization

Section II of the Sherman Act was harder to interpret. It provides that:

> Every person who shall monopolize, or attempt to monopolize, or combine or conspire to monopolize any part of the trade or commerce among the several states, or with foreign nations, shall be deemed guilty of a misdemeanor. . . .

The verb "to monopolize" did not have a judicial history as "contract . . . in restraint of trade" did. The impact of Section II only became apparent with the Standard Oil case in 1911. As analyzed in that and subsequent decisions (with the possible exception of the Alcoa case of 1945), it appeared that merely being a dominant firm was not enough to violate the law. The company involved must have done something unreasonable to get or retain its powerful position. In legal jargon, the courts were inserting a "rule of reason" into the Sherman Act. Monopoly was not automatically illegal; it required unreasonable acts to come under the law. Chapter 4 contains excerpts from several decisions that developed this interpretation of the law.

THE FEDERAL TRADE COMMISSION AND CLAYTON ACTS

During the "Progressive Era" in the years between 1900 and World War I, there was a good deal of concern that the Sherman Act, especially Section II, was inadequate to prevent the development of new monopolies. Many people hoped to "nip monopoly in the bud" rather than wait to dissolve it after it was well established, as in Standard Oil. This concern became more serious after the Standard Oil decision because of its rule of reason.

Two different approaches were proposed. Theodore Roosevelt advocated an agency that would investigate competitive practices and report on those that might lessen competition. Another group in the Senate wanted to spell out practices that were to be prohibited due to their expected anticompetitive effects. Congress used both approaches in 1914.

---

[1] *U.S. v. E. C. Knight,* 156 U.S. 1 (1895).

[2] *U.S. v. Northern Securities,* 193 U.S. 197 (1903).

The merger involved the Northern Pacific, Great Northern, and Burlington Railroads. Ironically, the Supreme Court permitted precisely the same merger in 1970; *U.S. v. ICC,* 396 U.S. 491 (Northern Lines Merger Cases). And, for further irony, the resulting firm (Burlington Northern) turned out to be a near monopoly in hauling coal from the northern plains to utilities in the South and East and showed signs of exercising that monopoly.

First, it set up the Federal Trade Commission with the investigation function proposed by Roosevelt. Rather logically, the new agency was given the function of prohibiting "unfair methods of competition," presumably those that it turned up in its investigations. As it turned out, "unfair methods of competition" embraced everything prohibited under the other antitrust laws plus false or misleading advertising and, in some product lines, labeling.

The list of prohibited practices appeared in the Clayton Antitrust Act passed in 1914. The practices affected were:

Section 2: price discrimination
Section 3: tying agreements and exclusive dealerships
Section 7: mergers among competing firms
Section 8: interlocking directorates

Again, all four prohibitions carried rules of reason, but this time they were based on the expected effect on competition rather than on the behavior of the defendant. More precisely, the practices prohibited by the Clayton Act were illegal where the effect "may be to substantially lessen competition or tend to create a monopoly." Here "may be" means a reasonable probability, not some possibility.

Sections 2, 3, and 7 have all had important judicial histories, and 2 and 7 further legislation. They will be discussed subsequently. Section 8 has been little used. It prohibits interlocking directorates where the same person is on the board of directors of competing firms. In recent years it has been extended to employees of the same firm (commonly a bank) being on the boards of competing firms. Every once in a while the FTC initiates a case, but the cases never go to trial. The director involved resigns from one of the boards before that can happen.

Price Discrimination

Section 2 made it illegal "to discriminate between different purchasers of commodities" but exempted discounts for different grade, quality, or quantity. In the 1920s the courts limited the prohibition to cases where discrimination had a reasonable chance of lessening competition in the "primary line" (the line of business of the discounter) and excluded "secondary line" effects (in the line of business of the firm receiving the discount). Moreover, the exemption of quantity discounts excluded many of the important cases. As a result, the original Section 2 was also little used.

Section 2 was amended in 1936 by the Robinson-Patman Act. One of its main objectives was to remove discriminatory advantages of large buyers, especially chain stores, so it explicitly applied to the secondary line and even to the tertiary line (the customers of firms that received the discounts). Discrimination was illegal in cases where it was likely "substantially to lessen competition or tend to create monopoly *or to injure, destroy or prevent competition.*" The first part of the statement was familiar, but the part in italics was new. It meant that someone was hurt by the discrimination, usually by being put at a competitive disadvantage.

In both the original Section 2 and the Robinson-Patman Act, price discrimination meant price differences for goods "of like grade or quality." In economics, a uniform price to all buyers even though it costs less to supply some buyers than others would clearly be discriminatory. But this is not the case at law. A seller can avoid the law completely by setting a single price for all buyers. Moreover, price differences of goods that are not of "like grade or quality" aren't discriminatory at law, although they may well be in economics. If Alcoa takes a 30 percent margin on aluminum sheet, but a 10 percent margin on aluminum screening, it will be discriminating by economic standards but not at law. The economic meaning is important because different customers get different signals about what their purchases cost society. The Robinson-Patman Act doesn't touch the largest part of economic discrimination.

The law does permit the discriminator to justify price discrimination by showing that the price differences "make only due allowance for differences in the cost of manufacture, sale, or delivery." The price difference can be less than the cost difference but not vice versa. In practice the cost defense was very hard to establish in the heyday of the Robinson-Patman Act because of the uncertainties of cost accounting (which is seldom set up to distinguish costs of supplying particular customers) and because of uncertainties of the FTC staff in evaluating the cost accounting. Few such defenses were accepted.

A seller can also justify his differences if he can show that his price was necessary to meet competition. Specifically:

> . . . nothing herein contained shall prevent a seller from rebutting the prima-facie case thus made by showing that his lower price . . . was made in good faith to meet an equally low price of a competitor. . . .

While the courts accept this as a defense, it has strict limits. The price being met must itself be lawful as far as the firm proposing the defense knows. The firm can meet, but not beat, the other price. And, these price cuts can be made to keep old customers but not to win new ones.

The provisions of the act are supposed to apply equally to buyers as well as to sellers:

> . . . it shall be unlawful for any person engaged in commerce, in the course of such commerce, knowingly to induce to receive a discrimination in price which is prohibited by this section.

However, this provision has been little used because buyers cannot usually know whether or not the price concessions they negotiate are discriminatory or capable of a cost defense.

There are other provisions of the act dealing with payment of brokerage commissions to buyers and provisions of advertising allowances that were inserted in response to practices of some chain stores in the 1930s. These clauses were important at that time but not today.

The Robinson-Patman Act was very actively enforced by the FTC in the 1940s, 1950s, and 1960s. In the 1960s it accounted for almost half of the FTC resources assigned to antitrust issues. In the 1970s the FTC greatly reduced its Robinson-Patman Act emphasis. It initiates only a few cases per year today. There are many private cases, however, and these are commonly brought by firms that are primarily objecting to price cutting by competitors. Many observers question whether such cases promote competition.

Mergers

Section 7 of the Clayton Act also had an uneven history. The original act was explicitly aimed at acquisitions of stock in competing firms. In the 1920s the courts concluded that the act did not apply to mergers in which the acquiring firm bought the assets of another firm rather than its stock. And, it appeared that the law did not consider the effects of mergers on markets other than those where the acquired and acquiring firms were direct competitors.

The law was finally amended by the Celler-Kefauver Act in 1950. The new act specified:

> that no corporation engaged in commerce shall acquire, directly or indirectly, the whole or any part of the stock or other share capital and no corporation subject to the jurisdiction of the Federal Trade Commission shall acquire the whole or any part of the assets of another corporation engaged also in commerce, where in any line of commerce in any section of the country, the effect of such acquisition may be substantially to lessen competition, or to tend to create a monopoly.

The new act closed the asset loophole and applied the merger rule to mergers where there was a reasonable probability that a merger would lead to a lessening of competition in any market, not just markets in which the merging parties competed.

The law clearly applied to horizontal mergers, that is, mergers between competing firms. These firms didn't have to compete in every market in which they sold; just one important market was enough for the laws to apply. For instance, the first important merger to reach the courts was between Bethlehem Steel, the second-largest steel producer, and Youngstown Sheet and Tube, the seventh-largest steel producer. Bethlehem sold mainly on the two coasts, while Youngstown sold in the Midwest. But they both made substantial shipments to the Detroit and Cleveland areas, and that was enough to overrule the merger. Much stronger precedents were set by the courts in later years.

The new law also applied to vertical mergers where a supplier merged with a buyer. The courts were primarily concerned with the likelihood of foreclosure—buyers being excluded from raw materials or sellers being excluded from outlets. Again, the courts set very strong precedents in the 1960s.

In spite of a very tough merger law, however, there was a huge merger wave in the late 1960s. Few of the mergers involved were horizontal or vertical. Most were conglomerate mergers, combinations of firms in different markets. Some were market extension mergers, when a firm doing business in one part of the country acquired a firm doing the same thing elsewhere. For instance, Atlantic Oil, which operated mainly in the East, merged with Richfield Oil, which sold mainly on the West Coast, and ARCO, the resulting firm, acquired Sinclair, which sold mainly in the Midwest. The Bethlehem-Youngstown merger was, in good part, a market extension merger. Another common type of merger was product extension mergers, where firms in related industries merged. For instance, Proctor and Gamble, the leading producer of soap and detergents, merged with Clorox, which sold half of the laundry bleach in the country.

In a few of the market and product extension mergers, the law was interpreted to apply because the merger resulted in the loss of important potential competition. The argument goes as follows: If one of the few most likely entrants into some market acquires a leading firm in that market, there will be a lessening of competition because an acquiring firm from outside might have actually entered the market. Or even if the outside firm had no such plans at that moment, it would be on the edge of the market and able to enter if prices rose relative to costs. For instance, when Bethlehem was prevented from acquiring Youngstown, it built a new plant near Chicago and the Midwest had a more competitive steel industry as a result. P & G claimed before the FTC that it had studied the bleach industry and found that it could not meet its profit goals if it went into bleach; it has not, in fact, entered the bleach industry since then. Does this mean that the potential competition argument in this case was invalid? On the other hand, some would argue that the fact that P & G acquired Clorox indicated that it was a potential entrant. Do you believe that? Could any market or product extension merger get by on that argument?

A substantial number of the mergers of the late 1960s were "pure conglomerate mergers," mergers between firms in different and unrelated markets, for instance, the acquisition of a coal firm by an aircraft company. The effect of the merger law on such mergers has never been established. The Justice Department started five cases against such mergers in 1969, but they were all settled out of court (apparently on orders from President Nixon in the case of three mergers involving International Telephone and Telegraph). Though the frantic pace of conglomerate mergers of the late 1960s has ended, quite a number of them are still going on— Mobil Oil and AMCOR (Montgomery Ward and Container Corporation of America), ARCO (oil) and Anacanda Copper, United Technologies (one of the two United States producers of aircraft engines) and Otis Elevator. None of these huge mergers was challenged. The impact of the law on this sort of case has not yet been established.

Vertical Restrictions on Competition

One more element of the Clayton Act deserves some mention. That is Section 3, which holds:

> that it shall be unlawful for a person engaged in commerce to lease or make a sale . . . on the condition, agreement, or understanding that the lessee or purchasers thereof shall not use the goods . . . of a competitor or competitors of the lessor or seller, where the effect . . . may be to substantially lessen competition or tend to create a monopoly. . . .

This prohibition has been interpreted to apply to tying sales (tie-in sales in legalese); that is, sales where the customer must buy the seller's A if he or she buys the seller's B. For instance, IBM used to require that users of its tab-machines (predecessors to computers) had to use cards produced by IBM. During most of the period since World War II, this prohibition was virtually per se, though in one recent case (the second Fortner decision on page 138) the Supreme Court refused to rule illegal a tie of building materials to construction loans, over which the seller certainly had no special power.

Section 3 has also been interpreted to prohibit exclusive dealerships on a virtual per se basis. For instance, oil companies used to prevent their gas stations from carrying other brands of gasoline. The courts ruled against this practice, and the formal provision no longer exists, but you still won't find many Shell stations that also sell Texaco products.

A related practice arises when the supplier specifies the type of customer or the territory a franchisee can sell, although such provisions have been attacked under Section 1 of the Sherman Act, rather than under the Clayton Act, Section 3, as preventing intrabrand competition. For instance, for years Coca Cola restricted its bottlers to strictly drawn, nonoverlapping territories. Many such provisions have been struck down, but the courts have been willing to permit them if the supplier itself is weak. Exclusive territories may be a way to secure dealers that the weak supplier could not get otherwise.

Finally, Section 3 has been read to prohibit requirements contracts where the buyer contracts for all its requirements of some good from a particular supplier. Such provisions can clearly have the same effect as exclusive dealerships. However, there are settings where such contracts are clearly necessary. When the courts were in the process of prohibiting tying and requirements contracts in the tin can industry, the canners asked for and were permitted to use one-year requirements contracts because they could not predict in advance the sizes of the crops they would have to pack. A mine-mouth power plant would not be built without an assured long-term supply of coal from the mine. Before a plant is built there are hundreds of coal mines available as potential suppliers, but once it is built, it is fully dependent on just one. The courts have applied a rule of reason to requirements contracts.

CHAPTER 3

RESTRAINT OF TRADE

Section 1 of the Sherman Act is the most straightforward part of antitrust law. Decisions applying Section 1 have been more consistent over time and clearer than those enforcing any other part of the law. Still there are ambiguities. The first two cases below are the main precedents in this field. The rest deal with issues that have arisen in applying Section 1.

The meaning of Section 1 of the Sherman Act was fairly easy to establish because "contracts in restraint of trade" had a long established meaning in common law. The Addyston Pipe and Steel decision spelled out that definition and its implications and established the longest standing precedent in American antitrust law. The opinion quoted here was reached by a three-judge panel in a Court of Appeals [and was delivered by Judge (later President) William Howard Taft]. It was subsequently affirmed by the Supreme Court. How did the court interpret "restraint of trade"? How did the Court believe that the Sherman Act changed the law? How did it treat evidence that the prices set were reasonable? Can any contract restraining trade be "reasonable" by the criterion set in this decision? Shortly after this decision *all* the firms in this case merged. No antitrust action was taken against the merger. Do you think the new firm restrained trade more or less than the agreement?

The rule in Addyston continues in effect today, but there were some aberrations along the way. The most serious occurred during the great depression. Congress passed the National Industrial Recovery Act (NIRA) in June 1933, which permitted industries to prepare "Codes of Fair Competition" which often involved obvious restraints of trade. The NIRA was declared unconstitutional in June 1935, but many of the restraints continued. A great deal of antitrust activity in the late 1930s was devoted to clearing these restraints out. The Socony Vacuum case was the most important of these cases. It set a very strong precedent. Do you think oil markets were demoralized and competition was destructive in the early 1930s? If you said yes, do you think that the scheme developed by the oil companies was the best way to deal with the problem? If the court had accepted the position that the industry could set reasonable restraints to prevent destructive competition, what standard should it set to judge what was reasonable? Do you think the courts are a good vehicle for determining which restraints are reasonable? What actually happened was that the oil producing states set up prorationing systems that limited oil production by means of output quotas. They were effective from about 1936 until 1973. Oil prices were certainly stabilized—and raised—by prorationing. Do you think this was a better approach to the problem?

While the principle in Addyson Pipe and Steel has been well established for almost a century, lawyers can still find something to argue about in Section 1 cases. An important issue has been what constitutes collusion. The last five cases in this chapter deal with this issue.

Interstate Circuit presents the question directly. Do you think the eight distributors actually colluded? No evidence was presented that they met together and agreed explicitly on policy. If they did, who gained? The distributors? The exhibitors? Why did the distributors change their policies? Who, if anyone, was hurt by these distributors?

The American Tobacco case also depends on collusion in part. There is much more to this case than what is presented here. We cover only collusion here. As you read the portion reproduced here, see if you agree with the Court's decision on conspiracy. Do you think that the major cigarette companies colluded to set their prices? Did they collude to raise prices in 1931 when most prices were falling? Do you think an explicit agreement was involved? Does it make any difference? What about the price cuts in 1932 and 1933? Was a formal agreement needed to make these stick? How about their instructions to their buyers in tobacco auctions? Would truly independent competitors act this way? If there were no more than this to the case (there *is* more), should they have been convicted under Section 1? What could they do to avoid another conviction twenty or thirty years later?

Theatre Enterprises also deals with parallel policies among oligopolists, mostly the same firms as in Interstate Circuit. Do you think they consciously colluded here? If you were distributing a movie would you put its first run in a neighborhood theatre? Maybe so now, but in the 1940s the downtown theatres were much larger and drew much bigger audiences. What did this decision do to Interstate Circuit and American Tobacco, especially the latter?

Cement Institute also involves skating on thin ice. The cement companies (and steel, rigid steel conduit, and corn product producers in other cases) were not charged with agreeing on price *levels* but on how they handled transportation costs. Do you think that they explicitly agreed to use a basing-point system? (There is actually good evidence that at least the steel companies did.) Would it make any difference if they hadn't? Could you imagine a workable decree that would end the conduct complained of in this case (or other cases directed toward the basing-point system)? Is it easier than in American Tobacco? The Cement Institute case led to the elimination of the basing-point system throughout American industry, but it still exists in Europe. Do you think we gained anything from the change?

The Container Corporation case depends on a milder issue. Cardboard boxmakers exchanged price information among themselves on an informal, intermittent basis. Did this mean they were colluding? Could it prevent prices from falling or make them rise? Conventional economic analysis says that better and more widespread information makes competitive markets more efficient. Is this true in cardboard boxes in the South? Why or why not?

The last case deals with the lawyers themselves. Professional associations have long engaged in collusive practices. They published fee schedules and made violations of them matters of professional ethics. They have worked through state licensing boards (typically made up of practitioners) to restrict entry into the affected professions. Starting in 1970, the Antitrust Division brought cases against professional association rules that controlled prices or advertising among real estate agents, accountants, architects, and engineers but, for some reason, ignored the lawyers. The Goldfarb case was initiated by an individual, but reached the Supreme Court anyway. Do you think the lawyers here colluded? Does the "advisory" function of the fee schedule mean it should not be counted as collusion? Do you think title examinations on personal residences is in interstate commerce? If it is, can you think of any economic activity that wouldn't be? *Should* title investigations be in interstate commerce? Do you think that fee schedules are essential for the maintenance of professional ethics? What could the Virginia lawyers do to get their fee schedules back?

United States v. Addyston Pipe & Steel Co.

85 Fed. 271 (1898)

TAFT, Circuit judge.

[An association of cast-iron pipe producers allocated cities to particular sellers, rigged bids on public contracts, and provided for bonuses paid by sellers to the association on sales in "pay territory" (the South and Midwest). The organization was a formal one (with regular meetings, minutes, and voting rules).]

Two questions are presented in this case for our decision: First. Was the association of the defendants a contract, combination, or conspiracy in restraint of trade, as the terms are to be understood in the act? Second. Was the trade thus restrained trade between the states? . . .

[I]t is certain that, if the contract of association which bound the defendants was void and unenforceable at the common law because in restraint of trade, it is within the inhibition of the statute if the trade it restrained was interstate. Contracts that were in unreasonable restraint of trade at common law were not unlawful in the sense of being criminal, or giving rise to a civil action for damages in favor of one prejudicially affected thereby, but were simply void, and were not enforced by the courts. . . . The effect of the act of 1890 is to render such contracts unlawful in an affirmative or positive sense, and punishable as a misdemeanor, and to create a right of civil action for damages in favor of those injured thereby, and a civil remedy by injunction in favor of both private persons and the public against the execution of such contracts and the maintenance of such trade restraints. . . .

[C]ovenants in partial restraint of trade are generally upheld as valid when they are agreements (1) by the seller of property or business not to compete with the buyer in such a way as to derogate from the value of the property or business sold; (2) by a retiring partner not to compete with the firm; (3) by a partner pending the partnership not to do anything to interfere, by competition or otherwise, with the business of the firm; (4) by the buyer of property not to use the same in competition with the business retained by the seller; and (5) by an assistant, servant, or agent not to compete with his master or employer after the expiration of his time of service. Before such agreements are upheld, however, the court must find that the restraints attempted thereby are reasonably necessary (1, 2 and 3) to the enjoyment by the buyer of the property, good will, or interest in the partnership bought; or (4) to the legitimate ends of the existing partnership; or (5) to the prevention of possible injury to the business of the seller from use by the buyer of the thing sold; or (6) to protection from the danger of loss to the employer's business caused by the unjust use on the part of the employees of the confidential knowledge acquired in such business. . . .

This very statement of the rule implies that the contract must be one in which there is a main purpose, to which the covenant in restraint of trade is merely ancillary. The covenant is inserted only to protect one of the parties from the injury which, in the execution of the contract or enjoyment of its fruits, he may suffer from the unrestrained competition of the other. The main purpose of the contract suggests the measure of protection needs, and furnishes a sufficiently uniform standard by which the validity of such restraints may be judicially determined. In such a case, if the restraint exceeds the necessity presented by the main purpose of the contract, it is void for two reasons: First, because it oppresses the covenantor, without any corresponding benefit to the coventee; and, because it tends to a monopoly. But where the sole object of both parties in making the contract as expressed therein is merely to restrain competition, and enhance or maintain prices, it would seem that there was nothing to justify or excuse the restraint, that it would necessarily have a tendency to monopoly, and therefore would be void. . . .

Much evidence is adduced upon affidavit to prove that defendants had no power arbitrarily to fix prices, and that they were always obliged to meet competition. To the extent that they could not impose prices on the public in excess of the price of pipe with freight from the Atlantic seaboard added, this is true; but, within that limit, they could fix prices as they chose. The most cogent evidence that they had this power is the fact, everywhere apparent in the record, that they exercised it.

It has been earnestly pressed upon us that the prices at which the cast-iron pipe was sold in pay territory were reasonable. We do not think the issue an important one, because, as already stated, we do not think at common law there is any question of reasonableness open to the courts with reference to such a contract. Its tendency was certainly to give defendants the power to charge unreasonable prices, had they chosen to do so. . . .

Another aspect of this contract of association brings it within the term used in the statute, "a conspiracy in restraint of trade." A conspiracy is a combination of two or more persons to accomplish an unlawful end by lawful means or a lawful end by unlawful means. In the answer of the defendants, it is averred that the chief way in which cast-iron pipe is sold is by contracts let after competitive bidding invited by the intending purchaser. It would have much interfered with the smooth working of defendant's association had its existence and purposes become known to the public. A part of the plan was a deliberate attempt to create in the minds of the members of the public inviting bids the belief that competition existed between the defendants. Several of the defendants were required to bid at every letting, and to make their bids at such prices that the one already selected to obtain the contract should have the lowest bid. It is well settled then at agreement between intending bidders at a public auction or a public letting not to bid against each other, and thus to prevent competition, is a fraud upon the intending vendor or contractor, and the ensuing sale or contract will be set aside. . . . No matter what the excuse for the combination by defendants in restraint of trade, the illegality of the means stamps it as a conspiracy, and so brings it within that term of the federal statute.

United States v. Socony-Vacuum Oil Co.

310 U.S. 150 (1940)

MR. JUSTICE DOUGLAS delivered the opinion for the Court.

[In the late 1920s and the early 1930s, large-scale discoveries of oil and the Great Depression brought about disastrously low prices for oil: 10 to 15 cents a barrel for crude and less than 3 cents a gallon for gasoline in Texas! Federal, state, and industry groups made strenuous efforts to "stabilize the market." The industry efforts were associated with its "Code of Fair Competition" under the NIRA. A Tank Car Stabilization Committee was established in 1934 to find ways of preventing shipments of "distress gasoline" from destabilizing gasoline prices in the Midwest. Major oil companies were assigned "dancing partners" among the independent refiners. Each major bought up the distress shipments of its partner or partners. Both federal and state officials knew of the arrangement and apparently approved of it. The practice continued after the NIRA was declared unconstitutional in June 1935. An antitrust suit was initiated in 1937. The major issue on appeal from the trial was the judge's charge to the jury.]

. . . The court charged the jury that it was a violation of the Sherman Act for a group of individuals or corporations to act together to raise the prices to be charged for the commodity which they manufactured where they controlled a substantial part of the interstate trade and commerce in that commodity. The court stated that where the members of a combination had the power to raise prices and acted together for that purpose, the combination was illegal; and that it was immaterial how reasonable or unreasonable those prices were or to what extent they had been affected by the combination. It further charged that if such illegal combination existed, it did not matter that there may also have been other factors which contributed to the raising of the prices. . . . The court then charged that, unless the jury found beyond a reasonable doubt that the price rise and its continuance were "caused" by the combination and not caused by those other factors, verdicts of "not guilty" should be returned. It also charged that there was no evidence of governmental approval which would exempt the buying programs from the prohibitions of the Sherman Act; and that knowledge or acquiescence of officers of the government or the good intentions of the members of the combination would not give immunity from prosecution under that Act.

The Circuit Court of Appeals held this charge to be reversible error, since it was based upon the theory that such a combination was illegal per se. In its view respondents' activities were not unlawful unless they constituted an unreasonable restraint of trade. . . .

[R]espondents contend that in the instant case there was no elimination in the spot tank car market of competition which prevented the prices in that market from being made by the play of competition in sales between independent refiners and their jobber and consumer customers; that during the buying programs those prices were in fact determined by such competition; that the purchases under those programs were closely related to or dependent on the spot market prices; that there was no evidence that the purchases of distress gasoline under those programs had any effect on the competitive market price beyond that flowing from the removal of a competitive evil; and that if respondents had tried to do more than free competition from the effect of distress gasoline and to set an arbitrary non-competitive price through their purchases, they would have been without power to do so.

But we do not deem those distinctions material.

In the first place, there was abundant evidence that the combination had the purpose to raise prices. And likewise, there was ample evidence that the buying programs at least contributed to the price rise and the stability of the spot markets, and to increases in the price of gasoline sold in the Mid-Western area during the indictment period. That other factors also may have contributed to that rise and stability of the markets is immaterial. . . .

Secondly, the fact that sales on the spot markets were still governed by some competition is of no consequence. For it is indisputable that that competition was restricted through the removal by respondents of a part of the supply which but for the buying programs would have been a factor in determining the going prices on those markets. But the vice of the conspiracy was not merely the restriction of supply of gasoline by removal of a surplus. As we have said, this was a well organized program. The timing and strategic placement of the buying orders for distress gasoline played an important and significant role. Buying orders were carefully placed so as to remove the distress gasoline from weak hands. . . .

The elimination of so-called competitive evils is no legal justification for such buying programs. The elimination of such conditions was sought primarily for its effect on the price structures. Fairer competitive prices, it is claimed, resulted when distress gasoline was removed from the market. But such defense is typical of the protestations usually made in price-fixing cases. Ruinous competition, financial disaster, evils of price cutting and the like appear throughout our history as ostensible justifications for price-fixing. If the so-called competitive abuses were to be appraised here, the reasonableness of prices would necessarily become an issue in every price-fixing case. In that event the Sherman Act would soon be emasculated; its philosophy would be supplanted by one which is wholly alien to a system of free competition; it would not be the charter of freedom which its framers intended.

The reasonableness of prices has no constancy due to the dynamic quality of the business facts underlying price structures. Those who fixed reasonable prices today would perpetuate unreasonable prices tomorrow, since those prices would not be subject to continuous administrative supervision and readjustment in light of changed conditions. Those who controlled the prices would control or effectively dominate the market. And those who were in that strategic position would have it in their power to destroy or drastically impair the competitive system. But the thrust of the rule is deeper and reaches more than monopoly power. Any combination which tampers with price structures is engaged in an unlawful activity. Even though the members of the price-fixing group were in no position to control the market, to the extent that they raised, lowered, or stabilized prices they would be directly interfering with the free play of market forces. The Act places all such schemes beyond the pale and protects that vital part of our economy against any degree of interference. . . . There was accordingly no error in the refusal to charge that in order to convict the jury must find that the resultant prices were raised and maintained at "high, arbitrary and non-competitive levels." The charge in the indictment to that effect was surplusage. . . .

Under the Sherman Act a combination formed for the purpose and with the effect of raising, depressing, fixing, pegging, or stabilizing the price of a commodity in interstate or foreign commerce is illegal per se. Where the machinery for price-fixing is an agreement on the prices to be charged or paid for the commodity in the interstate or foreign channels of trade, the power to fix prices exists if the combination has control of a substantial part of the commerce in that commodity. Where the means for price-fixing are purchases or sales of the commodity in a market operation or, as here, purchases of a part of the supply of the commodity for the purpose of keeping it from having a depressive effect on the markets, such power may be found to exist though the combination does not control a substantial part of the commodity.

Interstate Circuit, Inc. v. United States

306 U.S. 208 (1939)

MR. JUSTICE STONE delivered the opinion of the Court.

Appellants comprise the two groups of defendants in the District Court. The members of one group of eight corporations which are distributors of motion picture films, and the Texas agents of two of them. The other group, corporations and individuals engaged in exhibiting motion pictures in Texas, and some of them in New Mexico. The distributor appellants are engaged in the business of distributing in interstate commerce motion picture films, copyrights on which they own or control, for exhibition in theatres throughout the United States. They distribute about 75 percent of all first-class feature films exhibited in the United States. They solicit from motion picture theatre owners and managers in Texas and other states applications for licenses to exhibit films, and forward the applications, when received from such exhibitors, to their respective New York offices, where they are accepted or rejected. If the applications are accepted, the distributors ship the films from points outside the states of exhibition to their exchanges within those states, from which, pursuant to the license agreements, the films are delivered to the local theatres for exhibition. After exhibition the films are reshipped to the distributors at points outside the state.

The exhibitor group of appellants consists of Interstate Circuit, Inc., and Texas Consolidated Theatres, Inc. The two corporations are affiliated with each other and with Paramount Pictures Distributing Co., Inc., one of the distributor appellants.

Interstate operates forty-three first-run and second-run motion picture theatres, located in six Texas cities.

Texas Consolidated operates sixty-six theatres, some first- and some subsequent-run houses, in various cities and towns in the Rio Grande Valley and elsewhere in Texas and in New Mexico. . . . At the time of the contracts in question Interstate and Consolidated each contributed more than 74 percent of all the license fees paid by the motion picture theatres in their respective territories to the distributor appellants.

On July 11, 1934, following a previous communication on the subject to the eight branch managers of the distributor appellants, O'Donnell, the manager of the Interstate and Consolidated, sent to each of them a letter on the letterhead of Interstate, each letter naming all of them as addressees, in which he asked compliance with two demands as a condition of Interstate's continued exhibition of the distributor's films in its 'A' or first-run theatres at a night admission of 40 cents or more. One demand was that the distributors "agree that in selling their product to subsequent runs, that this 'A' product will never be exhibited at any time or in any theatre at a smaller admission price than 25¢ for adults in the evening." The other was that "on 'A' pictures which are exhibited at a night admission of 40¢ or more—they shall never be exhibited in conjunction with another feature picture under the so-called policy of double features." The letter added that with respect to the "Rio Grande Valley situation," with which Consolidated alone was concerned, "We must insist that all pictures exhibited in our 'A' theatres at a maximum night admission price of 35¢ must also be restricted to subsequent runs in the Valley at 25¢."

The admission price customarily charged for preferred seats at night in independently operated subsequent-run theatres in Texas at the time of these letters was less than 25 cents. In seventeen of the eighteen independent theatres of this kind whose operations were described by witnesses the admission price was less than 25 cents. In one only was it 25 cents. In most of them the admission was 15 cents or less. It was also the general practice in those theatres to provide double bills either on certain days of the week or with any feature picture which was weak in drawing power. The distributor appellants had generally provided in their license contracts for a minimum admission price of 10 or 15 cents, and three of them had included provisions restricting double-billing. But none was at any time previously subject to contractual compulsion to continue the restrictions. The trial court found that the proposed restrictions constituted an important departure from prior practice.

The local representatives of the distributors, having no authority to enter into the proposed agreements, communicated the proposal to their home offices. Conferences followed between Hoblitzelle and O'Donnell, acting for Interstate and Consolidated, and the representatives of the various distributors. In these conferences each distributor was represented by its local branch manager and by one or more superior officials from outside the state of Texas. In the course of them each distributor agreed with Interstate for the 1934-35 season to impose both the demanded restrictions upon their subsequent-run licensees in the six Texas cities served by Interstate, except Austin and Galveston. While only two of the distributors incorporated the agreement to impose the restrictions in their license contracts with Interstate, the evidence establishes, and it is not denied, that all joined in the agreement, four of them after some delay in negotiating terms other than the restrictions and not now material. These agreements for the restrictions—with the immaterial exceptions noted—were carried into effect by each of the distributors' imposing them on their subsequent-run licensees in the four Texas cities during the 1934-35 season. One agreement, that of Metro-Goldwyn-Mayer Distributing Corporation, was for three years. The others were renewed in the two following seasons and all were in force when the present suit was begun. . . .

The trial court found that the distributor appellants agreed and conspired among themselves to take uniform action upon the proposals made by Interstate, and that they agreed and conspired with each other and with Interstate to impose the demanded restrictions upon all subsequent-run exhibitors in Dallas, Fort Worth, Houston and San Antonio; that they carried out the agreement by imposing the restrictions upon their subsequent-run licensees in those cities, causing some of them to increase their admission price to 25 cents, either generally or when restricted pictures were shown, and to abandon double-billing of all such pictures, and causing the other subsequent-run exhibitors, who were either unable or unwilling to accept the restrictions, to be deprived of any opportunity to exhibit the restricted pictures, which were the best and most popular of all new feature pictures; that the effect of the restrictions upon "low-income members of the community" patronizing the theatres of these exhibitors was to withhold from them altogether the "best entertainment furnished by the motion picture industry;" and that the restrictions operated to increase the income of the distributors and of Interstate and to deflect attendance from later-run exhibitors who yielded to the restrictions to the first-run theatres of Interstate.

The court concluded as matters of law that the agreement of the distributors with each other and those with Interstate to impose the restrictions upon subsequent-run exhibitors and the carrying of the agreements into effect, with the aid and participation of Hoblitzelle and O'Donnell, constituted a combination and conspiracy in restraint of interstate commerce in violation of the Sherman Act. It also concluded that each separate agreement between Interstate and a distributor that Interstate should subject itself to the restrictions in its subsequent-run theatres and that the distributors should impose the restrictions on all subsequent-run theatres in the Texas cities as a condition of supplying them with its feature pictures, was likewise a violation of the Act.

It accordingly enjoined the conspiracy and restrained the distributors from enforcing the restrictions in their license agreements with subsequent-run exhibitors and from enforcing the contracts on any of them. . . .

While the District Court's finding of an agreement of the distributors among themselves is supported by the evidence, we think that in the circumstances of this case such agreement for the imposition of the restrictions upon subsequent-run exhibitors was not a prerequisite to an unlawful conspiracy. It was enough that, knowing that concerted action was contemplated and invited, the distributors gave their adherence to the scheme and participated in it. Each distributor was advised that the others were asked to participate; each knew that cooperation was essential to successful operation of the plan. They knew that the plan, if carried out, would result in a restraint of commerce, which, we will presently point out, was unreasonable within the meaning of the Sherman Act, and knowing it, all participated in the plan. The evidence is persuasive that each distributor early became aware that the others had joined. With that knowledge they renewed the arrangement and carried it into effect for the two successive years.

It is elementary that an unlawful conspiracy may be and often is formed without simultaneous action or agreement on the part of the conspirators. . . . Acceptance by competitors, without previous agreement, of an invitation to participate in a plan, the necessary consequence of which, if carried out, is restraint of interstate commerce, is sufficient to establish an unlawful conspiracy under the Sherman Act. . . .

American Tobacco Co. v. United States

328 U.S. 781 (1946)

MR. JUSTICE BURTON delivered the opinion for the Court.

The petitioners are The American Tobacco Company, Liggett & Myers Tobacco Company, R. J. Reynolds Tobacco Company, American Suppliers, Inc., a subsidiary of American, and certain officials of the respective companies who were convicted by a jury.

Each petitioner was convicted on four counts: (1) Conspiracy in restraint of trade, (2) monopolization, (3) attempt to monopolize, and (4) conspiracy to monopolize. Each count related to interstate and foreign trade and commerce in tobacco.

The following record of price changes is circumstantial evidence of the existence of a conspiracy and of a power and intent to exclude competition coming from cheaper grade cigarettes. On June 23, 1931, Reynolds, without previous notification or warning to the trade or public, raised the list price of Camel cigarettes, constituting its leading cigarette brand, from $6.40 to $6.85 a thousand. The same day, American increased the list price for Lucky Strike cigarettes, its leading brand, and Liggett, the price for Chesterfield cigarettes, its leading brand, to the identical price of $6.85 a thousand. No economic justification for this raise was demonstrated. This general price increase soon resulted in higher retail prices and in a loss in volume of sales. Yet in 1932, in the midst of the national depression with the sales of the petitioner's cigarettes falling off greatly in number, the petitioners still were making tremendous profits as a result of the price increase.

Their net profits in that year amounted to more than $100,000,000. This was one of the three biggest years in their history.

Before 1931, certain smaller companies had manufactured cigarettes retailing at 10 cents a package, which was several cents lower than the retail price for the leading brands of the petitioners. Up to that time, the sales of the 10 cents cigarettes were negligible. However, after the above described increase in list prices of the petitioners in 1931, the 10 cents brands made serious inroads upon the sales of the petitioners. These cheaper brands of cigarettes were sold at a list price of $4.75 a thousand and from 1931 to 1932, the sales of these cigarettes multiplied 30 times, rising from 0.28% of the total cigarette sales of the country in June, 1931, to 22.78% in November, 1932. In response to this threat of competition from the manufacturers of the 10 cent brands, the petitioners, in January, 1933, cut the list price of their three leading brands from $6.85 to $6 a thousand. In February, they cut again to $5.50 a thousand. The evidence tends to show that this cut was directed at the competition of the 10 cent cigarettes. . . . Following the first price cut by petitioners, the sales of the 10 cent brands fell off considerably. After the second cut they fell off to a much greater extent. When the sale of the 10 cent brands had dropped from 22.78% of the total cigarette sales in November, 1932, to 6.43% in May, 1933, the petitioners, in January, 1934, raised the list price of their leading brands from $5.50 back up to $6.10 a thousand. . . .

The verdicts show that the jury found that the petitioners conspired to fix prices and to exclude undesired competition against them in the purchase of the domestic type of flue-cured tobacco and of burley tobacco. . . .

Petitioners refused to purchase tobacco on these [auction] markets unless the other petitioners were also represented thereon. There were attempts made by others to open new tobacco markets but none of the petitioners would participate in them unless the other petitioners were present. Consequently, such markets were failures due to the absence of buyers. . . . In this way the new tobacco markets and their locations were determined by the unanimous consent of the petitioners and, in arriving at their determination, the petitioners consulted with each other as to whether or not a community deserved a market.

The Government presented evidence to support its claim that, before the markets opened, the petitioners placed limitations and restrictions on the prices which their buyers were permitted to pay for tobacco. None of the buyers exceeded these price ceilings. Grades of tobacco were formulated in such a way as to result in the absence of competition between the petitioners. There was manipulation of the price of lower grade tobaccos in order to restrict competition from manufacturers of the lower priced cigarettes. Methods used included the practice of the petitioners of calling their respective buyers in, prior to the opening of the annual markets, and giving them instructions as to the prices to be paid for leaf tobacco in each of the markets. These instructions were in terms of top prices or price ranges. The price ceilings thus established for the buyers were the same for each of them. . . .

Where one or two of the petitioners secured their percentage of the crop on a certain market or were not interested in the purchase of certain offerings of tobacco, their buyers, nevertheless, would enter the bidding in order to force the other petitioners to bid up to the maximum price. The petitioners were not so much concerned with the prices they paid for the leaf tobacco as that each should pay the same price for the same grade. . . .

. . . There was evidence that when dealers received an announcement of the price increase from one of the petitioners and attempted to purchase some of the leading brands of cigarettes from the other petitioners at their unchanged prices before announcement of a similar change, the latter refused to fill such orders until their prices were also raised, thus bringing about the same result as if the changes had been precisely simultaneous.

It was on the basis of such evidence that the Circuit Court of Appeals found that the verdicts of the jury were sustained by sufficient evidence on each count.

It is not the form of the combination or the particular means used but the result to be achieved that the statute condemns. It is not of importance whether the means used to accomplish the unlawful objective are in themselves lawful or unlawful. Acts done to give effect to the conspiracy may be in themselves wholly innocent acts. Yet, if they are part of the sum of the acts which are relied upon to effectuate the conspiracy which the statute forbids, they come within its prohibition. No formal agreement is necessary to constitute an unlawful conspiracy. Often crimes are a matter of inference deduced from the acts of the person accused and done in pursuance of a criminal purpose. Where the conspiracy is proved, as here, from the evidence of the action taken in concert by the parties to it, it is all the more convincing proof of an intent to exercise the power of exclusion acquired through that conspiracy. The essential combination or conspiracy in violation of the Sherman Act may be found in a course of dealings or other circumstances as well as in any exchange of words. Where the circumstances are such as to warrant a jury in finding that the conspirators had a unity of purpose or a common design and understanding, or a meeting of minds in an unlawful arrangement, the conclusion that a conspiracy is established is justified.

Theatre Enterprises, Inc. v. Paramount Film Distributing Corp.

346 U.S. 537 (1954)

MR. JUSTICE CLARK delivered the opinion for the court.

Petitioner brought this suit for treble damages and an injunction . . . alleging that respondent motion picture producers and distributors had violated the antitrust laws, by conspiring to restrict "first-run" pictures to downtown Baltimore theatres, thus confining its suburban theatre to subsequent runs and unreasonable "clearances." After hearing the evidence a jury returned a general verdict for respondents. The Court of Appeals for the Fourth Circuit affirmed the judgment based on the verdict. 201 F.2d 306. We granted certiorari.

Petitioner now urges, as it did in the Court of Appeals, that the trial judge should have directed a verdict in its favor and submitted to the jury only the question of the amount of damages. . . .

Petitioner owns and operates the Crest Theatre, located in a neighborhood shopping district some six miles from the downtown shopping center in Baltimore, Maryland. The Crest, possessing the most modern improvements and appointments, opened on February 26, 1949. Before and after the opening, petitioner, through its president, repeatedly sought to obtain first-run features for the theatre. . . . But respondents uniformly rebuffed petitioner's efforts and adhered to an established policy of restricting first-runs in Baltimore to the eight downtown theatres. Admittedly there is no direct evidence of illegal agreement between the respondents and no conspiracy is charged as to the independent exhibitors in Baltimore, who account for 63% of first-run exhibitions. The various respondents advanced much the same reasons for denying petitioner's offers. Among other reasons they asserted that . . . first-runs are normally granted only to noncompeting theatres. Since the Crest is in "substantial competition" with the downtown theatres . . . [a first-run] arrangement would be economically unfeasible. And even if respondents wished to grant petitioner such a license, no downtown exhibitor would waive his clearance rights over the Crest and agree to a simultaneous showing. As a result, if petitioner were to receive first-runs, the license would have to be an exclusive one. However, an exclusive license would be economically unsound because the Crest is a suburban theatre, located in a small shopping center, and served by limited public transportation facilities; and, with a drawing area of less than one-tenth that of a downtown theatre, it cannot compare with those easily accessible theatres in the power to draw patrons. Hence the downtown theatres offer far greater opportunities for the widespread advertisement and exploitation of newly released features, which is thought necessary to maximize the overall return from subsequent runs as well as first-runs. The respondents, in the light of these conditions, attacked the guaranteed offers of petitioner, one of which occurred during the trial, as not being made in good faith. Respondents Loew's and Warner refused petitioner an exclusive license because they owned the three downtown theatres receiving their first-run product.

The crucial question is whether respondents' conduct toward petitioner stemmed from independent decision or from an agreement, tacit or express. To be sure, business behavior is admissible circumstantial evidence from which the fact finder may infer agreement. But this Court has never held that proof of parallel business behavior conclusively establishes agreement or, phrased differently, that such behavior itself constitutes a Sherman Act offense. Circumstantial evidence of consciously parallel behavior may have made heavy inroads into the traditional judicial attitude toward conspiracy; but "conscious parallelism" has not yet read conspiracy out of the Sherman Act entirely.

Federal Trade Commission v. Cement Institute

333 U.S. 683 (1948)

MR. JUSTICE BLACK delivered the opinion of the Court.

The proceedings were begun by a Commission complaint of two counts. The first charged that certain alleged conduct set out at length constituted an unfair method of competition in violation of Section 5 of the Federal Trade Commission Act. The core of the charge was that the respondents had restrained and hindered competition in the sale and distribution of cement by means of a combination among themselves made effective through mutual understanding or agreement to employ a multiple basing point system of pricing. It was alleged that this system resulted in the quotation of identical terms of sale and identical prices for cement by the respondents at any given point in the United States. This system had worked so successfully, it was further charged, that for many years prior to the filing of the complaint, all cement buyers throughout the nation, with rare exceptions, had been unable to purchase cement for delivery in any given locality from any one of the respondents at a lower price or on more favorable terms than from any of the other respondents.

The second count of the complaint, resting chiefly on the same allegations of fact set out in Count I, charged that the multiple basing point system of sales resulted in systematic price discriminations between the customers of each respondent. These discriminations were made, it was alleged, with the purpose of destroying competition in price between the various respondents. . . .

Since the multiple basing point delivered price system of fixing prices and terms of cement sales is the nub of this controversy, it will be helpful at this preliminary stage to point out in general what it is and how it works. A brief reference to the distinctive characteristics of "factory" or "mill prices" and "delivered prices" is of importance to an understanding of the basing point delivered price system here involved.

Goods may be sold and delivered to customers at the sellers' mill or warehouse door or may be sold free on board (f.o.b.) trucks or railroad cars immediately adjacent to the seller's mill or warehouse. In either event the actual cost of the goods to the purchaser is, broadly speaking, the seller's "mill price" plus the purchaser's cost of transportation. However, if the seller fixes a price at which he undertakes to deliver goods to the purchaser where they are to be used, the cost to the purchaser is the "delivered price." A seller who makes the "mill price" identical for all purchasers of like amount and quality simply delivers his goods at the same place (his mill) and for the same price (price at the mill). He thus receives for all f.o.b. mill sales an identical net amount of money for like goods from all customers. But a "delivered price" system creates complications which may result in a seller's receiving different net returns from the sale of like goods. The cost of transporting 500 miles is almost always more than the cost of transporting 100 miles. Consequently if customers 100 to 500 miles away pay the same "delivered price," the seller's net return is less from the more distant customer. This difference in the producer's net return from sales to customers in different localities under a "delivered price" system is an important element in the charge under Count I of the complaint and is the crux of Count II.

The best known early example of a basing point price system was called "Pittsburgh plus." It related to the price of steel. The Pittsburgh price was the base price, Pittsburgh being therefore called a price basing point. In order for the system to work, sales had to be made only at delivered prices. Under this system the delivered price of steel from anywhere in the United States to a point of delivery anywhere in the United States was in general the Pittsburgh price plus the railroad freight rate from Pittsburgh to the point of delivery. Take Chicago, Illinois, as an illustration of the operation and consequences of the system. A Chicago steel producer was not free to sell his steel at cost plus a reasonable profit. He must sell it at the Pittsburgh price plus the railroad freight rate from Pittsburgh to the point of delivery. Chicago steel customers were by this pricing plan thus arbitrarily required to pay for Chicago produced steel the Pittsburgh base price plus what it would have cost to ship the steel by rail from Pittsburgh to Chicago had it been shipped. The theoretical cost of this fictitious shipment became known as "phantom freight." But had it been economically possible under this plan for a Chicago producer to ship his steel to Pittsburgh, his "delivered price" would have been merely the Pittsburgh price, although he actually would have been required to pay the freight from Chicago to Pittsburgh. Thus the "delivered price" under these latter circumstances required a Chicago (non-basing point) producer to "absorb" freight costs. That is, such a seller's net returns became smaller and smaller as his deliveries approached closer and closer to the basing point.

Several results obviously flow from use of a single basing point system such as "Pittsburgh plus" originally was. One is that the "delivered prices" of all producers in every locality where the deliveries are made are always the same regardless of the producers' different freight costs. Another is that sales made by a non-base mill for delivery at different localities result in net receipts to the seller which vary in amounts equivalent to the "phantom freight" included in, or the "freight absorption" taken from the "delivered price."

As commonly employed by respondents, the basing point system is not single but multiple. That is, instead of one basing point, like that in "Pittsburgh plus," a number of basing point localities are used. In the multiple basing point system, just as in the single basing point system, freight absorption or phantom freight is an element of the delivered price on all sales not governed by a basing point actually located at the seller's mill. And all sellers quote identical delivered prices in any given locality regardless of their different costs of production and their different freight expenses. Thus the multiple and single systems function in the same general manner and produce the same consequences—identity of prices and diversity of net returns.

It is strongly urged that the Commission failed to find, as charged in both counts of the complaint, that the respondents had by combination, agreements, or understandings among themselves utilized the multiple basing point delivered price system as a restraint to accomplish uniform prices and terms of sale. A subsidiary contention is that assuming the Commission did so find, there is no substantial evidence to support such a finding. We think that adequate findings of combination were made and that the findings have support in the evidence. . . .

Thus we have a complaint which charged collective action by respondents designed to maintain a sales technique that restrained competition, detailed findings of collective activities by groups of respondents to achieve that end, then a general finding that respondents maintained the combination, and finally an order prohibiting the continuance of the combination. It seems impossible to conceive that anyone reading these findings in their entirety could doubt that the Commission found that respondents collectively maintained a multiple basing point delivered price system for the purpose of suppressing competition in cement sales. The findings are sufficient. . . .

When the Commission rendered its decision there were about 80 cement manufacturing companies in the United States operating about 150 mills. Ten companies controlled more than half of the mills and there were substantial corporate affiliations among many of the others. This concentration of productive capacity made concerted action far less difficult than it would otherwise have been. The belief is prevalent in the industry that because of the standardized nature of cement, among other reasons, price competition is wholly unsuited to it. That belief is historic. It has resulted in concerted activities to devise means and measures to do away with competition in the industry. Out of those activities came the multiple basing point delivered price system. Evidence shows it to be a handy instrument to bring about elimination of any kind of price competition. The use of the multiple basing point delivered price system by the cement producers has been coincident with a situation whereby for many years, with rare exceptions, cement has been offered for sale in every given locality at identical prices and terms by all producers. Thousands of secret sealed bids have been received by public agencies which corresponded in prices of cement down to a fractional part of a penny. . . .

The Commission did not adopt the views of the economists produced by the respondents. It decided that even though competition might tend to drive the price of standardized products to a uniform level, such a tendency alone could not account for the almost perfect identity in prices, discounts, and cement containers which had prevailed for so long a time in the cement industry.

The Commission held that the uniformity and absence of competition in the industry were the results of understandings or agreements entered into or carried out by concert of the Institute and the other respondents. It may possibly be true, as respondents' economists testified, that cement producers will, without agreement express or implied and without understanding explicit or tacit, always and at all times (for such has been substantially the case here) charge for their cement precisely, to the fractional part of a penny, the price their competitors charge. Certainly it runs counter to what many people have believed, namely, that without agreement, prices will vary—that the desire to sell will sometimes be so strong that a seller will be willing to lower his prices and take his chances. We therefore hold that the Commission was not compelled to accept the views of respondents' economist-witnesses that active competition was bound to produce uniform cement prices. . . .

The Commission's order should not have been set aside by the Circuit Court of Appeals. Its judgment is reversed and the case is remanded to that court with directions to enforce the order.

United States v. Container Corp. of America

393 U.S. 333 (1969)

MR. JUSTICE DOUGLAS delivered the Opinion of the Court.

This is a civil antitrust action charging a price-fixing agreement in violation of §1 of the Sherman Act. The District Court dismissed the complaint. . . .

Here all that was present was a request by each defendant of its competitor for information as to the most recent price charged or quoted, whenever it needed such information and whenever it was not available from another source. Each defendant on receiving that request usually furnished the data with the expectation that it would be furnished reciprocal information when it wanted it. That concerted action is of course sufficient to establish the combination or conspiracy, the initial ingredient of a violation of §1 of the Sherman Act.

There was of course freedom to withdraw from the agreement. But the fact remains that when a defendant requested and received price information, it was affirming its willingness to furnish information in return.

There was to be sure an infrequency and irregularity of price exchanges between the defendants; and often the data were available from the records of the defendants or from the customers themselves. Yet the essence of the agreement was to furnish price information whenever requested.

Moreover, although the most recent price charged or quoted was sometimes fragmentary, each defendant had the manuals with which it could compute the price charged by a competitor on a specific order to a specific customer.

Further, the price quoted was the current price which a customer would need to pay in order to obtain products from the defendant furnishing the data.

The defendants account for about 90% of the shipment of corrugated containers from plants in the Southeastern United States. While containers vary as to dimensions, weight, color, and so on, they are substantially identical, no matter who produces them, when made to particular specifications. The prices paid depend on price alternatives. Suppliers when seeking new or additional business or keeping old customers, do not exceed a competitor's price. It is common for purchasers to buy from two or more suppliers concurrently. A defendant supplying a customer with containers would usually quote the same price on additional orders, unless costs had changed. Yet where a competitor was charging a particular price, a defendant would normally quote the same price or even a lower price.

The exchange of price information seemed to have the effect of keeping prices within a fairly narrow ambit. Capacity has exceeded the demand from 1955 to 1963, the period covered by the complaint, and the trend of corrugated container prices has been downward. Yet despite this excess capacity and the downward trend of prices, the industry has expanded in the Southeast from 30 manufacturers with 49 plants to 51 manufacturers with 98 plants. An abundance of raw materials and machinery makes entry into the industry easy with an investment of $50,000 to $75,000. . . .

Price information exchanged in some markets may have no effect on a truly competitive price. But the corrugated container industry is dominated by relatively few sellers. The product is fungible and the competition for sales is on price. The demand is inelastic, as buyers place orders only for immediate, short-run needs. The exchange of price data tends toward price uniformity. For a lower price does not mean a larger share of the available business but a sharing of the existing business at a lower return. Stabilizing prices as well as raising them is within the ban of §1 of the Sherman Act. . . . The inferences are irresistible that the exchange of price information has had an anticompetitive effect in the industry, chilling the vigor of price competition.

Goldfarb v. Virginia State Bar

421 U.S. 773 (1975)

MR. CHIEF JUSTICE BURGER delivered the opinion of the Court.

We granted certiorari to decide whether a minimum-fee schedule for lawyers published by the Fairfax County Bar Association and enforced by the Virginia State Bar violates Section 1 of the Sherman Act. . . .

In 1971 petitioners, husband and wife, contracted to buy a home in Fairfax County, Va. The financing agency required them to secure title insurance; this required a title examination, and only a member of the Virginia State Bar could legally perform that service. . . . Petitioners therefore contacted a lawyer who quoted them the precise fee suggested in a minimum-fee schedule published by respondent Fairfax County Bar Association; the lawyer told them that it was his policy to keep his charges in line with the minimum-fee schedule which provided for a fee of 1% of the value of the property involved. Petitioners then tried to find a lawyer who would examine the title for less than the fee fixed by the schedule. They sent letters to 36 other Fairfax County lawyers requesting their fees. Nineteen replied, and none indicated that he would charge less than the rate fixed by the schedule; several stated that they knew of no attorney who would do so.

The fee schedule the lawyers referred to is a list of recommended minimum prices for common legal services. Respondent Fairfax County Bar Association published the fee schedule although, as a purely voluntary association of attorneys, the County Bar has no formal power to enforce it. Enforcement has been provided by respondent Virginia State Bar which is the administrative agency through which the Virginia Supreme Court regulated the practice of law in that State; membership in the State Bar is required in order to practice in Virginia. Although the State Bar has never taken formal disciplinary action to compel adherence to any fee schedule, it has published reports condoning fee schedules, and has issued two ethical opinions indicating that fee schedules cannot be ignored. The most recent opinion states that "evidence that an attorney habitually charges less than the suggested minimum fee schedule adopted by his local bar Association, raises a presumption that such lawyer is guilty of misconduct. . . ." (Virginia State Bar Committee on Legal Ethics. Opinion No. 170, May 29, 1971.)

Because petitioners could not find a lawyer willing to charge a fee lower than the schedule dictated, they had their title examined by the lawyer they had first contacted. They then brought this class action against the State Bar and the County Bar alleging that the operation of the minimum-fee schedule, as applied to fees for legal services relating to residential real estate transactions, constitutes price fixing in violation of §1 of the Sherman Act. . . .

Our inquiry can be divided into four steps: did respondents engage in price fixing? If so, are there activities in interstate commerce or do they affect interstate commerce? If so, are the activities exempt from the Sherman Act because they involve a "learned profession"? If not, are the activities "state action" within the meaning of *Parker v. Brown,* 317 U.S. 341 (1943), and therefore exempt from the Sherman Act?

The County Bar argues that because the fee schedule is merely advisory, the schedule and its enforcement mechanism do not constitute price fixing. Its purpose, the argument continues, is only to provide legitimate information to aid member lawyers in complying with Virginia professional regulations. . . .

A purely advisory fee schedule issued to provide guidelines, or an exchange of price information without a showing of an actual restraint on trade, would present us with a different question. . . . The fee schedule was enforced through the prospect of professional discipline from the State Bar, and the desire of attorneys to comply with announced professional norms. . . . The County Bar makes much of the fact that it is a voluntary organization; however, the ethical opinions issued by the State Bar provide that any lawyer, whether or not a member of his county bar association, may be disciplined for "habitually charg[ing] less than the suggested minimum fee schedule adopted by his local bar Association. . . ." These factors coalesced to create a pricing system that consumers could not realistically escape. On this record respondents' activities constitute a classic illustration of price fixing.

The County Bar argues, that any effect on interstate commerce caused by the fee schedule's restraint on legal services was incidental and remote. In its view the legal services, which are performed wholly intrastate, are essentially local in nature and therefore a restraint with respect to them can never substantially affect interstate commerce. Further, the County Bar maintains, there was no showing here that the fee schedule and its enforcement mechanism increased fees, and that even if they did there was no showing that such an increase deterred any prospective homeowner from buying in Fairfax County.

As the District Court found, "a significant portion of funds furnished for the purchasing of homes in Fairfax County comes from without the State of Virginia," and "significant amounts of loans on Fairfax County real estate are guaranteed by the United States Veterans Administration and Department of Housing and Urban Development, both headquartered in the District of Columbia." Given the substantial volume involved, and the inseparability of this particular legal service from the interstate aspects of real estate transactions, we conclude that interstate commerce has been sufficiently affected.

The fact that there was no showing that home buyers were discouraged by the challenged activities does not mean that interstate commerce was not affected. Otherwise, the magnitude of the effect would control, and our cases have shown that, once an effect is shown, no specific magnitude need be proved.

The County Bar argues that Congress never intended to include the learned professions within the terms "trade or commerce" in Section 1 of the Sherman Act, and therefore the sale of professional services is exempt from the Act. No explicit exemption or legislative history is provided to support this contention; also, the County Bar maintains that competition is inconsistent with the practice of a profession because enhancing profit is not the goal of professional activities; the goal is to provide services necessary to the community. That indeed, is the classic basis traditionally advanced to distinguish professions from trades, businesses, and other occupations, but it loses some of its force when used to support the fee control activities involved here.

In arguing that learned professions are not "trade or commerce" the County Bar seeks a total exclusion from antitrust regulation. Whether state regulation is active or dormant, real or theoretical, lawyers would be able to adopt anticompetitive practices with impunity. We cannot find support for the proposition that Congress intended any such sweeping exclusion. Congress intended to strike as broadly as it could in Section 1 of the Sherman Act, and to read into it so wide an exemption as that urged on us would be at odds with that purpose.

In *Parker v. Brown,* 317 U.S. 341 (1943), the Court held that an anticompetitive marketing program which "derived its authority and its efficacy from the legislative command of the state" was not a violation of the Sherman Act because the Act was intended to regulate private practices and not to prohibit a State from imposing a restraint as an act of government. Respondent State Bar and respondent County Bar both seek to avail themselves of this so-called state-action exemption.

Through its legislature Virginia has authorized its highest court to regulate the practice of law. That court has adopted ethical codes which deal in part with fees, and far from exercising state power to authorize binding price fixing, explicitly directed lawyers not "to be controlled" by fee schedules. The County Bar, although it is a voluntary association and not a state agency, claims that the ethical codes and the activities of the State Bar "prompted" it to issue fee schedules and thus its actions, too, are state action for Sherman Act purposes. . . . The Supreme

Court's ethical codes mention advisory fee schedules, they do not direct either respondent to supply them, or require the type of price floor which arose from respondents' activities. It is not enough that, as the County Bar puts it, anticompetitive conduct is "prompted" by state action; rather, anticompetitive activities must be compelled by direction of the State acting as a sovereign. . . .

We recognize that the states have a compelling interest in the practice of professions within their boundaries, and that as part of their power to protect the public health, safety, and other valid interests they have broad power to establish standards for licensing practitioners and regulating the practice of professions. . . . In holding that certain anticompetitive conduct by lawyers is within the reach of the Sherman Act we intend no diminution of the authority of the State to regulate its professions.

The judgment of the Court of Appeals is reversed and the case is remanded to that court with orders to remand to the District Court for further proceedings consistent with this opinion.

CHAPTER 4

MONOPOLIZATION

Section 2 of the Sherman Act is much less clear in meaning than Section 1. Here is where the spectacular dissolution cases arise. They are usually very long and costly and the government often loses. Moreover, even when the government does win, there is often no dissolution. Still many people feel that here is where the monopoly problem is most severe.

The Standard Oil case of 1911 was probably the most important decision in antitrust history. It was the first "monopolization" case—it told us what Section 2 meant. It was also the first (and still is one of a few) dissolution case in antitrust history. And it transformed what is now our most important industry. It provided for the distribution of shares in the Standard Oil subsidiaries to the stockholders of the parent companies. Since the Rockefellers had a major interest in Standard Oil of New Jersey, they had a controlling interest in the successor companies when they were set up. As a result, one could reasonably doubt how strenuously the companies competed among themselves in the 1920s and 1930s. However, the Rockefellers' interest in these companies is minor today: Chase Manhattan (traditionally the Rockefeller bank), the Rockefellers, and their various foundations had 2.08 percent of the voting stock of Exxon (formerly Standard Oil of New Jersey) and smaller shares in the other successor companies in 1976.[1] They have entered each others' territories and have competed actively among themselves. The decision is the most important reason why we have fifteen major oil companies while most of the other countries in the world have one or two, or at least had that few until the "independents" entered in the postwar years. Most of those

---

[1] U.S. Senate, Committee on Governmental Affairs, Subcommittee on Reports, Accounting and Management, *Voting Rights in Major Corporations,* General Printing Office, 1978, pp. 30–251.

"independents" were U.S. firms including a number of the Standard Oil successor companies. In 1972 the major successor firms (Exxon, Standard Oil of California, Standard Oil of Indiana, Mobil, ARCO, SOHIO, Conoco, and Marathon) had 37 percent of U.S. refining capacity. The largest of them, Exxon, had only 9 percent.[2] The old Standard Oil had 82 percent at the turn of the century and about 64 percent in 1911 at the time of this decision.[3]

More than any other case, Standard Oil determined what was necessary for a successful Section 2 suit. What did it take? If your great grandfather had developed a superior way to make gimlets and had, as a result, kept the field to himself, would he have lost a Section 2 case in 1911? Should he have lost from an economic point of view? It is widely believed that predation played a major role in Standard Oil's dominant position: that is, that Standard Oil had often cut prices below cost and held them there until its rivals succumbed or joined the trust. Some economists have concluded that this didn't happen.[4] They argue that collusion or merger is always cheaper than predation and that in fact there is very little evidence of predation. In fact, some firms sold out to Standard Oil and then reentered the industry. Actually, predation got only minor attention in the 1911 decision. The Court's main emphasis was on mergers and on discriminatory rebates the firm had won from the railroads. Do you think such mergers and rebates were against the public interest?

The Alcoa case is another Section 2 case of Standard Oil proportions. At the time that it was decided it was hailed as a harbinger of the "New Sherman Act." A major issue was the market definition. How do you feel about the way the issue was resolved? In particular, how do you feel about the treatment of secondary aluminum? If we had a monopolization case against General Motors, how would you react to a proposal that the market should be defined to include secondhand cars, including those that GM produced in the past (about half of them)? How can monopoly be "thrust upon" a firm? Try the newspapers. In a majority of cities today there is only one newspaper publisher. A generation ago there were two or more in most large cities. Was monopoly thrust upon the survivors? Are they sitting ducks for a series of Alcoa cases?

Monopolization cases are famous for being long and costly. Suppose Congress passed a law saying that any firm with more than 65 percent of a market should be dissolved unless it could show that it got its position due to "superior skill, foresight, and industry." Do you think that cases would be shorter and less costly? If you were in charge of such a case at the Antitrust Division, how would you answer evidence that monopoly was due to superior skill, foresight, and industry?

The United Shoe Machinery case is a district court decision, but it was affirmed by the Supreme Court in the following year. Unlike Alcoa, it emphasized practices of the firm as well as its large market share. Do its practices strike you as abnor-

---

[2] T. D. Duchesneau, *Competition in the U.S. Energy Industry*, Ballinger, 1975, p. 44.

[3] H. F. Williamson et al., *The American Petroleum Industry, 1899–1959*, Northwestern University Press, Chicago, 1963, p. 7.

[4] J. S. McGee, "Predatory Pricing: The Standard Oil (N.J.) Case," *Journal of Law and Economics*, vol. I, October 1958, pp. 137–169.

mal? If a smaller firm such as Compo had used them, should they have been subject to antitrust prohibitions? Why is their use by United Shoe Machinery different? Or do you think it should be different?

The United Shoe Machinery case is more representative of postwar Section 2 cases than is Alcoa. Section 2 cases typically revolve around market share and anticompetitive practices.

The *FTC v. Du Pont* (titanium dioxide) case was an attempt to apply the Alcoa criteria directly. The trial staff's only charge was that Du Pont, with a temporary technical advantage, set out to attain a dominant position in the market. Is that a satisfactory basis for an antitrust case? What effect would a decision against Du Pont have had on competition? On consumer welfare? Do you think that the Alcoa precedent is dead in view of this decision?

Section 2 of the Sherman Act also prohibits "attempts to monopolize." The meaning of this phrase is even murkier than the verb "to monopolize." The last two cases in this chapter shed a little light on the subject.

In the *Lorain Journal* case, an attempt to monopolize seemed to depend on a particular practice on the part of a firm with a powerful position in local advertising media. Do you think it was really trying to attain monopoly? Does it make any difference?

Klors is different. Klors was an annoying discounter next to a Broadway-Hale store. What do you think made the suppliers behave as they did? Did Broadway-Hale have a chance of attaining monopoly? Do you approve of its actions? Do you think they lessened competition? Should they be prohibited?

Standard Oil Company of New Jersey v. United, States

221 U.S. 1 (1911)

MR. CHIEF JUSTICE WHITE delivered the opinion of the Court:

The Standard Oil Company of New Jersey and thirty-three other corporations, John D. Rockefeller, William Rockefeller, and five other individual defendants, prosecute this appeal to reverse a decree of the court below. . . .

Reiterating in substance the averments that both the Standard Oil Trust from 1882 to 1899, and the Standard Oil Company of New Jersey, since 1899, had monopolized and restrained interstate commerce in petroleum and its products, the bill at great length additionally set forth various means by which, during the second and third periods [1882–1899 and after 1899], in addition to the effect occasioned by the combination of alleged previously independent concerns, the monopoly and restraint complained of were continued. Without attempting to follow the elaborate averments on these subjects, spread over fifty-seven pages of the printed record, it suffices to say that such averments may properly be grouped under the following heads: Rebates, preferences, and other discriminatory practices in favor of the combination by railroad companies; restraint and monopolization by control of pipe lines, and unfair practices against competing pipe lines; contracts with competitors in restraint of trade; unfair methods of competition, such as local price cutting at the points where necessary to suppress competition; espionage of the business of competitors, the operation of bogus independent companies, and payment of rebates on oil, with the like intent; the division of the United States into districts, and the limiting the operations of the various subsidiary corporations as to such districts so that competition in the sale of petroleum products between such corporations had been entirely eliminated and destroyed; and finally reference was made to what was alleged to be the "enormous and unreasonable profits" earned by the Standard Oil Trust and the Standard Oil Company as a result of the alleged monopoly; which presumably was averred as a means of . . . inferring the scope and power acquired by the alleged combination. . . .

In view of the common law and the law in this country as to restraint of trade, which we have reviewed, and the illuminating effect which that history must have under the rule to which we have referred, we think it results:

a. That the context manifests that the statute was drawn in the light of the existing practical conception of the law of restraint of trade, because it groups as within that class, not only contracts which were in restraint of trade in the subjective sense, but all contracts or acts which theoretically were attempts to monopolize, yet which in practice had come to be considered as in restraint of trade in a broad sense.

b. That in view of the many new forms of contracts and combinations which were being evolved from existing economic conditions, it was deemed essential by an all-embracing enumeration to make sure that no form of contract or combination by which an undue restraint of interstate or foreign commerce, but to protect that commerce from being restrained by methods, whether old or new, which would constitute an interference—that is, an undue restraint.

c. And as the contracts or acts embraced in the provision were not expressly defined, since the enumeration addressed itself simply to classes of acts, those classes being broad enough to embrace every conceivable contract or combination which could be made concerning trade or commerce or the subjects of such commerce, and thus caused any act done by any of the enumerated methods anywhere in the whole field of human activity to be illegal if in restraint of trade, it inevitably follows that the provision necessarily called for the exercise of judgment which required that some standard should be resorted to for the purpose of determining whether the prohibition contained in the statute had or had not in any given case been violated. Thus not specifying, but indubitably contemplating and requiring a standard, it follows that it was intended that the standard of reason which had been applied at the common law and in this country in dealing with subjects of character embraced by the statute was intended to be the measure used for the purpose of determining whether, in a given case, a particular act had or had not brought about the wrong against which the statute provided.

And a consideration of the text of the 2nd section serves to establish that it was intended to supplement the 1st, and to make sure that by no possible guise could the public policy embodied in the 1st section be frustrated or evaded. The prohibition of the 2nd embraces "every person who shall monopolize, or attempt to monopolize, or combine or conspire with any other person or persons to monopolize, any part of the trade or commerce among the several states or with foreign nations. . . ."

Undoubtedly, the words "to monopolize" and "monopolize," as used in the section, reach every act bringing about the prohibited results. The ambiguity, if any, is involved in determining what is intended by monopolize. But this ambiguity is readily dispelled in the light of the previous history of the law of restraint of trade to which we have referred and the indication which it gives of the practical evolution by which monopoly and the acts which produce the same result as monopoly, that is, an undue restraint of the course of trade, all came to be spoken of as, and to be indeed synonymous with, restraint of trade. In other words, having by the 1st section forbidden all means of monopolizing trade, that is, unduly restraining it by means of every contract, combination, etc., the 2d section seeks, if possible, to make the prohibitions of the act all the more complete and perfect by embracing all attempts to reach the end prohibited by the 1st section, that is, restraints of trade, by any attempt to monopolize, or monopolization thereof, even although the acts by which such results are attempted to be brought about or are brought about be not embraced within the general enumeration of the 1st section. And, of course, when the 2d section is thus harmonized with and made, as it was intended to be, the complement of the 1st, it becomes obvious that the criteria to be resorted to in any given case for the purpose of ascertaining whether violations of the section have been committed is the rule of reason guided by the established law and by the plain duty to enforce the prohibitions of the act, and thus the public policy which its restrictions were obviously enacted to subserve. . . .

Giving to the facts just stated the weight which it was deemed they were entitled to, in the light afforded by the proof of other cognate facts and circumstances, the court below held that the acts and dealings established by the proof operated to destroy the "potentiality of competition" which otherwise would have existed to such an extent as to cause the transfers of stock which were made to the New Jersey corporation and the control resulted over the many and various subsidiary corporations to be a combination or conspiracy in restraint of trade, in violation of the 1st section of the act, but also to be an attempt to monopolize and monopolization bringing about a perennial violation of the 2d section. . . .

a. Because the unification of power and control over petroleum and its products which was the inevitable result of the combining in the New Jersey corporation by the increase of its stock and the transfer to it of the stocks of so many other corporations, aggregating so vast a capital, gives rise, in and of itself, in the absence of countervailing circumstances, to say the least, to the prima facie presumption of intent and purpose to maintain the dominancy over the oil industry, not as a result of normal methods of industrial development, but by new means of combination which were resorted to in order that greater power might be added than would otherwise have arisen had normal methods been followed, the whole with the purpose of excluding others from the trade, and thus centralizing in the combination a perpetual control of the movements of petroleum and its products in the channels of interstate commerce.

b. Because the prima facie presumption of intent to restrain trade, to monopolize and to bring about monopolization, resulting from the act of expanding the stock of the New Jersey corporation and vesting it with such vast control of the oil industry, is made conclusive by considering (1) the conduct of the persons or corporations who were mainly instrumental in bringing about the extension of power in the New Jersey corporation before the consummation of that result and prior to the formation of the trust agreements of 1879 and 1882; (2) by considering the proof as to what was done under those agreements and the acts which immediately preceded the vesting of power in the New Jersey corporation, as well as by weighing the modes in which the power vested in that corporation has been exerted and the results which have arisen from it.

Recurring to the acts done by the individuals or corporations who were mainly instrumental in bringing about the expansion of the New Jersey corporation during the period prior to the formation of the trust agreements of 1879 and 1882, including those agreements, not for the purpose of weighing the substantial merit of the numerous charges of wrongdoing made during which period, but solely as an aid for discovering intent and purpose, we think no disinterested mind can survey the period in question without being irresistibly driven to the conclusion that the very genius for commercial development and organization which would seem was manifested from the beginning soon begot an intent and purpose to exclude others which was frequently manifested by acts and dealings wholly inconsistent with the theory that they were made with the single conception of advancing the development of business power by usual methods, but which, on the contrary, necessarily involved the intent to drive others from the field and to exclude them from their right to trade, and thus accomplish the mastery which was the end in view. . . .

We are thus brought to the last subject which we are called upon to consider, viz.:

. . . The remedy to be administered.

It may be conceded that ordinarily where it was found that acts had been done in violation of the statute, adequate measure of relief would result from restraining the doing of such acts in the future. But in a case like this, where the condition which has been brought about in violation of the statute, in and of itself is not only a continued attempt to monopolize, but also a monopolization, the duty to enforce the statute requires the application of broader and more controlling remedies. As penalties which are not authorized by law may not be inflicted by judicial authority, it follows that to meet the situation with which we are confronted the application of remedies two-fold in character becomes essential: 1st. To forbid the doing in the future of acts like those which we have found to have been done in the past which would be violative of the statute. 2d. The exertion of such measure of relief as will effectually dissolve the combination found to exist in violation of the statute, and thus neutralize the extension and continually operating force which the possession of the power unlawfully obtained has brought and will continue to bring about.

The court below . . . adjudged that the New Jersey corporation, in so far as it held the stock of the various corporations recited in . . . the decree, or controlled the same, was a combination in violation of the 1st section of the act, and an attempt to monopolize or a monopolization contrary to the 2d section of the act. It commanded the dissolution of the combination, and therefore in effect directed the transfer by the New Jersey corporation back to the stockholders of the various subsidiary corporations entitled to the same of the stock which had been turned over to the New Jersey company in exchange for its stock. . . . So far as the owners of the stock of the subsidiary corporations and the corporations themselves were concerned after the stock had been transferred, Section 6 of the decree enjoined them from in any way conspiring or combining to violate the act, or to monopolize or attempt to monopolize in virtue of their ownership of the stock transferred to them, and prohibited all agreements between the subsidiary corporations or other stockholders in the future, tending to produce or bring about further violations of the act.

So far as the decree held that the ownership of the stock of the New Jersey corporation constituted a combination in violation of the 1st section and an attempt to create a monopoly or to monopolize under the 2d section, and commanded the dissolution of the combination, the decree was clearly appropriate. And this also is true of Section 5 of the decree, which restrained both the New

Jersey corporation and the subsidiary corporations from doing anything which would recognize or give effect to further ownership in the New Jersey corporation of the stocks which were ordered to be retransferred. . . .

Our conclusion is that the decree below was right and should be affirmed, except as to the minor matters concerning which we have indicated the decree should be modified. Our order will therefore be one of affirmance with directions, however, to modify the decree in accordance with this opinion. The court below to retain jurisdiction to the extent necessary to compel compliance in every respect with its decree. And it is so ordered.

United States v. Aluminum Co. of America

148 F.2nd 416 (1945)

L. HAND, Circuit Judge.

[This case was heard on appeal at a Court of Appeals rather than at the Supreme Court. The Supreme Court did not have a quorum because five of its members disqualified themselves due to their earlier involvement in the case. Special legislation of 1944 provided that in such cases the Court of Appeals would make the final decision. The decision in this case was cited as a relevant precedent in the American Tobacco case decided by the Supreme Court in the following year.]

"Alcoa," is a corporation, organized under the laws of Pennsylvania on September 18, 1888; . . . It has always been engaged in the production and sale of "ingot" aluminum, and since 1895 also in the fabrication of the metal into many finished and semi-finished articles.

[Alcoa had a legally enforced monopoly based on patents until 1909. The corporation entered into a number of agreements to buy large amounts of electricity on condition that the suppliers would not sell to any other producer of aluminum. Alcoa or its subsidiaries joined with foreign producers in four successive "cartels" that controlled or prohibited their sales in the United States. These agreements and cartels were struck down in a consent degree in 1912. On at least three occasions after 1912, Alcoa acquired the properties of other firms attempting to enter the aluminum industry in the United States or in Canada.]

None of the foregoing facts are in dispute, and the most important question in the case is whether the monopoly in "Alcoa's" production of "virgin" ingot, secured by the two patents until 1909, and in part perpetuated between 1909 and 1912 by the unlawful practices, forbidden by the decree of 1912, continued for the ensuing twenty-eight years; and whether, if it did, it was unlawful under Section 2 of the Sherman Act. It is undisputed that throughout this period "Alcoa" continued to be the single producer of "virgin" ingot in the United States; and the plaintiff argues that this without more was enough to make it an unlawful monopoly. It also takes an alternative position; that in any event during this period "Alcoa" consistently pursued unlawful exclusionary practices, which made its dominant position certainly unlawful, even though it would not have been, had it been retained only by "natural growth." Finally, it asserts that many of these practices were of themselves unlawful, as contracts in restraint of trade under Section 1 of the Act. "Alcoa's" position is that the fact that it alone continued to make "virgin" ingot in this country did not, and does not, give it a monopoly of the market; that it was always subject to the competition of imported "virgin" ingot, and of what is called "secondary" ingot; and that even if it had not been, its monopoly would not have been retained by unlawful means, but would have been the result of a growth which the Act does not forbid, even when it results in a monopoly. We shall first consider the amount and character of this competition; next, how far it established a monopoly; and finally, if it did, whether that monopoly was unlawful under Section 2 of the Act.

From 1902 onward until 1928 "Alcoa" was making ingot in Canada through a wholly owned subsidiary; so much of this as it imported into the United States it is proper to include with what it produced here. In the year 1912 the sum of these two items represented nearly ninety-one percent of the total amount of "virgin" ingot available for sale in this country. This percentage varied year by year up to and including 1938: in 1913 it was about seventy-two percent; in 1921 about sixty-eight percent; in 1922 about seventy-two; with these exceptions it was always over eighty percent of the total and for the last five years 1934–1938 inclusive it averaged over ninety percent. The effect of such a proportion of the production upon the market we reserve for the time being, for it will be necessary first to consider the nature and uses of "secondary" ingot, the name by which the industry knows ingot made from aluminum scrap. . . .

There are various ways of computing "Alcoa's" control of the aluminum market—as distinct from its production—depending upon what one regards as competing in that market. The judge figured its share—during the years 1929–1938, inclusive—as only about thirty-three percent; to do so he included "secondary," and excluded that part of "Alcoa's" own production which it fabricated and did not therefore sell as ingot. If, on the other hand, "Alcoa's" total production, fabricated and sold, be included, and balanced against the sum of imported "virgin" and "secondary," its share of the market was in the neighborhood of sixty-four percent for that period. The percentage we have already mentioned—over ninety—results only if we both include all "Alcoa's" production and exclude "secondary." That percentage is enough to constitute a monopoly; it is doubtful whether sixty or sixty-four percent would be enough; and certainly thirty-three percent is not. Hence it is necessary to settle what we shall treat as competing in the ingot market. That part of its production which "Alcoa" itself fabricates, does not of course ever reach the market as ingot; and we recognize that it is only when a restriction of production either inevitably affects prices, or is intended to do so, that it violates Section 1 of the Act. However, even though we were to assume that a monopoly is unlawful under Section 2 only in case it controls prices, the ingot fabricated by "Alcoa," necessarily had a direct effect upon the ingot market. All ingot—with trifling exceptions—is used to fabricate intermediate, or end, products; and therefore all intermediate, or end, products which "Alcoa" fabricates and sells, pro tanto reduce the demand for ingot itself. . . .

As to "secondary," . . . for certain purposes the industry will not accept it at all; but for those for which it will, the difference in price is ordinarily not very great; the judge found that it was between one and two cents a pound, hardly enough margin on which to base a monopoly. Indeed, there are times when all differential disappears, and "secondary" will actually sell at a higher price: i.e., when there is a supply available which contains just the alloy that a fabricator needs for the article which he proposes to make. Taking the industry as a whole, we can say nothing more definite than that, although "secondary" does not compete at all in some uses, (whether because of "sales resistance" only, or because of actual metallurical inferiority), for most purposes it competes upon a substantial equality with "virgin." On these facts the judge found that "every pound of secondary or scrap aluminum which is sold in commerce displaces a pound of virgin aluminum which otherwise would, or might have been, sold." We agree: so far as "secondary" supplies the demand of such fabricators as will accept it, it increases the amount of "virgin" which must seek sale elsewhere; and it therefore results that the supply of that part of the demand which will accept only "virgin" becomes greater in proportion as "secondary" drives away "virgin" from the demand which will accept "secondary." At any given moment therefore "secondary" competes with "virgin" in the ingot market; further, it can, and probably does, set a limit or "ceiling" beyond which the price of "virgin" cannot go, for the cost of its production will in the end depend only upon the expense of scavenging and reconditioning. It might seem for this reason that in estimating "Alcoa's control over the ingot market, we ought to include the supply of "secondary," as the judge did. . . .

In the case of a monopoly of any commodity which does not disappear in use and which can be salvaged, the supply seeking sale at any moment will be made up of two components: (1) the part which the putative monopolist can immediately produce and sell; and (2) the part which has been, or can be, reclaimed out of what he has produced and sold in the past. By hypothesis he presently controls the first of these components; the second, he has controlled in the past, although he no longer does. During the period when he did control the second, if he was aware of his interest, he was guided not alone by its effect at that time upon the market, but by his knowledge that some part of it was likely to be reclaimed and seek the future market. That consideration will to some extent always affect his production. . . . Thus, in the case at bar "Alcoa" always knew that the future supply of ingot would be made up in part of what it produced at the time, and, if it was as farsighted as it proclaims itself, that consideration must have had its share in determining how much to produce. . . . The competition of "secondary" must therefore be disregarded, as soon as we consider the position of "Alcoa" over a period of years; it was as much within "Alcoa's" control as was the production of the "virgin" from which it had been derived. . . .

We conclude therefore that "Alcoa's" control over the ingot market must be reckoned at over ninety percent; that being the proportion which its production bears to imported "virgin" ingot. If the fraction which it did not supply were the product of domestic manufacture there could be no doubt that this percentage gave it a monopoly—lawful or unlawful, as the case might be. The producer of so large a proportion of the supply has complete control within certain limits. It is true that, if by raising the price he reduces the amount which can be marketed— as always, or almost always, happens—he may invite the expansion of the small producers who will try to fill the place left open; nevertheless, not only is there an inevitable lag in this, but the large producer is in a strong position to check such competition. . . .

The judge found that, over the whole half century of its existence, "Alcoa's" profits upon capital invested, after payment of income taxes, had been only about ten percent, and, although the plaintiff puts this figure a little higher, the difference is negligible. . . . [I]t would be hard to say that "Alcoa" had made exorbitant profits on ingot, if it is proper to allocate the profit upon the whole business proportionately among all its products—ingot, and fabrications from ingot. . . .

It may be retorted that it was for the plaintiff to prove what was the profit upon ingot in accordance with the general burden of proof. We think not. Having proved that "Alcoa" had a monopoly of the domestic ingot market, the plaintiff had gone far enough; if it was an excuse, that "Alcoa" had not abused its power, it lay upon "Alcoa" to prove that it had not. But the whole issue is irrelevant anyway for it is no excuse for "monopolizing" a market that the monopoly has not been used to extract from the consumer more than a "fair" profit. The Act has wider purposes. Indeed, even though we disregarded all but economic considerations, it would by no means follow that such concentration of producing power is to be desired, when it has not been used extortionately. Many people believe that possession of unchallenged economic power deadens initiative, discourages thrift and depresses energy; that immunity from competition is a narcotic, and rivalry is a stimulant, to industrial progress; that the spur of constant stress is necessary to counteract an inevitable disposition to let well enough alone. Such people believe that competitors, versed in the craft as no consumer can be, will be quick to detect opportunities for saving and new shifts in production, and be eager to profit by them. In any event the mere fact that a producer, having command of the domestic market, has not been able to make more than a "fair" profit, is no evidence that a "fair" profit could not have been made at lower prices. True, it might have been thought adequate to condemn only those monopolies which could not show that they had exercised the highest possible ingenuity, had adopted every possible economy, had anticipated every conceivable improvement, stimulated every possible demand. No doubt, that would be one way of dealing with the matter, although it would imply constant scrutiny and constant supervision, such as courts are unable to provide. Be that as it may, that was not the way that Congress chose; it did not condone "good trusts" and condemn "bad" ones; it forbad all. Moreover, in so doing it was not necessarily actuated by economic motives alone. It is possible, because of its indirect social or moral effect, to prefer a system of small producers each dependent for his success upon his own skill and character, to one in which the great mass of those engaged must accept the direction of a few. These considerations, which we have suggested only as possible purposes of the Act, we think the decisions prove to have been in fact its purposes. . . .

The only possible difference between them [price fixing agreements] and a monopoly is that while a monopoly necessarily involves an equal, or even greater, power to fix prices, its mere existence might be thought not to constitute an exercise of that power. That distinction is nevertheless purely formal; it would be valid only so long as the monopoly remained wholly inert; it would disappear as soon as the monopoly began to operate; for, when it did—that is, as soon as it began to sell at all—it must sell at some price and the only price at which it could sell is a price which it itself fixed. Thereafter the power and its exercise must needs coalesce. Indeed it would be absurd to condemn such contracts unconditionally, and not to extend the condemnation to monopolies; for the contracts are only steps toward that entire control which monopoly confers: they are really partial monopolies. . . .

[T]here can be no doubt that the vice of restrictive contracts and of monopoly is really one, it is the denial to commerce of the supposed protection of competition. To repeat, if the earlier stages are proscribed, when they are parts of a plan, the mere projecting of which condemns them unconditionally, the realization of the plan itself must also be proscribed. . . .

It does not follow because "Alcoa" had such a monopoly, that it "monopolized" the ingot market: it may not have achieved monopoly; monopoly may have been thrust upon it. If it had been a combination of existing smelters which united the whole industry and controlled the production of all aluminum ingot, it would certainly have "monopolized" the market. In several decisions the Supreme Court has decreed the dissolution of such combinations, although they had engaged in no unlawful trade practices. Nevertheless, it is unquestionably true that from the very outset the courts have at least kept in the reserve the possibility that the origin of a monopoly may be critical in determining its legality; and for this they had warrant in some of the congressional debates which accompanied the passage of the Act. This notion has usually been expressed by saying that size does not determine guilt; that there must be some "exclusion" of competitors; that the growth must be something else than "natural" or "normal;" that there must be a "wrongful intent," or some other specific intent; or that some "unduly" coercive means must be used. At times there has been emphasis upon the use of the active verb, "monopolize," as the judge noted in the case at bar. . . . What engendered these compunctions is reasonably plain; persons may unwittingly find themselves in possession of monopoly, automatically so to say: that is, without having intended either to put an end to existing competition, or to prevent competition from arising when none had existed; they may become monopolists by force of accident. Since the Act makes "monopolizing" a crime, as well as a civil wrong, it would be not only unfair, but presumably contrary to the intent of Congress, to include such instances. A market may, for example, be so limited that it is impossible to produce at all and meet the cost of production except by a plant large enough to supply the whole demand. Or there may be changes in taste or in cost which drive out all but one purveyor. A single producer may be the survivor out of a group of active competitors, merely by virtue of his superior skill, foresight and industry. In such cases a strong argument can be made that, although the result may expose the public to the evils of monopoly, the Act does not mean to condemn the resultant of those very forces which it is its prime object to foster: finis opus coronat. The successful competitor, having been urged to compete, must not be turned upon when he wins.

It would completely misconstrue "Alcoa's" position in 1940 to hold that it was the passive beneficiary of a monopoly, following upon an involuntary elimination of competitors by automatically operative economic forces. Already in 1909, when its last lawful monopoly ended, it sought to strengthen its position by unlawful practices, and these concededly continued until 1912. In that year it had two plants in New York, at which it produced less than 42 million pounds of ingot; in 1934 it had five plants (the original two, enlarged; one in Tennessee; one in North Carolina; one in Washington), and its production has risen to about 327 million pounds, an increase of almost eight-fold. Meanwhile not a pound of ingot had been produced by anyone else in the United States. This increase and this continued and undisturbed control did not fall undesigned into "Alcoa's" lap; obviously it could not have done so. It could only have resulted, as it did result, from a persistent determination to maintain the control, with which it found itself vested in 1912. . . . True, it stimulated demand and opened new uses for the metal, but not without making sure that it could supply what it had evoked. There is no dispute to this; "Alcoa" avows it as evidence of the skill, energy and initiative with which it has always conducted its business; as a reason why, having won its way by fair means, it should be commended, and not dismembered. We need charge it with no moral derelictions after 1912; we may assume that all it claims for itself is true. The only question is whether it falls within the exception established in favor of those who do not seek, but cannot avoid, the control of a market. It seems to us that that question scarcely survives its statement. It was not inevitable that it should always anticipate increases in the demand for ingot and be prepared to supply them. Nothing compelled it to keep doubling and redoubling its capacity before others entered the field. It insists that it never excluded competitors; but we can think of no more effective exclusion than progressively to embrace each new opportunity as it opened, and to face every newcomer with new capacity already geared into a great organization, having the advantage of experience, trade connections and the elite of personnel. Only in case we interpret "exclusion" as limited to manuevers not honestly industrial, but actuated solely by a desire to prevent competition, can such a course, indefatigably pursued, be deemed not "exclusionary." So to limit it would in our judgment emasculate the Act; would permit just such consolidations as it was designed to prevent.

In order to fall within Section 2, the monopolist must have both the power to monopolize, and the intent to monopolize. To read the passage as demanding any "specific" intent, makes nonsense of it, for no monopolist monopolizes unconscious of what he is doing. So here, "Alcoa" meant to keep, and did keep, that complete and exclusive hold upon the ingot market with which it started. That was to "monopolize" that market, however innocently it otherwise proceeded. So far as the judgment held that it was not within Section 2, it must be reversed. . . .

Nearly five years have passed since the evidence was closed; during that time the aluminum industry, like most other industries, has been revolutionized by the nation's efforts in a great crisis. That alone would make it impossible to dispose of the action upon the basis of the record as we have it; and so both sides agree; both appeal to us to take "judicial notice" of what has taken place meanwhile, though they differ as to what should be the result. The plaintiff wishes us to enter a judgment that "Alcoa" shall be dissolved, and that we shall direct it presently to submit a plan, whose execution, however, is to be deferred until after the war. It also asks a termination of all shareholding in common between "Alcoa" and "Limited;" and that injunctions shall go against any resumption of the putative unlawful practices. On the other hand, "Alcoa" argues that, when we look at the changes that have taken place—particularly the enormous capacity of plaintiff's aluminum plants—it appears that, even though we should conclude that it had "monopolized" the ingot industry up to 1941, the plaintiff now has in its hands the means to prevent any possible "monopolization" of the industry after the war, which it may use as it wills; and that the occasion has therefore passed forever which might call for, or justify, a dissolution.

[The decision went on to say that final relief should wait until the disposal of the many aluminum plants built by the government during the war was determined. As it turned out, none of them went to Alcoa but went rather to two new entrants, Reynolds and Kaiser, perhaps because of the court's decision. The District Court did require that the common owners of Alcoa and Aluminum, Ltd. dispose of their stock in one of the two firms. Aluminum, Ltd. is the Canadian company created in 1928 to operate the Canadian properties of Alcoa and those owned by J. B. Duke (of American Tobacco). Technically it was a separate company. Actually, it was owned mainly by the Dukes, the Mellons, and the Davises, who also controlled Alcoa. The chairmen of the boards of the two companies were brothers. This "dissolution" established a fourth independent North American aluminum producer with almost as much ingot capacity as Alcoa and one whose natural market was U.S. aluminum fabricators. Today there are nine producers of "virgin" aluminum in the United States, far more than in any other country in the world.]

United States v. United Shoe Machinery Corp.

110 F. Supp. 295 (1953)

WYZANSKI, District Judge.

December 15, 1947 the Government filed a complaint against United Shoe Machinery Corporation under Section 4 of the Sherman Act, in order to restrain alleged violations of Sections 1 and 2 of that Act.

Stripped to its essentials, the complaint charged, first, that since 1912 United had been "monopolizing interstate trade and commerce in the shoe machinery industry of the United States. . . ." The second principal charge laid by the complaint was that United had been (a) "monopolizing the distribution in inter-state commerce of numerous . . . shoe factory supplies" and (b) "attempting to monopolize the distribution in interstate commerce of . . . other such supplies." Third, the complaint alleged United was "attempting to monopolize and monopo-lizing the manufacture and distribution in interstate commerce of tanning machin-ery used in the manufacture of shoe leather. . . ."

There are 18 major processes for the manufacturing of shoes by machine. Some machine types are used in one process, but others are used in several; and the relationship of machine types to one another may be competitive or sequential. The approximately 1460 shoe manufacturers themselves are highly competitive in many respects, including their choice of processes and other technological aspects of production. Their total demand for machine services, apart from those ren-dered by dry thread sewing machines in the upper-fitting room, constitutes an identifiable market which is a "part of the trade or commerce among the several States."

United, the largest source of supply, is a corporation lineally descended from a combination of constituent companies, adjudged lawful by the Supreme Court of the United States in 1918. . . .

Supplying different aspects of that market are at least 10 other American manufacturers and some foreign manufacturers, whose products are admitted to the United States free of tariff duty. Almost all the operations performed in the 18 processes can be carried out without the use of any of United's machines, and (at least in foreign areas, where patents are no obstacle), a complete shoe factory can be efficiently organized without a United machine.

Nonetheless, United at the present time is supplying over 75%, and probably 85% of the current demand in the American shoe machinery market, as heretofore defined. This is somewhat less than the share it was supplying in 1915. In the meantime, one important competitor, Compo Shoe Machinery Corporation, be-came the American innovator of the cement process of manufacture. In that sub-market Compo roughly equals United. . . .

United is the only machinery enterprise that produces a long line of machine types and covers every major process. It is the only concern that has a research laboratory covering all aspects of the needs of shoe manufacturing; though Compo has a laboratory concentrating on the needs of those in the cement pro-cess. United's heavy research expenditures, over $3 million annually, have been pro-rated roughly according to those fields where maximum revenue has been or could be attained, and, except in the cement process, often in inverse proportion to actual competition. Through its own research, United has developed inventions many of which are not patented. Roughly 95% of its 3915 patents are attributable to the ideas of its own employees.

Although at the turn of the century, United's patents covered the fundamentals of shoe machinery manufacture, those fundamental patents have expired. Current patents cover for the most part only minor developments, so that it is possible to "invent around" them, to use the words of United's chief competitor. However, the aggregation of patents does to some extent block potential competition. It furnishes a trading advantage. It leads inventors to offer their ideas to United, on the general principle that new complicated machines embody numerous patents. And it serves as a hedge of insurance for United against unforeseen competitive developments.

In the last decade and a half, United has not acquired any significant patents, inventions, machines, or businesses from any outside source, and has rejected many offers made to it. Before then, while it acquired no going businesses, in a period of two decades it spent roughly $3,500,000 to purchase inventions and machines. . . .

In supplying its complicated machines to shoe manufacturers, United, like its more important American competitors, has followed the practice of never selling, but only leasing. Leasing has been traditional in the shoe machinery field since the Civil War. So far as this record indicates, there is virtually no expressed dissatisfaction from consumers respecting that system; and Compo, United's principal competitor, endorses and uses it. Under the system, entry into shoe manufacture has been easy. The rates charged for all customers have been uniform. The machines supplies have performed excellently. United has, without separate charge, promptly and efficiently supplied repair service and many kinds of other service useful to shoe manufacturers. . . . The cost to the average shoe manufacturer of its machines and services supplied to him has been less than 2% of the wholesale price of his shoes.

However, United's leases, in the context of the present shoe machinery market, have created barriers to the entry by competitors into the shoe machinery field.

First, the complex of obligations and rights accruing under United's leasing system in operation deter a shoe manufacturer from disposing of a United machine and acquiring a competitor's machine. He is deterred more than if he owned that same United machine, or if he held it on a short lease carrying simple rental provisions and a reasonable charge for cancellation before the end of the term. The lessee is now held closely to United by the combined effect of the 10 year term, the requirement that if he has work available he must use the machine to full capacity, and by the return charge which can in practice, through the right of a deduction fund, be reduced to insignificance if he keeps this and other United machines to the end of the periods for which he leased them.

Second, when a lessee desires to replace a United machine, United gives him more favorable terms if the replacement is by another United machine than if it is by a competitive machine.

Third, United's practice of offering to repair, without separate charges, its leased machines, has had the effect that there are no independent service organizations to repair complicated machines. In turn, this has had the effect that the manufacturer of a complicated machine must either offer repair service with his machine, or must face the obstacle of marketing his machine to customers who know that repair service will be difficult to provide.

Through its success with its principal and more complicated machines, United has been able to market more successfully its other machines, whether offered only for sale, or on optional sale or lease terms. In ascending order of importance, the reasons for United's success with these simpler types are these. These other, usually more simple, machines are technologically related to the complex leased machines to which they are auxiliary or preparatory. Having business relations with, and a host of contacts with, shoe factories, United seems to many of them the most efficient, normal, and above all, convenient supplier. Finally, United has promoted the sale of these simple machine types by the sort of price discrimination between machine types, about to be stated.

Although maintaining the same nominal terms for each customer, United has followed, as between machine types, a discriminatory pricing policy. Clear examples of this policy are furnished by the nine selected instances reviewed in detail in the findings. Other examples of this policy can be found in the wide, and relatively permanent, variations in the rates of return United secures upon its long line of machine types. United's own internal documents reveal that these sharp and relatively durable differentials are traceable, at least in large part, to United's policy of fixing a higher rate of return where competition is of minor significance, and a lower rate of return where competition is of major significance. . . .

The facts show that (1) defendant has, and exercises, such overwhelming strength in the shoe machinery market that it controls that market, (2) this strength excludes some potential, and limits some actual, competition, and (3) this strength is not attributable solely to defendant's ability, economies of scale, research, natural advantages, and adaptation to inevitable economic laws.

In estimating defendant's strength, this Court gives some weight to the 75 plus percentage of the shoe machinery market which United serves. But the Court considers other factors as well. In the relatively static shoe machinery market where there are no sudden changes in the style of machines or in the volume of demand, United has a network of long-term, complicated leases with over 90% of the shoe factories. These leases assure closer and more frequent contacts between United and its customers than would exist if United were a seller and its customers were buyers. Beyond this general quality, these leases are so drawn and so applied as to strengthen United's power to exclude competitors. Moreover, United offers a long line of machine types, while no competitor offers more than a short line. Since in some parts of its line United faces no important competition, United has the power to discriminate, by wide differentials and over long periods of time, in the rate of return it procures from different machine types. Furthermore, being by far the largest company in the field, with by far the largest resources in dollars, in patents, in facilities, and in knowledge, United has a marked capacity to attract offers of inventions, inventors' services, and shoe machinery businesses. And, finally, there is no substantial substitute competition from a vigorous secondhand market in shoe machinery.

To combat United's market control, a competitor must be prepared with knowledge of shoemaking, engineering skill, capacity to invent around patents, and financial resources sufficient to bear the expense of long developmental and experimental processes. The competitor must be prepared for consumers' resistance founded on their long-term, satisfactory relations with United, and on the cost to them of surrendering United's leases. Also, the competitor must be prepared to give, or point to the source of, repair and other services, and to the source of supplies for machine parts, expendable parts, and the like. Indeed, perhaps a competitor who aims at any large scale success must also be prepared to lease his machines. These considerations would all affect potential competition, and have not been without their effect on actual competition.

Not only does the evidence show United has control of the market, but also the evidence does not show that the control is due entirely to excusable causes. The three principal sources of United's power have been the original constitution of the company, the superiority of United's products and services, and the leasing system. The first two of these are plainly beyond reproach. The original constitution of United in 1899 was judicially approved in *United States v. United Shoe Machinery Company of New Jersey,* 247 U.S. 32 (1918). . . . Likewise beyond criticism is the high quality of United's products, its understanding of the techniques of shoemaking and the needs of shoe manufacturers, its efficient design and improvement of machines, and its prompt and knowledgeable service. These have illustrated in manifold ways that "superior skill, foresight and industry" of which Judge Hand spoke in Aluminum.

But United's control does not rest solely on its original constitution, its ability, its research, or its economies of scale. There are other barriers to competition, and these barriers were erected by United's own business policies. Much of United's market power is traceable to the magnetic ties inherent in its system of leasing, and not selling, its more important machines. The lease-only system of distributing complicated machines has many "partnership" aspects, and it has exclusionary features such as the 10-year term, the full capacity clause, the return charges, and the failure to segregate service charges from machine charges. Moreover, the leasing system has aided United in maintaining a pricing system which discriminates between machine types. . . .

In one sense, the leasing system and the miscellaneous activities just referred to (except United's purchase in the secondhand market) were natural and normal, for they were, in Judge Hand's words, "honestly industrial." They are the sort of activities which would be engaged in by other honorable firms. And, to a large extent, the leasing practices conform to long-standing traditions in the shoe machinery business. Yet, they are not practices which can be properly described as the inevitable consequences of ability, natural forces, or law. They represent something more than the use of accessible resources, the process of invention and innovation, and the employment of those techniques of employment, financing, production, and distribution, which a competitive society must foster. They are contracts, arrangements, and policies which, instead of encouraging competition based on pure merit, further the dominance of a particular firm. In this sense, they are unnatural barriers; they unnecessarily exclude actual and potential competition; they restrict a free market. While the law allows many enterprises to use such practices, the Sherman Act is now construed by superior courts to forbid the continuance of effective market control based in part upon such practices. Those courts hold that market control is inherently evil and constitutes a violation of

Section 2 unless economically inevitable, or specifically authorized and regulated by law. . . .

Defendant seems to suggest that even if its control of the market is not attributable exclusively to its superior performance, its research, and its economies of scale, nonetheless, United's market control should not be held unlawful, because only through the existence of some monopoly power can the thin shoe machinery market support fundamental research of the first order, and achieve maximum economies of production and distribution.

To this defense the shortest answer is that the law does not allow an enterprise that maintains control of a market through practices not economically inevitable, to justify that control because of its supposed social advantage. It is for Congress, not for private interests, to determine whether a monopoly, not compelled by circumstances, is advantageous. And it is for Congress to decide on what conditions, and subject to what regulations, such a monopoly shall conduct its business.

Moreover, if the defense were available, United has not proved that monopoly is economically compelled by the thinness of the shoe machinery market. It has not shown that no company could undertake to develop, manufacture, and distribute certain types of machines, unless it alone met the total demand for those types of machines.

Nor has United proved that it has achieved spectacular results at amazing rates of speed, nor has it proved that comparable research results and comparable economies of production, distribution, and service could not be achieved as well by, say, three important shoe machinery firms, as by one. Compo with a much smaller organization indicates how much research can be done on a smaller scale. . . .

From the opinion on defendant's violations it follows that some form of relief regarding defendant's leases and leasing practices is proper and necessary.

The Government does not propose that United should cease leasing machines. It does suggest that this Court order defendant to eliminate from the leases those provisions found to be restrictive, to offer for sale every type of machine which it offers for lease, and to make the sales terms somewhat more advantageous to customers, than the lease terms. . . .

Although leasing should not now be abolished by judicial decree, the Court agrees with the Government that the leases should be purged of their restrictive features. In the decree filed herewith, the term of a lease is shortened, the full capacity clause is eliminated, the discriminatory commutative charges are removed, and United is required to segregate its charges for machines from its charges for repair service. For the most part, the decree speaks plainly enough upon these points. Yet, on two matters, a further word is in order. . . .

The Court also agrees with the Government that if United chooses to continue to lease any machine type, it must offer that type of machine for sale also. The principal merit of this proposal does not lie in its primary impact, that is, in its effect in widening the choices open to shoe factories. For present purposes it may be assumed that the anti-trust laws are not designed, chiefly, if at all, to give a customer choice as to the selling methods by which his supplier offers that supplier's own products. The merit of the Government's proposal is in its secondary impact. Insofar as United's machines are sold rather than leased, they will ultimately, in many cases, reach a second-hand market. From that market, United will face a type of substitute competition which will gradually weaken the prohibited market power which it now exercises. Moreover, from that market, or from United itself, a competitor of United can acquire a United machine in order to study it, to copy its unpatented features, and to experiment with improvements in, or alterations of, the machine. Thus, in another and more direct way, United's market power will be diminished.

United States of America before Federal Trade Commission

In the Matter of

E. I. du Pont de Nemours & Co., a corporation

Docket No. 9108 (1980)

OPINION OF THE COMMISSION, by Clanton, commissioner:

Introduction

In challenging the legality of an expansion strategy adopted and carried out by respondent, E. I. du Pont de Nemours & Company ("Du Pont"), in its titanium pigments business, this case addresses issues that are fundamental to antitrust policy. The complaint, issued April 5, 1978, charges Du Pont in a two-part count with unfair methods of competition and unfair acts and practices by using its dominant position in an attempt to monopolize the production of titanium dioxide pigments ("TiO_2") in the United States, in violation of Section 5 of the Federal Trade Commission Act. . . .

Respondent and the Market

In 1976, Du Pont had sales exceeding $8.3 billion, assets exceeding $7 billion and net income exceeding $459 million. It is engaged in the manufacture and sale of diverse chemical and related products, among them pigments and dyes including titanium dioxide pigment. . . .

TiO_2 is a white chemical pigment used in the manufacture of such products as paint and paper to make them whiter or opaque. In manufacturing TiO_2, there are two basic processes: the "sulfate" process and the "chloride" process. Essentially, the sulfate process involves the reaction of sulfuric acid with relatively low-grade feedstock, while the chloride processes entail the reaction of chlorine either with a high-grade titanium ore or with lower grades of feedstock. During the relevant time frame, only Du Pont used the latter chloride process. . . .

The complaint charges Du Pont with an attempt to monopolize the TiO_2 market by the adoption and implementation of a strategy of plan to expand its domestic TiO_2 production capacity to capture substantially all of the growth in domestic demand for TiO_2 through the mid 1980's. Crucial to the plan was Du Pont's undisputed cost advantage over its rivals in production of TiO_2, which stemmed both from economies of scale and from Du Pont's unique technological ability to use lower-grade (and lower cost) ilmenite ore. In this respect, complaint counsel contend that Du Pont's cost advantage was "fortuitous," conferred upon it accidentally by the increases in the price of rutile and the costs of waste disposal in the sulfate process.

As alleged, Du Pont's growth strategy consists of three interrelated elements: a) expansion of capacity by construction of a large-scale plant; b) exploitation of its cost advantage by pricing its products high enough to finance its own expanded capacity, yet low enough to discourage rivals from expanding; and c) refusal to license its cost-saving ilmenite chloride technology with which rivals could learn to take advantage of the economics of scale inherent in the low-grade ore technology. In addition, the allegedly strategic behavior of Du Pont consisted of premature expansion of its TiO_2 capacity and exaggerated announcements of its expansion intentions, all for the primary purpose of preempting competitors' expansion plans. . . .

Du Pont admits that it sought to capitalize on its cost advantage in order to capture or serve the major portion of the growth in demand for TiO_2 well into the 1980's. Even so, it denies that the cost advantage was "fortuitous," claiming instead that it was due to its costly innovations in low-grade ilmenite chloride technology in earlier years. It further denies that its capacity expansion had any purpose other than to satisfy the expected increase in demand for TiO_2.

Furthermore, Du Pont claims that it was under no duty to license its ilmenite chloride technology to any competitor, and contends that its competitors, all large corporations engaged in TiO_2 manufacture, are not prevented from developing their own low-grade ore technology or constructing large-scale plants if they choose to make such investments. . . .

There is no evidence that Du Pont planned to build excess capacity or that its plans to fulfill the foreseen demand with new and expanded plants were inconsistent with scale economies.

As for Du Pont's individual pricing decisions throughout the period 1972–1977, there is some additional evidence to suggest that those decisions took account of the effect upon competitive expansion. At the same time the record indicates that respondent's pricing strategy underwent periodic adjustment due to variations in market forces, including cost inflation and amended demand forecasts.

Complaint counsel cite several events that allegedly reveal Du Pont's pricing policy to prevent competitors from earning sufficient funds to expand. In one such instance, Kerr-McGee increased its TiO_2 price by 3¢ in June, 1972, an action that Du Pont personnel understood to be related to the desire of certain competitors to expand. Complaint counsel contend that it was Du Pont's unilateral refusal to follow the price increase, not market forces, that prevented the price hike. However, Du Pont proved unable to prevent an increase—because of lack of excess capacity, Du Pont could not force a rollback of prices to its level, and two-tier pricing resulted.

While an interest in discouraging expansions by competitors could be inferred from the totality of the pricing policies and conduct, substantial alternative reasons attributable to external market forces were also evident, and neither of the explanations is necessarily inconsistent with what occurred in each instance. In reviewing the strategy, the 1975 Task Force inferred that, from the outset, the pricing policy had the dual purpose of providing cash for expansion and limiting competitors' ability to expand. On the other hand, as we discuss further below, it appears that independent market factors may have led Du Pont and competitors to price at levels below the expansion-inducing (or limit) price that would have prevailed under more favorable market conditions.

Complaint counsel also contend that Du Pont strategically announced its intentions to build new capacity and actually began such expansions prematurely, for the primary purpose of preempting and discouraging competitors' expansion opportunities. . . .

[I]t appears that the scope and timing of Du Pont's announcements of its intentions regarding DeLisle [a new plant in Mississippi] were related to legitimate business considerations.

Complaint counsel also allege that Du Pont's decision on the timing of DeLisle's start-up amounted to another of the strategic decisions aimed at preventing competitive expansion, and that Du Pont eventually decided to bring DeLisle onstream "early." Yet complaint counsel acknowledge that an accelerated start-up would not result in oversupply. From the outset, the start-up of DeLisle was planned to coincide with the increase in demand that the economic recovery of the late 70's was expected to bring. . . . [T]he decisions regarding the commencement of production at DeLisle were consistent with both a desire to respond to market opportunities and a desire to expand before competitors expanded.

In 1975, a general economic recession led the Du Pont Executive Committee to reevaluate about ten capital projects, and a slump in TiO_2 sales in particular led it to review the DeLisle construction plans. The Pigments Department found its DeLisle project competing for funds with several other corporate projects. To make its case for the DeLisle project, the Task Force devised two alternative ten-year TiO_2 business strategies—one an aggressive "growth" plan calling for completion of DeLisle and aiming toward 60% of the market, the other a "maintain" strategy aimed at a 43% share with no new plant until 1985. To convince the Executive Committee not to abandon or delay DeLisle, the Task Force focused on the long-run profitability of the TiO_2 business with the added capacity and a larger market share. Much attention in the parties' briefs is devoted to the extent to which the Executive Committee was exposed to and adopted the plans and recommendations of the reconstituted TiO_2 Task Force.

In attempting to estimate the effect of TiO_2 prices on Du Pont's ability to sell out DeLisle within three or four years of the plant's opening, the Task Force performed the following calculations: price that would trigger competitive expansion, price that would trigger imports, price at which TiO_2 substitutes occur, price that will sink any firm. (CX 85B) The express pricing goal under the "growth" strategy was to price as high as possible to generate expansion funds without a major competitive expansion or foreign entry. Under the "maintain" strategy, the pricing policy would be "to balance profit with limited competitive expansion and foreign entry." . . .

The Task Force also prepared several comparative long-range projections of the price and profit expectations under the two proposed strategies, projections that are referred to in the briefs as the "welfare analysis." These projections showed that, while TiO_2 prices would be lower in 1980 under the growth plan than under the "maintain" strategy, after 1984 the prices, and thus the total profitability out to 1992, would be higher under the expansion plan. The welfare analysis itself contains no explanation of the different price assumptions used, but other documents referred generally to the value of a larger market share. . . .

[T]he Executive Committee decided to continue as planned with construction of the 150 MT DeLisle plant, to commence operation in 1979. . . .

As originally conceived, the growth strategy did not call for Du Pont to take market share or existing sales away from competitors; rather, the plant was to capture the forecast growth in demand. As it turned out, over the course of the strategy, Du Pont did take some market share from its competitors. Despite Du Pont's early forecasts and expectations, between 1972 and 1977 there was no net increase in total demand for TiO_2 and competitor's sulfate plants did not close. While it fell well short of its earlier market share goals, Du Pont nevertheless increased its sales over the period by 80 MT, at the expense of competitors.

We have here a remarkably clear blueprint of Du Pont's plan to capture all or most of the increased demand for TiO_2 after 1972. Although Du Pont has fallen somewhat short of its 1972 market share goals—51.8% planned vs. 43% actual for 1978—it nevertheless has continued to follow the early strategy. The principal setbacks resulted from a slowdown in demand growth and the continued operation of sulfate plants that Du Pont thought would be closed due to pollution problems. These circumstances also forced Du Pont to cancel (or at least indefinitely postpone) a second line at DeLisle. As to much of the evidence there is little dispute about the precise events that occurred or the sequence of these events. Where the parties diverge sharply is over the inferences to be drawn from Du Pont's conduct and, more specifically, over the justifications offered in defense of the expansion and pricing decisions. . . .

Complaint counsel do not contend that Du Pont overbuilt its capacity relative to anticipated demand; rather they argue that respondent met its growth objectives only by preempting competitive expansion through strategic announcement and start-up of the DeLisle plant as well as pricing to deter competitive growth. As examples of strategic timing, complaint counsel cite Du Pont's 1974 announcement of its plan to build DeLisle, which occurred before funds were actually appropriated, and the 1975 recommendation to the Executive Committee urging that start-up of DeLisle not be delayed for two years (despite a market slump) because of competitive ramifications.

On the pricing side, two interrelated issues are involved: Du Pont's influence over price and the rationale for both the firm's individual pricing decisions and its overall pricing strategy. Central to complaint counsel's case is the allegation that Du Pont deliberately sought to deter competitive expansion, and simultaneously effect its own expansion plans, by using its cost advantage to price at a level that would make it unattractive for competitors to enlarge their capacity. In support of their position, complaint counsel rely on Task Force statements as well as four instances where Du Pont forced a rollback in competitors' price hikes by refusing to go along. . . .

The evidence of Du Pont's cost advantage and its pricing behavior clearly indicates that it exercised some degree of price leadership in the industry. For example, internal company documents reveal Du Pont's own belief in 1975 that if price increases were to occur it would have to lead the way. Moreover, Du Pont's ability to force a rollback of price hikes in early 1975, to initiate successfully a lesser price increase several months later, and to force further rollbacks in 1976 and 1977, points strongly to the conclusion that respondent had a measure of power over price. . . .

As for the Task Force recommendations concerning deterrent or limit pricing, it is hard to reach any conclusion other than that such an objective was part and parcel of the overall growth strategy. To be sure, the 1972 plan presented to the Executive Committee did not expressly refer to a limit pricing policy. Nevertheless, that objective was viewed by the Task Force in 1975 as an element of the plan and later Task Force reports reiterated this feature. . . . There is no evidence, however, that Du Pont priced below its costs and complaint counsel do not attempt to make such a showing.

In sum, the facts show rather unequivocally that Du Pont, with a 30% market share in 1972 and a substantial cost advantage over its rivals, sought to exploit this opportunity by embarking on a long-term expansion project to capture the demand growth anticipated over the following decade. In pursuing this objective, Du Pont foresaw that this plan would significantly enhance its market share, possibly giving the firm a 65% share by 1985. In addition, Du Pont took into account the impact of its actions on expansion by competitors, with particular emphasis on the effects of its pricing decisions and the competitive consequences of delaying DeLisle when the market turned downward in the mid-1970's. At the same time, Du Pont's pricing and construction decisions were also influenced by intervening market factors. Lastly, Du Pont refused to license its technology, preferring instead to reap the rewards of its low-cost technology by direct application rather than by sharing it with competitors.

Whether this conduct violates the antitrust laws is the critical issue to which we turn next.

This case raises fundamental questions about the extent to which dominant firms may aggressively pursue competitive opportunities, especially where they enjoy some form of cost or technological advantage over their rivals. More specifically, the crucial issue facing us is not whether such firms may legitimately compete or capitalize on their advantages, but whether those opportunities are exploited in an unreasonable fashion. In other words, how much latitude should be afforded a major, well-established firm when it seizes a competitive edge and attempts to enhance significantly its market position? In the context of this case the question is not so much whether Du Pont had the right to expand but whether it did so by measures that went beyond what were justified by its cost advantage.

Section 5 of the Federal Trade Commission Act empowers the Federal Trade Commission to prohibit certain unfair methods of competition, and that section has been construed to cover conduct that violates either the prohibitions of the Clayton Act and the Sherman Act or conduct that could lead to unreasonable restraints on competition if not prohibited.

As a general matter, it seems unwise to find that a firm has the requisite specific intent for anticipating the exclusionary consequences of successful competitive behavior which leads, or may lead, to a monopoly, so long as that behavior is reasonable. To suggest otherwise would be to proscribe all acts in which firms conjure up some thoughts of achieving monopoly irrespective of the actual character of the means employed to gain that end.

We come now to the critical element of an attempt to monopolize for purposes of this case: the reasonableness of Du Pont's conduct in formulating and executing its expansion strategy. Few antitrust issues of late have sparked more interest and debate than has the subject of predation and strategic deterrent behavior. At stake is the extent to which dominant firms should be permitted to compete aggressively, and the standards by which conduct should be deemed predatory (and therefore unreasonable).

Such an approach is reflected even in the far-reaching, landmark decision in *United States v. Aluminum Company of America,* 148 F.2d 416 (2d Cir. 1945). ("Alcoa"), the progenitor of the cases on exclusionary expansion, as well as complaint counsel's theory here. In that case Alcoa, with its 90 percent market share, confronted rivals with repeated increases in capacity in anticipation of demand, thereby excluding competitors from profitable opportunities to grow. In condemning this action and finding that Alcoa was not the "passive beneficiary of a monopoly," Judge Hand nonetheless concluded that not all monopolies were proscribed by Section 2. In addition to natural monopolies and those created by "force of accident," he cited the situation where "[a] single producer may be the survivor out of a group of active competitors merely by virtue of his superior skill, foresight and industry." Thus, Judge Hand felt that some evaluation of the justifications for the monopolist's behavior and the resulting market structure was called for, although, as applied to Alcoa, he believed that its capacity expansions were not "inevitable" and that they did not reflect the actions of firms "who do not seek, but cannot avoid, the control of a market."

As for *Alcoa,* it superficially at least provides a much closer analogy to the facts of this case. But there are differences, not the least of which is the fact that Alcoa was a monopolist that had maintained its hold over the market through repeated additions to capacity over a long period of time. Moreover, the circumstances and justifications surrounding those increases in output are not detailed. In light of more recent precedents and literature on exclusionary conduct, discussed below,

Alcoa leaves unanswered a number of important questions that are especially relevant in the context of the attempt case now before us.

There is little doubt that many of these considerations can be of great help in judging the lawfulness of single-firm conduct. Actions that promote innovation or improve efficiency, for instance, should generally be encouraged, not inhibited. But we believe it would be unwise policy, especially in the face of actual or threatened monopoly, to focus solely on the benefit side of the equation while ignoring the adverse effects of dominant firm behavior. For example, a firm's conduct might consist largely of ordinary business practices, yet be highly exclusionary because of the industry structure and the firm's market power. So too, the actions of the would-be monopolist may enhance efficiency or product performance, albeit marginally, although the overall competitive effect is decidedly negative. In a similar vein, there are shortcomings in a test which relies exclusively on determining whether the conduct would have been rational for a smaller firm. On the one hand, it might be logical and necessary for a new or recent entrant to engage in below cost pricing as a means of achieving market penetration. On the other hand, size and efficiency may coalesce so that it is difficult, if not impossible, to ascertain precisely whether an effective marketing tactic owes its success to greater efficiency or the naked exercise of market power. Moreover, behavior that is rational for a firm with little or no market power may nevertheless produce substantial and unnecessary anticompetitive effects when wielded by a firm with considerable market clout.

In the present case, Du Pont's conduct appears to be justified by respondent's cost superiority over its rivals, demand forecasts and scale economies. There is no evidence that Du Pont's pricing or capacity strategies were unprofitable (regardless of the cost test employed) and, as discussed later, the plant announcements do not appear to be misleading. Yet, that is not the end of our inquiry. As we have suggested, the proper test for measuring the reasonableness of Du Pont's conduct takes account of overall competitive effects—pro and con—within the relevant market setting. . . .

To summarize, the focus of much of the literature centers on strategic responses to new entry, or, as characterized by [one article], response "of a gaming variety—now it's there, now it isn't, depending on whether an entrant has appeared or perished. . . ." Such behavior hardly typifies Du Pont's expansion plan, which contemplated a permanent increase in plant capacity and output. Even as to respondent's pricing objectives—generating funds for its own expansion while discouraging similar efforts by competitors—those objectives were consistent with Du Pont's cost advantage and undertaken in conjunction with the firm's long-term growth in response to demand projections; they were not undertaken simply as a device to retard entry without regard to independent market forces.

In applying these principles to the facts of this case, it is useful to restate complaint counsel's fundamental objection to Du Pont's growth plan. In essence, complaint counsel contend that it was logical for Du Pont to do what it did only if monopoly power could be attained in the future. It is argued that Du Pont's construction/pricing/non-licensing policy involved a current foregoing of available profits, that Du Pont recognized that it could recoup those profits down the road through high volume and higher prices, and that Du Pont's policy only made sense if those excess profits would become available at a later date.

Put differently, Du Pont presumably would not have tried to capture all future demand growth, and thereby risked the costs of operating a plant the size of DeLisle at less than capacity, unless it was reasonably assured that other competitors could not expand. Du Pont obtained this assurance, it is claimed, not through normal market forces, but rather through its own efforts, as evidenced by the combination of expansion, announcement, pricing and licensing policies. As further proof of the overall strategy, complaint counsel cite to Du Pont's pricing forecasts, which it is argued clearly reveal respondent's plan to sacrifice short-term profits for long-term monopoly gains.

We simply cannot accept this analysis. The rationality of Du Pont's program hardly seems dependent on its ability to extract monopoly profits in the future. Du Pont had a highly efficient process, indeed the most efficient in the industry, and it anticipated expanding market demand. To serve that demand, Du Pont enlarged its existing facilities to optimal levels and built a new plant of efficient scale (but not above efficient levels and no larger than necessary to satisfy predicted demand) to serve the market it expected would develop. Given respondent's level of efficiency, expansion of the magnitude undertaken would make sense, regardless of whether the firm would eventually be able to raise prices above competitive levels. Moreover, Du Pont's pricing policies were entirely consistent with its cost advantage and apparently (for there is no suggestion that it engaged in predatory pricing) were profitable, even during the '70s when respondent was arguably foregoing additional profits.

It may be that Du Pont ultimately will achieve a monopoly share of the market. As its share increases, other firms may find it harder to capture the efficiencies enjoyed by Du Pont due to the scale economies associated with the ilmenite process. Those effects should be weighed carefully, and we have done so. Antitrust policy wisely disfavors monopoly, but it also seeks to promote vigorous competitive behavior. Indeed, the essence of the competitive process is to induce firms to become more efficient and to pass the benefits of the efficiency along to consumers. That process would be ill-served by using antitrust to block hard, aggressive competition that is solidly based on efficiencies and growth opportunities, even if monopoly is a possible result. Such a view, we believe, is entirely consistent with the "superior skill, foresight and industry" exception in *Alcoa* and subsequent cases, for those decisions clearly indicate that monopolies may be lawfully created by superior competitive ability.

As we have previously indicated, Du Pont engaged in conduct consistent with its own technological capacity and market opportunities. It did not attempt to build excess capacity or to expand temporarily as a means of deterring entry. Nor did respondent engage in other conduct that might tip the scales in the direction of liability, such as pricing below cost, making false announcements about future expansion plans, or attempting to lock up customers in requirements contracts to assure the success of its growth plans. In short, we find Du Pont's conduct to be reasonable. Accordingly, we affirm the ALJ's dismissal of the complaint.

Lorain Journal Co. v. United States

342 U.S. 143 (1951)

MR. JUSTICE BURTON read the decision for the Court.

This is a civil action, instituted by the United States in the District Court for the Northern District of Ohio, against The Lorain Journal Company, an Ohio corporation, publishing, daily except Sunday, in the City of Lorain, Ohio, a newspaper here called the Journal. The complaint alleged that the corporation, together with four of its officials, was engaging in a combination and conspiracy in restraint of interstate commerce in violation of Section 1 of the Sherman Antitrust Act, and in a combination and conspiracy to monopolize such commerce in violation of Section 2 of the Act, as well as attempting to monopolize such commerce in violation of Section 2. The District Court declined to issue a temporary injunction but, after trial, found that the parties were engaging in an attempt to monopolize as charged. Confining itself to that issue, the court enjoined them from continuing the attempt. . . .

The court below describes the position of the Journal, since 1933, as "a commanding and an overpowering one. It has a daily circulation in Lorain of over 13,000 copies and it reaches ninety-nine per cent of the families in the city." Lorain is an industrial city on Lake Erie with a population of about 52,000 occupying 11,325 dwelling units. The Sunday News, appearing only on Sundays, is the only other newspaper published there. . . .

From 1933 to 1948 the publisher enjoyed a substantial monopoly in Lorain of the mass dissemination of news and advertising, both of a local and national character. However, in 1948 the Elyria-Lorain Broadcasting Company, a corporation independent of the publisher, was licensed by the Federal Communications Commission to establish and operate in Elyria, Ohio, eight miles south of Lorain, a radio station whose call letters, WEOL, stand for Elyria, Oberlin and Lorain. Since then it has operated its principal studio in Elyria and a branch studio in Lorain. Lorain has about twice the population of Elyria and is by far the largest community in the station's immediate area. Oberlin is much smaller than Elyria and eight miles south of it. . . .

The court below found that appellants knew that a substantial number of Journal advertisers wished to use the facilities of the radio station as well. For some of them it found that advertising in the Journal was essential for the promotion of their sales in Lorain County. It found that at all times since WEOL commenced broadcasting, appellants had executed a plan conceived to eliminate the threat of competition from the station. Under this plan the publisher refused to accept local advertisements in the Journal from any Lorain County advertiser who advertised or who appellants believed to be about to advertise over WEOL. The court found expressly that the purpose and intent of this procedure was to destroy the broadcasting company.

The publisher's attempt to regain its monopoly of interstate commerce by forcing advertisers to boycott a competing radio station violated Section 2. The findings and opinion of the trial court describe the conduct of the publisher upon which the Government relies. The surrounding circumstances are important. The most illuminating of these is the substantial monopoly which was enjoyed in Lorain by the publisher from 1933 to 1948, together with a 99% coverage of Lorain families. Those factors made the Journal an indispensable medium of advertising for many Lorain concerns. Accordingly, its publisher's refusals to print Lorain advertising for those using WEOL for like advertising often amounted to an effective prohibition of the use of WEOL for that purpose. Numerous Lorain advertisers wished to supplement their local newspaper advertising with local radio advertising but could not afford to discontinue their newspaper advertising in order to use the radio.

WEOL's greatest potential source of income was local Lorain advertising. Loss of that was a major threat to its existence. The court below found unequivocally that appellants' conduct amounted to an attempt by the publisher to destroy WEOL and, at the same time, to regain the publiisher's pre-1948 substantial monopoly over the mass dissemination of all news and advertising.

To establish this violation of §2 as charged, it was not necessary to show that success rewarded appellants' attempt to monopolize. While appellants' attempt to monopolize did succeed insofar as it deprived WEOL of income, WEOL has not yet been eliminated. The injunction may save it. . . .

Assuming the interstate character of the commerce involved, it seems clear that if all the newspapers in a city, in order to monopolize the dissemination of news and advertising by eliminating a competiting radio station, conspired to accept no advertisements from anyone who advertised over that station, they would violate Sections 1 and 2 of the Sherman Act. . . . It is consistent with that result to hold here that a single newspaper, already enjoying a substantial monopoly in its area, violates the "attempt to monopolize" clause of §2 when it uses its monopoly to destroy threatened competition.

Klor's, Inc. v. Broadway-Hale Stores, Inc.
359 U.S. 207 (1959)

MR. JUSTICE BLACK delivered the opinion of the Court.

Klor's, Inc., operates a retail store on Mission Street, San Francisco, California; Broadway-Hale Stores, Inc., a chain of department stores, operates one of its stores next door. The two stores compete in the sale of radios, television sets, refrigerators and other household appliances. Klor's brought this action for treble damages and injunction in the United States District Court.

In support of its claim Klor's made the following allegations: George Klor started an appliance store some years before 1952 and has operated it ever since either individually or as Klor's, Inc. Klor's is as well equipped as Broadway-Hale to handle all brands of appliances. Nevertheless, manufacturers and distributors of such well-known brands as General Electric, RCA, Admiral, Zenith, Emerson and others have conspired among themselves and with Broadway-Hale either not to sell to Klor's or to sell to it only at discriminatory prices and highly unfavorable terms. Broadway-Hale has used its "monopolistic" buying power to bring about this situation. The business of manufacturing, distributing and selling household appliances is in interstate commerce. The concerted refusal to deal with Klor's has seriously handicapped its ability to compete and has already caused it a great loss of profits, goodwill, reputation and prestige.

The defendants did not dispute these allegations, but sought summary judgment and dismissal of the complaint for failure to state a cause of action. They submitted unchallenged affidavits which showed that there were hundreds of other household appliance retailers, some within a few blocks of Klor's who sold many competing brands of appliances, including those the defendant's refused to sell to Klor's. From the allegations of the complaint, and from the affidavits supporting the motion for summary judgment, the District Court concluded that the controversy was a "purely private quarrel" between Klor's and Broadway-Hale, which did not amount to a "public wrong proscribed by the [Sherman] Act." On this ground the complaint was dismissed and summary judgment was entered for the defendants. The Court of Appeals for the Ninth Circuit affirmed the summary judgment. It stated that "a violation of the Sherman Act requires conduct of defendants by which the public is or conceivably may be ultimately injured." It held that here the required public injury was missing since "there was no charge or proof that by any act of defendants the price, quantity, or quality offered the public was affected, nor that there was any intent or purpose to effect a change in, or an influence on, prices, quantity, or quality. . . ." The holding, if correct, means that unless the opportunities for customers to buy in a competitive market are reduced, a group of powerful businessmen may act in concert to deprive a single merchant, like Klor, of the goods he needs to compete effectively. . . .

Group boycotts, or concerted refusals by traders to deal with other traders, have long been held to be in the forbidden category. . . . Even when they operated to lower prices or temporarily to stimulate competition they were banned. . . .

Plainly the allegations of this complaint disclose such a boycott. This is not a case of a single trader refusing to deal with another, nor even of a manufacturer and a dealer agreeing to an exclusive distributorship. Alleged in this complaint is a wide combination consisting of manufacturers, distributors and a retailer. This combination takes from Klor's its freedom to buy appliances in an open competitive market and drives it out of business as a dealer in the defendant's products. It deprives the manufacturers and distributors of their freedom to sell to Klor's at the same prices and conditions made available to Broadway-Hale and in some instances forbids them from selling to it on any terms whatsoever. It interferes with the natural flow of interstate commerce. It clearly has, by its "nature" and "character," a "monopolistic tendency." As such it is not to be tolerated merely because the victim is just one merchant whose business is so small that his destruction makes little difference to the economy. Monopoly can as surely thrive by the elimination of such small businessmen, one at a time, as it can by driving them out in large groups. In recognition of this fact the Sherman Act has consistently been read to forbid all contracts and combinations "which 'tend to create a monopoly,' " whether "the tendency is a creeping one" or "one that proceeds at full gallop."

The judgment of the Court of Appeals is reversed and the cause is remanded to the District Court for trial.

CHAPTER 5

HORIZONTAL MERGERS

Our rules with respect to mergers are probably the most important part of the antitrust laws today, but they had very limited effect before 1950. Presumably a merger between competitors could be a "combination in restraint of trade" under Section 1 of the Sherman Act, but the first successful merger case under the act, Northern Securities, was decided in 1904, fourteen years after the act was passed. Do you think the merger would have been a "combination in restraint of trade"? There was widespread surprise when the decision was announced. It may be of some interest that precisely the same merger was allowed by the ICC and the Supreme Court in 1969 over the objections of the Justice Department. Why do you think the Court reversed itself sixty-five years later? Does Burlington-Northern (the merged firm) have less monopoly than the same firm would have had in 1904? Actually, it did turn out to be the only railroad serving most of the coal producers of the northern plains, and its unilateral increases in freight rates in delivery of coal to utilities in the East, Midwest, and South came close to killing legislation for regulatory reform in the railroad industry in 1980.

Section 7 of the Clayton Act (1914) explicitly prohibited horizontal mergers, but its effect was nil because of decisions in the early 1920s that opened a large loophole. The merger rules finally got some teeth when Section 7 was amended in 1950.

Brown Shoe was the first case decided by the Supreme Court under the newly amended Section 7. It set strong precedents for horizontal and vertical mergers. The horizontal part of the decision is discussed here, and the vertical part is presented in Chapter 6.

Do you worry much about monopoly in the shoe store business? Would you if you lived in one of the generally small cities where Brown and Kinney together sold more than 20% of the shoes? If such a merger was illegal, what horizontal merger would get by? Can you see why Brown Shoe was considered such a strong precedent?

The Von's Grocery decision set even a more restrictive horizontal merger standard than Brown Shoe set. Los Angeles is one of the nation's most competitive retail food markets. In 1963 (after the Von's-Market Basket merger but before this decision) the four largest food chains in the area made 30 percent of the food store sales in Los Angeles.[1] The Court put a great deal of emphasis on the trend toward fewer and larger food stores in the area. Between 1950 and 1963 Los Angeles lost 1775, or about one-third, of its single store firms. Some 126 or fewer of these firms went into mergers. Where do you think the others went? Do you think mergers like those in the Von case brought these closings about? Do you think stopping mergers such as Von's would affect the rate at which single stores disappeared? If this or similar mergers would have accelerated the trend, was it in consumers' interests to stop the mergers? On the other hand, what mergers in Los Angeles could the Court have stopped if it let this one get by? It could still have stopped many mergers in other cities since food store concentration was much higher in most cities than in Los Angeles. In the average metropolitan area the four largest food chains had 50 percent of sales in 1963.[2]

The main issue in the Continental Can case is market definition. Continental Can wanted glass and metal containers to be treated as two different markets. The Justice Department advocated a whole series of markets: containers for baby food, containers for beer, containers for soft drinks, and so forth. The Supreme Court didn't take either route. What did it do? Which makes the most sense to you? For each of the three alternatives, try to imagine how future similar cases would have been argued if the Court had gone each route in turn. Would a merger of Continental Can (33 percent of tin cans) and National Can (5 percent of tin cans) have been easier or harder for the courts to decide? Do you think the acquisition of National by Continental would lessen competition more or less than its acquisition of Hazel Atlas?

All of the decisions covered so far were made by the "Warren Court" of the 1950s and 1960s. General Dynamics is the work of the "Burger Court." It seems to provide an exception to the general horizontal merger rule. Do you think the Warren Court would have accepted this special argument? What conditions would have to be present for another merger between two mining companies to be illegal under the new rules? Since General Dynamics, the FTC and the Justice Department have brought fewer horizontal merger cases to court. And, as of 1981, they have not appealed any of these cases to the Supreme Court. Why do you think this has happened?

---

[1] National Commission on Food Marketing, *Organization and Competition in Food Retailing*, Government Printing Office, 1966, pp. 44-51.
[2] Ibid.

Northern Securities Co. v. United States

193 U.S. 197 (1904)

MR. JUSTICE HARLAN delivered the following decision.

This suit was brought by the United States against the Northern Securities Company, a corporation of New Jersey; the Great Northern Railway Company, a corporation of Minnesota; the Northern Pacific Railway Company, a corporation of Wisconsin; James J. Hill, a citizen of Minnesota; and William P. Clough, D. Willis James, John S. Kennedy, J. Pierpont Morgan, Robert Bacon, George F. Baker, and Daniel S. Lamont, citizens of New York.

Its general object was to enforce, as against the defendants, the provisions of the statute of July 2d, 1890, commonly known as the anti-trust act. . . .

The Great Northern Railway Company and the Northern Pacific Railway Company owned, controlled, and operated separate lines of railway—the former road extending from Superior, and from Duluth and St. Paul, to Everett, Seattle and Portland, with a branch line to Helena; the latter extending from Ashland, and from Duluth and St. Paul, to Helena, Spokane, Seattle, Tacoma and Portland. The two lines, main and branches, about 9000 miles in length, were and are parallel and competing lines across the continent through the northern tier of states between the Great Lakes and the Pacific, and the two companies were engaged in active competition for freight and passenger traffic, each road connecting at its respective terminals with lines of railway, or with lake and river steamers, or with seagoing vessels. . . .

Early in 1901 the Great Northern and Northern Pacific Railway Companies, having in view the ultimate placing of their two systems under a common control, united in the purchase of the capital stock of the Chicago, Burlington, & Quincy Railway Company, giving in payment, upon an agreed basis of exchange, the joint bonds of the Great Northern and Northern Pacific Railway Companies, payable in twenty years from date, with interest at 4 per cent per annum. . . .

Prior to November 13th, 1901, defendant Hill and associate stockholders of the Great Northern Railway Company, and defendant Morgan and associate stockholders of the Northern Pacific Railway Company, entered into a combination to form under the laws of New Jersey, a holding corporation to be called the Northern Securities Company, with a capital stock of $400,000,000 and to which company, in exchange for its own capital stock upon a certain basis and at a certain rate, was to be turned over the capital stock, or a controlling interest in the capital stock, of each of the constituent railway companies, with power in the holding corporation to vote such stock and in all respects to act as the owner thereof. . . .

Necessarily by this combination or arrangement the holding company in the fullest sense dominates the situation in the interest of those who were stockholders of the constituent companies; as much so, for every practical purpose, as if it had been itself a railroad corporation which had built, owned, and operated both lines for the exclusive benefit of its stockholders. . . .

The result of the combination is that all the earnings of the constituent companies make a common fund in the hands of the Northern Securities Company, to be distributed, not upon the basis of the earnings of the respective constituent companies, each acting exclusively in its own interests, but upon the basis of the certificates of stock issued by the holding company. No scheme or device could more certainly come within the words of the act—"combination in the form of a trust or otherwise. . . . in restraint of commerce among the several states or with foreign nations"—or could more effectively and certainly suppress free competition between the constituent companies. . . .

We will not encumber this opinion by extended extracts from the former opinions of this court. It is sufficient to say that from the decisions in the above cases certain propositions are plainly deducible and embrace the present case. Those propositions are:

. . . That the act is not limited to restraints of interstate and international trade or commerce that are unreasonable in their nature, but embraces all direct restraints imposed by combination, conspiracy, or monopoly upon such trade or commerce;

That railroad carriers engaged in interstate or international trade or commerce are embraced by the act;. . . .

That every combination or conspiracy which would extinguish competition between otherwise competing railroads engaged in interstate trade or commerce, and which would in that way restrain such trade or commerce, is made illegal by the act;

That the natural effect of competition is to increase commerce, and an agreement whose direct effect is to prevent this play of competition restrains instead of promoting trade and commerce;

That to vitiate a combination such as the act of Congress condemns, it need not be shown that the combination, in fact, results or will result, in a total suppression of trade or in a complete monopoly, but it is only essential to show that, by its necessary operation, it tends to restrain interstate or international trade or commerce or tends to create a monopoly in such trade or commerce. . . .

[The Court affirmed the lower-court decision that ordered the dissolution of the merger.]

Brown Shoe Co. v. United States

370 U.S. 294 (1962)

MR. CHIEF JUSTICE WARREN delivered the opinion for the Court.

This suit was initiated in November 1955, when the Government filed a civil action in the United States District Court for the Eastern District of Missouri alleging that a contemplated merger between the G. R. Kinney Company, Inc.

(Kinney) and the Brown Shoe Company, Inc. (Brown), through an exchange of Kinney for Brown stock, would violate §7 of the Clayton Act. . . .

In the District Court, the Government contended that the effect of the merger of Brown—the third largest seller of shoes by dollar volume in the United States, a leading manufacturer of men's, women's, and children's shoes, and a retailer with over 1,230 owned, operated or controlled retail outlets—and Kinney—the eighth largest company, by dollar volume, among those primarily engaged in selling shoes, itself a large manufacturer of shoes, and a retailer with over 350 retail outlets—"may be substantially to lessen competition or to tend to create a monopoly" by eliminating actual or potential competition in the production of shoes for the national wholesale shoe market and in the sale of shoes at retail in the Nation, by foreclosing competition from "a market represented by Kinney's retail outlets whose annual sales exceed $42,000,000" and by enhancing Brown's competitive advantage over other producers, distributors and sellers of shoes. The Government argued that the "line of commerce" affected by this merger is "footwear," or alternatively, that the "line[s]" are "men's," "women's," and "children's" shoes, separately considered, and that the "section of the country," within which the anticompetitive effect of the merger is to be judged, is the Nation as a whole, or alternatively, each separate city or city and its immediate surrounding area in which the parties sell shoes at retail. . . .

This case is one of the first to come before us in which the Government's complaint is based upon allegations that the appellant has violated §7 of the Clayton Act, as that section was amended in 1950. . . .

What were some of the factors, relevant to a judgment as to the validity of a given merger, specifically discussed by Congress in redrafting §7?

First, there is no doubt that Congress did wish to "plug the loophole" and to include within the coverage of the Act the acquisition of assets no less than the acquisition of stock.

Second, by the deletion of the "acquiring-acquired" language in the original text, it hoped to make plain that §7 applied not only to mergers between actual competitors, but also to vertical and conglomerate mergers whose effect may tend to lessen competition in any line of commerce in any section of the country.

Third, it is apparent that a keystone in the erection of a barrier to what Congress saw was the rising tide of economic concentration, was its provision of authority for arresting mergers at a time when the trend to a lessening of competition in a line of commerce was still in its incipiency. . . .

Fourth, and closely related to the third, Congress rejected, as inappropriate to the problem it sought to remedy, the application to §7 cases of the standards for judging the legality of business combinations adopted by the courts in dealing with cases arising under the Sherman Act, and which may have been applied to some early cases arising under original §7.

Fifth, at the same time that it sought to create an effective tool for preventing all mergers having demonstrable anticompetitive effects, Congress recognized the stimulation to competition that might flow from particular mergers. When concern as to the Act's breadth was expressed, supporters of the amendments indicated that it would not impede, for example, a merger between a corporation which is financially healthy and a failing one which no longer can be a vital competitive factor in the market. . . .

Sixth, Congress neither adopted nor rejected specifically any particular tests for measuring the relevant markets, either as defined in terms of product or in terms of geographic locus of competition, within which the anticompetitive effects of a merger were to be judged. Nor did it adopt a definition of the word "substantially," whether in quantitative terms of sales or assets or market shares or in designated qualitative terms, by which a merger's effects on competition were to be measured.

Seventh, while providing no definite quantitative or qualitative tests by which enforcement agencies could gauge the effects of a given merger to determine whether it may "substantially" lessen competition or tend toward monopoly, Congress indicated plainly that a merger had to be functionally viewed, in the context of its particular industry. That is, whether the consolidation was to take place in an industry that was fragmented rather than concentrated, that had seen a recent trend toward domination by a few leaders or had remained fairly consistent in its distribution of market shares among the participating companies, that had experienced easy access to markets by suppliers and easy access to suppliers by buyers or had witnessed foreclosure of business, that had witnessed the ready entry of new competition or the erection of barriers to prospective entrants, all were aspects, varying in importance with the merger under consideration, which would properly be taken into account.

Eighth, Congress used the words "*may* be substantially to lessen competition" (emphasis supplied), to indicate that its concern was with probabilities, not certainties. . . .

An economic arrangement between companies performing similar functions in the production or sale of comparable goods or services is characterized as "horizontal." The effect on competition of such an arrangement depends, of course, upon its character and scope. Thus, its validity in the face of the antitrust laws will depend upon such factors as: the relative size and number of the parties to the arrangement; whether it allocates shares of the market among the parties; whether it fixes prices at which the parties will sell their product; or whether it absorbs or insulates competitors. Where the arrangement effects a horizontal merger between companies occupying the same product and geographic market, whatever competition previously may have existed in that market between the parties to the merger is eliminated. . . .

[T]he proper definition of the market is a "necessary predicate" to an examination of the competition that may be affected by the horizontal aspects of the merger. The acquisition of Kinney by Brown resulted in a horizontal combination at both the manufacturing and retailing levels of their businesses. Although the District Court found that the merger of Brown's and Kinney's manufacturing facilities was economically too insignificant to come within the prohibitions of the Clayton Act, the Government has not appealed from this portion of the lower court's decision. Therefore, we have no occasion to express our views with respect to that finding. On the other hand appellant does contest the District Court's finding that the merger of the companies' retail outlets may tend substantially to lessen competition.

Shoes are sold in the United States in retail shoe stores and in shoe departments of general stores. These outlets sell: (1) men's shoes, (2) women's shoes, (3) women's or children's shoes, or (4) men's, women's or children's shoes. Prior to the merger, both Brown and Kinney sold their shoes in competition with one another through the enumerated kinds of outlets characteristic of the industry. . . .

The criteria to be used in determining the appropriate geographic market are essentially similar to those used to determine the relevant product market. . . .

[J]ust as a product submarket may have Section 7 significance as the proper "line of commerce," so may a geographic submarket be considered the appropriate "section of the country." . . . The geographic market selected must, therefore, both "correspond to the commercial realities" of the industry and be economically significant. Thus, although the geographic market in some instances may encompass the entire Nation, under other circumstances it may be as small as a single metropolitan area. . . .

The fact that two merging firms have competed directly on the horizontal level in but a fraction of the geographic markets in which either has operated, does not, in itself, place their merger outside the scope of Section 7. That section speaks of "any. . . . section of the country," and if anticompetitive effects of a merger are probable in "any" significant market, the merger—at least to that extent—is proscribed.

The parties do not dispute the findings of the District Court that the Nation as a whole is the relevant geographic market for measuring the anticompetitive effects of the merger viewed vertically or of the horizontal merger of Brown's and Kinney's manufacturing facilities. As to the retail level, however, they disagree. . . .

We believe, however, that the record fully supports the District Court's findings that shoe stores in the outskirts of cities compete effectively with stores in central downtown areas, and that while there is undoubtedly some commercial intercourse between smaller communities within a single "standard metropolitan area," the most intense and important competition in retail sales will be confined to stores within the particular communities in such an area and their immediate environs.

We therefore agree that the District Court properly defined the relevant geographic markets in which to analyze this merger as those cities with a population exceeding 10,000 and their environs in which both Brown and Kinney retailed shoes through their own outlets. Such markets are large enough to include the downtown shops and suburban shopping centers in areas contiguous to the city, which are the important competitive factors, and yet are small enough to exclude stores beyond the immediate environs of the city, which are of little competitive significance.

An analysis of undisputed statistics of sales of shoes in the cities in which both Brown and Kinney sell shoes at retail, separated into the appropriate lines of commerce, provides a persuasive factual foundation upon which the required prognosis of the merger's effect may be built. Although Brown objects to some details in the Government's computations used in drafting these exhibits, appellant cannot deny the correctness of the more general picture they reveal. . . . They show, for example, that during 1955 in 32 separate cities, ranging in size and location from Topeka, Kansas, to Batavia, New York, and Hobbs, New Mexico, the combined share of Brown and Kinney sales of women's shoes (by unit volume) exceeded 20%. In 31 cities—some the same as those used in measuring the effect of the merger in the women's line—the combined share of children's shoes sales exceeded 20%; in 6 cities their share exceeded 40%. In Dodge City, Kansas, their combined share of the market for women's shoes was over 57%; their share of the children's shoe market in that city was 49%. In the 7 cities in which Brown's and Kinney's combined shares of the market for women's shoes were greatest (ranging from 33% to 57%) each of the parties alone, prior to the merger, had captured substantial portions of those markets (ranging from 13% to 34%); the merger intensified this existing concentration. . . .

The market share which companies may control by merging is one of the most important factors to be considered when determining the probable effects of the combination on effective competition in the relevant market. In an industry as fragmented as shoe retailing, the control of substantial shares of the trade in a city may have important effects on competition. If a merger achieving 5% control were now approved, we might be required to approve future merger efforts by Brown's competitors seeking similar market shares. The oligopoly Congress sought to avoid would then be furthered and it would be difficult to dissolve the combinations previously approved. Furthermore, in this fragmented industry, even if the combination controls but a small share of a particular market, the fact that this share is held by a large national chain can adversely affect competition. Testimony in the record from numerous independent retailers, based on their actual experience in the market, demonstrates that a strong, national chain of stores can insulate selected outlets from the vagaries of competition in particular locations and that the large chains can set and alter styles in footwear to an extent that renders the independents unable to maintain competitive inventories. A third significant aspect of this merger is that it creates a large national chain which is integrated with a manufacturing operation. The retail outlets of integrated companies, by eliminating wholesalers and by increasing the volume of purchases from the manufacturing division of the enterprise, can market their own brands at prices below those of competing independent retailers. Of course, some of the results of large integrated or chain operations are beneficial to consumers. Their expansion is not rendered unlawful by the mere fact that small independent stores may be adversely affected. It is competition, not competitors, which the Act protects. But we cannot fail to recognize Congress' desire to promote competition through the protection of viable, small, locally-owned businesses. Congress appreciated that occasional higher costs and prices might result from the maintenance of fragmented industries and markets. It resolved these competing considerations in favor of decentralization. We must give effect to that decision.

Other factors to be considered in evaluating the probable effects of a merger in the relevant market lend additional support to the District Court's conclusion that this merger may substantially lessen competition. One such factor is the history of tendency toward concentration in the industry. As we have previously pointed out, the shoe industry has, in recent years, been a prime example of such a trend. Most combinations have been between manufacturers and retailers, as each of the larger producers has sought to capture an increasing number of assured outlets for its wares. Although these mergers have been primarily vertical in their aim and effect, to the extent that they have brought ever greater numbers of retail outlets within fewer and fewer hands, they have had an additional important impact on the horizontal plane. By the merger in this case, the largest single group of retail stores still independent of one of the large manufacturers was absorbed into an already substantial aggregation of more or less controlled retail outlets. As a result of this merger, Brown moved into second place nationally in terms of retail stores directly owned. . . .

On the basis of the record before us, we believe the Government sustained its burden of proof. We hold that the District Court was correct in concluding that this merger may tend to lessen competition substantially in the retail sale of men's, women's, and children's shoes in the overwhelming majority of those cities and their environs in which both Brown and Kinney sell through owned or controlled outlets.

United States v. Von's Grocery Co.

384 U.S. 270 (1966)

MR. JUSTICE BLACK delivered the opinion of the Court.

On March 25, 1960, the United States brought this action charging that the acquisition by Von's Grocery Company of its direct competitor Shopping Bag Food Stores, both large retail grocery companies in Los Angeles, California, violated §7 of the Clayton Act. After hearing evidence on both sides, the District Court made findings of fact and concluded as a matter of law that there was "not a reasonable probability" that the merger would tend "substantially to lessen competition" or "create a monopoly" in violation of §7. For this reason the District Court entered judgment for the defendants. The Government appealed directly. . . . The sole question here is whether the District Court properly concluded on the facts before it that the Government had failed to prove a violation of §7.

The record shows the following facts relevant to our decision. The market involved here is the retail grocery market in the Los Angeles area. In 1958 Von's retail sales ranked third in the area and Shopping Bag's ranked sixth. In 1960 their sales together were 7.5% of the total two and one-half billion dollars of retail groceries sold in the Los Angeles market each year. For many years before the merger both companies had enjoyed great success as rapidly growing companies. From 1948 to 1958 the number of Von's stores in the Los Angeles area practically doubled from 14 to 27, while at the same time the number of Shopping Bag's stores jumped from 15 to 34. During that same decade, Von's sales increased fourfold and its share of the market almost doubled while Shopping Bag's sales multiplied seven times and its share of the market tripled. The merger of these two highly successful, expanding and aggressive competitors created the second largest grocery chain in Los Angeles with sales of almost $172,488,000 annually. In addition the findings of the District Court show that the number of owners operating single stores in the Los Angeles retail grocery market decreased from 5,365 in 1950 to 3,818 in 1961. By 1963, three years after the merger, the number of single-store owners had dropped still further to 3,590. During roughly the same period, from 1953 to 1962, the number of chains with two or more grocery stores increased from 96 to 150. While the grocery business was being concentrated into the hands of fewer and fewer owners, the small companies were continually being absorbed by the larger firms through mergers. Figures of a principal defense witness, set out below, illustrate the many acquisitions and mergers in the Los Angeles grocery industry from 1954 through 1961 including acquisitions made by Food Giant, Alpha Beta, Fox, and Mayfair, all among the 10 leading chains in the area. Moreover, a table prepared by the Federal Trade Commission appearing in the Government's reply brief, but not a part of the record here, shows that acquisitions and mergers in the Los Angeles retail grocery market have continued at a rapid rate since the merger. These facts alone are enough to cause us to conclude contrary to the District Court that the Von's-Shopping Bag merger did violate §7. Accordingly, we reverse. . . .

Like the Sherman Act in 1890 and the Clayton Act in 1914, the basic purpose of the 1950 Celler-Kefauver Act was to prevent economic concentration in the American economy by keeping a large number of small competitors in business. In stating the purposes of their bill, both of its sponsors, Representative Celler and Senator Kefauver, emphasized their fear, widely shared by other members of Congress, that this concentration was rapidly driving the small businessman out of the market. By using these terms in §7 which look not merely to the actual present effect of a merger but instead to its effect upon future competition, Congress sought to preserve competition among many small businesses by arresting a trend toward concentration in its incipiency before that trend developed to the point that a market was left in the grip of a few big companies. Thus, where concentration is gaining momentum in a market, we must be alert to carry out Congress' intent to protect competition against ever-increasing concentration through mergers.

The facts of this case present exactly the threatening trend toward concentration which Congress wanted to halt. The number of small grocery companies in the Los Angeles retail grocery market had been declining rapidly before the merger and continued to decline rapidly afterwards. This rapid decline in the number of grocery store owners moved hand in hand with a large number of significant absorptions of the small companies by the larger ones. In the midst of this steadfast trend toward concentration, Von's and Shopping Bag, two of the most successful and largest companies in the area, jointly owning 66 grocery stores merged to become the second largest chain in Los Angeles. This merger cannot be defended on the ground that one of the companies was about to fail or that the two had to merge to save themselves from destruction by some larger and more powerful competitor. What we have on the contrary is simply the case of two already powerful companies merging in a way which makes them even more powerful than they were before. If ever such a merger would not violate §7, certainly it does when it takes place in a market characterized by a long and continuous trend toward fewer and fewer owner-competitors which is exactly the sort of trend which Congress, with power to do so, declared must be arrested.

Appellees' primary argument is that the merger between Von's and Shopping Bag is not prohibited by §7 because the Los Angeles grocery market was competitive before the merger, has been since, and may continue to be in the future. . . . It is enough for us that Congress feared that a market marked at the same time by both a continuous decline in the number of small businesses and a large number of mergers would slowly but inevitably gravitate from a market of many small competitors to one dominated by one or a few giants, and competition would thereby be destroyed.

United States v. Continental Can Co.

378 U.S. 441 (1964)

MR. JUSTICE WHITE delivered the opinion of the Court.

Continental Can is a New York corporation organized in 1913 to acquire all the assets of three metal container manufacturers. Since 1913 Continental has acquired 21 domestic metal container companies as well as numerous others engaged in the packaging business, including producers of flexible packaging; a manufacturer of polyethylene bottles and similar plastic containers; 14 producers of paper containers and paperboard; four companies making closures for glass containers; and one—Hazel-Atlas—producing glass containers. In 1955, the year prior to the present merger, Continental, with assets of $382 million, was the second largest company in the metal container field, shipping approximately 33% of all such containers sold in the United States. It and the largest producer, American Can Company, accounted for approximately 71% of all metal container shipments. National Can Company, the third largest, shipped approximately 5%, with the remaining 24% of the market being divided among 75 to 90 other firms. . . .

Hazel-Atlas was a West Virginia corporation which in 1955 had net sales in excess of $79 million and assets of more than $37 million. Prior to the absorption of Hazel-Atlas into Continental the pattern of dominance among a few firms in the glass container industry was similar to that which prevailed in the metal container field. Hazel-Atlas, with approximately 9.6% of the glass container shipments in 1955, was third. Owens-Illinois Glass Company had 34.2% and Anchor-Hocking Glass Company 11.6%, with the remaining 44.6% being divided among at least 39 other firms. . . .

We deal first with the relevant market. It is not disputed here, and the District Court held, that the geographical market is the entire United States. As for the product market, the court found, as was conceded by the parties, that the can industry and the glass container industry were relevant lines of commerce. Beyond these two product markets, however, the Government urged the recognition of various other lines of commerce, some of them defined in terms of the end uses for which tin and glass containers were in substantial competition. These end-use claims were containers for the beer industry, containers for the soft drink industry, containers for the canning industry, containers for the toiletry and cosmetic industry, containers for the medicine and health industry, and containers for the household and chemical industry. . . .

It is quite true that glass and metal containers have different characteristics which may disqualify one or the other, at least in their present form, from this or that particular use; that the machinery necessary to pack in glass is different from that employed when cans are used; that a particular user of cans or glass may pack in only one of the other containers and does not shift back and forth from day to day as price and other factors might make desirable; and that the competition between metal and glass containers is different from the competition between the can companies themselves or between the products of the different glass companies. These are relevant and important considerations but they are not sufficient to obscure the competitive relationships which this record so compellingly reveals.

Baby food was at one time packed entirely in metal cans. Hazel-Atlas played a significant role in inducing the shift to glass as the dominant container by designing "what has become the typical baby food jar." According to Continental's estimate, 80% of the Nation's baby food now moves in glass containers.

In the soft drink business, a field which has been, and is, predominantly glass territory, the court recognized that the metal can industry has "[a]fter considerable initial difficulty developed a can strong enough to resist the pressures generated by carbonated beverages" and "made strenuous efforts to promote the use of metal cans for carbonated beverages as against glass bottles." . . .

The District Court found that "[a]lthough at one time almost all packaged beer was sold in bottles, in a relatively short period the beer can made great headway and may well have become the dominant beer container." . . .

In the light of this record and these findings, we think the District Court employed an unduly narrow construction of the "competition" protected by §7 and of "reasonable interchangeability of use or the cross-elasticity of demand" in judging the facts of this case. We reject the opinion below insofar as it holds that these terms as used in the statute or in Brown Shoe were intended to limit the competition protected by §7 to competition which exists, for example, between the metal containers of one company and those of another, or between the several manufacturers of glass containers. Certainly, that the competition here involved may be called "inter-industry competition" and is between products with distinctive characteristics does not automatically remove it from the reach of §7. . . .

In our view there is and has been a rather general confrontation between metal and glass containers and competition between them for the same end uses which is insistent, continuous, effective and quantity-wise very substantial. Metal has replaced glass and glass has replaced metal as the leading container for some important uses; both are used for other purposes; each is trying to expand its share of the market at the expense of the other; and each is attempting to preempt for itself every use for which its product is physically suitable, even though some such uses have traditionally been regarded as the exclusive domain of the competing industry. In differing degrees for different end uses manufacturers in each industry take into consideration the price of the containers of the opposing industry in formulating their own pricing policy. Thus, though the interchangeability of use may not be so complete and the cross-elasticity of demand not so immediate as in the case of most intraindustry mergers, there is over the long run the kind of customer response to innovation and other competitive stimuli that brings the competition between these two industries within §7's competition-preserving proscriptions. . . .

Based on the evidence thus far revealed by this record we hold that the interindustry competition between glass and metal containers is sufficient to warrant treating as a relevant product market the combined glass and metal container industries and all end uses for which they compete. There may be some end uses for which glass and metal do not and could not compete, but complete interindustry competitive overlap need not be shown. We would not be true to the purpose of the Clayton Act's line of commerce concept as a framework within which to measure the effect of mergers on competition were we to hold that the existence of noncompetitive segments within a proposed market area precludes its being treated as a line of commerce. . . .

The evidence so far presented leads us to conclude that the merger between Continental and Hazel-Atlas is in violation of §7. The product market embracing the combined metal and glass container industries was dominated by six firms having a total of 70.1% of the business. Continental, with 21.9% of the shipments, ranked second within this product market, and Hazel-Atlas, with 3.1%, ranked sixth. Thus, of this vast market—amounting at the time of the merger to almost $3 billion in annual sales—a large percentage already belonged to Continental before the merger. By the acquisition of Hazel-Atlas stock Continental not only increased its own share more than 14% from 21.9% to 25%, but also reduced from five to four the most significant competitors who might have threatened its dominant position. . . .

Continental insists, however, that whatever the nature of interindustry competition in general, the types of containers produced by Continental and Hazel-Atlas at the time of the merger were for the most part not in competition with each other and hence the merger could have no effect on competition. . . .

A merger between the second and sixth largest competitors in a gigantic line of commerce is significant not only for its intrinsic effect on competition but also for its tendency to endanger a much broader anticompetitive effect by triggering other mergers by companies seeking the same competitive advantages sought by Continental in this case . . . .

It is not at all self-evident that the lack of current competition between Continental and Hazel-Atlas for some important end uses of metal and glass containers significantly diminished the adverse effect of the merger on competition. Continental might have concluded that it could effectively insulate itself from competition by acquiring a major firm not presently directing its market acquisition efforts toward the same end uses as Continental, but possessing the potential to do so. Two examples will illustrate. Both soft drinks and baby food are currently packed predominantly in glass, but Continental has engaged in vigorous and imaginative promotional activities attempting to overcome consumer preferences for glass and secure a larger share of these two markets for its tin cans. Hazel-Atlas was not at the time of the merger a significant producer of either of these containers, but with comparatively little difficulty, if it were an independent firm making independent business judgments, it could have developed its soft drink and baby food capacity. The acquisition of Hazel-Atlas by a company engaged in such intense efforts to effect a diversion of business from glass to metal in both of these lines cannot help but diminish the likelihood of Hazel-Atlas realizing its potential as a significant competitor in either line. It would make little sense for one entity within the Continental empire to be busily engaged in persuading the public of metal's superiority over glass for a given end use, while the other is making plans to increase the Nation's total glass container output for the same end use. Thus, the fact that Continental and Hazel-Atlas were not substantial competitors of each other for certain end uses at the time of the merger may actually enhance the long-run tendency of the merger to lessen competition.

We think our holding is consonant with the purpose of Section 7 to arrest anticompetitive arrangements in their incipiency. Some product lines are offered in both metal and glass containers by the same packer. In such areas the interchangeability of use and immediate interindustry sensitivity to price changes would approach that which exists between products of the same industry. In other lines, as where one packer's products move in one type container while his competitor's move in another, there are inherent deterrents to customer diversion of the same type that might occur between brands of cans or bottles. But the possibility of such transfers over the long run acts as a deterrent against attempts by the dominant members of either industry to reap the possible benefits of their position by raising prices above the competitive level or engaging in other comparable practices. And even though certain lines are today regarded as safely within the domain of one or the other of those industries, this pattern may be altered, as it has in the past. From the point of view not only of the static competitive situation but also the dynamic long-run potential, we think that the Government has discharged its burden of proving prima facie anticompetitive effect. Accordingly the judgment is reversed and the case remanded for further proceedings consistent with this opinion.

United States v. General Dynamics Corp.

415 U.S. 487 (1974)

MR. JUSTICE STEWART delivered the opinion of the Court.

On September 22, 1967, the Government commenced this suit in the United States District Court for the Northern District of Illinois, challenging as violative of §7 of the Clayton Act the acquisition of the stock of United Electric Coal Companies by Material Service Corp. and its successor, General Dynamics Corp. . . .

At the time of the acquisition involved here, Material Service Corp. was a large midwest producer and supplier of building materials, concrete, limestone, and coal. All of its coal production was from deep-shaft mines operated by it or its affiliate, appellee Freeman Coal Mining Corp., and production from these operations amounted to . . . 8.4 million tons in 1967. In 1954, Material Service began to acquire the stock of United Electric Coal Companies. United Electric at all relevant times operated only strip or open pit mines in Illinois and Kentucky; . . .by 1967, it had increased this output to 5.7 million tons. Material Service's purchase of United Electric stock continued until 1959. At this point Material's holdings amounted to more than 34% of United Electric's outstanding shares and—all parties are now agreed on this point—Material had effective control of United Electric. . . .

Some months after this takeover, Material Service was itself acquired by the appellee General Dynamics Corp. General Dynamics is a large diversified corporation, much of its revenues coming from sales of aircraft, communications, and marine products to government agencies. . . .

The thrust of the Government's complaint was that the acquisition of United Electric by Freeman and Material Service in 1959 violated §7 of the Clayton Act because the takeover substantially lessened competition in the production and sale of coal in either or both of two geographical markets. It contended that a relevant "section of the country" within the meaning of §7 was, alternatively, the State of Illinois or the Eastern Interior Coal Province Sales Area, the latter being one of four major coal distribution areas recognized by the coal industry and comprising Illinois and Indiana, and parts of Kentucky, Tennessee, Iowa, Minnesota, Wisconsin, and Missouri.

At trial controversy focused on three basic issues: the propriety of coal as a "line of commerce," the definition of Illinois or the Eastern Interior Coal Province Sales Area as a relevant "section of the country," and the probability of a lessening of competition within these or any other product and geographic markets resulting from the acquisition. The District Court decided against the Government on each of these issues. . . .

Finally, and, for purposes of this appeal most significantly, the District Court found that the evidence did not support the Government's contention that the 1959 acquisition of United Electric substantially lessened competition in any product or geographic market. This conclusion was based on four determinations made in the court's opinion. . . . In particular, the court found that virtually all of United Electric's proven coal reserves were either depleted or already committed by long-term contracts with large customers, and that United Electric's power to affect the price of coal was thus severely limited and steadily diminishing. On the basis of these considerations, the court concluded: "Under these circumstances, continuation of the affiliation between United Electric and Freeman is not adverse to competition, nor would divestiture benefit competition even were this court to accept the Government's unrealistic product and geographic market definitions."

The Government sought to prove a violation of §7 of the Clayton Act principally through statistics showing that within certain geographic markets the coal industry was concentrated among a small number of large producers; that this concentration was increasing; and that the acquisition of United Electric would materially enlarge the market share of the acquiring company and thereby contribute to the trend toward concentration.

The concentration of the coal market in Illinois and, alternatively, in the Eastern Interior Coal Province was demonstrated by a table of the shares of the largest two, four, and 10 coal producing firms in each of these areas and for both 1957 and 1967 that revealed the following:

	Eastern interior coal province		Illinois	
	1957	1967	1957	1967
Top 2 firms	29.8	48.6	37.8	52.9
Top 4 firms	43.0	62.9	54.5	75.2
Top 10 firms	65.5	91.4	84.0	98.0

	1959			1967		
	Share of top 2 but for merger	Share of top 2 given merger	Percent increase	Share of top 2 but for merger	Share of top 2 given merger	Percent increase
Province	33.1	37.9	14.5	45.0	48.6	8.0
Illinois	36.6	44.3	22.4	44.0	52.9	20.2

Finally, the Government's statistics indicated that the acquisition increased the share of the merged company in the Illinois and Eastern Interior Coal Province coal markets by significant degrees:

	Province		Illinois	
	Rank	Share (percent)	Rank	Share (percent)
1959				
Freeman	2	7.6	2	15.1
United Electric	6	4.8	5	8.1
Combined	2	12.4	1	23.2
1967				
Freeman	5	6.5	2	12.9
United Electric	9	4.4	6	8.9
Combined	2	10.9	2	21.8

While the statistical showing proffered by the Government in this case, the accuracy of which was not discredited by the District Court or contested by the respondents, would under this approach have sufficed to support a finding of "undue concentration" in the absence of other considerations, the question before us is whether the District Court was justified in finding that other pertinent factors affecting the coal industry and the business of the respondents mandated a conclusion that no substantial lessening of competition occurred or was threatened by the acquisition of United Electric. We are satisfied that the court's ultimate finding was not in error. . . .

[T]he court discerned a number of clear and significant developments in the industry. First, it found that coal had become increasingly less able to compete with other sources of energy in many segments of the energy market. . . . [C]oal's share of the energy resources consumed in this country fell from 78.4% in 1920 to 21.4% in 1963. . . .

Second, the court found that to a growing extent since 1954, the electric utility industry has become the mainstay of coal consumption. While electric utilities consumed only 15.76% of the coal produced nationally in 1947, their share of total consumption increased every year thereafter, and in 1968 amounted to more than 59% of all the coal consumed throughout the Nation.

Third, and most significantly, the court found that to an increasing degree, nearly all coal sold to utilities is transferred under long-term requirements contracts, under which coal producers promise to meet utilities' coal consumption requirements for a fixed period of time, and at predetermined prices. . . . These developments in the patterns of coal distribution and consumption, the District Court found, have limited the amounts of coal immediately available for "spot" purchases on the open market, since "[t]he growing practice by coal producers of expanding mine capacity only to meet long-term contractual commitments and the gradual disappearance of the small truck mines has tended to limit the production capacity available for spot sales."

Because of these fundamental changes in the structure of the market for coal, the District Court was justified in viewing the statistics relied on by the Government as insufficient to sustain its case. Evidence of past production does not, as a matter of logic, necessarily give a proper picture of a company's future ability to compete. In most situations, of course, the unstated assumption is that a company that has maintained a certain share of a market in the recent past will be in a position to do so in the immediate future. Thus, companies that have controlled sufficiently large shares of a concentrated market are barred from merger by §7 not because of their past acts, but because their past performances imply an ability to continue to dominate with at least equal vigor. In markets involving groceries or beer, as in Von's Grocery, and Pabst, statistics involving annual sales naturally indicate the power of each company to compete in the future. Evidence of the amount of annual sales is relevant as a prediction of future competitive strength, since in most markets distribution systems and brand recognition are such significant factors that one may reasonably suppose that a company which has attracted a given number of sales will retain that competitive strength.

In the coal market, as analyzed by the District Court, however, statistical evidence of coal production was of considerably less significance. The bulk of the coal produced is delivered under long-term requirements contracts, and such sales thus do not represent the exercise of competitive power but rather the obligation to fulfill previously negotiated contracts at a previously fixed price. The focus of competition in a given time-frame is not on the disposition of coal already produced but on the procurement of new long-term supply contracts. In this situation, a company's past ability to produce is of limited significance, since it is in a position to offer for sale neither its past production nor the bulk of the coal it is presently capable of producing, which is typically already committed under a long-term supply contract. A more significant indicator of a company's power effectively to compete with other companies lies in the state of a company's uncommitted reserves of recoverable coal. . . .

The testimony and exhibits in the District Court revealed that United Electric's coal reserve prospects were "unpromising." United's relative position of strength in reserves was considerably weaker than its past and current ability to produce. While United ranked fifth among Illinois coal producers in terms of annual production, it was 10th in reserve holdings, and controlled less than 1% of the reserves held by coal producers in Illinois, Indiana, and western Kentucky. Many of the reserves held by United had already been depleted, at the time of trial, forcing the closing of some of United's midwest mines. Even more significantly, the District Court found that of the 52,033,304 tons of currently mineable reserves in Illinois, Indiana, and Kentucky controlled by United, only four million tons had not already been committed under long-term contracts. United was found to be facing the future with relatively depleted resources at its disposal, and with the vast majority of those resources already committed under contracts allowing no further adjustments in price. In addition, the District Court found that "United Electric has neither the possibility of acquiring more [reserves] nor the ability to develop deep coal reserves," and thus was not in a position to increase its reserves to replace those already depleted or committed. . . .

One factual claim by the Government, however, goes to the heart of the reasoning of the District Court and thus is worthy of explicit note here. The Government asserts that the paucity of United Electric's coal reserves could not have the significance perceived by the District Court, since all companies engaged in extracting minerals at some point deplete their reserves and then acquire new reserves or the new technology required to extract more minerals from their existing holdings. United Electric, the Government suggests, could at any point either purchase new strip reserves or acquire the expertise to recover currently held deep reserves.

But the District Court specifically found new strip reserves not to be available: "Evidence was presented at trial by experts, by state officials, by industry witnesses and by the Government itself indicating that economically mineable strip reserves that would permit United Electric to continue operations beyond the life of its present mines are not available. The Government failed to come forward with evidence that such reserves are presently available." In addition, there was considerable testimony at trial, apparently credited by the District Court, indicating that United Electric and others had tried to find additional strip reserves not already held for coal production, and had been largely unable to do so.

Moreover, the hypothetical possibility that United Electric might in the future acquire the expertise to mine deep reserves proves nothing—or too much. As the Government pointed out in its brief and at oral argument, in recent years a number of companies with no prior experience in extracting coal have purchased coal reserves and entered the coal production business in order to diversify and complement their current operations. The mere possibility that United Electric, in common with all other companies with the inclination and the corporate treasury to do so, could some day expand into an essentially new line of business does not depreciate the validity of the conclusion that United Electric at the time of the trial did not have the power to compete on a significant scale for the procurement of future long-term contracts, nor does it vest in the production statistics relied on by the Government more significance than ascribed to them by the District Court. . . .

The judgment of the District Court is affirmed.

CHAPTER 6

VERTICAL AND CONGLOMERATE MERGERS

The Celler-Kefauver amendment to Section 7 of the Clayton Act did more than just plug the loophole. It also expanded the law's coverage. The original act prohibited mergers where the effect "may be to substantially lessen competition between the corporation whose stock is so acquired and the corporation making the acquisition. . . ." The courts read this to mean that the law applied to horizontal mergers only. The 1950 amendment said a merger was illegal if it was likely to lessen competition "in any line of commerce in any section of the country. . . ." This was read by the Court to include vertical mergers (between suppliers and buyers) and conglomerate mergers (between firms in different lines of business). The first two cases in this chapter deal with vertical mergers and the last three, with conglomerate mergers.

Brown Shoe, the first merger to reach the Supreme Court under the new law, set a very strong precedent for vertical as well as for horizontal mergers. Can you see why? If you were a nonintegrated shoe manufacturer would you have been worried by the Brown-Kinney merger? Why or why not? The Court made much of the disappearance of Kinney as a buyer from independent shoe producers, but Brown's shoe sales were removed from the open market to the same extent. Does this imply that independents were unlikely to be hurt by the merger? The Court was especially concerned about the trend toward vertical integration. Should it have been? What shoe mergers could it have stopped if it had let this one get by? The decision contains extensive discussion about market definition. Why is market definition relevant to a vertical merger case?

In the second case, the trend turned into a race. In the 1960s the cement companies were frantically buying up ready-mix producers. Why? What does this behavior suggest about cement producers' beliefs about foreclosure? So what?

Would an integrated cement-ready mix industry be less competitive than the two industries separately?

"Potential competition" is the most important issue in Procter and Gamble, but its influence is hard to pin down. Did the Court cover all the bases needed to justify its decision here? Do you think Procter and Gamble was the most likely entrant in liquid bleach? Did it have a substantial advantage in making and marketing bleach over such firms as Colgate, Lever Brothers, General Foods, and General Mills? P & G officers said they had studied the market and decided against entering "de novo" (by building their own plants and introducing their own new product) or by acquiring a smaller bleach producer. What do you make of this? In fact, they never have entered the business in the thirteen years since they were required to give up Clorox. Does this imply the Court was wrong? Do you think P & G has an effect on the bleach industry, even if it never enters the industry?

It's often hard to decide, after the fact, whether a firm is one of a few most likely entrants into an industry or not. It is certainly wrong to use the fact that a firm merged into an industry as indicating that it was the most likely entrant, but it is hard to keep the fact of the merger out of your mind when evaluating such a claim.

The Court also emphasized the huge size of P & G compared with the independent bleach makers. This comparison is often described as entrenchment. Do you think that the bleach industry would be more or less competitive with a billion dollar firm and 200 firms with sales of $1,000,000 each or with a $50 million firm and 200 firms in the million dollar category? Suppose that Colgate then acquired Purex. Would that mean more entrenchment?

Finally, the Court spoke of the discounts P & G received from the media in advertising, but there is a twist here. If P & G had economies of scale in advertising, isn't it in the public interest to let the merger go through to save advertising costs?

The fourth case has to do with banking. During the 1960s and early 1970s a large number of mergers occurred in banking as many of the leading firms in various states sought to establish statewide branch banking or bank holding-company systems. The Justice Department initiated suits in Mississippi, Idaho, Maryland, Colorado, Connecticut, and Washington in an attempt to prevent these systems from acquiring the leading independent banks in cities where they did not operate. It was hoped that these cases could divert the big systems into entry de novo or by merger with small banks. Then concentration would decline and the markets would become more competitive. The Marine Bancorporation case was Justice's strongest one because banking is more concentrated there than in most states, because Spokane is the second largest city in the state, and because the bank being acquired was the leading independent bank in town. The Court emphasized the regulatory restrictions on entry and branching. Do you think these restrictions are in the public's interest? If the Antitrust Division had won the case, might not the result have been pressure on the banking authorities to reduce their branching and entry restrictions? Finally, how do you think new potential entry cases are likely to fare before the Burger court in the future?

The last case takes another tact, reciprocity: I'll buy from you if you buy from me. Can you see why large conglomerate firms might have an advantage in such transactions? Would they still have this advantage if explicit reciprocity agreements were outlawed? Consolidated's response to the decision was to sell off its food stores and keep Gentry. Did that solve the problem? Do you think competition was advanced as a result?

Brown Shoe Co. v. United States (continued)

370 U.S. 29 (1962)

MR. CHIEF JUSTICE WARREN delivered the opinion of the Court.

Economic arrangements between companies standing in a supplier-customer relationship are characterized as "vertical." The primary vice of a vertical merger or other arrangement tying a customer to a supplier is that by foreclosing the competitors of either party from a segment of the market otherwise open to them, the arrangement may act as a "clog on competition which deprive(s) . . . rivals of a fair opportunity to compete." Every extended vertical arrangement by its very nature, for at least a time, denies to competitors of the supplier the opportunity to compete for part or all of the trade of the customer-party to the vertical arrangement. However, the Clayton Act does not render unlawful all such vertical arrangements, but forbids only those whose effect "may be substantially to lessen competition, or to tend to create a monopoly" "in any line of commerce in any section of the country." . . .

The outer boundaries of a product market are determined by the reasonable interchangeability of use or the cross-elasticity of demand between the product itself and substitutes for it. However, within this broad market, well-defined submarkets may exist which, in themselves, constitute product markets for antitrust purposes. . . . The boundaries of such a submarket may be determined by examining such practical indicia as industry or public recognition of the submarket as a separate economic entity, the product's peculiar characteristics and uses, unique production facilities, distinct customers, distinct prices, sensitivity to price changes, and specialized vendors. Because Section 7 of the Clayton Act prohibits any merger which may substantially lessen competition "in any line of commerce," it is necessary to examine the effects of a merger in each such economically significant submarket to determine if there is a reasonable probability that the merger will substantially lessen competition. If such a probability is found to exist, the merger is proscribed.

Applying these considerations to the present case, we conclude that the record supports the District Court's finding that the relevant lines of commerce are men's, women's, and children's shoes. These product lines are recognized by the public; each line is manufactured in separate plants; each has characteristics peculiar to itself rendering it generally noncompetitive with the others; and each is, of course, directed toward a distinct class of customers.

Appellant, however, contends that the District Court's definitions fail to recognize sufficiently "price/quality" and "age/sex" distinctions in shoes. Brown argues that the predominantly medium-priced shoes which it manufactures occupy a product market different from the predominantly low-priced shoes which Kinney sells. But agreement with that argument would be equivalent to holding that medium-priced shoes do not compete with low-priced shoes. We think the District

Court properly found the facts to be otherwise. It would be unrealistic to accept Brown's contention that, for example, men's shoes selling below $8.99 are in a different product market from those selling above $9.00.

This is not to say, however, that "price/quality" differences, where they exist, are unimportant in analyzing a merger; they may be of importance in determining the likely effect of a merger. But the boundaries of the relevant market must be drawn with sufficient breadth to include the competing products of each of the merging companies and to recognize competition where, in fact, competition exists. Thus we agree with the District Court that in this case a further division of product lines based on "price/quality" differences would be "unrealistic."

Brown's contention that the District Court's product market definitions should have recognized further "age/sex" distinctions raises a different problem. Brown's sharpest criticism is directed at the District Court's finding that children's shoes constituted a single line of commerce. Brown argues, for example, that "a little boy does not wear a little girl's black patent leather pump" and that "[a] male baby cannot wear a growing boy's shoes." Thus Brown argues that "infants' and babies'" shoes, "misses' and children's" shoes and "youths' and boys'" shoes should each have been considered a separate line of commerce. Assuming, arguendo, that little boys' shoes, for example, do have sufficient peculiar characteristics to constitute one of the markets to be used in analyzing the effects of this merger, we do not think that in this case the District Court was required to employ finer "age/sex" distinctions than those recognized by its classifications of "men's," "women's," and "children's" shoes. . . . Appellant can point to no advantage it would enjoy were finer divisions than those chosen by the District Court employed. Brown manufactures significant, comparable quantities of virtually every type of nonrubber men's, women's, and children's shoes, and Kinney sells such quantities of virtually every type of men's, women's, and children's shoes. Thus, whether considered separately or together, the picture of this merger is the same. . . .

We agree with the parties and the District Court that insofar as the vertical aspect of this merger is concerned, the relevant geographic market is the entire Nation. The relationships of product value, bulk, weight and consumer demand enable manufacturers to distribute their shoes on a nationwide basis, as Brown and Kinney, in fact, do. The anticompetitive effects of the merger are to be measured within this range of distribution. . . .

Since the diminution of the vigor of competition which may stem from a vertical arrangement results primarily from a foreclosure of a share of the market otherwise open to competitors, an important consideration in determining whether the effect of a vertical arrangement "may be substantially to lessen competition, or to tend to create a monopoly" is the size of the share of the market foreclosed. However, this factor will seldom be determinative. If the share of the market foreclosed is so large that it approaches monopoly proportions, the Clayton Act will, of course, have been violated; but the arrangement will also have run afoul of the Sherman Act. And the legislative history of §7 indicates clearly that the tests for measuring the legality of any particular economic arrangement under the Clayton Act are to be less stringent than those used in applying the Sherman Act. On the other hand, foreclosure of a de minimus share of the market will not tend "substantially to lessen competition."

Between these extremes, in cases such as the one before us, in which the foreclosure is neither of monopoly nor de minimus proportions, the percentage of the market foreclosed by the vertical arrangement cannot itself be decisive. In such cases, it becomes necessary to undertake an examination of various economic and historical factors in order to determine whether the arrangement under review is of the type Congress sought to proscribe. . . .

The present merger involved neither small companies nor failing companies. In 1955, the date of this merger, Brown was the fourth largest manufacturer in the shoe industry with sales of approximately 25 million pairs of shoes and assets of over $72,000,000 while Kinney had sales of about 8 million pairs of shoes and assets of about $18,000,000. Not only was Brown one of the leading manufacturers of men's, women's, and children's shoes, but Kinney, with over 350 retail outlets, owned and operated the largest independent chain of family shoe stores in the Nation. Thus, in this industry, no merger between a manufacturer and an independent retailer could involve a larger potential market foreclosure. Moreover, it is apparent both from past behavior of Brown and from the testimony of Brown's President, that Brown would use its ownership of Kinney to force Brown shoes into Kinney stores. Thus, in operation this vertical arrangement would be quite analogous to one involving a tying clause.

Another important factor to consider is the trend toward concentration in the industry. It is true, of course, that the statute prohibits a given merger only if the effect of that merger may be substantially to lessen competition. But the very wording of Section 7 requires a prognosis of the probable future effect of the merger.

The existence of a trend toward vertical integration, which the District Court found, is well substantiated by the record. Moreover, the court found a tendency of the acquiring manufacturers to become increasingly important sources of supply for their acquired outlets. The necessary corollary of these trends is the foreclosure of independent manufacturers from markets otherwise open to them. And because these trends are not the product of accident but are rather the result of deliberate policies of Brown and other leading shoe manufacturers, account must be taken of these facts in order to predict the probable future consequences of this merger. It is against this background of continuing concentration that the present merger must be viewed. . . .

Moreover, as we have remarked above, not only must we consider the probable effects of the merger upon the economics of the particular markets affected but also we must consider its probable effects upon the economic way of life sought to be preserved by Congress. Congress was desirous of preventing the formation of further oligopolies with their attendant adverse effects upon local control of industry and upon small business. Where an industry was composed of numerous independent units, Congress appeared anxious to preserve this structure. . . .

The District Court's findings, and the record facts . . . convince us that the shoe industry is being subjected to just such a cumulative series of vertical mergers which, if left unchecked, will be likely "substantially to lessen competition."

We reach this conclusion because the trend toward vertical integration in the shoe industry, when combined with Brown's avowed policy of forcing its own shoes upon its retail subsidiaries, may foreclose competition from a substantial share of the markets for men's, women's, and children's shoes, without producing any countervailing competitive, economic, or social advantages. . . .

[After reviewing the horizontal aspects of the merger as laid out in Chapter 5 of this book, the Court concluded that both the vertical and horizontal aspects of the Brown-Kinney merger were likely to lessen competition substantially. It therefore prohibited the merger.]

Federal Trade Commission, Commission Enforcement Policy with Respect to Vertical Mergers in the Cement Industry

Processed, January 17, 1967

Vertical mergers and acquisitions are today the most significant, critical and important problem faced by the cement and ready-mixed concrete industries. Beginning in the late nineteen-fifties a trend of acquisitions of leading ready-mixed concrete producers by cement manufacturers began which now threatens to transform the structures of both industries. . . .

The Commission early became concerned with vertical mergers in the cement industry in the course of carrying out its statutory duties in the enforcement of the antitrust laws. Complaints were issued at the outset initiating a series of adjudicative cases. The trend of acquisitions, however, continued. By the end of 1965 no fewer than 40 ready-mixed concrete companies had been acquired by leading cement companies, while several large ready-mixed companies had entered into the manufacture of cement. Many cement companies had indicated that while they were opposed to this development, they might be forced in the future to acquire major customers to protect their outlets from further foreclosure. Various segments of the industry requested the Commission to clarify, as soon as possible, the legal status of such mergers.

The Federal Trade Commission has concluded that vertical mergers and acquisitions involving cement manufacturers and consumers of cement, particularly ready-mixed concrete companies, can have substantial adverse effects on competition in the particular market areas where they occur. . . .

[The] urban markets, within which vertical mergers and acquisitions take place, are often highly concentrated on both the supply and demand sides. Cement is a heavy, bulky product economically impractical to ship very far except by water.

For this reason, almost all cement is sold and used comparatively near the site of production. Cement production is decentralized and is based upon a network of geographically scattered plants which ship directly, or through terminals, to consumers in adjacent markets. Most urban markets therefore are served by comparitively few producers. Out of the fifty largest metropolitan markets in the United States, 19 had five or fewer cement companies soliciting sales, and an additional 19 had only five to ten suppliers. . . .

Similarly, although there are well over 4,000 ready-mixed concrete producers in the United States, the major needs of most urban areas are supplied by a few sizeable ready-mix firms. Concrete is a highly perishable commodity of great bulk and weight and, even more crucially than in the case of cement, high transportation costs in comparison with the selling price limit the area serviceable from a particular plant. Concrete is normally not transported more than five to ten miles from the production site to the construction job of the purchase. Any given metropolitan area would therefore appear to be a definitive market for concrete production and sale. . . . In most urban centers, the ready-mixed concrete industry is quite concentrated. . . .

Out of a total 1964 cement production in the United States of 368,633,000 barrels, ready-mixed concrete companies purchased about 60 percent. The importance of the ready-mixed concrete firms as cement consumers is even greater in metropolitan centers where there is reason to believe that they account for 70 percent or more of cement purchases. . . . When one or more major ready-mixed concrete firms are tied through ownership to particular cement suppliers, the resulting foreclosure not only may be significant in the short run, but may impose heavy long-run burdens on the disadvantaged cement suppliers who continue selling in markets affected by integration. Acquisitions of leading cement consumers in markets containing comparatively few volume buyers may have the effect of substantially disrupting the competitive situation at the cement level, and, in fact, may set off a "chain" reaction of acquisitions.

Unintegrated ready-mixed concrete producers furthermore may be at a disadvantage in competing with rivals who are integrated cement and concrete manufacturers. This is true not only because of disparities in size and access to capital, and the advantages inherent in product and market diversification, but also because of the potential "price squeeze" latent in competition with integrated companies.

The more extensive vertical integration becomes in the cement and concrete industries, the higher tends to be the level of entry barriers in individual metropolitan markets and in larger geographic regions. This can result from a number of causes. Higher capital requirements are necessitated by entry into the production of cement and ready-mixed concrete on an integrated basis. The capital requirements for entry on an integrated basis appear to be double the cost of entry into the production of cement only. But the need for far more capital is not the only problem. Industry executives at the public hearings were unanimous in stating the difficulty of penetrating the ready-mixed concrete industry on a significant scale in markets containing long established ready-mixed concrete producers. New entrants in ready-mixed concrete in integrated markets, of course, may face the additional deterring effect of competition with very large, diversified and integrated rivals.

[T]his Commission wishes to make abundantly clear, insofar as possible, its future enforcement policy with regard to vertical mergers in the cement and ready-mixed concrete industries. In so doing it is expected that needless litigation may be forestalled. At the same time however it should be noted that the issues in any proceeding instituted by the Commission will be decided on the merits of that case.

I. The Commission has determined as a matter of general enforcement policy to use all the legal weapons at its disposal to proceed against and order the divestiture of those vertical acquisitions which it believes may unlawfully lessen competition in any market. Specifically, the Commission intends to investigate expeditiously every future acquisition by a cement producer of any substantial ready-mixed concrete firm in any market to which such acquiring producer is an actual or potential supplier. Whenever such an investigation reveals the market circumstances described below, the Commission shall issue a complaint challenging the acquisition under Section 7 of the Clayton Act, unless unusual circumstances in a particular case dictate the contrary.

II. In general, the acquisition of any ready-mixed concrete firm ranking among the leading four nonintegrated ready-mixed concrete company, or other cement consumer, which regularly purchases 50,000 barrels of cement or more annually, will be considered to constitute a substantial acquisition.

Federal Trade Commission v. Procter & Gamble Co.

386 U.S. 569 (1967)

MR. JUSTICE DOUGLAS delivered the opinion of the Court.

This is a proceeding initiated by the Federal Trade Commission charging that respondent, Procter & Gamble Co., had acquired the assets of Clorox Chemical Co. in violation of Section 7 of the Clayton Act. The charge was that Procter's acquisition of Clorox might substantially lessen competition or tend to create a monopoly in the production and sale of household liquid bleaches.

As indicated by the Commission in its painstaking and illuminating report, it does not particularly aid analysis to talk of the merger in conventional terms, namely, horizontal or vertical or conglomerate. This merger may most appropriately be described as a "product-extension merger," as the Commission stated. The facts are not disputed, and a summary will demonstrate the correctness of the Commission's decision.

At the time of the merger, in 1957, Clorox was the leading manufacturer in the heavily concentrated household liquid bleach industry. It is agreed that household liquid bleach is the relevant line of commerce. The product is used in the home as a germicide and disinfectant, and, more importantly, as a whitening agent in washing clothes and fabrics. It is a distinctive product with no close substitutes. Liquid bleach is a low-price, high-turnover consumer product sold mainly through grocery stores and super-markets. The relevant geographical market is the Nation and a series of regional markets. Because of high shipping costs and low sales price, it is not feasible to ship the product more than 300 miles from its point of manufacture. Most manufacturers are limited to competition within a single region since they have but one plant. Clorox is the only firm selling nationally; it has 13 plants distributed throughout the Nation. Purex, Clorox's closest competitor in size, does not distribute its bleach in the northeast or mid-Atlantic States; in 1957, Purex's bleach was available in less than 50% of the national market.

At the time of the acquisition, Clorox was the leading manufacturer of household liquid bleach, with 48.8% of the national sales—annual sales of slightly less than $40,000,000. Its market share had been steadily increasing for the five years prior to the merger. Its nearest rival was Purex, which manufactures a number of products other than household liquid bleaches, including abrasive cleaners, toilet soap, and detergents. Purex accounted for 15.7% of the household liquid bleach market. The industry is highly concentrated; in 1957, Clorox and Purex accounted for almost 65% of the Nation's household liquid bleach sales, and, together with four other firms, for almost 80%. . . . The remaining 20% was divided among over 200 small producers. . . .

Since all liquid bleach is chemically identical, advertising and sales promotion are vital. In 1957 Clorox spent almost $3,700,000 on advertising, imprinting the value of its bleach in the mind of the consumer. In addition, it spent $1,700,000 for other promotional activities. The Commission found that these heavy expenditures went far to explain why Clorox maintained so high a market share despite the fact that its brand, though chemically indistinguishable from rival brands, retailed for a price equal to or, in many instances, higher than its competitors.

Procter is a large, diversified manufacturer of low-price, high-turnover household products sold through grocery, drug, and department stores. Prior to its acquisition of Clorox, it did not produce household liquid bleach. Its 1957 sales were in excess of $1,100,000,000 from which it realized profits of more than $67,000,000; its assets were over $500,000,000. Procter has been marked by rapid growth and diversification. It has successfully developed and introduced a number of new products. Its primary activity is in the general area of soaps, detergents, and cleansers; in 1957, of total domestic sales, more than one-half (over $500,000,000) were in this field. Procter was the dominant factor in this area. It accounted for 54.4% of all packaged detergent sales. The industry is heavily concentrated—Procter and its nearest competitors, Colgate-Palmolive and Lever Brothers account for 80% of the market.

In the marketing of soaps, detergents, and cleansers, as in the marketing of household liquid bleach, advertising and sales promotion are vital. In 1957, Procter was the Nation's largest advertiser, spending more than $80,000,000 on advertising and an additional $47,000,000 on sales promotion. Due to its tremendous volume, Procter receives substantial discounts from the media. As a multi-product producer Procter enjoys substantial advantages in advertising and sales promotion. Thus, it can and does feature several products in its promotions, reducing the printing, mailing, and other costs for each product. It also purchases network programs on behalf of several products, enabling it to give each product network exposure at a fraction of the cost per product that a firm with only one product to advertise would incur.

Prior to the acquisition, Procter was in the course of diversifying into product lines related to its basic detergent-soap-cleanser business. Liquid bleach was a distinct possibility since packaged detergents—Procter's primary product line— and liquid bleach are used complementarily in washing clothes and fabrics, and in general household cleaning. . . .

The decision to acquire Clorox was the result of a study conducted by Procter's promotion department designed to determine the advisability of entering the liquid bleach industry. The initial report noted the ascendancy of liquid bleach in the large and expanding household bleach market, and recommended that Procter purchase Clorox rather than enter independently. Since a large investment would be needed to obtain a satisfactory market share, acquisition of the industry's leading firm was attractive. . . . The initial report predicted that Procter's "sales, distribution and manufacturing setup" could increase Clorox's share of the markets in areas where it was low. The final report confirmed the conclusions of the initial report and emphasized that Procter would make more effective use of Clorox's advertising budget and that the merger would facilitate advertising economies. A few months later, Procter acquired the assets of Clorox. . . .

The Commission . . . found that the substitution of Procter with its huge assets and advertising advantages for the already dominant Clorox would dissuade new entrants and discourage active competition from the firms already in the industry due to fear of retaliation by Procter. The Commission thought it relevant that retailers might be induced to give Clorox preferred shelf space since it would be manufactured by Procter, which also produced a number of other products marketed by the retailers. There was also the danger that Procter might underprice Clorox in order to drive out competition, and subsidize the underpricing with revenue from other products. . . . Further, the merger would seriously diminish potential competition by eliminating Procter as a potential entrant into the industry. Prior to the merger, the Commission found, Procter was the most likely prospective entrant, and absent the merger would have remained on the periphery, restraining Clorox from exercising its market power. If Procter had actually entered, Clorox's dominant position would have been eroded and the concentration of the industry reduced. The Commission stated that it had not placed reliance on post-acquisition evidence in holding the merger unlawful. . . .

The anticompetitive effects with which this product-extension merger is fraught can easily be seen: (1) the substitution of the powerful acquiring firm for the smaller, but already dominant, firm may substantially reduce the competitive structure of the industry by raising entry barriers and by dissuading the smaller firms from aggressively competing; (2) the acquisition eliminates the potential competition of the acquiring firm.

The liquid bleach industry was already oligopolistic before the acquisition, and price competition was certainly not as vigorous as it would have been if the industry were competitive. Clorox enjoyed a dominant position nationally, and its position approached monopoly proportions in certain areas. The existence of some 200 fringe firms certainly does not belie that fact. Nor does the fact, relied upon by the court below, that, after the merger, producers other than Clorox "were selling more bleach for more money than ever before." In the same period, Clorox increased its share from 48.8% to 52%. The interjection of Procter into the market considerably changed the situation. There is every reason to assume that the smaller firms would become more cautious in competing due to their fear of retaliation by Procter. It is probable that Procter would become the price leader and that oligopoly would become more rigid.

The acquisition may also have the tendency of raising the barriers to new entry. The major competitive weapon in the successful marketing of bleach is advertising. Clorox was limited in this area by its relatively small budget and its inability to obtain substantial discounts. By contrast, Procter's budget was much larger; and, although it would not devote its entire budget to advertising Clorox, it could divert a large portion to meet the short-term threat of a new entrant. Procter would be able to use its volume discounts to advantage in advertising Clorox. Thus, a new entrant would be much more reluctant to face the giant Procter than it would have been to face the smaller Clorox.

Possible economies cannot be used as a defense to illegality. Congress was aware that some mergers which lessen competition may also result in economies but it struck the balance in favor of protecting competition.

The Commission also found that the acquisition of Clorox by Procter eliminated Procter as a potential competitor. The Court of Appeals declared that this finding was not supported by evidence because there was no evidence that Procter's management had ever intended to enter the industry independently and that Procter had never attempted to enter. The evidence, however, clearly shows that Procter was the most likely entrant. Procter had recently launched a new abrasive cleaner in an industry similar to the liquid bleach industry, and had wrested leadership from a brand that had enjoyed even a larger market share than had Clorox. Procter was engaged in a vigorous program of diversifying into product lines closely related to its basic products. Liquid bleach was a natural avenue of diversification since it is complementary to Procter's products, is sold to the same customers through the same channels, and is advertised and merchandised in the same manner. Procter had substantial advantages in advertising and sales promotion which, as we have seen, are vital to the success of liquid bleach. No manufacturer had a patent on the product or its manufacture, necessary information relating to manufacturing methods and processes were readily available, there was no shortage of raw material, and the machinery and equipment required for a plant of efficient capacity were available at reasonable cost. Procter's management was experienced in producing and marketing goods similar to liquid bleach. Procter had considered the possibility of independently entering but decided against it because the acquisition of Clorox would enable Procter to capture a more commanding share of the market.

It is clear that the existence of Procter at the edge of the industry exerted considerable influence on the market. First, the market behavior of the liquid bleach industry was influenced by each firm's predictions of the market behavior of its competitors, actual and potential. Second, the barriers to entry by a firm of Procter's size and with its advantages were not significant. There is no indication that the barriers were so high that the price Procter would have to charge would be above the price that would maximize the profits of the existing firms. Third, the number of potential entrants was not so large that the elimination of one would be insignificant. Few firms would have the temerity to challenge a firm as solidly entrenched as Clorox. Fourth, Procter was found by the Commission to be the most likely entrant. These findings of the Commission were amply supported by the evidence.

The judgment of the Court of Appeals is reversed and remanded with instructions to affirm and enforce the Commission's order.

United States v. Marine Bancorporation, Inc.
418 U.S. 602 (1974)

MR. JUSTICE POWELL delivered the opinion of the Court.

The United States brought this civil antitrust action under §7 of the Clayton Act to challenge a proposed merger between two commercial banks. The acquiring bank is a large, nationally chartered bank based in Seattle, Washington, and the acquired bank is a medium-size, state-chartered bank located at the opposite end of the State in Spokane. The banks are not direct competitors to any significant degree in Spokane or any other part of the State. They have no banking offices in each other's home cities. The merger agreement would substitute the acquiring bank for the acquired bank in Spokane and would permit the former for the first time to operate as a direct participant in the Spokane market. . . .

The acquiring bank, National Bank of Commerce (NBC), is a national banking association with its principal office in Seattle, Washington. . . . NBC is a wholly owned subsidiary of a registered bank holding company, Marine Bancorporation, Inc. (Marine), and in terms of assets, deposits, and loans is the second largest banking organization with headquarters in the State of Washington. . . . It operates 107 branch banking offices within the state, 59 of which are located in the Seattle metropolitan area and 31 of which are in lesser developed sections of eastern Washington. . . .

The target bank, Washington Trust Bank (WTB), founded in 1902, is a state bank with headquarters in Spokane. . . .

WTB has seven branch offices. . . . WTB is the eighth largest banking organization with headquarters in Washington and the ninth largest banking organization in the State. . . .

WTB is well managed and profitable. From December 31, 1966, to June 30, 1972, it increased its percentage of total deposits held by banking organizations in the Spokane metropolitan area from 16.6 percent to 18.6 percent. . . .

As of June 30, 1972, there were 91 national and state banking organizations in Washington. The five largest in the State held 74.3 percent of the State's total commercial bank deposits and operated 61.3 percent of its banking offices. At that time, the two largest in the State, Seattle-First National Bank and NBC, held 51.3 percent of total deposits and operated 36.5 percent of the banking offices in Washington. There are six banking organizations operating in the Spokane metropolitan area. . . . The target bank held 18.6 percent of total deposits at that time, placing it third in the Spokane area behind Washington Bancshares, Inc., and Seattle-First National Bank. Thus, taken together, Washington Bancshares, Seattle-First National Bank and WTB hold approximately 92 percent of total deposits in the Spokane area. None of the remaining three commercial banks in Spokane holds a market share larger than 3.1 percent. . . .

The degree of concentration of the commercial banking business in Spokane may well reflect the severity of Washington's statutory restraints on de novo geographic expansion by banks. Although Washington permits branching, the restrictions placed on that method of internal growth are stringent. . . . Since federal law subjects nationally chartered banks to the branching limitations imposed on their state counterparts, . . . national and state banks in Washington are restricted to mergers or acquisitions in order to expand into cities and towns with preexisting banking organizations.

The ability to acquire existing banks is also limited by a provision of state law requiring that banks incorporating in Washington include in their articles of incorporation a clause forbidding a new bank from merging with or permitting its assets to be acquired by another bank for a period of at least ten years, without the consent of the state supervisor of banking. . . . [O]nce a bank acquires or takes over one of the banks operating in a city or town other than the acquiring bank's principal place of business, it cannot branch from the acquired bank. . . . Thus, an acquiring bank that enters a new city or town containing banks other than the acquired bank is restricted to the number of bank offices obtained at the time of the acquisition. Moreover, multibank holding companies are prohibited in Washington. . . . Accordingly, it is not possible in Washington to achieve the rough equivalent of free branching by aggregating a number of unit banks under a bank holding company.

In February 1971, Marine, NBC, and WTB agreed to merge the latter into NBC. NBC, as the surviving bank, would operate all eight banking offices of WTB as branches of NBC. In March 1971, NBC and WTB applied to the Comptroller of the Currency pursuant to the Bank Merger Act of 1966 for approval of the merger. . . .

The Comptroller approved the merger in a report issued September 24, 1971. He concluded that state law precluded NBC from branching in Spokane and "effectively prevented" NBC from causing a new Spokane bank to be formed which could later be treated as a merger partner. . . . The Comptroller relied heavily on the view that the merger would contribute to the convenience and needs of bank customers in Spokane by bringing to them services not previously provided by WTB. . . .

[T]he United States then commenced this action in the United States District Court for the Western District of Washington, challenging the legality of the merger under §7 of the Clayton Act. . . . The United States sought to establish that the merger "may . . . substantially . . . lessen competition" within the meaning of §7 in three ways: by eliminating the prospect that NBC, absent acquisition of the market share represented by WTB, would enter Spokane de novo or through acquisition of a smaller bank and thus would assist in deconcentrating that market over the long run; by ending present procompetitive effects allegedly produced in Spokane by NBC's perceived presence on the fringe of the Spokane market; and by terminating the alleged probability that WTB as an independent entity would develop through internal growth or through mergers with other medium-size banks into a regional or ultimately statewide counterweight to the market power of the State's largest banks. . . .

The District Court found that the relevant product market "within which the competitive effect of the merger is to be judged" is the "business of commercial banking (and the cluster of products and services denoted thereby). . . ."

The District Court found that the relevant geographic market is the Spokane metropolitan area, "consisting of the City of Spokane and the populated areas immediately adjacent thereto. . . ." It contains all eight of the target bank's offices. On the basis of the record, we have no reason to doubt that it constitutes a reasonable approximation of the "localized" banking market in which Spokane banks offer the major part of their services and to which local consumers can practicably turn for alternatives. . . . [W]e affirm the District Court's holding that the Spokane metropolitan area is the appropriate geographic market for determining the legality of the merger. . . .

[T]he Government contends that the entire state is also an appropriate "section of the country" in this case. It is conceded that the state is not a banking market. But the Government asserts that the state is an economically differentiated region, because its boundaries delineate an area within which Washington banks are insulated from most forms of competition by out-of-state banking organizations. The Government further argues that this merger, and others it allegedly will trigger, may lead eventually to the domination of all banking in the state by a few large banks, facing each other in a network of local, oligopolistic banking markets. . . .

The Government's proposed reading of the "any section of the country" phrase of §7 is at variance with this Court's §7 cases, and we reject it. Without exception the Court has treated "section of the country" and "relevant geographic market" as identical. . . . In cases in which the acquired firm markets its products or services on a local, regional, and national basis, the Court has acknowledged the existence of more than one relevant geographic market. But in no previous §7 case has the Court determined the legality of a merger by measuring its effects on areas where the acquired firm is not a direct competitor. . . . We hold that in a potential-competition case like this one, the relevant geographic market or appropriate section of the country is the area in which the acquired firm is an actual, direct competitor. . . .

The term potential competitor appeared for the first time in a §7 opinion of this Court in *United States v. El Paso Natural Gas Co.,* 376 U.S. 651, 659 (1964). El Paso was in reality, however, an actual-competition rather than a potential-competition case. . . . Unequivocal proof that an acquiring firm actually would have entered de novo but for a merger is rarely available. . . .

[T]he principal focus of the doctrine is on the likely effects of the premerger position of the acquiring firm on the fringe of the target market. In developing and applying the doctrine, the Court has recognized that a market extension merger may be unlawful if the target market is substantially concentrated, if the acquiring firm has the characteristics, capabilities, and economic incentive to render it a perceived potential de novo extrant, and if the acquiring firm's premerger presence on the fringe of the target market in fact tempered oligopolistic behavior on the part of existing participants in that market. In other words, the Court has interpreted §7 as encompassing what is commonly known as the "wings effect"— the probability that the acquiring firm prompted premerger procompetitive effects within the target market by being perceived by the existing firms in that market as likely to enter de novo. . . . The elimination of such present procompetitive effects may render a merger unlawful under §7.

Although the concept of perceived potential entry has been accepted in the Court's prior §7 cases, the potential-competition theory upon which the Government places principal reliance in the instant case has not. The Court has not previously resolved whether the potential-competition doctrine proscribes a market extension merger solely on the ground that such a merger eliminates the prospect for long-term deconcentration of an oligopolistic market that in theory might result if the acquiring firm were forbidden to enter except through a de novo undertaking or through the acquisition of a small existing entrant (a so-called foothold or toehold acquisition).

The Government's potential-competition argument in the instant case proceeds in five steps. First, it argues that the potential-competition doctrine applies with full force to commercial banks. Second, it submits that the Spokane commercial banking market is sufficiently concentrated to invoke that doctrine. Third, it urges us to resolve in its favor the question [of potential competition. . . .] Fourth, it contends that without regard to the possibility of future deconcentration of the Spokane market, the challenged merger is illegal under established doctrine because it eliminates NBC as a perceived potential entrant. Finally, it asserts that the merger will eliminate WTB's potential for growth outside Spokane. We shall address those points in the order presented. . . .

Although the Court's prior bank merger cases have involved combinations between actual competitors operating in the same geographic markets, an element that distinguishes them factually from this case, they nevertheless are strong precedents for the view that §7 doctrines are applicable to commercial banking. In accord with the general principles of those cases, we hold that geographic market extension mergers by commercial banks must pass muster under the potential-competition doctrine. We further hold, however, that the application of the doctrine to commercial banking must take into account the unique federal and state regulatory restraint on entry into that line of commerce. . . .

Unlike for example, the beer industry. . . . entry of new competitors into the commercial banking field is "wholly a matter of governmental grace. . . ." and "far from easy." . . . Beer manufacturers are free to base their decisions regarding entry and the scale of entry into a new geographic market on nonregulatory considerations, including their own financial capabilities, their long-range goals as to markets, the cost of creating new production and distribution facilities, and above all the profit prospects in the target market. They need give no thought to public needs and convenience. No comparable freedom exists for commercial banks. . . . [E]ntry into and exit from the commercial banking business have been extensively regulated by the Federal and State Governments. . . .

In Philadelphia National Bank [374 U.S. 321 (1963), a horizontal merger case], the Court relied on regulatory barriers to entry to support its conclusion that mergers between banks in direct competition in the same market must be scrutinized with particular care under §7. . . . But the same restrictions on new entry render it difficult to hold that a geographic market extension merger by a commercial bank is unlawful under the potential-competition doctrine. Such limitations often significantly reduce, if they do not eliminate, the likelihood that the acquiring bank is either a perceived potential de novo entrant or a source of future competitive benefits through de novo or foothold entry. . . .

Since the legality of the challenged merger must be judged by its effects on the relevant product and geographic markets, commercial banking in the Spokane metropolitan area, it is imperative to determine the competitive characteristics of commercial banking in that section of the country. The potential-competition doctrine has meaning only as applied to concentrated markets. That is, the doctrine comes into play only where there are dominant participants in the target market engaging in interdependent or parallel behavior and with the capacity effectively to determine price and total output of goods or services. If the target market performs as a competitive market in traditional antitrust terms, the participants in the market will have no occasion to fashion their behavior to take into account the presence of a potential entrant. The present procompetitive effects that a perceived potential entrant may produce in an oligopolistic market will already have been accomplished if the target market is performing competitively. Likewise, there would be no need for concern about the prospects of long-term deconcentration of a market which is in fact genuinely competitive.

In an effort to establish that the Spokane commercial banking market is oligopolistic, the Government relied primarily on concentration ratios indicating that three banking organizations (including WTB) control approximately 92 percent of total deposits in Spokane. . . . neither the Government nor the appellees undertook any significant study of the performance, as compared to the structure, of the commercial banking market in Spokane.

We conclude that by introducing evidence of concentration ratios of the magnitude of those present here the Government established a prima facie case that the Spokane market was a candidate for the potential-competition doctrine. On this aspect of the case, the burden was then upon appellees to show that the concentration ratios, which can be unreliable indicators of actual market behavior, see *United States v. General Dynamics Corp.,* 415 U.S. 486 (1974), did not accurately depict the economic characteristics of the Spokane market. In our view, appellees did not carry this burden. . . .

. . . The Government contends that the challenged merger violates §7 because it eliminates the alleged likelihood that, but for the merger, NBC would enter Spokane de novo or through a foothold acquisition. Utilization of one of these methods of entry, it is argued, would be likely to produce deconcentration of the Spokane market over the long run or other procompetitive effects, because NBC would be required to compete vigorously to expand its initially insignificant market share.

Two essential preconditions must exist before it is possible to resolve whether the Government's theory, if provided, establishes a violation of §7.

It must be determined: (1) that in fact NBC has available feasible means for entering the Spokane market other than by acquiring WTB; and (2) that those means offer a substantial likelihood of ultimately producing deconcentration of that market or other significant precompetitive effects. . . .

It is undisputed that under state law NBC cannot establish de novo branches in Spokane and that its parent holding company cannot hold more than 25 percent of the stock of any other bank. Entry for NBC into Spokane therefore must be by acquisition of an existing bank. The Government contends that NBC has two distinct alternatives for acquisition of banks smaller than WTB and that either alternative would be likely to benefit the Spokane commercial banking market.

First, the Government contends that NBC could arrange for the formation of a new bank (a concept known as sponsorship), insure that the stock for such a new bank is placed in friendly hands, and then ultimately acquire that bank. Appellees respond that this approach would violate the spirit if not the letter of state law restrictions on bank branching. . . .

Although we note that the intricate procedure for entry by sponsorship espoused by the Government can scarcely be compared to the de novo entry opportunities available to unregulated enterprises such as beer producers, we will assume, arguendo, that NBC conceivably could succeed in sponsoring and then acquiring a new bank in Spokane at some indefinite time in the future. It does not follow from this assumption, however, that this method of entry would be reasonably likely to produce any significant procompetitive benefits in the Spokane commercial banking market. To the contrary, it appears likely that such a method of entry would not significantly affect that market.

State law would not allow NBC to branch from a sponsored bank after it was acquired. NBC's entry into Spokane therefore would be frozen at the level of its initial acquisition. Thus, if NBC were to enter Spokane by sponsoring and acquiring a small bank, it would be trapped into a position of operating a single branch office in a large metropolitan area with no reasonable likelihood of developing a significant share of that market. . . . This assumed method of entry therefore would offer little realistic hope of ultimately producing deconcentration of the Spokane market.

As a second alternative method of entry, the Government proposed that NBC could enter by a foothold acquisition of one of two small, state-chartered commercial banks that operate in the Spokane metropolitan area. Appellees reply that one of those banks is located in a suburb and has no offices in the city of Spokane, that after an acquisition NBC under state law could not branch from the suburb into the city, and that such a peripheral foothold cannot be viewed as an economically feasible method of entry into the relevant market. . . .

Granting the Government the benefit of the doubt that these two small banks were available merger partners for NBC, or were available at some not too distant time, it again does not follow that an acquisition of either would produce the long-term market-structure benefits predicted by the Government. Once NBC acquired either of these banks, it could not branch from the acquired bank. This limitation strongly suggests that NBC would not develop into a significant participant in the Spokane market. . . .

In sum, with regard to either of its proposed alternative methods of entry, the Government has offered an unpersuasive case on the [third issue]—that feasible, alternative methods of entry in fact existed. Putting these difficulties aside, the Government simply did not establish the second precondition. It failed to demonstrate that the altnerative means offer a reasonable prospect of long-term structural improvement or other benefits in the target market. In fact, insofar as competitive benefits are concerned, the Government is in the anomalous position of opposing a geographic market extension merger that will introduce a third full-service banking organization to the Spokane market, where only two are now operating, in reliance on alternative means of entry that appear unlikely to have any significant procompetitive effect. . . .

The Government's failure to establish that NBC has alternative methods of entry that offer a reasonable likelihood of producing procompetitive effects is determinative of the fourth step of its argument. Rational commercial bankers in Spokane, it must be assumed, are aware of the regulatory barriers that render NBC an unlikely or an insignificant potential entrant except by merger with WTB. In light of those barriers, it is improbable that NBC exerts any meaningful procompetitive influence over Spokane banks by standing "in the wings." . . .

In the final step of its argument, the Government challenges the merger on the ground that it will eliminate the prospect that WTB may expand outside its base in Spokane and eventually develop into a direct competitor with large Washington banks in other areas of the State. At no time in its 70-year history has WTB established branches outside the Spokane metropolitan area. Nor has it ever acquired another bank . . . or received a merger offer other than the one at issue here. . . . In sum, the Government's argument about the elimination of WTB's potential for expansion outside Spokane is little more than speculation. . . .

In applying the doctrine of potential competition to commercial banking, courts must, as we have noted, take into account the extensive federal and state regulation of banks. Our affirmance of the District Court's judgment in this case rests primarily on state statutory barriers to de novo entry and to expansion following entry into a new geographic market. In states where such stringent barriers exist and in the absence of a likelihood of entrenchment, the potential-competition doctrine—grounded as it is on relative freedom of entry on the part of the acquiring firm—will seldom bar a geographic market extension merger by a commercial bank. In states that permit free branching or multibank holding companies, courts hearing cases involving such mergers should take into account all relevant factors, including the barriers to entry created by state and federal control over the issuance of new bank charters. . . . If regulatory restraints are not determinative, courts should consider the factors that are pertinent to any potential-competition case, including the economic feasibility and likelihood of de novo entry, the capabilities and expansion history of the acquiring firm, and the performance as well as the structural characteristics of the target market.

Federal Trade Commission v. Consolidated Foods Corp.

380 U.S. 592 (1965)

MR. JUSTICE DOUGLAS delivered the opinion of the Court.

The question presented involves an important construction and application of §7 of the Clayton Act. Consolidated Foods Corp.—which owns food processing plants and a network of wholesale and retail food stores—acquired Gentry, Inc., in 1951. Gentry manufactures principally dehydrated onion and garlic. The Federal Trade Commission held that the acquisition violated §7 because it gave respondent the advantage of a mixed threat and lure of reciprocal buying in its competition for business and "the power to foreclose competition from a substantial share of the markets for dehydrated onion and garlic." It concluded, in other words, that the effect of the acquisition "may be substantially to lessen competition" within the meaning of §7, and it ordered divestiture and gave other relief. The Court of Appeals, relying mainly on 10 years of post-acquisition experience, held that the Commission had failed to show a probability that the acquisition would substantially lessen competition. . . .

We hold at the outset that the "reciprocity" made possible by such an acquisition is one of the congeries of anticompetitive practices at which the antitrust laws are aimed. The practice results in "an irrelevant and alien factor," intruding into the choice among competing products, creating at the least "a priority on the business at equal prices." Reciprocal trading may ensue not from bludgeoning or coercion but from more subtle arrangements. A threatened withdrawal of orders if products of an affiliate cease being bought, as well as a conditioning of future purchases on the receipt of orders for products of that affiliate, is an anticompetitive practice. Section 7 of the Clatyon Act is concerned "with probabilities, not certainties." Reciprocity in trading as a result of an acquisition violates §7, if the probability of a lessening of competition is shown. . . .

Consolidated is a substantial purchaser of the products of food processors who in turn purchase dehydrated onion and garlic for use in preparing and packaging their food. Gentry, which as noted is principally engaged in the manufacture of dehydrated onion and garlic, had in 1950, immediately prior to its acquisition by Consolidated, about 32% of the total sales of the dehydrated garlic and onion industry and, together with its principal competitor, Basic Vegetable Products, Inc., accounted for almost 90% of the total industry sales. The remaining 10% was divided between two other firms. By 1958 the total industry output of both products had doubled, Gentry's share rising to 35% and the combined share of Gentry and Basic remaining at about 90%.

After the acquisition Consolidated (though later disclaiming adherence to any policy of reciprocity) did undertake to assist Gentry in selling. An official of Consolidated wrote as follows to its distributing divisions:

> Oftentimes, it is a great advantage to know when you are calling on a prospect, whether or not that prospect is a supplier of someone within your own organization. Everyone believes in reciprocity providing all things are equal. . . .

Food processors who sold to Consolidated stated they would give their onion and garlic business to Gentry for reciprocity reasons if it could meet the price and quality of its competitors' products. . . .

Some suppliers responded and gave reciprocal orders. Some who first gave generous orders later reduced them or abandoned the practice. It is impossible to recreate the precise anatomy of the market arrangements following the acquisition, though respondent offers a factual brief seeking to prove that "reciprocity" either failed or was not a major factor in the post-acquisition history.

The Commission found, however, that "merely as a result of its connection with Consolidated, and without any action on the latter's part, Gentry would have an unfair advantage over competitors enabling it to make sales that otherwise might not have been made." . . .

The Court of Appeals, on the other hand, gave post-acquisition evidence almost conclusive weight. It pointed out that, while Gentry's share of the dehydrated onion market increased by some 7%, its share of the dehydrated garlic market decreased 12%. It also relied on apparently unsuccessful attempts at reciprocal buying. The Court of Appeals concluded that "Probability can best be gauged by what the past has taught." . . .

The Court of Appeals was not in error in considering the post-acquisition evidence in this case. But we think it gave too much weight to it. No group acquiring a company with reciprocal buying opportunities is entitled to a "free trial" period. To give it such would be to distort the scheme of §7. The "mere possibility" of the prohibited restraint is not enough. Probability of the proscribed evil is required, as we have noted. If the post-acquisition evidence were given conclusive weight or allowed to override all probabilities, then acquisitions would go forward willy-nilly, the parties biding their time until reciprocity was allowed fully to bloom. . . . But the force of §7 is still in probabilities, not in what later transpired. That must necessarily be the case, for once the two companies are united no one knows what the fate of the acquired company and its competitors would have been but for the merger.

Moreover, the post-acquisition evidence here tends to confirm, rather than cast doubt upon, the probable anticompetitive effect which the Commission found the merger would have. The Commission found that Basic's product was superior to Gentry's—as Gentry's president freely and repeatedly admitted. Yet Gentry, in a rapidly expanding market, was able to increase its share of onion sales by 7% and to hold its losses in garlic to a 12% decrease. Thus the Commission was surely on safe ground in reaching the following conclusion:

> If reciprocal buying creates for Gentry a protected market, which others cannot penetrate despite superiority of price, quality, or service, competition is lessened whether or not Gentry can expand its market share. It is for this reason that we reject respondent's argument that the decline in its share of the garlic market proves the ineffectiveness of reciprocity. We do not know that its share would not have fallen still farther, had it not been for the influence of reciprocal buying. This loss of sales fails to refute the likelihood that Consolidated's reciprocity power, which it has shown a willingness to exploit to the full, will not immunize a substantial segment of the garlic market from normal quality, price, and service competition.

We do not go so far as to say that any acquisition, no matter how small, violates §7 if there is a probability of reciprocal buying. Some situations may amount only to de minimus. But where, as here, the acquisition is of a company that commands a substantial share of a market, a finding of probability of reciprocal buying by the Commission, whose expertise the Congress trusts, should be honored, if there is substantial evidence to support it.

The evidence is in our view plainly substantial. Reciprocity was tried over and over again and it sometimes worked. The industry structure was peculiar, Basic being the leader with Gentry closing the gap. Moreover there is evidence, as the Commission found, "that many buyers have determined that their source of supply may best be protected by a policy of buying from two suppliers." When reciprocal buying—or the inducement of it—is added, the Commission observed:

> Buyers are likely to lean toward Basic on the ground of quality, but, in seeking a second, protective supply channel, to purchase from Gentry in the belief that this will further their sales to Consolidated. Not only does Gentry thus obtain sales that might otherwise go to Basic or Puccinelli, but the two-firm oligopoly structure of the industry is strengthened and solidified and new entry by others is discouraged. . . .

We conclude that there is substantial evidence to sustain that conclusion and that the order of the Commission should not have been denied enforcement.

CHAPTER 7

PRICE DISCRIMINATION

The Robinson-Patman Act was passed in 1936. It was intensively enforced by the FTC in the late 1930s, but its authoritative interpretation by the Supreme Court came only after World War II. Its meaning was not at all clear because the act was the largest and most complex piece of legislation in the antitrust laws.

The first case in this chapter has to do primarily with "injury to competition." What did the Supreme Court decide that this means? Do you think that the fact that all buyers were charged according to the same discount schedule should solve the problem? What must the FTC do to prove injury to competition? Do you think that the discount schedule might reflect differences in costs in serving the different customers involved? For instance, what about the discount for carload lots compared with less than carload lots? The law specifically permits a "cost justification," but cost accounting is hard. Who has the burden of proof here? Who should have it?

The Robinson-Patman Act provides for two defenses for a seller who is charged with discrimination. One was a cost defense: The seller can defend his or her "discrimination" by showing that the price differences were no greater than differences in the costs of serving the customers involved. This defense has been difficult to establish because of the uncertainties of cost accounting.

The second defense arises where the seller in good faith cuts price to meet a lawful and equally low price of a competitor. It is often referred to as the "good faith" defense. It also was difficult to apply, but it was finally established in the Standard Oil (of Indiana) case seventeen years after the complaint involved was issued. Some people felt that the act opened a large loophole in the law, because sellers seldom give discounts except in response to competition. In fact, the hole wasn't very large. Subsequently it turned out that the seller could meet, but not beat, the rival's price. The rival's price must be lawful—for example, it can't be part of a systematically discriminatory scheme such as a basing-point system. And it can be used to keep old customers but not to get new ones. What do you think these restrictions do to price competition? If the FTC's position in the Standard Oil case had been affirmed, would competition have been enhanced?

The A&P case was brought by the FTC in 1965. At that time the FTC was still very actively enforcing the act. The case finally reached the Supreme Court in 1979. The crucial legal issue was how to interpret Section 2(f) of the Robinson-Patman Act, which reads as follows:

(2)(f) That it shall be unlawful for any person engaged in commerce, in the course of such commerce, knowingly to induce or receive a discrimination in price which is prohibited in this section.

"This section" means the whole of the Robinson-Patman Act.

Do you think A&P violated this provision? If you answer yes, and if the courts agreed with you, how would you advise buyers for large chain stores to act in the future to comply with 2(f)? Would there be more or less competition among suppliers of the chains if the law were interpreted that way? If you think that A & P did *not* violate 2(f), would it ever be possible for a chain store to violate 2(f)? What, if any, type of buyer behavior would still be illegal under Section 2(f)?

The FTC cut back drastically on its enforcement of the Robinson-Patman Act after 1969, but the act continued to have an active life in the courts because of private suits. The last decision in this chapter arose from such a suit. In all the other cases reported here (and in FTC cases generally), the emphasis was on injury to competition in the secondary line—that is, in the line of business of the buyers. This case deals with primary line injury, the line of business of the sellers who discriminated. The criterion is the same as in the secondary line cases—price discrimination that results in injury to competition for a seller who competes with the discriminating firm. Do you think that Pet, Continental Banking, and Carnation discriminated? Do you think Utah Pie was hurt by their pricing practices? Was competition increased or decreased by their pricing in Salt Lake? How do you feel about a rule that says that such firms must sell at the same price in all markets? Or, a rule that prices must be equal to prices in regions where they produce, plus transport costs to other areas? If you are doubtful about such rules, what alternative can you suggest to deal with situations like those in Utah Pie?

Federal Trade Commission v. Morton Salt Co.

334 U.S. 37 (1948)

MR. JUSTICE BLACK delivered the opinion of the Court.

The Federal Trade Commission, after a hearing, found that the respondent, which manufactures and sells table salts in interstate commerce, had discriminated in price between different purchases of like grades and qualities, and concluded that such discriminations were in violation of §2 of the Clayton Act, as amended by the Robinson-Patman Act. It accordingly issued a cease and desist order. Upon petition of the respondent the Circuit Court of Appeals, with one judge dissenting, set aside the Commission's findings and order, directed the Commission to dismiss its complaint. . . .

Respondent manufactures several different brands of table salt and sells them directly to (1) wholesalers or jobbers, who in turn resell to the retail trade, and (2) large retailers, including chain store retailers. Respondent sells its finest brand of table salt, known as Blue Label, on what it terms a standard quantity discount system available to all customers. Under this system the purchasers pay a delivered price and the cost to both wholesale and retail purchasers of this brand differs according to the quantities bought. These prices are as follows, after making allowance for rebates and discounts:

	Per case
Less-than-carload purchases	$1.60
Carload purchases	1.50
5,000-case purchases in any consecutive 12 months	1.40
50,000-case purchases in any consecutive 12 months	1.35

Only five companies have ever bought sufficient quantities of respondent's salt to obtain the $1.35 per case price. These companies could buy in such quantities because they operate large chains of retail stores in various parts of the country. As a result of this low price these five companies have been able to sell Blue Label salt at retail cheaper than wholesale purchasers from respondent could reasonably sell the same brand of salt to independently operated retail stores, many of whom competed with the local outlets of the five chain stores.

Respondent's table salts, other than Blue Label, are also sold under a quantity discount system differing slightly from that used in selling Blue Label. Sales of these other brands in less-than-carload lots are made at list price plus freight from plant to destination. Carload purchasers are granted approximately a 5 per cent discount; approximately a 10 per cent discount is granted to purchasers who buy as much as $50,000 worth of all brands of salt in any consecutive twelve-month period. Respondent's quantity discounts on Blue Label and on other table salts were enjoyed by certain wholesalers and retailers who competed with other wholesalers and retailers to whom these discounts were refused.

In addition to these standard quantity discounts, special allowances were granted certain favored customers who competed with other customers to whom they were denied.

First. Respondent's basic contention, which it argues this case hinges upon, is that its "standard quantity discounts, available to all on equal terms, as contrasted for example, to hidden or special rebates, allowances, prices or discounts, are not discriminatory, within the meaning of the Robinson-Patman Act." Theoretically, these discounts are equally available to all, but functionally they are not. For as the record indicates (if reference to it on this point were necessary) no single independent retail grocery store, and probably no single wholesaler, bought as many as 50,000 cases or as much as $50,000 worth of table salt in one year. Furthermore, the record shows that, while certain purchasers were enjoying one or more of respondent's standard quantity discounts, some of their competitors made purchases in such small quantities that they could not qualify for any of respondent's discounts, even those based on carload shipments. The legislative history of the Robinson-Patman Act makes it abundantly clear that Congress considered it to be an evil that a large buyer could secure a competitive advantage over a small buyer solely because of the large buyer's quantity purchasing ability. The Robinson-Patman Act was passed to deprive a large buyer of such advantages except to the extent that a lower price could be justified by reason of a seller's diminished costs due to quantity manufacture, delivery or sale, or by reason of the seller's good faith effort to meet a competitor's equally low price.

Second. The Government interprets the opinion of the Circuit Court of Appeals as having held that in order to establish "discrimination in price" under the Act the burden rested on the Commission to prove that respondent's quantity discount differentials were not justified by its cost savings. Respondent does not so understand the Court of Appeals decision, and furthermore admits that no such burden rests on the Commission. We agree that it does not. . . . The Act specifically imposes the burden of showing justification upon one who is shown to have discriminated in prices. . . .

Third. It is argued that the findings fail to show that respondent's discriminatory discounts had in fact caused injury to competition. There are specific findings that such injuries had resulted from respondent's discounts although the statute does not require the Commission to find that injury has actually resulted. The statute requires no more than that the effect of the prohibited price discriminations "may be substantially to lessen competition . . . or to injure, destroy, or prevent competition." . . . Here the Commission found what would appear to be obvious, that the competitive opportunities of certain merchants were injured when they had to pay respondent substantially more for their goods than their competitors had to pay. The findings are adequate.

Fourth. It is urged that the evidence is inadequate to support the Commission's findings of injury to competition. As we have pointed out, however, the Commission is authorized by the Act to bar discriminatory prices upon the "reasonable possibility" that different prices for like goods to competing purchasers may have the defined effect on competition. That respondent's quantity discounts did result in price differentials between competing purchasers sufficient in amount to influence their resale price of salt was shown by evidence. This showing in itself is adequate to support the Commission's appropriate findings that the effect of such price discriminations "may be substantially to lessen competition . . . or to injure, destroy and prevent competition."

The adequacy of the evidence to support the Commission's findings of reasonably possible injury to competition from respondent's price differentials between competing carload and less-than-carload purchasers is singled out for special attacks here. It is suggested that in considering the adequacy of the evidence to show injury to competition respondent's carload discounts and its other quantity discounts should not be treated alike. The argument is that there is an obvious saving to a seller who delivers goods in carload lots. Assuming this to be true, that fact would not tend to disprove injury to the merchant compelled to pay the less-than-carload price. For a ten-cent carload price differential against a merchant would injure him competitively just as much as a ten-cent differential under any other name. However relevant the separate carload argument might be to the question of justifying a differential by cost savings, it has no relevancy in determining whether the differential works an injury to a competitor. Since Congress has not seen fit to give carload discounts any classification we cannot do so. Such discounts, like all others, can be justified by a seller who proves that the full amount of the discount is based on his actual savings in cost. The trouble with this phase of respondent's case is that it has thus far failed to make such proof. . . .

[I]n enacting the Robinson-Patman Act, Congress was especially concerned with protecting small businesses which were unable to buy in quantities, such as the merchants here who purchased in less-than-carload lots. To this end it undertook to strengthen this very phase of the old Clayton Act. . . .

Apprehension is expressed in this Court that enforcement of the Commission's order against respondent's continued violations of the Robinson-Patman Act might lead respondent to raise table salt prices to its carload purchasers. Such a conceivable, though, we think, highly improbable, contingency, could afford us no reason for upsetting the Commission's findings and declining to direct compliance with a statute passed by Congress.

The Commission here went much further in receiving evidence than the statute requires. It heard testimony from many witnesses in various parts of the country to show that they had suffered actual financial losses on account of respondent's discriminatory prices. Experts were offered to prove the tendency of injury from such prices. The evidence covers about two thousand pages, largely devoted to this single issue—injury to competition. It would greatly handicap effective enforcement of the Act to require testimony to show that which we believe to be self-evident, namely, that there is a "reasonable possibility" that competition may be adversely affected by a practice under which manufacturers and producers sell their goods to some customers substantially cheaper than they sell like goods to the competitors of these customers. This showing in itself is sufficient to justify our conclusion that the Commission's findings of injury to competition were adequately supported by evidence. . . .

The judgment of the Circuit Court of Appeals is reversed and the proceedings are remanded to that court to be disposed of in conformity with this opinion.

Federal Trade Commission v. Standard Oil Co. (of Indiana)

335 U.S. 395 (1958)

MR. JUSTICE CLARK delivered the opinion of the Court.

[This case grew out of a complaint issued by the FTC in 1941, and it went to the Supreme Court twice. Standard was charged with giving discounts to four "jobbers" in the Detroit area. The first case (*Standard Oil Company* [of Indiana] *v. FTC*—340 U.S. 231 [1951]) described them as follows:

> Each of petitioner's so-called "jobber" customers has been free to resell its gasoline at retail or wholesale. Each, at some time, has resold some of it at retail. One now resells it only at retail. The others now resell it largely at wholesale. As to resale prices, two of the "jobbers" have resold their gasoline only at the prevailing wholesale or retail rates. The other two, however, have reflected, in varying degrees, petitioner's reductions in the cost of the gasoline to them by reducing their resale prices of that gasoline below the prevailing rates. . . .

> The distinctive characteristics of these "jobbers" are that each (1) maintains sufficient bulk storage to take delivery of gasoline in tank-car quantities (of 8,000 to 12,000 gallons) rather than in tank-wagon quantities (or 700 to 800 gallons) as is customary for service stations; (2) owns and operates tank wagons and other facilities for delivery of gasoline to service stations; (3) has an established business sufficient to insure purchases of from one to two million gallons a year; and (4) has adequate credit responsibility. While the cost of petitioner's sales and deliveries of gasoline to each of these four "jobbers" is no doubt less, per gallon, than the cost of its sales and deliveries of like gasoline to its service station customers in the same area, there is no finding that such difference accounts for the entire reduction in price made by petitioner to these "jobbers," and we proceed on the assumption that it does not entirely account for that difference.

Excerpts from the final decision in 1958 are shown below:]

This case is a sequel to *Standard Oil Co. v. Federal Trade Comm'n*, 340 U.S. 231 (1951), wherein the Court held that Section 2(b) of the Clayton Act . . . as amended by the Robinson-Patman Act . . . afforded a seller a complete defense to a charge of price discrimination if its lower price was "made in good faith to meet a lawful and equally low price of a competitor." . . . We remanded the case with instructions that the Federal Trade Commission make findings on Standard's contention that its discriminatory prices were so made. The subsequent findings are not altogether clear. The Commission, acting on the same record, seemingly does not contest the fact that Standard's deductions were made to meet the equally low prices of its competitors. However, Standard was held not to have acted in good faith, and the Section 2(b) defense precluded, because of the Commission's determination that Standard's reduced prices were made pursuant to a price system rather than being "the result of departures from a nondiscriminatory price scale." . . . The Court of Appeals found no basis in the record for such a finding and vacated the order of the Commission, holding that Standard's " 'good faith' defense was firmly established." . . .

The Commission urges us to examine its 8-volume record of over 5,500 pages and determine if its finding that Standard reduced prices to four "jobbers" pursuant to a pricing system was erroneous, as held by the Court of Appeals. The Commission contends that a Section 2(b) defense is precluded if the reductions were so made. If wrong in this, it maintains that the "good faith" element of a Section 2(b) defense is not made out by showing that competitors employ such a pricing system, and in any event is negatived by Standard's failure to make a bona fide effort to review its pricing system upon passage of the Robinson-Patman Act.

On the present posture of the case we believe that further review of the evidence is unwarranted. . . . We do no more on the issue of insubstantiality than decide that the Court of Appeals has made a "fair assessment" of the record.

Both parties acknowledge that discrimination pursuant to a price system would preclude a finding of "good faith." . . . The sole question then is one of fact: were Standard's reduced prices to four "jobber" buyers—Citrin-Kolb, Stikeman, Wayne, and Ned's—made pursuant to a pricing system rather than to meet individual competitive situations? . . .

It appears to us that the crucial inquiry is not why reduced prices were first granted to Citrin-Kolb, Stikeman, and Wayne, but rather why the reduced price was continued subsequent to passage of the Act in 1936. The findings show that both major and local suppliers made numerous attempts in the 1936-1941 period to lure these "jobbers" away from Standard with cut-rate prices, oftentimes much lower than the one-and-one-half-cent reduction Standard was giving them. It is uncontradicted . . . that Standard lost three of its seven "jobbers" by not meeting competitors' pirating offers in 1933-1934. All of this occurred in the context of a major gasoline price war in the Detroit area, created by an extreme overabundance of supply—a setting most unlikely to lend itself to general pricing policies. . . .

The findings as to Ned's, the only one of the "jobbers" initially to receive the tank-car price post Robinson-Patman, are highly significant. After a prolonged period of haggling, during which Ned's pressured Standard with information as to numerous more attractive price offers made by other suppliers, Standard responded to an ultimatum from Ned's in 1936 with a half-cent-per-gallon reduction from the tank-wagon price. The Commission concedes that this first reduction occurred at a time when Ned's did not meet the criteria normally insisted upon by Standard before giving any reduction. Two years later, after a still further period of haggling and another Ned's ultimatum, Standard gave a second reduction of still another cent.

In determining that Standard's prices to these four "jobbers" were reduced as a response to individual competitive situations rather than pursuant to a pricing system, the Court of Appeals considered the factors just mentioned, all of which weigh heavily against the Commission's position. The Commission's own findings thus afford ample witness that a "fair assessment" of the record has been made. Standard's use here of two prices, the lower of which could be obtained under the spur of threats to switch to pirating competitors, is a competitive deterrent far short of the discriminatory pricing of Staley, Cement, and National Lead [three cases where price discrimination was found illegal because it was part of a systematic, industrywide scheme such as basing-point systems], and one which we believe within the sanction of Section 2(b) of the Robinson-Patman Act.

Great Atlantic and Pacific Tea Co., Inc. v. Federal Trade Commission

440 U.S. 69 (1979)

MR. JUSTICE STEWART delivered the opinion of the Court.

The question presented in this case is whether the petitioner, the Great Atlantic and Pacific Tea Company (A & P), violated Section 2(f) of the Robinson-Patman Act, by knowingly inducing or receiving illegal price discriminations from the Borden Company (Borden).

The alleged violation was reflected in a 1965 agreement between A & P and Borden under which Borden undertook to supply "private label" milk to more than 200 A & P stores in a Chicago area that included portions of Illinois and Indiana. This agreement resulted from an effort by A & P to achieve cost savings by switching from the sale of "brand label" milk (milk sold under the brand name of the supplying dairy) to the sale of "private label" milk (milk sold under the A & P label).

To implement this plan, A & P asked Borden, its longtime supplier, to submit an offer to supply under private label certain of A & P's milk and other dairy product requirements. After prolonged negotiations, Borden offered to grant A & P a discount for switching to private label milk provided A & P would accept limited delivery service. Borden claimed that this offer would save A & P $410,000 a year compared to what it had been paying for its dairy products. A & P, however, was not satisfied with this offer and solicited offers from other dairies. A competitor of Borden, Bowman Dairy, then submitted an offer which was lower than Borden's.

At this point, A & P's Chicago buyer contacted Borden's chain store sales manager and stated, "I have a bid in my pocket. You [Borden] people are so far out of line it is not even funny. You are not even in the ball park." When the Borden representative asked for more details, he was told nothing except that a $50,000 improvement in Borden's bid "would not be a drop in the bucket."

Borden was thus faced with the problem of deciding whether to rebid. A & P at the time was one of Borden's largest customers in the Chicago area. Moreover, Borden had just invested more than five million dollars in a new dairy facility in Illinois. The loss of the A & P account would result in underutilization of this new plant. Under these circumstances, Borden decided to submit a new bid which doubled the estimated annual savings to A & P, from $410,000 to $820,000. In presenting its offer, Borden emphasized to A & P that it needed to keep A & P's business and was making the new offer in order to meet Bowman's bid. A & P then accepted Borden's bid after concluding that it was substantially better than Bowman's.

Based on these facts, the Federal Trade Commission filed a three-count complaint against A & P. Count I charged that A & P had violated Section 5 of the Federal Trade Commission Act by misleading Borden in the course of negotiations for the private label contract, in that A & P had failed to inform Borden that its second offer was better than the Bowman bid. Count II, involving the same conduct, charged that A & P had violated Section 2(f) of the Robinson-Patman Act by knowingly inducing or receiving price discriminations from Borden. Count III charged that Borden and A & P had violated Section 5 of the Federal Trade Commission Act by combining to stabilize and maintain the retail and wholesale prices of milk and other dairy products.

An Administrative Law Judge found, after extended discovery and a hearing that lasted over 110 days, that A & P had acted unfairly and deceptively in accepting the second offer from Borden and had therefore violated Section 5 of the Federal Commission Act as charged in Count I. The Administrative Law Judge similarly found that this same conduct had violated Section 2(f) of the Robinson-Patman Act. Finally, he dismissed Count III on the ground that the Commission had not satisfied its burden of proof.

On review, the Commission reversed the Administrative Law Judge's finding as to Count I. Pointing out that the question at issue was what amount of disclosure is required of the buyer during contract negotiations, the Commission held that the imposition of a duty of affirmative disclosure would be "contrary to normal business practice and, we think, contrary to the public interest." Despite this ruling, however, the Commission held as to Count II that the identical conduct on the part of A & P had violated Section 2(f) of the Robinson-Patman Act, finding that Borden had discriminated in price between A & P and its competitors, that the discrimination had been injurious to competition, and that A & P had known or should have known that it was the beneficiary of unlawful price discrimination. The Commission rejected A & P's defenses that the Borden bid had been made to meet competition and was cost justified.[1]

A & P filed a petition for review of the Commission's order in the Court of Appeals for the Second Circuit. The court held that substantial evidence sup-

---

[1] With respect to the meeting competition defense, the Commission stated that even though Borden as the seller might have had a meeting competition defense, A & P as the buyer did not have such a defense, because it knew that the bid offered was, in fact, better than the Bowman bid.

ported the findings of the Commission, and, that as a matter of law A & P could not successfully assert a meeting competition defense because it, unlike Borden, had known that Borden's offer was better than Bowman's. Finally, the court held that the Commission had correctly determined that A & P had no cost justification defense. . . .

The Robinson-Patman Act was passed in response to the problem perceived in the increased market power and coercive practices of chain stores and other big buyers that threatened the existence of small independent retailers. Notwithstanding this concern with buyers, however, the emphasis of the Act is in Section 2(a), which prohibits price discriminations by sellers. . . . Section 2(f) of the Act, making buyers liable for inducing or receiving price discriminations by sellers, was the product of a belated floor amendment near the conclusion of the Senate debates.

As finally enacted, Section 2(f) provides:

That it shall be unlawful for any person engaged in commerce, in the course of such commerce, knowingly to induce or receive a discrimination in price which is prohibited by this section. . . .

The petitioner argues that it cannot be liable under Section 2(f) if Borden had a valid meeting competition defense. The respondent, on the other hand, argues that the petitioner may be liable even assuming that Borden had such a defense. The meeting competition defense, the respondent contends, must in these circumstances be judged from the point of view of the buyer. Since A & P knew for a fact that the final Borden bid beat the Bowman bid, it was not entitled to assert the meeting competition defense even though Borden may have honestly believed that it was simply meeting competition. . . .

The short answer to these contentions of the respondent is that Congress did not provide in Section 2(f) that a buyer can be liable even if the seller has a valid defense. The clear language of Section 2(f) states that a buyer can be liable only if he receives a price discrimination "prohibited by this section." If a seller has a valid competition defense, there is simply no prohibited price discrimination.

In the Automatic Canteen case, the Court warned against interpretations of the Robinson-Patman Act which "extend beyond the prohibitions of the Act, and, in so doing, help give rise to a price uniformity and rigidity in open conflict with the purposes of other antitrust legislation." Imposition of Section 2(f) liability on the petitioner in this case would lead to just such price uniformity and rigidity.

In a competitive market, uncertainty among sellers will cause them to compete for business by offering buyers lower prices. Because of the evils of collusive action, the Court has held that the exchange of price information by competitors violates the Sherman Act. United States v. Container Corp. (393 U.S. 33, 1969). Under the view advanced by the respondent, however, a buyer, to avoid liability, must either refuse a seller's bid or at least inform him that his bid has beaten competition. Such a duty of affirmative disclosure would almost inevitably frustrate competitive bidding and, by reducing uncertainty, lead to price matching and anticompetitive cooperation among sellers. . . .

Faced with a substantial loss of business and unable to find out the precise details of the competing bid, Borden made another offer stating that it was doing so in order to meet competition. Under these circumstances, the conclusion is virtually inescapable that in making that offer Borden acted in a reasonable and good-faith effort to meet its competition, and therefore was entitled to a meeting competition defense.

Since Borden had a meeting competition defense and thus could not be liable under Section 2(b) the petitioner who did no more than accept that offer cannot be liable under Section 2(f).

Accordingly, the judgment is reversed.

It is so ordered.

Utah Pie Co. v. Continental Baking Co.

386 U.S. 685 (1967)

MR. JUSTICE WHITE delivered the opinion of the Court.

This suit for treble damages and injuction under Sections 4 and 16 of the Clayton Act was brought by petitioner, Utah Pie Company, against respondents, Continental Baking Company, Carnation Company and Pet Milk Company. The complaint charged a conspiracy under Sections 1 and 2 of the Sherman Act, and violations by each respondent of Section 2(a) of the Clayton Act as amended by the Robinson-Patman Act. The jury found for respondents on the conspiracy charge and for petitioner on the price discrimination charge. Judgment was entered for petitioner for damages and attorneys' fees and respondents appealed on several grounds. The Court of Appeals reversed, addressing itself to the single issue of whether the evidence against each of the respondents was sufficient to support a finding of probable injury to competition within the meaning of Section 2(a) and holding that it was not. . . .

The product involved is frozen dessert pies—apple, cherry, boysenberry, peach, pumpkin, and mince. The period covered by the suit comprised the years 1958, 1959, and 1960 and the first eight months of 1961. Petitioner is a Utah corporation which for 30 years had been baking pies in its plant in Salt Lake City and selling them in Utah and surrounding States. It entered the frozen pie business in late 1957. It was immediately successful with its new line and built a new plant in Salt Lake City in 1958. The frozen pie market was a rapidly expanding one: 57,060 dozen frozen pies were sold in the Salt Lake City market in 1958, 111,729 dozen in 1960, and 266,908 dozen in 1961. Utah Pie's share of this market in those years was 66.5%, 34.3%, 45.5%, and 45.3% respectively, its sales volume steadily increasing over the four years. Its financial position also improved. Petitioner is not, however, a large company. At the time of the trial, petitioner operated with only 18 employees, nine of whom were members of the Rigby family, which controlled the business. Its net worth increased from $31,651.98 on October 31, 1957, to $68,802.13 on October 31, 1961. Total sales were $238,000 in the year ending

October 31, 1957, $353,000 in 1958, $430,000 in 1959, $504,000 in 1960 and $589,000 in 1961. Its net income or loss for these same years was a loss of $6,461 in 1957, and net income in the remaining years of $7,090, $11,987, $7,636, and $9,216.

Each of the respondents is a large company and each of them is a major factor in the frozen pie market in one or more regions of the country. Each entered the Salt Lake City frozen pie market before petitioner began freezing dessert pies. None of them had a plant in Utah. . . . The Salt Lake City market was supplied by respondents chiefly from their California operations. They sold primarily on a delivered price basis. . . .

The major competitive weapon in the Utah market was price. The location of petitioner's plant gave it natural advantages in the Salt Lake City marketing area and it entered the market at a price below the then going prices for respondents' comparable pies. For most of the period involved here its prices were the lowest in the Salt Lake City market. It was, however, challenged by each of the respondents at one time or another and for varying periods. There was ample evidence to show that each of the respondents contributed to what proved to be a deteriorating price structure over the period covered by this suit, and each of the respondents in the course of the ongoing price competition sold frozen pies in the Salt Lake market at prices lower than it sold pies of like grade and quality in other markets considerably closer to its plants. . . .

We deal first with petitioner's case against the Pet Milk Company. Pet entered the frozen pie business in 1955, acquired plants in Pennsylvania and California. . . .

First, Pet successfully concluded an arrangement with Safeway, which is one of the three largest customers for frozen pies in the Salt Lake market, whereby it would sell frozen pies to Safeway under the latter's own "Bel-air" label at a price significantly lower than it was selling its comparable "Pet-Ritz" brand in the same Salt Lake market and elsewhere. The initial price on "Bel-air" pies was slightly lower than Utah's price for its "Utah" brand of pies at the time, and near the end of the period the "Bel-air" price was comparable to the "Utah" price but higher than Utah's "Frost 'N' Flame" brand. Pet's Safeway business amounted to 22.8%, 12.3% and 6.3% of the entire Salt Lake City market for the years 1959, 1960, and 1961. . . .

Second, it introduced a 20-ounce economy pie under the "Swiss Miss" label and began selling the new pie in the Salt Lake market in August 1960 at prices ranging from $3.25 to $3.30 for the remainder of the period. This pie was at times sold at a lower price in the Salt Lake City market than it was sold in other markets.

Third, Pet became more competitive with respect to the prices for its "Pet-Ritz" proprietary label. . . . According to the Court of Appeals, in seven of the 44 months Pet's prices in Salt Lake were lower than prices charged in the California markets. This was true although selling in Salt Lake involved a 30- to 35-cent freight cost.

The Court of Appeals first concluded that Pet's price differential on sales to Safeway must be put aside in considering injury to competition because in its view of the evidence the differential has been completely cost justified and because Utah would not in any event have been able to enjoy the Safeway custom. Second, it concluded that the remaining discriminations on "Pet-Ritz" and "Swiss Miss" pies were an insufficient predicate on which the jury could have found a reasonably possible injury either to Utah Pie as a competitive force or to competition generally.

We disagree with the Court of Appeals in several respects. First, there was evidence from which the jury could have found considerably more price discrimination by Pet with respect to "Pet-Ritz" and "Swiss Miss" pies than was considered by the Court of Appeals. In addition to the seven months during which Pet's prices in Salt Lake were lower than prices in the California markets, there was evidence from which the jury could reasonably have found that in 10 additional months the Salt Lake City prices for "Pet-Ritz" pies were discriminatory as compared with sales in western markets other than California. Likewise, with respect to "Swiss Miss" pies, there was evidence in the record from which the jury could have found that in five of the 13 months during which the "Swiss Miss" pies were sold prior to the filing of this suit, prices in Salt Lake City were lower than those charged by Pet in either California or some other western market.

Second, with respect to Pet's Safeway business, the burden of proving cost justification was on Pet and, in our view, reasonable men could have found that Pet's lower priced, "Bel-air" sales to Safeway were not cost justified in their entirety. Pet introduced cost data for 1961 indicating a cost saving on the Safeway business greater than the price advantage extended to that customer. These statistics were not particularized for the Salt Lake market, but assuming that they were adequate to justify the 1961 sales, they related to only 24% of the Safeway sales over the relevant period. . . . It was insufficient to take the defense of cost justification from the jury, which reasonably could have found a greater incidence of unjustified price discrimination than that allowed by the Court of Appeals' view of the evidence. . . .

Third, the Court of Appeals almost entirely ignored other evidence which provides material support for the jury's conclusion that Pet's behavior satisfied the statutory test regarding competitive injury. This evidence bore on the issue of Pet's predatory intent to injure Utah Pie. As an initial matter, the jury could have concluded that Pet's discriminatory pricing was aimed at Utah Pie; Pet's own management, as early as 1959, identified Utah Pie as an "unfavorable factor," one which "d[u]g holes in our operation" and posed a constant "check" on Pet's performance in the Salt Lake City market. Moreover, Pet candidly admitted that during the period when it was establishing its relationship with Safeway, it sent into Utah Pie's plant an industrial spy to seek information that would be of use to Pet in convincing Safeway that Utah Pie was not worthy of its custom. . . . Finally, Pet does not deny that the evidence showed it suffered substantial losses on its frozen pie sales during the greater part of the time involved in this suit, and there was evidence from which the jury could have concluded that the losses Pet sustained in Salt Lake City were greater than those incurred elsewhere. It would not have been an irrational step if the jury concluded that there was a relationship between price and the losses.

It seems clear to us that the jury heard adequate evidence from which it could have concluded that Pet had engaged in predatory tactics in waging competitive warfare in the Salt Lake City market. Coupled with the incidence of price discrimination attributable to Pet, the evidence as a whole established, rather than negated, the reasonable possibility that Pet's behavior produced a lessening of competition proscribed by the Act. . . .

Petitioner's case against Continental is not complicated. Continental was a substantial factor in the market in 1957. But its sales of frozen 22-ounce dessert pies, sold under the "Morton" brand, amounted to only 1.3% of the market in 1958, 2.9% in 1959, and 1.8% in 1960. Its problems were primarily that of cost and in turn that of price, the controlling factor in the market. In late 1960 it worked out a co-packing arrangement in California by which fruit would be processed directly from the trees into the finished pie without large intermediate packing, storing, and shipping expenses. Having improved its position, it attempted to increase its share of the Salt Lake City market by utilizing a local broker and offering short-term price concessions in varying amounts. Its efforts for seven months were not spectacularly successful. Then in June, 1961, it took the steps which are the heart of petitioner's complaint against it. Effective for the last two weeks of June it offered its 22-ounce frozen apple pies in the Utah area at $2.85 per dozen. It was then selling the same pies at substantially higher prices in other markets. The Salt Lake City price was less than its direct cost plus an allocation for overhead. Utah's going price at the time for its 24-ounce "Frost 'N' Flame" apple pie sold to Associated Grocers was $3.10 per dozen, and for its "Utah" brand $3.40 per dozen. . . . Utah's response was immediate. It reduced its price on all of its apple pies to $2.75 per dozen. Continental refused Safeway's request to match Utah's price, but renewed its offer at the same prices effective July 31 for another two-week period. Utah filed suit on September 8, 1961. Continental's total sales of frozen pies increased from 3,350 dozen in 1960 to 18,800 in 1961. Its market share increased from 1.8% in 1960 to 8.3% in 1961. The Court of Appeals concluded that Continental's conduct had had only minimal effect, that it had not injured or weakened Utah Pie as a competitor, that it had not substantially lessened competition and that there was no reasonable possibility that it would do so in the future.

We again differ with the Court of Appeals. Its opinion that Utah was not damaged as a competitive force apparently rested on the fact that Utah's sales volume continued to climb in 1961 and on the court's own factual conclusion that Utah was not deprived of any pie business which it otherwise might have had. But this retrospective assessment fails to note that Continental's discriminatory below-cost price caused Utah Pie to reduce its price to $2.75. The jury was entitled to consider the potential impact of Continental's price reduction absent any responsive price cut by Utah Pie. . . . The jury could rationally have concluded that had

Utah not lowered its price, Continental, which repeated its offer once, would have continued it. . . . It could also have reasonably concluded that a competitor who is forced to reduce his price to a new all-time low in a market of declining prices will in time feel the financial pinch and will be a less effective competitive force. . . .

The Carnation Company entered the frozen dessert pie business in 1955 through the acquisition of "Mrs. Lee's Pies" which was then engaged in manufacturing and selling frozen pies in Utah and elsewhere under the "Simple Simon" label. Carnation also quickly found the market extremely sensitive to price. Carnation decided, however, not to enter an economy product in the market, and during the period covered by this suit it offered only its quality "Simple Simon" brand. Its primary method of meeting competition in its markets was to offer a variety of discounts and other reductions, and the technique was not unsuccessful. In 1958, for example, Carnation enjoyed 10.3% of the Salt Lake City market, and although its volume of pies sold in that market increased substantially in the next year, its percentage of the market temporarily slipped to 8.6%. However, 1960 was a turnaround year for Carnation in the Salt Lake City market; it more than doubled its volume of sales over the preceding year and thereby gained 12.1% of the market. And while the price structure in the market deteriorated rapidly in 1961 Carnation's position remained important.

We need not dwell long upon the case against Carnation, which in some respects is similar to that against Continental and in others more nearly resembles the case against Pet. After Carnation's temporary setback in 1959 it instituted a new pricing policy to regain business in the Salt Lake City market. The new policy involved a slash in price of 60¢ per dozen pies, which brought Carnation's price to a level admittedly well below its costs, and well below the other prices prevailing in the market. . . . Carnation's banner year, 1960, in the end involved eight months during which the prices in Salt Lake City were lower than prices charged in other markets. The trend continued during the eight months in 1961 that preceded the filing of the complaint in this case. In each of those months the Salt Lake City prices charged by Carnation were well below prices charged in other markets, and in all but August 1961 the Salt Lake City delivered price was 20¢ to 50¢ lower than the prices charged in distant San Francisco. The Court of Appeals held that only the early 1960 prices could be found to have been below cost. That holding, however, simply overlooks evidence from which the jury could have concluded that throughout 1961 Carnation maintained a below-cost price structure and that Carnation's discriminatory pricing, no less than that of Pet and Continental, had an important effect on the Salt Lake City market. We cannot say that the evidence precluded the jury from finding it reasonably possible that Carnation's conduct would injure competition. . . .

Section 2(a) does not forbid price competition which will probably injure or lessen competition by eliminating competitors, discouraging entry into the market or enhancing the market shares of the dominant sellers. But Congress has established some ground rules of the game. Sellers may not sell like goods to different purchasers at different prices if the result may be to injure competition in either the sellers' or the buyers' market unless such discriminations are justified as permitted by the Act. This case concerns the sellers' market. In this context, the Court of Appeals placed heavy emphasis on the fact that Utah Pie constantly increased its sales volume and continued to make a profit. But we disagree with its apparent view that there is no reasonably possible injury to competition as long as the volume of sales in a particular market is expanding and at least some of the competitors in the market continue to operate at a profit. Nor do we think that the Act only comes into play to regulate the conduct of price discriminators when their discriminatory prices consistently undercut other competitors. It is true that many of the primary line cases that have reached the courts have involved blatant predatory price discriminations employed with the hope of immediate destruction of a particular competitor. On the question of injury to competition such cases present courts with no difficulty, for such pricing is clearly within the heart of the proscription of the Act. Courts and commentators alike have noted that the existence of predatory intent might bear on the likelihood of injury to competition. In this case there was some evidence of predatory intent with respect to each of these respondents. There was also other evidence upon which the jury could rationally find the requisite injury to competition. The frozen pie market in Salt Lake City was highly competitive. At times Utah Pie was a leader in moving the general level of prices down, and at other times each of the respondents also bore responsibility for the downward pressure on the price structure. We believe that the Act reaches price discrimination that erodes competition as much as it does price discrimination that is intended to have immediate destructive impact. In this case, the evidence shows a drastically declining price structure which the jury could rationally attribute to continued or sporadic price discrimination. The jury was entitled to conclude that "the effect of such discrimination," by each of these respondents, "may be substantially to lessen competition . . . or to injure, destroy, or prevent competition with any person who either grants or knowingly receives the benefit of such discrimination. . . ." The statutory test is one that necessarily looks forward on the basis of proven conduct in the past. Proper application of that standard here requires reversal of the judgment of the Court of Appeals.

CHAPTER 8

RESTRICTIVE PRACTICES

Section 3 of the Clayton Act prohibits contracts that prevent the buyer from using other sellers' goods where the effect may be substantially to lessen competition. Before World War II the courts read this to mean that such agreements were illegal if the firm that imposed them had monopoly power, but since the war the courts have set much stronger rules. Not all the cases in this chapter derive from the Clayton Act. Some were brought under Section I of the Sherman Act. But they all involve limits on sales or purchases imposed by one firm on others in the market.

Northern Pacific deals with tying agreements. The court talked about the appropriateness of per se rules. Suppose a particular practice served no useful social purpose but was harmless in 80 percent of the cases. Should the court prohibit it in a per se rule? Does it make any difference if the firm with the tying clause has monopoly power or not? Do you think Northern Pacific had monopoly power in the relevant market? What was the relevant market? Why do you think Northern Pacific wrote the preference clause into its contracts? Do you think it had an anticompetitive effect?

The Fortner decision seems to deviate from previous Supreme Court rulings concerning tying contracts. Is the difference due to the special circumstances of the case, or would Northern Pacific be treated differently in the Burger court? Do you believe that U. S. Steel was able to raise capital on better terms than Fortner? Than other billion-dollar steel companies (there are eight)? What, if any, difference does your answer to the last question make? Do you think U. S. Steel's contracts of the sort it had with Fortner were likely to lessen competition?

The Standard Oil Company of California (or Standard Stations) case is a little different. There was no tying clause here, but there was an exclusive requirements contract. Is that different in its effect on competition? Would it have been logical for the Court to make a per se rule in tying, but base a requirements contract decision on whether Standard had monopoly power? Did Standard Oil have monopoly power? Does it make any difference that the other major West Coast oil companies had similar provisions in their contracts? There are no exclusive requirements contracts any more in gasoline. Why don't you see many gas stations selling more than one brand of gasoline? What would it take to make the oil companies compete for the business of gas stations? What would you think of a rule that allowed stations to buy gasoline anywhere they wanted and sell it under the Standard Oil (or any other) brand? Would that make such competition effective? Would it be fair?

The Tampa Electric case also deals with exclusive requirements contracts, but with a twist. The supplier is trying to use the antitrust laws to break a contract. Do you think competition or monopoly had anything to do with the real case here? The case does point out a way in which requirements contracts can have a useful social function. Might not Tampa Electric have been reluctant to invest heavily in coal-fueled equipment if they had not had an assured supply of coal at a good price?

In the Schwinn case the issue is restrictions set by a manufacturer on its distributors as to where and to whom they can sell. Do you think such restrictions lessen competition? Can you imagine situations where they might increase competition? You should read the Sylvania case in this connection. Actually, the Court tried to walk a narrow line in the Schwinn case, distinguishing possible situations according to the status of the manufacturer, the market in which he or she sold, and the ownership status of the product. Do you think its rule made sense? In particular, can you see good economic reasons for distinguishing between items on consignment and those sold outright to the distributors?

The Sealy case might plausibly be considered as a collusion case, but it also fits well with Schwinn, which was decided the same day. What sort of organization is Sealy? Do you believe the firms involved were engaged in collusion? Do you think that consumers would benefit from competition between Sealy licensees in, say, Ohio and Pennsylvania? In 1963 the four largest producers of mattresses and bedsprings in Massachusetts accounted for 39 percent of total shipments. Similar concentration ratios were 32 in New York, 39 in Pennsylvania, 72 in Ohio, 46 in Texas, and 37 in California.[1] Sealy was not the leading brand on a nationwide basis. Do these facts affect your judgment about the appropriateness of the decision?

The Sylvania case finds the court eliminating a previous per se rule again. Is its new rule worth the cost in terms of uncertainty, legal expense, and less effective enforcement? Do you think that Sylvania in the television set market reduced competition importantly by its franchise provisions? Do you think its franchise provisions enhanced its ability to compete with other firms such as RCA, Zenith, and Sony? Does an increase in Sylvania's ability to compete with other television producers (if that does result) mean more competition for society as a whole?

---

[1] Bureau of the Census, *Concentration Ratios in Manufacturing Industry, 1963,* Government Printing Office (Washington: 1967), Part II, p. 324.

Northern Pacific Railway Co. v. United States

356 U.S. 1 (1958)

MR. JUSTICE BLACK delivered the opinion of the Court.

In 1864 and 1870 Congress granted the predecessor of the Northern Pacific Railway Company approximately forty million acres of land in several Northwestern States and Territories to facilitate its construction of a railroad line from Lake Superior to Puget Sound. In general terms, this grant consisted of every alternate section of land in a belt 20 miles wide on each side of the track through States and 40 miles wide through Territories. . . . By 1949 the Railroad had sold about 37,000,000 acres of its holdings, but had reserved mineral rights in 6,500,000 of those acres. Most of the unsold land was leased for one purpose or another. In a large number of its sales contracts and most of its lease agreements the Railroad had inserted "preferential routing" clauses which compelled the grantee or lessee to ship over its lines all commodities produced or manufactured on the land, provided that its rates (and in some instances its service) were equal to those of competing carriers. . . .

In 1949 the Government filed suit . . . seeking a declaration that the defendant's "preferential routing" agreements were unlawful as unreasonable restraints of trade under §1 of that Act. After various pretrial proceedings the Government moved for summary judgment contending that on the undisputed facts it was entitled, as a matter of law, to the relief demanded. The district judge . . . granted the Government's motion. He issued an order enjoining the defendant from enforcing the existing "preferential routing" clauses or from entering into any future agreements containing them. . . .

[T]here are certain agreements or practices which because of their pernicious effect on competition and lack of any redeeming virtue are conclusively presumed to be unreasonable and therefore illegal without elaborate inquiry as to the precise harm they have caused or the business excuse for their use. This principle of per se unreasonableness not only makes the type of restraints which are proscribed by the Sherman Act more certain to the benefit of everyone concerned, but it also avoids . . . prolonged economic investigation into the entire history of the industry involved, as well as related industries, in an effort to determine at large whether a particular restraint has been unreasonable—an inquiry so often wholly fruitless when undertaken. Among the practices which the courts have heretofore deemed to be unlawful in and of themselves are price fixing, *United States v. Socony-Vacuum Oil Co.;* division of markets, *United States v. Addyston Pipe & Steel Co.;* group boycotts, *Fashion Originators' Guild of America v. Federal Trade Comm.;* and tying arrangements, *International Salt Co. v. United States.*

For our purposes a tying arrangement may be defined as an arrangement by a party to sell one product but only on the condition that the buyer also purchases a different (or tied) product, or at least agrees that he will not purchase that product from any other supplier. Where such conditions are successfully exacted competition on their merits with respect to the tied product is inevitably curbed.

Indeed "tying agreements serve hardly any purpose beyond the suppression of competition. . . ." They deny competitors free access to the market for the tied product, not because the party imposing the tying requirements has a better product or a lower price but because of his power or leverage in another market. At the same time buyers are forced to forego their free choice between competing products. . . . They are unreasonable in and of themselves whenever a party has sufficient economic power with respect to the tying product to appreciably restrain free competition in the market for the tied product and a "not insubstantial" amount of interstate commerce is affected. Of course where the seller has no control or dominance over the tying product so that it does not represent an effectual weapon to pressure buyers into taking the tied item any restraint of trade attributable to such tying arrangements would obviously be insignificant at most. . . .

In this case we believe the district judge was clearly correct in entering summary judgment declaring the defendant's "preferential routing" clauses unlawful restraints of trade. We wholly agree that the undisputed facts established beyond any genuine question that the defendant possessed substantial economic power by virtue of its extensive landholdings which it used as leverage to induce large numbers of purchasers and lessees to give it preference, to the exclusion of its competitors, in carrying goods or produce from the land transferred to them. Nor can there be any real doubt that a "not insubstantial" amount of interstate commerce was and is affected by these restrictive provisions.

As pointed out before, the defendant was initially granted large acreages by Congress in the several Northwestern States through which its lines now run. This land was strategically located in checkerboard fashion amid private holdings and within economic distance of transportation facilities. . . . In disposing of its holdings the defendant entered into contracts of sale or lease covering at least several million acres of land which included "preferential routing" clauses. The very existence of this host of tying arrangements is itself compelling evidence of the defendant's great power, at least where, as here, no other explanation has been offered for the existence of these restraints. The "preferential routing" clauses conferred no benefit on the purchasers or lessees. While they got the land they wanted by yielding their freedom to deal with competing carriers, the defendant makes no claim that it came any cheaper than if the restrictive clauses had been omitted.

United States Steel Corp. v. Fortner Enterprises, Inc.

429 U.S. 610 (1977)

MR. JUSTICE STEVENS delivered the opinion of the Court.

[In an earlier decision concerning the same case—394 U.S. 495 (1969)—the Supreme Court required a lower court to hear the case and seemed to say that the tie involved was illegal. Eight years later, the case reached the Supreme Court once more, and this time the Court saw things differently.]

In exchange for respondent's promise to purchase prefabricated houses to be erected on land near Louisville, KY., petitioners agreed to finance the cost of acquiring and developing the land. Difficulties arose while the development was in progress, and respondent (Fortner) commenced this treble-damages action, claiming that the transaction was a tying arrangement forbidden by the Sherman Act. Fortner alleged that competition for prefabricated houses (the tied product) was restrained by petitioners' abuse of power over credit (the tying product). A summary judgment in favor of petitioners was reversed by this Court. *Fortner Enterprises v. United States Steel Co.,* 394 U.S. 495, (Fortner I). We held that the agreement affected a "not insubstantial" amount of commerce in the tied product and that Fortner was entitled to an opportunity to prove that petitioners possessed "appreciable economic power" in the market for the tying product. The question now presented is whether the record supports the conclusion that petitioners had such power in the credit market. . . .

Only the essential features of the arrangement between the parties need be described. Fortner is a corporation which was activated by an experienced real estate developer for the purpose of buying and improving residential lots. One petitioner, United States Steel Corp., operates a "Home Division" which manufactures and assembles components of prefabricated houses; the second petitioner, the "Credit Corp.," is a wholly owned subsidiary, which provides financing to customers of the Home Division in order to promote sales. Although their common ownership and control make it appropriate to regard the two as a single seller, they sell two separate products—prefabricated houses and credit. The credit extended to Fortner was not merely for the price of the homes. Petitioners agreed to lend Fortner over $2,000,000 in exchange for Fortner's promise to purchase the components of 210 homes for about $689,000. The additional borrowed funds were intended to cover Fortner's cost of acquiring and developing the vacant real estate, and the cost of erecting the houses.

The impact of the agreement on the market for the tied product (prefabricated houses) is not in dispute. On the one hand, there is no claim—nor could there be—that the Home Division had any dominance in the prefabricated housing business. We . . . confine our attention to the source of the tying arrangement—petitioners' "economic power" in the credit market.

The Credit Corp. was established in 1954 to provide financing for customers of the Home Division. The United States Steel Corp. not only provided the equity capital, but also allowed the Credit Corp. to use its credit in order to borrow money from banks at the prime rate.

The Credit Corp.'s loan policies were primarily intended to help the Home Division sell its products. It extended credit only to customers of the Home Division, and over two-thirds of the Home Division customers obtained such financing. With few exceptions, all the loan agreements contained a tying clause comparable to the one challenged in this case. . . .

One witness testified that the Home Division's price was $455 higher than the price of comparable components in a conventional home; another witness testified that the Home Division's price was $443 higher than a comparable prefabricated product.

The finding that the credit extended to Fortner was unique was based on factors emphasized in the testimony of Fortner's expert witness who testified that mortgage loans equal to 100% of the acquisition and development cost of real estate were not otherwise available in the Kentucky area; that even though Fortner had a deficit of $16,000, its loan was not guaranteed by a shareholder, officer, or other person interested in its business; and that the interest rate of 6% represented a low rate under prevailing economic conditions . . . and concluded that the terms granted to respondent by the Credit Corp. were so unusual that it was almost inconceivable that the funds could have been acquired from any other source. It is a fair summary of his testimony, and of the District Court's findings, to say that the loan was unique because the lender accepted such a high risk and the borrower assumed such a low cost. . . .

Accordingly, the District Court concluded "that all of the required elements of an illegal tie-in agreement did exist since the tie-in itself was present, a not insubstantial amount of interstate commerce in the tied product was restrained and the Credit Corporation did possess sufficient economic power or leverage to effect such restraint."

Without the finding that the financing provided to Fortner was "unique," it is clear that the District Court's findings would be insufficient to support the conclusion that the Credit Corp. possessed any significant economic power in the credit market.

Although the Credit Corp. is owned by one of the Nation's largest manufacturing corporations . . . the affiliation (with U.S. Steel) was significant only because the Credit Corp. provided a source of funds to customers of the Home Division. That fact tells us nothing about the extent of petitioners' economic power in the credit market. . . .

If, as some economists have suggested, the purpose of a tie-in is often to facilitate price discrimination, such evidence would imply the existence of power that a free market would not tolerate. But in this case Fortner was only required to purchase houses for the number of lots for which it received financing. The tying product produced no commitment from Fortner to purchase varying quantities of the tied product over an extended period of time. This record, therefore, does not describe the kind of "leverage" found in some of the Court's prior decisions condemning tying arrangements.

The fact that Fortner—and presumably other Home Division customers as well—paid a noncompetitive price for houses also lends insufficient support to the judgment of the lower court. Proof that Fortner paid a higher price for the tied product is consistent with the possibility that the financing was unusually inexpensive and that the price for the entire package was equal to, or below, a competitive price. And this possibility is equally strong even though a number of Home Division customers made a package purchase of homes and financing. . . .

As the Court plainly stated in its prior opinion in this case, these decisions do not require that the defendant have a monopoly or even a dominant position throughout the market for a tying product. They do, however, focus attention on the question whether the seller has the power, within the market for the tying product, to raise prices or to require purchasers to accept burdensome terms that would not be exacted in a completely competitive market. In short, the question is whether the seller has some advantage not shared by his competitors in the market for the tying product.

Without any such advantage differentiating his product from that of his competitors, the seller's product does not have the kind of uniqueness considered relevant in prior tying-clause cases. . . .

Quite clearly, if the evidence merely shows that credit terms are unique because the seller is willing to accept a lesser profit—or to incur greater risks—than its competitors, that kind of uniqueness will not give rise to any inference of economic power in the credit market. Yet this is, in substance, all that the record in this case indicates.

The unusual credit bargain offered to Fortner proves nothing more than a willingness to provide cheap financing in order to sell expensive houses. Without any evidence that the Credit Corp. had some cost advantage over its competitors—or could offer a form of financing that was significantly differentiated from that which other lenders could offer if they so elected—the unique character of its financing does not support the conclusion that petitioners had the kind of economic power which Fortner had the burden of proving in order to prevail in this litigation.

The judgment of the Court of Appeals is reversed.

Standard Oil Co. of California v. United States

337 U.S. 293 (1949)

MR. JUSTICE FRANKFURTER delivered the opinion of the Court.

This is an appeal to review a decree enjoining the Standard Oil Company of California and its wholly-owned subsidiary, Standard Stations, Inc., from enforcing or entering exclusive supply contracts with any independent dealer in petroleum products and automobile accessories. The use of such contracts was successfully assailed by the United States as violative of §1 of the Sherman Act and §3 of the Clayton Act.

The Standard Oil Company of California, a Delaware corporation, owns petroleum-producing resources and refining plants in California and sells petroleum products in what has been termed in these proceedings the "Western area"—Arizona, California, Idaho, Nevada, Oregon, Utah and Washington. It sells through its own service stations, to the operators of independent service stations, and to industrial users. . . . It is the largest seller of gasoline in the area. In 1946 its combined sales amounted to 23% of the total taxable gallonage sold there in that year: sales by company-owned service stations constituted 6.8% of the total, sales under exclusive dealing contracts with independent service stations, 6.7% of the total; the remainder were sales to industrial users. It is undisputed that Standard's major competitors employ similar exclusive dealing arrangements. In 1948 only 1.6% of retail outlets were what is known as "split-pump" stations, that is, sold the gasoline of more than one supplier. . . .

[I]n all about 8,000 exclusive supply contracts are here in issue. These are of several types, but a feature common to each is the dealer's undertaking to purchase from Standard and all his requirements of one or more products. . . .

The District Court held that the requirement of showing an actual or potential lessening of competition or a tendency to establish monopoly was adequately met by proof that the contracts covered "a substantial number of outlets and a substantial amount of products, whether considered comparatively or not." Given such quantitative substantiality, the substantial lessening of competition—so the court reasoned—is an automatic result, for the very existence of such contracts denied dealers opportunity to deal in the products of competing suppliers and excludes suppliers from access to the outlets controlled by those dealers. . . .

The issue before us, therefore, is whether the requirement of showing that the effect of the agreements "may be to substantially lessen competition" may be met simply by proof that a substantial portion of commerce is affected or whether it must also be demonstrated that competitive activity has actually diminished or probably will diminish. . . .

In the International Business Machines case, the defendants were the sole manufacturers of a patented tabulating machine requiring the use of unpatented cards. The lessees of the machines were bound by tying clauses to use in them only the cards supplied by the defendants, who, between them, divided the whole of the $3,000,000 annual gross of this business also.

The Court concluded:

> These facts, and others, which we do not stop to enumerate, can leave no doubt that the effect of the condition in appellant's leases 'may be to substantially lessen competition,' and that it tends to create monopoly, and has in fact been an important and effective step in the creation of monopoly.

The Fashion Originators' Guild case involved an association of dress manufacturers which sold more than 60% of all but the cheapest women's garments. In rejecting the relevance of evidence that the Guild's use of requirements contracts was a "reasonable and necessary" measure of protection against "the devastating evils growing from the pirating of original designs," the Court again emphasized the presence and the consequences of economic power:

> The purpose and object of this combination, its potential power, its tendency to monopoly, the coercion it could and did practice upon a rival method of competition, all brought it within the policy of the prohibition declared by the Sherman and Clayton Acts.

It is thus apparent that none of these cases controls the disposition of the present appeal, for Standard's share of the retail market for gasoline, even including sales through company-owned stations, is hardly large enough to conclude as a matter of law that it occupies a dominant position, nor did the trial court so find. The cases do indicate, however, that some sort of showing as to the actual or probable economic consequences of the agreements, if only the inferences to be drawn from the fact of dominant power, is important, and to that extent they tend to support appellant's position. . . .

But then came *International Salt Co. v. United States.* That decision, at least as to contracts tying the sale of a nonpatented to a patented product, rejected the necessity of demonstrating economic consequences once it has been established that "the volume of business affected" is not "insignificant or insubstantial" and that the effect of the contracts is to "foreclose competitors from [a] substantial market." Upon that basis we affirmed a summary judgment granting an injunction against the leasing of machines for the utilization of salt products on the condition that the lessee use in them only salt products supplied by defendant. It was established by pleadings or admissions that defendant was the country's largest producer of salt for industrial purposes, that it owned patents on the leased machines, that about 900 leases were outstanding, and that in 1944 defendant sold about $500,000 worth of salt for use in these machines. It was not established that equivalent machines were unobtainable, it was not indicated what proportion of the business of supplying such machines was controlled by defendant, and it was deemed irrelevant that there was no evidence as to the actual effect of the tying clauses upon competition. It is clear, therefore, that unless a distinction is to be drawn for purposes of the applicability of §3 between requirements contracts and contracts tying the sale of a nonpatented to a patented product, the showing that Standard's requirements contracts affected a gross business of $58,000,000 comprising 6.7% of the total in the area goes far toward supporting the inference that competition has been or probably will be substantially lessened.

In favor of confining the standard laid down by the International Salt case to tying agreements, important economic differences may be noted. Tying agreements serve hardly any purpose beyond the suppression of competition. The justification most often advanced in their defense—the protection of the good will of the manufacturer of the tying device—fails in the usual situation because specification of the type and quality of the product to be used in connection with the tying device is protection enough. If the manufacturer's brand of the tied product is in fact superior to that of competitors, the buyer will presumably choose it anyway. The only situation, indeed, in which the protection of good will may necessitate the use of tying clauses is where specifications for a substitute would be so detailed that they could not practicably be supplied. In the usual case only the prospect of reducing competition would persuade a seller to adopt such a contract and only his control of the supply of the tying device, whether conferred by patent monopoly or otherwise obtained, could induce a buyer to enter one. The existence of market control of the tying device, therefore, affords a strong foundation for the presumption that it has been or probably will be used to limit competition in the tied product also.

Requirements contracts, on the other hand, may well be of economic advantage to the consuming public. In the case of the buyer, they may assure supply, afford protection against rises in price, enable long-term planning on the basis of known costs, and obviate the expense and risk of storage in the quantity necessary for a commodity having a fluctuating demand. From the seller's point of view, requirements contracts may make possible the substantial reduction of selling expense, give protection against price fluctuations, and—of particular advantage to a newcomer to the field to whom it is important to know what capital expenditures are justified—offer the possibility of a predictable market. . . .

Yet serious difficulties would attend the attempt to apply these tests. We may assume, as did the court below, that no improvement of Standard's competitive position has coincided with the period during which the requirements-conract system of distribution has been in effect. We may assume further that the duration of the contracts is not excessive and that Standard does not by itself dominate the market. But Standard was a major competitor when the present system was adopted, and it is possible that its position would have deteriorated but for the adoption of that system. When it is remembered that all the other major suppliers have also been using requirements contracts, and when it is noted that the relative share of the business which fell to each has remained about the same during the period of their use, it would not be farfetched to infer that their effect has been to enable the established suppliers individually to maintain their own standing and at the same time collectively, even though not collusively, to prevent a late arrival from wresting away more than an insignificant portion of the market. If, indeed, this were a result of the system, it would seem unimportant that a short-run by-product of stability may have been greater efficiency and lower costs, for it is the theory of the antitrust laws that the long-run advantage of the community depends upon the removal of restraints upon competition. . . .

If in fact it is economically desirable for service stations to confine themselves to the sale of the petroleum products of a single supplier, they will continue to do so though not bound by contract, and if in fact it is important to retail dealers to assure the supply of their requirements by obtaining the commitment of a single supplier to fulfill them, competition for their patronage should enable them to insist upon such an arrangement without binding them to refrain from looking elsewhere.

We conclude, therefore, that the qualifying clause of §3 is satisfied by proof that competition has been foreclosed in a substantial share of the line of commerce affected. It cannot be gainsaid that observance by a dealer of his requirements contract with Standard does effectively foreclose whatever opportunity there might be for competing suppliers to attract his patronage, and it is clear that the affected proportion of retail sales of petroleum products is substantial. In view of the widespread adoption of such contracts by Standard's competitors and the availability of alternative ways of obtaining an assured market, evidence that competitive activity has not actually declined is inconclusive. Standard's use of the contracts creates just such a potential clog on competition as it was the purpose of §3 to remove whatever, were it to become actual, it would impede a substantial amount of competitive activity.

The judgment below is affirmed.

Tampa Electric Co. v. Nashville Coal Co.

365 U.S. 320 (1961)

MR. JUSTICE CLARK delivered the opinion of the Court.

We granted certiorari to review a declaratory judgment holding illegal under §3 of the Clayton Act a requirements contract between the parties providing for the purchase by petitioner of all the coal it would require as boiler fuel at its Gannon Station in Tampa, Florida, over a 20-year period. Both the District Court and the Court of Appeals agreed with respondents that the contract fell within the proscription of §3 and therefore was illegal and unenforceable. We cannot agree that the contract suffers the claimed antitrust illegality and, therefore, do not find it necessary to consider respondents' additional argument that such illegality is a defense to the action and a bar to enforceability. . . .

Petitioner Tampa Electric Company is a public utility located in Tampa, Florida. As of 1954 petitioner operated two electrical generating plants comprising a total of 11 individual generating units, all of which consumed oil in their burners. In 1955 Tampa Electric decided to expand its facilities by the construction of an additional generating plant. . . .

[I]t contracted with the respondents to furnish the expected coal requirements for the units. The agreement, dated May 23, 1955, embraced Tampa Electric's "total requirements of fuel . . . for the operation of its first two units to be installed at the Gannon Station . . . not less than 225,000 tons of coal per unit per year," for a period of 20 years. The minimum price was set at $6.40 per ton delivered, subject to an escalation clause based on labor cost and other factors. Deliveries were originally expected to begin in March 1957, for the first unit, and for the second unit at the completion of its construction.

In April 1957, soon before the first coal was actually to be delivered and after Tampa Electric, in order to equip its first two Gannon units for the use of coal, had expended some $3,000,000 more than the cost of constructing oil-burning units, and after respondents had expended approximately $7,500,000 readying themselves to perform the contract, the latter advised petitioner that the contract was illegal under the antitrust laws, would therefore not be performed, and no coal would be delivered. . . .

We are persuaded that on the record in this case, neither peninsular Florida, nor the entire State of Florida, nor Florida and Georgia combined constituted the relevant market of effective competition. We do not believe that the pie will slice so thinly. By far the bulk of the overwhelming tonnage marketed from the same producing area as serves Tampa is sold outside of Georgia and Florida, and the producers were "eager" to sell more coal in those States. While the relevant competitive market is not ordinarily susceptible to a "metes and bounds" definition. . . . [I]t is of course the area in which respondents and the other 700 producers effectively compete. . . . The record shows that, like the respondents, they sold bituminous coal . . . mined in parts of Pennsylvania, Virginia, West Virginia,

Kentucky, Tennessee, Alabama, Ohio and Illinois. We take notice of the fact that the approximate total bituminous coal (and lignite) product in the year 1954 from the districts in which these 700 producers are located was 359,289,000 tons, of which some 290,567,000 tons were sold on the open market. From these statistics it clearly appears that the proportionate volume of the total relevant coal product as to which the challenged contract pre-empted competition, less than 1%, is, conservatively speaking, quite insubstantial. A more accurate figure, even assuming pre-emption to the extent of the maximum anticipated total requirements, 2,250,000 tons a year, would be .77%. . . .

The 20-year period of the contract is singled out as the principal vice, but at least in the case of public utilities the assurance of a steady and ample supply of fuel is necessary in the public interest. Otherwise consumers are left unprotected against service failures owing to shutdowns; and increasingly unjustified costs might result in more burdensome rate structures eventually to be reflected in the consumer's bill. The compelling validity of such considerations has been recognized fully in the natural gas public utility field. This is not to say that utilities are immunized from Clayton Act proscriptions, but merely that, in judging the term of a requirements contract in relation to the substantiality of the foreclosure of competition, particularized considerations of the parties' operations are not irrelevant. In weighing the various factors, we have decided that in the competitive bituminous coal marketing area involved here the contract sued upon does not tend to foreclose a substantial volume of competition. . . .

The judgment is reversed and the case remanded to the District Court for further proceedings not inconsistent with this opinion.

United States v. Arnold, Schwinn & Co.

388 U.S. 365 (1967)

MR. JUSTICE FORTAS delivered the opinion of the Court.

The United States brought this appeal to review the judgment of the District Court in a civil antitrust case alleging violations of §1 of the Sherman Act. . . . The complaint charged a continuing conspiracy since 1952 between defendants and other alleged co-conspirators involving price fixing, allocation of exclusive territories to wholesalers and jobbers, and consignment of merchandise to franchised dealers.

At trial, the United States asserted that not only the price fixing but also Schwinn's methods of distribution were illegal per se under §1 of the Sherman Act. . . .

The District Court rejected the charge of price fixing. With respect to the charges of illegal distribution practices, the court held that the territorial limitation was unlawful per se as respects products sold by Schwinn to its distributors;

but that the limitation was not unlawful insofar as it was incident to sales by Schwinn itself to franchised retailers where the wholesaler or jobber (hereinafter referred to as the distributor) functioned as agent or consignee, including distribution pursuant to the "Schwinn Plan" described below.

The United States did not appeal from the District Court's rejection of its price-fixing charge. The appellees did not appeal from the findings and order invalidating restraints on resale by distributors who purchase products from Schwinn.

In this Court, the United States has abandoned its contention that the distribution limitations are illegal per se. Instead we are asked to consider these limitations in light of the "rule of reason," and, on the basis of the voluminous record below, to conclude that the limitations are the product of "agreement" between Schwinn and its wholesale and retail distributors and that they constitute an unreasonable restraint of trade.

Appellee Schwinn is a family-owned business which for many years has been engaged in the manufacture and sale of bicycles and some limited bicycle parts and accessories. Appellee SCDA is an association of distributors handling Schwinn bicycles and other products. The challenged marketing program was instituted in 1952. In 1951 Schwinn had the largest single share of the United States bicycle market—22.5%. In 1961 Schwinn's share of the market had fallen to 12.8% although its dollar and unit sales had risen substantially. In the same period, a competitor, Murray Ohio Manufacturing Company, which is now the leading United States bicycle producer, increased its market share from 11.6% in 1951 to 22.8% in 1961. Murray sells primarily to Sears, Roebuck & Company and other mass merchandisers. By 1962 there were nine bicycle producers in the Nation, operating 11 plants. Imports of bicycles amounted to 29.7% of sales in 1961. . . .

Schwinn sells its products primarily to or through 22 wholesale distributors, with sales to the public being made by a large number of retailers. In addition, it sells about 11% of its total to B. F. Goodrich for resale in B. F. Goodrich retail or franchised stores. There are about 5,000 to 6,000 retail dealers in the United States which are bicycle specialty shops, generally also providing servicing. About 84% of Schwinn's sales are through such specialized dealers. Schwinn sells only under the Schwinn label, never under private label, while about 64% of all bicycles are sold under private label. Distributors and retailers handling Schwinn bicycles are not restricted to the handling of that brand. They may and ordinarily do sell a variety of brands.

The United States does not contend that there is in this case any restraint on interbrand competition, nor does it attempt to sustain its charge by reference to the market for bicycles as a whole. Instead, it invites us to confine our attention to the intrabrand effect of the contested restrictions. It urges us to declare that the method of distribution of a single brand of bicycles, amounting to less than one-seventh of the market, constitutes an unreasonable restraint of trade or commerce among the several States.

Schwinn's principal methods of selling its bicycles are as follows: (1) sales to distributors, primarily cycle distributors, B. F. Goodrich and hardware jobbers;

(2) sales to retailers by means of consignment or agency arrangements with distributors; and (3) sales to retailers under the so-called Schwinn Plan which involves direct shipment by Schwinn to the retailer with Schwinn invoicing the dealers, extending credit, and paying a commission to the distributor taking the order. Schwinn fair-traded certain of its models at retail in States permitting this, and suggested retail prices for all of its bicycles in all States. During the 1952-1962 period, as the District Court found, "well over half of the bicycles sold by Schwinn have been sold direct to the retail dealer (not to a cycle distributor) by means of Schwinn Plan sales and consignment and agency sales." Less than half were sold to distributors.

After World War II, Schwinn had begun studying and revamping its distribution pattern. As of 1951-52, it had reduced its mailing list from about 15,000 retail outlets to about 5,500. It instituted the practice of franchising approved retail outlets. The franchise did not prevent the retailer from handling other brands, but it did require the retailer to promote Schwinn bicycles and to give them at least equal prominence with competing brands. The number of franchised dealers in any area was limited, and a retailer was franchised only as to a designated location or locations. Each franchised dealer was to purchase only from or through the distributor authorized to serve that particular area. He was authorized to sell only to consumers and not to unfranchised retailers. . . .

Schwinn assigned specific territories to each of its 22 wholesale cycle distributors. These distributors were instructed to sell only to franchised Schwinn accounts and only in their respective territories which were specifically described and allocated on an exclusive basis. The District Court found "that certain cycle distributors have in fact not competed with each other . . . and that in so doing they have conspired with Schwinn to unreasonably restrain competition contrary to the provisions of Section 1 of the Sherman Act." The court, however, restricted this finding and its consequent order to transactions in which the distributor purchased the bicycles from Schwinn for resale, as distinguished from sales by the distributor or agent or consignee of Schwinn or on the Schwinn Plan. The United States urges that this Court should require revision of the decree in this respect to forbid territorial exclusivity regardless of the technical form by which the products are transferred from Schwinn to the retailer or consumer.

The District Court rejected the Government's contention that Schwinn had in fact canceled the franchises of some retailers because of sales to discount houses or other unfranchised dealers, nor did it find that distributors have been cut off because of sales to unfranchised retailers or violation of territorial limitations. The United States urges that this is "clearly erroneous." In any event, it is clear and entirely consistent with the District Court's findings that Schwinn has been "firm and resolute" in insisting upon observance of territorial and customer limitations by its bicycle distributors and upon confining sales by franchised retailers to consumers, and that Schwinn's "firmness" in these respects was grounded upon the communicated danger of termination. Our analysis will embrace this conclusion, rather than the finding which is urged by the Government and which was refused by the trial court that Schwinn actually terminated retail franchises or cut off distributors for the suggested reasons.

We come, then, to the legal issues in this case. We are here confronted with challenged vertical restrictions as to territory and dealers. The source of the restrictions is the manufacturer. . . .

Schwinn was not a newcomer, seeking to break into or stay in the bicycle business. It was not a "failing company." On the contrary, at the initiation of these practices, it was the leading bicycle producer in the Nation. Schwinn contends, however, and the trial court found, that the reasons which induced it to adopt the challenged distribution program were to enable it and the small, independent merchants that made up its chain of distribution to compete more effectively in the marketplace. Schwinn sought a better way of distributing its product: a method which would promote sales, increase stability of its distributor and dealer outlets, and augment profits. But this argument, appealing as it is, is not enough to avoid the Sherman Act proscription; because, in a sense, every restrictive practice is designed to augment the profit and competitive position of its participants. Price fixing does so, for example, and so may a well-calculated division of territories. The antitrust outcome does not turn merely on the presence of sound business reason or motive. Here, for example, if the test of reasonableness were merely whether Schwinn's restrictive distribution program and practices were adopted "for good business reasons" and not merely to injure competitors, or if the answer turned upon whether it was indeed "good business practice," we should not quarrel with Schwinn's eloquent submission of the finding of the trial court. But our inquiry cannot stop at that point. Our inquiry is whether, assuming nonpredatory motives and business purposes and the incentive of profit and volume considerations, the effect upon competition in the marketplace is substantially adverse. The promotion of self-interest alone does not invoke the rule of reason to immunize otherwise illegal conduct. It is only if the conduct is not unlawful in its impact in the marketplace or if the self-interest coincides with the statutory concern with the preservation and promotion of competition that protection is achieved. . . .

As noted above, appellees have not appealed from the District Court's order, and, accordingly, we have before us only the Government's pleas: (1) that the decree should not be confined to sale transactions between Schwinn and wholesalers but should reach territorial restrictions upon distributors whether they are incident to sale and resale transactions or to consignment, agency or Schwinn-Plan relationship between Schwinn and the distributors; (2) that agreements requiring distributors to limit their distribution to only such retailers as are franchised should be enjoined; and (3) that arrangements preventing franchised retailers from supplying nonfranchised retailers, including discount stores, should also be forbidden.

As to point (2), the Government argues that it is illogical and inconsistent to forbid territorial limitations on resales by distributors where the distributor owns the goods, having bought them from Schwinn, and, at the same time, to exonerate arrangements which require distributors to confine resales of the goods they have bought to "franchised" retailers. It argues that requiring distributors, once they have purchased the product, to confine sales to franchised retailers is indistinguishable in law and principle from the division of territory which the decree condemns. Both, the Government argues, are in the nature of restraints upon alienation which are beyond the power of the manufacturer to impose upon its vendees and which, since the nature of the transaction includes an agreement, combination or understanding, are violations of §1 of the Sherman Act. . . . We agree, and upon remand, the decree should be revised to enjoin any limitation upon the freedom of distributors to dispose of the Schwinn products, which they have bought from Schwinn, where and to whomever they choose. The principle is, of course, equally applicable to sales to retailers, and the decree should similarly enjoin the making of any sales to retailers upon any condition, agreement or understanding limiting the retailer's freedom as to where and to whom it will resell the products.

The appellant vigorously argues that, since this remedy is confined to situations where the distributor and retailer acquire title to the bicycles, it will provide only partial relief; that to prevent the allocation of territories and confinement to franchised retail dealers, the decree can and should be enlarged to forbid these practices, however effected—whether by sale and resale or by agency, consignment, or the Schwinn Plan. But we are dealing here with a vertical restraint embodying the unilateral program of a single manufacturer. We are not dealing with a combination of manufacturers, or of distributors. We are not dealing with a "division" of territory in the sense of an allocation by and among the distributors, or an agreement among distributors to restrict their competition. We are here concerned with a truly vertical arrangement, raising the fundamental question of the degree to which a manufacturer may not only select the customers to whom he will sell, but also allocate territories for resale and confine access to his product to selected, or franchised, retailers. We conclude that the proper application of §1 of the Sherman Act to this problem requires differentiation between the situation where the manufacturer parts with title, dominion, or risk with respect to the article, and where he completely retains ownership and risk of loss.

As the District Court held, where a manufacturer sells products to his distributor subject to territorial restrictions upon resale, a per se violation of the Sherman Act results. And, as we have held, the same principle applies to restrictions of outlets with which the distributors may deal and to restraints upon retailers to whom the goods are sold. Under the Sherman Act, it is unreasonable without more for a manufacturer to seek to restrict and confine areas or persons with whom an article may be traded after the manufacturer has parted with dominion over it. Such restraints are so obviously destructive of competition that their mere existence is enough. If the manufacturer parts with dominion over his product or transfers risk of loss to another, he may not reserve control over its destiny or the conditions of its resale. To permit this would sanction franchising and consignment of distribution as the ordinary instead of the unusual method which may be permissible in an appropriate and impelling competitive setting, since most merchandise is distributed by means of purchase and sale. On the other hand . . . we are not prepared to introduce the inflexibility which a per se rule might bring if it were applied to prohibit all vertical restrictions of territory and all franchising, in the sense of designating specified distributors and retailers as the chosen instruments through which the manufacturer, retaining ownership of the goods, will distribute them to the public. Such a rule might severely hamper smaller enterprises resorting to reasonable methods of meeting the competition of giants and of merchandising through independent dealers, and it might sharply accelerate the trend towards vertical integration of the distribution process. But to allow this freedom where the manufacturer has parted with dominion over the goods—the usual marketing situation—would violate the ancient rules against restraints on alienation and open the door to exclusivity of outlets and limitation of territory further than prudence permits. . . .

On this record, we cannot brand the District Court's finding as clearly erroneous and cannot ourselves conclude that Schwinn's franchising of retailers and its confinement of retail sales to them—so long as it retains all indicia of ownership, including title, dominion, and risk, and so long as the dealers in question are indistinguishable in function from agents or salesmen—constitute an "unreasonable" restraint of trade. Critical in this respect are the facts: (1) that other competitive bicycles are available to distributors and retailers in the marketplace, and there is no showing that they are not in all respects reasonably interchangeable as articles or competitive commerce with the Schwinn product; (2) that Schwinn distributors and retailers handle other brands of bicycles as well as Schwinn's; (3) in the present posture of the case we cannot rule that the vertical restraints are unreasonable because of their intermixture with price fixing; and (4) we cannot disagree with the findings of the trial court that competition made necessary the challenged program; that it was justified by, and went no further than required by, competitive pressures; and that its net effect is to preserve and not to damage competition in the bicycle market. Application of the rule of reason here cannot be confined to intrabrand competition. When we look to the product market as a whole, we cannot conclude that Schwinn's franchise system with respect to products as to which it retains ownership and risk constitutes an unreasonable restraint of trade. This does not, of course, excuse or condone the per se violations which, in substance, consist of the control over the resale of Schwinn's products after Schwinn has parted with ownership thereof. . . .

Accordingly, the judgment of the District Court is reversed and the case remanded for the entry of a decree in accordance with this question.

United States v. Sealy, Inc.

388 U.S. 350 (1967)

MR. JUSTICE FORTAS delivered the opinion of the Court.

Appellee and its predecessors have, for more than 40 years, been engaged in the business of licensing manufacturers of mattresses and bedding products to make and sell such products under the Sealy name and trademarks. In this civil action the United States charged that appellee had violated §1 of the Sherman Act by conspiring with its licensees to fix the prices at which the retail customers of the licensees might resell bedding products bearing the Sealy name, and to allocate mutually exclusive territories among such manufacturer-licensees.

After trial, the District Court found that the appellee was engaged in a continuing conspiracy with its manufacturer-licensees to agree upon and fix minimum retail prices on Sealy products and to police the prices so fixed. It enjoined the appellee from such conduct. . . . Appellee did not appeal the finding or order relating to price-fixing.

With respect to the charge that appellee conspired to allocate mutually exclusive territory among its manufacturers, the District Court held that the United States had not proved conduct "in unreasonable restraint of trade in violation of Section 1 of the Sherman Act." The United States appealed. . . .

There is no dispute that exclusive territories were allotted to the manufacturer-licensees. Sealy agreed with each licensee not to license any other person to manufacture or sell in the designated area; and the licensee agreed not to manufacture or sell "Sealy products" outside the designated area. A manufacturer could make and sell his private label products anywhere he might choose. . . .

If we look at substance rather than form, there is little room for debate. These must be classified as horizontal restraints. . . .

There are about 30 Sealy "licensees." They own substantially all of its stock. Sealy's bylaws provide that each director must be a stockholder or a stockholder-licensee's nominee. Sealy's business is managed and controlled by its board of directors. Between board meetings, the executive committee acts. It is composed of Sealy's president and five board members, all licensee-stockholders. Control does not reside in the licensees only as a matter of form. It is exercised by them in the day-to-day business of the company including the grant, assignment, reassignment, and termination of exclusive territorial licenses. Action of this sort is taken either by the board of directors or the executive committee of Sealy, both of which, as we have said, are manned, wholly or almost entirely, by licensee-stockholders.

Appellee argues that "there is no evidence that Sealy is a mere creature or instrumentality of its stockholders." In support of this proposition, it stoutly asserts that "the stockholders and directors wore a 'Sealy hat' when they were acting on behalf of Sealy." But the obvious and inescapable facts are that Sealy was a joint venture of, by, and for its stockholder-licensees; and the stockholder-licensees are themselves directly, without even the semblance of insulation, in charge of Sealy's operations.

It is true that the licensees had an interest in Sealy's effectiveness and efficiency, and, as stockholders, they welcomed its profitability—at any rate within the limits set by their willingness as licensees to pay royalties to the joint venture. But that does not determine whether they as licensees are chargeable with action in the name of Sealy. We seek the central substance of the situation, not its periphery; and in this pursuit, we are moved by the identity of the persons who act, rather than the label of their hats. The arrangements for exclusive territories are necessarily chargeable to the licensees of appellee whose interests such arrangements were supposed to promote and who, through select members, guaranteed or withheld and had the power to terminate licenses for inadequate performance. The territorial arrangements must be regarded as the creature of horizontal action by the licensees. It would violate reality to treat them as equivalent to territorial limitations imposed by a manufacturer upon independent dealers as incident to the sale of a trademarked product. Sealy, Inc., is an instrumentality of the licensees for purposes of the horizontal territorial allocation. It is not the principal.

Appellee has not appealed the order of the District Court enjoining continuation of this price-fixing, but the existence and impact of the practice cannot be ignored in our appraisal of the territorial limitations. In the first place, this flagrant and pervasive price-fixing in obvious violation of law, was, as the trial court found, the activity of the "stockholder representatives" acting through and in collaboration with Sealy mechanisms. This underlines the horizontal nature of the enterprise, and the use of Sealy, not as a separate entity, but as an instrumentality of the individual manufacturers. In the second place, this unlawful resale price-fixing activity refutes appellee's claim that the territorial restraints were mere incidents of a lawful program of trademark licensing. The territorial restraints were a part of the unlawful price-fixing and policing. As specific findings of the District Court show, they gave to each licensee an enclave in which it could and did zealously and effectively maintain resale prices, free from the danger of outside incursions. It may be true, as appellee vigorously argues, that territorial exclusivity served many other purposes. But its connection with the unlawful price-fixing is enough to require that it be condemned as an unlawful restraint and that appellee be effectively prevented from its continued or further use.

It is urged upon us that we should condone this territorial limitation among manufacturers of Sealy products because of the absence of any showing that it is unreasonable. It is argued, for example, that a number of small grocers might allocate territory among themselves on an exclusive basis as incident to the use of a common name and common advertisements, and that this sort of venture should be welcomed in the interests of competition, and should not be condemned as per se unlawful. But condemnation of appellee's territorial arrangements certainly does not require us to go so far as to condemn that quite different situation, whatever might be the result if it were presented to us for decision. For here, the arrangements for territorial limitations are part of "an aggregation of trade restraints" including unlawful price-fixing and policing. Within settled doctrine, they are unlawful under Section 1 of the Sherman Act without the necessity for an inquiry in each particular case as to their business or economic justification, their impact in the marketplace, or their reasonableness. Accordingly, the judgment of the District Court is reversed and the case remanded for the entry of an appropriate decree.

Continental TV, Inc. v. GTE Sylvania Inc.

433 U.S. 36 (1977)

MR. JUSTICE POWELL delivered the opinion of the Court.

Franchise agreements between manufacturers and retailers frequently include provisions barring the retailers from selling franchised products from locations other than those specified in the agreements. This case presents important questions concerning the appropriate antitrust analysis of these restrictions. . . .

Respondent GTE Sylvania Inc. (Sylvania) manufactures and sells television sets through its Home Entertainment Products Division. Prior to 1962, like most other television manufacturers, Sylvania sold its televisions to independent or company-owned distributors who in turn resold to a large and diverse group of retailers. Prompted by a decline in its market share to a relatively insignificant 1% to 2% of national television sales, Sylvania conducted an intensive reassessment of its marketing strategy, and in 1962 adopted the franchise plan challenged here. Sylvania phased out its wholesale distributors and began to sell its televisions directly to a smaller and more select group of franchised retailers. An acknowledged purpose of the change was to decrease the number of competing Sylvania retailers in the hope of attracting the more aggressive and competent retailers thought necessary to the improvement of the company's market position. To this end, Sylvania limited the number of franchises granted for any given area and required each franchisee to sell his Sylvania products only from the location or locations at which he was franchised. A franchise did not constitute an exclusive territory, and Sylvania retained sole discretion to increase the number of retailers in an area in light of the success or failure of existing retailers in developing their market. The revised marketing strategy appears to have been successful during the period at issue here, for by 1965 Sylvania's share of national television sales had increased to approximately 5%, and the company ranked as the Nation's eighth largest manufacturer of color television sets.

This suit is the result of the rupture of a franchiser-franchisee relationship that had previously prospered under the revised Sylvania plan. Dissatisfied with its sales in the City of San Francisco, Sylvania decided in the spring of 1965 to franchise Young Brothers, an established San Francisco retailer of televisions, as an additional San Francisco retailer. The proposed location of the new franchise was approximately a mile from a retail outlet operated by petitioner Continental T.V., Inc. (Continental) protested that the location of the new franchise violated Sylvania's marketing policy, but Sylvania persisted in its plans. Continental then canceled a large Sylvania order and placed a large order with Phillips, one of Sylvania's competitors.

During this same period, Continental expressed a desire to open a store in Sacramento, Cal., a desire Sylvania attributed at least in part to Continental's displeasure over the Young Brothers decision. Sylvania believed that the Sacramento market was adequately served by the existing Sylvania retailers and denied the request. In the face of this denial, Continental advised Sylvania in early September 1965, that it was in the process of moving Sylvania merchandise from its San Jose, Cal. warehouse to a new retail location that it had leased in Sacramento. . . .

The antitrust issues before us originated in cross-claims brought by Continental against Sylvania. . . . Most important for our purposes was the claim that Sylvania had violated Section 1 of the Sherman Act by entering into and enforcing franchise agreements that prohibited the sale of Sylvania products other than from specified locations. . . .

[The District Court instructed the jury as follows:]

> Therefore, if you find by a preponderance of the evidence that Sylvania entered into a contract, combination or conspiracy with one or more of its dealers pursuant to which Sylvania exercised dominion or control over the products sold to the dealer, after having parted with title and risk to the products, you must find any effort thereafter to restrict outlets or store locations from which its dealers resold the merchandise which they had purchased from Sylvania to be a violation of Section 1 of the Sherman Act, regardless of the reasonableness of the location restrictions.

On appeal, the Court of Appeals for the Ninth Circuit, sitting en banc, reversed by a divided vote. The court acknowledged that there is language in Schwinn that could be read to support the District Court's instruction but concluded that Schwinn was distinguishable on several grounds. Contrasting the nature of the restrictions, their competitive impact, and the market shares of the franchisers in the two cases, the court concluded that Sylvania's location restriction had less potential for competitive harm than the restrictions invalidated in Schwinn and thus should be judged under the "rule of reason" rather than the per se rule stated in Schwinn. The court found support for its position in the policies of the Sherman Act and in the decisions of other federal courts involving nonprice vertical restrictions. . . .

In the present case, it is undisputed that title to the television sets passed from Sylvania to Continental. Thus, the Schwinn per se rule applies unless Sylvania's restriction on locations falls outside Schwinn's prohibition against a manufacturer's attempting to restrict a "retailer's freedom as to where and to whom it will resell the products." . . .

Both Schwinn and Sylvania sought to reduce but not to eliminate competition among their respective retailers through the adoption of a franchise system. Although it was not one of the issues addressed by the District Court or presented on appeal by the Government, the Schwinn franchise plan included a location restriction similar to the one challenged here. These restrictions allowed Schwinn and Sylvania to regulate the amount of competition among their retailers by preventing a franchisee from selling franchised products from outlets other than the one covered by the franchise agreement. To exactly the same end, the Schwinn franchise plan included a companion restriction, apparently not found in the Sylvania plan, that prohibited franchised retailers from selling Schwinn products to nonfranchised retailers. In Schwinn the Court expressly held that this restriction was impermissible under the broad principle stated here. In intent and competitive impact, the retail-customer restriction in Schwinn is indistinguishable from the location restriction in the present case. . . .

Sylvania argues that if Schwinn cannot be distinguished, it should be reconsidered. Although Schwinn is supported by the principle of stare decisis, we are convinced that the need for clarification of the law in this area justifies reconsideration. . . . In our view, the experience of the past 10 years should be brought to bear on this subject of considerable commercial importance.

The traditional framework of analysis under Section 1 of the Sherman Act is familiar and does not require extended discussion. Section 1 prohibits "[e]very contract, combination . . . or conspiracy, in restraint of trade or commerce." Since the early years of this century a judicial gloss on this statutory language has established the "rule of reason" as the prevailing standard of analysis. *Standard Oil Co. v. United States,* 221 U.S. 1 (1911). Under this rule, the factfinder weighs all of the circumstances of a case in deciding whether a restrictive practice should be prohibited as imposing an unreasonable restraint on competition. Per se rules of illegality are appropriate only when they relate to conduct that is manifestly anticompetitive. As the Court explained in *Northern Pac. R. Co. v. United States,* 56 U.S. 1, 5 (1958), "there are certain agreements or practices which because of their pernicious effect on competition and lack of any redeeming virtue are conclusively presumed to be unreasonable and therefore illegal without elaborate inquiry as to the precise harm they have caused or the business excuse for their use."

In essence, the issue before us is whether Schwinn's per se rule can be justified under the demand standards of Northern Pac. R. Co. . . .

The market impact of vertical restrictions is complex because of their potential for a simultaneous reduction of intrabrand competition and stimulation of interbrand competition. Significantly, the Court in Schwinn did not distinguish among the challenged restrictions on the basis of their individual potential for intrabrand harm or interbrand benefit. Restrictions that completely eliminated intrabrand competition among Schwinn distributors were analyzed no differently from those that merely moderated intrabrand competition among retailers. The pivotal factor was the passage of title: All restrictions were held to be per se illegal where title had passed, and all were evaluated and sustained under the rule of reason where it had not. The location restriction at issue here would be subject to the same pattern of analysis under Schwinn.

It appears that this distinction between sale and nonsale transactions resulted from the Court's effort to accommodate the perceived intrabrand harm and interbrand benefit of vertical restrictions. The per se rule for sale transactions reflected the view that vertical restrictions are "so obviously destructive" of intrabrand competition that their use would "open the door to exclusivity of outlets and limitation of territory further than prudence permits." Conversely, the continued adherence to the traditional rule of reason for nonsale transactions reflected the view that the restrictions have too great a potential for the promotion of interbrand competition to justify complete prohibition. The Court's opinion provides

no analytical support for these contrasting positions. Nor is there even an assertion in the opinion that the competitive impact of vertical restrictions is significantly affected by the form of the transaction. Nonsale transactions appear to be
excluded from the per se rule, not because of a greater danger of intrabrand harm
or a greater promise of interbrand benefit, but rather because of the Court's
unexplained belief that a complete per se prohibition would be too "inflexibl[e]."

Vertical restrictions reduce intrabrand competition by limiting the number of
sellers of a particular product competing for the business of a given group of
buyers. Location restrictions have this effect because of practical constraints on
the effective marketing area of retail outlets. . . .

Vertical restrictions promote interbrand competition by allowing the manufacturer to achieve certain efficiencies in the distribution of his products. These "redeeming virtues" are implicit in every decision sustaining vertical restrictions under the rule of reason. Economists have identified a number of ways in which
manufacturers can use such restrictions to compete more effectively against other
manufacturers. For example, new manufacturers and manufacturers entering new
markets can use the restrictions in order to induce competent and aggressive
retailers to make the kind of investment of capital and labor that is often required
in the distribution of products unknown to the consumer. Established manufacturers can use them to induce retailers to engage in promotional activities or to
provide service and repair facilities necessary to the efficient marketing of their
products. Service and repair are vital for many products, such as automobiles and
major household appliances. The availability and quality of such services affect a
manufacturer's goodwill and the competitiveness of his product. Because of market imperfections such as the so-called "free rider" effect, these services might not
be provided by retailers in a purely competitive situation, despite the fact that
each retailer's benefit would be greater if all provided the services than if none did.

Economists also have argued that manufacturers have an economic interest in
maintaining as much intrabrand competition as is consistent with the efficient
distribution of their products. Although the view that the manufacturer's interest
necessarily corresponds with that of the public is not universally shared, even the
leading critic of vertical restrictions concedes that Schwinn's distinction between
sale and nonsale transactions is essentially unrelated to any relevant economic
impact. Indeed, to the extent that the form of the transaction is related to intrabrand benefits, the Court's distinction is inconsistent with its articulated concern
for the ability of smaller firms to compete effectively with larger ones. Capital
requirements and administrative expenses may prevent smaller firms from using
the exception for nonsale transactions.

We conclude that the distinction drawn in Schwinn between sale and nonsale
transactions is not sufficient to justify the application of a per se rule in one
situation and a rule of reason in the other. The question remains whether the per
se rule stated in Schwinn should be expanded to include nonsale transactions or
abandoned in favor of a return to the rule of reason. We have found no persuasive
support for expanding the per se rule. . . . Certainly, there has been no showing in
this case, either generally or with respect to Sylvania's agreements, that vertical

restrictions have or are likely to have a "pernicious effect on competition" or that they "lack . . . any redeeming virtue." Ibid. Accordingly, we conclude that the per se rule stated in Schwinn must be overruled. In so holding we do not foreclose the possibility that particular applications of vertical restrictions might justify per se prohibition under Northern Pac. R. Co. But we do make clear that departure from the rule-of-reason standard must be based upon demonstrable economic effect rather than—as in Schwinn—upon formalistic line drawing.

In sum, we conclude that the appropriate decision is to return to the rule of reason that governed vertical restrictions prior to Schwinn. When anticompetitive effects are shown to result from particular vertical restrictions they can be adequately policed under the rule of reason, the standard traditionally applied for the majority of anticompetitive practices challenged under Section 1 of the Act. Accordingly, the decision of the Court of Appeals is Affirmed.

CHAPTER 9

PATENTS

The patent is much older than the antitrust laws. It existed in late medieval Europe and was explicitly provided for in the Constitution. The first patent law was passed by the first Congress.

The patent is a major exception to the antitrust laws. The courts have long had to reconcile the two areas of law. In the 1920s and 1930s, the courts tended to strengthen the patent at the expense of competition. In such fields as light bulbs and glass containers, elaborate cartels developed based on patents.

The General Electric case illustrates this period. Technically, the precedent set there still applies, but many observers feel that if a major firm took full advantage of it, the rule would change. Should it? Is the General Electric rule necessary to give incentive for invention? What about a pharmaceutical house that licenses another firm for veterinary applications only, keeping human applications for itself? Or an eastern firm that licenses another firm to produce in the West but prohibits the firm from selling east of the Mississippi? Both practices are legal today.

The patent has become a much more limited grant of monopoly. Hartford Empire made the most important change. Why was the outcome of this case so different from that of General Electric? What did the firms in Hartford Empire do what General Electric did not? Were the restrictions in Hartford Empire more anticompetitive than those in General Electric? One difference is that General Electric involved one firm licensing another with restrictions while Hartford Empire involved cross-licensing—several firms licensing one another with restrictions. Is this an economically relevant distinction?

International Salt involves the use of patents on two products to restrict competition in a third. Such restrictions had been struck down in other cases, but

International Salt offered a stronger precedent. An important aspect of such cases is that such practices are often treated as "patent misuse" and can lead to the loss of patent rights for the patentee. Are the restrictions serious enough from a public point of view to warrant such a drastic penalty?

There is an extensive body of law dealing with patents that has grown out of private infringment suits and countersuits charging patent misuse or challenging patent validity. That body of law is represented in this chapter by one important case, *Lear v. Adkins.*

Patent licensees had traditionally been prevented from challenging the validity of the patents they were licensed to use by the judicial doctrine of estoppel. This doctrine held that a licensee was made ineligible by that agreement to challenge the patent. The Court changed this in *Lear v. Adkins.* Do you think the decision was fair? Do you think it lessened the incentive to invent?

United States v. General Electric Co.

272 U.S. 476 (1926)

MR. CHIEF JUSTICE TAFT delivered the opinion of the Court.

This is a bill in equity brought by the United States in the District Court for the Northern District of Ohio to enjoin the General Electric Company, the Westinghouse Electric and Manufacturing Company, and the Westinghouse Lamp Company from further violation of the Anti-Trust Act of July 2, 1890. The bill made two charges, one that the General Electric Company in its business of making and selling incandescent electric lights had devised and was carrying out a plan for their distribution throughout the United States by a number of so-called agents, exceeding 21,000, to restrain interstate trade in such lamps and to exercise a monopoly of the sale thereof; and, second, that it was achieving the same illegal purpose through a contract of license with the defendants, the Westinghouse Electric and Manufacturing Company and the Westinghouse Lamp Company. . . . [The distribution system was really a means by which General Electric controlled retail prices—it got by the court in 1926 but was abandoned in 1973 after another antitrust suit. It will be omitted here.]

The second question in the case involves the validity of a license granted March 1, 1912, by the Electric Company to the Westinghouse Company to make, use and sell lamps under the patents owned by the former. It was charged that the license in effect provided that the Westinghouse Company would follow prices and terms of sale from time to time fixed by the Electric Company and observed by it, and that the Westinghouse Company would, with regard to lamps manufactured by it under the license, adopt and maintain the same conditions of sale as observed by the Electric Company in the distribution of lamps manufactured by it. . . .

The Electric Company is the owner of three patents—one of 1912 to Just & Hanaman, the basic patent for use of tungsten filaments in the manufacture of electric lamps; the Coolidge patent of 1913, covering a process of manufacturing tungsten filaments by which their tensile strength and endurance are greatly increased; and, third, the Langmuir patent of 1916, which is for the use of gas in the bulb by which the intensity of the light is substantially heightened. These three patents cover completely the making of the modern electric lights with the tungsten filaments, and secure to the Electric Company the monopoly of their making, using and vending. . . .

Had the Electric Company, as the owner of the patents entirely controlling the manufacture, use and sale of the tungsten incandescent lamps, in its license to the Westinghouse Company, the right to impose the condition that its sales should be at prices fixed by the licensor and subject to change according to its discretion? The contention is also made that the license required the Westinghouse Company not only to conform in the matter of the prices at which it might vend the patented articles, but also to follow the same plan as that which we have already explained the Electric Company adopted in its distribution. It does not appear that this provision was express in the license, because no such plan was set out therein; but even if the construction urged by the Government is correct, we think the result must be the same.

The owner of a patent may assign it to another and convey, (1) the exclusive right to make, use and vend the invention through the United States, or, (2) an undivided part or share of that exclusive right, or (3) the exclusive right under the patent within and through a specific part of the United States. But any assignment or transfer short of one of these is a license, giving the licensee no title in the patent and no right to sue at law in his own name for an infringment. Conveying less than title to the patent, or part of it, the patentee may grant a license to make, use and vend articles under the specifications of his patent for any royalty or upon any condition the performance of which is reasonably within the reward which the patentee by the grant of the patent is entitled to secure. It is well settled, as already said, that where a patentee makes the patented article and sells it, he can exercise no future control over what the purchaser may wish to do with the article after his purchase. It has passed beyond the scope of the patentee's rights. But the question is a different one which arises when we consider what a patentee who grants a license to one to make and vend the patented article may do in limiting the licensee in the exercise of the right to sell. The patentee may make and grant a license to another to make and use the patented articles, but withhold his right to sell them. The licensee in such a case acquires an interest in the articles made. He owns the material of them and may use them. But if he sells them, he infringes the right of the patentee, and may be held for damages and enjoined. If the patentee goes further, and licenses the selling of the articles, may he limit the selling by limiting the method of sale and the price? We think he may do so, provided the conditions of sale are normally and reasonably adapted to secure pecuniary reward for the patentee's monopoly. One of the valuable elements of the exclusive right of a patentee is to acquire profit by the price at which the article is sold. The higher the price, the greater the profit, unless it is prohibitory. When the patentee licenses another to make and vend, and retains the right to continue to make and vend on his own account, the price at which his licensee will sell will necessarily affect the price at which he can sell his own patented goods. It would seem entirely reasonable that he should say to the licensee, "Yes, you may make and sell articles under my patent, but not so as to destroy the profit that I wish to obtain by making them and selling them myself." He does not thereby sell outright to the licensee the articles the latter may make and sell, or vest absolute ownership in them. He restricts the property and interest the licensee has in the goods he makes and proposes to sell.

Hartford-Empire Co. v. United States

323 U.S. 386 (1945)

MR. JUSTICE ROBERTS delivered the opinion of the Court.

These are appeals from a decree awarding an injunction against violations of §§1 and 2 of the Sherman Act, as amended, and §3 of the Clayton Act. Two questions are presented. Were violations proved? If so, are the provisions of the decree right? . . .

In 1912 Hartford-Fairmont Company was organized to combine the activities of two existing companies interested in glass manufacture with those of a group of engineers who desired to obtain and exploit patents for automatic glassmaking machinery. The defendant Corning Glass Works' . . . field may be defined roughly as the pressed and blown field, or the noncontainer field. In 1909 persons interested in Corning organized Empire Machine Company as a patent holding and developing company.

The defendant Owens-Illinois Glass Company (hereinafter called Owens) is a large manufacturer of glass. Mr. Owens of that company produced the first fully automatic machine for blowing bottles, which is known as a suction type machine. . . . From about 1904 the Owens group followed the policy of granting exclusive licenses, in limited fields, for the manufacture of glassware by the suction process. Owens itself was, and is, mainly interested in what is known as narrow neck container ware. . . .

June 30, 1916, Hartford-Fairmont and Empire made an agreement whereby Empire was given an exclusive license to use Hartford-Fairmont's patents for pressed and blown glassware and Hartford-Fairmont was given an exclusive license to use Empire's patents for production of containers. Thus Corning obtained exclusive rights, under the patents, for Corning's line of ware—pressed and blown glass—and Hartford obtained the patent rights of both companies in respect of other glassware. Negotiations led to agreements, October 6, 1922, whereby Hartford-Empire (hereinafter called Hartford) was formed and took over all assets of Hartford-Fairmont and of Empire relating to glass machinery. . . .

As a result of negotiations for a settlement of their disputes, they [Owens and Hartford] entered into an agreement April 9, 1924, whereby Owens granted Hartford an exclusive license under Owens' patents for gob feeder and forming machines and Hartford granted Owens a nonexclusive, nonassignable, and nondivisible license to make and use machines and methods embodying patents then or thereafter owned or acquired by Hartford for the manufacture of glassware, but Owens was not to sell or license gob feeding machinery and was excluded from the pressed and blown field previously reserved to Corning.

As soon as the agreement had been made, Hartford and Owens combined to get control of all other feeder patents. In this endeavor they pooled the efforts of their legal staffs and contributed equally to the purchase of patents and the expenses of litigation.

Hazel-Atlas Glass Company (hereinafter called Hazel) was second to Owens in the manufacture and sale of glass containers. It had been using feeders of its own design and manufacture. To build up further patent control, to discourage use of machinery not covered by their patents, and to influence glassmakers to take licenses under Hartford's inventions, Hartford and Owens desired that Hazel should become a partner-licensee. . . . As of June 1, 1932, Hartford, Owens, and Hazel executed a series of agreements. Hartford licensed Hazel under all its glass machinery patents, present and future, to January 3, 1945. Owens and Hazel had the option, on notice, to terminate their contracts with Hartford but agreed mutually to protect each other in such event. The result of this combination was that resistance to Hartford's licensing campaign disappeared and practically the entire industry took licenses from Hartford.

Thatcher Manufacturing Company, a large manufacturer of milk bottles, early obtained an exclusive license to manufacture them on the Owens suction machine. In 1920 Thatcher secured the exclusive right to manufacture milk bottles on Hartford's paddle needle feeder and milk bottle forming machine. . . . In 1936 a new agreement was made whereby Hartford agreed that, so long as Thatcher manufactured 750,000 gross per annum, Hartford would grant no other license for manufacture of milk bottles.

Ball Brothers, the largest manufacturer of domestic fruit jars, had used machines of its own design as well as the Owens suction machines under license, but had never taken any license from Hartford. In 1933 Ball took a license from Hartford, obtaining all the residual rights of Hartford for the manufacture of fruit jars, and, inter alia, granted Hartford an option to take licenses on all Ball's patents for glass machinery then owned or thereafter acquired. After discussion as to the rights of Hazel and Owens to manufacture fruit jars, it was proposed that they be limited by written agreement, Hazel to 300,000 gross and Owens to 100,000 gross annually. It was decided not to have a written agreement but both have generally kept within these limits. . . .

In granting licenses under the pooled patents Hartford always reserved the rights within Corning's field. Further, it not only limited its licensees to certain portions of the container field but, in many instances, limited the amount of glassware which might be produced by the licensee and, in numerous instances, as a result of conferences with Owens, Hazel, Thatcher and Ball, refused licenses to prevent overstocking the glassware market and to "stabilize" the prices at which such ware was sold. . . .

Several forming machines not covered by Hartford patents were on the market. Without going into detail, it is sufficient to say that, by purchases of patents and manufacturing plants, and by an agreement with Hartford's principal competitor, Lynch Manufacturing Company, the field was divided between Hartford and Lynch under restrictions which gave Hartford control. In the upshot it became impossible to use Hartford feeders with any other forming machine than one licensed by Hartford or used by its consent. . . .

In 1919 the Glass Container Association of America was formed. Prior to 1933 its members produced 82% of the glass containers made in the United States and since have produced 92%. Since 1931 . . . the Association has had a statistical committee of seven, on which Owens, Hazel, Thatcher, and since 1933, Ball were represented. These appellants also were represented on the Board of Directors. Hartford, though not a member, has closely cooperated with the officers of the association in efforts to discourage outsiders from increasing production of glassware and newcomers from entering the field. The court below, on sufficient evidence, has found that the association, through its statistical committee, assigned production quotas to its members and that they and Hartford were zealous in seeing that these were observed.

In summary, the situation brought about in the glass industry, and existing in 1938, was this: Hartford, with the technical and financial aid of others in the conspiracy, had acquired, by issue to it or assignment from the owners, more than 600 patents. These, with over 100 Corning controlled patents, over 60 Owens patents, over 70 Hazel patents, and some 12 Lynch patents, had been, by cross-licensing agreements, merged into a pool which effectually controlled the industry. This control was exercised to allot production in Corning's field to Corning, and that in restricted classes within the general container field to Owens, Hazel, Thatcher, Ball, and such other smaller manufacturers as the group agreed should be licensed. The result was that 94% of the glass containers manufactured in this country on feeders and formers were made on machinery licensed under the pooled patents.

The District Court found that invention of glassmaking machinery had been discouraged, that competition in the manufacture and sale or licensing of such machinery had been suppressed, and that the system of restricted licensing had been employed to suppress competition in the manufacture of unpatented glassware and to maintain prices of the manufactured product. The findings are full and adequate and are supported by evidence, much of it contemporary writings of corporate defendants or their officers and agents. . . .

We affirm the District Court's findings and conclusions that the corporate appellants combined in violation of the Sherman Act, that Hartford and Lynch contracted in violation of the Clayton Act, and that the individual appellants with exceptions to be noted participated in the violations in their capacities as officers and directors of the corporations.

[The rest of the decision was devoted to a long and careful review of the District Court's order. It tried to end the complex "conspiracy" in the glassware industry without eliminating the patent's incentive effect on invention and innovation. Licenses were to be granted to all applicants without restrictions as to field of use or quantities produced, but Hartford was allowed to retain its patents, to collect royalties on them, and to place machinery embodying the patented technology on a lease-only basis. The Glass Container Association changed its statistics so that they could not serve as output quotas. These changes had mostly been made "voluntarily" while the case was pending.]

International Salt Co., Inc. v. United States

332 U.S. 392 (1947)

MR. JUSTICE JACKSON delivered the opinion of the Court.

The Government brought this civil action to enjoin the International Salt Company, appellant here, from carrying out provisions of the leases of its patented machines to the effect that lessees would use therein only International's salt products. The restriction is alleged to violate §1 of the Sherman Act, and §3 of the Clayton Act. Upon appellant's answer and admissions of fact, the Government moved for summary judgment under Rule 56 of the Rules of Civil Procedure, upon the ground that no issue as to a material fact was presented and that, on the admissions, judgment followed as matter of law. Neither party submitted affidavits. Judgment was granted and appeal was taken directly to this Court.

It was established by pleadings or admissions that the International Salt Company is engaged in interstate commerce in salt, of which it is the country's largest producer for industrial uses. It also owns patents on two machines for utilization of salt products. One, the "Lixator," dissolves rock salt into a brine used in various industrial processes. The other, the "Saltomat," injects salt, in tablet form, into canned products during the canning process. The principal distribution of each of these machines is under leases which, among other things, require the lessees to purchase from appellant all unpatented salt and salt tablets consumed in the leased machines. . . .

The appellant's patents confer a limited monopoly of the invention they reward. From them appellant derives a right to restrain others from making, vending, or using the patented machines. But the patents confer no right to restrain use of, or trade in, unpatented salt. By contracting to close this market for salt against competition, International has engaged in a restraint of trade for which its patents afford no immunity from the antitrust laws.

Appellant contends, however, that summary judgment was unauthorized because it precluded trial of alleged issues of fact as to whether the restraint was unreasonable within the Sherman Act or substantially lessened competition or tended to create a monopoly in salt within the Clayton Act. We think the admitted facts left no genuine issue. Not only is price-fixing unreasonable, per se, but also it is unreasonable, per se, to foreclose competitors from any substantial market. The volume of business affected by these contracts cannot be said to be insignificant or insubstantial and the tendency of the arrangement to accomplishment of monopoly seems obvious. Under the law, agreements are forbidden which "tend to create a monopoly," and it is immaterial that the tendency is a creeping one rather than one that proceeds at full gallop; nor does the law await arrival at the goal before condemning the direction of the movement.

Appellant contends, however, that the "Lixator" contracts are saved from unreasonableness and from the tendency to monopoly because they provided that if any competitor offered salt of equal grade at a lower price, the lessee should be free to buy in the open market, unless appellant would furnish the salt at an equal price; and the "Saltomat" agreements provided that the lessee was entitled to benefit of any general price reduction in lessor's salt tablets. The "Lixator" provision does, of course, afford a measure of protection to the lessee, but it does not avoid the stifling effect of the agreement on competition. The appellant had at all times a priority on the business at equal prices. A competitor would have to undercut appellant's price to have any hope of capturing the market, while appellant could hold that market by merely meeting competition. We do not think this concession relieves the contract of being a restraint of trade, albeit a less harsh one than would result in the absence of such a provision. The "Saltomat" provision obviously has no effect of legal significance since it gives the lessee nothing more than a right to buy appellant's salt tablets at appellant's going price. All purchases must in any event be of appellant's product.

Appellant also urges that since under the leases it remained under an obligation to repair and maintain the machines, it was reasonable to confine their use to its own salt because its high quality assured satisfactory functioning and low maintenance cost. The appellant's rock salt is alleged to have an average sodium chloride content of 98.2%. Rock salt of other producers, it is said, "does not run consistent in sodium chloride content and in many instances runs as low as 95% of sodium chloride." This greater percentage of insoluble impurities allegedly disturbs the functioning of the "Lixator" machine. A somewhat similar claim is pleaded as to the "Saltomat."

Of course, a lessor may impose on a lessee reasonable restrictions designed in good faith to minimize maintenance burdens and to assure satisfactory operation. We may assume, as matter of argument, that if the "Lixator" functions best on rock salt of average sodium chloride content of 98.2%, the lessee might be required to use only salt meeting such a specification of quality. But it is not pleaded, nor is it argued, that the machine is allergic to salt of equal quality produced by anyone except International. If others cannot produce salt equal to reasonable specifications for machine use, it is one thing; but it is admitted that, at times, at least, competitors do offer such a product. They are, however, shut out of the market by a provision that limits it, not in terms of quality, but in terms of a particular vendor. Rules for use of leased machinery must not be disguised restraints of free competition, though they may set reasonable standards which all suppliers must meet.

Appellant urges other objections to the summary judgment. The tying clause has not been insisted upon in all leases, nor has it always been enforced when it was included. But these facts do not justify the general use of the restriction which has been admitted here. . . .

Lear, Inc. v. Adkins

395 U.S. 653 (1969)

MR. JUSTICE HARLAN delivered the opinion of the Court.

In January of 1953, John Adkins, an inventor and mechanical engineer, was hired by Lear Incorporated for the purpose of solving a vexing problem the company had encountered in its efforts to develop a gyroscope which would meet the increasingly demanding requirements of the aviation industry. . . . Shortly after Adkins was hired, he developed a method of construction at the company's California facilities which improved gyroscope accuracy at a low cost. Lear almost immediately incorporated Adkins' improvements into its production process to its substantial advantage.

The question that remains unsettled in this case, after eight years of litigation in the California courts, is whether Adkins will receive compensation for Lear's use of those improvements which the inventor has subsequently patented. At every stage of this lawsuit, Lear has sought to prove that, despite the grant of a patent by the Patent Office, none of Adkins' improvements were sufficiently novel to warrant the award of a monopoly under the standards delineated in the governing federal statutes. Moreover, the company has sought to prove that Adkins obtained his patent by means of a fraud on the Patent Office. In response, the inventor has argued that since Lear had entered into a licensing agreement with Adkins, it was obliged to pay the agreed royalties regardless of the validity of the underlying patent. . . .

The uncertain status of licensee estopped [prohibited because of the license from challenging the patent] in the case law is a product of judicial efforts to accommodate the competing demands of the common law of contracts and the federal law of patents. On the one hand, the law of contracts forbids a purchaser to repudiate his promises simply because he later becomes dissatisfied with the bargain he has made. On the other hand, federal law requires that all ideas in general circulation be dedicated to the common good unless they are protected by a valid patent. When faced with this basic conflict in policy, both this Court and courts throughout the land have naturally sought to develop an intermediate position which somehow would remain responsive to the radically different concerns of the two different worlds of contract and patent. The result has been a failure. Rather than creative compromise, there has been a chaos of conflicting case law, proceeding on inconsistent premises. Before renewing the search for an elusive middle ground, we must reconsider on their own merits the arguments which may properly be advanced on both sides of the estoppel question.

It will simplify matters greatly if we first consider the most typical situation in which patent licenses are negotiated. In contrast to the present case, most manufacturers obtain a license after a patent has issued. Since the Patent Office makes an inventor's ideas public when it issues its grant of a limited monopoly, a potential licensee has access to the inventor's ideas even if he does not enter into an agreement with the patent owner. Consequently, a manufacturer gains only two benefits if he chooses to enter a licensing agreement after the patent has issued. First, by accepting a license and paying royalties for a time, the licensee may have avoided the necessity of defending an expensive infringement action during the period when he may be least able to afford one. Second, the existence of an unchallenged patent may deter others from attempting to compete with the licensee.

Under ordinary contract principles the mere fact that some benefit is received is enough to require the enforcement of the contract, regardless of the validity of the underlying patent. Nevertheless, if one tests this result by the standard of good-faith commercial dealing, it seems far from satisfactory. For the simple contract approach entirely ignores the position of the licensor who is seeking to invoke the court's assistance on his behalf. Consider, for example, the equities of the licensor who has obtained his patent through a fraud on the Patent Office. It is difficult to perceive why good faith requires that courts should permit him to recover royalties despite his licensee's attempts to show that the patent is invalid.

Even in the more typical cases, not involving conscious wrongdoing, the licensor's equities are far from compelling. A patent, in the last analysis, simply represents a legal conclusion reached by the Patent Office. Moreover, the legal conclusion is predicated on factors as to which reasonable men can differ widely. Yet the Patent Office is often obliged to reach its decision . . . without the aid of the arguments which could be advanced by parties interested in proving patent invalidity. Consequently, it does not seem to us to be unfair to require a patentee to defend the Patent Office's judgment when his licensee places the question in issue, especially since the licensor's case is buttressed by the presumption of validity which attaches to his patent. Thus, although licensee estoppel may be consistent with the letter of contractual doctrine, we cannot say that it is compelled by the spirit of contract law, which seeks to balance the claims of promisor and promisee in accord with the requirements of good faith.

Surely the equities of the licensor do not weigh very heavily when they are balanced against the important public interest in permitting full and free competition in the use of ideas which are in reality a part of the public domain. Licensees may often be the only individuals with enough economic incentive to challenge the patentability of an inventor's discovery. If they are muzzled, the public may continually be required to pay tribute to would-be monopolists without need for justification. We think it plain that the technical requirements of contract doctrine must give way before the demands of the public interest in the typical situation involving the negotiation of a license after a patent has issued. . . .

The case before us, however, presents a far more complicated estoppel problem than the one which arises in the most common licensing context. The problem arises out of the fact that Lear obtained its license in 1955, more than four years before Adkins received his 1960 patent. Indeed, from the very outset of the relationship, Lear obtained special access to Adkins' ideas in return for its promise to pay satisfactory compensation.

Thus, during the lengthy period in which Adkins was attempting to obtain a patent, Lear gained an important benefit not generally obtained by the typical licensee. For until a patent issues, a potential licensee may not learn his licensor's ideas simply by requesting the information from the Patent Office. During the time the inventor is seeking patent protection, the governing federal statute requires the Patent Office to hold an inventor's patent application in confidence. If a potential licensee hopes to use the ideas contained in a secret patent application, he must deal with the inventor himself, unless the inventor chooses to publicize his ideas to the world at large. By promising to pay Adkins royalties from the very outset of their relationship, Lear gained immediate access to ideas which it may well have not learned until the Patent Office published the details of Adkins' invention in 1960. At the core of this case, then, is the difficult question whether federal patent policy bars a State from enforcing a contract regulating access to an unpatented secret idea. . . .

The California Supreme Court did not address itself to this issue with precision, for it believed that the venerable doctrine of estoppel provided a sufficient answer to all of Lear's claims based upon federal patent law. Thus, we do not know whether the Supreme Court would have awarded Adkins recovery even on his pre-patent royalties if it had recognized that previously established estoppel doctrine could no longer be properly invoked with regard to royalties accruing during the 17-year patent period. . . .

The judgment of the Supreme Court of California is vacated and the case is remanded to that court for further proceedings not inconsistent with this opinion.

PART THREE

ECONOMIC REGULATION

THE ISSUES OF REGULATION

This section deals with conventional regulation in the United States. In a broad sense, all private enterprises are regulated today. They must comply with federal and state laws establishing minimum wage rates, safe working conditions, zoning restrictions, environmental standards, truth-in-packaging requirements, and so on. A businessperson from the turn of the century would be amazed at the degree of government "interference" in private business activity today. Yet for most of American industry, individual businesspeople still make the important decisions that determine price, output, and investment. We rely on competition to prevent monopoly pricing, to provide the goods that consumers want, and to ensure utilization of productive resources.

THE REGULATED INDUSTRIES

In an important minority of industries, however, the government actively intervenes and regulates business decisions in much greater detail. Table 10.1 lists the most important industries that are usually thought of as "regulated" and their shares of national income in 1978. Altogether these industries accounted for 9.7 percent of national income in 1978. A number of them are slated for deregulation in the mid-1980s. This is true of oil and natural gas production, oil refining, and airlines. Less comprehensive regulation has also been mandated for the trucking, railroad, and broadcasting industries.

Characteristics of Regulated Industries

Regulated industries differ from most unregulated industries in a number of respects. First, the regulated sector has grown much faster than the economy as a

TABLE 10-1
THE IMPORTANCE OF REGULATED INDUSTRIES

Industry	National income accruing in 1978 (millions of dollars)	Percentage of 1978 national income
Oil and gas:		
Oil and gas extraction	14,298	0.8
Petroleum refining	16,103*	0.9
Transportation:		
Railroad	14,217	0.8
Local & interurban transit	3,771	0.2
Trucking and warehousing	28,608	1.6
Water transportation	4,673	0.3
Air transportation	12,054	0.7
Pipelines, except natural gas	1,336	0.1
Communications:		
Telegraph and telephone	35,792	2.0
Radio and television broadcasting	4,741	0.3
Electric, gas, and sanitary services	34,912	2.0
Total	170,505	9.7

*Based on "petroleum and coal products" ($20,303 million $\times$ .793). Petroleum refining accounted for 79.3% of value added in this industry group in 1977.
Source: Survey of Current Business, July 1979, p. 53.

whole. One reason for this is the extension of regulation to new industries. At the turn of the century only the railroads and some local electric, gas, water, and transit industries were regulated. Since then, industries that accounted for 4.7 percent of 1978 national income have been added to the regulated category. Most of the additions occurred during the 1930s, but oil, natural gas production, and cable television have been added since then. Another reason for the growth of the regulated sector is that many, though not all, of the regulated industries have grown much faster than the economy as a whole. This is true of electric power, natural gas, telephone, broadcasting, and airlines.

Second, practically all of the regulated industries sell services rather than goods. Electric power, communications, and transportation are services that can only be provided for the customer on demand. They cannot be produced for inventory and stored until purchased. As a result, most regulated industries maintain excess capacity most of the time so they will be able to serve the customers whenever they throw a switch or pick up a phone.

A third feature of regulated industries is that they are generally very capital-intensive. In general, manufacturing industries have total investments of less than one year's sales. Many of the regulated industries, however, have invested capital equivalent to several years' sales. The high capital requirements of these industries has made the valuation of invested capital and the rates of return major isues of regulation.

WHY REGULATE?

Decreasing Costs

Another special feature of some, though not all, regulated industries provides one of the main justifications for regulation. Economists have labeled these industries "decreasing-cost" industries. That is, cost per unit of output declines continuously as output increases. This concept is illustrated in Figures 10-1 and 10-2. Figure 10-1 shows the long-run average cost curve for a typical firm in the unregulated sector. As the firm expands, cost per unit declines up to a production level often referred to as minimum efficient scale. Beyond that point, cost per unit is roughly constant regardless of firm size. In most industries minimum efficient scale is quite small compared to the size of the market. Existing markets could support five or ten efficient producers in automobiles, a dozen or two efficient steel or oil companies, and hundreds of producers of textiles or shoes.

The contrasting case shown in Figure 10-2, where cost per unit falls continuously, is found in some regulated industries. An industry with continuously decreasing costs is apt to be a monopoly. Even if two or more producers do compete at some point, competition among them is not likely to last; the largest firm can set its price below its competitors' cost and win its competitors' customers. The larger the firm becomes, the greater is its advantage over its rivals. Ultimately it will be a monopoly. Even if we could maintain more than one firm in the market, we would still be worse off: cost per unit for two firms would be higher than for one.

FIGURE 10-1

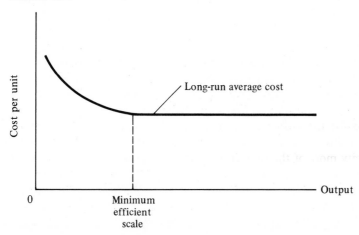

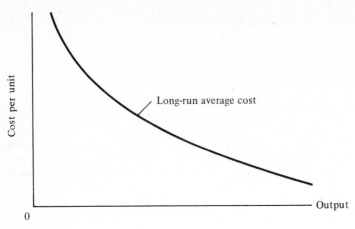

FIGURE 10-2

"Natural Monopoly"

Many regulated industries have been described as "natural monopolies" because they are supposed to be decreasing-cost industries. This is undoubtedly true of some of them, most notably local electric, gas, telephone, and cable TV, where competition would require duplicate distribution systems. This implies that the most efficient way to provide these services is with a single distribution network of high capacity.[1]

Some, though not all, modes of intercity transportation and communication also have decreasing costs over a wide range. The railroads' costs per ton-mile are lower with two tracks than with one, and lower yet with a third track, *provided* they have enough business to keep all that capacity in use. Nevertheless, in the railroads' heyday before World War I, there seems to have been room for two or more reasonably efficient lines connecting most major cities. Today there is only one line for many major city pairs; its main competition is from trucks and barges.

Electric transmission lines and oil and gas pipelines have sharply decreasing costs. The cost of a pipeline is roughly proportional to its circumference and therefore to its radius, but pipeline capacity depends on its cross-section area and therefore on the square of its radius. Similarly, the cost of electric transmission lines is roughly proportional to voltage, while capacity rises with the square of voltage. This means that the cheapest way to transmit oil, gas, or electricity be-

---

[1] Decreasing cost is not the only condition that will yield "natural monopoly." Another may be "economies of scope"—cost reductions that arise when two or more services are rendered jointly. It might be implied that monopoly would have lower cost if one of the services involved is a natural monopoly for other reasons. A possible example is local service and long-distance telephone service, though many economists are doubtful about that case. A third case where natural monopoly might arise would be where one firm had significantly lower costs than other firms, regardless of its size.

tween two points is with one large pipeline or transmission line. There may be some room for competition if a city is supplied from two or more sources or if the first line installed is fully used and a second one is still needed, but competition among pipelines or electric transmission lines seems bound to be quite limited.

The same used to be the case with long-distance telephone service. However, modern microwave transmission systems have proved efficient at quite a small scale. There are a number of private microwave systems operated by railroads and pipelines, and independent microwave companies have been able to compete with Ma Bell quite effectively in long-distance service between large cities.

In electric generation (about half of total electric costs) there are two or more electric power generating firms capable of supplying most large cities, so some competition would be feasible if all generating companies could bid for the business of independent distribution systems. In fact, most transmission and distribution systems are owned by generating companies, so competition is bound to be quite limited short of a major reorganization of the industry.

That leaves a number of regulated industries where competition is clearly possible. On the routes connecting large cities, there is usually a choice of more than one airline. We seldom see more than a few airlines on a given route, but the threat of entry by other airlines serving other routes serves to keep rates within bounds.

Truckers are even more susceptible to competition. Trucking requires minimal capital and can be carried on efficiently on a very small scale, as indicated by the success of small firms in hauling exempt agricultural products. The situation in ocean and inland water transportation is very similar. And there are thousands of successful producers of oil and natural gas, many of them very small. Even in broadcasting, where the number of broadcasters must be limited to avoid interference, there is room for substantial competition in the larger cities.

"Ruinous Competition"

It is sometimes maintained by proponents of regulation that competition in certain industries would be "ruinous" without regulation. Presumably this means that price competition in such industries would bring about periodic price cuts substantially below cost, resulting in many bankruptcies. This may or may not be true in the decreasing-cost industries with high capital-output ratios, but it seems highly unlikely in trucking, where "ruinous competition" is most often cited as a reason for regulation. Capital costs are relatively small compared to variable costs, so that unregulated truckers would not be likely to operate at prices much below cost. Also, the labor and capital resources employed in trucking can easily be shifted to alternative uses. In other industries with low fixed costs, such as retailing, prices seldom fall much below cost, and adjustments for changing market conditions are made quickly and with little disruption. In fact, this has been the case in trucking's unregulated sector, which carries agricultural products and has been quite free of "ruinous competition."

The Demand for Regulation

Some economists believe that the real reason we regulate certain industries is that the firms involved *want* to be regulated. Regulation normally restricts entry and often prevents price competition as well. Advocates of this position feel that the industries involved submit to regulatory control in return for the protection from competition which it affords.

There is some historical evidence in support of this view. In the years immediately following the Civil War most railroads opposed state regulation. But after several bouts of severe rate competition on major routes, some railroad men became active supporters of regulations prohibiting price competition. The legislation that established the Interstate Commerce Commission (ICC) seems to have been passed by a coalition of farm and small-town representatives with some railroad support. At any rate, there is little doubt that the railroads lobbied for and benefited from the Elkins Act of 1903, the Hepburn Act of 1906, and the Mann-Elkins Act of 1910, which strengthened ICC control over railroad rates.

With the appearance of trucks, the railroads and the ICC campaigned hard for their regulation. Bills were introduced in every Congress from 1925 on to provide for such regulation, but while prosperity continued, the bills were defeated by the combined opposition of truckers and shippers. After several years of the great depression, however, many of the larger trucking firms supported regulation. The Motor Carrier Act of 1935 gave the ICC control over which trucking firms could haul particular products between specific locations and over the rates they could charge. Whatever their stance had been before the passage of that bill, the common carrier truckers and the Teamsters Union that bargains with them are currently the most ardent advocates of regulation.

The origins of regulation will undoubtedly be debated for many years. In most cases any initial legislation establishing regulatory controls had support from groups besides the affected industries and contained provisions important to those groups. Sometimes a substantial sector of the industry favored regulation and sometimes it strongly opposed regulation. Whatever the stance of the industry when regulation was introduced, however, most regulated firms have since found ways to live quite comfortably in a regulatory environment.

THE REGULATORS

The first attempts at regulation in this country were through municipal franchises, which usually established monopoly electric, gas, and trolley companies and specified the terms of service. This placed the regulatory function in the hands of the city council, which was seldom prepared for the task. Franchise awards and their terms became political matters, making the regulatory process a fertile area for corruption.

Regulatory Commissions

We still have franchises, but in most states regulatory decisions are made by state public utility commissions. In most cases the members of these commissions are

TABLE 10-2
ECONOMIC REGULATORY AGENCIES AND THEIR JURISDICTIONS

Agency	Economic activities regulated and date of initial federal regulation
Interstate Commerce Commission (ICC)	Interstate railroads (1887) Interstate motor carriers (1935) Interstate water carriers (1940) Interstate telepnone (1910–1934) Interstate oil pipelines (1906–1977)
State Regulatory Commissions	Established in 35 states, 1907–1920 and in all by 1973. Local electric service (46 states in 1973) Local gas service (47 states in 1973) Local telephone service (48 states in 1973)
Federal Communications Commission (FCC)	Interstate telephone service (1934) Broadcasting (1934)* Cable television (1968–1980)
Federal Power Commission (FPC), to 1977	Interstate electricity (1935) Interstate natural gas pipelines (1938)
Federal Energy Regulatory Commission (FERC), since 1977	Field production and pricing of natural gas (1954) Oil pipelines (1977)
Civil Aeronautics Board (CAB)	Interstate airlines (1938)†
Federal Energy Administration (FEA) and Economic Regulatory Administration (ERA)	Established 1973. Name changed and shifted to Department of Energy, 1977. Oil and oil product prices and allocations (1973)

*Regulated by Federal Radio Commission (1907–1934)
†Regulated by ICC and Post Office (1934–1938)

appointed by the Governor, usually for long and overlapping terms. The main concerns of the state commissions are the local electric, gas, telephone, water, and transit utilities.

There is another set of regulatory commissions at the federal level that is primarily concerned with interstate industries. Table 10-2 lists the major regulatory agencies, the industries they regulate, and the dates on which regulation began. Federal commissioners are appointed by the President with the advice and consent of the Senate for long and overlapping terms.

Both the federal and state commissions have civil service staffs that collect data on the industries involved, prepare cases, and argue them before the commissions. These staffs are appointed and supervised by the chairpersons of the commissions.

Regulatory Cases

Cases may be initiated by the staff and/or affected firms. The full commission may hear a case, but more commonly it is heard by a trial examiner (administrative law judge in the federal commissions). The trial examiner is a lawyer appointed by the commission to hear evidence presented by the staff, the affected firms, and any intervenors admitted to the proceeding. For instance, in recent years environmental interest groups have been frequent intervenors.

The hearing is similar to a court proceeding with prepared testimony, cross-examination of witnesses, and the usual rules of procedure. The participants complete the case by submitting briefs, which summarize their arguments, the relevant evidence, and appropriate precedents. The trial examiner then prepares a proposed decision, which he or she turns over to the commission. The commission reviews the case record and reaches its own decision, which may or may not be the same as the trial examiner's. Commission decisions are reached by a majority vote. Some of the cases in this book are excerpts from these decisions.

Commission decisions may be appealed on questions of law or procedure to the courts—initially to a Court of Appeals and ultimately to the Supreme Court in decisions on federal commissions or to individual state supreme courts in the case of state commissions. Most court decisions in regulatory cases involve interpreting the legislative mandate that established a particular commission, defined its jurisdiction, and set its guiding principles. These principles are normally very general, giving the commissions wide latitude in their actions, while inviting judicial review. For instance, the ICC is required not only to set "just and reasonable" rates for all the transportation modes under its jurisdiction, but also to "recognize and preserve the inherent advantages of each. . . ." As illustrated later in this book, the actual principles which commissions follow are frequently determined in court decisions.

The Regulators in Practice

The behavior of the commissions is heavily influenced by the individual commissioners. Membership on regulatory commissions has often been considered one of the less attractive jobs in government. Some commissioners possess great ability and dedication, especially immediately after the commission is established or reformed, but the positions are frequently awarded to defeated legislators or congressmen, members of their staffs, or other persons to whom the Governor or the President has a political obligation. Occasionally someone is appointed who has had a previous connection with the regulated industries—for instance, a broadcaster on the Federal Communications Commission. Senate confirmation of federal commissioners is almost guaranteed. Hearings are often perfunctory, and from 1950 to 1973, no such nomination was rejected by the Senate. The affected industries play an important role here. Their views on proposed appointments are solicited, and if they strongly oppose a particular nomination, it will probably be withdrawn.

Once appointed, commissioners become involved in long, complex cases that are little noticed and even less understood by the public. They regularly hear representatives of affected industries and become very familiar wiih their positions on issues before the commission. The general public is usually represented by the staff, but the consumer's interest isn't always emphasized. The most heated arguments are usually intraindustry squabbles between affected firms.

Regulatory commissions were designed to be independent agencies, but in fact they depend on Congress or the Legislature for funds and on the President or Governor for reappointment. The commissions are consequently quite responsive to pressure from the administration and/or congressional committees that deal with regulatory issues. The administration and Congress, in turn, are often beholden to the regulated firms, their trade associations, and unions. Friendly Congress members on important committees can usually count on large campaign contributions from these sources.

In addition, commissioners are commonly courted on an informal basis by representatives of the regulated industries. The big broadcasting and airline companies maintain high-paid lobbyists in Washington who regularly socialize with commissioners. Occasionally the press or congressional committees uncover stories of commissioners enjoying golfing weekends in Bermuda as guests of the airlines or travelling to Florida in private railroad cars provided by the railroads. After serving on the commissions, many commissioners and staff members are subsequently employed by regulated firms.

Some commissioners successfully resist these pressures and prove to be devoted and effective regulators. (Fairly often the most effective regulators are hired away to become officers of regulated firms.) Probably few commissioners feel that they have been compromised by pressures brought to bear on them. But persons who study regulation have repeatedly concluded that commissions see many things from the point of view of the regulated. This is not to say that all commission decisions are in the interests of the regulated firms. The FCC licensed independent microwave carriers over the strong opposition of Ma Bell, the SEC required the competitive determination of brokerage fees, and the FPC consistently set natural gas prices below their levels in unregulated intrastate transactions. Even in the common cases where commissions have forestalled entry, prevented price competition, or increased rates in the presence of excess capacity, they often required additional actions that the regulated firms opposed. Still, the typical commissioner seems to feel that a major part of his job is to keep his or her industry financially healthy.

THE PROBLEMS OF RATE MAKING

The bread-and-butter regulatory case is concerned with "rate making"—establishing prices for the services provided by regulated firms. The traditional standard is that the commission should set rates that will cover costs and yield a "fair return on a fair value" of the firm's capital. While this is not the language of economics, it can be given a reasonable economic meaning. But first, a brief review of pricing in unregulated markets may be helpful.

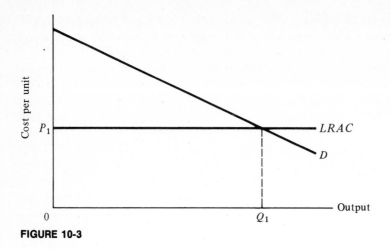

FIGURE 10-3

Competitive and Monopoly Prices

Figure 10-3 shows the demand and long-run average cost curves for an industry. It is again convenient to assume constant costs—that is, cost per unit of output will be the same regardless of the level of output in the long run.

Suppose that the particular industry depicted in Figure 10-3 is competitive. In the short run, price could settle above long-run average cost or below it, depending upon total industry capacity. In the long run, however, price will settle at P_1 where it equals long-run average cost. At this price any exceptional profits or losses disappear. The last unit produced was worth as much to consumers as the other goods that the resources employed here would produce in their best alternative uses. Moreover, surviving producers are virtually forced to use minimum cost methods of production. Most observers find this outcome both efficient and equitable.

By contrast, a monopolist faced with the same demand and cost curves, as in Figure 10-4, would produce too little and charge too much for it. At P_2 in that figure, consumers are willing to pay more for another unit than the opportunity cost of the inputs needed to produce it; resources are misallocated. We would get more output from our scarce resources if the monopolist would cut price and expand output. In addition, a monopolist is rarely *forced* to use minimum cost methods, as competitive producers are. A profit maximizer would do so, anyway, but many people believe that the lack of competitive pressure results in lethargic management. Finally, monopoly often results in exceptional profits, which many people find unfair.

Regulatory Goals in Rate Making

Now we can try translating the "fair return on fair value" principle into economic jargon. If the regulated firm were the monopolist in Figure 10-4, this principle

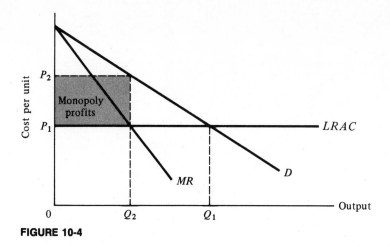

FIGURE 10-4

would imply setting price equal to minimum long-run average cost. This price would cover operating costs and provide a return on capital as high as any alternative available in the long run.

Note that in this case a regulated *reduction* in price from the unregulated monopoly level leads to an *increase* in output. In a competitive market a fall in price will induce suppliers to offer less, not more, but this is not a competitive market. The monopolist in Figure 10-4 restricts output to Q_2 in order to keep the price up. If he or she cannot raise the price above P_1 because of regulation, he or she no longer has any incentive to restrict output. Most regulatory commissions can require a utility to supply all comers at a specified price, but this is seldom necessary. It is normally in a utility's own interest to meet all the demand at the allowed price.

Rate Making in the Presence of Decreasing Costs

The above story is too simple, however. In real rate cases problems arise that aren't even hinted at in Figure 10-4. As we saw earlier, a number of regulated firms display decreasing costs in the long run. The larger their capacity, the lower their unit cost. They have production-cost curves like those shown in Figure 10-5.

When average cost falls as output increases, marginal cost must be less than average cost. This presents a problem for regulators. If they set price at P_1, equal to marginal cost, then the last unit produced costs just as much to produce as consumers are willing to pay for it, and resources are optimally allocated. But the price will be less than average cost, and the firm will lose money. On the other hand, if the commission sets price at P_2, equal to average cost, the utility will earn a normal rate of return, but price will exceed marginal cost.

One possible solution to this dilemma is to subsidize the utility. We do subsidize a few regulated industries, such as local-service airlines and mass transit, but

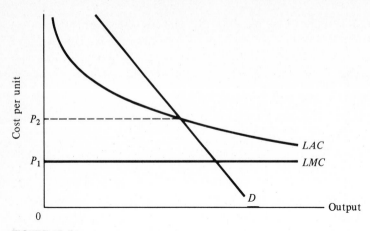

FIGURE 10-5

in most cases regulatory commissions do not have the authority to grant subsidies. Besides, it is not at all clear that a subsidy would be optimal, since the taxes needed to finance it would introduce additional distortions into the economic system. These distortions could possibly be as great as those that come from the deviation between price and marginal cost in the regulated industry.[1] A more viable alternative is to set discriminatory prices. This alternative will be discussed on page 190.

The Level of Costs

In a competitive market average cost must be at its minimum level in the long run. This will not automatically occur in a regulated industry. Theoretically a commission can set rates to cover only "prudent costs," so that an inefficient utility will incur losses. However, in practice commissions don't have the expertise to require cost minimization by regulated firms. As a result, firms might not minimize costs, especially since lower costs would just lead to lower regulated prices and *not* higher profits.

In the past regulatory cases occurred infrequently, so a utility that reduced costs would experience increased profits until the next rate case. Similarly, a utility with poor cost control would suffer losses for some time. As a result of the inflation of recent years, regulation cases now occur more frequently, so the incentive effects of "regulatory lag" have been weakened.

There are real problems in determining the costs of providing a particular service. Accountants must make judgments in recording depreciation costs, inven-

---

[1] This story does imply that we should *not* impose special taxes on decreasing-cost utilities. Such taxes raise prices and decrease output, which in turn means higher costs per unit of output. In practice, state and local governments frequently impose heavy taxes on utilities since, unlike other industries, they cannot move their plants to low tax jurisdictions.

tory valuation, and customer accounts, and will report different figures, depending on which of a variety of widely used accounting conventions they employ. Most commissions impose uniform accounting procedures in an attempt to deal with this problem, but the procedures adopted are not necessarily the economically correct ones.

Rate Base

Since capital is such an important input in most regulated industries, the issue of how to determine the "fair value" of that capital—the "rate base"—is a major one in regulatory proceedings. Until the 1940s that issue was the basis for repeated appeals of regulatory decisions to the courts. The courts ruled that a commission that undervalued a utility's assets was, in effect, confiscating part of that property. The issue is no longer a major constitutional question, but it still presents a serious economic problem.

The main issue is how the commission should value long-lasting assets in the presence of inflation. If it values the company's assets at "original cost" (what it originally paid for them less subsequent depreciation), and if there has been inflation since they were installed, then the assets will have an unrealistically low value. An alternative is to use "reproduction cost" (what it would cost to install the same equipment today), which will exceed original cost if there has been inflation since the time of installation. The federal commissions and a majority of state commissions currently use original cost, but a number of states use "fair value." Fair value generally turns out to be an average of original and reproduction cost, where the weights given to each concept differ from state to state.

What is the economically correct valuation? In a competitive industry price will settle in the long run at a level that just covers variable costs plus a normal return on a *new* plant. This means that long-run equilibrium price in competitive industries will yield a normal return on "replacement cost"—the cost of replacing an existing plant at present prices with the most efficient technology available. A firm with an old plant carried on its books at original cost will show profits as long as the old plant is used. No entrant will be able to compete those profits away.

Replacement cost is not the same as reproduction cost. No sensible utility would actually reproduce an old plant with outdated equipment. Replacement cost is normally less than reproduction cost because of technological progress. Replacement cost would not be easy to determine in a rate-making case; the utilities and the commission staff could argue for years about what a hypothetical new, best-practice plant would cost at current prices. A workable compromise that some of the "fair value" states use is to estimate reproduction cost (usually based on price indexes for the detailed elements of utility plants) and then to write off some percentage of those costs for obsolescence. The end result is obviously somewhat arbitrary, but if recent inflation rates continue, original cost valuations will be even more arbitrary.

To dramatize this last point, imagine an economy where the price level doubled every year. If regulators insisted on original cost valuation, a utility's book value would soon be very small. If the commission permitted only a normal return on that value, the price of the utility's product would be far below the opportunity costs of its inputs. At this low price consumers would purchase too much of this product compared with products of unregulated competitive industries whose prices reflected their inputs' full opportunity costs. In the long run a utility in such a situation would go out of business.

Fair Return

After determining the rate base, the commission must decide what return to allow on it. Economic theory suggests that it should be a normal return—what the utility could earn on its capital in a competitive industry in long-run equilibrium. This figure should be about the same as the utility's cost of capital—the rate of return necessary to attract the required capital into the industry.

In practice most commissions allow for the interest and dividends actually paid by the utility on its bonds and preferred stock plus a "fair return" on its common stock. Many utilities' interest payments are much less than current rates, since many of their bonds were issued when interest rates were lower.

The rate of return allowed on equity varies from commission to commission. In recent years many commissions have had to increase this rate of return to enable utilities to raise new capital. The rapid growth of many regulated industries makes regular bond offerings necessary, and bond ratings depend importantly on the ratio between the borrowing firms' earnings and their interest obligations. With new bonds bearing very high interest rates, the earnings required to assure good bond ratings have risen sharply. If a commission insists on the old lower rates of return on equity, it is apt to force its utilities to borrow at higher interest rates, if they can find funds at all. Of course they could sell more stock, but many utilities resist doing so because their stock is selling for less than their equity per share so that new stock issues would reduce the present stockholders' equity per share. A common allowed rate of return on equity in recent years has been 14 percent after tax, though the actual return received was less, approximately 12 percent. This is less than the average for the manufacturing sector of the economy (13.9 percent for 1974–78).

A commission's determination of a "fair return" can at best only be a rough approximation of the cost of capital. If it is less than the cost of capital, it will discourage utility investment. As a result, utilities may not have sufficient capacity to meet all of their customers' demands in the future.

On the other hand, if a commission allows a return greater than the cost of capital, utilities will have an incentive to overinvest. If a utility increased its rate base, it would add more to permitted revenue than to its capital cost, thereby increasing its value to its owners. A utility can overinvest by carrying more spare reserves than it really needs and investing in very capital-intensive production processes (for example, nuclear power plants instead of fossil fuel plants). A commission could exclude items from the utility's rate base if it felt that they were not "prudent investments," but commissions seldom know enough to second-guess utility investment decisions.

RATE STRUCTURE

Few regulated firms charge a single price for their services. Ordinarily there are different prices for different classes of customers, different amounts of service purchased, and even different times of day and year. In the past commissions were most concerned about a utility's overall revenue and worried little about the particular set of prices charged. In recent years, however, commissions have become increasingly interested in the rate structure used to achieve the allowed rate level.

Peak-Load Pricing

Some rate differences merely reflect differences in the cost of providing service. For instance, many industrial electric customers take power at high voltages and transform it themselves. They often make little or no use of the utility's distribution system. For the rate per kilowatt hour to reflect properly the cost of serving them, it should be less than rates that reflect all the costs of providing service to residential customers.

An important case in which the costs of servicing customers differ is when one customer buys when the system is running at peak levels and the other buys when the system has substantial excess capacity. A utility must build at least enough capacity to satisfy total peak demand. In the case of off-peak customers, the plant is already there, so the additional cost of providing service for them is much less.

Figure 10–6 shows the *short-run* marginal cost curve for a utility and the de-

FIGURE 10-6

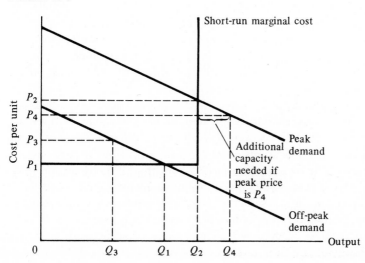

mand curves it faces during peak and off-peak periods. For a telephone company peak demand is during business hours, while off-peak demand is at night and on weekends. For a gas pipeline, peak demand occurs during the winter heating season and off-peak demand is in the summer. For electric utilities in most of the country, peak demand comes on hot summer working days when air conditioners are running full blast. Winter is typically an off-peak season except in the Pacific Northwest and parts of the South, where electric heat is common.

Figure 10–6 shows spare capacity during the off-peak period. If this were an electric utility, the cost of serving the off-peak customers would be fuel burned and such things as metering and billing. The cost of serving the peak-period customer, however, would include those expenses plus the full cost of the depreciation, maintenance, and return allowed on the utility's generating plant and transmission lines. Many economists argue that efficient pricing requires charging rates equal to these costs. In Figure 10–6 this would mean rates of P_1 for off-peak customers and P_2 for peak customers. If P_2 yields more revenue than necessary to cover costs, the price of service to peak customers should be reduced and more capacity should be installed to provide the additional service they will demand at the lower price. On the other hand, if P_2 does not yield sufficient revenue, then there is too much plant, the peak period price should be higher, and the amount of plant should be reduced (more realistically, no additional capacity should be built until peak-period demand at the higher price requires more capacity).

Such a pricing system could imply peak-period rates several times higher than off-peak rates. Some people feel that such prices would be unfair since off-peak customers use the same plant as peak customers. Therefore, to be equitable, shouldn't off-peak users pay part of its costs? Not if you want to fully utilize a plant's facilities. Suppose we increased the off-peak rate in Figure 10-6 from P_1 to P_3 and reduced the peak rate from P_2 to P_4. The utility would have to build more plant to meet the peak-period demand at the lower price. At the same time, off-peak customers would buy less power, so the utility's plant would be less fully used, even though off-peak consumers are willing to pay more than the marginal cost of additional output. In general, peak-load pricing will minimize a utility's total investment while insuring a higher utilization rate than under other pricing schemes.

What if the peak is shifted by the low off-peak price? Figure 10–7 illustrates such a situation. If off-peak customers are charged no more than P_1, they will demand so much electricity that capacity will have to be expanded to serve them. *They* would then become the peak customers. In such a case the off-peak customers *should* pay part of the equipment cost (P_3), though still less than the peak-period customers (P_2). If rates like P_2 and P_3 yield enough revenue to cover plant costs, then no adjustment is necessary. If they yield more, they should both be reduced and capacity should be expanded. If they yield less, they should both be raised and plant should be reduced. When things settle down, the utility's plant will be fully utilized, both on peak and off.

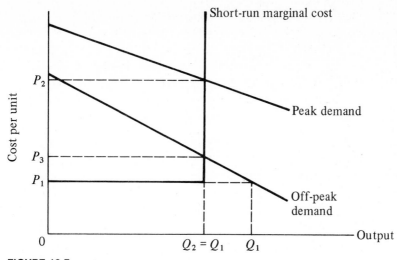

FIGURE 10-7

In practice, rates that charge each customer the marginal cost of providing service have several components:

1 A fixed charge per month to cover the cost of metering, billing, connection, distribution, and any special equipment needed to serve the customer (such as the telephone in the case of telephone service). These costs are incurred as soon as the customer is connected to the system and do not vary with the amount of service.

2 Other plant costs assigned to the customer in proportion to the amount of service used at the peak period. The peak that counts here is the period of peak demand for the system as a whole, which need not be the same as the customer's own peak. This charge covers the amount of capacity that must be built to serve her.

3 A charge per unit of service (per kilowatt hour in electricity) to cover the costs which vary with output (such as fuel costs in the case of electricity).

With such a pricing system, an off-peak customer would pay her customer cost and the variable costs involved in serving her. If she took no service during the peak period and if the system had spare capacity off-peak, she wouldn't have to pay any of the plant costs in the second category. But if the utility's plant is fully used during both peak and off-peak periods, she would have to pay some of the plant costs as well.

Quite a few commissions and utilities have adopted peak-load pricing policies in recent years. The telephone company charges more for long-distance calls made during business hours than for the same calls made at night and on weekends, when the circuits are not fully utilized. Natural gas pipelines charge less for inter-ruptible gas, which is not available during peak periods, than for firm gas supplied during the heating period. Some transit companies charge less at midday or at night than they do at rush hour. And an increasing number of electric companies charge more for electricity in summer than in winter. In England and France (the pioneer in peak-load pricing), and in some states, large users of electricity are charged more during working hours than at night and on weekends.

Price Discrimination

Not all rate differences are due to differences in the cost of providing service. The regulated industries often engage in price discrimination as well.

A common practice of regulated firms is to discriminate by class of customer. They set low rates for classes where demand is more elastic and high rates where it is less elastic. For instance, electric utilities usually have low rates for industrial customers because at higher rates such users will generate their own electricity or move out of town to areas where electricity is cheaper. Industrial rates are generally lower than residential and commercial rates, even after allowance is made for the different costs of serving these groups. The telephone company, on the other hand, charges higher rates for commercial than for residential service. A household can do without a phone, but a business cannot. Similarly, the airlines have many especially low fares designed to attract tourists away from their family cars, but the conditions to get those low fares are set so that most people travelling on business are kept from using them. Business travellers are often on expense accounts; they are usually unwilling to extend their trips over weekends; and they seldom time to travel by other modes. Business demand is much less elastic than the demands of those travelling for pleasure.

A reasonable case can be made for price discrimination for a utility with long-run decreasing costs, as illustrated in Figure 10-8. If the utility charges a single price of P_1, the largest attainable output is Q_1. Yet consumers are willing to pay

FIGURE 10-8

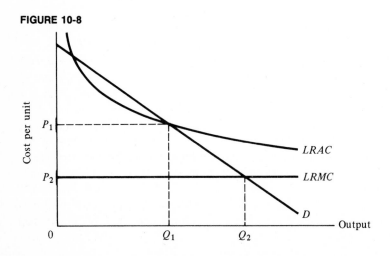

more for additional output than it would add to costs right out to Q_2. A general reduction in price to P_2 would result in losses, but if the utility can discriminate it could expand output to Q_2 and still get enough revenue to cover its full costs. For instance, it might charge P_1 for the first Q_1 units consumed and P_2 for any subsequent units. The charge for the initial Q_1 units would cover the utility's overhead, while the price of additional units would just cover their marginal cost.

If you look at your next electric or gas bill you may discover just such a pricing system. You're apt to pay something like the following:

kwh per month	Price per kwh
0–100	5.0¢
101–500	4.0¢
501–1,000	3.5¢
1,001–2,000	3.0¢
more than 2,000	2.8¢

Such a price schedule is designed to get you to buy a lot of electricity and still make you pay the full cost of the service.

The case for discrimination on the basis of decreasing costs goes only so far, however. It is certainly not in the public's best interest for the price of additional service to be less than the marginal cost of providing it. And in industries with constant costs, such as trucking, there is really no economic justification for discrimination at all.

In recent years some commissions have made serious efforts to estimate "long-run incremental costs" of serving various customer classes. This is an operational approximation to long-run marginal cost. Estimates of long-run incremental cost are based on the usual customer costs per customer, current commodity costs per unit of service (such as fuel cost per kilowatt hour), and the estimated current cost per unit of capacity that the utility expects to add in the near future (allocated to customers according to their expected future demand for service at peak periods). Ideally, rates would be based on these estimated long-run incremental costs, but such rates might not yield enough revenue to cover total costs if the utility has decreasing costs. The distortions that result will be minimized if the rate increases are inversely proportional to the elasticities of demand for different customers. Those with inelastic demands (for example, electricity for lighting or refrigeration) won't change their consumption very much in spite of higher prices, so the price increase imposed upon them can be relatively large with little distortion of consumption patterns. On the other hand, those with more elastic demands (for example, electricity used for heating where there are many close substitutes) will change their consumption patterns greatly with a price change. Efficient consumption decisions require that the price for customers with elastic demands be quite close to long-run incremental cost.

Rapid inflation can turn this story on its ear. Figure 10-9 shows how long-run average costs have changed for electric utilities from 1970 to 1980. There are decreasing costs in both years, but the whole long-run average cost curve is higher

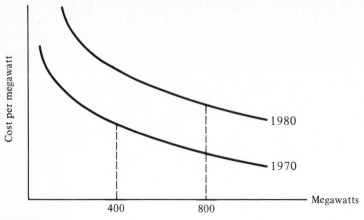

FIGURE 10-9

in 1980 than in 1970. The typical plant built in 1980 (about 800 megawatts) is larger than the typical one built in 1970 (about 400 megawatts), but because of inflation the unit cost of the new plants exceeds that of plants built a decade earlier. Thus, costs per unit of additional capacity have increased over time even though most electric utilities still have economies of scale that have yet to be realized.

If long-run incremental costs are to yield prices that give the customer correct signals about what society sacrifices by serving him or her, then rates must be based on the current cost of expected additions to capacity. One effect of rapid inflation has been that each major addition to capacity in recent years has added more than proportionally to total cost and has therefore led to an increase in average cost and, usually, in rates. Basically this has resulted from the inflated input prices and the fact that most utilities must value their old plants in original cost terms.

As a result of inflation, long-run incremental cost can easily exceed average cost based on original cost today. If rates are set equal to long-run incremental cost, they may yield more than the allowed total revenue to the utility. If this is the case, some rates must be set below long-run incremental costs to reduce total revenue to the level allowed by the commission. To minimize the distorting effect of deviations from long-run incremental costs, the rate *reductions* should go to customers with relatively inelastic demands. They won't consume much more if their price is reduced. But it is still important to charge prices close to long-run incremental costs for customers with elastic demands. If these customers are charged much less than the additional costs they impose on the system, they will consume a lot more and a great deal of uneconomic expansion in capacity will result.

Quite a few commissions have "flattened" their rate schedules in recent years in response to such arguments. That is, they have reduced the difference in rates between customers who buy little service (mainly for lighting and refrigeration among residential customers) and those who buy a lot (for example, for air conditioning). A few commissions have even established "inverted rates" which have customers pay more per kilowatt hour the more they consume.

SPECIAL REGULATORY PROBLEMS IN CERTAIN INDUSTRIES

Unprofitable Utilities

The problems of the regulators are even greater when the firms they control are unprofitable. This has been the situation with railroads and transit companies since World War II.

When the firm involved is unprofitable, the commission has little choice but to permit high rates. The end result is illustrated in Figure 10-10. In this case there is no single price that will yield normal profits. If only one price can be charged, the commission has no choice but to permit the utility to charge its profit-maximizing (or loss-minimizing) price of P. An unregulated monopolist with the same pattern of costs would charge the same price.

One way to deal with such a problem is to discriminate in pricing once more. For instance, as shown in Figure 10-11, the firm might charge P_1 for the first Q_1 units of service, P_2 from Q_1 to Q_2, and P_3 for service beyond that. Then the firm would receive revenue associated with the single price P_2 *plus* the revenue represented by the shaded rectangles. The extra revenue from discrimination might be enough to make the overall operation profitable. Similarly, the firm could increase its receipts by setting high prices for customers with relatively inelastic demand and low prices where demand is elastic. Again, an unregulated monopolist would discriminate in about the same fashion.

The price-discrimination route to profitability can be a trap, however. The railroads have engaged in blatant price discrimination over the years, traditionally charging "what the traffic would bear"—low freight rates for shippers of cheap

FIGURE 10-10

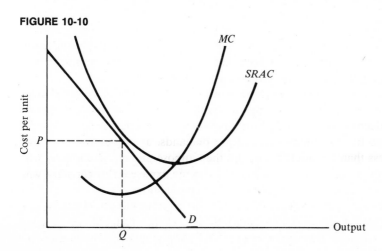

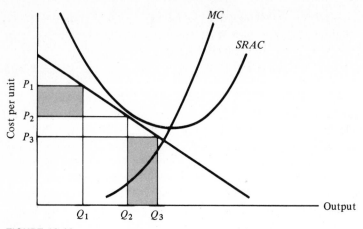

FIGURE 10-11

products like coal and high rates on expensive products like machinery. By discriminating, they were able in the nineteenth century to extend service to sparsely populated areas, when such service would not have been profitable without this practice. However, rate discrimination backfired with the appearance of trucks in the 1920s. Truckers earned hefty profits by undercutting railroad rates on high-value commodities. This was one of the main reasons railroads supported regulation of trucks, but regulation didn't solve their problem. For one thing, not all trucks are regulated. Private trucking (manufacturers hauling their own products and materials) and trucks hauling agricultural produce are exempt from regulation. Second, the regulated common carrier truckers have continued to take high-value freight from the railroads because they offer quicker and more convenient service.

Certification and Licensing

A related issue in prosperous industries is the question of who is to get the available business. Almost all regulators have the authority to certify or license new suppliers. This power leads to many regulatory headaches.

Truckers in business in 1935 were certified to go on carrying the same commodities over the same routes. After that a "certificate of public convenience and necessity" from the ICC was required for a new firm to become a common carrier or for an existing firm to acquire new routes or haul new commodities. Issuances of new certificates were predictably opposed by existing common carriers, who would face increased competitive pressures from the licensees. Under this pressure, the ICC turned down the majority of such applications.

The restrictive licensing practices of the ICC, along with mergers among carriers and construction of new highways and industrial plants, resulted in high costs for the common carriers. They often had to drive circuitous routes, bypass potentially profitable stops along their routes, and drive many of their trucks empty on return hauls, even though cargos of goods that they were not certified to transport were available. Regulation thus led to higher costs, and the rates that covered those high costs encouraged the rapid expansion of private trucking (even though many of the firms that maintained their own truck fleets also had empty back hauls).

Certification issues also absorbed a large part of the CAB's time, since it had to determine who could fly between particular pairs of cities.

On the routes connecting large cities there were usually a great many major airlines eager to serve. The CAB had to choose among several qualified airlines, but it didn't have terribly compelling reasons to certify one over another. Fairly commonly it chose among the contenders on the basis of which airline most needed the new route in order to improve its profitability. The agency consistently refused to give Pan American any domestic routes, even though Pan Am is one of the most experienced airlines and has been unprofitable during the early 1970s. For a long time the CAB also refused to give the local-service airlines long routes, but in the 1960s it did award them a few, in the hope of reducing the subsidy they received. A common result was that these airlines put their best efforts into those profitable long routes and slighted the smaller cities they were supposed to serve.

Once they were awarded routes, the airlines were free to operate as many or as few flights as they wanted on those routes. On the dense routes connecting the largest cities, the airlines competed for customers by offering many departures. The result was many half-empty flights, high costs, and airline profit rates that usually fell far below the CAB's goals.

The FCC has also had to determine which broadcasting companies would have the right to provide service. In the larger cities it usually had to choose among many applicants for its valuable gifts. The situation again became one of establishing rules for choosing between Tweedledee and Tweedledum. The FCC began by limiting the number of television licenses owned by one firm to one in a given community and to seven in total. It emphasized local ownership and diversity of ownership so that many voices could be heard. But it also tried to choose experienced firms in order to get good service. These criteria were often in conflict. The owners of the local newspapers and radio stations had the desired experience, but if they were awarded the television channels, fewer voices would be heard. In practice, many of the licenses were awarded to owners of newspapers or radio stations—often to owners of both. The general criteria used by the FCC still left many applicants for licenses in the larger cities. After long hearings and much pressure, the commission made a decision. As it turned out, more than two dozen broadcasting licenses went to firms owned in full or in part by members of Congress or their close families.

Once awarded, licenses must be renewed every three years, and the FCC can cancel a license if it doesn't approve of how it has been used. Cancelling a license imposes a tremendous financial penalty on the owners, since licenses are worth millions of dollars in the larger metropolitan areas. In practice, though, very few licenses have been cancelled. One station in Mississippi lost its license because its programming did not adequately serve the large black population in its area, a license owned by a Boston newspaper was transferred to another applicant to ensure greater diversity in media ownership, and RKO General lost a license because of illegal payments made by its parent corporation. But these are the exceptions. In most cases broadcasters have had little difficulty in renewing their licenses. One indication of the security of license holders is that licenses are often sold—for many millions of dollars in the large cities. The FCC has usually approved the new owner without much consideration of what the alternatives might have been. Yet the threat of cancellation, though distant, still exists. During the Nixon years there was widespread concern that this threat would be used to censor programming critical of the administration.

Certification or licensing issues take less of the regulators' time in other areas, but they do come up. The FCC must decide who, if anyone, can offer microwave service in competition with AT&T's long lines department. The FERC must occasionally decide whether an additional gas pipeline should be permitted to serve certain cities. And state commissions or the courts must often decide which utility has the right to serve newly developed areas. These battles are frequently decided on the basis of some notion of fairness among the contenders rather than on the basis of who would best serve the consumers.

REGULATORY REFORM

Regulation was repeatedly criticized by economists in the postwar years. By the 1970s the chorus had become quite loud. The Brookings Institution published a shelf full of scholarly studies on regulation in particular fields. The American Enterprise Institute put out even more studies. But it seemed for a long time that no one was listening.

It turned out that some people were listening. Presidents Nixon, Ford, and Carter all made important proposals to Congress for regulatory reform meant to eliminate, or at least to lessen, the inefficiencies and anticompetitive effects of regulation. And their staffs added to the flood of paper on the subject. Several Congressional committees did further studies that yielded more paper. Yet nothing much seemed to happen. The groups in society that benefitted from regulation—often including those who were being regulated—appeared to be just too strong.

But something did happen. Early in 1977 Senators Kennedy and Cannon introduced a bill to reform airline regulation. As usual, most of the airlines opposed the bill strongly. At the same time, President Carter appointed two well-known economists, Alfred E. Kahn and Elizabeth Bailey, to the five-member CAB (Kahn was made chairman). During the next two years the board went a long way toward adopting the proposed legislation directly. Airlines were permitted to cut fares by as much as 50 percent without going to the CAB for explicit permission. The board became far less restrictive in awarding new routes and licensed three new trunk carriers, the first since its establishment in 1938.

The result was amazing. Fares for tourists (but not for most business travellers) fell drastically, a novel experience in the inflationary years of the late 1970s. Most of the empty seats on the planes disappeared and airline profits rose. By the time the Kennedy-Cannon Bill came to a vote in late 1978, most of the opposition had evaporated, and the bill passed easily. In 1979, when fuel prices more than doubled, airfares rose again, though by less than fuel costs rose. Airline profits declined partly because of rising fuel costs and partly because of the 1980 recession.

Nevertheless, the lesson from airline deregulation was obvious to many in Washington. In the next two years changes were made to phase out or greatly relax regulation in such fields as natural gas, oil, trucking, railroads, and cable TV.

Even the bastion of old-line regulation, the ICC, gave way. In late 1979 President Carter appointed two more economists, Darius Gaskins and Marcus Alexis, to the commission, making Gaskins its chairman. Again, controls on rate cutting were weakened and entry was made far easier. Congress passed new legislation before 1980 was out, permitting truckers to cut rates by as much as 10 percent a year, greatly easing entry, and eliminating many restrictions that resulted in circuitous routes and empty backhauls. By the end of 1980 the value of ICC certificates, in which there had previously been quite a brisk market, were reported to have virtually fallen to zero. The regulatory reform movement seems to have gotten somewhere after all, and economists played a big role in bringing about its progress.

SOME CONCLUSIONS

Altogether, regulators face enormously complex problems that no one has to solve in competitive markets. They must determine what costs are and what prices will cover them—issues that are settled automatically where competitive forces are strong. The regulators must also decide among contending suppliers, something the customers do for themselves in competitive markets. And finally, regulators must decide on the right degree of price discrimination, something that cannot occur in unregulated industries if markets are fully competitive.

Regulating economic activity leads to long and tedious arguments in real life. The vague mandates that commissions receive from the legislative branch rarely provide them with much guidance. And the decisions that are made typically result from hearings that are little noticed and less understood. Altogether, the job of the regulator is not a very attractive one. With some impressive exceptions, it generally does not attract the most able public administrators. Once in office, the regulators are courted and pressured by the firms they are supposed to regulate, while the consumer often receives little representation. Arguments are frequently settled on the basis of apparent fairness among the contending parties. As a result, commission decisions sometimes, though not always, stray far from economic good sense.

The alternative of completely eliminating regulation and depending instead on competition appeals to many observers. In some fields, such as trucking and natural gas production, this alternative is readily available by simply turning the regulators off. These industries contain large numbers of firms and entry is easy. By 1980 we had gone a surprisingly long way along that road.

In industries with decreasing costs, such as local electric, gas, telephone, transit, and cable television, competition is a very doubtful alternative. The probable result of deregulation would be unregulated monopoly. If competition did arise it would most likely be wasteful. Some people feel that deregulation would still be desirable, but most don't.

In between are pipelines, electric generation, and long lines telephone service, where some competition seems possible, but only if care is taken in organizing the industries. Whether the result would be better than regulation is an unsettled issue.

In sum, we seem certain to have at least some regulation with us for many years. The procedures and precedents of regulation are surely important now, and most of them will be important for years to come. The cases covered in this part will give you an idea of the problems faced by regulators and their wards, and how they have been solved in the past.

11

THE MANDATE FOR REGULATION

The question of whether or not to regulate a particular industry is really two separate questions. First, is regulation constitutional? And second, does regulation make good economic sense? The cases in this chapter deal with these two basic questions.

The first two cases mark the beginning and the end of a half-century debate over what industries could be constitutionally regulated. The Fourteenth Amendment to the Constitution, among other things, prohibited states from taking private property without "due process of law." Before long some clever lawyer noticed that regulating a firm reduced its prospective profits, thereby depriving it of property. Thus, the question became, "Is regulation consistent with due process of law?" Since some industries had been regulated for generations, presumably it could be. In *Munn v. Illinois* the Supreme Court faced this issue for the first time and used common law precedents to uphold state regulation of grain storage rates. In so doing, the Court asserted that industries "affected with a public interest" were subject to regulation. Unfortunately this decision did not spell out the criteria to be used in determining if an industry was sufficiently affected with a public interest to warrant regulation. As a result, the courts struggled with this question again and again. The *Nebbia v. New York* decision contains lists of industries where the Court concluded regulation was constitutional and of those where it wasn't. Can you see any logical basis on which to distinguish among the industries on the two lists? Finally, the Nebbia decision has been widely interpreted as stating that states could, in effect, regulate whatever economic activity they so desired. Does this mean that there are *no* legal restrictions on state extensions of regulation?

Since the Nebbia decision, attention has shifted from the constitutional question of what *can* be regulated to the economic question of what *should* be regulated. In short, when does regulation make good economic sense? The last two cases are illustrative of decisions to extend regulation to previously unregulated areas of the economy.

The extension of regulation to motor carriers was a decision of Congress. You will read excerpts from the Federal Coordinator of Transportation's report in which he argues in favor of regulating entry and freight rates in the motor carrier industry. His report was one of the major reasons for the Congressional decision. His analysis raises many questions. Why is regulation necessary to ensure the efficient operation of the trucking industry? How can the flour, bread, and retailing industries reliably and efficiently coordinate *their* productive activities without the aid of regulatory controls? Is trucking different from them in this respect? Also, if regulators set rates based on "what the traffic will bear," is this in the public's interest? Finally, if regulators also prohibit entry of new firms, what will force existing trucking firms to provide good service to shippers?

The last case in this chapter concerns a recent court-mandated extension of regulation. The Federal Communications Commission had been given the job of regulating over-the-air broadcasters in the Communications Act of 1934. The need for government intervention arose from the possibility of interference due to two firms broadcasting at the same wavelength to overlapping territories. Three decades later their legislative mandate became the center of a major controversy in the broadcasting industry. Did the FCC have the authority to regulate cable television companies that distributed television programs to customers over cable where the interference problem did not arise? The Supreme Court said yes, thereby setting the groundwork for extensive regulation of cable television, which we will discuss later in Chapter 16. But for the present, what was the Court's basis for determining the FCC's jurisdiction? Does it sound like a reasonable interpretation of their legislative charter? Do you think television viewers were helped or hurt by this decision? How about advertisers? Television stations?

Munn v. Illinois

94 U.S. 113 (1877)

[The 1870 Illinois Constitution declared all elevators or storehouses where grain was stored for a fee to be "public warehouses" and provided for their regulation by the state. In 1871 the General Assembly passed a law that, among other things, fixed maximum fees for such warehouses located in cities with populations of over 100,000. Munn & Scott were the managers and proprietors of the "Northwestern Elevator," which was located in Chicago, the only Illinois city with more than 100,000 inhabitants.]

Munn & Scott had complied in all respects with said act, except in two particulars: first, they had not taken out a license, nor given a bond, as required by sects. 3 and 4; and, second, they had charged for storage and handling grain the rates established and published in January, 1872, which were higher than those fixed by sect. 15.

The defendants were found guilty, and fined $100.

The judgment of the Criminal Court of Cook County having been affirmed by the Supreme Court of the State, Munn & Scott sued out this writ, and assign for error.

MR. CHIEF JUSTICE WAITE delivered the opinion of the Court.

The question to be determined in this case is whether the general assembly of Illinois can, under the limitations upon the legislative power of the States imposed by the Constitution of the United States, fix by law the maximum of charges for the storage of grain in warehouses at Chicago and other places in the State having not less than one hundred thousand inhabitants, "in which grain is stored in bulk, and in which the grain of different owners is mixed together, or in which grain is stored in such a manner that the identity of different lots or parcels cannot be accurately preserved."

It is claimed that such a law is repugnant.

This brings us to inquire as to the principles upon which this power of regulation rests, in order that we may determine what is within and what without its operative effect. Looking, then, to the common law, from whence came the right which the Constitution protects, we find that when private property is "affected with a public interest, it ceases to be juris privati only." . . . Property does become clothed with a public interest when used in a manner to make it of public consequence, and affect the community at large. When, therefore, one devotes his property to a use in which the public has an interest, he, in effect, grants to the public an interest in that use, and must submit to be controlled by the public for the common good, to the extent of the interest he has thus created. He may withdraw his grant by discontinuing the use; but, so long as he maintains the use, he must submit to the control.

. . . Enough has already been said to show that, when private property is devoted to a public use, it is subject to public regulation. It remains only to ascertain whether the warehouses of these plaintiffs in error, and the business which is carried on there, come within the operation of this principle.

For this purpose we accept as true the statements of fact contained in the elaborate brief of one of the counsel of the plaintiffs in error. From these it appears that "the great producing region of the West and North-west sends its grain by water and rail to Chicago, where the greater part of it is shipped by vessel for transportation to the seaboard by the Great Lakes, and some of it is forwarded by railway to the Eastern ports. . . . This business has created a demand for means by which the immense quantity of grain can be handled or stored, and these have been found in grain warehouses, which are commonly called elevators, because the grain is elevated from the boat or car, by machinery operated by steam, into the bins prepared for its reception, and elevated from the bins, by a like process, into the vessel or car which is to carry it on. . . . In this way the largest traffic between the citizens of the country north and west of Chicago and the citizens of the country lying on the Atlantic coast north of Washington is in grain which passes through the elevators of Chicago. . . . The railways have found it impracticable to own such elevators, and public policy forbids the transaction of such business by the carrier; the ownership has, therefore, been by private individuals, who have embarked their capital and devoted their industry to such business as a private pursuit."

In this connection it must also be borne in mind that, although in 1874 there were in Chicago fourteen warehouses adapted to this particular business, and owned by about thirty persons, nine business firms controlled them, and that the prices charged and received for storage were such "as have been from year to year agreed upon and established by the different elevators or warehouses in the city of Chicago, and which rates have been annually published in one or more newspapers printed in said city, in the month of January in each year, as the established rates for the year then next ensuing such publication." Thus it is apparent that all the elevating facilities through which these vast productions "of seven or eight great States of the West" must pass on the way "to four or five of the States on the seashore" may be a "virtual" monopoly.

. . . They stand, to use again the language of their counsel, in the very "gateway of commerce," and take toll from all who pass. Their business most certainly "tends to common charge, and is become a thing of public interest and use." Every bushel of grain for its passage "pays a toll, which is a common charge," and, therefore, according to Lord Hale, [an English Chief Justice] every such warehouseman "ought to be under public regulation, viz., that he . . . take but reasonable toll." Certainly, if any business can be clothed "with a public interest, and cease to be juris privati only," this has been. It may not be made so by the operation of the Constitution of Illinois or this statute, but it is by the facts.

It matters not in this case that these plaintiffs in error had built their warehouses and established their business before the regulations complained of were adopted. What they did was from the beginning subject to the power of the body politic to require them to conform to such regulations as might be established by the proper authorities for the common good. They entered upon their business and provided themselves with the means to carry it on subject to this condition. If they did not wish to submit themselves to such interference, they should not have clothed the public with an interest in their concerns.

It is insisted, however, that the owner of property is entitled to a reasonable compensation for its use, even though it be clothed with a public interest, and that what is reasonable is a judicial and not a legislative question.

As has already been shown, the practice has been otherwise. In countries where the common law prevails, it has been customary from time immemorial for the legislature to declare what shall be a reasonable compensation under such circumstances, or, perhaps more properly speaking, to fix a maximum beyond which any charge made would be unreasonable. Undoubtedly, in mere private contracts, relating to matters in which the public has no interest, what is reasonable must be ascertained judicially. But this is because the legislature has no control over such a contract. So, too, in matters which do affect the public interest, and as to which legislative control may be exercised, if there are no statutory regulations upon the subject, the courts must determine what is reasonable. The controlling fact is the power to regulate at all. If that exists, the right to establish the maximum of charge, as one of the means of regulation, is implied. In fact, the common-law rule, which requires the charge to be reasonable, is itelf a regulation as to price. Without it the owner could make his rates at will, and compel the public to yield to his terms, or forego the use.

We know that this is a power which may be abused; but there is no argument against its existence. For protection against abuses by legislatures the people must resort to the polls, not to the courts.

We conclude, therefore, that the statute in question is not repugnant to the Constitution of the United States, and that there is no error in the judgment.

Judgment affirmed.

Nebbia v. New York

291 U.S. 502 (1934)

MR. JUSTICE ROBERTS delivered the opinion of the Court.

The Legislature of New York established, by Chapter 158 of the Laws of 1933, a Milk Control Board with power, among other things, to "fix minimum and maximum . . . retail prices to be charged by . . . stores to consumers for consumption off the premises where sold." The Board fixed nine cents as the price to be charged by a store for a quart of milk. Nebbia, the proprietor of a grocery store in Rochester, sold two quarts and a five cent loaf of bread for eighteen cents; and was convicted for violating the Board's order. At his trial he asserted the statute and order contravene the equal protection clause and the due process clause of the Fourteenth Amendment, and renewed the contention in successive appeals to the county court and the Court of Appeals. Both overruled his claim and affirmed the conviction.

The question for decision is whether the Federal Constitution prohibits a state from so fixing the selling price of milk.

The Fifth Amendment, in the field of federal activity, and the Fourteenth, as respects state action, do not prohibit governmental regulation for the public welfare. They merely condition the exertion of the admitted power, by securing that the end shall be accomplished by methods consistent with due process. And the guaranty of due process, as has often been held, demands only that the law shall not be unreasonable, arbitrary or capricious, and that the means selected shall have a real and substantial relation to the object sought to be attained. It results that a regulation valid for one sort of business, or in given circumstances, may be invalid for another sort, or for the same business under other circumstances, because the reasonableness of each regulation depends upon the relevant facts.

The court has repeatedly sustained curtailment of enjoyment of private property, in the public interest. The owner's rights may be subordinated to the needs of other private owners whose pursuits are vital to the paramount interests of the community.

The milk industry in New York has been the subject of long-standing and drastic regulation in the public interest. The legislative investigation of 1932 was persuasive of the fact that for this and other reasons unrestricted competition aggravated existing evils, and the normal law of supply and demand was insufficient to correct maladjustments detrimental to the community. The inquiry disclosed destructive and demoralizing competitive conditions and unfair trade practices which resulted in retail price-cutting and reduced the income of the farmer below the cost of production. We do not understand the appellant to deny that in these circumstances the legislature might reasonably consider further regulation and control desirable for protection of the industry and the consuming public. That body believed conditions could be improved by preventing destructive price-cutting by stores which, due to the flood of surplus milk, were able to buy at much lower prices than the larger distributors and to sell without incurring the delivery costs of the latter. In the order of which complaint is made the Milk Control Board fixed a price of ten cents per quart for sales by a distributor to a consumer, and nine cents by a store to a consumer, thus recognizing the lower costs of the store, and endeavoring to establish a differential which would be just to both. In the light of the facts the order appears not to be unreasonable or arbitrary, or without relation to the purpose to prevent ruthless competition from destroying the wholesale price structure on which the farmer depends for his livelihood, and the community for an assured supply of milk.

But we are told that because the law essays to control prices it denies due process. . . . The argument runs that the public control of rates or prices is per se unreasonable and unconstitutional, save as applied to businesses affected with a public interest; that a business so affected is one in which property is devoted to an enterprise of a sort which the public itself might appropriately undertake, or one whose owner relies on a public grant or franchise for the right to conduct the business, or in which he is bound to serve all who apply; in short, such as is commonly called a public utility; or a business in its nature a monopoly. The milk industry, it is said, possesses none of these characteristics, and, therefore, not being affected with a public interest, its charges may not be controlled by the state. Upon the soundness of this contention the appellant's case against the statute depends.

. . . The thought seems nevertheless to have persisted that there is something peculiarly sacrosanct about the price one may charge for what he makes or sells, and that, however able to regulate other elements of manufacture or trade, with incidental effect upon price, the state is incapable of directly controlling the price itself. This view was negatived many years ago. *Munn v. Illinois,* 94 U.S. 113.

The true interpretation of the court's language is claimed to be that only property voluntarily devoted to a known public use is subject to regulation as to rates. But obviously Munn and Scott had not voluntarily dedicated their business to a public use. They intended only to conduct it as private citizens, and they insisted that they had done nothing which gave the public an interest in their transactions or conferred any right of regulation. The statement that one has dedicated his property to a public use is, therefore, merely another way of saying that if one embarks in a business which public interest demands shall be regulated, he must know regulation will ensue.

In the same volume the court sustained regulation of railroad rates. After referring to the fact that railroads are carriers for hire, are incorporated as such, and given extraordinary powers in order that they may better serve the public, it was said that they are engaged in employment "affecting the public interest," and therefore, under the doctrine of the Munn case, subject to legislative control as to rates. And in another of the group of railroad cases then heard it was said that the property of railroads is "clothed with a public interest" which permits legislative limitation of the charges for its use. Plainly the activities of railroads, their charges and practices, so nearly touch the vital economic interests of society that the police power may be invoked to regulate their charges, and no additional formula of affection or clothing with a public interest is needed to justify the regulation. And this is evidently true of all business units supplying transportation, light, heat, power and water to communities, irrespective of how they obtain their powers.

The touchstone of public interest in any business, its practices and charges, clearly is not the enjoyment of any franchise from the state, *Munn v. Illinois,* supra. Nor is it the enjoyment of a monopoly; for in *Brass v. North Dakota,* 153 U.S. 391, a similar control of prices of grain elevators was upheld in spite of overwhelming and uncontradicted proof that about six hundred grain elevators existed along the line of the Great Northern Railroad, in North Dakota; that at the very station where the defendant's elevator was located two others operated; and that the business was keenly competitive throughout the state.

In *German Alliance Insurance Co. v. Lewis,* 233 U.S. 389, a statute fixing the amount of premiums for fire insurance was held not to deny due process. Though the business of the insurers depended on no franchise or grant from the state, and there was no threat of monopoly, two factors rendered the regulation reasonable. These were the almost universal need of insurance protection and the fact that while the insurers competed for the business, they all fixed their premiums for similar risks according to an agreed schedule of rates. The court was at pains to point out that it was impossible to lay down any sweeping and general classification of businesses as to which price-regulation could be adjudged arbitrary or the reverse.

Many other decisions show that the private character of a business does not necessarily remove it from the realm of regulation of charges or prices. The usury laws fix the price which may be exacted for the use of money, although no business more essentially private in character can be imagined than that of loaning one's personal funds. *Griffith v. Connecticut,* 218 U.S. 563. Insurance agents' compensation may be regulated, though their contracts are private, because the business of insurance is considered one properly subject to public control. *O'Gorman & Young v. Hartford Fire Ins. Co.,* 282 U.S. 251. Statutes prescribing in the public interest the amounts to be charged by attorneys for prosecuting certain claims, a matter ordinarily one of personal and private nature, are not a deprivation of due process. *Frisbie v. United States,* 157 U.S. 160. . . . A stockyards corporation, "while not a common carrier, nor engaged in any distinctively public employment, is doing a work in which the public has an interest," and its charges may be controlled. *Cotting v. Kansas City Stockyards Co.,* 183 U.S. 79, 85. Private contract carriers, who do not operate under a franchise, and have no monopoly of the carriage of goods or passengers, may, since they use the highways to compete with railroads, be compelled to charge rates not lower than those of public carriers for corresponding services, if the state, in pursuance of a public policy to protect the latter, so determines.

So far as the requirement of due process is concerned, and in the absence of other constitutional restriction, a state is free to adopt whatever economic policy may reasonably be deemed to promote public welfare, and to enforce that policy by legislation adapted to its purpose. The courts are without authority either to declare such policy, or, when it is declared by the legislature, to override it. If the laws passed are seen to have a reasonable relation to a proper legislative purpose, and are neither arbitrary nor discriminatory, the requirements of due process are satisfied, and judicial determination to that effect renders a court functus officio. "Whether the free operation of the normal laws of competition is a wise and wholesome rule for trade and commerce is an economic question which this court need not consider or determine." *Northern Securities Co. v. United States,* 193 U.S. 197, 337–8. And it is equally clear that if the legislative policy be to curb unrestrained and harmful competition by measures which are not arbitrary or discriminatory it does not lie with the courts to determine that the rule is unwise. With the wisdom of the policy adopted, with the adequacy or practicability of the law enacted to forward it, the courts are both incompetent and unauthorized to deal. The course of decision in this court exhibits a firm adherence to these principles.

Tested by these considerations we find no basis in the due process clause of the

Fourteenth Amendment for condemning the provisions of the Agriculture and Markets Law here drawn into question.

The judgment is Affirmed.

Separate opinion of MR. JUSTICE McREYNOLDS

Is the milk business so affected with public interest that the Legislature may prescribe prices for sales by stores? This Court has approved the contrary view; has emphatically declared that a State lacks power to fix prices in similar private businesses. *United States v. Cohen Grocery Co.,* 255 U.S. 81 [food retailing]; *Adkins v. Children's Hospital,* 261 U.S. 525 [minimum wage law]; *Wolff Packing Co. v. Industrial Court,* 262 U.S. 522 [meat packing]; *Tyson & Bro. v. Banton,* 273 U.S. 418 [ticket brokers]; *Fairmont Creamery C. v. Minnesota,* 274 U.S. 1 [dairy]; *Ribnik v. McBride,* 277 U.S. 350 [employment agency]; *Williams v. Standard Oil Co.,* 278 U.S. 235 [gasoline]; *New State Ice Co. v. Liebmann,* 285 U.S. 262 [ice manufacturing]; *Sterling v. Constantin,* 287 U.S. 378, 396 [oil production].

Wolff Packing Co. v. Industrial Court, 262 U.S. 522, 537.—Here the State's statute undertook to destroy the freedom to contract by parties engaged in so-called "essential" industries. This Court held that she had no such power. "It has never been supposed, since the adoption of the Constitution, that the business of the butcher, or the baker, the tailor, the woodchopper, the mining operator or the miner was clothed with such a public interest that the price of his product or his wages could be fixed by State regulation. . . . An ordinary producer, manufacturer or shopkeeper may sell or not sell as he likes." On a second appeal, 267 U.S. 552, 569, the same doctrine was restated:—"The system of compulsory arbitration which the Act establishes is intended to compel, and if sustained will compel, the owner and employees to continue the business on terms which are not of their making. . . . Such a system infringes the liberty of contract and rights of property guaranteed by the due process of law clause of the Fourteenth Amendment. 'The established doctrine is that this liberty may not be interfered with, under the guide of protecting the public interest, by legislative action which is arbitrary or without reasonable relation to some purpose within the competency of the State to effect.' "

Williams v. Standard Oil Co., 278 U.S. 235, 239.—The State of Tennessee was declared without power to prescribe prices at which gasoline might be sold. "It is settled by recent decisions of this Court that a state legislature is without constitutional power to fix prices at which commodities may be sold, services rendered, or property used, unless the business or property involved is 'affected with a public interest.' " Considered affirmatively, "it means that a business or property, in order to be affected with a public interest, must be such or be so employed as to justify the conclusion that it has been devoted to a public use and its use thereby in effect granted to the public. . . . Negatively, it does not mean that a business is affected with a public interest merely because it is large or because the public are warranted in having a feeling of concern in respect of its maintenance."

New State Ice Co. v. Liebmann, 285 U.S. 262, 277.—Here Oklahoma undertook the control of the business of manufacturing and selling ice. We denied the power so to do. "It is a business as essentially private in its nature as the business of the grocer, the dairyman, the butcher, the baker, the shoemaker, or the tailor, . . . And this court has definitely said that the production or sale of food or clothing cannot be subjected to legislative regulation on the basis of a public use."

Munn v. Illinois (1877), 94 U.S. 113, has been much discussed in the opinions referred to above. And always the conclusion was that nothing there sustains the notion that the ordinary business of dealing in commodities is charged with a public interest and subject to legislative control. The contrary has been distinctly announced. To undertake now to attribute a repudiated implication to that opinion is to affirm that it means what this Court has declared again and again was not intended. The painstaking effort there to point out that certain businesses like ferries, mills, &c. were subject to legislative control at common law and then to show that warehousing at Chicago occupied like relation to the public would have been pointless if "affected with a public interest" only means that the public has serious concern about the perpetuity and success of the undertaking. That is true of almost all ordinary business affairs.

But plainly, I think, this Court must have regard to the wisdom of the enactment. At least, we must inquire concerning its purpose and decide whether the means proposed have reasonable relation to something within legislative power— whether the end is legitimate, and the means appropriate.

The court below has not definitely affirmed this necessary relation; it has not attempted to indicate how higher charges at stores to impoverished customers when the output is excessive and sale prices by producers are unrestrained, can possibly increase receipts at the farm. The Legislative Committee pointed out as the obvious cause of decreased consumption, notwithstanding low prices, the consumers' reduced buying power. Higher store prices will not enlarge this power; nor will they decrease production. Low prices will bring less cows only after several years. The prime causes of the difficulties will remain. Nothing indicates early decreased output. Demand at low prices being wholly insufficient, the proposed plan is to raise and fix higher minimum prices at stores and thereby aid the producer whose output and prices remain unrestrained!

The somewhat misty suggestion below that condemnation of the challenged legislation would amount to holding "that the due process clause has left milk producers unprotected from oppression," I assume, was not intended as a material contribution to the discussion upon the merits of the cause. Grave concern for embarrassed farmers is everywhere; but this should neither obscure the rights of others nor obstruct judicial appraisement of measures proposed for relief. The ultimate welfare of the producer, like that of every other class, requires dominance of the Constitution.

The judgment of the court below should be reversed.

Federal Regulation of Motor Carriers

[The decision of Congress to expand the ICC's jurisdiction to include interstate trucking was taken with only limited Congressional investigation. The Congressional committee reports on the Motor Carrier Act of 1935 totaled ten pages, citing as the main evidence the reports of the Federal Coordinator of Transportation. The most relevant portion of his analysis is given below.]

Extracts from Second Report of Federal Coordinator of Transportation, Senate Document No. 152, Seventy-third Congress, second session [1934]:

CONTROLLING PRINCIPLES

It is clear that no regulation or restrictions should be imposed upon any form of transportation merely for the purpose of benefiting some other form of transportation. The test must be the public interest. On the other hand, whatever the public interest may require ought to be done no matter how it may affect private interests. These are principles which no one is likely to gainsay. Yet they need emphasis, because private interests are vitally involved. Much of the demand for regulation and restriction of the other transportation agencies has come from the railroads, for their own protection. Equally selfish interests are uppermost in the opposition. The controversy has been largely between private interests, but it is the public interest which must be paramount and controlling.

In the final analysis the public interest requires a national transportation system so administered and controlled that service can be furnished at the lowest possible charges consistent with adequate maintenance and ability to provide the modern facilities and the character of service which the best interests of commerce and industry demand.

THE MOTOR-TRANSPORT INDUSTRY

Motor transport entered the field as a competitor of rail transport about a decade and a half ago. For convenience, the term "intercity" will be used to identify such motor transport and distinguish it from the kind which substitutes in local service for the old horse-drawn vehicle. During its short life, intercity motor transport has grown with extraordinary rapidity, without any Federal control and until recently with comparatively little effective State control. The question for consideration is the present need for Federal control.

What the public interest requires is the essential thing, but in determining where that interest lies the welfare of the industry itself must be taken into account, and also the welfare of other transport agencies. The vital public need is a national transportation system in which, so far as possible, all the parts will coordinate in a smoothly running whole and which can furnish the best service at the lowest cost consistent with sound credit conditions. In diagnosing the present situation, therefore, the internal problems of the motor-transport industry will first be discussed, then its relations with other transportation agencies, and finally the public interest in its entirety.

Conditions within the industry.—Intercity trucking is disorganized and much of it is in an economically unsound condition. The reasons are familiar, and a brief summary will suffice.

The small scale of operations, the presence of three more or less distinctive but highly competitive types of operators, and the ease of entering the business are the basic reasons. As yet there are comparatively few well-organized, large-scale operations, and these are small when judged by rail standards. There are thousands of little operators, with a very few trucks or even a single truck. The law makes a distinction between common carriers and contract carriers and attaches greater responsibilities, or gives lesser opportunities, to the former than to the latter. Both, but especially the common carrier, are continually faced with actual or potential competition from private truck operation, whether it be by industries, commercial or shipper organizations, or farmers.

It has been and is easy to enter the business, especially on a contract or private basis, and may require little capital expenditure. The efforts of the States to control entrance, summarized elsewhere, have not been very successful, owing, however, in part to the lack of supporting interstate regulation. A small sum, and often only a down payment on a single truck, is enough in many instances for a start. Use is made of a publicly owned highway, the construction and maintenance of which impose a charge through some form of taxation upon the operation but no capital expenditure.

This ease of starting small-scale operations has the natural result that many truck operators are poorly trained and inadequately financed, and some are irresponsible. The lack of training means hardships for the individual trucker and difficulties for his competitors, both those of equally low qualifications and those who, with greater experience and larger resources, try to conduct their operations on a businesslike basis. Too often rates have been demoralized by operators with little or no knowledge of costs or by those who have been driven by sheer financial necessity to quote rates which they know to be unremunerative. The situation is very like, but worse than, that which existed in the early days of railroading.

The depression has increased the difficulties of the industry. It has drawn many unemployed into the business, has made thousands of second-hand trucks available at low prices, and by low labor, fuel, and tire costs has invited their purchase. The abundance of labor to be had at low wages has stimulated cut-throat competition between operators who have wanted to maintain high or reasonable standards of employment and those who have been willing to exploit labor, either as a matter of deliberate policy or from necessity. In brief, the depression has lowered the standard of living of the industry.

Relations with other transportation agencies.—Competition between motor, rail, and water transport is now widespread and much of it is destructive. The motor trucks fill a need for expeditious, frequent, and specialized short-haul intercity service which the railroads were unable to meet. For this better service the trucks at first charged rates which often exceeded rail rates, and this is still true to some extent. The railroads, for the most part, were not greatly concerned by this competition in the beginning, or at least took no immediate steps to meet it. The loss was chiefly in short-haul, less-than-carload traffic, and it has long been railroad doctrine that such traffic was unprofitable.

However, with the rapid improvement of trucks and the lowering of their first costs and expense of operation, and with the tremendous expansion of the system of hard-surface highways, the number of truck operators and the range of their operations greatly increased. They were helped by the railroad rate structure. Prior to regulation, a very important factor in railroad rates was "what the traffic will bear." This was modified by regulation, but the principle was retained in the recognition in railroad rate making of the value as well as the cost of the service. The result of this, and also of market competition, has been that in general the higher-valued commodities and the shorter hauls pay higher rates, relatively, than the lower-valued commodities and the longer hauls.

The country has in general approved this method of making railroad rates, believing that it tended to place the burden where it could best be borne; and much the same method has been followed all over the world. It will readily be seen, however, that this deviation from cost of service favored truck competition, since it made the traffic vulnerable on which the relatively higher rates are charged. This is what the railroads mean when they say that the trucks are taking the "cream of the traffic," although this comment does not apply to much of the short-haul, merchandise traffic.

The great and rapid increase in truckers brought sharp competition in the industry itself, and a progressive lowering of rate levels. The railroad response was tardy, because the menace was not at first perceived. Even as late as 1931, the railroads were proposing a horizontal increase of 15 percent in all rates. Sporadic reductions to meet truck competition date back for several years, but drastic and widespread reductions have largely been confined to the past 2 or 3 years. At the present time, however, the tendency in that direction is so pronounced that it is causing serious concern to the truckers, especially since the operations of the National Recovery Administration have set minimum limits to wages and maximum limits to hours of service. In making these reductions, the railroads proceed on the theory that any rates necessary to regain traffic can be justified, if they more than cover so-called "out-of-pocket" expense.

Having no noncompetitive traffic to furnish reserve strength, the trucks cannot apply that theory as fully or as effectively as the railroads. Yet they do apply it to some extent. The most familiar example is that of back-haul traffic, where the operator accepts loads moving against the general direction of traffic at very low rates, on the theory that otherwise the truck would go back empty. . . . This "out-of-pocket" cost theory is, it may be said, an element of great danger to the entire transportation industry, particularly as competition becomes general rather than incidental.

The relative advantages of the rail and motor carriers in competition were somewhat fully discussed in Coordination of Motor Transportation, 182 I.C.C. 263, 300–309. The advantages of trucks were thus summarized at page 301:

> The advantages of truck transportation from a service standpoint are to be found mainly in the speed, the completeness, and the flexibility of the service rendered. The area in which the truck has most effectively supplanted rail traffic is that which can be served one or more times during the day; the area within which overnight delivery can be made is a fertile field for the truck; to points more distant the service advantages of

the truck are lessened until a zone of indifference or disadvantage is reached. Coupled with this phase of service is the ability or willingness of truck operators to take shipments at a later hour than the railroads ordinarily do and yet make earlier morning delivery.

In the case of some shippers an even greater advantage of truck transportation is the completed service it renders. Only one transportation agency needs to be dealt with for given shipments and pick-up and delivery service is usually provided. There is also more flexibility about truck than rail service in moving emergency and irregular shipments.

From the standpoint of cost of service, the great advantage of the trucks is in the much lower cost of terminal operations. The great advantage of the railroads is in line-haul cost, more particularly when the traffic loads heavily and moves in volume. It follows that net advantage for the trucks is ordinarily to be found in the shorter hauls and disappears when a certain varying limit is reached.

Apart from cost of service, the principal disadvantages of the trucks are to be found in the lack of known and stable rates and dependable service and in lesser financial responsibility, although there has been considerable improvement of late in the latter respects.

The situation may be summarized by saying that the truck has distinctive cost and service advantages for many classes of traffic within a considerable zone; that it also endeavors, sporadically or otherwise, to reach beyond this zone; and that the railroads, once indifferent to the loss of short-haul traffic, are fighting to hold or regain both it and the moderate and long-distance traffic for which trucks are now bidding.

The extent of truck competition with rail service is difficult to measure. No definite and accurate figures are available. The aggregate volume of truck traffic can only be estimated and with difficulty, and much of it has been developed by the trucks. Estimates in the Coordination case . . . placed the volume of truck traffic in 1929 at 18.3 percent of rail traffic in terms of tons originated, and at 5.8 percent in terms of ton-miles.

An estimate of the aggregate volume of motor-truck traffic handled outside the strictly local haulage area indicates that in 1932 truck traffic was about 44 percent of rail in terms of tons originated, and 12.7 percent in terms of ton-miles. This comparison understates, however, the influence of the truck on the rail and water carriers, as the latter are suffering severe losses in revenue on much of the traffic which they carry, owing to reductions of rates made to keep or regain traffic. There is also the fact that, on the whole, truck traffic is of the higher revenue-producing types. All told, the losses to rail and water carriers probably amount to several hundred millions of revenue per year.

The question of public interest.—In the past 10 or 15 years of transportation development in this country, we have followed, unconsciously for the most part, a policy of encouraging an oversupply of transportation service.

In consequence, transportation charges have been lowered for many shippers but these savings are in part only apparent, as diversions of traffic have played a part in holding noncompetitive rail rates on a high level, and the costs borne by the public as a whole may, in the aggregate, be insufficiently met by the payments which the shippers make. Moreover, there have been large losses in capital returns. An important part of the capital put by individuals into the trucking business, for example, has yielded no returns and has frequently been entirely lost. Duplication of facilities was for the most part inevitable. The costs which it represents are widely diffused and difficult of assignment.

The public has also a decided interest in an orderly functioning of the entire transportation mechanism. While some shippers gain temporary advantage from unstable and unpublished rates, the greater present good and the long-run good of all require that the transportation factor in the cost of doing business be known and predictable. The truck has changed a situation in which substantially all these requirements were met to one of widespread uncertainty, instability, distrust among shippers, and undue discrimination and prejudice, particularly in favor of the large shipper. Trucks have done much to break down a system of rate control which was subject to deliberate adjustment to changed conditions, but a system whose very deliberateness and openness were in fact substantial virtues.

Many groups of shippers complain against the uncertainties and vagaries of the present situation. Dealers in fruits and vegetables, coal, cotton, grain, lumber, and many other commodities are most critical. They find their own marketing processes disintegrating without, at least in their view, better ones taking their place. Small shippers feel the effects of the competition of larger ones who can employ contract trucks at less than common-carrier rates or who operate their own motor equipment. The greater burden of taxation upon the common carrier-truck is also said to be an adverse competitive factor.

There are certain service requirements to which the public attaches importance. One of these is responsibility on the part of the operator. Although improvement has occurred . . . there still is complaint against the failure of the truck and bus industries to measure up in all respects to the standards of responsibility expected of a public servant. Loss and damage claims are not always met, c.o.d. collections promptly or fully returned, schedules maintained, or contracts lived up to.

A broader aspect of responsibility also deserves mention. This relates to the maintenance of truck or bus service on which the shipper or traveler has come, perhaps entirely, to depend. Certainly no responsibility is felt by the motor-transport industry today to maintain unprofitable or relatively unprofitable service, such as the railroads have maintained, frequently voluntarily, although sometimes by order of public authorities. The highway operator assumes a lesser degree of responsibility for a complete coverage of the transportation needs of the area he sets out to serve. Truck and bus operators tend commonly to concentrate their efforts on the profitable avenues of traffic.

Finally, so long certainly as private capital is the mainstay of the transportation system, the public interest requires conditions which will enable the carriers to maintain good credit. Loss of investment means wasted human effort, and the effect of such waste permeates the entire community. Moreover, financially weak carriers are bound to become poor public servants. Good equipment, good facilities, and good service cannot be maintained indefinitely without financial stability.

The public interest in transportation may, then, be summarized as requiring at least the following: (1) A minimum of outright duplication of facilities or services; (2) a transportation system which is well organized and functions in an orderly, dependable way, rather than one which is unstable, uncertain, and a breeder of discriminations; (3) responsibility, in both the narrow and the broad sense indicated above; and (4) financial stability and good credit.

Need for regulation.—There are some who think that the thing to do is to let down the bars and allow the competitors to fight it out to the finish. This would, of course, require practical abandonment of railroad regulation, leaving redress of grievances to the courts. The eventual result might be a kind of coordinated system of transportation, achieved through survival of the fittest, but the greater competitive strength of the railroads would be likely to distort the results. The fact is that this plan of free-for-all competition has never worked successfully, either here or elsewhere. It has been tried and found wanting.

On the other hand, a partial and incomplete system of regulation such as we have had, will not work. The phase through which transportation has been passing in the last decade and a half was doubtless inevitable, for it is difficult to regulate new forms of transportation until they have passed the experimental stage. But the time has arrived for effective control. There is the same need for bringing some degree of order out of chaos as there was in 1887, when Federal regulation of railroads became clearly necessary. Unless competition is brought under greater restraint, it can bring only widespread losses to shippers, to communities and sections of the country, to investors in rail, water, and motor facilities, and to the public generally. Competition between the different forms of transportation will continue to have an important part to play, but it must be held within reasonable limits and kept from assuming destructive and wasteful forms. The transportation system must be knit together and coordinated. This can only be done under the guiding hand of the Federal Government. The primary objective should be to use each form of transportation to the best long-run advantage of the public.

* * *

The report of the Joint Committee of Railroads and Highway Users, made on January 30, 1933, is also significant. The committee agreed that motor common carriers should be required to obtain certificates of public convenience and necessity designed to assure financial responsibility, and reasonable protection of existing carriers, to keep proper accounts and file reports, and to observe such regulations as to qualifications and hours of service of drivers as the administrative authority might prescribe in the interest of public safety on the highways. Regulation of security issues also was favored. It was further agreed that contract carriers should be required to obtain permits, observe regulations as to qualifications and hours of drivers, keep records and file reports, and make adequate provision for financial responsibility. There was no agreement, however, on rate control. The representatives of the highway users agreed that "Adequate requirements should be imposed upon common-carrier trucks in interstate commerce to insure just and reasonable rates, with provision for publication thereof and adherence thereto, and proper inhibition against undue discrimination, if and when sufficient data have been collected to indicate the desirability of such regulation in the public interest." They also attached a similar qualification to their acceptance of the recommendation that contract trucks in interstate commerce should "observe minimum rates fixed by regulatory authority and comply with rules and practices applying to rates and service, as may be prescribed by such authority."

It is reasonable to conclude that there is a rather general demand for Federal regulation of motor carriers, although views differ as to how far control of truck rates should go and to numerous details of regulation.

Practicability of Federal regulation.—The most serious argument against Federal regulation of motor carriers is that, to be effective it would require a large, costly, and bureaucratic establishment with a small army of agents and investigators, the remedy being worse than the disease. The enforcement of the eighteenth amendment is used by way of horrible example.

It would be foolish to deny that serious practical difficulties will be encountered in Federal regulation of the trucks; but it would be equally foolish to believe that they are insurmountable. The chief difficulties will be met in securing adherence to published rates, particularly by contract carriers; in preventing private carriers from engaging in for-hire operations without proper authorization; in securing accurate accounting and records; in the granting of certificates and permits; and in prescribing minimum rates, where that proves necessary.

Considerable difficulty is to be expected in connection with the granting of certificates and permits. The information now in the hands of the States and that which is being collected under the auspices of the National Recovery Administration will be a great aid. The so-called "grandfather" clause in the proposed legislation will simplify matters at the start, as it will permit all carriers in operation on a specified date to continue and, in general, will require only proof of such operation and of proper qualifications as a prerequisite to an initial certificate or permit. The task thereafter will not be easy, owning to the rather frequent shifts in personnel and operations in the trucking industry and the controversies which will arise in determining "public convenience and necessity."

The fixing of minimum rates, when necessary, for either railroads, trucks, or any other transportation agency, is not a simple or an easy duty. That it is necessary and not impracticable in the trucking industry is attested by the fact that provision for such minimum rates has been included, at the insistence of the industry, in the trucking code. The task should, on the whole, be less difficult than the fixing of maximum reasonable rates on all sorts and conditions of railroad freight traffic, a duty which the Commission has performed for many years.

Probable effects of regulation.—The demand for regulation of the motor-transport industry began with the railroads, spread at length to the industry itself, and is now voiced by an important section of public opinion. The probable effects, however, will be considered in a different order.

It is likely that regulation of the kind proposed will somewhat lessen the flexibility of truck operations and set up requirements which small or poorly financed operators will not be able to meet. But it should confer benefits on the trucking industry which will more than compensate for these losses, by promoting a more orderly conduct of the business, lessening irresponsible competition and undue internal strife, encouraging the organization of stronger units, and otherwise enabling the industry to put itself on a sounder and more generally profitable basis. It will also enable the common carrier to strive more effectively for his share of the business, through proper recognition of the greater responsibility which he assumes and by reducing the number of pseudo-contract operations, which in the past have sought the more profitable business, leaving to the common carrier more generally the small freight and the responsibility of furnishing scheduled service the year around.

It may be urged that regulation will encourage private trucking and thereby work a serious injury to the for-hire sections of the industry. There is little reason to believe that important injury would result. As the legislation proposed would debar the private operator from transporting freight for hire, unless he submits to the regulation proposed for for-hire operators, his opportunity to fill up outbound loads and to pack up for-hire traffic on return trips would be materially limited. Such a restriction is justified for the protection of the common carriers upon whom the general public must depend.

This change would reduce the radius of operation of the strictly private carrier, except where, for example, he can carry his own products out and bring back raw or semifinished products or other supplies for his own use. There is also the likelihood that, by making the rates of common and contract carriers both stable and known, regulation will discourage such private operations as have been entered into because of the uncertainties and irresponsibility attaching to much of the existing for-hire service. The possibility of private operation will, however, set limits to rates, both for the railroads and for the common carrier and contract trucks, and if these limits are not observed, there will be a material increase in private operation.

Regulation will be of substantial advantage to shippers and the public generally. While certain shippers will lose the unreasonably low rates and the privilege of driving hard bargains which they have enjoyed, especially of late, all will gain the advantages of fair, known, and stable rates. The smaller shipper, mainly dependent on common-carrier service, will be relieved from some of his present handicaps, so that he can compete to better advantage with the shipper who has secured special-rate privileges through volume of traffic.

Public advantage will also result from the opportunities which regulation will create for coordinating rail, water, and motor services. There is no other way to prevent unnecessary duplication and waste and to give each form of transportation a chance to develop in the field where it can function the best, without destructive competition from inferior forms. Such coordination is the foundation for financial stability and lower transportation costs and rates. It will raise two questions, however, which will require serious consideration.

As already indicated, the railroad rate structure has been influenced to a considerable extent by the value-of-the service theory. The theory is of long standing and was stated by the Commission in its first report in 1887 as follows:

"The public interest is best served when the rates are so apportioned as to encourage the largest practicable exchange of products between different sections of our country and with foreign countries; and this can only be done by making value an important consideration, and by placing upon the higher classes of freight some share of the burden that on a relatively equal apportionment, if service alone were considered, would fall upon those of less vaue."

The motor truck is threatening this theory all over the world, for it has provided the truck with one of its best competitive opportunities. Under free and uncontrolled competition, cost of service would inevitably be the controlling factor, and rates would tend to seek that level. The same thing would occur under a plan of coordination which aims to utilize each agency for the purpose of securing transportation at the lowest possible cost. The result in either event is likely to compel a far-reaching readjustment of the rate structure, if transportation costs prove to be what they are commonly supposed to be. The present knowledge of costs is sufficiently imperfect and the possibility of lowering them is sufficiently great, so that it is impossible to prophesy with certainty in regard to this matter, but it is obviously of the utmost importance.

This likely tendency to a radical change in the rate structure might be tempered and controlled under public regulation to an extent impossible under free competition. However, the private truck sets definite limits to any policy of modification, for railroad rates and common carrier or contract truck rates cannot go beyond the mark set by the cost of transportation in trucks privately operated by the shipper. The prospects are that there will be disruption of the rate structure in any event, but there is more chance of keeping this tendency within reasonable limits with comprehensive regulation than without.

The second question which will arise is how far coordination should be accomplished under the auspices of the railroad companies. Beyond question they can use trucks and busses to great advantage to supplement or substitute for their rail service, both at terminals and on the line. Already they are doing this to a very considerable extent . . . and the movement is plainly one which should be encouraged, for it means both greater efficiency and greater economy in service. Some believe that they should definitely become transportation systems, rather than railroad systems, and assume control over all means of transportation. Others strongly oppose this idea, on the ground that railroad personnel is too prone to work along traditional lines and would use railroad methods poorly adapted to the operation of trucks, that it would quickly dissipate the benefits in the way of personal contacts with shippers which truckers have achieved, and that monopolistic tendencies would set in.

While railroads should be permitted to use trucks freely in connection with their rail service, there appears to be no present need for encouraging a movement toward the absorption by them of truck, bus, and water operations. Railroad credit conditions permit of no such movement at the present time, and a more or less independent development of the rival agencies is plainly desirable. It is possible that experience may later furnish occasion for changing this view, but that is a bridge which need not be crossed now.

Turning to the effect of motor transport regulation on the railroad, it should result in clarifying and stabilizing competitive conditions, and in preventing much unnecessary duplication and waste. The railroads will also benefit from the impetus which it will give to coordination. However, such regulation is in no way to be regarded as a panacea for railroad ills. The railroads have spent too much time and attention on plans for the restriction of their competitors and too little on the development and improvement of their own service and the readjustment of their own rates. Regulation of their competitors is desirable, but it is from self-help that the railroads have most to gain. This has been the experience all over the world, so far as motor transport competition with the railroads is concerned. Included in railroad self-help is, of course, the proper utilization as an adjunct of rail service of all other means of transportation. These other agencies cannot be legislated out of existence; they perform useful and necessary functions; and they are here to stay.

United States v. Southwestern Cable Co.
392 U.S. 157 (1968)

MR. JUSTICE HARLAN delivered the opinion of the Court.

These cases stem from proceedings conducted by the Federal Communications Commission after requests by Midwest Television for relief under the rules promulgated by the Commission for the regulation of community antenna television (CATV) systems. Midwest averred that respondents' CATV systems transmitted the signals of Los Angeles broadcasting stations into the San Diego area, and thereby had, inconsistently with the public interest, adversely affected Midwest's San Diego station. Midwest sought an appropriate order limiting the carriage of such signals by respondents' systems. After consideration of the petition and of various responsive pleadings, the Commission restricted the expansion of respondents' service in areas in which they had not operated on February 15, 1966, pending hearings to be conducted on the merits of Midwest's complaints. On petitions for review, the Court of Appeals for the Ninth Circuit held that the Commission lacks authority under the Communications Act of 1934, to issue such an order. We granted certiorari to consider this important question of regulatory authority. For reasons that follow, we reverse.

I

CATV systems receive the signals of television broadcasting stations, amplify them, transmit them by cable or microwave, and ultimately distribute them by wire to the receivers of their subscribers. CATV systems characteristically do not produce their own programming, and do not recompense producers or broadcasters for use of the programming which they receive and redistribute. Unlike ordinary broadcasting stations, CATV systems commonly charge their subscribers installation and other fees.

The CATV industry has grown rapidly since the establishment of the first commercial system in 1950. In the late 1950's, some 50 new systems were established each year; by 1959, there were 550 "nationally known and identified" systems serving a total audience of 1,500,000 to 2,000,000 persons. It has been more recently estimated that "new systems are being founded at the rate of more than one per day, and . . . subscribers . . . signed on at the rate of 15,000 per month." By late 1965, it was reported that there were 1,847 operating CATV systems, that 758 others were franchised but not yet in operation, and that there were 938 applications for additional franchises. The statistical evidence is incomplete, but, as the Commission has observed, "whatever the estimate, CATV growth is clearly explosive in nature."

CATV systems perform either or both of two functions. First, they may supplement broadcasting by facilitating satisfactory reception of local stations in adjacent areas in which such reception would not otherwise be possible; and second, they may transmit to subscribers the signals of distant stations entirely beyond the range of local antennae. As the number and size of CATV systems have increased, their principal function has more frequently become the importation of distant signals. In 1959, only 50 systems employed microwave relays, and the maximum distance over which signals were transmitted was 300 miles; by 1964, 250 systems used microwave, and the transmission distances sometimes exceeded 665 miles. Thus, "while the CATV industry originated in sparsely settled areas and areas of adverse terrain . . . it is now spreading to metropolitan centers. . . ." CATV systems, formerly no more than local auxiliaries to broadcasting, promise for the future to provide a national communications system, in which signals from selected broadcasting centers would be transmitted to metropolitan areas throughout the country.

The Commission has on various occasions attempted to assess the relationship between community antenna television systems and its conceded regulatory functions. Although it found that CATV is "related to interstate transmission," the Commission reasoned that CATV systems are neither common carriers nor broadcasters, and therefore are within neither of the principal regulatory categories created by the Communications Act. The Commission declared that it had not been given plenary authority over "any and all enterprises which happen to be connected with one of the many aspects of communications." It refused to premise regulation of CATV upon assertedly adverse consequences for broadcasting, because it could not "determine where the impact takes effect, although we recognize that it may well exist."

The Commission instead declared that it would forthwith seek appropriate legislation "to clarify the situation."

Despite its inability to obtain amendatory legislation, the Commission has, since 1960, gradually asserted jurisdiction over CATV. It first placed restrictions upon the activities of common carrier microwave facilities that serve CATV systems. Finally, the Commission in 1962 conducted a rule-making proceeding in which it re-evaluated the significance of CATV for its regulatory responsibilities. The proceeding was explicitly restricted to those systems that are served by microwave, but the Commission's conclusions plainly were more widely relevant. The Commission found that "the likelihood or probability of [CATV's] adverse impact upon potential and existing service has become too substantial to be dismissed." It reasoned that the importation of distant signals into the service areas of local stations necessarily creates "substantial competition" for local broadcasting. The Commission acknowledged that it could not "measure precisely the degree of . . . impact," but found that "CATV competition can have a substantial negative effect upon station audience and revenues. . . ."

The Commission attempted to "accommodat[e]" the interests of CATV and of local broadcasting by the imposition of two rules. First, CATV systems were required to transmit to their subscribers the signals of any station into whose service area they have brought competing signals. Second, CATV systems were forbidden to duplicate the programming of such local stations for periods of 15 days before and after a local broadcast. These carriage and nonduplication rules were expected to "insur[e] many stations' ability to maintain themselves as their areas' outlets for highly popular network and other programs. . . ."

The Commission in 1965 issued additional notices of inquiry and proposed rule-making, by which it sought to determine whether all forms of CATV, including those served only by cable, could properly be regulated under the Communications Act. After further hearings, the Commission held that the Act confers adequate regulatory authority over all CATV systems. It promulgated revised rules, applicable both to cable and to microwave CATV systems, to govern the carriage of local signals and the nonduplication of local programming. Further, the Commission forbade the importation by CATV of distant signals into the 100 largest television markets, except insofar as such service was offered on February 15, 1966, unless the Commission has previously found that it "would be consistent with the public interest," . . . "particularly the establishment and healthy maintenance of television broadcast service in the area." . . . Thirteen days after the Commission's adoption of the Second Report, Midwest initiated these proceedings by the submission of its petition for special relief.

II

We must first emphasize that questions as to the validity of the specific rules promulgated by the Commission for the regulation of CATV are not now before the Court. The issues in these cases are only two: whether the Commission has authority under the Communications Act to regulate CATV systems, and, if it has, whether it has, in addition, authority to issue the prohibitory order here in question.

The Commission's authority to regulate broadcasting and other communications is derived from the Communications Act of 1934, as amended. The Act's provisions are explicitly applicable to "all interstate and foreign communication by wire or radio. . . ." The Commission's responsibilities are no more narrow: it is required to endeavor to "make available . . . to all the people of the United States a rapid, efficient, Nation-wide, and world-wide wire and radio communication service. . . ." The Commission was expected to serve as the "single Government agency" with "unified jurisdiction" and "regulatory power over all forms of electrical communication, whether by telephone, telegraph, cable, or radio." It was for this purpose given "broad authority." As this Court emphasized in an earlier case, the Act's terms, purposes, and history all indicate that Congress "formulated a unified and comprehensive regulatory system for the [broadcasting] industry."

Respondents do not suggest that CATV systems are not within the term "communication by wire or radio." . . . Nor can we doubt that CATV systems are engaged in interstate communication, even where, as here, the intercepted signals emanate from stations located within the same State in which the CATV system operates. We may take notice that television broadcasting consists in very large part of programming devised for, and distributed to, national audiences; respondents thus are ordinarily employed in the simultaneous retransmission of communications that have very often originated in other States. The stream of communication is essentially uninterrupted and properly indivisible. To categorize respondents' activities as intrastate would disregard the character of the television industry, and serve merely to prevent the national regulation that "is not only appropriate but essential to the efficient use of radio facilities."

Nonetheless, respondents urge that the Communications Act, properly understood, does not permit the regulation of CATV systems. First, they emphasize that the Commission in 1959 and again in 1966 sought legislation that would have explicitly authorized such regulation, and that its efforts were unsuccessful. In the circumstances here, however, this cannot be dispositive. The Commission's requests for legislation evidently reflected in each instance both its uncertainty as to the proper width of its authority and its understandable preference for more detailed policy guidance than the Communications Act now provides. We have recognized that administrative agencies should, in such situations, be encouraged to seek from Congress clarification of the pertinent statutory provisions.

Second, respondents urge that Section 152(a) does not independently confer regulatory authority upon the Commission, but instead merely prescribes the forms of communication to which the Act's other provisions may separately be made applicable. Respondents emphasize that the Commission does not contend either that CATV systems are common carriers, and thus within Title II of the Act, or that they are broadcasters, and thus within Title III. They conclude that CATV, with certain of the characteristics both of broadcasting and of common carriers, but with all of the characteristics of neither, eludes altogether the Act's grasp.

We cannot construe the Act so restrictively. Nothing in the language of Section 152(a), in the surrounding language, or in the Act's history or purposes limits the Commission's authority to those activities and forms of communication that are specifically described by the Act's other provisions. The section itself states merely that the "provisions of [the Act] shall apply to all interstate and foreign communication by wire or radio. . . ." Similarly, the legislative history indicates that the Commission was given "regulatory power over all forms of electrical communication. . . ." Certainly Congress could not in 1934 have foreseen the development of community antenna television systems, but it seems to us that it was precisely because Congress wished "to maintain, through appropriate administrative control, a grip on the dynamic aspects of radio transmission" that it conferred upon the Commission a "unified jurisdiction" and "broad authority." Thus, "[u]nderlying the whole [Communications Act] is recognition of the rapidly fluctuating factors characteristic of the evolution of broadcasting and of the corresponding requirement that the administrative process possess sufficient flexibility to adjust itself to these factors." . . . We have found no reason to believe that Section 152 does not, as its terms suggest, confer regulatory authority over "all interstate . . . communication by wire or radio."

Moreover, the Commission has reasonably concluded that regulatory authority over CATV is imperative if it is to perform with appropriate effectiveness certain of its other responsibilities. Congress has imposed upon the Commission the "obligation of providing a widely dispersed radio and television service," with a "fair, efficient, and equitable distribution" of service among the "several States and communities." The Commission has, for this and other purposes, been granted authority to allocate broadcasting zones or areas, and to provide regulations "as it may deem necessary" to prevent interference among the various stations. The Commission has concluded, and Congress has agreed, that these obligations require for their satisfaction the creation of a system of local broadcasting stations, such that "all communities of appreciable size [will] have at least one television station as an outlet for local self-expression." In turn, the Commission has held that an appropriate system of local broadcasting may be created only if two subsidiary goals are realized. First, significantly wider use must be made of the available ultra-high frequency channels. Second, communities must be encouraged "to launch sound and adequate programs to utilize the television channels now reserved for educational purposes." These subsidiary goals have received the endorsement of Congress.

The Commission has reasonably found that the achievement of each of these purposes is "placed in jeopardy by the unregulated explosive growth of CATV." Although CATV may in some circumstances make possible "the realization of some of the [Commission's] most important goals," its importation of distant signals into the service areas of local stations may also "destroy or seriously degrade the service offered by a television broadcaster," and thus ultimately deprive the public of the various benefits of a system of local broadcasting stations. In particular, the Commission feared that CATV might, by dividing the available audiences and revenues, significantly magnify the characteristically serious financial difficulties of UHF and educational television broadcasters. The Commission acknowledged that it could not predict with certainty the consequences of unregulated CATV, but reasoned that its statutory responsibilities demand that it "plan in advance of foreseeable events, instead of waiting to react to them." We are aware that these consequences have been variously estimated, but must conclude that there is substantial evidence that the Commission cannot "discharge its over-all responsibilities without authority over this important aspect of television service."

The Commission has been charged with broad responsibilities for the orderly development of an appropriate system of local television broadcasting. The significance of its efforts can scarcely be exaggerated, for broadcasting is demonstrably a principal source of information and entertainment for a great part of the Nation's population. The Commission has reasonably found that the successful performance of these duties demands prompt and efficacious regulation of community antenna television systems. We have elsewhere held that we may not, "in the absence of compelling evidence that such was Congress' intention . . . prohibit administrative action imperative for the achievement of an agency's ultimate purposes." There is no such evidence here, and we therefore hold that the Commission's authority over "all interstate . . . communication by wire or radio" permits the regulation of CATV systems.

There is no need here to determine in detail the limits of the Commission's authority to regulate CATV. It is enough to emphasize that the authority which we recognize today under Section 152(a) is restricted to that reasonably ancillary to the effective performance of the Commission's various responsibilities for the regulation of television broadcasting. The Commission may, for these purposes, issue "such rules and regulations and prescribe such restrictions and conditions, not inconsistent with law," as "public convenience, interest, or necessity requires."

III

We must next determine whether the Commission has authority under the Communications Act to issue the particular prohibitory order in question in these proceedings. . . .

The Commission has acknowledged that, in this area of rapid and significant change, there may be situations in which its generalized regulations are inadequate, and special or additional forms of relief are imperative. It has found that the present case may prove to be such a situation, and that the public interest demands "interim relief . . . limiting further expansion," pending hearings to determine appropriate Commission action. Such orders do not exceed the Commission's authority. . . . In these circumstances, we hold that the Commission's order limiting further expansion of respondents' service pending appropriate hearings did not exceed or abuse its authority under the Communications Act. And there is no claim that its procedure in this respect is in any way constitutionally infirm.

The judgments of the Court of Appeals are reversed, and the cases are remanded for further proceedings consistent with this opinion.

It is so ordered.

12

RATE MAKING

Once the decision to regulate has been made, what standards should the regulator apply, and what procedures should he or she follow? It is appropriate to ask two basic questions: first, what is constitutional? and second, what makes good economic sense?

The constitutional argument was almost as longlasting as the argument that began with *Munn v. Illinois.* The question was what constituted due process. In an industry where the right to regulate was well established, there was still a question about what the regulators could do constitutionally. The primary issue was the setting of rates—rate making. Early in the game it was noticed that a regulator who set rates so low that the utility yielded no return on its capital or even a terribly low return (say 2 percent) was, in effect, confiscating the utility's property—taking property without due process—and could therefore be attacked under the Fourteenth Amendment.

Smyth v. Ames is the classic precedent on this issue. The Supreme Court conceived the crucial question to be the proper valuation of the utility's investment. The Court proceeded to rule that railroads were entitled to earn a "fair return on the fair value" of their resources devoted to intrastate use in Nebraska. Unfortunately, this decision was not as definitive as it might at first appear. Do the criteria for determining "fair value" in *Smyth v. Ames* make sense to you (for example, should the value of the utility's property depend on the market value of its stocks and bonds)? All of them? Any of them? Are they consistent with each other? Can you see why the *Smyth v. Ames* ruling became the basis for many subsequent appeals in rate-making cases?

We argued about the constitutionally correct answer for forty-six years until the *Federal Power Commission v. Hope Natural Gas* case was decided (the second case in this chapter). In this case the Court concluded that if due process is followed and if the resulting rates are "just and reasonable," then it is not necessary to examine the specific rate-making rules used. In reading the Hope case try to decide how you would determine whether the overall impact of a rate decision was "just and reasonable." Could you make such a decision without deciding how to evaluate the utility's property?

The Hope decision ended the constitutional issue, but it did not settle the question of what rate-making rules are economically appropriate. The regulatory agencies have gone in various directions in this respect. The federal commissions and the majority of states adopted original cost valuations of utility plants after the Hope decision. A minority of states evaluate utility capital in terms of "fair value," which generally turns out to be a weighted average of original cost and reproduction cost with the regulatory commission determining the weights. Illinois was a "fair value" state until 1973 when it joined the original cost majority. The third case presents excerpts from an amicus curiae (friend of the court) brief before the Illinois Commerce Commission. It discusses both the "fairness to investors" and "ability to raise capital" arguments. Do you believe the stockholders of Illinois utilities were unfairly treated by the Commission's shift to original cost valuation? More so than bondholders who explicitly opted for fixed income securities? In the presence of inflation, which valuation would be most efficient: original cost or fair value? Suppose that a firm was still able to raise all the capital that it needed to finance its expansion plans. Would you still worry about fairness to investors?

Once a utility's rate base has been estimated, the regulators must determine the rate of return that they will allow the utility to earn on its rate base. This process is illustrated by the Federal Communications Commission's regulation of American Telephone and Telegraph (AT&T). The FCC will allow AT&T a rate of return that will cover the costs of its two types of capital—debt (bonds) and equity (stocks). The cost of debt is simply the coupon interest rates for the bonds and is quickly calculated. The primary issue is thus the cost of equity. Since equity is riskier than debt, stockholders require a higher return than bondholders. The difference between the two rates is known as a "risk premium." AT&T contends that it needs a 50 percent risk premium since its business operations are as risky as those of other industrial companies in the economy. Does this seem reasonable? Is AT&T subject to the same uncertainties and competitive pressures as unregulated industrial firms? The FCC concluded that AT&T was entitled to an overall rate of return of 9.5 to 10.0 percent on its capital. What is the rationale for allowing a range of acceptable rates instead of a single rate such as 9.5 percent?

Smyth v. Ames

169 U.S. 466 (1898)

[In 1893 the state legislature of Nebraska passed a law establishing "reasonable maximum rates" for intrastate railroad service. A Board of Transportation was created and empowered to lower these rates if the resulting rates would be "just and reasonable." Stockholders of the Union Pacific took the initiative in appealing to the courts for an injunction against enforcement of the above statute.]

MR. JUSTICE HARLAN, after stating the case as above reported, delivered the opinion of the court.

In these cases the plaintiffs, stockholders in the corporations named, ask a decree enjoining the enforcement of certain rates for transportation upon the ground that the statute prescribing them is repugnant to the Constitution of the United States.

In view of the [several previous railroad] adjudications these principles must be regarded as settled:

1 A railroad corporation is a person within the meaning of the Fourteenth Amendment declaring that no State shall deprive any person of property without due process of law, nor deny to any person within its jurisdiction the equal protection of the laws.

2 A state enactment, or regulations made under the authority of a state enactment, establishing rates for the transportation of persons or property by railroad that will not admit of the carrier earning such compensation as under all the circumstances is just to it and to the public, would deprive such carrier of its property without due process of law and deny to it the equal protection of the laws, and would therefore be repugnant to the Fourteenth Amendment of the Constitution of the United States.

3 While rates for the transportation of persons and property within the limits of a State are primarily for its determination, the question whether they are so unreasonably low as to deprive the carrier of its property without such compensation as the Constitution secures, and therefore without due process of law, cannot be so conclusively determined by the legislature of the State or by regulations adopted under its authority, that the matter may not become the subject of judicial inquiry.

The cases before us directly present the important question last stated.

We turn now to the evidence in the voluminous record before us for the purpose of ascertaining whether—looking at the cases in the light of the facts as they existed when the decrees were rendered—the Nebraska statute, if enforced, would, by its necessary operation, have deprived the companies whose stockholders and bondholders here complain, of the right to obtain just compensation for the services rendered by them.

The first and most important contention of the plaintiffs is that, if the statute had been in force during any one of the three years preceding its passage, the defendant companies would have been compelled to use their property for the public substantially without reward or without the just compensation to which it was entitled. We think this mode of calculation for ascertaining the probable effect of the Nebraska statute upon the railroad companies in question is one that may be properly used.

The conclusion reached by the Circuit Court was that the reduction made by the Nebraska statute in the rates for local freight was so unjust and unreasonable as to require a decree staying the enforcement of such rates against the companies named in the bill.

The tariff which was in force at the time of the passage of this act has been, for some three or more years, fixed by the voluntary action of the railroad companies, and the reduction of 29½ percent was from their rates. It must be remembered that these roads are competing roads; that competition tends to a reduction of rates—sometimes, as the history of the country has shown, below that which affords any remuneration to those who own the property.

It appears, from what has been said, that if the rates prescribed by the act of 1893 had been in force during the years ending June 30, 1891, 1892 and 1893 . . . the Union Pacific Company, in the years ending June 30, 1892, and June 30, 1893, would have received more than enough to pay operating expenses. Do those facts affect the general conclusion as to the probable effect of the act of 1893? In the discussion of this question, the plaintiffs contended that a railroad company is entitled to exact such charges for transportation as will enable it, at all times, not only to pay operating expenses, but also to meet the interest regularly accruing upon all its outstanding obligations, and justify a dividend upon all its stock; and that to prohibit it from maintaining rates or charges for transportation adequate to all those ends will deprive it of its property without due process of law, and deny to it the equal protection of the laws.

In our opinion, the broad proposition advanced by counsel involves some misconception of the relations between the public and a railroad corporation. It is unsound in that it practically excludes from consideration the fair value of the property used, omits altogether any consideration of the right of the public to be exempt from unreasonable exactions, and makes the interests of the corporation maintaining a public highway the sole test in determining whether the rates established by or for it are such as may be rightfully prescribed as between it and the public. . . . It cannot, therefore, be admitted that a railroad corporation maintaining a highway under the authority of the State may fix its rates with a view solely to its own interests, and ignore the rights of the public. But the rights of the public would be ignored if rates for the transportation of persons or property on a railroad are exacted without reference to the fair value of the services rendered, but in order simply that the corporation may meet operating expenses, pay the interest on its obligations, and declare a dividend to stockholders.

If a railroad corporation has bonded its property for an amount that exeeds its fair value, or if its capitalization is largely fictitious, it may not impose upon the public the burden of such increased rates as may be required for the purpose of realizing profits upon such excessive valuation or fictitious capitalization; and the apparent value of the property and franchises used by the corporation, as represented by its stocks, bonds and obligations, is not alone to be considered when determining the rates that may be reasonably charged.

We hold, however, that the basis of all calculations as to the reasonableness of rates to be charged by a corporation maintaining a highway under legislative sanction must be the fair value of the property being used by it for the convenience of the public. And in order to ascertain that value, the original cost of construction, the amount expended in permanent improvements, the amount and market value of its bonds and stock, the present as compared with the original cost of construction, the probable earning capacity of the property under particular rates prescribed by statute, and the sum required to meet operating expenses, are all matters for consideration, and are to be given such weight as may be just and right in each case. We do not say that there may not be other matters to be regarded in estimating the value of the property. What the company is entitled to ask is a fair return upon the value of that which it employs for the public convenience. On the other hand, what the public is entitled to demand is that no more be exacted from it for the use of a public highway than the services rendered by it are reasonably worth. But even upon this basis, and determining the probable effect if it had been in operation during the three years immediately preceding its passage, we perceive no ground on the record for reversing the decree of the Circuit Court. On the contrary we are of opinion that as to most of the companies in question there would have been, under such rates as were established by the act of 1893, an actual loss in each of the years ending June 30, 1891, 1892 and 1893; and that, in the exceptional cases above stated, when two of the companies would have earned something above operating expenses, in particular years, the receipts or gains, above operating expenses, would have been too small to affect the general conclusion that the act, if enforced, would have deprived each of the railroad companies involved in these suits of the just compensation secured to them by the Constitution. Under the evidence there is no ground for saying that the operating expenses of any of the companies were greater than necessary.

Federal Power Commission
v. Hope Natural Gas Co.

320 U.S. 591 (1944)

MR. JUSTICE DOUGLAS delivered the opinion of the Court.

The primary issue in these cases concerns the validity under the Natural Gas Act of 1938 of a rate order issued by the Federal Power Commission reducing the rates chargeable by Hope Natural Gas Co. On a petition for review of the order made pursuant to §19(b) of the Act, the Circuit Court of Appeals set it aside, one judge dissenting. The cases are here on petitions for writs of certiorari which we granted because of the public importance of the questions presented.

Hope is a West Virginia corporation organized in 1898. It is a wholly owned subsidiary of Standard Oil Co. (N.J.). Since the date of its organization, it has been in the business of producing, purchasing and marketing natural gas in that state. It sells some of that gas to local consumer companies which receive it at the West Virginia line and distribute it in Ohio and in Pennsylvania. In July 1938 the cities of Cleveland and Akron filed complaints with the Commission charging that the rates collected by Hope from East Ohio Gas Co. (an affiliate of Hope which distributes gas in Ohio) were excessive and unreasonable. Later in 1938 the Commission on its own motion instituted an investigation to determine the reasonableness of all of Hope's interstate rates.

On May 26, 1942, the Commission entered its order and made its findings. Its order required Hope to decrease its future interstate rates so as to reflect a reduction, on an annual basis, of not less than $3,609,857 in operating revenues. And it established "just and reasonable" average rates per m.c.f. for each of the five customer companies.

Hope contended that it should be allowed a return of not less than 8%. The Commission found that an 8% return would be unreasonable but that 6½% was a fair rate of return. The rate of return, applied to the rate base of $33,712,526, would produce $2,191,314 annually, as compared with the present income of not les than $5,801,171.

The Circuit Court of Appeals set aside the order of the Commission for the following reasons. (1) It held that the rate base should reflect the "present fair value" of the property, that the Commission in determining the "value" should have considered reproduction cost and trended original cost, and that "actual legitimate cost" (prudent investment) was not the proper measure of "fair value" where price levels had changed since the investment. (2) It concluded that the well-drilling costs and overhead items in the amount of some $17,000,000 should have been included in the rate base. (3) It held that accrued depletion and depreciation and the annual allowance for that expense should be computed on the basis of "present fair value" of the property, not on the basis of "actual legitimate cost."

Order Reducing Rates. Congress has provided in §4(a) of the Natural Gas Act that all natural gas rates subject to the jurisdiction of the Commission "shall be just and reasonable, and any such rate or charge that is not just and reasonable is hereby declared to be unlawful." Sec. 5(a) gives the Commission the power, after hearing, to determine the "just and reasonable rate" to be thereafter observed and to fix the rate by order. Sec. 5(a) also empowers the Commission to order a "decrease where existing rates are unjust . . . unlawful, or are not the lowest reasonable rates." And Congress has provided in §19(b) that on review of these rate orders the "finding of the Commission as to the facts, if supported by substantial evidence, shall be conclusive." Congress, however, has provided no formula by which the "just and reasonable" rate is to be determined.

When we sustained the constitutionality of the Natural Gas Act in the Natural

Gas Pipeline Co. case, we stated that the "authority of Congress to regulate the prices of commodities in interstate commerce is at least as great under the Fifth Amendment as is that of the States under the Fourteenth to regulate the prices of commodities in intrastate commerce."

We held in *Federal Power Commission v. Natural Gas Pipeline Co.*, supra, that the Commission was not bound to the use of any single formula or combination of formulae in determining rates. Its rate-making function, moreover, involves the making of "pragmatic adjustments." And when the Commission's order is challenged in the courts, the question is whether that order "viewed in its entirety" meets the requirements of the Act. Under the statutory standard of "just and reasonable" it is the result reached not the method employed which is controlling. . . . It is not theory but the impact of the rate order which counts. If the total effect of the rate order cannot be said to be unjust and unreasonable, judicial inquiry under the Act is at an end. The fact that the method employed to reach that result may contain infirmities is not then important. Moreover, the Commission's order does not become suspect by reason of the fact that it is challenged. It is the product of expert judgment which carries a presumption of validity. And he who would upset the rate order under the Act carries the heavy burden of making a convincing showing that it is invalid because it is unjust and unreasonable in its consequences.

The rate-making process under the Act, i.e., the fixing of "just and reasonable" rates, involves a balancing of the investor and the consumer interests. Thus we stated in the Natural Gas Pipeline Co. case that "regulation does not insure that the business shall produce net revenues." But such considerations aside, the investor's interest has a legitimate concern with the financial integrity of the company whose rates are being regulated. From the investor or company point of view it is important that there be enough revenue not only for operating expenses but also for the capital costs of the business. These include service on the debt and dividends on the stock. By that standard the return to the equity owner should be commensurate with returns on investments in other enterprises having corresponding risks. That return, moreover, should be sufficient to assure confidence in the financial integrity of the enterprise, so as to maintain its credit and to attract capital. . . . The conditions under which more or less might be allowed are not important here. Nor is it important to this case to determine the various permissible ways in which any rate base on which the return is computed might be arrived at. For we are of the view that the end result in this case cannot be condemned under the Act as unjust and unreasonable from the investor or company viewpoint.

As we have noted, the Commission fixed a rate of return which permits Hope to earn $2,191,314 annually. In determining that amount it stressed the importance of maintaining the financial integrity of the company. It considered the financial history of Hope and a vast array of data bearing on the natural gas industry, related businesses, and general economic conditions. It noted that the yields on better issues of bonds of natural gas companies sold in the last few years were "close to 3 per cent." It stated that the company was a "seasoned enterprise whose risks have been minimized" by adequate provisions for depletion and depreciation (past and present) with "concurrent high profits," by "protected established markets, through affiliated distribution companies, in populous and industrialized areas," and by a supply of gas locally to meet all requirements, "except on certain peak days in the winter, which it is feasible to supplement in the future with gas from other sources." The Commission concluded, "The company's efficient management, established markets, financial record, affiliations, and its prospective business place it in a strong position to attract capital upon favorable terms when it is required."

In view of these various considerations we cannot say that an annual return of $2,191,314 is not "just and reasonable" within the meaning of the Act. Rates which enable the company to operate successfully, to maintain its financial integrity, to attract capital, and to compensate its investors for the risks assumed certainly cannot be condemned as invalid, even though they might produce only a meager return on the so-called "fair value" rate base. In that connection it will be recalled that Hope contended for a rate base of $66,000,000 computed on reproduction cost new. The Commission points out that if that rate base were accepted, Hope's average rate of return for the four-year period from 1937–1940 would amount to 3.27%. During that period Hope earned an annual average return of about 9% on the average investment. It asked for no rate increases. Its properties were well maintained and operated. As the Commission says, such a modest rate of 3.27% suggests an "inflation of the base on which the rate has been computed." The incongruity between the actual operations and the return computed on the basis of reproduction cost suggests that the Commission was wholly justified in rejecting the latter as the measure of the rate base.

In The Supreme Court of Illinois May Term, 1973

Brief Amicus Curiae of Central Illinois Light Company, Central Illinois Public Service Company, Commonwealth Edison Company and Illinois Power Company

INTRODUCTION

The Amici Curiae are Central Illinois Light Company, an electric and gas utility, Central Illinois Public Service Company, an electric and gas utility, Commonwealth Edison Company, an electric utility, and Illinois Power Company, an electric and gas utility.

Each of the Amici provides service within the State of Illinois and is regulated as to its retail electric and gas rates by the Commission. The Amici served at year-end 1972 approximately 3.5 million electric and 660 thousand gas customers. At June 1, 1973, the Amici had outstanding approximately $2.8 billion of bonds and other long-term debt, $600 million in preferred stock, and 82 million shares of common stock which on that date had a market value of about $2.4 billion. These utilities estimate that they must during the next five years raise more than $4 billion dollars from the public sale of securities in order to meet the demands of their customers for utility services.

One of the issues raised in the case at bar is whether there should be a change in the requirement of Illinois law that utilities be allowed to earn a fair rate of return on the fair value of their property devoted to public service. Chicago has urged that they be limited to a fair rate of return on the original cost of that property. The issue is one of major importance to the Amici, other private utilities regulated as to rates by the Commission, the customers they serve, and investors. It is the position of the Amici that the fair value concept should and must be retained.

In the case before the Court, the Commission employed the fair value concept. Chicago, in its appeal to the Court, acknowledges that the concept has long been the law in Illinois, but asserts that Chicago has continuously objected to the concept since at least 1953, and urges the Court to overrule its earlier decisions requiring a fair value rate base.

Chicago relies upon the order of the Commission in CIPS (Central Illinois Public Service Company, Docket 57300, March 13, 1973). Commencing with CIPS, the Commission has in five cases made it abundantly clear that, insofar as the Commission is concerned, the fair value concept has been discarded and has been replaced with the original cost method, the precedents of the Court and the legislative history of the Utilities Act notwithstanding.

Because the Commission's adoption of original cost will affect all pending and future rate cases if allowed to stand, the Amici urge that the Court once more affirm that the law in Illinois is that rates shall be determined on the basis of fair value of the properties used and useful in rendering utility services.

The removal of the uncertainties created by the Commission's recent orders and the affirmation of the fair value principle are of immediate and substantial importance to the utilities, consumers and investors. Investors have purchased the securities of Illinois public utilities on the apparently safe assumption that fair value would not overnight disappear from the law of rate-making in Illinois. While obviously neither the utilities nor any agency of this State could or should guarantee that this or any other law may not be changed in the public interest, nevertheless investors might reasonably expect that such a change would not occur except in an orderly manner and certainly not in the absence of proceedings, whether administrative, judicial or legislative, in which they and other interested persons would have an opportunity to be heard and in which the question could be resolved on a complete record. No such hearings have been held. The Commission's holding in CIPS was not foreshadowed. Suddenly there was the decision and suddenly original cost replaced fair value for rate-making purposes.

The immediate and harsh economic reality of the Commission's new position is that the rate bases of Illinois utilities have been substantially reduced. From the standpoint of the investment community, the sudden disappearance of these real values represents a shattering and wholly unexpected occurrence. And it is in this community that Illinois utilities must compete with other utilities and businesses for enormous amounts of capital in order to fulfill their obligations to meet necessary demands for their services. Utilities cannot defer or forego expenditures for this purpose even if they were to choose to do so; as a matter of law they are obligated to provide services upon request. But while Illinois utilities must, therefore, constantly seek additional capital, there is no corresponding obligation on the part of investors to purchase their securities.

CONTINUANCE OF FAIR VALUE RATE-MAKING IS CRITICAL TO MEETING THE PROBLEM OF INFLATION PRESENTLY FACED BY REGULATED PUBLIC UTILITIES

The importance of the fair value rate base as a means of dealing with inflation is the subject which the Amici wish to bring to the attention of the Court.

Regulation requires the use of some standard to establish rates which will produce an adequate return to investors in the enterprise. Telephone, electric and gas distribution utilities, and some others, are regulated by the rate base—rate of return method, a method suited to one of their unique economic characteristics— they are capital intensive.

There are three basic approaches to rate base valuation: original cost, reproduction cost new less depreciation, and fair value. An original cost rate base is established by reference to the historic cost of the utility plant less the amount of depreciation charged as recorded on the books of the company. A reproduction cost new rate base reflects the current cost of the utility plant less the actual depreciation of the existing plant determined by observation and engineering evaluation. Fair value is a composite method which considers original cost less book depreciation and reproduction cost new less actual depreciation with each factor given the weight judged appropriate in the individual case. The most important difference in the original cost and fair value rate-making methods lies in the manner in which price inflation is treated.

The Impact of Inflation

Utilities are required to make substantial investments in plant in order to conduct their business. They are, in economic terms, highly capital intensive. For example, electric utilities typically have in the order of five times as much investment per revenue dollar as the oil and steel industries and twenty times that of the automotive and electrical [equipment] industries.

Utility plant tends to be long-lived—in the thirty-year range for certain electric and telephone plant and in excess of fifty years for certain gas plant. Consequently there is a slower turn-over of the plant or earnings base than in industries whose earnings base—such as the inventory in a dry-goods business—is being sold and replaced at current prices at a rapid pace. The dry-goods merchant, with rapid turn-over, recovers his investment in his inventory very soon after he makes it and, therefore, receives dollars with approximately the same purchasing power as those he spent to acquire it. The utility, on the other hand, being capital intensive, recovers its investment only over a very long period of time. In 1973, for example, it will still have substantial unrecovered investments reflecting dollars spent, say, in 1950. If the utility is allowed 1973 earnings, measured in terms of 1950 dollars, it will obviously be receiving much cheaper and less valuable dollars than it originally received.

The economic reality, therefore, is that the risks of inflation are greater for utilities than for almost any other industry.

At the same time that a high rate of inflation is occurring, utilities are faced with growing demands for service. These demands the utilities must meet. They are not free as are other industries to defer investment in plant expansion to a future date when profitability would not be impaired by adverse economic conditions. Price increases, and therefore rate cases, are necessary if utilities are to preserve the value of existing investment and attract the necessary capital to finance the expansion of their plants.

The Need To Consider Inflation in Rate Cases

The principal objective of utility regulation is to achieve the beneficial results of competition in terms of good service and reasonable rates. Preservation of the real capital of public utilities during long-term inflation does not conflict with the intent of regulation to emulate the constructive results of competition. To the contrary, preservation of utility real capital by recognition of inflation in the regulatory process is entirely consistent with the competitive standard, and this policy will have an important effect on the ability of the regulated utility to attract new capital in competitive money markets.

The physical resources of successful competitive industries will increase in both nominal value and nominal earning power during inflation. Regulatory treatment of utility resources, to be consistent with the competitive economic standard in this respect, should provide for protection from inflation akin to that available to comparable resources in the competitive area. To require utilities to sustain impairment of real capital during inflation, by relying upon nominal dollar values in the regulatory process, would be a departure from the competitive standard and wholly unrelated to the principal objective of utility regulation.

There are many instances of formal recognition of long-term inflation in the unregulated sector. Collective bargaining agreements have provided for cost of living wage adjustments, pegged to the Consumer Price Index, for some years. Congress has included a similar price-level adjustment in the statute covering military retirement pensions. Commercial lease rentals, construction contracts and a host of commodity-supply agreements, for example, make provision for future price adjustment to reflect changes in such variables as the prime rate of interest, specified price indexes, materials costs, and wage rates.

The Difference in Methods

Original cost or book cost is a permanently fixed dollar figure which remains unchanged over the life of a unit of property. An original cost rate base is obtained by deducting book depreciation charges from the original cost of the property. Book depreciation is charged each year over the estimated life of the property without regard to its actual condition. Any dollar recorded in the property accounts is the equal of any other dollar so recorded. Original cost disregards, or is incapable of reflecting, differences in the purchasing power of dollars invested over a long period of years at varying price levels.

Original cost ceases to be an economically valid measurement during long-term inflation, because as plant additions are made at different times and at different price levels, book cost will be comprised of a diverse collection of dollars of widely differing purchasing power—each of which is considered the equal of all of the others for rate-making purposes. As inflation advances, there is a widening excess of current cost over book cost and the value of dollars received currently is sharply less than the value of the dollars originally invested in plant.

In contrast, reproduction cost or current cost, which is the equivalent of original cost in today's purchasing power, is given weight in fair value rate-making. The translation of original cost dollars into current cost dollars does not add to or subtract from the purchasing power actually invested. Reproduction cost less actual depreciation only reflects the total purchasing power of each of the remaining dollars invested at earlier dates and under differing price levels. In the fair value process, the deduction of actual depreciation will reflect the deterioration, including obsolescence, experienced by the existing plant.

In public utility rate cases, the effects of inflation on investors are treated differently, depending on the types of securities issued and the ratio of each in the capital structure. Bondholders and preferred stockholders are limited by contract to a specific return measured in dollars. Investors in such fixed income senior securities have no claim for protection from all of the economic effects of inflation. The principal effort of the utility for holders of its senior securities during a period of continuing inflation will be to maintain earnings at a sufficient level to provide the margins of protection, or coverages of fixed charges, needed to preserve the investment quality or market ratings of those securities.

The status of the common stock capital is materially different. Common stock is sold and purchased with the reasonable expectation that earnings will be sufficient to offset the economic effects of inflation or to be competitive with the earnings performance of alternative investments of generally comparable quality.

The inflation hazard to the common stock capital is dealt with by according reproduction cost or current cost less actual depreciation a weight which takes into consideration the ratio of common stock to total capital. Stating the investment of the common equity holder in terms of reproduction cost new less depreciation gives some weight, within the limits of advances in technology, to going levels of prices, whereas historic original cost does not. As explained by Mr. Justice Schaefer in *City of Alton v. Commerce Commission,* the fair value concept "provides a flexible rate-making standard which is equally applicable in periods of rising and falling price levels" and that "the significant figure is the rate of return on common stock valued at fair value."

The original cost rate base was initially proposed in the 1920's and 1930's. The extensive literature on this subject makes clear that advocates of the original cost rate base in the 1920's and 1930's had no expectation of long-term inflation. There is really no reason why they should have anticipated this. For more than half a century, the U.S. economy had experienced largely stable or relative depressed price levels.

Price inflation was generally considered to be only a short-term problem, associated with the wartime economies of 1861–1865 and 1916–1920 and with occasional short-lived "boom" periods. The then prevailing view contemplated cyclical price behavior under the theory that what goes up must come down.

Advocates of the book cost rate base generally agreed that an inability to cope with a prolonged period of inflation was its major weakness. Professor Emeritus James C. Bonbright of Columbia University, originally one of the advocates of the original cost rate base, has since endorsed recognition of current costs in the rate base. In his 1961 book, *Principles of Public Utility Rates,* pp. 274, 280 (Columbia University Press) Professor Bonbright favored the restatement of book cost in terms of current cost because of inflation.

A principal advantage often ascribed to original cost (and one that the Commission relied on in CIPS) is that costs are based on verifiable accounting data, and cost determinations can be made with ease, speed and definiteness. On economic grounds, however, conventionally administered original cost treatment disregards changes in value. Justice Jackson in his dissent in *Federal Power Commission v. Hope Natural Gas Co.,* 320 U.S. 591, 643 (1944) stated:

> To make a fetish of mere accounting is to shield from examination the deeper forces, movements, and conditions which should govern rates. Even as a recording of current transactions, bookkeeping is hardly an exact science. As a representation of the condition and trend of a business, it uses symbols of certainty to express values that actually are in constant flux. . . . However, our quest for certitude is so ardent that we pay an irrational reverence to a technique which uses symbols of certainty, even though, experience again and again warns us that they are delusive. . . .

While the inexactness of various reproduction cost estimates as a means of measuring inflation is sometimes criticized (and exaggerated), the proposed substitute is an addition to rate of return to take into account the effects of inflation. Determination of that added increment which must be based on a judgment of the effect of inflation on others is frequently far more inexact and less explicit than the reproduction cost estimates which it proposes to displace.

Since the Court last considered these arguments, no changes have occurred in theory or in practice which in any way bestow current validity to them. The alleged problems have if anything become less difficult. The statistical data with respect to costs, trends, and inflation are now available in greater quantity and have been refined and improved in quality and accuracy. Trend factors are available which simplify deriving reproduction costs. Modern statistical sampling methods reduce greatly the work involved in determining the amount of actual depreciation. Data processing in conjunction with modern computers facilitates the collection, analysis and verification of the reproduction cost data.

What the Commission substituted for reproduction cost studies of the actual property being considered in CIPS was its judgment of the rate of return necessary to reflect "current economic conditions." The Commission's order in CIPS does not set forth any findings which show the basis for its judgment. It is impossible to determine what if any portion of the rate of return on original cost allowed in that case takes into account the effects of inflation on the common stock investment which supports the utility plant.

Difficulties in according proper weight to reproduction cost studies of actual property are insignificant when compared to the difficulty of *verifying* and *reviewing* a determination of a rate of return which apparently treats the effect of inflation on existing investment as well as allows for the attraction of new investment. The practical effect in most original cost jurisdictions is that a rate of return which serves both functions is neither reviewable nor reviewed.

From the standpoint of the consumer, the investor and the utilities, the *fair value concept is proof positive that regulatory consideration will be given to the effect of inflation*—and of deflation should this economic event again occur. That reproduction values are given weight in arriving at the appropriate rate base provides some assurance that the utility will, when the time comes, have resources to replace aging facilities. Also, in determining the fair value of a utility's rate base, consideration is given to the condition of its properties, the extent to which they have in fact depreciated, and the presence or absence of obsolescence—all matters of importance to consumers and investors.

The fair value rate base provides the Commission with a practical approach to the problem of long-term and continuing inflation. The strength of the fair value rate base is that it lies somewhere between the lowest and highest possible valuations so it is essentially a balancing of consumer and investor interests. Each must be recognized and given consideration in the rate-making process.

In the Matter of

American Telephone & Telegraph Co.

57 F.C.C. 2d 960 (1976)

BY THE COMMISSION:

This case comes before us on exceptions to the Initial Decision (ID) of the presiding Administrative Law Judge (ALJ) released October 14, 1975. It was designated for hearing . . . following a tariff filing made by the American Telephone and Telegraph Company and the Bell System Operating Companies (AT&T or

Bell), respondents herein, seeking a rate increase and an increase in the prescribed rate of return. . . .

INTRODUCTION

This proceeding represents the third time the Commission has considered the fair rate of return of the Bell System for interstate and foreign operations. . . . we determined in 1967 that a fair rate of return for Bell was 7–7-½ percent and ordered rate reductions to reduce the return to this level. Five years later, in our Decision on the first phase of Docket No. 19129 (1972–hereinafter the Phase I decision), we prescribed a rate of return of 8-½ percent and permitted Bell to increase rates by an amount designed to realize this return. In both of these proceedings, we indicated our view that the cost of capital was as real as other necessary business costs and decided that the most appropriate manner by which to regulate the overall earnings from AT&T's jurisdictional activities was through a determination of the cost of capital, expressed as a percent rate of return. The overall rate of return was found to be the weighted average of the cost of embedded debt and the cost of equity based upon a debt-equity ratio (capital structure) fixed in such a way as to raise capital "at the lowest possible cost consistent with [the Bell System's] overall responsibility to provide modern, efficient service at reasonable rates and to maintain the financial integrity of the enterprise." Since the cost of debt can be calculated, based upon the weighted average of the coupon interest rates of all outstanding long- and short-term debt issues, the principal determination to be made in calculating the fair rate of return is the current cost of equity.

. . . [W]e instituted the present investigation to determine what increases, if any, had occurred in AT&T's cost of equity capital since the Phase I decision. At that time, the cost of equity was found to be 10-½ percent. . . . [We] confined the issues in this proceeding to the present cost of equity and the fair overall rate of return of the Bell System. . . .

CAPITAL STRUCTURE

In designating this case for hearing, we indicated that the capital structure of AT&T which then existed was 49 percent debt, 51 percent equity. This represented an increase in debt both over the ratio in 1967 and in 1972 (45-55). . . .

AT&T now contends, however, that the increased debt ratio in its existing capital structure renders its securities more risky than would be the case with a 45-55 debt-equity ratio. This is one of several factors, Bell asserts, which endanger its Aaa bond rating. Downgrading of its bonds, AT&T claims, will be detrimental to the rate payer, as it will cause interest rates on new debt issues to rise. Accordingly, AT&T states, we should impute a 45-55 percent debt-equity ratio and permit it a higher return on equity so it can achieve this figure. In further support of its contention, Bell points to our recent decision in the Comsat Rate Case, Docket

No. 16070, FCC 75-1304 in which we imputed a debt ratio of 45 percent to a company which had no outstanding debt.

While the ALJ used the 49-51 ratio in his rate of return calculations, he also made a finding that the percent of debt should be reduced in order to give Bell greater flexibility in choosing debt or equity financing at a given point in time. We disagree that the record demonstrates this to be the case. While any substantial increase in leverage over a 50 percent debt ratio might affect the company's bond ratings, we cannot agree with Bell that the present capital structure is inappropriate. If the company intends to issue additional equity to return to a 45-55 ratio, this is a management decision, but we cannot find that either a 45-55 or 49-51 ratio subjects the rate payers to unreasonable high costs of capital or the company's investors to unreasonable risks. Accordingly, we shall use the present capital structure of 49 percent debt, 51 percent equity for purposes of this proceeding.

COST OF EQUITY

We now turn to the principal issue for consideration, the Bell System's cost of equity. Unlike embedded debt, this is not a figure which can be objectively calculated or for which there is any one methodology of measurement. For this reason, three of the parties herein presented the testimony of a total of 8 expert witnesses on the issue of cost of equity. These witnesses proposed several methodologies for determination of this issue and arrived at conclusions as much as five percentage points apart.

Bell's principal proposed methodology is based on the proposition that equity investments are for the most part riskier than debt investments in the same company. Accordingly, AT&T asserts that investors require a "risk premium" on their equity funds. It claims that, based upon three "representative" groups of equity investments (the 425 Standard and Poor's industrial firms, the quality growth series, and the institution holdings series), the minimum spread between bond yields and equity market returns is over five percentage points. When this risk premium is applied to an 8-1/2 percent bond yield, for example, the minimum market return on equity would be 13-1/2 percent. Bell recognizes, however, that in a period of inflation the 5 percent premium may be difficult to achieve. In any event, AT&T maintains that investors require a minimum equity return which is about 50 percent above current bond yields, or 12-3/4 to 13-1/2 percent on bond yields in the 8-1/2–9 percent range.

AT&T further alleges it requires a minimum of 50 percent premium based upon the relative risk of its equity compared to Standard and Poor's 425 industrials and the other series listed above. . . . Accordingly, it concludes that its equity risk premium must be at least as high as that which it claims institutional investors require for these series investments.

This result, AT&T contends, is also supported through use of a discounted cash flow (DCF) approach. DCF purports to measure the cost of equity by adding a projected growth factor to the current dividend yield on common stock. Using this approach, Bell adds a 7 percent expected growth factor to its 7 percent current dividend yield to produce a 14 percent cost of equity. The growth factor is derived not from Bell's own corporate historical growth but from the aggregate historical growth of Standard and Poor's 425 industrials.

The ID also dismissed Bell's 50 percent risk premium approach as unsupported in the record, although the ALJ found that equity investors do require some premium for risk. The Trial Staff supports his conclusion but also indicates that, even if the institutional investor would normally require at least a 50 percent risk premium, AT&T's shareholders include a high percentage of non-institutional investors. It asserts that there is no indication that private investors require such a risk premium.

Essentially, the ALJ endorsed the views of the opponents of each method and rejected each one out of hand. Rather than adopting any of these methods, then, the ALJ considered the views of each expert witness in light of his background and the biases caused by that background. By balancing these biases, the ALJ concluded that the rate of return should be set no higher than 10 percent. As indicated above, he made no findings as to the cost of equity.

We cannot agree that each of the methods proposed by the expert witnesses should be completely dismissed. Nor can we find any one computational approach so superior that we should adopt it as the only appropriate method for determining AT&T's cost of equity. However, this is not to say that a combination of approaches cannot be helpful in determining the cost of equity capital. For example, while we agree with the ALJ that the record does not support the 50 percent premium advocated by AT&T, it is clear from the record evidence that some premium is required to account for the additional risk associated with equity over that associated with debt realized by investors in the same company. Accordingly, we agree with all parties here in that equity investors generally require a greater return than investors in the same company's debt, but we cannot put a specific figure on this premium.

In this we are consistent with the findings in our Phase I decision. Debt is senior to equity in claim on assets and income, and accordingly investors require a higher return on equity to compensate for this additional risk. However, even assuming arguendo that the record supported Bell's claim that institutional investors require this premium to be 50 percent, this is not determinative of the risk premium associated with Bell's common stock. Although the record is not entirely undisputed on this point, it is clear that a substantial number of AT&T's shares are held by non-institutional investors for whom the risk premium may be somewhat different. Therefore, we cannot accept AT&T's assertion of a 50 percent risk premium.

Furthermore, contrary to Bell's position, we believe the record demonstrates that investment in Bell's common stock is significantly less risky than the aggregate of Standard and Poor's 425 industrials or the other series which are listed above. . . . Risk-averting investors are interested in stability of earnings and preservation of principal. The record shows that the earnings volatility of AT&T as measured by the standard deviation in the earned return over a period of years, is considerably less than the aggregates of the Standard and Poor's equity series proposed by Bell. In addition, experience has shown that Bell stock has provided better protection against downside price loss than the market as a whole.

One method used in the Comsat Rate Case, but which has no record support here, is to determine the value of a risk-free investment, such as U.S. Government bonds, and to add to this a risk factor based upon the increment of risk which a company has over a riskless investment. While AT&T discussed this approach in the oral argument of this case, there is no record evidence which would support a holding as to the relative risk of AT&T. . . . In sum, while we believe the risk premium approach as used in the Comsat case, or a variation thereof, may have some validity as an alternative approach for the determination of Bell's cost of equity, we have no record evidence here which would permit us to utilize this methodology.

CONCLUSIONS ON THE CURRENT COST OF EQUITY

In the preceding paragraphs it has been shown that changes in economic and financial conditions since our 1972 Decision . . . dictate a higher return on Bell's equity capital than was allowed at that time. However, for the reasons discussed above, none of Bell's contentions, taken individually or collectively, support Bell's claim that it requires a return on equity of 13-½ to 14-½ percent.

The ALJ did not make a finding as to the cost of equity capital in his determination of Bell's overall rate of return, although he rendered findings regarding some of the specific contentions of the parties in support of their claimed cost of equity. Our conclusion as to the cost of Bell's equity capital is based on consideration of the ALJ's findings, all testimony and other record evidence, proposed findings, exceptions, briefs, and the record of the oral argument.

We have indicated that no individual method can be determinative of the appropriate return on Bell's equity capital. In the final analysis we must apply our informed judgment to the range of estimates which we have found to be helpful indicators of the cost of equity. In particular, on the strength of the composite of the methods proposed by Dr. Carleton, considered in the light of the entire record of this proceeding, we conclude that 12.0 percent is the cost of Bell's equity capital. This return on equity reflects the changed economic and financial conditions since our 1972 Decision in Phase I of Docket 19129. We believe that a 12.0 percent return will enable Bell to attract additional equity capital at terms that are fair to existing shareholders and, at the same time, this return will provide for rate levels that are just and reasonable and in the public interest. In addition, the increased earnings resulting from this higher return on equity will help arrest the decline in, if not improve, Bell's post-tax interest coverage level.

Summarizing our findings, then . . . the cost of embedded debt is 6.9 percent and the capital structure is 49 percent debt, 51 percent equity with preferred stock included with common for this purpose. . . . The cost of equity is found to be 12.0 percent.

CONCLUSIONS ON RATE OF RETURN

From these findings, it is a routine calculation to determine the fair rate of return to be prescribed for the interstate and foreign services of the Bell System:

Item	Proportion of capital (percent)	Cost rate (percent)	Proportion of total cost (percent)
Debt	49	6.9	3.38
Total equity	51	12.0	6.12
Total cost			9.50

This 9.5 percent figure represents a fair rate of return to be prescribed for AT&T's interstate and foreign operations. It will allow Bell to compete in the capital market and give existing stockholders a reasonable return on their investment. It will also, we believe, help prevent the downgrading of the company's bonds and preclude further erosion in its interest coverage. Accordingly, we prescribe this figure, and Bell may set its rates in order to yield a 9.5 percent overall rate of return from interstate and foreign operations.

As in our decisions in 1967 and 1972 on rate of return, we believe that a range of rate of return should be established in order to provide an incentive to increase productivity and efficiency. In both of these earlier proceedings, the range was set at .5 percent above the prescribed return. From the record evidence, our analysis of present economic conditions, and the testimony of the parties at oral argument, we believe this range is appropriate here. This is also consistent with the finding of the ALJ as to rate of return, which we affirm, that AT&T should be permitted "a level or range of interstate earnings not to exceed 10%." Accordingly, we shall not require any downward adjustment of AT&T's overall interstate rates provided its overall rate of return does not exceed 10 percent.

Accordingly, IT IS ORDERED, pursuant to Section 205 of the Communications Act of 1934, as amended, That the fair rate of return of the Bell System respondents from interstate and foreign services IS PRESCRIBED at 9.5 percent.

IT IS FURTHER ORDERED, That the provisions of Section 61.58 of the Commission's Rules and Regulations, 47 C.F.R. 61.58 ARE WAIVED, and tariff revisions necessary to increase AT&T's rate of return to prescribed levels may be effective not less than 30 days from the filing thereof.

CHAPTER 13

RATE STRUCTURE

Once the rate base and rate of return have been established, the regulators must establish the rate structure. What rates will be charged for the different types of customers (for example, residential, commercial, and industrial) served by a utility? For many years regulators did little more than endorse the rate structures devised by the utilities provided that the expected revenues did not exceed the utility's revenues requirements. Recently, more and more commissions have concerned themselves with the design of rate structures.

One of the major issues of rate structure has been the amount that peak and off-peak users should be charged. The Atlantic Seaboard case examined this important issue for interstate natural gas pipelines. A pipeline's capacity is largely determined by the northern states' winter heating needs. Pipelines do transmit natural gas during the summer for industrial users, however. The price to be charged these off-peak users was decided by the Federal Power Commission (FPC) in this case. The FPC allocated Atlantic Seaboard's overhead element fifty-fifty between demand (depending on time of use) and commodity (per unit consumed) charges. If the FPC had assigned more of the basic capital costs of the pipeline to winter heating uses, would this have encouraged or discouraged the construction of pipeline capacity? Would Atlantic Seaboard's existing pipeline capacity be used more during the summer months? Based on your answers to these questions, do you feel the Commission's allocation rule is consistent with economic efficiency?

The Madison Gas and Electric case is one of the most sophisticated rate structure cases. It takes explicit account of the incremental (marginal) costs of serving customers in various classes and distinguishes between serving them during peak and off-peak periods. The problems of setting rates on the basis of marginal costs are not small, however. The commissions that have legislated in this direction still have quite a way to go. For instance, the marginal cost of serving customers at night is much lower than during the day. Why is this so? It may not be worthwhile to adopt time-of-day metering because of the cost of installing and operating the necessary meters. Where would the savings to offset the increased costs of metering come from?

The United States Postal Service case concerns the establishment of postal rates for different classes of mail (for example, first class, second class). A major issue is the proper role of delivery priority in the rate structure. This is illustrated by the Postal Service's proposal for a new mail category—citizens' rate mail. The rate for "personal" correspondence would be 13¢ compared to the 16¢ rate for first-class mail. Citizen's rate mail would be separated from first-class mail and deferred if there were delivery problems. Does this difference in service justify the 3¢ rate difference? Would the Postal Service incur less costs in order to process the citizens' rate mail? Even if this mail was deferred on only a few days of the year? Finally, this new mail rate was supported by greeting card companies, but opposed by magazine publishers. What do you think accounts for the different positions of these companies?

In the Matters of

Atlantic Seaboard Corporation and Virginia Gas Transmission Corporation

11 F.P.C. 43 (1952)

These matters are before the Commission on appeal from the decision, 11 F.P.C. 486, and accompanying order filed herein by the presiding examiner on November 7, 1951. In such decision and order the presiding examiner found, among other things, that the rates contained in the presently effective tariffs of Atlantic Seaboard Corp. (Seaboard) and Virginia Gas Transmission Corp. (Virginia Gas) are, each of them, unjust, unreasonable, and unduly discriminatory. And, after finding that which was conceived by him to be the just and reasonable rates and charges, "coupled with a proper heat content adjustment provision," the presiding examiner ordered Seaboard and Virginia Gas to file new schedules setting forth the rates and charges so found proper.

Prior to 1950, applicants owned and operated a natural-gas transmission pipeline system consisting principally of a high-pressure, 20-inch continuous pipeline some 420 miles in length extending from Seaboard's Boldman (Kentucky) compressor station, through West Virginia, Virginia, and Maryland, to a point of connection with the facilities of The Manufacturers Light & Heat Co. (Manufacturers) at a point on the Maryland-Pennsylvania boundary. On January 7, 1950, applicants commenced the operation of a newly constructed 26-inch pipeline some 268 miles in length extending from the vicinity of the Cobb (West Virginia) compressor station of United Fuel Gas Co. (United Fuel) through Virginia to Rockville, Md., where it is interconnected with the 20-inch line. The portions of the two lines, with their respective appurtenant facilities, including compressor stations and measuring and regulating stations, which are situated in the States of Kentucky, West Virginia, and Maryland are owned and operated by Seaboard, and the portions which lie in the State of Virginia are owned and operated by Virginia Gas. The last-named company is a wholly owned subsidiary of Seaboard, and both are subsidiaries of Columbia Gas System, Inc. (Columbia).

All natural gas transported by applicants through these facilities is sold by them at wholesale for resale to consumers in the District of Columbia, and the States of West Virginia, Virginia, Maryland, and Pennsylvania. No sales are made by applicants directly to the consumers. Practically all of the gas so sold is purchased from United Fuel, an affiliate in the Columbia system.

In this, as in most of our natural gas rate proceedings, we are confronted with a cost allocation problem. Applicants, the staff, and Washington each introduced evidence showing that which they conceived to be the proper method of allocation. The examiner in his intermediate decision did not agree with any of them in respect to all items.

Because this question of proper allocation of costs is of such great importance in practically all rate proceedings before us—and usually, as here, is one of the most controversial of issues—we consider it appropriate to set out at some length our views as to proper methods of cost allocation so that all may be informed and guided in situations, which may be substantially similar to the conditions here present.

The controversy generally engendered in rate proceedings as to the proper method for allocation of costs stems largely from the fact that the relative importance of the demand (capacity) and commodity (volume) functions cannot be measured with scientific accuracy. In the final analysis the allocations of cost to these respective functions are and must be largely dictated by informed judgment.

The three witnesses who testified on this subject in this proceeding generally divided costs between demand and commodity factors or elements. Demand costs were characterized as those which are associated with capacity of the facilities, whereas commodity costs were deemed associated with the volume or quantity of gas delivered.

A natural-gas transmission facility performs both a capacity and a volumetric function. In this sense, it is a joint facility, which thus presents the problem, always difficult, of allocating joint costs.

In this present case, applicants, generally speaking, allocated fixed costs or expenses, except return on investment and related income taxes, to the capacity, or demand, function. Return and income taxes were allocated equally between the demand and volume. Variable costs were assigned to the volumetric or commodity function. The staff, on the other hand, apportioned all fixed costs or expenses equally between demand and volume, but, like applicants' witness, assigned variable expenses to commodity.

In brief, applicants' witness holds to the theory that the capital outlay for a transmission facility varies with the size or the capacity of the facility; that the fixed expenses associated with this capital outlay do not vary with the volume of gas transported; and, therefore, such expenses should be assigned to the demand or capacity function. All other annual relatively nonvariable costs were treated by such witness the same as the fixed expenses on the capital outlay. As noted before, an important exception to this theory is made in respect to return on investment and income taxes, both of which are allocated equally between the demand and volumetric functions.

We are unable, however, to accept the premise that merely because certain costs do not vary with use they automatically become in toto demand or capacity costs. A pipeline would not normally be built to supply peak service, that is to say, service on the peak days only. We know from our administration of section 7 of the Natural Gas Act, which involves the issuance of certificates of public convenience and necessity, that pipelines are built to supply service not only on the few peak days but on all days throughout the year. In proving the economic feasibility of the project in certificate proceedings, reliance is placed upon the annual as well as the peak deliveries. Stated another way, the capital outlay for the pipeline facility is made—and justified—not only for service on the peak days but for service throughout the year. Both capacity and annual use are important considerations in the conception of the project and in the issuance of certificates of public convenience and necessity. Both capacity and volume, therefore, are what are known as cost factors or incidences in respect to the capital outlay for a pipeline project. It follows that reasonably accurate results can be achieved only by allocating the fixed expenses flowing from the capital outlay to both operating functions, viz., capacity and volume.

The soundness of the foregoing conclusion will be made clear by a simple illustration. If fixed expenses are assigned wholly to the demand or capacity function, then gas service which is interrupted on peak days will not share in any of the fixed costs. Conceivably under such an allocation large quantities of natural gas could be sold to industrials 360 days of the year and interrupted on five or so peak days, and such gas would bear none of the costs incurred in constructing the pipeline facility. In other words, under a strict application of this theory, the interruptible service would not bear any depreciation expense, return, income taxes, or any part of the other fixed expenses associated with the capital outlay. This would be so even though the capital outlay made the interruptible service possible by providing the means of transportation used extensively by such assumed interruptible service. As pointed out in the Colorado Interstate case, this would result in free transportation for the interruptible gas. Under such a procedure, as has been demonstrated in our rate proceedings, the interruptible gas would be charged nothing for return (compensation of capital) while, at the same time, the failure to allocate any of the fixed expenses to that service would result in very high profit (return) therefrom.

Applicants' witness assigned 50 percent of the return and 50 percent of income taxes, which follows return, to the volume of gas transported, that is to the commodity function. It must be evident that as far as cost incidence is concerned return and depreciation are alike as two peas in a pod. In the public utility sense return is compensation for the use of capital during the service life of the pipeline or other plant facility, whereas depreciation expense represents the return of capital outlay to the natural-gas company during that same service life. One is a return on capital whereas the other is a return of capital. Clearly, consistency requires that both costs be treated alike. Both costs are incurred in respect to capacity and volumetric functions, and, therefore, should be apportioned to both functions.

Similarly the other fixed expenses are incurred in respect to both capacity and volumetric functions. Thus, the labor involved in operating transmission mains may not vary greatly in the course of a year, but this does not mean that the costs thereof are incurred solely for demand or capacity service. Quite the contrary is true. The costs are incurred in connection with the operation of the mains throughout the year. The operation of mains is necessary to get all the gas transported, hence all sales should bear a share of this item of expense.

To reiterate—and emphasize—fixed costs or expenses are incurred for both peak use and annual use in respect to both demand and volumetric functions. They are important cost factors in respect to both services. To achieve a reasonable equitable result—they must be apportioned to both services.

The determination of how much of the fixed costs is assignable to each function, demand or volume, involves judgment. It can only be done by judgment

inasmuch as the facts upon which the determination must be made are not susceptible to mathematical computation. We know that both functions are very significant. This is not a case where one form of joint use greatly predominates. It is our
opinion that these significant cost factors should be weighted equally, that is to
say, 50 percent should be assigned to demand and 50 percent to commodity. In
this manner all gas transported by the pipeline will share in all of the various
kinds of expenses incurred to transport the gas. Gas which is associated with
delivery on the peak day or a group of peak days will share in the total expenses
including the total of the fixed charges. That gas which is not associated with
deliveries on the peak day or group of peak days will not share in 50 percent of the
fixed costs. This solution recognizes the principle that costs associated with peak
service are higher than those which are associated with interruptible or off-peak
service. In our opinion it reasonably assigns these heavier costs to the service
associated with peak deliveries. By the same token, while relieving off-peak service
from sharing in 50 percent of the fixed expenses, it, nevertheless, assigns to that
service some or all of the costs incurred to construct and operate the pipeline. As
stated previously, the equal weighting assigned to the two cost factors of demand
and commodity for the purpose of allocating fixed cost or expenses is a judgment
determination. It can never be otherwise for the allocation of joint costs is not and
cannot be an exact science.

Therefore, for the reasons set forth in the foregoing discussion, we find that the
examiner erred in allocating the following items of operating expense wholly to
the demand component of the costs: measuring and regulating station—supplies
and expenses; operation of transmission mains—labor; operation of transmission
mains—supplies and expenses; and transmission maps and records. Similarly, we
find that the examiner erred in allocating the following items of maintenance
expenses wholly to the demand component: pumping station structures; measuring and regulating station structures; other transmission system structures; mains;
and measuring and regulating station equipment. For the same reasons, we also
find that the examiner erroneously allocated to the demand factor substantially all
taxes other than income taxes. It is our judgment that each of such above-enumer-
ated items of expense should be weighted equally; that is, 50 percent to demand
and 50 percent to commodity.

In thus setting forth principles which we believe should be applied in the allocation of costs, we have explained why we have reversed the examiner as to his
findings and conclusions with respect to the allocation of those items of expense
heretofore specified. As to all other items, we approve the several findings and
conclusions of the examiner and believe that they adequately and properly support the allocations made. Further, in addition to the reasons hereinbefore set
forth as to why, in our judgment, depreciation expense should be allocated to the
demand and commodity components equally, we also approve and adopt the
findings and conclusions of the examiner as to this item.

Case 2-U-7423

Application of Madison Gas and Electric Company for Authority to Increase its Electric and Gas Rates

(1974)

Madison Gas and Electric Company (Applicant) filed an application with the [Wisconsin Public Service] Commission on March 3, 1972 . . . to increase its rates for electric and gas service . . . .
. . . Intervenors offered evidence relating to electric rate structure.

DISCUSSION OF ISSUES

Inasmuch as the hearings on the matter of electric rate design for Madison Gas and Electric Company in this docket involved considerable presentation and discussion, these matters will be discussed in general terms in this section of the Order. These principles, in general, apply to other electric utilities under this Commission's jurisdiction facing similar operating conditions and are not limited to MG&E in this docket. Specific findings of fact on these issues will follow.

I Principles and Practices of Rate Design

Many witnesses in this case have testified on the subject of basic principles of rate design. The suggested basic principles alluded to most frequently in this proceeding are:

1 Rates should promote an efficient allocation of resources, thus discouraging wasteful use of energy.
2 Rates should not be discriminatory.
3 Rates should lead to stable revenues.
4 Rates should reflect a sense of historical continuity.

There was reasonably general agreement among all parties that the first principle enumerated above implies that rates should properly reflect the marginal cost of providing service to a given customer.

The widely prevailing practice among electric utilities today concerning rate structures calls for recovery of customer costs, i.e., costs which do not vary with use—in the first one or two consumption blocks. Often, a portion of the customer costs are collected through a fixed charge. The third and following blocks generally exhibit a declining price level with increased sales in order to reflect the economies of scale which result from increased output. This typical profile of a rate schedule will be referred to herein as a "declining block rate structure." This order covers the first comprehensive hearing testing the appropriateness of these traditional rate designs in view of new and different conditions faced by the public utility industry.

II Long-Run Incremental Costs

A modification of current practice was advocated by Dr. Stelzer, appearing as a witness for the Applicant. He suggests that the economic principle of marginal cost pricing be adopted and implemented in the form of rates based on long-run incremental costs—hereinafter often referred to as "LRIC."

The "marginal cost" of an item refers to the change in cost that occurs with infinitesimally small changes in output. A central proposition of economic theory is that when prices of goods and services are set equal to their marginal costs of production, an optimum allocation of resources results. This occurs because the price will reflect the cost to society of producing one more unit of the good. The consumer will compare this price to the value to him of one more unit and will then buy the extra unit if, and only if, it is worth at least as much to him as it costs society to produce it.

A major obstacle to the application of marginal cost pricing to electric utilities is the problem of measuring marginal cost. In order to discuss the measurement, it is necessary to carefully determine and define exactly what is to be measured. Theoretically, the economically efficient price, as discussed above, is set at the short-run marginal cost (SRMC) of the smallest possible additional unit of sale. However, rather than short-run marginal cost, long-run incremental cost has been suggested as the logical surrogate for marginal cost. Long-run incremental cost is the incremental cost of the capacity and output which can reasonably be expected to be added in the next several years. There are two reasons for looking to LRIC. The first is practicality. Long-run incremental cost lends itself to measurement while short-run marginal cost does not. The second, and more basic reason, is that if electric utility rates were tied to short-run marginal costs they would be extremely volatile. Such rapidly fluctuating rates would deprive consumers of those expectations of reasonable continuity of rates on which they must rely in order to make rational advance preparations for the use of services.

Applicant has provided estimates of MGE's LRIC in this proceeding. The study divides LRIC into the three following components:

1 *Customer Cost* This component includes meter reading, billing, connection costs, and that part of distribution costs that has been designated as varying only with number of customers.

2 *Demand Costs* This component includes generation, transmission and distribution capacity costs that vary with total kilowatt demand. These future costs are estimated on the basis of expected expenses adjusted to the current price level of actual additions to plant anticipated by the utility. These costs do not vary with number of customers but equal the sum of the capacity commitments made by the utility when providing service to customers. These costs are the same whether the customer buys energy only at system peak or buys the same amount continuously over the year.

3 *Energy Costs* This component includes the operating and maintenance costs associated with supplying a given number of kilowatt-hours of energy. These costs vary directly with the amount of energy consumed by the customer's facilities. [Operating costs include fuel costs, the largest element of variable costs.]

The record shows a general acceptance of the principle of basing rate design on long-run incremental cost. . . .

We believe that the appropriate benchmark for the design of electric rates in the case is marginal cost as represented by the practical variant, long-run incremental cost. If electric rates are designed to promote a[n] efficient allocation of resources, this is a logical starting point.

It must be understood that the "long-run" concept is pursued as the most appropriate and most practicable cost measurement. The fact that "long-run" incremental cost is being used does not imply that the resulting rates will be valid for a long time into the future, nor that they will compensate for inflationary cost increases. The primary objective that LRIC-based rates are intended to accomplish is to guarantee an efficient allocation of resources directed toward the production of electricity. Applicant's estimate of future costs in terms of current dollars is consistent with the economic definition of long-run costs. If it is desired that there be a guard against the attrition of earnings which might result from future inflation, the appropriate mechanism for such allowance must be embodied in the calculation of the overall revenue requirement.

III Peak-Load Pricing

A fully implemented application of LRIC pricing would be reflected in price differentiation for on- and off-peak sales. A first approximation to such peak-load pricing is the winter/summer differential which has been proposed by the Applicant. The winter/summer price differential reflects the costs of a seasonably peaking electric utility better than a year-round rate. The application of the winter/summer differential to a summer-peaking utility such as MG&E does not charge the space-heating customer for the cost of additional summer capacity, since the space-heating customer is using excess capacity.

Another type of peak-load pricing discussed in this record is interruptible service. Under such a rate, customers could avoid being charged for additions to capacity by agreeing to use electricity only at off-peak times. Interruptible rates have been made available by various Wisconsin electric utilities at various times. Such rates have not proven popular.

Full peak-load pricing applied to electric rates must take the form of time-of-day metering. Under such a plan, rates would vary with the time of day in order to reflect the true cost of peak demand. Customers are compelled to pay for the actual cost they are imposing on society and are rewarded for shifting consumption to an off-peak time, thereby improving the utility's load factor. The winter/summer differential does not offer such an alternative. Summer air-conditioning use cannot be postponed until winter.

The cost associated with the installation and use of the equipment necessary to implement time-of-day metering is not known, nor was any evidence submitted on this point. Whether the improvement in system-load factor warrants any additional outlay for metering depends on the elasticity of demand at various times of day. However, the recording-type metering equipment already in use for many commercial and industrial customers lends itself to time-of-day metering at a negligible cost. In this area an investigation into the possible benefits of such a pricing system would begin without delay. Such a pricing system could result in lower costs to the large users as well as an improved system-load factor for the utility.

The Applicant will be ordered herein to investigate the feasibility of such a pricing system . . . .

IV Cost Structure

Applicant's witnesses calculated the revenue that would be derived if rates for all classes were set so that class revenues were equal to their respective incremental costs. This was compared to Applicant's total revenue requirement. This comparison showed that revenues which would be generated by the rates set equal to LRIC would be approximately equal to the company's revenue requirement. The implication of this result is that Applicant cannot be experiencing "increasing costs" as defined by economists since "increasing costs" would imply that the rates set equal to LRIC exceeded the revenue requirement.

The reasons initially cited in support of the claim that MG&E is in an "increasing cost" situation centered on arguments showing historical increases in generating cost per kwh, which confounds the notions of "increasing costs" due to increased production vs. "cost increases" due to other factors such as inflation. Intervenors accepted this distinction later in the proceedings but still suggested that the inclusion of external costs as a part of total LRIC would result in the conclusion that MG&E is an "increasing cost" industry. They asserted that this conclusion would follow, since external costs increase disproportionately more than associated increases in output.

For the reasons outlined under heading VI below, the Commission does not consider it appropriate to include external costs in the cost study. Thus, analysis of the facts presented indicated that the claims that Applicant is in an "increasing cost" situation are not correct. . . .

VI External Costs

There was much discussion in this record concerning external or social costs. These costs are imposed on society but are not borne directly by the transacting parties. The discussion in this proceeding regarding external costs dealt primarily with the practicality of charging for these costs.

[An] expert witness appearing for [the intervenors] suggested that external costs could only be reflected by imposing a tax on the utility. It is, of course, beyond the province of this Commission to impose such a tax. Dr. Stelzer has stated that these external costs should be reflected in the incremental costs on which rates are based to the limited extent to which they are quantifiable, but he warned that including such costs for the purpose of electric rates, but not including them in the rates of its substitutes, could cause an uneconomic *shift* of resources rather than simply more efficient use of electricity. Professor Cicchetti has observed that, due to the problems involved in accurately reflecting external costs in rates, it might be more plausible to simply try to reduce such costs.

Although we intend to explore Dr. Stelzer's view we feel that, in general, taxation is the most appropriate vehicle for recognizing externalities. This issue involves broad questions of policy crossing multiple industrial and energy lines. To recover external costs solely from utility customers through their rates without assessing similar costs in the prices of other energy and industrial products would probably discriminate against utility customers.

VII Rate Structure

A central issue raised in this case was the appropriateness of the declining block rate structure. Alternatives to the declining block structure discussed are "flat rates" and "inverted rates." A "flat rate" structure consists of a fixed charge plus one rate per kilowatt-hour applied to all consumption. The "inverted rate" structure imposes higher energy charges for greater levels of consumption.

Factors relating to the appropriateness of the declining block rate structure that have been presented in this case include the following:

1 The relationship of LRIC to the revenue requirement.
2 The importance of stability of rate structure.
3 The treatment of customer-related costs.
4 The relationship between load factor and level of consumption.

The relationship between LRIC and the revenue requirement was discussed in part IV where it was determined that rates equal to LRIC would approximately equal Applicant's revenue requirement. This relationship points to the desirability of flattening the rate structure.

Customers of public utilities are entitled to rates for service which are reasonable and just. They therefore expect that the structure of rates will remain reasonably stable and make purchases of durable goods on this assumption. While we consider this to be an important factor in rate design, we do not feel that our approval of a flat summer residential rate in this case is contrary to the customers' reasonable expectations of stability.

Customer-related costs are costs which remain constant with respect to changes in either consumption or demand. They ostensibly vary only as the number of customers vary. These costs are currently recovered in part through a fixed charge, and the remainder is spread over the early consumption blocks. A strictly cost-related approach to customer costs calls for such costs to be recovered entirely by a fixed charge. Applicant, however, has suggested several reasons for not recovering all customer-related costs through a fixed charge. These reasons include the fact that customers strongly object to payments not associated with the quantity of electricity used. Also, if customer costs are overestimated, a spreading of these costs will tend to offset the impact of any overestimation.

Intervenors claim that such spreading of customer costs is inappropriate as a matter of economic logic, and that it magnifies the differential between the early blocks and the tail block, fostering the belief that electricity is cheap when used in large amounts.

It is our opinion that, inasmuch as rates are to be based on costs, it is appropriate that fixed monthly charges reflect customer-related costs to the extent to which they have been reliably established.

Since current fixed charges are considerably below customer-related costs, the resulting increase would appear too great to accomplish at one time. However, a reasonable step in this direction can be taken at this time and the customer should be aware that further adjustment of fixed monthly charges toward total cost levels will be a consideration of this Commission in future proceedings.

If load factor improves with the level of monthly consumption in a given customer class or sub-class, then this fact, coupled with LRIC theory, would be reflected by declining block rates. There is no evidence demonstrating such a relationship, or lack of it, in this docket. We consider it important that in future rate cases electric utilities provide empirical information demonstrating a relationship between annual system peak-load factors and amount of usage by class, subclass or by individual customer.

CONCLUSIONS OF LAW

THE COMMISSION CONCLUDES:

That the Commission is empowered . . . to authorize Applicant to establish rates in accordance with the above Findings of Fact; and that such an order should be issued.

National Association of Greeting Card Publishers v. United States Postal Service

607 F.2d 392 (1979)

Opinions for the Court filed by Circuit Judges LEVENTHAL and TAMM.

In this case the court again has occasion to consider the response of the United States Postal Service ("USPS" or "Postal Service") to the "special, and quite demanding, ratemaking requirements" of the Postal Reorganization Act of 1970 ("Act") and to this court's views concerning those requirements.

. . . Our principal focus here. . . . is on the methods by which the Postal Service, in setting the rates for the various classes of mail, allocates its costs among those classes. In particular, we must assess the Postal Service's "service related cost" methodology, by which it undertook. . . . to assign to certain classes of mail fixed delivery costs deemed to result from the maintenance of a six-day-a-week, as opposed to a three-day-a-week, mail delivery schedule.

In its first two rate proceedings under the Act, the Commission adopted a two-step approach to the allocation of the costs of operation of the Postal Service among the classes of mail. The Commission first "attributed" to the various mail classes and postal services only those costs demonstrably caused by providing the particular service, thereby establishing a rate floor for each class and service. The key to determining causation was a strict requirement of a showing of cost variability—that a particular cost varied with a change in volume of the service provided. . . .

In the second step, the costs remaining—after the attribution in the first step—were "assigned" to the various classes under a "value of service" or demand theory approach. Specifically, the Commission developed an "inverse elasticity rule," under which final rates were derived "by assigning to the various classes of mail different markups (above attributed costs) in inverse proportion to the relative elasticity of demand for each of the classes." In this way, the Commission purported to "assign costs in a manner that fully takes into account the noncost factors of the statute."

It is useful to start with a brief sketch of the various mail classifications as they are defined in the Domestic Mail Classification Schedule. First-class consists of letters and sealed parcels weighing 12 ounces or less, plus postal cards and post cards. Priority mail is a high priority service akin to first-class for sealed parcels weighing more than 12 ounces.

Second-class and controlled circulation are available for magazines, newspapers and other periodicals.

Third-class is a service for single pieces and bulk mail, consisting of matter that is not mailed or required to be mailed as first-class, is not entered as second-class or controlled circulation, or weighs too little to qualify as fourth-class.

Fourth-class includes parcel post (merchandise weighing 16 ounces or more) bound advertising matter; books, films, sound recordings and other matter entitled to a "special rate"; and library rate mail.

As its first step, the PRC determined USPS's revenue requirement by projecting its costs for each of 20 "cost segments" based on estimates of the volume of mail that would be generated at the proposed rates. The PRC determined the revenue requirement to be $17,585 million, modifying USPS's calculation slightly.

Within each cost segment, the PRC then determined the percentage of costs that could be said to vary with volume—over either the short or long run. This percentage was then available for attribution to the various classes by application of an appropriate "distribution key." . . .

The PRC's assignment of service related costs proceeded from differences in service accorded the various classes of mail. The Postal Service Manual commits the Service to different standards of service for different types of mail, based on USPS's perception of customer needs, and transportation and distribution capabilities. For first-class mail and for newspapers (a "service category" within the second-class regular rate classification, also known as "red tag" mail), the Manual requires delivery on the "first delivery trip" if the mail is received at a "distribution facility" prior to the cut-off time. For third and fourth-class parcels, USPS is required to deliver on the next delivery trip all parcels, received prior to the cutoff. For all other mail, including third-class mail and second-class publications not entitled to red tag service, the regulations provide for "delivery not later than the second day after receipt."

In considering the various challenges to the assignment of service related costs, we recall that we judge a particular ratemaking methodology by whether it is reasoned, nonarbitrary and congruent with the statutory mandate. We do not insist on mathematical precision in developing new ratemaking methods; mere articulation of imperfections in a new scheme will not alone defeat it. . . .

With this overview, we conclude that the service related cost method reflects a reasonable inference of causation and, despite the imperfections identified by the parties, represents an acceptable first effort. . . .

The newspaper publishers attack the assignment of service related costs as arbitrary and unreasonable on the ground that nonpreferential mail is rarely, if ever, deferred in the delivery function. . . . On heavy volume days, delivery service managers may use overtime or auxiliary help, but deferral is discouraged. Instead, it is argued, most deferral occurs not at the delivery stage, but in mail processing units before reaching the delivery unit. Based on these facts, the publishers submit that "it is arbitrary and unreasonable to apportion costs upon the basis of a theoretical differential between preferential and nonpreferential mail in the delivery function."

In general we agree with the first-class users that there is good reason, in economics and common sense, to call upon nonpreferential classes to contribute to the capacity costs used in providing them a benefit. However, as applied to the costs entailed in maintaining a six-day system, the question is not a simple one. There is a question whether and to what extent the users of this nonpreferential mail receive a benefit of value. On the record, we cannot hold that the PRC abused its discretion in choosing as of this ratemaking proceeding not to require the nonpreferential classes to contribute to the differential in capacity costs ascribable to a six-day system.

. . . [Finally] the United States Postal Service (Postal Service) . . . [requested] . . . a recommended decision on a change in the classification schedule that would lead to the adoption of a new subclass for citizens' rate mail [CRM], with appropriate rates. CRM, as proposed by the Postal Service, would be a separate first-class service to be used by individuals for the mailing of their personal correspondence. Users of CRM would be entitled to a lower rate of thirteen cents in exchange for service inferior, to some degree, to regular first-class service, which would be available at a higher rate of sixteen cents. CRM would have to comply with standard size restrictions and be fully zip coded, and would be denoted by a special stamp.

According to the Postal Service's proposal, all first-class mail would be treated alike prior to the delivery stage of the mail process. However, CRM would be "deferrable" in the delivery function. If exigencies required, mail carriers would separate the CRM mail from the first-class mail at the delivery unit, and set aside sufficient CRM to alleviate the immediate delivery problem. While delivery of the remaining regular first-class mail would be accomplished on the first delivery trip, delivery of the segregated CRM would be deferred until the second delivery trip.

The PRC [Postal Rate Commission] held prolonged hearings on the CRM proposal, and considered briefs, comments filed, and oral argument by the parties to the proceedings and numerous intervenors. The PRC concluded that the evidentiary record did not support the implementation of a CRM [subclass]. . . . In contrast to its finding on nonpreferential mail, the PRC found that the infrequency of deferral of CRM and the resultant minimal delay, did not support the necessary finding that CRM could be deferred on an operational basis. . . .

. . . [W]e affirm the . . . PRC recommendation to reject the CRM proposal.

. . . Our affirmation of the PRC's rejection of this CRM proposal does not imply that future CRM proposals, supported by a fuller, more substantial record, should be rejected. By contrast, we echo Chairman DuPont's encouragement to the Postal Service to restudy the CRM concept and offer a new proposal in future proceedings.

CHAPTER 14

SURFACE TRANSPORTATION

The Interstate Commerce Commission is the oldest federal regulatory commission. Initially it was primarily concerned with regulating the interstate activities of the nation's railroads. Its regulatory authority was subsequently expanded to include, among other things, interstate truck transport (1935) and inland and coastal waterway common carriers (1940).

A major responsibility of the Commission has been to determine the number of trucking companies that can serve a given transportation market. For example, out of the thousands of trucking firms the Commission decided which ones would be allowed to enter new markets. The first two cases illustrate the ICC's changing position toward entry controls.

In *ICC v. J-T Transport,* the issue was whether a contract carrier would be allowed to haul new products that could potentially be hauled by common carriers. (Contract carriers haul a limited range of items for a limited number of shippers, whereas common carriers can generally haul a greater number of commodities for any firm shipping along their routes. Both types of carriers must be licensed by the ICC, but the rates set by contract carriers are not controlled, while those of common carriers are controlled.) In this case, the ICC and the courts, presented with the same facts, reached quite different conclusions. Whose decision made more sense in terms of creating an efficient trucking industry? On equity grounds? Why do you think the Commission's perspective was so different from that of the courts? The Motor Carrier Act of 1980 has since made it easier for carriers to enter new markets. Is this change in the public interest?

The second case, Toto Purchasing, concerns the role of private trucking companies in the nation's transportation system. These firms transport their products with their own trucks, instead of relying on common or contract carriers. They themselves are not contract or common carriers, however. The primary issue in this case is the right of private firms to act as for-hire carriers. This would enable them to reduce empty backhauls—driving empty trucks on their return trips. In this case, the Commission overrules its previous policy against private carriers acting in a for-hire capacity. Is this decision consistent with the public interest? Will it lead to a more efficient trucking sector? Who will gain and who will lose from this decision?

The third and fourth cases illustrate the Commission's rate-making policies in situations where there has been intermodal competition. Since the Transportation Act of 1940, its instructions have been to set rates that preserve the "inherent service advantages" of the competing transport modes. Consequently, most controversy has centered on the determination of inherent advantage. Truckers contend that inherent advantage should be determined by comparing "fully allocated costs," while railroads prefer the use of long-run "out of pocket costs" (both terms are defined in the footnotes of the Ingot Molds case). Which cost concept most closely corresponds to marginal cost? Are marginal cost concepts appropriate for determining inherent advantage?

If allowable rates are set equal to "fully allocated costs" in the Ingot Molds case, truckers will receive most of the contested traffic. On the other hand, if rates are based on long-run "out of pocket costs," the railroads will receive most of the business. Why is there such a substantial difference between the railroads' fully allocated and out of pocket costs? Would you expect a similarly large difference for trucks and barges? A number of economic studies show that if rates are set according to marginal costs, the railroads will have an advantage on hauls of more than 200 miles. As the railroads acquire more and more control over their rates, how do you think the structure of the transportation industry will change? Will the railroads drive truck and barge companies out of business? If they do, should we be concerned about it? Are you also concerned about the many firms that go out of business in competitive industries such as textiles and retailing? Since this decision, new legislation has given both the railroads and the trucking companies some rate flexibility, enabling them to raise and lower rates to some degree without ICC approval.

The Big John Hopper case also deals with intermodal rate competition, which in this instance arises due to a major technological innovation in rail service. It took Southern Railway four years and two trips to the Supreme Court to get ICC approval of substantially lower rates for its new, low-cost freight car—the Big John Hopper. ICC rate-making policies have seriously delayed implementation of other rail innovations such as piggybacking and unit trains. The Commission's response in these situations is illustrative of a serious problem in regulation—how to create an atmosphere conducive to technological change in a regulatory environment. Many economists feel that ICC policy has systematically impeded technical change. Why should this be? The carriers can still adopt the low-cost methods regardless of whether or not the ICC approves their rate requests. Would firms do this? Why or why not?

Interstate Commerce Commission v. J-T Transport Co.

368 U.S. 81 (1961)

MR. JUSTICE DOUGLAS delivered the opinion of the Court.

These are appeals from judgments of three-judge district courts, which set aside orders of the Interstate Commerce Commission denying applications for permits as contract carriers.

Appellee J-T Transport Company asked to expand its present operations as an irregular-route contract carrier of airplane parts to include carriage of aircraft landing gear bulkheads for Boeing Airplane Co. Boeing supported the application. Common carriers opposed the application, as did another carrier, U.S.A.C. Transport, Inc. Boeing indicated it preferred the applicant over the other because of its unsatisfactory experience with the latter in other operations. Boeing indicated that contract carriage was more practicable in its experience than common carriage, as a contract carrier's operations could be better integrated with a manufacturer's production. Though the examiner recommended a grant of the permit, the Commission denied it saying that no attempt had been made to ascertain if the existing services were capable of meeting the needs of the shipper. It ruled that "There is, in effect, a presumption that the services of existing carriers will be adversely affected by a loss of 'potential' traffic, even if they may not have handled it before." It held that the applicant had not established a need for this contract service and that the applicant had not shown "the existing service" of the other carrier to be "inadequate." It indicated that a service "not needed" cannot be found consistent with the public interest or the National Transportation Policy, as those terms are used in . . . the Interstate Commerce Act. . . . It said that the shippers did not require a distinct type of service that could not be provided by the protesting carrier, which was indeed in a position to provide any service needed and which would be adversely affected by a grant of this application, even though it never had the business in question.

Appellee Reddish made applications to carry canned goods as a contract carrier from three points in Arkansas and one in Oklahoma to various points in thirty-three States and to carry other goods on return. His application was supported by his prospective shippers and opposed by motor common carriers, and by rail common carriers.

Reddish showed that he delivered to customers who ordered goods in less-than-truckload amounts. These customers maintained low inventories and needed expedited deliveries in small quantities and on short notice. Some accepted deliveries only on certain days, a requirement calling for integration and coordination between shipper and customer. The shippers said that common carriage was an inadequate service for these shipments, as they were in such small lots that they often had to be carried in consolidated loads which caused delays in shipments. Moreover, it was shown that not all points would be served by one common carrier, making it necessary to unload the shipments and reload them on another carrier causing delays, misconsignment, and damage to goods. The shippers also testified that the cost of common carriage was prohibitive for less-than-truckload shipments and that if the Reddish application were denied they would use private carriage. The protesting motor common carriers testified they could render adequate service for these shipments and provide multiple pick-up and delivery services to most of the points by tranferring the shipments to other carriers. The Examiner recommended that the application be granted. The Commission denied it, saying, *inter alia,* that the services needed by the shippers could be performed by existing common carriers, that they would be injured by the loss of potential traffic, and that the shipper's desire to obtain lower rates for less-than-truckload shipments was the primary reason for their support of the application, but was not a sufficient basis to justify a grant of authority to this contract carrier.

The cases turn on the meaning of language added to the Act in 1957.

Our decision in *United States v. Contract Steel Carriers,* held that a contract carrier, rendering a specialized service in the sense that it hauled only a limited group of commodities over irregular routes, did not become a common carrier because it reached for new business within the limits of its license. That decision caused concern to the Commission which proposed amendments to the Act. It proposed . . . to define a contract carrier as one who engages in transportation by motor vehicle "under continuing contracts with one person or a limited number of persons for the furnishing of transportation services of a special and individual nature required by the customer and not provided by common carriers." It also proposed that [the act] be amended by adding an additional requirement for issuance of a contract carrier permit, viz., "the existing common carriers are unwilling or unable to provide the type of service for which a need has been shown."

These amendments were vigorously opposed in some quarters. [One group objected] on the ground that many contract carriers would be driven out of business because they could not meet the test of performing a service "not provided by common carriers." [It was also] opposed because it would be impossible for a contact carrier to prove that competing common carriers were "unwilling" to render the service and very difficult for it to prove that common carriers were "unable" to render the service, as the applicant would have no intimate knowledge of the business of the opposing carriers.

The Commission bowed to these objections; and the bill as it passed eliminated the proposed changes. . . . [However, the act] was amended, so far as material here, by adding to the description of the term "contract carrier by motor vehicle" one who furnishes "transporation services designed to meet the distinct need of each individual customer" . . . and by adding a sentence which sets forth five factors the Commission shall consider in determining whether the permit should issue:

> In determining whether issuance of a permit will be consistent with the public interest and the national transportation policy declared in this Act, the Commission shall consider (1) the number of shippers to be served by the applicant, (2) the nature of the service proposed, (3) the effect which granting the permit would have upon the services

of the protesting carriers and (4) the effect which denying the permit would have upon the applicant and/or its shipper and (5) the changing character of that shipper's requirements. (Numerals added.)

It seems clear from these provisions that the adequacy of existing services is a criterion to be considered by the Commission, as it is instructed to consider "the effect which granting the permit would have upon the services of the protesting carriers," as well as the effect of a denial upon the shippers. Or to put the matter otherwise, the question of the need of the shipping public for the proposed service necessarily includes the question whether the extent, nature, character, and suitability of existing, available service makes the proposed service out of line with the requirements of the national transportation policy. But the adequacy of existing facilities or the willingness or ability of existing carriers to render the new service is not determinative. The "effect which denying the permit would have upon the applicant and/or its shipper and the changing character of that shipper's requirements" have additional relevance. This is a phase of the problem reflected in the broadened definition of a "contract carrier by motor vehicle"—one who furnishes transportation services "designed to meet the distinct need of each individual customer." It means, we think, that the "distinct need" of shippers for the new contract carrier service must be weighed against the adequacy of existing services. The Commission indulged in "a presumption that the services of existing carriers will be adversely affected by a loss of 'potential' traffic, even if they may not have handled it before." The effect of the presumption is in substance to limit competing contract carriage to services "not provided" by existing carriers—a provision that the Commission sought unsuccessfully to have incorporated into the Act. We see no room for a presumption in favor of, or against, any of the five factors on which findings must be made. . . . The effect on protesting carriers of a grant of the application and the effect on shippers of a denial are factors to be weighed in determining on balance where the public interest lies. The aim of the 1957 amendments, as we read the legislative history, was not to protect the *status quo* of existing carriers but to establish a regime under which new contract carriage could be allowed if the "distinct need" of shippers indicated it was desirable.

We cannot assume that Congress, in amending the statute, intended to adopt the administrative construction which prevailed prior to the amendment.

By adding the five criteria which it directed the Commission to consider, Congress expressed its will that the Commission should not manifest special solicitude for that criterion which directs attention to the situation of protesting carriers, at the expense of that which directs attention to the situation of supporting shippers, when those criteria have contrary implications. Such a situation doubtless exists in these cases, for granting the permits might well have produced some consequences adverse to the protesting supporting shippers. Had the Commission, having drawn out and crystallized these competing interests, attempted to judge them with as much delicacy as the prospective nature of the inquiry permits, we should have been cautious about disturbing its conclusion.

But while such a determination is primarily a responsibility of the Commission, we are under no compulsion to accept its reading where, as here, we are convinced that it has loaded one of the scales. By indulging in a presumption "that the services of existing carriers will be adversely affected by a loss of 'potential' traffic, even if they may not have handled it before," and by assigning to the applicants the burden of proving the inadequacy of existing services, the Commission favored the protestants' interests at the expense of the shippers' in a manner not countenanced by anything discoverable in Congress' delegation to it of responsibility.

The proper procedure, we conclude, is for the applicant first to demonstrate that the undertaking it proposes is specialized and tailored to a shipper's distinct need. The protestants than may present evidence to show they have the ability as well as the willingness to meet that specialized need. If that is done, then the burden shifts to the applicant to demonstrate that it is better equipped to meet the distinct needs of the shipper than the protestants.

Moreover, as we read the Act, as amended in 1957, the standard is not whether existing services are "reasonably adequate." It is whether a shipper has a "distinct need" for a different or a more select or a more specialized service. The protesting carriers must show they can fill that "distinct need," not that they can provide a "reasonably adequate service."

In the *Reddish* case the Commission ruled that the desire for lower rates offered by the applicant was irrelevant to a shipper's needs, that if the rates of existing carriers were too high, shippers would seek relief for their reduction. We think the matter of rates is one factor to be weighed in determining the need for the new service. In a contest between carriers by motor vehicles and carriers by rail, we held in *Schaffer Transportation Co. v. United States,* 355 U.S. 83, that the ability of a particular mode of transportation to operate with a lower rate is one of the "inherent advantages" that one type may have over another within the meaning of the Act. By analogy, contract carriage may be more "economical" than common carriage by motor or rail within the framework of the national transportation policy, as it is defined in the Act—"the Commission's guide" to the public interest. It would seem hardly contestable that if denial of the application meant, for example, that a shipper's costs of transportation would be prohibitive, the shipper had established a "need" for the more "economical" service. This does not mean that the lawfulness of rates would be injected into certificate proceedings. The issue of whether such advantage establishes a "need" for the service that overrides counterbalancing considerations presents issues that fall far short of a rate proceeding.

We agree with the court in the J-T Transport Co. case that, while the 1957 amendments changed the result of our decision in *United States v. Contract Steel Carriers,* supra, by giving the Commission power to limit the number of contracts which a contract carrier can maintain, the amendments in other respects put the contract carrier on a firmer footing. That court said, "Under the statute a shipper is entitled to have his distinct needs met." We agree. We also agree that though common carrier service is reasonably adequate and though another carrier is willing and able to furnish the service, a permit to a contract carrier to furnish this particular service still might be wholly consistent with the national transportation policy defined in the Act. For it is "the distinct need of each individual customer" that the contract carrier is designed to fill. And "the changing character" of the shipper's "requirements" is a factor to be weighed before denying the application. Hence the adequacy of existing carrier for normal needs and willingness and ability of an existing carrier to render the service are not the end of the matter. The "distinct need" of the shipper may nonetheless not be served by existing services, if the new service is better tailored to fit the special requirements of a shipper's business, the length of its purse, or the select nature of the delivery service that is desired. The fact that the protesting carriers do not presently perform the service being tendered and that the grant of the application would not divert business from them does not necessarily mean that the grant would have no effect "upon the services" of protesting carriers. . . . But where the protesting carriers do not presently have the business, it would seem that the grant of it to a newcomer would have an adverse effect on them only in the unusual case.

We intimate no opinion on the merits, for it is the Commission, not the courts, that brings an *expertise* to bear on the problem, that makes the findings, and that grants the applications. Yet that *expertise* is not sufficient by itself. Findings supported by substantial evidence are required.

Since the standards and criteria employed by the Commission were not the proper ones, the causes must be remanded for further consideration and for new findings. Accordingly the judgments below are

Affirmed.

Toto Purchasing & Supply Co., Inc., Common Carrier Application

128 M.C.C. 873 (1978)

GRESHAM, Commissioner:

By application filed February 4, 1976. . . . Toto Purchasing & Supply Co., Inc. (Toto), of Las Vegas, Nev., seeks a certificate of public convenience and necessity authorizing operation, in interstate or foreign commerce, as a common carrier by motor vehicle. . . . By report and order of Review Board Number 1, dated March 31, 1977, the application was denied on the basis of this Commission's long-established policy, first articulated and enforced in *Geraci Contract Carrier Application*, 7 M.C.C. 369 (1938), not to grant a certificate or permit to an applicant who intends to use it primarily as an incident to carriage of its own goods and its own nontransportation business. Upon consideration of applicant's one petition for reconsideration . . . the title proceeding was. . . . reopened for reconsideration. . . .

FACTS

Toto Purchasing & Supply Co., Inc., . . . is not primarily a for-hire motor carrier, but, rather, is primarily a wholesaler and retailer of various kinds of building materials. Its offices, warehouse, and terminal are located in Las Vegas, Nev. Toto, using its three truck-tractors and four flat-bed semitrailers, engages in private carriage of its building materials from points in southern California to its Las Vegas warehouse and to various jobsites in Nevada. It proposes to serve the supporting shippers by using equipment which would otherwise be deadheaded from Las Vegas to points in southern California for the purpose of picking up its building materials. Essentially, applicant would provide its shippers with common carriage for a one-way movement from points in Clark County, Nev., to points in the four named destination counties in California. Afterwards, it would deadhead the equipment from 5 to 25 miles until it would arrive at the origin of its own supplies, and would then engage in private carriage on a return movement back to Nevada. . . .

DISCUSSION AND CONCLUSIONS

The *Geraci* case involved an individual applicant who was primarily engaged in the purchase and sale of fruits and vegetables, and, as an incident to that business, conducted a private carrier operation, transporting fruits and vegetables in his own trucks from points in Florida to Cincinnati, Ohio. His vehicles were operated empty in the reverse direction. He, therefore, filed an application seeking motor contract carrier operating authority to transport bottled beverages from Covington, Ky., to certain points in Florida, in order to provide revenue traffic for his southbound trips and to round out his entire operations. The Commission . . . noting that the "applicant intends to conduct the proposed contract carrier operation as an incident to his regular business and in order to help defray the expenses of such business," found that the operation proposed by applicant, "in connection with operation as a private carrier in the reverse direction" would not be consistent with the public interest, and that, therefore, the application should be denied. . . .

The *Geraci* rule was soon extended . . . to applications seeking motor common carrier operating authority, and in the ensuing 40 years numerous common and contract carrier applications have been denied on *Geraci* grounds.

On the other hand, the *Geraci* rule has been distinguished in numerous cases. Exceptions have been carved into it over the years. . . . *Geraci* has been distinguished, and authority granted, in instances where the proposed for-hire operation would be in the same direction as the existing private carrier operation, so that the for-hire movement could not provide a backhaul for the private carrier movement. For-hire motor carrier operating authority has been granted to a private carrier applicant that used its own vehicles in a private carrier movement during one-half of the year only, on the basis of the applicant's need to find a use for its vehicles during the remaining part of the year. . . . Authority has been granted to private carrier applicants which were already engaged in for-hire motor carriage, provided that the circumstances were such that the private carrier operation was clearly incidental to, and much less significant than, the for-hire operations. A private carrier was granted operating authority upon a finding that its proposed service would not be competitive with the existing service of any for-hire motor carrier.

There is another notable exception to the *Geraci* rule. The rule has been interpreted so as not to prohibit a contract carrier subsidiary from serving its corporate parent. . . .

The continued validity of the *Geraci* rule has been questioned frequently in recent years. We have reexamined the rule twice in the past two decades and have affirmed its continued operation. . . . We now reexamine the rule again, but this time we opt against its continued existence.

The issues noted in *Geraci* and its progeny reflect serious concerns. However, there are other countervailing considerations which also need to be weighed. In addition, the Commission's increased emphasis on the need for efficient operations as a result of the continuing "energy crisis" casts previous policies in a new light. The issues noted in *Geraci* may be viewed as follows:

1. *The difficulties with references to accounting, statistics, issue of securities, unifications, and the like.*—The concern is that the applicant would integrate the records of its transportation operation into the books of its primary, nontransportation business. Without the ability to see clearly the records of the transportation aspects of the enterprise, the Commission would arguably be unable properly to regulate the carrier.

However, the Commission has faced this problem in those cases in which authority has been granted to private carrier applicants. A satisfactory solution has been found. The imposition of conditions requiring the applicant to conduct its for-hire motor carrier activities and its other activities independently and to maintain separate records for each would seem to preclude applicant from integrating its records in such a manner as to defeat our regulatory supervision. . . .

2. *The potential for undue preference and prejudice between the carrier's own traffic and that of its customers.*—When a private carrier seeks for-hire motor carrier operating authority, a theoretical potential for preference and prejudice may be created, for it is to be expected that the private carrier would be naturally inclined to give first priority to its own shipments, as opposed to the traffic tendered to it by other shippers. However, the theoretical potential for preference and prejudice may be eliminated when the for-hire authority complements rather than conflicts with the private carriage. When a private carrier seeks to acquire for-hire authority which would allow it to backhaul on its existing private carrier routes, the two kinds of motor carrier operations would appear to complement one another and to provide little danger of undue preference and prejudice. . . .

Even when the operations are uncomplementary, there are good reasons to authorize the services. . . . We can find little to be realistically concerned about when the shippers intending to use the applicant's services are aware that the carrier is controlled by another shipper. The shipper presumably knows the theoretical risks involved in using a carrier which also hauls its own goods. Some deference must be accorded to the business judgment of the shipper in deciding to use the service. Indeed, we believe it entirely possible that the shipper's judgment in such matters may be better than ours. Perpetuation of *Geraci,* unfortunately, precludes shippers from exercising any choice in the matter. For the shipper, this may be disastrous; he may be left with inadequate or no for-hire service. . . .

3. *Granting private carrier operating authority as for-hire carriers gives them an unfair advantage over regulated carriers.*—The general public may be dependent upon the common carrier's obligations to provide service within the limits of their authority to everyone who tenders them traffic. However, it is not this Commission's purpose to provide protection for regulated carriers when the public's interest in more adequate transportation service could best be served by authorization of a new, competitive carrier.

The Commission in *Geraci* pointed out that the private carrier has the advantage of being free from the expenses that regulation entails. However, to the extent that a private carrier receives operating authority from this agency, it too faces those expenses. The regulated traffic of a company which also conducts private carriage would, all things being equal, bear the same expenses of regulation as a similar amount of traffic carried by a company that engaged solely in for-hire carriage. . . .

The Commission in *Geraci* also noted that the private carrier often has the advantage of an overhead or management expense shared with the nontransportation side of the enterprise. However, such an arrangement would benefit the private carrier only if it were assumed that the transportation operation did not contribute its proportionate share to the total revenue of the enterprise. The argument assumes the existence of a cross-subsidy which is not inherent in such an arrangement. To the contrary, it is general business practice to extract from each segment of an enterprise at least sufficient productivity to meet its costs. Any part of a business that cannot contribute enough to the overall operation to meet its costs is usually eliminated.

Another theoretical problem is the temptation of the private carrier to price its for-hire backhaul at less than variable cost, in order to fill up an otherwise empty haul. However, the incentive for the carrier to price its return haul at out-of-pocket costs would apply equally to for-hire carriers seeking backhaul traffic. In any event, the Commission can police any threatened abuses in this area through its ratemaking functions.

This analysis . . . persuades us that the long-established and supposedly inflexible (although riddled with exceptions) *Geraci* rule, that motor carrier operating authority is not to be granted to an applicant who intends to use it primarily as an incident to carriage of its own goods and its own business, should be rejected. . . . *Geraci* [is], therefore, overruled. It is our expectation that implementation of the new policy will enable private carrier applicants . . . to provide for-hire service to shippers which do not have adequate for-hire service available, and will also provide for increased efficiency in the transportation system by filling up otherwise empty backhauls. We are convinced that the high cost of energy, now and into the foreseeable future, requires us to pay close attention to the need for greater operating efficiency, not only in the for-hire sector, but in all interstate surface transportation.

FINDINGS

On further consideration in the title proceeding, we find that the present and future public convenience and necessity require operation by Toto, in interstate or foreign commerce, as a common carrier by motor vehicle, over irregular routes, of gypsum wallboard and gypsum lath, from points in Clark County, Nev., to points in Los Angeles, Orange, Riverside, and San Bernardino Counties, Calif., subject to the condition that Toto conduct its for-hire motor carrier activities and its other activities separately and maintain separate records for each. Toto is fit, willing, and able properly to perform such service and to conform to the requirements of the Interstate Commerce Act and the Commission's rules and regulations. A certificate authorizing such operation should be granted. . . .

American Commercial Lines, Inc. v. Louisville & Nashville Railroad Co.

392 U.S. 571 (1968) (The "Ingot Molds" Case)

MR. JUSTICE MARSHALL delivered the opinion of the Court.

The basic issue in these cases is whether the action of the Interstate Commerce Commission in disallowing a rate reduction proposed by the appellee railroads, [in 1965], was consistent with the provisions of Section 15a (3) of the Interstate Commerce Act, [added by Congress in 1958]. . . . which governs ratemaking in situations involving intermodal competition. A subsidiary but related issue is whether the Commission adequately articulated its reasons for disallowing the proposed rate. A statutory three-judge court, upon appeal of the Commission's decision was erroneous on both of the foregoing grounds. For the reasons detailed below, we conclude that the District Court erred in its rejection of the Commission's decision, and the grounds on which it was based, and we reverse.

I

Since 1953 the movement of ingot molds from Neville Island and Pittsburgh, Pennsylvania, to Steelton, Kentucky, has been almost exclusively by combination barge-truck service, and since 1960 the overall charge for this service has been $5.11 per ton. In 1963 the Pennsylvania Railroad and the Louisville & Nashville Railroad lowered their joint rate for this same traffic from $11.86 to $5.11 per ton. The competing barge lines, joined by intervening trucking interests, protested to the ICC that the new railroad violated Section 15a (3) of the Interstate Commerce Act because it impaired or destroyed the "inherent advantage" then enjoyed by the barge-truck service. The Commission thereupon undertook an investigation of the rate reduction.

In the course of the administrative proceedings that followed, the ICC made the following factual findings about which there is no real dispute among the parties. The fully distributed cost[1] to the railroads of this service was $7.59 per ton, and the "long term out-of-pocket costs"[2] were $4.69 per ton. The fully distributed cost to the barge-truck service[3] was $5.19 per ton.[4] The out-of-pocket cost[5] of the barge-truck service was not separately computed, but was estimated without contradiction, to be approximately the same as the fully distributed cost and higher, in any event, than the out-of-pocket cost of the railroads. The uncontroverted shipper testimony was to the effect that price was virtually the sole determinant of which service would be utilized, but that, were the rates charged by the railroads and the barge-truck combination the same, all the traffic would go to the railroads.

The railroads contended that they should be permitted to maintain the $5.11 rate, once it was shown to exceed the out-of-pocket cost attributable to the service, on the ground that any rate so set would enable them to make a profit on the traffic. The railroads further contended that the fact that the rate was substantially below their fully distributed cost for the service was irrelevant, since that cost in no way reflected the profitability of the traffic to them. The barge-truck interests, on the other hand, took the position that Section 15a (3) required the Commission to look to the railroads' fully distributed costs in order to ascertain which of the

---

[1] Fully distributed costs are defined broadly by the ICC as the "out-of-pocket costs plus a revenue-ton and revenue ton-mile distribution of the constant cost, including deficits, [that] indicate the revenue necessary to a fair return on the traffic, disregarding ability to pay." *New Automobiles in Interstate Commerce,* 259 I.C.C. 475, 513 (1945).

[2] The long-term out-of-pocket costs were computed under an ICC-sponsored formula which generally holds that 80% of rail operating expenses, rents and taxes are out-of-pocket in that they will vary with traffic. To this is added a return element of 4% on a portion of the investment (all the equipment and 50% of the road property), which is apportioned to all traffic on a proportional basis. Compare n. 1, *supra.*

[3] This figure is not precisely a cost figure. Rather it is the barge fully distributed cost, plus the charge made for the truck portion of the service and the charge for barge-truck transfer. Since all parties seem willing to treat the figure as one of fully distributed cost for the barge-truck combination, no further mention will be made of its disparate elements.

[4] Because the barge-truck rate of $5.11 was below the fully distributed cost of the service, Division 2 of the ICC initially concluded that the barge-truck combination had forfeited its right to claim that its inherent advantage of lower fully distributed cost was being impaired by the railroads' setting of a matching rate. On reconsideration, the full Commission reversed this ruling by Division 2, observing that there was no evidence that the failure of the barge-truck rate to equal fully distributed cost was due to anything but the barge lines' ignorance of the precise amount of their fully distributed cost for this service. This determination is not challenged here by any party and we express no opinion on it.

[5] Out-of-pocket costs have been regarded generally in these cases as equivalent to what economists refer to as "incremental" or "marginal" costs. Accordingly we shall equate the terms likewise, although we have no intention of vouching for the accuracy of that equation as a matter of pure economics. Cf. n. 2, *supra.* Such costs are defined generally as the costs specifically incurred by the addition of each new unit of output and do not include any allocation to that unit of pre-existing overhead expenses.

competing modes had the inherent cost advantage on the traffic at issue. They argued that the fact that the railroads' rate would be profitable was merely the minimum requirement under the statute. The railroads in response contended that inherent advantage should be determined by a comparison of out-of-pocket rather than fully distributed costs, and they produced several economists to testify that, from the standpoint of economic theory, the comparison of out-of-pocket, or incremental, costs was the only rational way of regulating competitive rates.

The ICC rejected the railroads' contention that out-of-pocket costs should be the basis on which inherent advantage should be determined. The Commission observed that it had in the past regularly viewed fully distributed costs as the appropriate basis for determining which of two competing modes was the lower cost mode as regards particular traffic. It further indicated that the legislative history of Section 15a (3) revealed that Congress had in mind a comparison of fully distributed costs when it inserted the reference to the National Transportation Policy into that section in place of language sought by the railroads.

Having decided to utilize a comparison between fully distributed costs to determine inherent advantage, the Commission then concluded that the rate set by the railroads would undercut the barge-truck combination's ability to exploit its inherent advantage because the rate would force the competing carriers to go well below their own fully distributed costs to recapture the traffic from the railroads. Moreover, since the result sought by the railroads was general permission to set rates on an out-of-pocket basis, the Commission concluded that eventually the railroads could take all the traffic away from the barge-truck combination because the out-of-pocket costs of the former were lower than those of the latter and, therefore, in any rate war the railroads would be able to outlast their competitors. Accordingly, the Commission ordered that the railroads' rate be canceled.

The District Court read the statute and its accompanying legislative history to reflect a congressional judgment that inherent advantage should be determined in most cases by a comparison of out-of-pocket costs and that, therefore, railroads should generally be permitted to set any individual rate they choose as long as that rate is compensatory.[6] The court also held that the Commission had failed adequately to articulate its reasons for deciding that the proper way of determining which mode of transportation was the more efficient was by comparison of fully distributed costs rather than out-of-pocket costs.

II

This Court has previously had occasion to consider the meaning and legislative history of Section 15a (3) of the Interstate Commerce Act in *ICC v. New York, N. H. & H. R. Co.,* 372 U.S. 744 (1963) ("New Haven"), and both the ICC and the District Court have relied heavily on that decision as support for the conflicting

---

[6] A rate is compensatory in the sense used by the District Court any time it is greater than the out-of-pocket cost of the service for which the rate is set. The term fully compensatory is sometimes used to describe a rate in excess of fully distributed costs.

results reached by them in these cases. Because the statute and its relevant legislative history were so thoroughly canvassed there, we shall not undertake any extended discussion of the same material here. Instead, we shall refer to that opinion for most of the relevant history.

So far as relevant here, Section 15a (3) provides that:

> [r]ates of a carrier shall not be held up to a particular level to protect the traffic of any other mode of transportation, giving due consideration to the objectives of the national transportation policy declared in this Act.

The National Transportation Policy, states that it is the intention of the Congress:

> to provide for fair and impartial regulation of all modes of transportation subject to the provisions of this act, so administered as to recognize and preserve the inherent advantages of each. . . .

The District Court apparently believed that the Commission was required to exercise its judgment in the direction of using out-of-pocket costs as the rate floor because that would encourage "hard" competition. We do not deny that the competition that would result from such a decision would probably be "hard." Indeed, from the admittedly scanty evidence in this record, one might well conclude that the competition resulting from out-of-pocket ratemaking by the railroads would be so hard as to run a considerable number of presently existing barge and truck lines out of business.

We disagree, however, with the District Court's reading of congressional intent. The language contained in Section 15a (3) was the product of a bitter struggle between the railroads and their competitors. One of the specific fears of those competitors that prompted the change from the original language used in the bill was that the bill as it then read would permit essentially unregulated competition between all the various transportation modes. It was argued with considerable force that permitting the railroads to price on an out-of-pocket basis to meet competition would result in the eventual complete triumph of the railroads in intermodal competition because of their ability to impose all their constant costs on traffic for which there was no competition.

The economists who testified for the railroads in this case all stated that such an unequal allocation of constant costs among shippers on the basis of demand for railroad service, i.e., on the existence of competition for particular traffic, was economically sound and desirable.

The simple fact is that Section 15a (3) was not enacted, as the railroads claim, to enable them to price their services in such a way as to obtain the maximum revenue therefrom. The very words of the statute speak of "preserv[ing]" the inherent advantages of each mode of transportation. If all that was meant by the statute was to prevent wholly noncompensatory pricing by regulated carriers, language that was a good deal clearer could easily have been used. And, as we have shown above, at least one version of such clear language was proposed by the railroads and rejected by the Congress. If the theories advanced by the economists who testified in this case are as compelling as they seem to feel they are, Congress is the body to whom they should be addressed. The courts are ill-qualified indeed to make the kind of basic judgments about economic policy sought by the railroads here. And it would be particularly inappropriate for a court to award a carrier, on economic grounds, relief denied it by the legislature. Yet this is precisely what the District Court has done in this case.

We do not mean to suggest by the foregoing discussion that the Commission is similarly barred from making legislative judgments about matters of economic policy. It is precisely to permit such judgments that the task of regulating transportation rates has been entrusted to a specialized administrative agency rather than to courts of general jurisdiction. Of course, the Commission must operate within the limits set by Congress in enacting the legislation it administers. But nothing we say here should be taken as expressing any view as to the extent that Section 15a (3) constitutes a categorical command to the ICC to use fully distributed costs as the only measure of inherent advantage in intermodal rate controversies. As was stated in the *New Haven* case, it "may be" that after due consideration another method of costing will prove to be preferable in such situations as the present one. All we hold here is that the initial determination of that question is for the Commission.

The Commission stated here that it intended to exercise its informed judgment by considering the issues presented here in the context of a rule-making proceeding where it could evaluate the alternatives on the basis of a consideration of the effects of a departure from a fully distributed cost standard on the transportation industry as a whole. Until that evaluation was completed, the Commission took the position that it would continue to follow the practice it had observed in the past of dealing with individual rate reductions on a fully distributed cost basis. The District Court, in effect, refused to permit the Commission to deal with the complex problems of developing a general standard of costing to use in determining inherent advantage in situations involving intermodal competition in the broad context of a rule-making proceeding. Instead, it ordered the Commission to resolve those problems in the narrow context of this individual rate reduction proceeding.

We have already observed that the District Court erred in interpreting the *New Haven* decision to require the Commission to permit out-of-pocket pricing in most instances. Given the fact that *New Haven* indicated that the Commission was to exercise its informed judgment in ultimately determining what method of costing was preferable, it is clear that the District Court also erred in refusing to permit the Commission to exercise that judgment in a proceeding it reasonably believed would provide the most adequate record for the resolution of the problems involved. We can see no justification for denying the Commission reasonable latitude to decide where it will resolve these complex issues, in addition to how it will resolve them. The action by the District Court here not only deprives the Commission of the opportunity to make the initial resolution of the issues but also prevents it from doing so in a more suitable context.

The District Court also objected to the failure of the Commission to explain why it permitted out-of-pocket ratemaking where the competing carrier was unregulated and not where the competitor was regulated. The short answer to this is that Section 15a (3) by its own terms applies only to "modes of transportation subject to this Act," which by definition means regulated carriers. As a result any arbitrariness that may flow from the distinction recognized by the Commission between regulated and unregulated carriers in situations of intermodal competition is the creation of Congress, not of the Commission.

The District Court also appears to have held that the Commission did not adequately explain how the rate set by the railroads would impair or destroy the barge-truck inherent advantage. Yet the Commission pointed out that the principle proposed by the railroads would, if recognized, permit the railroads to capture all the traffic here that is presently carried by the barge-truck combination because the railroads' out-of-pocket costs were lower than those of the combined barge-truck service. The District Court seems to have been impressed by the fact that the railroads were merely meeting the barge-truck rate, despite the uncontroverted evidence that given equal rates all traffic would move by train. Given a service advantage, it seems somewhat unrealistic to suggest that rate parity does not result in undercutting the competitor that does not possess the service advantage. In any event, regardless of the label used, it seems self-evident that a carrier's "inherent advantage" of being the low cost mode on a fully distributed cost basis is impaired when a competitor sets a rate that forces the carrier to lower its own rate below its fully distributed costs in order to retain the traffic. In addition, when a rate war would be likely to eventually result in pushing rates to a level at which the rates set would no longer provide a fair profit, the Commission has traditionally, and properly, taken the position that such a rate struggle should be prevented from commencing in the first place. Certainly there is no suggestion here that the rate charged by the barge-truck combination was excessive and in need of being driven down by competitive pressure. We conclude, therefore, that the Commission adequately articulated its reasons for determining that the railroads' rate would impair the inherent advantage enjoyed by the barge-truck service.

The judgment of the District Court is reversed and the cases are remanded to that court with directions to enter a judgment affirming the Commission's order.

It is so ordered.

The Cincinnati, New Orleans & Texas Pacific Railway Co. v. United States
229 F. Supp. 572 (1964) (The "Big John Hopper" Case)

JOHN W. PECK, District Judge.

This suit is brought to set aside and annul an order issued by the Interstate Commerce Commission on July 1, 1963. . . . A temporary restraining order was granted on August 21, 1963, and has remained in effect since that time. . . .

FINDINGS OF FACT

This cause arises upon a complaint filed by the Cincinnati, New Orleans & Texas Pacific Railway Company and other corporate members of the Southern Railway System seeking to set aside the Report and Order entered by the Interstate Commerce Commission in *Grain in Multiple Car Shipments—River Crossings to the South,* decided on July 1, 1963, by the entire Commission.

The Southern Governors Conference, the Southeastern Association of Railroad and Utilities Commissioners, the City of Cincinnati, and the Secretary of Agriculture of the United States intervened as plaintiffs and adopted the position of Southern. The Department of Justice filed an answer in which it admitted certain of the allegations of Southern. The Louisville and Nashville Railroad Company and other principal railroads serving the southeastern states of the United States filed an intervening complaint seeking review of the Commission's *Report and Order* in part.

The proceedings before the Commission arose from the proposal of Southern to reduce rates on shipments of grain by an average of sixty (60%) percent to specified points in the Southeast. The reduced rates would apply only to multiple car shipments of not less than 450 tons of grain from one consignor to one consignee on one bill of lading. The rates were for bare transportation service only and would not cover transit privileges, absorption of connecting line switching charges, and the usual free time for loading and unloading.

The rates as proposed were constructed on a formula of forty-two (42¢) cents per ton for terminal services and .573 cents per ton-mile for line haul services. In addition a minimum rate of $2.40 (240 cents) per ton was established. This had the effect of fixing the application of the minimum rate on all shipments traveling less than 346 miles. These rates are available to shippers from Tennessee River ports on the same basis as to shippers from Ohio and Mississippi River gateways.

Southern contemplated the use of five of the newly developed jumbo aluminum covered hopper cars known as "Big Johns" for each 450 ton shipment of grain. Southern owns five hundred of these cars each of which is capable of handling more than one hundred tons of grain, offer a much higher ratio of payload to deadweight than the conventional boxcar equipment, and thus these cars make it possible to transport grain at far less cost. The Commission characterized the development of these cars as "a major breakthrough in the control of cost and a notable advance in the art of railroading."

Promptly after Southern's publication of these rates and in order to remain competitive with Southern, other railroads serving the Southeast (intervening plaintiffs herein), published comparable reduced multiple-car rates on grain shipment carried in conventional equipment, requiring nine cars (instead of five "Big Johns") to carry the minimum load.

These reduced rates were designed to capture for the railroads an increased share of the expanding grain traffic moving from the Middle West into the Southeast, a grain deficit area. In 1960 the movement of at least four million and probably as much as six million tons (estimated sixty (60%) percent of the entire traffic) into the Southeast was accounted for by long haul itinerant truckers. These truckers transport grain into the Southeast as a regulation-exempt backhaul movement after delivering other commodities in the Middle West. These backhaul truckers have complete flexibility in making their transportation charges and may, depending on market conditions, charge as little as expense or gasoline money. From 1955 to 1960 the participation of these backhaul truckers in the long distance movement of grain to the Southeast increased steadily and tremendously while the rail carriers' share of the total volume declined.

The other methods of transporting grain into the Southeast are by rail from the producing areas, by barge to the Tennessee River ports and thence by truck or rail to the consuming markets in the Southeast which are generally located less than 346 miles from the port cities.

The reduced rates proposed by Southern and the other railroads serving the Southeast were scheduled to become effective on August 10, 1961. Upon protest by certain interested parties and under the authority of the Interstate Commerce Act, (hereinafter referred to as the Act), the effective date of the proposed rates was suspended by the Commission, subsequently the suspension was voluntarily extended by Southern, and the Commission undertook an investigation into the lawfulness of the proposed rate reduction.

. . . On July 1, 1963, the Commission issued its Report and Order. . . . [It] found that the proposed 240 cent minimum had an effect which would be unduly prejudicial to the Tennessee River ports and unduly preferential to the Ohio and Mississippi River ports in violation of Section 3(1) of the Act.[1] The Commission also found that the level of the proposed rates would be inadequately compensatory, unjust and unreasonable, and thus violative of Section 1(5) of the Act.[2] The Commission concluded that this violation could be cured by a sixteen (16%) percent increase in the proposed rates, which would be fifty-three (53%) percent lower than the pre-existing rate level.

This action was subsequently brought asking that the Commission's order be set aside, annulled and enjoined as not supported by adequate subsidiary findings, as not supported by the substantial evidence of record, as in excess of the Com-

[1] Section 3(1) of the Act provides:

> It shall be unlawful for any common carrier subject to the provisions of this chapter to make, give, or cause any undue or unreasonable preference or advantage to any particular person, company, firm, corporation, association, locality, port, port district, gateway, transit point, region, district, territory, or any particular description of traffic, in any respect whatsoever; or to subject any particular person, company, firm, corporation, association, locality, port, port district, gateway, transit point, region, district, territory, or any particular description of traffic to any undue or unreasonable prejudice or disadvantage in any respect whatsoever: *Provided, however,* That this paragraph shall not be construed to apply to discrimination, prejudice, or disadvantage to the traffic of any other carrier of whatever description.

[2] Section 1(5) of the Act provides:

> All charges made for any service rendered or to be rendered in the transportation of passengers or property as aforesaid, or in connection therewith, shall be just and reasonable, and every unjust and unreasonable charge for such service or any part thereof is prohibited and declared to be unlawful.

mission's statutory authority, as arbitrary and capricious and as constituting an abuse of discretion. Southern also alleged that the Commission's order violated Section 15a(3) of the Act.[3]

On August 21, 1963, this Court granted a temporary restraining order suspending the effectiveness of the Commission's order pending a final determination of this suit. Southern's rates have been in continuous effect since May 11, 1963.

CONCLUSIONS OF LAW

This Court has jurisdiction of the subject matter and the parties in this action. . . .

A conclusion by the Interstate Commerce Commission that Section 3(1) of the Interstate Commerce Act has been violated must be supported by several findings, including that of the discriminatory treatment under substantially similar transportation and competitive conditions.

The Commission's purported finding on this essential element is inadequate to support the conclusion of a violation under Section 3(1) and is not itself supported by substantial evidence in the record. The conclusion constitutes an abuse of discretion in that it was made despite other findings by the Commission that transportation conditions, as between the points of origin allegedly unduly preferred and those allegedly unduly prejudiced, are in fact not similar. The conclusion that Section 3(1) of the Act has been violated being invalid must be set aside.

The conclusion by the Interstate Commerce Commission that the rates are unlawful as violative of Section 1(5) of the Interstate Commerce Act is invalid and must be set aside because it is based on the invalid premise that Section 3(1) of the Act has been violated and on findings as to car utilization and costing procedures which are not supported by substantial evidence in the record.

The conclusion of the Interstate Commerce Commission that the proposed rates must be increased in order to avoid unfair and destructive competition in violation of the National Transportation Policy is invalid and must be set aside because the conclusion violates Section 15a(3) of the Interstate Commerce Act; it exceeds the statutory authority granted to the Commission; and it is not supported by substantial evidence in the record.

The Order of the Interstate Commerce Commission in *Grain in Multiple Car Shipments—River Crossing to the South* is accordingly null and void, and must be enjoined and set aside.

[The Supreme Court vacated the District Court's decision and remanded the case to the I.C.C. for reconsideration—379 U.S. 642 (1965). The Commission finally approved Southern's rates for the Big John Hopper in August, 1965, four years after the initial rate proposal.]

---

[3] Section 15a(3) of the Act provides:

> In a proceeding involving competition between carriers of different modes of transportation. . . . the Commission, in determining whether a rate is lower than a reasonable minimum rate, shall consider the facts and circumstances attending the movement of the traffic by the carrier or carriers to which the rate is applicable. Rates of a carrier shall not be held up to a particular level to protect the traffic of any other mode of transportation, giving due consideration to the objectives of the national transportation policy. . . .

CHAPTER 15

AIR TRANSPORTATION

The Civil Aeronautics Board (CAB) was established in 1938 to regulate the nation's air carriers. The CAB was empowered to control entry into the airline industry and the rates that could be charged by the airlines. Since 1958, airline safety has been under the jurisdiction of the Federal Aviation Administration (FAA).

The first case examines the CAB's old rate-making policy. It presents excerpts from one phase of a domestic passenger-fare investigation conducted by the CAB. The primary issue in this phase is the relation of airline fares to costs for economy, coach, and first-class service. In short, what are the costs of serving different passengers and do the fares reflect those costs? Who, if anyone, gained from the CAB's decision? The airlines? Which ones: the long-distance trunk lines or the local service carriers? Did airline passengers gain? If so, which ones? There is a well-established basis for price discrimination in regulated firms such as electric utilities and telephone companies because of decreasing costs. Does the same argument apply to the airlines? Since 1977 the airlines have been free to provide almost any discount they want on economy fares. The result has been much larger fare differentials than this decision overruled. Do you think the public is better or worse off because of these discount fares?

The airline regulatory environment has been altered dramatically since the CAB's Domestic Passenger Fare Investigation. Through CAB decisions and the Airline Deregulation Act of 1978, controls over entry and fares have been substantially reduced. Prior to deregulation, it was feared that these changes would deprive small towns of airline service, lessen competition, and generally not promote the public interest. The second and third cases in this chapter examine the limited empirical evidence on the effects of deregulation. Has deregulation improved or worsened performance in the airline industry? Has the industry become more or less efficient? Under the Airline Deregulation Act, the CAB will be abolished in 1985. Is this step warranted by our experience with deregulation?

In the last case, the CAB approves the proposed merger between Pan American and National Airlines. For years, Pan American applied for domestic routes, but was continually turned down by the CAB. The merger with National Airlines would enable Pan Am to quickly acquire a domestic route system. The Administrative Law Judge decided that the merger would be anticompetitive, but was overruled by the Board. Do you think that the Board's decision was correct? Would you reach the same conclusion if the airline industry was not being deregulated?

Domestic Passenger-Fare Investigation
Phase 9—Fare Structure

Decided: March 18, 1974
Docket 21866-9

By the Board: The instant Phase 9 dealing with the fare structure represents the culmination of the proceeding. The preceding phases of the investigation have been, for the most part, concerned with issues relating to the fare level, *i.e.,* the determination of the total revenue necessary for the industry to recover its costs including a reasonable rate of return. The present phase is concerned with the manner in which the total costs of operations should be distributed to, and recouped from, the myriad of passenger services operated by the domestic certificated carriers. Thus, the issues in this phase are concerned with the cost of service at various mileage blocks; the development of an appropriate fare formula for the determination of coach fares for service at varying mileages; the proper relationship between coach fares and other classes of normal fares; and finally, determination of the appropriate form of the final order herein establishing the lawful future fares.

I OVERVIEW

The major issue in the proceeding involves the evaluation of the coach fare structure, coach service being the predominant mode of domestic air transportation. . . . Airline operating costs are characterized by a significant "taper." That is, the costs per passenger-mile decline materially as distance increases. On the other hand, coach fares under the present fare structure are also tapered but not to the same degree as are costs. This means that the fares charged for short trips are currently below the full costs of providing the service, whereas the fares for long trips are in excess of the cost of service. To some extent the present fare structure is explicable on historical grounds: it still retains a bias inherited from the age of piston aircraft when the cost taper was much less than it is today. And the structure has generally been defended on the ground that short-haul fares cannot be increased to the level of costs whereas long-haul traffic will bear fares in excess of costs and that it is reasonable in the interest of maintaining an overall air transportation system to set fares so as to achieve a cross-subsidization of short-haul services by long-haul fares.

We conclude . . . that the fare structure should be more closely aligned to the cost structure than it presently is, and, indeed, that our long-term goal should be the creation of a fare structure which is entirely cost based. Our conclusions in this regard are consistent with those in other phases of this proceeding. A fare structure based on the cost of providing adequate and efficient service should, in the long run, equalize the opportunities of all carriers to achieve reasonable returns on their investment. As a result of our decision short-haul fares will be slightly increased and long-haul fares will be modestly reduced. The increased yield which will be realized in the short-haul markets will encourage carriers to furnish adequate short-haul service, while at the same time reduction of yields in long-haul markets should reduce the incentives to provide excessive long-haul service, or to engage in uneconomical forms of competition.

In reaching these conclusions we have considered the arguments advanced in favor of cross-subsidization and find that they are essentially unsupported by the record, that short-haul fares *can* be moderately increased without endangering the nationwide air transportation network, and that because of the multi-carrier structure of the industry, the cross-subsidization tool can never work effectively in any event.

Turning to the relationship between coach fares and those for other classes of service, our basic conclusion again is that these relationships should be based upon cost differences. We find . . . that first-class fares today do not bear their fair share of total costs. Whereas the costs of providing first-class service range up to 163 percent of coach-service costs, the first-class fares are generally no higher than 130 percent of coach fares. It is plain that, in the interests of revenue maximization, the coach passenger has been subsidizing the first-class passenger. Our decision herein is designed to correct this situation over a two-year period.

We also find that economy fares are presently under-priced in relation to coach fares and, as in the case of first-class fares, burden the coach passenger. Since the only material difference in the two classes of service is the provision of free meals on some coach flights, we have determined that economy-service fares may reflect only the difference in meal costs on those flights in which free meals are served to coach passengers, an amount which we calculate at $4.00. Carriers are, of course, free to institute lower-cost types of service at commensurate fare reductions.

Finally, we have considered the question of the extent to which fares should be prescribed by the Board. Many parties have urged that carriers be given freedom to fix individual fares within a range of plus or minus 15 percent of the cost-related fares found reasonable herein. Adoption of these proposals would, in our judgment, virtually undo all of the progress which we have made in this investigation to devise a rational system of passenger fares and would, moreover, inevitably result in excessive fares. Accordingly, we are directing the cancellation of all tariffs that are inconsistent with our findings herein and the filing of new tariffs at the precise fares and fare relationships specified herein. On the other hand, we recognize the need for flexibility in responding to changes in carrier costs and operations and, accordingly, we will, with certain exceptions, leave the carriers free to file tariffs in the future proposing changes in the fare level and/or improvements in the cost/fare relationship subject only to our power to suspend and investigate those tariffs. We will, however, evaluate all such tariffs on the basis of the standards and guidelines developed in this and other phases of the investigation.

Ultimate Findings and Conclusions

On the basis of all of the foregoing facts and considerations, it is found that:

In the long-run, the coach-fare structure should be based upon the costs of service, but this policy should be implemented only on a partial basis at this time.

Trunkline coach fares should be based upon a multi-element formula consisting of a terminal charge and a variable line-haul charge as follows:

| | Line-haul charge | |
Terminal charge	Mileage	Cents per mile
$12.56	0–500	7.06
	501–1500	5.39
	1501 and over	5.18

Local service carriers may file fares ranging from 100 to 130 percent of the otherwise applicable trunkline coach fare.

The fare-basing mileage for both trunklines and local service carriers should be the shortest authorized mileage from the airport of origin to the airport of destination.

Passengers making trips involving stopovers may be charged the combination of the local fares.

The various proposals for establishment of a range of maximum and minimum fares within which fares would be deemed reasonable *per se* are rejected.

The minimum first-class fares should be based upon the fully allocated cost of service, this determination to be implemented on a phased basis over a period of two years . . . .

An appropriate order will be entered.

Presentation of the U.S. Civil Aeronautics Board before the Subcommittee on Aviation, Committee on Public Works and Transportation

House of Representatives, July 25, 1979

INTRODUCTION

. . . Since the President signed the Airline Deregulation Act into law on October 24 last year, we have seen many changes in the way airlines serve the American public and in the way they price their product. . . .

While not all communities have benefitted during this period of change, by almost every aggregate measure the results of change have been good. More communities are receiving more service. Since last year, the number of certificated carriers is up; the aircraft utilization of all the certificated carriers is up. More passengers are flying more miles than any time in the nation's history. And they are flying for less money. The price of air travel has declined for many passengers over the past year. We estimate that 40 percent of all travelers now fly at discount prices. We are also witnessing the advent of real price competition in the industry—competition which promises lower fares for regular coach seats, rather than the limited price cutting of restricted discount fares.

These benefits to consumers have not come at the expense of the industry. The airlines as a group are making more money than they ever have, though they're probably working harder at making it. The expansion of service has also meant more jobs. Total employment has increased 3.4 percent between January 1978 and January 1979, from 347,800 to 359,500 people.

PRICE COMPETITION AND LOWER FARES

The relaxation of government control of market entry and the easing of the requirements for approval of fares have, *in combination,* resulted in real price competition in the airline industry for the first time in many years. This has meant real benefits to consumers—lower prices for air transportation and less restrictive conditions on the discount fares. During 1978 average fares declined by 1.4 percent in all domestic markets. We have estimated that consumers have saved almost $2.5 billion over the past year. . . .

Fare reductions have been most pronounced in the long-haul, high density markets, like New York-Los Angeles and Washington-San Francisco, although there are exceptions. . . .

We know that the price of air travel in most of the small markets, especially those served by monopoly carriers, has not decreased. However, the benefits of reductions in major markets like New York-Los Angeles are shared by all passengers who travel over the segment, not just the passengers that begin and end their journeys in New York and Los Angeles. Connecting passengers whose trips include markets for which unrestricted low fares are available need not pay more than the sum of the low fare plus the local fare on the connecting segment. . . .

Some critics have argued that fares from small and medium size cities . . . are too high, and, since they're often higher on a per mile basis than the fares in major markets, that they are being discriminated against. However, there is usually a cost-based reason for the difference. . . .

CHANGES IN AIR SERVICE

Most travelers are aware of the explosion in service at many of the nation's large cities; however, service levels at the nation's smaller airports are also increasing. . . .

While average service levels were up significantly . . . some communities did experience reductions in air service during the April 1978–April 1979 period. In virtually every state, some communities are losing service, but most are gaining. We also know that the certificated carriers have opened up almost 100 new stations in the past year . . . [F]rom April 1978 to April 1979, 393 communities had increases or no change in service, measured by departures, while 284 had decreases. In general, it appears that service is increasing at the points which have the greatest demand for it.

NEW AUTHORITY ISSUED

Before the passage of the Deregulation Act, an air carrier could receive certificate authority to operate large aircraft only after notice and hearing, a legal battle to prove that its services were the most desirable so that it should be selected for a new route from among a group of competing applicants. We could also grant temporary authority to carriers by exemption in exceptional circumstances. We rarely did so, especially if more than one carrier had applied for the authority. The route certification process often took from 18 to 24 months to complete. Now, since it is no longer necessary to select from among competing applicants, we are able to issue a final decision in about four to five months.

The relaxed entry policy has not had the disruptive impact on the industry feared by some of its opponents. Multiple awards—the award of authority in a market to more carriers than the market can possibly support—has not resulted in the chaos predicted by its opponents who argued that the failure to maintain exclusive or semi-exclusive franchises would mean that either all authorized carriers would rush into a market and ruin the opportunity for profitable operations by anyone, or the reverse would obtain, and no carrier would enter when multiple carriers had been authorized because the opportunity for profitable operations had been reduced. Neither result has occurred. Aviation industry officials are quite as capable as businessmen in other industries of weighing the competitive risks before committing the resources of their firm to a new market and in seizing the best opportunities for profitable service. A number of civic parties complained that multiple awards would mean less service, but this is not what has happened. . . .

A REVIEW OF THE STATUTORY CHANGES THAT AFFECT REDUCTIONS AND TERMINATIONS OF SERVICE

The Airline Deregulation Act has changed the rules for reducing service. Certificated carriers are required to provide 90-days notice of their intent to suspend all of their service *at a point.* Under the old Act, they were required to apply for permission to terminate all service and we would permit a suspension if we found it to be in the public interest. Full notice and a costly evidentiary hearing were usually required before we took any action. In fact, we did approve 129 deletions or suspensions at single carrier cities in the period from 1968 to 1978 and these cities lost all federally guaranteed service. Now our power is more limited; carriers may suspend after notice period unless we stop them; we may prohibit a suspension after the ninetieth day if we find that the suspension will result in a loss of essential air service and we are unable to find a willing replacement. Even in these circumstances, we may prohibit a suspension only for 30-day intervals while we search for a substitute.

There are two major differences between the old Act and the new as it affects the termination of service by a carrier at a point. First, a community's access to the national air transportation system is no longer at risk since the government has guaranteed that access for at least 10 years, and second, the Board is required to act quickly, and is free to act informally, to find substitute service for a carrier that wants to terminate its service at a point.

REDUCTIONS AND TERMINATIONS OF SERVICE AT LARGER COMMUNITIES

We have not routinely blocked suspensions of service at large and medium-size communities. We are authorized to prohibit the termination, suspension or reduction of air transportation at a point only when it reasonably appears to deprive the point of essential air transportation. In the case of communities which retain multiple jet services from a number of certificated carriers, we see no threat to the maintenance of the community's essential air service. Interference with the carriers' plans to reduce air service at larger communities is likely to be counterproductive both for the airlines and the passengers.

The industry is engaged in a sifting and sorting of considerable proportions as the airlines seek the markets which best fit their equipment and route systems. The large trunk carriers are using ever-larger equipment and moving it to markets where it can be operated at maximum efficiency. The local service carriers are expanding into the markets vacated by the trunks, and commuters are expanding into markets abandoned by the locals. This is a natural process which has been going on for decades. Between the original certification of the local service carriers in the mid-1940s and 1969, 211 points were transferred from the trunks to the local service carriers. Between 1969 and 1976, the trunks ceased service at another 45 points. There were also 179 points that lost all certificated service between 1960 and 1976. A number of these receive commuter service, which is voluntarily provided or underwritten in some form by the certificated carrier. The trunk and local service carriers' continuing investment in larger jet equipment increases the costs of providing short-haul, small community service and thereby reduces their incentive to provide it.

. . . It is our job during this transition to encourage a competitive system in which the carriers' interests and the public interest coincide as closely as possible. . . . Blocking suspensions and interfering with the process wouldn't really work to the public's benefit in most cases. The carrier that wanted to suspend would be stopped from moving its equipment to markets where it sees a greater need for its service. The community would probably not receive satisfactory service from the carrier whose suspension we prohibited since long experience suggests that unwilling carriers provide unsatisfactory service. Prohibiting suspensions at these cities would discourage experiments with new service by other carriers at other cities of a similar size. A carrier won't enter a point as quickly if it fears it may be stuck there indefinitely. Finally, prohibiting suspensions of this kind would destroy the efficiencies that permit carriers to reduce costs and lower prices throughout their systems.

Report on Airline Service, Fares, Traffic, Load Factors and Market Shares Service Status on July 1, 1979

Civil Aeronautics Board, Washington, D.C. 20428, August 1979

EXPLANATION OF ANALYSIS

This report, the sixth in a series, summarizes service changes that have occurred since the passage of the Airline Deregulation Act in October 1978. It also includes data on fares, traffic, load factors, market shares and airlines efficiency indicators.

Overview—Departures and System-Wide City-Pair Analysis

Total domestic departures showed an increase of 9.1 percent from July 1978 to July 1979. Weekly seats available increased 5.9 percent from 11.5 million to 12.1 million. . . .

Traffic and Traffic-Related Performance

Actual departures and available seats increased between 4 and 5 percent for all market groups during June 1979 vs. June 1978. This is a reversal of the downward trend in departures and seats over the last several months in comparison to the same months a year earlier and occurred despite the DC-10 aircraft grounding on June 6. . . .

Load factors for June 1979 compared with June 1978 increased across all market groups. The gains ranged from 0.7 points in monopoly markets to 3.2 points in four-carrier markets. . . .

Average Fare Per Mile or Yield Comparisons

Beginning with the third quarter of 1978, carriers . . . were directed to report the dollar fare on each ticket included in the survey sample. These data allow the Board and staff to construct average prices per mile or yield and evaluate the effect of pricing flexibility . . . allowing the carriers to separately price each market.

Yield by Market Category

Average fares per mile or yield, during the first quarter of 1979 are shown in the following table:

Market group	Yields in cents per mile			
	Average	First class	Coach	Discount
One carrier authorized	10.67	12.72	11.85	7.72
Two or three carriers authorized	9.59	12.32	10.60	7.13
Four or more carriers authorized	9.80	11.91	10.53	7.48
Average (all markets)	9.79	12.19	10.76	7.31

Higher fares in monopoly markets reflect several factors, particularly shorter average trip lengths (that is, fares increase at a decreasing rate with distance) and less intense competitive pressures. In two-and-three-carrier and four-or-more-carrier markets, average yields were similar for all classes of service considering differential trip lengths.

[Previously], normal fares were prescribed by mileage. Now, however, carriers have the ability to price slightly above and substantially below the normal level as competition and market conditions dictate. This was expected to produce a variety of price/quality options for normal fare as well as discount fare travelers. As of the first quarter of 1979, however, different price/quality options for the normal fare passengers have not appeared. Normal coach fares (including night coach and economy) were running between 85 and 90 percent of formula fares. . . . First-class fares were also fairly constant, running at about 30 percent above formula coach fares at all distances.

Upward Pricing Flexibility

Upward pricing flexibility granted under the new pricing policies is a function of competition. Carriers can raise fares by: (1) 5% above the normal coach level in monopoly markets for 58 days of the year; (2) 5% above the normal coach level for all days of the year in markets with two or three carriers authorized to provide nonstop service; and, (3) 10% above the normal coach level for all days of the year in markets where four or more carriers are authorized to provide nonstop service. A concern expressed against offering upward flexibility was that carriers would take all increases possible and that, at least by implication, the competitive marketplace would not function to police such action. This concern, as of the first quarter of 1969, appears to have been unwarranted. . . . Currently, however, the situation is changing. In September, all carriers are taking 5 percent upward flexibility across all markets. This is the maximum allowable in monopoly and two-or-three-carrier markets and is one-half the allowable 10 percent in four-or-more-carrier markets.

Input/Output Analysis

Three simple efficiency or "input/output" ratios—operating costs per revenue ton-mile in real terms; operating costs per available ton-mile in real terms; and revenue ton-miles per employee—are presented to measure changes in efficiency as the industry moves from protective regulation to market regulation.

Operating costs per revenue ton-mile, adjusted for inflation, declined markedly during 1978. . . . Operating costs per available ton-mile, also adjusted, have remained relatively constant over the last four years. Revenue ton-miles per employee have grown at a much faster rate particularly the last three years than has output per man-hour in the general economy. Because input costs increased at about the same rate as in the general economy, the gains have come exclusively from capital and labor productivity improvements deriving principally from higher load factors, and higher seating density and aircraft utilization rates.

Had the general economy enjoyed the same productivity gains the inflation rate would have been about zero. In calendar year 1978 the inflation rate was 7.7%, whereas airline yield declined by 1.8% in inflated dollars. . . .

United States of America Civil Aeronautics Board, Washington, D.C.

Pan American-Acquisition of Control of, and Merger with National, Docket 33283
Decided: October 24, 1979

BY THE BOARD:

INTRODUCTION

On August 24, 1978, Pan American World Airways (Pan American) filed an application requesting the right to acquire and merge with National and to have National's certificates of public convenience and necessity transferred to it. Shortly thereafter, on September 6, 1978, Pan American and National entered into an agreement to merge. . . .

A . . . hearing was held before Administrative Law Judge William H. Dapper. . . . Judge Dapper recommended that [the merger] . . . be denied on the grounds that [it was] . . . anticompetitive and otherwise inconsistent with the public interest. In its order instituting this proceeding the Board determined that it would review the decision of the administrative law judge in its entirety. . . .

Pan American is our leading international carrier and its operations have been traditionally confined to international and overseas markets. It principally operates a fleet of 4-engine wide and narrow bodied aircraft and has on order a substantial number of 3-engine Boeing 727 and Lockheed L-1011 equipment. Recently it has begun to conduct its domestic operations through the use of fill-up rights and other licensing provisions made available by the Airline Deregulation Act. Its application for acquisition of National is said to be in furtherance of its long term objective of obtaining a fully competitive domestic system.

Market Definition: United States-Western Europe

At the outset we note that the Judge appeared to be concerned with the need to draw market boundaries as precisely as possible, whereas we place considerably less importance on establishing the exact limits of the relevant market. Again, this difference in emphasis is based on fundamental differences in our respective approaches to the analysis of the competitive effects of a merger: in the Judge's view, concentration ratios and other market share data are major tools for assessing the effects of the merger on competition; in our view, the most crucial factors are those which determine the nature of competition in the market—for example, ease of entry, traffic density, the number of actual competitors and the likelihood of new entry. Precision in delineating the market is important if concentration ratios and market shares will determine whether the merger is found to be anticompetitive. Since our focus, however, is on the specific forces which shape transatlantic competition, we do not think it is crucial to establish precisely where market boundaries lie. . . .

As to geographic market Pan American argued for "international service" (service between different nations) as the international market, with North America-Europe as a defensible submarket. . . . Judge Dapper designated the relevant international market as United States-Western Europe, with United States-London as a relevant submarket. The Judge, noting that the relevant geographic market must accord with commercial reality, found that National's international route system is constituted almost entirely of transatlantic flights, and that within Europe National serves Western European points only. In addition, he found that within Europe Pan American serves primarily Western Europe, and that it was therefore only within that zone that the two carriers' international systems were in actual competition.

Competitive Effects of the Merger: United States-Western Europe

Judge Dapper found that the merger would result in a substantial lessening of competition in the United States-Western Europe market. The Judge concluded that a merger between the two carriers would violate section 7 of the Clayton Act by a loss of actual competition in the United States-Western Europe market. . . .

The Judge found that Pan American and National engage in actual competition in the United States-Western Europe market on the following basis: Pan American serves London, Frankfurt and Rome from New York; London and Frankfurt from Washington, Los Angeles and San Francisco; and Madrid from Miami. National serves London, Paris and Amsterdam from Miami; Frankfurt from New Orleans and Miami; and Amsterdam from New York. The Judge also found that the respective market shares of the carriers in the United States-Western Europe market were 2.1% for National (excluding New York-Amsterdam service, for which data were unavailable), and 16.3 percent for Pan American. The combined market share of the carriers was thus found to be 18.4 percent of the transatlantic market.

With regard to the level of concentration, the Judge found that TWA and Pan American account for 37.2 percent of the market; the four-firm concentration (adding British Airways and Lufthansa) was found to be 57 percent; and the eight-firm concentration (including Air France, KLM, SAS and Swissair) was 76 percent.

. . . [We] find that, with the exception of the United States-London market discussed below, competition in those transatlantic markets which would be affected by the merger is healthy and can be expected to increase. The markets now served by National—Amsterdam, Zurich, Frankfurt and Paris—are markets in which multiple designations of United States carriers are permitted. Moreover, in the Amsterdam and Frankfurt markets, innovative fares and price competition are a fact of life. Although the merger will result in the loss of one United States carrier in those markets, we do not anticipate a substantial reduction in competition when both United States and foreign carriers are free to enter the relevant markets and, in at least some markets, to charge competitive fares. It is our view that liberalized entry and recent route awards for foreign and United States carriers are sufficient to compensate for the loss of competition occasioned by the merger.

United States-London: Competitive Effects of the Merger

There was little dispute among the parties over the designation of a United States-London submarket. . . .

The Judge found that the United States-London market is highly concentrated: the three-firm concentration ratio was found to be 95.5 percent. Judge Dapper also found significant barriers to entry in the United States-London market due to Bermuda 2, which restricts the numbers of United States carriers permitted to enter London from United States gateways. Because of the bilateral agreement, the Judge reasoned, there is no possibility for deconcentration or a trend towards deconcentration in the market. He found that the merged carriers' share of the market would be about 35 percent. Pan American had 31 percent of the market, and National, about 4 percent. The Judge concluded that the market share of the combined carrier in a market that is highly concentrated would be presumptively illegal under antitrust case law. He found, therefore, that the proposed merger violated section 7 of the Clayton Act as a result of the loss of actual competition in the United States-London market.

We find that the effect of adding another gateway, Miami, to Pan American's already sizeable share of this market may substantially lessen competition in the United States-London market. . . . This finding is based on the following considerations.

The United States-London market is a restricted entry market. As the Judge found, the Bermuda 2 bilateral agreement between the United States and the United Kingdom limits the number of United States carriers serving London to two U.S. carriers at two cities, and only one U.S. carrier serving London at all of the other twelve U.S. points. With the exception of the two cities selected for service by two U.S. carriers, there can be no competition among U.S. carriers at the individual gateway; and since new entrants are prohibited by the bilateral agreement, there is no threat of new entry to discipline pricing behavior. Under these circumstances price and service options, if they are to exist, must come from competition among and between gateways.

We have found that carriers recently designated to serve the United States-London market have succeeded in creating competition where virtually none existed before. Until Sir Freddie Laker's Skytrain service from New York was introduced in 1977, the incumbents Pan American and Trans World Airways offered first class, standard coach and advance purchase excursion (APEX) fares. In 1978, Pan American responded to Laker's low-fare service with its first standby/budget fare to London. The lower fare offered by Pan American was initially limited to the New York gateway, the only gateway served by Laker. The fare offerings at the other gateways served by Pan American or TWA remained the same. It was clear that Laker's low-fare service had induced a competitive response, but only in that city-pair (New York-London) where the competition was direct.

For the reasons given above, we are transferring National's certificate to engage in foreign air transportation to Pan American, but deleting that segment which authorizes National to engage in foreign air transportation between the coterminal point Miami, Florida, and the terminal point London, England. New authority for the Miami-London route is the subject of a separate route proceeding. For the interim, that is, between the time this merger is effected and the time a carrier has been selected to serve Miami-London in Docket 36764, we will issue exemption authority to Pan American to serve the Miami-London route.

Potential Competition

The Judge found that the proposed merger would violate section 7 of the Clayton Act as a result of the loss of potential competition in five domestic city-pair markets. The five markets selected by the Judge were those currently served by National and where Pan American was considered an actual potential entrant. It has been established above that the use of the actual potential entrant doctrine requires that the target market show indications of interdependent oligopolistic behavior and that the merging firm be a likely entrant. As also discussed above the loss of one potential entrant is not significant when a sufficient number of others remain.

As we discussed above, our analysis of the competitiveness of a given market goes beyond market share and concentration ratio data. The two-firm concentration ratios used by Judge Dapper do not tell us, for example, whether the concentration is entrenched, or whether on the contrary entry and exit are relatively easy. The concentration statistics also do not disclose whether there are sufficient numbers of other potential entrants or special entry barriers that Pan American is uniquely capable of overcoming. We have examined these additional questions and conclude that there is no probability of a substantial loss of potential competition in any of the markets.

The markets are substantial in terms of passengers and revenue potential, and consequently profit opportunities, should they arise, are not likely to be ignored by the remaining potential competitors. Each market would have, assuming a merger between National and Pan American, at least seven carriers which either provide some service in the market or have existing facilities at both terminal points. . . . Furthermore, in many instances the potential entrants are major domestic carriers with equipment, marketing experience and route systems that clearly establish them as realistic threats to the incumbents. In short, we find a sufficient number of able competitors, potential and actual, for each of these markets.

ORDER

Subject to the conditions listed below, we approve (1) the application of Pan American World Airways, Inc. for acquisition of control of, and merger with, National Airlines, Inc., and (2) the transfer to Pan American of National's certificate of public convenience and necessity for route 31 and such other domestic certificate and exemption authority as National holds at the time of implementation of the merger;

Our approval is further subject to the condition that Pan American agree to operate the Miami-London portion of Route 168 and maintain National's Heathrow Airport facilities for the benefit of the successful applicant in Docket 36764;

We direct that this order become effective 65 days after transmittal to the President or five days after receipt by the Board of notification from the President that he will not disapprove the transfer of National's foreign route certificate to Pan American, whichever is sooner.

By the Civil Aeronautics Board.

CHAPTER 16

COMMUNICATIONS

The Federal Communications Commission was established in 1934 to regulate interstate communications utilities (mainly the American Telephone and Telegraph Company, or "Ma Bell") and to license firms to use particular electromagnetic frequencies for radio, television, microwave communications, and other activities. The first two cases in this chapter deal with the Commission's regulation of AT&T.

In the Carterfone decision, the main issue was whether other firms could supply equipment which would hook into the Bell system. Ma Bell naturally objected, maintaining that these "foreign attachments" would impair the reliability of the entire telephone system. Try to decide if the ultimate decision of the FCC was in the consumers' interest. Would it have been in their interest if the Bell system had superior equipment? If that were the case, would the issue of "foreign attachments" ever arise? It might. Can you see why?

The Carterfone decision was the first of several that opened up the input market to competition. Of most importance to consumers was the FCC's subsequent ruling that AT&T's rate for special interface equipment (used for connecting non-Bell equipment to the Bell system) unnecessarily restricted consumers' rights to install their own non-Bell telephone. By requiring users of non-Bell phones to rent interconnection devices, AT&T had apparently made it uneconomical to purchase these devices. AT&T responded to the Commission's decision with a request that every household must have at least one phone—a "primary" instrument—provided by the local telephone company. The FCC rejected this request, thereby permitting users to choose whatever equipment they desired. Carterfone was the decision that opened the market for the great flowering of new telephone styles in the late 1970s. More importantly, it also led to the installation of non-Bell telephone exchanges (PBXs) in many offices. Can you see why?

The MCI case (for Microwave Communications, Inc.) represented more of a threat to Ma Bell. In this case, MCI proposed to compete with AT&T in providing long-distance microwave service for business firms. The initial reaction of most observers was one of astonishment, even though MCI's proposal was technically quite feasible. Whether or not it was within the law was for the FCC to decide. Since this decision, more firms have entered into competition with AT&T. As it turns out, long-distance microwave service is less of a "natural monopoly" than most economists thought—at least on routes between major cities. More recently, the FCC has authorized firms, including MCI, to offer long-distance telephone services in competition with AT&T over many routes.

Independent microwave common carriers have generally stuck to the high-density routes and left the high-cost, low-density routes to Bell. With rates distinctly lower than Bell's, MCI has acquired a large share of the leased line service on the routes it chose to serve. Bell's natural response was to reduce rates where it faced competition and raise rates on other routes. Do you think that Bell's new rates more accurately reflect the marginal costs of providing service? The new rates are clearly a departure from Bell's average cost rate-making principle, whereby users in low-cost areas subsidized users in high-cost areas. Do you believe this subsidy was desirable from an efficiency perspective? From an equity perspective?

The third case concerns the FCC's regulation of the electromagnetic frequency spectrum. The most spectacular part of this job was the assignment of frequencies to particular radio or television stations. Most of these licenses were issued during the 1930s, 1940s, and 1950s. Receiving a radio license in the 1930s or a television license in the 1940s and 1950s with network affiliation was roughly comparable to inheriting a gold mine. As a result, the number of applicants far exceeded the number of licenses available.

At issue in this case are the Commission's rules regarding the joint ownership of local newspapers and local broadcast stations. The Commission was concerned that common ownership of these media would reduce the diversity of program and service viewpoints. As a result, it issued a rule preventing the formation of new broadcast-newspaper combinations in the same market and requiring the dissolution of existing combinations in some communities. Do you think that the FCC's decision was in the public interest? Even if it resulted in the sale of a television station to someone from another state who had no prior broadcasting experience? Some people have proposed that the Commission simply sell each broadcast frequency to the highest bidder at a public auction, thereby solving the problem of choosing among competing applicants. Would the public be harmed by such a selection process?

The fourth case deals with cable television. After *U.S. v. Southwestern Cable* (see Chapter 11), the FCC clearly had responsibility for regulating cable companies. Initially, these companies distributed distant television signals in small, remote towns. Cable television was not controversial in those days. But by the late 1960s, cable companies were beginning to distribute distant (as well as local) signals in the larger cities. The over-the-air broadcasters were very concerned about this development. The FCC responded by adopting rules that required cable systems to carry all local stations and placed a limit on the number of imported channels that could be carried.

The FCC's main concern was with cable television's impact on local stations. In particular, cable systems may divert viewers from local stations, thereby reducing these stations' profitability and their future as outlets for local self-expression. In this case, the FCC announced a proposed rulemaking to evaluate its rules that restrict the number and composition of programs that can be imported. Who would benefit if these restrictions were eliminated:—television viewers? Cable television companies? Over-the-air broadcasters?

The last case is another proposed rulemaking by the FCC with regard to broadcast radio. The focus is on FCC rules requiring a minimum amount of nonentertainment programming (news and public affairs) and a maximum amount of advertising. In a major break with past regulation, the Commission subsequently decided to adopt its proposed rules to rely on the marketplace to regulate programming instead of the government. What factors will determine whether or not competition among radio stations for the listening audience will make these regulations unnecessary? How would you determine whether or not radio deregulation has been successful one year from now?

In the Matter of

Use of The Carterfone Device in Message Toll Telephone Service

13 F.C.C. 420 (1968)

BY COMMISSIONER JOHNSON FOR THE COMMISSION:

This proceeding involves the application of American Telephone and Telegraph Co. tariffs to the use by telephone subscribers of the Carterfone.

The Carterfone is designed to be connected to a two-way radio at the base station serving a mobile radio system. When callers on the radio and on the telephone are both in contact with the base station operation, the handset of the operator's telephone is placed on a cradle in the Carterfone device. A voice control circuit in the Carterfone automatically switches on the radio transmitter when the telephone caller is speaking; when he stops speaking, the radio returns to a receiving condition. A separate speaker is attached to the Carterfone to allow the base station operator to monitor the conversation, adjust the voice volume, and hang up his telephone when the conversation has ended.

The Carterfone device, invented by Thomas F. Carter, has been produced and marketed by the Carter Electronics Corp., of which Mr. Carter is president, since 1959. From 1959 through 1966 approximately 4,500 Carterfones were produced and 3,500 sold to dealers and distributors throughout the United States and in foreign countries.

The defendant telephone companies, acting in accordance with their interpretation of tariff FCC No. 132, filed April 16, 1957, by American Telephone and Telegraph Co., advised their subscribers that the Carterfone, when used in conjunction with the subscriber's telephone, is a prohibited interconnecting device, the use of which would subject the user to the penalties provided in the tariff. The tariff provides that:

> No equipment, apparatus, circuit or device not furnished by the telephone company shall be attached to or connected with the facilities furnished by the telephone company, whether physically, by induction or otherwise.

A private antitrust action was brought by Carter against American Telephone and Telegraph Co. and General Telephone Co. of the Southwest. The District Court held that because of its "special competence and 'expertise' " in the technical and complex matter of telephone communication, the Federal Communications Commission, under the doctrine of primary jurisdiction, is vested with the right to determine the "justness, reasonableness, validity, application, and effect of the tariff and practices here involved." The court reserved jurisdiction to pass ultimately upon the antitrust issues after proceedings before the Commission should be concluded. The United States Court of Appeals for the Fifth Circuit affirmed the District Court's decision. On October 20, 1966, the Commission on its own motion ordered that a public hearing be held to resolve "the question of the justness, reasonableness, validity, and effect of the tariff regulations and practices complained of."

Thomas F. Carter and Carter Electronics Corporation (hereafter Carter), American Telephone and Telegraph Co. and 22 associated Bell Systems companies (AT&T), and General Telephone Co. of the Southwest (General) were named parties respondent.

On December 21, 1966, Carter filed a formal complaint against General and certain of the Bell companies, and further proceedings were held in abeyance pending disposition of the complaint.

By order released March 8, 1967, the complaint was consolidated for hearing . . . and the following issues were added:

1 Whether, with respect to the period from February 6, 1957, to December 21, 1966, the regulations and practices in tariff FCC No. 132 of the American Telephone and Telegraph Co. were properly construed and applied to prohibit any telephone user from attaching the Carterfone device to the facilities of the telephone companies for use in connection with interstate and foreign message toll telephone service; and if so

2 Whether, during the aforesaid period, such regulations and practices were unjust and unreasonable, and therefore unlawful within the meaning of section 201(b) of the Communications Act of 1934, as amended, or were unduly discriminatory or preferential in violation of section 202(a) of said Act.

The examiner found that there was a need and demand for a device to connect the telephone landline system with mobile radio systems which could be met in part by the Carterfone. He also found that the Carterfone had no material adverse effect upon use of the telephone system. He construed the tariff to prohibit attachment of the Carterfone whether or not it harmed the telephone system, and determined that future prohibition of its use would be unjust and unreasonable. He also found that it would be unduly discriminatory under section 202(a) of the Act, since the telephone companies permit the use of their own interconnecting devices. However, he did not find the tariff prohibitions to have been unlawful in the past, largely because the harmless nature of the Carterfone was not known to the telephone companies, and he did not find that a general prohibition against nontelephone company supplied interconnecting devices was unjust or unwise, because of the risk he saw of "serious harm to the heart of the nation's communications network."

We agree with and adopt the examiner's findings that the Carterfone fills a need and that it does not adversely affect the telephone system. They are fully supported by the record. We also agree that the tariff broadly prohibits the use of interconnection devices, including the Carterfone. Its provisions are clear as to this. Finally, in view of the above findings, we hold, as did the examiner, that application of the tariff to bar the Carterfone in the future would be unreasonable and unduly discriminatory. However, for the reasons to be given, we also conclude that the tariff has been unreasonable, discriminatory, and unlawful in the past, and that the provisions prohibiting the use of customer-provided interconnecting devices should accordingly be stricken.

We hold that the tariff is unreasonable in that it prohibits the use of interconnecting devices which do not adversely affect the telephone system. See *Hush-A-Phone Corp. v. U.S.,* [238 F.2d 266 (1956)] . . . holding that a tariff prohibition of a customer supplied "foreign attachment" was "in unwarranted interference with the telephone subscriber's right reasonably to use his telephone in ways which are privately beneficial without being publicly detrimental." The principle of Hush-A-Phone is directly applicable here, there being no material distinction between a foreign attachment such as the Hush-A-Phone and an interconnection device such as the Carterfone, so far as the present problem is concerned. Even if not compelled by the Hush-A-Phone decision, our conclusion here is that a customer desiring to use an interconnecting device to improve the utility to him of both the telephone system and a private radio system should be able to do so, so long as the interconnection does not adversely affect the telphone company's operations or the telephone system's utility for others. A tariff which prevents this is unreasonable; it is also unduly discriminatory when, as here, the telephone company's own interconnecting equipment is approved for use. The vice of the present tariff, here as in Hush-A-Phone, is that it prohibits the use of harmless as well as harmful devices.

A.T. & T. has urged that since the telephone companies have the responsibility to establish, operate and improve the telephone system, they must have absolute control over the quality, installation, and maintenance of all parts of the system in order effectively to carry out that responsibility. Installation of unauthorized equipment, according to the telephone companies, would have at least two negative results. First, it would divide the responsibility for assuring that each part of the system is able to function effectively and, second, it would retard development of the system since the independent equipment supplier would tend to resist changes which would render his equipment obsolete.

There has been no adequate showing that nonharmful interconnection must be prohibited in order to permit the telephone company to carry out its system responsibilities. The risk feared by the examiner has not been demonstrated to be substantial, and no reason presents itself why it should be. No one entity need provide all interconnection equipment for our telephone system any more than a single source is needed to supply the parts for a space probe. We are not holding that the telephone companies may not prevent the use of devices which actually cause harm, or that they may not set up reasonable standards to be met by interconnection devices. These remedies are appropriate; we believe they are also adequate to fully protect the system.

Nor can we assume that the telephone companies would be hindered in improving telephone service by any tendency of the manufacturers and users of interconnection devices to resist change. The telephone companies would remain free to make improvements to the telephone system and could reflect any such improvements in reasonable revised standards for nontelephone company provided devices used in connection with the system. Manufacturers and sellers of such devices would then have the responsibility of offering for sale or use only such equipment as would be in compliance with such revised standards. An owner or user of a device which failed to meet reasonable revised standards for such devices, would either have to have the device rebuilt to comply with the revised standards or discontinue its use. Such is the risk inherent in the private ownership of any equipment to be used in connection with the telephone system.

The present unlawfulness of the tariff also permeates its past. It has been unreasonable and unreasonably discriminatory since its inception, for the reasons given above. That the telephone companies may not have known prior to the proceedings herein that the Carterfone was in fact harmless is irrelevant, since they barred its use without regard to its effect upon the telephone system. Furthermore, the tariff was the carrier's own. It was not prescribed by the Commission. It has remained subject to complaint and to a finding that it had been unlawful since its inception.

A Commission-prescribed rate or practice must be followed by the carrier. It becomes the lawful rate or practice. But where the carrier itself initiates the rate or practice its lawfulness remains open, not only to a prospective finding but also to a retroactive one.

In view of the unlawfulness of the tariff there would be no point in merely declaring it invalid as applied to the Carterfone and permitting it to continue in operation as to other interconnection devices. This would also put a clearly improper burden upon the manufacturers and users of other devices. The appropriate remedy is to strike the tariff and permit the carriers, if they so desire, to propose new tariff provisions in accordance with this opinion. We make no rulings as to damages since that relief has not been requested. As noted above, the carriers may submit new tariffs which will protect the telephone system against harmful devices, and may specify technical standards if they wish.

Accordingly, we find that tariff FCC No. 263, paragraphs 2.6.1 and 2.6.9 are, and have since their inception been, unreasonable, unlawful and unreasonably discriminatory under sections 201(b) and 202(a) of the Communications Act of 1934, as amended.

In Re Applications of

Microwave Communications, Inc.

18 F.C.C. 953 (1969)

COMMISSIONER BARTLEY FOR THE COMMMISSION:

This proceeding involves applications filed by Microwave Communications, Inc. (MCI), for construction permits for new facilities in the Domestic Public Point-to-Point Radio Service at Chicago, Ill., St. Louis, Mo., and nine intermedi-

ate points. MCI proposes to offer its subscribers a limited common carrier microwave radio service, designed to meet the interoffice and interplant communications needs of small business. . . . MCI, however, does not plan to provide its
subscribers with a complete microwave service. The proposed service would be
limited to transmissions between MCI's microwave sites, making it incumbent
upon each subscriber to supply his own communications link between MCI's sites
and his place of business (loop service).

MCI contends that it will offer its subscribers substantially lower rates than
those charged for similar services by the established carriers and that subscribers
with less than full-time communication needs will be able to achieve additional
savings through the channel sharing and half-time use provisions of its proposed
tariff. Up to five subscribers will be permitted to share each channel on a party-
line basis with a pro-rata reduction in rates. . . . MCI further asserts that its
proposed tariff contains fewer restrictions than those of the existing common
carriers, so that greater flexibility of use will be possible, particularly with respect
to channel bandwidth, splitting channels for voice and data transmissions, and in
the attachment of customer equipment.

MCI's applications are opposed by Western Union Telegraph Co. (Western
Union), General Telephone Co. of Illinois (General), and the Associated Bell
System Cos., American Telephone & Telegraph Co., Illinois Bell Telephone Co.,
and Southwestern Bell Telephone Co. (Bell), which presently provide microwave
services to the geographical area which MCI proposes to serve. In a memorandum
opinion and order, on February 11, 1966, we designated the MCI applications for
hearing on issues to determine inter alia: (a) whether the established common
carriers offer services meeting the needs which MCI proposes to meet in the area
which MCI proposes to serve; (b) whether the grant of MCI's applications would
result in wasteful duplication of facilities; (c) whether MCI is financially qualified
to construct and operate its proposed facilities; (d) whether there is need for
MCI's proposal; and (e) whether operation of MCI's proposed system would
result in interference to existing common carrier services.

The evidentiary hearings commenced on February 13, 1967, and were concluded on April 19, 1967. In an initial decision, Hearing Examiner Herbert Sharf-
man recommended the grant of MCI's applications. The examiner found that the
proposed MCI system would not generate harmful electrical interference to the
receivers of the existing carriers or receive harmful interference from their stations. Although he indicated that serious questions exist concerning the reliability
of MCI's proposal, the examiner nevertheless found no reason to believe that the
system would not work, and he concluded that MCI had established that it is
technically qualified. The examiner also found that MCI is financially qualified
and that it would offer its subscribers a more economical rate structure, additional
savings through the utilization of the shared and half-time use provisions of its
tariff, and greater flexibility of use which would permit MCI's subscribers to adapt
the system to their particular needs. The examiner noted that the proposed Chi-
cago-St. Louis route is served by a wide range of common carrier services, that
there is a duplication of facilities, and that the MCI proposal would result in

additional duplication. However, he concluded that MCI's lower rates and more flexible use would enable it to serve a market whose needs are unfulfilled by the available common carrier services; that consequently there would be no unnecessary or wasteful duplication; and that the public interest would be served by authorizing MCI's proposed microwave system.

Upon release of the initial decision, we recognized that the questions raised at the hearing involved important policy considerations respecting the entry of new licensees into the communications common carrier field. . . . We have considered the initial decision in light of the record, pleadings, and oral argument. Except as modified below and in the attached appendix, we adopt the hearing examiner's findings and conclusions.

The principal contentions advanced by Bell, General, and Western Union against the grant of MCI's applications are: (1) That MCI is not financially qualified to construct and operate the proposed facilities; (2) that no need has been shown for the common carrier services proposed; (3) that MCI will be unable to provide a reliable communications service; (4) that the proposal represents an inefficient utilization of the frequency spectrum; and (5) that the proposal is not technically feasible. Each of these contentions will be considered below.

MCI'S FINANCIAL QUALIFICATIONS

The examiner found that MCI's estimate of its construction costs at $564,000 is reasonable, and that there is consumer interest in, and a market for, a communications service with the features MCI proposes. Based on the foregoing, the funds presently available to MCI and his finding that MCI could reasonably expect to procure additional funds, the examiner concluded that MCI is financially qualified. The carriers argue that the examiner erred in finding MCI financially qualified since MCI: (1) Underestimated its construction costs; (2) omitted essential items from its estimates; and (3) will be unable to market a sufficient number of channels to be able to raise the revenues necessary to operate its system. . . .

The further arguments advanced by the carriers that MCI's showing is deficient because it has not budgeted for emergency generators, proper equipment housing, and efficient maintenance, are predicated upon their views of what is essential to achieve an adequate common carrier communications service. For reasons which are discussed in later portions of this decision, we have determined that the MCI proposal reasonably may be expected to provide a reliable and adequate common carrier service so that the lack of funds for such equipment and maintenance does not constitute a deficiency in its financial showing. We conclude that MCI is financially qualified to construct and to operate its proposed microwave system, and the examiner's determination to this effect is affirmed.

NEED FOR MCI'S PROPOSALS

Relying upon a market survey conducted by the Spindletop Research Center of Lexington, Ky., and upon the testimony of witnesses produced at the hearing by

MCI, the examiner found that there is a market for microwave service of acceptable quality at lower rates than offered by the existing carriers, that MCI is offering such a service, and he concluded that a need exists for the service proposed by MCI. The carriers challenge these findings and the conclusions of need based thereon upon a number of grounds, including, inter alia, claims that rates will not be lower, that the service proposed is not of acceptable quality or reliability, and that no service not previously available is being offered.

This is not a rate proceeding . . . and we are not called upon to make specific findings concerning the reasonableness of MCI's proposed rates or whether they are compensatory. . . .

The significant fact remains that the existing carriers do not offer a 2-kc. voice channel and MCI will; so that a subscriber may achieve a substantial savings in his communications costs by utilizing MCI's services. Further savings may be effected by the sharing and part-time provision of MCI's proposal. MCI will permit up to five subscribers to share one channel with a pro-rata reduction in costs; and for those subscribers with less than full-time needs, use from 6 a.m. to 6 p.m. is offered at a 25-percent reduction in rate. No comparable offerings are made by the existing common carriers. Thus, a grant of the applications under consideration will make microwave service available to potential users who have no need for and cannot afford the full-time, nonsharing, and more sophisticated service to which they are limited under present tariffs. . . .

Additional advantages to MCI's subscribers are afforded by the flexibility of its system. In contrast to the protesting carriers which will lease no less than a nominal 4-kc. channel for voice use, MCI will lease and subdivide its channel into bandwidths in increments of 2 kc. and permit multiple terminations of channels. Furthermore, MCI imposes fewer restrictions on the nature of the subscribers' terminal equipment and on the use of its channels. The absence of restrictions gives each MCI subscriber the same flexibility to vary its stations' capability and use as if it were its own private system. Thus, each subscriber may adapt the system to its particular needs and equipment, lease shelter and tower space from MCI, and use the MCI trunk system for the carriage of voice, fascimile, and high speed or lower speed data transmissions, or a combination thereof in a manner which best suits its business requirements. No comparable degree of flexibility is offered by the existing carriers. Thus, while no new technology is involved in MCI's proposal, it does present a concept of common carrier microwave offerings which differs from those of the established carriers. Therefore, in determining the question of need, the controlling consideration is not whether existing communications services are being utilized by potential subscribers of MCI, but whether the proposed operation would better meet the particular needs of potential subscribers. We believe that MCI's offering would enable such subscribers to obtain a type of service not presently available and would tend to increase the efficiency of operation of the subscribers' businesses. . . .

The record evidence thus establishes that there are members of the public who require the microwave communications service proposed by MCI; that there exists, at the very least, a reasonable expectancy that one or more of such persons will avail themselves of the said facilities if they are authorized, and we conclude that MCI has demonstrated a need for the common carrier communications service which it proposes.

The carriers argue that even if lower rates for MCI communications services have been shown, that factor may not properly be considered in resolving the issue of need. They assert that they are required by the Commission to serve both high-density high-profit and low-density low-profit areas and in order to maintain rates which are relatively uniform, all rates are based on a cost averaging principle. Claiming that MCI is "cream skimming," i.e., proposing to operate solely on high-density routes where lower fixed costs per channel permit lower rates with higher profits, the carriers state that in order to compete with MCI they will be forced to abandon their cost averaging policies with a resultant increase in rates for subscribers on lightly used routes.

MCI is offering a service intended primarily for interplant and interoffice communications with unique and specialized characteristics. In these circumstances we cannot perceive how a grant of the authorizations requested would pose any serious threat to the established carriers' price averaging policies. Lower rates for the service offered is not the sole basis for our determination that MCI has demonstrated a need for the proposed facilities, but the flexibility available to subscribers, and the sharing and the part-time features of the proposal have been considered to be significant factors as well. . . . It may be, as the telephone companies and Western Union argue, that some business will be diverted from the existing carriers upon the grant of MCI's applications, but that fact provides no sufficient basis for depriving a segment of the public of the benefits of a new and different service.

Moreover, if we were to follow the carriers' reasoning and specify as a prerequisite to the establishment of a new common carrier service that it be so widespread as to permit cost averaging, we would in effect restrict the entry of new licensees into the common carrier field to a few large companies which are capable of serving the entire Nation. Such an approach is both unrealistic and inconsistent with the public interest. Innovations in the types and character of communications services offered or economies in operation which could not at once be instituted on a nationwide basis would be precluded from ever being introduced. In the circumstances of this case, we find the cream skimming argument to be without merit. . . .

The conclusion that a public need exists for the services proposed by MCI is adequately supported by the evidence of record and we have relied solely upon that evidence in reaching our determination. Consequently, it is unnecessary to take official notice of A.T.&T.'s aforementioned statements or to place any reliance thereon in connection with the resolution of the public need issue; and we shall not do so. . . .

RELIABILITY OF SERVICE

While some of MCI's potential subscribers indicated a willingness to compromise on reliability of service in order to obtain the benefits of lower rates, a common carrier communications system will be of little value if it fails to provide its customers with a substantial degree of reliability in the transmission of messages. The carriers argue that MCI will be unable to supply a reliable communications service since its physical plant and facilities, system maintenance, and signal beam clearance are inadequate. . . .

No specific standards have been enunciated by the Commission as to what constitutes a minimum degree of reliability which is acceptable for a common carrier communications service, and we believe it would be inconsistent with the public interest, in view of the need for the proposed service and the valuable information to be obtained from the operation of the system, to defer action in this proceeding until such standards are adopted. On the basis of the evidence before us, however, we find that the MCI proposal may reasonably be expected to achieve a degree of reliability which, while not matching the high degree of reliability claimed by the major carriers, will provide an acceptable and a marketable common carrier service. . . .

EFFICIENT UTILIZATION OF THE FREQUENCY SPECTRUM

We recognize, as the carriers argue, that MCI will not make the fullest possible use of the frequencies which it seeks. . . .

In view of the limited frequencies available for common carrier use, the increasing demand for such frequencies, and the possibility that the grant of an application might limit a future assignment to a carrier which proposes a heavier loading or a better service, efficient utilization of the common carrier frequency spectrum by an applicant is a matter of serious concern to the Commission. . . .

. . . In determining whether there is a frequency wastage we may take into account the benefits to be derived by the public from the proposed common carrier facilities, and to weigh these benefits against the disadvantages alleged by the opposing carriers. We have found that by reason of its low-cost, sharing, and part-time use provisions, MCI can reasonably be expected to furnish an economical microwave communications service to a segment of the public which presently cannot avail itself of such a service; and that its flexibility features will enable potential users to make more efficient use of their business equipment. These are substantial benefits which, in our view, outweigh the fact that MCI will not make the fullest possible use of its frequencies. When frequencies are used to meet a significant unfulfilled communications need, we do not believe that such use may be considered as "inefficient."

THE FEASIBILITY OF LOOP SERVICE

The testimony of MCI's public witnesses and the findings of the Spindletop survey show that, in general, MCI's potential subscribers have no interest in providing their own communications link between their facilities and MCI's transmitter sites. Therefore, MCI's ability to market its services will be dependent on the ability of its subscribers to secure loop service from the other common carriers serving the service area.

We are not unmindful of the fact that the carriers maintain that loop service is not technically feasible and that there is no provision for such service in their tariffs. However, insufficient evidence is contained in this record to support a conclusion that the proposed interconnection is not feasible, and we are disposed to deny MCI's application on the basis of the unsubstantiated allegations which have been advanced herein by the telephone companies and Western Union. What seems a more likely obstacle to interconnection is, as the hearing examiner indicated, the "carriers' intransigence, manifested in this case. . . . " In these circumstances, the carriers are not in a position to argue that consideration of the interconnection question is premature. Since they have indicated that they will not voluntarily provide loop service we shall retain jurisdiction of this proceeding in order to enable MCI to obtain from the Commission a prompt determination on the matter of interconnection. Thus, at such time as MCI has customers and the facts and details of the customers' requirements are known, MCI may come directly to the Commission with a request for an order of interconnection. We have already concluded that a grant of MCI's proposal is in the public interest. We likewise conclude that, absent a significant showing that interconnection is not technically feasible, the issuance of an order requiring the existing carriers to provide loop service is in the public interest.

SUMMARY

This is a very close case and one which presents exceptionally difficult questions. We have found MCI to be financially qualified but we realize that any unforeseen circumstances requiring a sizable expenditure may impair the applicant's financial capacity. We have found, based on the weight of the evidence, that there is a substantial likelihood that the communications of its subscribers will arrive promptly, in accurate form, and without extended interruptions due to failures in the system. We wish to make clear, therefore, that the findings and conclusions reached herein apply only to the frequencies specified, and for the areas described, in the applications now pending before us. Should MCI seek to obtain additional frequencies or to extend its microwave service to new areas, our action on its application will be based on a close scrutiny of its operations, the rules then governing the grant of applications for common carrier microwave frequencies and all other applicable policy considerations. Likewise, in connection with an application for renewal of license, we may deny the application if circumstances so warrant or grant renewal on such conditions as we deem essential to insure that MCI's subscribers receive a reliable transmission service of acceptable quality. However, it would be inconsistent with the public interest to deny MCI's applications and thus deprive the applicant of an opportunity to demonstrate that its proposed microwave facilities will bring to its subscribers the substantial benefits which it predicts and which we have found to be supported by the evidence in this proceeding. We conclude, on the basis of the record as a whole, that the public interest will be served by a grant of MCI's application.

Federal Communications Commission v. National Citizens Committee for Broadcasting

436 U.S. 775 (1978)

MR. JUSTICE MARSHALL delivered the opinion of the Court.

At issue in the cases are Federal Communications Commission regulations governing the permissibility of common ownership of a radio or television broadcast station and a daily newspaper located in the same community. The regulations, adopted after a lengthy rule making proceeding, prospectively bar formation or transfer of co-located newspaper-broadcast combinations. Existing combinations are generally permitted to continue in operation. However, in communities in which there is common ownership of the only daily newspaper and the only broadcast station, or (where there is more than one broadcast station) of the only daily newspaper and the only television station, divestiture of either the newspaper or the broadcast station is required within five years, unless grounds for waiver are demonstrated.

The questions for decision are whether these regulations either exceed the Commission's authority under the Communications Act of 1934, or violate the First or Fifth Amendment rights of newspaper owners; and whether the lines drawn by the Commission between new and existing newspaper-broadcast combinations, and between existing combinations subject to divestiture and those allowed to continue in operation, are arbitrary or capricious within the meaning of 10(e) of the Administrative Procedure Act. For the reasons set forth below, we sustain the regulations in their entirety.

I

Under the regulatory scheme established by the Radio Act of 1927 and continued in the Communications Act of 1934, no television or radio broadcast station may operate without a license granted by the Federal Communications Commission. Licensees who wish to continue broadcasting may apply for renewal of their licenses every three years, and the Commission may grant an initial license or a renewal only if it finds that the public interest, convenience, and necessity will be served thereby.

In setting its licensing policies, the Commission has long acted on the theory that diversification of mass media ownership serves the public interest by promoting diversity of program and service viewpoints, as well by preventing undue concentration of economic power. This perception of the public interest has been implemented over the years by a series of regulations imposing increasingly stringent restrictions on multiple ownership of broadcast stations. . . .

Against this background, the Commission began the instant rule making proceeding in 1970 to consider the need for a more restrictive policy toward newspaper ownership of radio and television broadcast stations. . . .

Citing studies showing the dominant role of television stations and daily newspapers as sources of local news and other information, the notice of rule making proposed adoption of regulations that would eliminate all newspaper broadcast combinations serving the same market, by prospectively banning formation or transfer of such combinations and requiring dissolution of all existing combinations within five years. The Commission suggested that the proposed regulations would serve "the purpose of promoting competition among the mass media involved, and maximizing diversification of service sources and view points." At the same time, however, the Commission expressed "substantial concern" about the disruption of service that might result from divestiture of existing combinations.

After reviewing the comments and studies submitted by the various parties during the course of the proceeding, the Commission then turned to an explanation of the regulations and the justifications for their adoption. The prospective rules, barring formation of new broadcast-newspaper combinations in the same market, as well as transfers of existing combinations to new owners, were adopted without change from the proposal set forth in the notice of rule making. While recognizing the pioneering contributions of newspaper owners to the broadcast industry, the Commission concluded that changed circumstances made it possible, and necessary, for all new licensing of broadcast stations to "be expected to add to local diversity."

With respect to the proposed across-the-board divestiture requirement, however, the Commission concluded that "a mere hoped for gain in diversity" was not a sufficient justification. Characterizing the divestiture issues as "the most difficult" presented in the proceeding, the Order explained that the proposed rules, while correctly recognizing the central importance of diversity considerations, "may have given too little weight to the consequences which could be expected to attend a focus on the abstract goal alone." Forced dissolution would promote diversity, but it would also cause "disruption for the industry and hardship for individual owners," . . . "resulting in losses or diminution of service to the public."

The Commission concluded that in light of these countervailing considerations divestiture was warranted only in "the most egregious cases," which it identified as those in which a newspaper-broadcast combination has an "effective monopoly" in the local marketplace of ideas as well as economically. It thus decided to require divestiture only where there was common ownership of the sole daily newspaper published in a community and either (1) the sole broadcast station providing that entire community with a clear signal, or (2) the sole television station encompassing the entire community with a clear signal.

The Order identified eight television-newspaper and ten radio-newspaper combinations meeting the divestiture criteria. Waivers of the divestiture requirement were granted sua sponte to one television and one radio combination, leaving a total of 16 stations subject to divestiture. The Commission explained that waiver requests would be entertained in the latter cases, but, absent waiver, either the newspaper or the broadcast station would have to be divested by January 1, 1980.

Various parties—including the National Citizens Committee for Broadcasting (NCCB), the National Association of Broadcasters (NAB), the American Newspaper Publishers Association (ANPA), and several broadcast licensees subject to the divestiture requirement—petitioned for review of the regulations in the United States Court of Appeals for the District of Columbia Circuit. NAB, ANPA, and the broadcast licensees subject to divestiture argued that the regulations went too far in restricting cross-ownership of newspapers and broadcast stations; NCCB and the Justice Department contended that the regulations did not go far enough and that the Commission inadequately justified its decision not to order divestiture on a more widespread basis.

Agreeing substantially with NCCB and the Justice Department, the Court of Appeals affirmed the prospective ban on new licensing of co-located newspaper-broadcast combinations but vacated the limited divestiture rules, and ordered the Commission to adopt regulations requiring dissolution of all existing combinations that did not qualify for a waiver under the procedure outlined in the Order.

II

Petitioners NAB and ANPA contend that the regulations promulgated by the Commission exceed its statutory rule making authority and violate the constitutional rights of newspaper owners. We turn first to the statutory, and then to the constitutional, issues.

Section 303(r) of the Communications Act, provides that "the Commission from time to time, as public convenience, interest, or necessity requires, shall . . . (m)ake such rules and regulations and prescribe such restrictions and conditions, not inconsistent with law, as may be necessary to carry out the provisions of (the Act)." As the Court of Appeals recognized, it is now well established that this general rule making authority supplies a statutory basis for the Commission to enact regulations codifying its view of the public interest licensing standard, so long as that view is based on consideration of permissible factors and is otherwise reasonable. . . .

The Court has specifically upheld this rule making authority in the context of regulations based on the Commission's policy of promoting diversification of ownership. . . .

Our past decisions have recognized, moreover, that the First Amendment and antitrust values underlying the Commission's diversification policy may properly be considered by the Commission in determining where the public interest lies. . . . And, while the Commission does not have power to enforce the antitrust laws as such, it is permitted to take antitrust policies into account in making licensing decisions pursuant to the public interest standard.

It is thus clear, that the regulations at issue are based on permissible public interest goals. . . .

Petitioners NAB and ANPA also argue that the regulations, though designed to further the First Amendment goal of achieving "the widest possible dissemination of information from diverse and antagonistic sources," nevertheless violate the First Amendment rights of newspaper owners. We cannot agree, for this argument ignores the fundamental proposition that there is no "unbridgeable First Amendment right to broadcast comparable to the right of every individual to speak, write, or publish."

The physical limitations of the broadcast spectrum are well known. Because of problems of interference between broadcast signals, a finite number of frequencies can be used productively; this number is far exceeded by the number of persons wishing to broadcast to the public. In light of this physical scarcity, government allocation and regulation of broadcast frequencies are essential, as we have often recognized. No one here questions the need for such allocation and regulation, and, given that need, we see nothing in the First Amendment to prevent the Commission from allocating licenses so as to promote the "public interest" in diversification of the mass communications media.

Finally, petitioners argue that the Commission has unfairly "singled out" newspaper owners for more stringent treatment than other license applicants. But the regulations treat newspaper owners in essentially the same fashion as other owners of the major media of mass communications were already treated under the Commission's multiple ownership rules; owners of radio stations, television stations, and newspapers alike are now restricted in their ability to acquire licenses for co-located broadcast stations.

In the instant case, far from seeking to limit the flow of information, the Commission has acted, in the Court of Appeals' words, "to enhance the diversity of information heard by the public without ongoing government surveillance of the content of speech." The regulations are a reasonable means of promoting the public interest in diversified mass communications; thus they do not violate the First Amendment rights of those who will be denied broadcast licenses pursuant to them. Being forced to "choose among applicants for the same facilities," the Commission has chosen on a "sensible basis," one designed to further, rather than contravene "the system of freedom of expression."

III

The Commission was well aware that separating existing newspaper-broadcast combinations would promote diversification of ownership. It concluded, however, that ordering widespread divestiture would not result in "the best practicable service to the American public." In particular, the Commission expressed concern that divestiture would cause "disruption for the industry" and "hardship to individual owners," both of which would result in harm to the public interest. Especially in light of the fact that the number of co-located newspaper-broadcast combinations was already on the decline as a result of natural market forces, and would decline further as a result of the prospective rules, the Commission decided that across-the-board divestiture was not warranted.

The Order identified several specific respects in which the public interest would or might be harmed if a sweeping divestiture requirement were imposed; the stability and continuity of meritorious service provided by the newspaper owners as a group would be lost; owners who had provided meritorious service would unfairly be denied the opportunity to continue in operation; "economic dislocations" might prevent new owners from obtaining sufficient working capital to maintain the quality of local programming; and local ownership of broadcast stations would probably decrease. We cannot say that the Commission acted irrationally in concluding that these public interest harms outweighed the potential gains that would follow from increasing diversification of ownership.

We also must conclude that the Court of Appeals erred in holding that it was arbitrary to order divestiture in the 16 "egregious cases" while allowing other existing combinations to continue in operation. The Commission's decision was based not—as the Court of Appeals may have believed—on a conclusion that divestiture would be more harmful in the grandfathered markets than in the 16 affected markets, but rather on a judgment that the need for diversification was especially great in cases of local monopoly. This policy judgment was certainly not irrational, and indeed was founded on the very same assumption that underpinned the diversification policy itself and the prospective rules upheld by the Court of Appeals and now by the Court—that the greater the number of owners in a market, the greater the possibility of achieving diversity of program and service viewpoints.

The judgment of the Court of Appeals is affirmed in part and reversed in part. It is so ordered.

Before the Federal Communications Commission

In the Matter of

Cable Television Syndicated Program Exclusivity Rules

Docket 20988

In the Matter of

Inquiry Into the Economic Relationship Between Television Broadcasting and Cable Television

Docket 21284

NOTICE OF PROPOSED RULE MAKING

Adopted: April 25, 1979

With this *Notice* we are commencing a proceeding that looks toward a complete re-evaluation of those of our rules that restrict cable television carriage of distant television broadcast stations' signals or syndicated programs constituting part of such signals.

INTRODUCTION

The Commission has been either directly or indirectly regulating the carriage of television broadcast signals by cable systems since 1962. The Commission began exercising direct jurisdiction over cable television signal carriage in 1966. The signal carriage rules were revised in major respects in 1972, and a number of less extensive revisions were made over the course of the next seven years. The rules affecting signals carried on cable now in force are of the following types:

rules that mandate carriage of particular signals,

rules that limit the carriage of distant commercial signals or noncommercial educational signals,

rules that require the deletion of particular network or syndicated programs from signals that are carried, and

rules that require deletion of particular sports programs from signals that are carried.

The need for these rules has been widely questioned and the economic facts underlying them challenged. Accordingly, in November of 1976 we issued our *Notice of Inquiry in Docket 20988* commencing a detailed review of the rules that limit cable television carriage of syndicated programs on distant signals. We followed this in June of 1977, with our *Notice of Inquiry in Docket 21284* which commenced a more general review of the economics of the relationship between television broadcasting and cable television.

We have also received petitions for rule making from the National Cable Television Association requesting the elimination of Commission signal carriage regulation, from the National Telecommunications and Information Administration of the Department of Commerce proposing changes in the syndicated exclusivity rules and the imposition of a requirement that new or expanded cable television operations only be permitted to carry distant signals with the consent of the originating station, and from the National Association of Broadcasters asking that we take some type of regulatory action with respect to what is described as the "superstation problem."[1] The rule making petitions and the two Inquiry proceedings all relate to the same general subject matter and will therefore be considered together. We do not propose to consider in this proceeding any changes in the network nonduplication, mandatory carriage, or sports blackout rules. Each of these may warrant review on its own merits but since different considerations are involved, we believe it administratively efficient to consider these rules separately.

* * *

Total pre-tax profits for the television broadcasting industry were $1.40 billion in 1977, consisting of $406.1 million (29%) from network operations, and $149.3 million (11%) from the 15 network owned stations, and $845.7 million (60%) from

---

[1] The term "superstation" is generally applied to a station whose signal is distributed by space satellite to cable television systems. It might also include any station whose signal is widely distributed on cable television systems outside its local service area.

all other commercial stations in the industry. Thirteen percent of all stations reporting showed no profits, including 32 percent of all independent UHF stations and 20 percent of all stations outside of the 100 largest television markets. Thirty-nine percent earned profits of over $1,000,000; 77% earned profits in excess of $100,000.

In contrast to broadcast television, where there is a central federal allocations plan to determine the distribution of facilities, cable television operations are franchised at the state or local level and have developed in response to consumer demands for better television reception and increased choice of television programming or, more probably, some combination of these.

Although the first cable television systems commenced operation in the late 1940's, the industry as a whole grew slowly at first and the million subscriber mark was not passed until about 1964. At approximately that point industry growth rates increased dramatically with the second million subscribers being connected in only three more years. Since that time, the number of systems commencing operation each year has varied with changing economic and regulatory conditions but the growth in absolute numbers of subscribers has been steady.

There are now some 3997 cable television systems in existence serving 9895 separate communities. Applications to commence cable television operations are pending in an additional 570 communities. These systems are estimated to provide service to some approximately 14.1 million households—perhaps 40 million people. Approximately 19 percent of all TV households receive cable TV service. Some 28 million households, or about one-third of all households, are estimated to have access to cable television service—that is, there is cable in their community and wires pass their homes.

BASIS FOR REGULATION

The competitive juxtaposition of these important elements of our economy's communications sector has produced numerous demands on the Congress and this Commission for the imposition of economic regulation. Broadcasters have sought limitations on both the broadcast and nonbroadcast activities of cable television systems. Program suppliers have pressed the Congress for changes in the copyright law and the Commission for copyright surrogates and other limitations on cable television signal carriage. Cable operators have sought, in the context of the existing regulatory structures, limitations on the contractual program exclusivity that broadcast stations and networks would be permitted to purchase.

The Commission's determination that cable television signal carriage should be restricted has historically been rationalized on one of four grounds: (1) as a means of assuring the public against a net loss of television service as a consequence of cable-created audience losses which would undermine the economic support of television stations and in the process deprive the poor and those living in areas unserved by cable of video service; (2) as necessary to support the broadcast television station allocations policy with its emphasis on local service; (3) as a means of eliminating what was perceived to be the unfair means by which cable television systems competed with local broadcasters; and (4) as necessary to assure against injury to the continued production of television programming.

Cable television growth, it was feared, would harm the public through its competitive effect on commercial broadcasting. At least three undesirable consequences of unrestricted cable television operations were identified:

1 Because cable television did not appear able to serve rural areas due to the high costs involved in providing cable in areas of low population density, urban cable subscribers might gain additional service from cable, but rural residents could lose service.

2 There are substantial numbers of people who either cannot afford or do not wish to pay for television service so that if cable television supplanted over-the-air service these persons would either lose service or be forced to pay for it.

3 Because cable television systems initially did not generally serve as an outlet for community self-expression, an adverse impact on local television broadcast service would have denied both cable subscribers and non-cable subscribers alike the benefits of programming designed to serve the needs and interests of the local area.

For these reasons, among others, the Commission tended to view cable as only a "supplementary" service to broadcast television which should be regulated to limit its impact on over-the-air service.

The Commission relied heavily on these considerations in asserting jurisdiction to regulate cable television. . . .

RESULTS OF THE INQUIRIES

In our *Economic Inquiry Report,* and our *Syndicated Exclusivity Report,* we articulated three criteria against which to measure the appropriateness of our cable television policies: consumer welfare, distributional equity, and external effects. The three criteria correspond in some respects to those used in earlier Commission decisions relating to cable television but frame the issues in somewhat more precise economic terms.

Briefly, our concern with localism in the context of broadcasting may be characterized as a concern with externalities—that is, the true value of local news and public affairs programming may not be reflected in the number of individuals who view it or the value they place on it but in the value it has to our society as a whole and especially in the functioning of our democratic institutions.

Distributional equity is related to the allocation between various segments of society of the costs and benefits of a particular policy. Cable television service, in contrast with broadcast service, must be paid for directly and is generally not available to residents of low population density areas or urban centers where demand is low and construction costs are high. Thus, even if the effect of a policy change to consumers as a whole proved beneficial, some groups might be less well off as a consequence of that policy change.

Consumer welfare is grounded in our responsibility to assure "efficient" communication service. It is reflected in our concern with assuring that policies adopted tend toward the creation of a communications system that increases the net video service supplied to the public or otherwise maximizes the value the public receives from society's overall investment in the video distribution system.

This set of values and the factual information developed in our *Syndicated Exclusivity* and *Economic Inquiry* proceedings provide the basic ingredients for a re-examination of our cable television policies.

The purpose of the *Economic Inquiry* was to permit qualitative and quantitative analysis into the competitive relationship of the television broadcasting and cable television industries. As our *Economic Inquiry Report* indicates, we feel the purpose has been accomplished. We have far better information now than has been available at previous important junctures in our broadcast-cable regulatory effort. The *Economic Inquiry* has permitted us to review and re-evaluate the theoretical concerns which led to our regulatory intervention in the light of experience and new quantitative information.

The *Syndicated Exclusivity Inquiry* overlapped with the *Economic Inquiry* in both purpose and scope. . . .

Both Reports note the significant sacrifices in consumer welfare occasioned by the distant signal and syndicated exclusivity limits and essentially inquire whether there are benefits which outweigh these costs. As the Reports make clear, all available evidence indicates that our rules limiting the quantity and composition of distant broadcast signals carried on cable systems are not only unnecessary, but counterproductive. No evidence has been adduced to indicate that the markets linking consumers with the cable, broadcasting, and program production industries would be unable to satisfactorily serve the interests of consumers of video service if we eliminated our regulatory restrictions. Finding no material benefits in the continuation of the distant signal and syndicated programming rules, we propose that they be eliminated.

We have carefully considered whether continuation of the limitations on cable carriage of distant broadcast signals is necessary to avoid undesirable distributional effects. As we explained in the *Economic Inquiry Report,* this consideration traditionally has been very important in our calculation of the public interest and was an important motivating element in our regulatory intervention in the cable-broadcast relationship. In Sections III and IV of the *Economic Inquiry Report* we assessed the effects of cable carriages of distant signals on the distribution of audiences within local television markets and found them to be far less significant than we imagined they would be when we first embarked upon the general regulation of cable television fourteen years ago. On the basis of econometric analysis and case studies of the actual experience of broadcast licensees confronting extensive cable competition, we were able to conclude that the risk that consumers dependent upon broadcast television by virtue of income level, location, or unwillingness to pay for video services would be harmed by the unrestricted cable carriage of broadcast signals is negligible. We believe that existing levels of service to the public are secure, "that it is extremely unlikely that any viewer will be significantly harmed" by elimination of the distant signal rules.

Finally, we have analyzed the desirability of continuing these restrictions in terms of their effect on the production of television programs in Section III of the *Syndicated Exclusivity Report*. Drawing upon quantitative analyses undertaken in the *Economic Inquiry*, we were able to conclude confidently that cable deregulation would visit no negative near-term effects upon the supply of television programming. We also estimated that there is little likelihood that the elimination of the rules requiring blackouts of syndicated programs under contract to local market broadcasters would adversely affect the supply of television programming at any point in the foreseeable future.

Overall, we have concluded on the basis of the data and analyses contained in the *Economic Inquiry Report* and *Syndicated Exclusivity Report* that the public interest would be better served by the deletion of the distant signal constraints and the syndicated exclusivity limitations. Our examination of the distant signal prohibitions, extending almost two years, and of the syndicated exclusivity limitations, extending well over two years, leads us to conclude in short that none of the four problems which these rules ostensibly address in fact exists. Under the circumstances, our obligation to rescind the rules is clear.

CONCLUSIONS

We have before us a wealth of information and analysis from our *Syndicated Exclusivity* and *Economic Inquiry* reports. We have, in addition, given careful consideration to the rule making petitions of the National Telecommunications and Information Administration and the National Association of Broadcasters and the comments filed in response thereto. We are now persuaded that the cable television distant signal and syndicated exclusivity rules can be deleted without undue risks and that the public will benefit by this action. We are, accordingly, issuing this *Notice of Proposed Rule Making* seeking comment on the proposed elimination of these rules.

[The FCC subsequently decided in July 1980 to abolish restrictions on the importation of distant signals, though cable systems must still carry all local stations. This decision is now being appealed in the courts.]

Inquiry and Proposed Rulemaking; Deregulation of Radio

Federal Communications Commission
47 CFR Parts 0, 73
October 5, 1979

In view of our forty-five years of experience in regulating broadcast radio, mindful of the legislative history of the Communications Act and our rules and policies as noted above, and in light of the data set forth below, we believe that it is appropriate for the Commission to initiate substantial deregulation of broadcast radio.

We note that circumstances have changed greatly since 1927. At that time there were but 681 broadcast radio stations. As of July 31, 1979, 8,654 such stations were comprised of 4,547 AM stations, 3,114 commercial FM stations, and 993 educational FM stations. This increase in stations has been steady and dramatic. . . . Additionally, since the advent of modern broadcast regulation, alternative sources of informational programming have arisen such as commercial television, public television, and cable television.

Traditionally, we have carried out our public interest mandate primarily by means of conduct related regulation. The First Amendment implications of such regulation have placed us in the difficult position of attempting to promote specific types of programming while at the same time avoiding supplanting of licensee discretion with the Commission's programming views. In addition to the content related approach, the Commission has also sought to achieve program diversity through structural means. Notable examples include our multiple ownership rules, which foster diversity of voices by limiting the number of outlets that any one source can control; our EEO and minority ownership rules and policies, which foster increased minority representation in the workforce and ownership of broadcast stations, thereby increasing the diversity of voices represented in broadcasting; and our efforts to increase or more efficiently use the broadcast radio spectrum. . . . We believe that in the future the emphasis of our regulatory effort should be shifted away where possible from content regulation and towards these types of structural vehicles. To do otherwise would continue to embroil unnecessarily the Commission in questions of what is, and is not, good or desirable radio programming.

It is of the highest importance that we begin to chart the course of the Commission's regulatory activity for the forseeable future. In the context of commercial AM and FM broadcasting, the course that appears in the public interest is the one that permits the market to dictate the programming decisions while the Commission regulates the structural aspects of that medium.

* * *

STRUCTURAL CHANGES IN RADIO MARKETS

Growth in the Number of Stations

Technological advances and increased demand have resulted in substantially greater use of the AM and FM radio spectrum. . . . This growth represents both an extension of radio service into previously unserved rural areas and a substantial increase in the number of stations in existing urban markets. . . . It should be noted that 17 markets have 30 or more radio stations; 46 have 20 or more; and 137 have 10 or more.

. . . [T]he growth in the number of radio stations in recent years has been most dramatic in the FM band. Technological improvements in transmission and reception and the development of FM stereo have been instrumental in this growth.

FM initially suffered two disadvantages—there were relatively few radio receivers with FM capability, and for a given transmitter power FM signals cannot be transmitted as far as AM signals. The advent of television, however, has partially changed the role of radio. Instead of being a "common denominator medium" reaching for a broad audience, radio, especially in the larger markets, has increasingly become a specialty medium reaching for a narrower audience. In this newer role, FM is no longer at a disadvantage with AM. In fact, FM can exploit its own technical advantages over AM, such as superior sound quality.

There is considerable evidence that FM radio has now attained competitive parity with AM. The October/November, 1978 Arbitron sweep data show, at least in the approximately 100 largest markets, many FM stations are equal competitors with AM stations. The fall 1978 and earlier Arbitron data have been available for analysis to many parties and a consensus has been reached that there is a strong trend toward parity. . . .

* * *

FAILURE TO PROVIDE SUFFICIENT INFORMATION PROGRAMMING

Perhaps the Commission's deepest concern during the last half century of broadcast regulation has been that the broadcast market might not provide sufficient informational programming (particularly news and public affairs programming).

A well-informed citizenry is necessary for the smooth functioning of the democratic process. Not only does an individual citizen benefit from the information he has received from broadcast programming, but so do other citizens in the community. Thus, there are social benefits as well as private benefits from informational broadcasting.

The Government presently employs two principal nonmarket mechanisms to try to increase informational programming: (1) It sets aside a large share of the radio spectrum for noncommercial use, and partially subsidizes noncommmercial station programming costs from the general treasury; and, (2) for all commercial radio stations, it suggests certain minimum quantitative programming guidelines for news and public affairs. At present, no matter how many stations are operating in a particular radio market, and no matter what the aggregate level of informational programming in the market, the licensing process for each station depends in part on these minimum guidelines.

Since these quantitative programming guidelines impose costs on the Commission, radio stations, and the public alike, it is essential that we determine whether or not they actually achieve their public interest objectives.

1 In markets with eight or more stations, more than 75% of the stations broadcast more than 6% news and public affairs programming (6% is the current Commission guideline for news, public affairs, and "other" programming for FM stations).

2 In markets with seven or fewer stations, over 96% of the stations broadcast more than 6% news and public affairs programming. More than 80% of these stations broadcast in excess of 10% news and public affairs programming.

3 As market size increases, the percentage of stations providing 10 to 25 percent news (or news and public affairs) programming decreases, while the percentage providing more than 50% news programming increases. This suggests that in markets with one or more stations providing listeners a steady diet of news programming, demand for such programming from other stations falls. These other stations can offer specialized programming formats because listeners can always switch to a news format station when they want news.

4 Excluding one and two station markets, the amount of public affairs programming provided falls greatly as market size falls, suggesting that this programming appeals to a minority audience, and such audiences can best be accommodated in large markets where individual stations seek small niches to serve.

The existence of many news-oriented commercial stations and of specialty radio news networks suggest that radio news programming may be profitable in large markets. If news programming is as profitable as entertainment formats, one can expect it to be provided even in the absence of Commission regulation.

Similarly, news programming greatly exceeds Commission guidelines in small markets, strongly suggesting that news is being provided in response to market forces, rather than to regulatory pressures, in these markets as well.

FAILURE TO PROVIDE MANY VOICES

The Commission's concern with informational programming is not limited to its nature and amount. The concern also relates to the diversity of the programming provided. A possible corollary to the "well-informed citizen" argument has been advanced as follows: Society as a whole benefits when its citizens have access to many points of view (or diversity of opinion or "voices") on both problem-oriented and issue-oriented matters of public interest, and the unregulated market may not take into account those social benefits. Similarly, there may be social costs if certain voices are excluded and those costs also may not be taken into account in the market. Nonetheless, as in the case of quantity of informational programming, though potential market failure may exist here, it is not clear how significant it is or whether government regulation can improve the situation.

While attempting to avoid direct First Amendment issues, the Commission has enunciated a number of rules and policies that touch, sometimes only tangentially, on the possible problem:

1 The first part of the Fairness Doctrine as administered by the Commission requires all stations to provide some coverage of controversial issues of public importance.

2 The second part of the Fairness Doctrine requires that, when a station covers controversial issues of public importance, it must provide diversity by presenting contrasting viewpoints.

3 Current quantitative processing guidelines for informational programming require *all* stations to meet minimum requirements or else justify the failure to do so.

4 Each station must meet certain community ascertainment requirements in order to learn about problems of importance to the community.

5 EEO requirements and minority ownership policies have been set, with the intention in part of making all stations aware of and sensitive to minority needs and points of view.

In general, the key to providing many voices remains the pursuit of policies that will maximize the number of stations on the air, coupled with the EEO and minority ownership policies. These provide the greatest opportunity for increasing the number of voices in radio markets by expanding radio ownership and management beyond its present confines. It is clear that the most effective method of encouraging equal employment opportunity and minority ownership goals may be to greatly expand the number of radio stations on the air and make it easier for minority groups to obtain new radio licenses or to buy existing stations.

COMMERCIAL PRACTICES

The Commission has imposed quantitative processing guidelines on the use of broadcast time for commercial messages based on the belief that the public airwaves should not be unduly used to further private commercial interests. The underlying presumption is that entertainment and informational programming better serve the public interest than do commercial messages. This is, of course, a value judgment. How many commercial minutes represent "too much" is a noneconomic judgment. There are no objective standards on which to base the decision.

Existing guidelines therefore cannot be subjected to any objective test. It is worth investigating, however, whether or not, absent the regulation, the market would have yielded more commercial minutes. Theory suggests there are strong limiting forces in the market.

Clearly, up to some point stations can increase their revenue if they increase the number of commercial messages broadcast. Advertising rates, however, depend on audience size and characteristics. If audiences prefer programming to commercial messages, they will desert stations that overcommercialize. This may be especially true of higher income audience members (those who may be most coveted by advertisers) who have more entertainment options available. Hence, audience pressure exists to limit commercial messages. At the same time, advertisers prefer that their messages not be lost [among all the other ads on] overcommercialized stations. Hence, sponsor pressure exists to limit commercial messages.

Fortunately, some data are available to test this theory. The actual commercial minutes reported by stations in the composite week logs of their license renewal applications can be compared to the Commission's guidelines. . . .

Data on stations in Georgia and Alabama are available from composite week logs filed with the license renewal applications. We have collected data from a sample of stations in large and small markets. . . . [T]he frequency with which the guidelines were met or exceeded generally was very low for large markets, increased somewhat for moderate sized markets (with 3 to 8 stations), and was very low again for small markets. Nonetheless, the overall incidence of "overcommercialization" was quite low, even in the "high incidence" markets.

There is an additional set of evidence suggesting that market forces will impose restrictions on the amount of commercial messages broadcast. Many if not most FM stations air far fewer commercial messages than do AM stations, and yet (or perhaps partially as a result) FM is far more viable today than it ever has been previously. Indeed, a growing number of FM stations in large urban markets present (and heavily promote) commercial-free hours or entire evenings of programming. Clearly, these stations believe that consumers do react positively to reduced commercial time.

It thus appears that at present the Commission's guidelines are unnecessary in that competitive forces in large markets and the lack of demand in small markets dictate even lower levels of commercialization. It is possible that, in the future, demand for advertising time will grow faster than supply (or than the demand for programming) and the market might then yield more commercial minutes, exceeding present guidelines. In this situation, however, more radio stations could be supported and pressures would build either to expand the amount of spectrum available for broadcast radio or reduce the spacing between AM stations and/or reallocate FM more efficiently. In the interim guidelines should be removed.

* * *

Our ultimate goal in this proceeding is to maximize the benefits of radio services to the public. If that goal can be achieved with a minimum of regulation on our part, we will increase the public benefit, for then we will have reduced the delays and costs of regulation without sacrificing service to the public. From this perspective, the option of eliminating the Commission's ascertainment obligations as well as the guidelines on nonentertainment programming and commercial matter is the most attractive. It offers the potential of a well-served public at greatly reduced regulatory cost. Moreover, the data presented in the previous section provides a strong indication that the marketplace can in fact be responsive to the public's needs and wants without Commission intervention. In other words, the evidence suggests that the Commission's statutory responsibility to protect the public interest can be honored if the Commission largely relies on the discretion of its broadcast licensees in the areas of ascertainment, nonentertainment programming, and commercial matter. If we should ultimately adopt this approach, however, we would not completely walk away from broadcast regulation in these areas. If we found that the marketplace had failed to serve the public adequately, we would have to be prepared to take appropriate action to remedy the situation. In addition, we must always keep in mind the Fairness Doctrine and how it will be enforced under the new regulatory procedures.

The approach we propose here is consistent with Congress' intent to permit commercial broadcasting to develop with the widest possible journalistic freedom consistent with its public obligations. Furthermore, it is entirely consistent with Congress' intent that the Commission have sufficient flexibility, through the "supple instrument" of the public interest, to respond to the rapid and dynamic changes that have characterized broadcasting throughout its history. . . .

CHAPTER 17

ENERGY

The energy sector of the economy has been subject to extensive government regulation at both the state and federal levels. A major activity for state governments has been the regulation of local electric and natural gas utilities (see Chapters 12 and 13), while the federal government has devoted considerable time to the regulation of oil and natural gas producers.

A major historical issue has been the regulation of the field price of natural gas. Under the Natural Gas Act of 1938 the Federal Power Commission (FPC) was empowered to regulate interstate gas pipelines. For the first decade the commission concerned itself only with the pipelines and did not try to regulate the prices the pipelines paid to gas producers in the gas fields. After World War II, consuming states argued that the commission should regulate field prices as well as the margin between the field price and the price the pipelines charged to local distributors. This issue was decided in favor of the consuming states in *Phillips v. Wisconsin,* the first case in this chapter.

After *Phillips v. Wisconsin,* the previously reluctant commission set out to find a basis for regulating the thousands of natural gas producers. The result was one of the largest and most complex rate cases in the history of regulation. Cost-based rates are difficult to establish in the natural gas industry because of the large numbers of producers and their different costs. The end product of almost a decade of investigation was the *Permian Basin* decision, the second in this chapter. (The Permian Basin is one of the largest American natural gas fields, covering nearly 100,000 square miles of Texas and New Mexico.)

As noted in the case, the Supreme Court had previously ruled that the FPC had the authority to regulate the field prices for natural gas produced by affiliates of the pipeline companies. That decision (*Interstate Natural Gas Co. v. FPC*) created little controversy. Can you see why? Could the commission have effectively regulated a pipeline company without control over the price the company charged itself for natural gas? Would the prices of pipeline affiliates be as hard to regulate as the prices of independent producers? Why or why not? Leaving aside the issue of congressional intent, do you feel that the decision was sensible? There are thousands of natural gas producers, many of them very small. The main element of monopoly in the gas fields is the limited number of pipelines—sometimes only one or two. Would you expect this monopoly element to raise or lower prices?

The FPC subsequently simplified the pricing of natural gas when it established a two-tier national price structure in 1974. This new approach was short-lived, however, as the Natural Gas Policy Act of 1978 established approximately two dozen different categories of natural gas for pricing purposes. This act also ordered the decontrol of the price of new natural gas on January 1, 1985. Not surprisingly, there is still substantial interest in the pricing of natural gas. Two different approaches are presented in the third case—rates based on accounting costs and economic costs. Will both cost standards forward the conservation of natural gas? Who will benefit? Industrial users? Residential consumers? Natural gas producers? Is the list of those benefitted and those harmed consistent with your notion of equity?

From 1971 until price controls were removed in 1981, the government also regulated the price of oil. In addition, it established numerous regulations concerning the allocation of oil supplies among users. One such program was the small refiner bias program which is evaluated in the fourth case. The ostensible purpose of this program was to maintain the competitive viability of small refiners. Do you believe that we should be concerned about the number of small refineries? Will their presence increase competition and promote efficiency in the petroleum industry? How long would you have maintained the subsidy program? Five years? Ten years? Forever? In fact, the program ended when the price of oil was decontrolled in 1981. Many small refiners subsequently left the business.

Finally, the last case presents excerpts from President Carter's energy program. This program consisted of a variety of measures to decrease the demand for energy while increasing the supply of energy. It supported the use of market prices to achieve these twin objectives. Does this seem efficient? Equitable? Would you favor rationing of energy supplies instead? If so, how would you allocate energy supplies? By the number of people in a household? By the number of cars or homes they owned? The energy plan also endorses the use of government regulations to force the development of energy-efficient buildings, appliances, and automobiles. Do you think these regulations are necessary? Why or why not?

The plan also called for research for many exotic fuels such as shale oil and the production of gas or oil from coal. Why can't we depend on the energy companies to do this without government help? They are getting *ten times* as much for a barrel of oil now as they did in 1972. If private development is not profitable at present prices, what kind of "solution" to our energy problem is shale oil or oil from coal?

Phillips Petroleum Co. v. Wisconsin

347 U.S. 672 (1954)

MR. JUSTICE MINTON delivered the opinion of the Court.

These cases present a common question concerning the jurisdiction of the Federal Power Commission over the rates charged by a natural-gas producer and gatherer in the sale in interstate commerce of such gas for resale. All three cases are an outgrowth of the same proceeding before the Power Commission and involve the same facts and issues.

The Phillips Petroleum Company is a large integrated oil company which also engages in the production, gathering, processing, and sale of natural gas. We are here concerned only with the natural-gas operations. Phillips is known as an "independent" natural-gas producer in that it does not engage in the interstate transmission of gas from the producing fields to consumer markets and is not affiliated with any interstate natural-gas pipeline company. As revealed by the record before us, however, Phillips does sell natural gas to five interstate pipeline transmission companies which transport and resell the gas to consumers and local distributing companies in fourteen states.

Approximately 50% of this gas is produced by Phillips, and the remainder is purchased from other producers. A substantial part is casinghead gas—i.e., produced in connection with the production of oil. The gas flows from the producing wells, in most instances at well pressure, through a network of converging pipelines of progressively larger size to one of twelve processing plants, where extractable products and impurities are removed. Of the nine such networks of pipelines involved in these cases, five are located entirely in Texas, one in Oklahoma, one in New Mexico, and two extend into both Texas and Oklahoma. After processing is completed, the gas flows from the processing plant through an outlet pipe, of varying lengths up to a few hundred feet, to a delivery point where the gas is sold and delivered to an interstate pipeline company. The gas then continues its flow through the interstate pipeline system until delivered in other states.

The Federal Power Commission, on October 28, 1948, instituted an investigation to determine whether Phillips is a natural-gas company within the jurisdiction of the Commission, and, if so, whether its natural-gas rates are unjust or unreasonable. . . . The Commission issued an opinion and order in which it held that Phillips is not a "natural-gas company" within the meaning of that term as used in the Natural Gas Act, and therefore is not within the Commission's jurisdiction over rates. Consequently, the Commission did not proceed to investigate the reasonableness of the rates charged by Phillips. On appeals, the decision of the Commission was reversed by the United States Court of Appeals for the District of Columbia Circuit, one judge dissenting. We granted certiorari.

The Power Commission is authorized by Section 4 of the Natural Gas Act to regulate the "rates and charges made, demanded, or received by any natural-gas company for or in connection with the transportation or sale of natural gas subject to the jurisdiction of the Commission. . . ." "Natural-gas company" is defined by Section 2(6) of the Act to mean "a person engaged in the transportation of natural gas in interstate commerce, or the sale in interstate commerce of such gas for resale." The jurisdiction of the Commission is set forth in Section 1(b) as follows:

> The provisions of this Act shall apply to the transportation of natural gas in interstate commerce, to the sale in interstate commerce of natural gas for resale for ultimate public consumption for domestic, commercial, industrial, or any other use, and to natural-gas companies engaged in such transportation or sale, but shall not apply to any other transportation or sale of natural gas or to the local distribution of natural gas or to the facilities used for such distribution or to the production or gathering of natural gas.

Petitioners admit that Phillips engages in "the sale in interstate commerce of natural gas for resale," as, of course, they must. They contend, however, that the affirmative grant of jurisdiction over such sales in the first clause of Section 1(b) is limited by the negative second clause of the section. In particular, the contention is made that the sales by Phillips are a part of the "production or gathering of natural gas" to which the Commission's jurisdiction expressly does not extend.

We do not agree. In our view, the statutory language, the pertinent legislative history, and the past decisions of this Court all support the conclusion of the Court of Appeals that Phillips is a "natural-gas company" within the meaning of that term as defined in the Natural Gas Act, and that its sales in interstate commerce of natural gas for resale are subject to the jurisdiction of and regulation by the Federal Power Commission.

The Commission found that Phillips' sales are part of the production and gathering process, or are "at least an exempt incident thereof." This determination appears to have been based primarily on the Commission's reading of legislative history and its interpretation of certain decisions of this Court. Also, there is some testimony in the record to the effect that the meaning of "gathering" commonly accepted in the natural-gas industry comprehends the sales incident to the physical activity of collecting and processing the gas. Petitioners contend that the Commission's finding has a reasonable basis in law and is supported by substantial evidence of record and therefore should be accepted by the courts, particularly since the Commission has "consistently" interpreted the Act as not conferring jurisdiction over companies such as Phillips. We are of the opinion, however, that the finding is without adequate basis in law, and that production and gathering, in the sense that those terms are used in Section 1(b), end before the sales by Phillips occur.

In *Federal Power Commission v. Panhandle Eastern Pipe Line Co.,* we observed that the "natural and clear meaning" of the phrase "production or gathering of natural gas" is that it encompasses "the producing properties and gathering facilities of a natural-gas company." Similarly, in *Colorado Interstate Gas Co. v. Federal Power Commission,* we stated that "[t]ransportation and sale do not include production or gathering," and indicated that the "production or gathering" exemption applies to the physical activities, facilities, and properties used in the production and gathering of natural gas.

Even more directly in point is our decision in *Interstate Natural Gas Co. v. Federal Power Commission,* 331 U.S. 682. The Interstate Company produced or purchased natural gas which it in turn sold and delivered to three interstate pipeline companies, all the activities occurring within the same state. We noted that "[e]xceptions to the primary grant of jurisdiction in the section [1(b)] are to be strictly construed," and held that Section 1(b) conferred jurisdiction over such sales on the Federal Power Commission. . . .

Petitioners attempt to distinguish the Interstate case on the grounds that the Interstate Company transported the gas in its pipelines after completion of gathering and before sale, and that the Interstate Company was affiliated with an interstate pipeline company and therefore subject to Commission jurisdiction in any event. This Court, however, refused to rely on such refinements and instead based its decision in Interstate on the broader ground that sales in interstate commerce for resale by producers to interstate pipeline companies do not come within the "production or gathering" exemption.

The Interstate case is also said to be distinguishable in that it did not involve an asserted conflict with state regulation, and federal control was not opposed by the state authorities, while in the instant cases there are said to be conflicting state regulations, and federal jurisdiction is vigorously opposed by the producing states. The short answer to this contention is that the jurisdiction of the Federal Power Commission was not intended to vary from state to state, depending upon the degree of state regulation and of state opposition to federal control. We expressly rejected any implication to the contrary, in the Interstate case.

The cases discussed above supply a ready answer to the determination of the Commission and also to petitioners' suggestion that "production or gathering" should be construed to mean the "business" of production and gathering, with the sale of the product considered as an integral part of such "business." We see no reason to depart from our previous decisions, especially since they are consistent with the language and legislative history of the Natural Gas Act.

In general, petitioners contend that Congress intended to regulate only the interstate pipeline companies since certain alleged excesses of those companies were the evil which brought about the legislation. If such were the case, we have difficulty in perceiving why the Commission's jurisdiction over the transportation or sale for resale in interstate commerce of natural gas is granted in the disjunctive. It would have sufficed to give the Commission jurisdiction over only those natural-gas companies that engage in "transportation" or "transportation and sale for resale" in interstate commerce, if only interstate pipeline companies were intended to be covered.

Rather, we believe that the legislative history indicates a congressional intent to give the Commission jurisdiction over the rates of all wholesales of natural gas in interstate commerce, whether by a pipeline company or not and whether occurring before, during, or after transmission by an interstate pipeline company. There can be no dispute that the overriding congressional purpose was to plug the "gap" in regulation of natural-gas companies resulting from judicial decisions prohibiting, on federal constitutional grounds, state regulation of many of the interstate commerce aspects of the natural-gas business. A significant part of this gap was created by cases holding that "the regulation of wholesale rates of gas and electrical energy moving in interstate commerce is beyond the constitutional powers of the States." The committee reports on the bill that became the Natural Gas Act specifically referred to two of these cases and to the necessity of federal regulation to occupy the hiatus created by them. Thus, we are satisfied that Congress sought to regulate wholesales of natural gas occurring at both ends of the interstate transmission systems.

Regulation of the sales in interstate commerce for resale made by a so-called independent natural-gas producer is not essentially different from regulation of such sales when made by an affiliate of an interstate pipeline company. In both cases, the rates charged may have a direct and substantial effect on the price paid by the ultimate consumers. Protection of consumers against exploitation at the hands of natural-gas companies was the primary aim of the Natural Gas Act. Attempts to weaken this protection by amendatory legislation exempting independent natural-gas producers from federal regulation have repeatedly failed, and we refuse to achieve the same result by a strained interpretation of the existing statutory language.

The judgment is Affirmed.

[Subsequent to this decision, an attempt was made to exempt gas producers from regulation by legislation, but the proposed revision of the Natural Gas Act was vetoed by the President and the veto was sustained. The Commission, thereafter, set out to control the field prices of natural gas in the following case].

Permian Basin Area Rate Cases

390 U.S. 747 (1968)

MR. JUSTICE HARLAN delivered the opinion of the Court.

These cases stem from proceedings commenced in 1960 by the Federal Power Commission under Section 5(a) of the Natural Gas Act, to determine maximum just and reasonable rates for sales in interstate commerce of natural gas produced in the Permian Basin. The Commission conducted extended hearings, and in 1965 issued a decision that both prescribed such rates and provided various ancillary requirements. On petitions for review, the Court of Appeals for the Tenth Circuit sustained in part and set aside in part the Commission's orders. Because these proceedings began a new era in the regulation of natural gas producers, we granted certiorari and consolidated the cases for briefing and extended oral argument. For reasons that follow, we reverse in part and affirm in part the judgments of the Court of Appeals, and sustain in their entirety the Commission's orders.

I

The circumstances that led ultimately to these proceedings should first be recalled. The Commission's authority to regulate interstate sales of natural gas is derived entirely from the Natural Gas Act of 1938. The Act's provisions do not specifically extend to producers or to wellhead sales of natural gas, and the Commission declined until 1954 to regulate sales by independent producers to interstate pipelines. Its efforts to regulate such sales began only after this Court held in 1954 that independent producers are "natural-gas compan[ies]."

The Commission initially sought to determine whether producers' rates were just and reasonable by examination of each producer's costs of service. Although this method has been widely employed in various rate-making situations, it ultimately proved inappropriate for the regulation of independent producers. Producers of natural gas cannot usefully be classed as public utilities. They enjoy no franchises or guaranteed areas of service. They are intensely competitive vendors of a wasting commodity they have acquired only by costly and often unrewarded search. Their unit costs may rise or decline with the vagaries of fortune. The value to the public of the services they perform is measured by the quantity and character of the natural gas they produce, and not by the resources they have expended in its search; the Commission and the consumer alike are concerned principally with "what [the producer] gets out of the ground, not . . . what he puts into it. . . ." *FPC v. Hope Natural Gas Co.* The exploration for and the production of natural gas are thus "more erratic and irregular and unpredictable in relation to investment than any phase of any other utility business." Moreover, the number both of independent producers and of jurisdictional sales is large, and the administrative burdens placed upon the Commission by an individual Company costs-of-service standard were therefore extremely heavy.

In consequence, the Commission's regulation of producers' sales became increasingly laborious, until, in 1960, it was described as the "outstanding example in the federal government of the breakdown of the administrative process." The Commission in 1960 acknowledged the gravity of its difficulties, and announced that it would commence a series of proceedings in which it would determine maximum producers' rates for each of the major producing areas. . . . These cases place in question the validity of the first such proceeding.

The perimeter of this proceeding was drawn by the Commission in its second Phillips decision and in its Statement of General Policy No. 61-1. The Commission in Phillips asserted that it possesses statutory authority both to determine and to require the application throughout a producing area of maximum rates for producers' interstate sales. It averred that the adoption of area maximum rates would appreciably reduce its administrative difficulties, facilitate effective regulation, and ultimately prove better suited to the characteristics of the natural gas industry.

The rate structure devised by the Commission for the Permian Basin includes two area maximum prices. The Commission provided one area maximum price for natural gas produced from gas wells and dedicated to interstate commerce after January 1, 1961. It created a second, and lower, area maximum price for all other natural gas produced in the Permian Basin. The Commission reasoned that it may employ price functionally, as a tool to encourage discovery and production of appropriate supplies of natural gas. It found that price could serve as a meaningful incentive to exploration and production only for gas-well gas committed to interstate commerce since 1960; the supplies of associated and dissolved gas, and of previously committed reserves of gas-well gas, were, in contrast, found to be relatively unresponsive to variations in price. The Commission expected that its adoption of separate maximum prices would both provide a suitable incentive to exploration and prevent excessive producer profits.

The Commission declined to calculate area rates from prevailing field prices. Instead, it derived the maximum just and reasonable rate for new gas-well gas from composite cost data, obtained from published sources and from producers through a series of cost questionnaires. This information was intended in combination to establish the national costs in 1960 of finding and producing gas-well gas; it was understood not to reflect any variations in cost peculiar either to the Permian Basin or to periods prior to 1960. The maximum just and reasonable rate for all other gas was derived chiefly from the historical costs of gas-well gas produced in the Permian Basin in 1960; the emphasis was here entirely local and historical. The Commission believed that the uncertainties of joint cost allocation made it difficult to compute accurately the cost of gas produced in association with oil. It held, however, that the costs of such gas could not be greater, and must surely be smaller, than those incurred in the production of flowing gas-well gas. In addition, the Commission stated that the exigencies of administration demanded the smallest possible number of separate area rates.

Each of the area maximum rates adopted for the Permian Basin includes a return to the producer of 12% on average production investment, calculated from the Commission's two series of cost computations. The Commission assumed for this purpose that production commences one year after investment, that gas wells deplete uniformly, and that they are totally depleted in 20 years. The rate of return was selected after study of the returns recently permitted to interstate pipelines, but, in addition, was intended to take fully into account the greater financial risks of exploration and production.

The allowances included in the return for the uncertainties of exploration were, however, paralleled by a system of quality and Btu adjustments. The Commission held that gas of less than pipeline quality must be sold at reduced prices, and it provided for this purpose a system of quality standards. The price reduction appropriate in each sale is to be measured by the cost of the processing necessary to raise the gas to pipeline quality; these costs are to be determined by agreement between the parties to the sale, subject to review and approval by the Commission.

The Commission acknowledged that area maximum rates derived from composite cost data might in individual cases produce hardship, and declared that it would, in such cases, provide special relief. It emphasized that exceptions to the area rates would not be readily or frequently permitted, but declined to indicate in detail in what circumstances relief would be given.

Second, the Commission imposed a moratorium until January 1, 1968, upon filings for prices in excess of the applicable area maximum rates. The Commission concluded that such a moratorium was imperative if the administrative benefits of an area proceeding were to be preserved. Further, it permanently prohibited the use of indefinite escalation clauses to increase prevailing contract prices above the applicable area maximum rate.

II

The parties before this Court have together elected to place in question virtually every detail of the Commission's lengthy proceedings. It must be said at the outset that, in assessing these disparate contentions, this Court's authority is essentially narrow and circumscribed.

Section 19(b) of the Natural Gas Act provides without qualification that the "finding of the Commission as to the facts, if supported by substantial evidence, shall be conclusive." More important, we have heretofore emphasized that Congress has entrusted the regulation of the natural gas industry to the informed judgment of the Commission, and not to the preferences of reviewing courts. A presumption of validity therefore attaches to each exercise of the Commission's expertise, and those who would overturn the Commission's judgment undertake "the heavy burden of making a convincing showing that it is invalid because it is unjust and unreasonable in its consequences." We are not obliged to examine each detail of the Commission's decision; if the "total effect of the rate order cannot be said to be unjust and unreasonable, judicial inquiry under the Act is at an end."

Moreover, this Court has often acknowleged that the Commission is not required by the Constitution or the Natural Gas Act to adopt as just and reasonable any particular rate level; rather, courts are without authority to set aside any rate selected by the Commission which is within a "zone of reasonableness." No other rule would be consonant with the broad responsibilities given to the Commission by Congress; it must be free, within the limitations imposed by pertinent constitutional and statutory commands, to devise methods of regulation capable of equitably reconciling diverse and conflicting interests. It is on these premises that we proceed to assess the Commission's orders.

III

The issues in controversy may conveniently be divided into four categories. In the first are questions of the Commission's statutory and constitutional authority to employ area regulation and to impose various ancillary requirements. In the second are questions of the validity of the rate structure adopted by the Commission for natural gas produced in the Permian Basin. The third includes questions of the accuracy of the cost and other data from which the Commission derived the two area maximum prices. In the fourth are questions of the validity of the refund obligations imposed by the Commission.

We turn first to questions of the Commission's constitutional and statutory authority to adopt a system of area regulation and to impose various supplementary requirements. The most fundamental of these is whether the Commission may, consistently with the Constitution and the Natural Gas Act, regulate producers' interstate sales by the prescription of maximum area rates, rather than by proceedings conducted on an individual producer basis.

It is plain that the Constitution does not forbid the imposition, in appropriate circumstances, of maximum prices upon commercial and other activities. . . . No more does the Constitution prohibit the determination of rates through group or class proceedings. This Court has repeatedly recognized that legislatures and administrative agencies may calculate rates for a regulated class without first evaluating the separate financial position of each member of the class; it has been thought to be sufficient if the agency has before it representative evidence, ample in quantity to measure with appropriate precision the financial and other requirements of the pertinent parties.

It is, however, plain that the "power to regulate is not a power to destroy," and that maximum rates must be calculated for a regulated class in conformity with the pertinent constitutional limitations. Price control is "unconstitutional . . . if arbitrary, discriminatory, or demonstrably irrelevant to the policy the legislature is free to adopt. . . ." Nonetheless, the just and reasonable standard of the Natural Gas Act "coincides" with the applicable constitutional standards, and any rate selected by the Commission from the broad zone of reasonableness permitted by the Act cannot properly be attacked as confiscatory. Accordingly, there can be no constitutional objection if the Commission, in its calculation of rates, takes fully into account the various interests which Congress has required it to reconcile. We do not suggest that maximum rates computed for a group or geographical area can never be confiscatory; we hold only that any such rates, determined in conformity with the Natural Gas Act, and intended to "balanc[e] . . . the investor and the consumer interests," are constitutionally permissible.

For the reasons indicated, we find no constitutional infirmity in the Commission's adoption of an area maximum rate system for the Permian Basin.

We consider next the claims that the Commission has exceeded the authority given it by the Natural Gas Act. The first and most important of these questions is whether, despite the absence of any constitutional deficiency, area regulation is inconsistent with the terms of the Act.

The Commission has asserted, and the history of producer regulation has confirmed, that the ultimate achievement of the Commission's regulatory purposes may easily depend upon the contrivance of more expeditious administrative methods. The Commission believes that the elements of such methods may be found in area proceedings. "[C]onsiderations of feasibility and practicality are certainly germane" to the issues before us. We cannot, in these circumstances, conclude that Congress has given authority inadequate to achieve with reasonable effectiveness the purposes for which it has acted.

Finally, we consider one additional question. Certain of the producers have urged that, having adopted a system of area regulation, the Commission improperly designated the Permian Basin as a regulatory area. It is contended that the Commission failed to provide appropriate opportunities for briefing and argument on questions of the size and composition of the area. We must, before considering the rate structure devised for the Permian Basin by the Commission, examine this contention.

We do not doubt that significant economic consequences may, in certain situations, result from the definition of boundaries among regulatory areas. The calculation of average costs might, for example, be influenced by the inclusion or omission of a given group of producers; and the loss or retention of a price differential between regulatory areas might prove decisive to the success of marginal producers. Nonetheless, we hold that the Commission did not abuse its statutory authority by its refusal to complicate still further its first area proceeding by inclusion of issues relating to the proper size and composition of the regulatory area.

It must first be emphasized that the regulatory area designated by the Commission was evidently both convenient and familiar. There is no evidence before us, and the producers have not alleged, that the Permian Basin, as it was defined by the Commission, does not fit either with prevailing industry practice or with other programs of state or federal regulation. Moreover, the Commission was already confronted by an extraordinary variety of difficult issues of first impression; it quite reasonably preferred to simplify, so far as possible, its proceedings. Finally, it is not amiss to note that the Commission evidently has more recently permitted consideration of similar questions in area proceedings. We assume that, consistent with this practice and with the terms of its Statement of General Policy, the Commission now would, upon an adequate request, permit interested parties to offer evidence and argument on the propriety of modification of the Permian Basin regulatory area. We hold only that the Commission was not obliged, in the circumstances of this case, to include among the disputed issues questions of the proper size and composition of the regulatory area.

We therefore conclude that the Commission did not, in these proceedings, violate pertinent constitutional limitations, and that its adoption of a system of area price regulation, supplemented by provisons for a moratorium upon certain price increases and for exceptions for smaller producers, did not abuse or exceed its authority.

IV

The motions for leave to adduce additional evidence are denied, the judgments of the Court of Appeals are affirmed in part and reversed in part, as herein indicated, and the cases are remanded to that court further proceedings consistent with this opinion.

It is so ordered.

Natural Gas Rate Design Study

Economic Regulatory Administration, U.S. Department of Energy (1980)

The study analyzes characteristics and effects of different approaches to rate design for natural gas utilities. It evaluates the impacts not only of those rate designs frequently authorized by State and Federal regulatory authorities, but also alternatives to those rate designs.

*   *   *

Natural gas supplies about one-fourth of all the energy consumed in the United States, ranking second only to oil as an energy source. It is particularly important in non-transportation uses, heating 55 percent of American residences and supplying a large part of industrial heating demand. The properties of natural gas—its clean flame and ease of delivery where gas pipes have been laid—make it especially attractive to many consumers. Another reason that gas is attractive is its price. On a Btu equivalent basis, natural gas is often less expensive than alternate fuels. In 1979, for example, the average price of gas to users was $2.52 per million Btu while the price of imported oil was $3.60 per million Btu. Since 1979, world oil prices have almost doubled, but the price of natural gas has changed only slightly.

Since 1954, the price that pipelines can pay producers for gas, known as the wellhead price, has been regulated by the FERC [Federal Energy Regulatory Commission, formerly the Federal Power Commission (FPC).] Though alternative energy sources, such as oil, have become much more costly in recent years, the prices paid for much of the natural gas delivered to pipelines, which in turn deliver it to distribution companies, have remained closer to levels set a decade or more ago, when gas was a plentiful by-product of oil exploration. Moreover, although new and more costly supplies of natural gas have been purchased by pipelines, the FERC has allowed the pipelines to roll in (average) the costs of this gas with the costs of their cheaper wellhead supplies. As a result, the gas prices charged by interstate pipelines to distribution companies do not fully reflect the cost consequences of supplying or conserving an additional cubic foot of natural gas.

At the State level, investor-owned distribution companies have also been required, in many instances, to base their rates on average costs. . . .

Because of these Federal and State rate policies, the demand for gas has in the past risen beyond the ability of the industry to supply everyone who wanted to use it at prevailing prices. Natural gas production peaked in the United States in the early 1970's and has since declined. When demand exceeded available supplies—particularly during long periods of unusually high demand caused by colder than normal winters—some customers were denied gas service and others received reduced deliveries. Administrative rationing under curtailment plans, rather than market mechanisms, was used to determine who received gas. These curtailments raised questions of equity, while the generally low prices of gas did little to encourage conservation or efficient use of utility resources.

Currently, the regulated prices of natural gas hold important implications for the solution of our national energy problems. These prices directly affect the levels of oil imports, because in many applications gas can be used instead of oil. Gas prices that encourage conservation of gas and increased use of domestically abundant fuels, such as coal, can free up gas supplies to replace imported oil. Yet, under present Federal and State regulatory procedures, the prices established for gas erroneously indicate to consumers that gas is far less valuable than oil. Consumers make their private decisions to use or conserve gas in light of prices which do not adequately reflect the value to the nation of importing less oil.

Two fundamentally different approaches may be used to develop the prices pipelines and distribution companies charge for natural gas. On the one hand, rates may be based on accounting costs or the costs recorded in a utility's financial books under regulatory accounting principles. Such rates reflect the consequences of past business decisions by pipelines and distributors. They reflect the costs of past investments in fixed facilities and the prices specified in previously negotiated contracts for natural gas. In addition, at the city gate and the burner tip, accounting cost rates reflect the effects of Federal regulation of pipelines and Federal wellhead price controls.

Alternatively, the rates charged for natural gas may be based on economic costs. Such rates would reflect the cost consequences of current decisions to use or conserve gas, rather than the cost consequences of decisions made in the past. Given that gas can be substituted for imported oil, this characteristic of economic cost rates is crucially important.

A. ACCOUNTING COST RATES

Currently, most State regulatory authorities permit distribution company rates to be developed on the basis of accounting costs. In addition, the FERC permits interstate pipeline rates to be based on accounting costs.

The establishment of rates based on accounting costs involves several steps. First, the total revenues needed by a company (its revenue requirement) are determined from an assessment of its fixed costs, its gas or commodity costs, and its other operating costs for a time period normally of one year's length. The fixed costs are determined primarily by the interest payments that the company must make on outstanding debt, return on equity capital, the depreciation charges it must recover on existing facilities, and any tax expenses, such as those for property taxes, which do not vary with net income. For pipelines, the commodity costs reflect the prices paid for gas as established by existing contracts with producers and other sources of supply. For distributors, the commodity costs include the price of gas from pipelines and other sources, as specified in existing contracts, as well as the costs of manufactured gas or gas stored locally. Operating costs include gas or gas stored locally. Operating costs include maintenance expenses and other expenses incurred in transporting or delivering gas.

A company's total revenue requirement is usually subdivided into several cost categories, such as demand costs, commodity costs, and customer costs. Either the sum of the costs in each category or the total revenue requirement is then apportioned to different customer classes, and rates are designed to recover the revenue assignment for each class. . . .

An essential characteristic of this approach to rate development is that it averages costs, thereby diluting the cost consequences of current usage decisions. The cost of high priced gas [imported gas, SNG (synthetic natural gas), LNG (liquified natural gas)] is added to the cost of low priced gas (from wells under Federal price controls) to obtain an average cost of gas. Depreciation charges for new plant and equipment may be added to similar charges based on the original cost of older plant and equipment, and the total then assigned to customer classes. Because of these averaging processes, rates based on accounting costs obscure the consequent costs and benefits of current decisions to consume or conserve natural gas.

A variety of rate structures has been developed on the basis of accounting costs. Of these, the declining block rate and the flat rate with customer charge are the most frequently used. Under a declining block structure, successive levels or blocks of consumption are priced at a lower rate than preceding levels. With flat rates, each unit of gas has the same price, although different customer classes may be charged different rates; in addition, there is a fixed charge, assessed in each billing period, which does not vary with the quantity of gas consumed. This charge may also vary by customer class. In approving these and other accounting cost rate structures, State regulatory authorities usually consider the results of "cost-of-service" studies which reflect accounting cost concepts. In some cases, State regulatory authorities have prescribed or adopted a specific type of cost-of-service procedure.

B. ECONOMIC COST RATES

Although the rates charged by regulated utilities have historically been based on accounting costs, they can also be based on economic costs. In the natural gas industry, economic costs are the consequences incurred if one more decatherm of gas is consumed or, alternatively, avoided if one less decatherm is consumed. Currently, Federal and State regulatory policies are a major impediment to the development of economic cost rates in the gas industry. Of the three types of costs a distribution company may incur in serving its customers, two (customer and capacity costs) are not encumbered or distorted by Federal regulatory policies. However, the commodity costs of gas, which in most instances constitute the majority of a distribution company's total costs, are fundamentally affected by Federal policies.

1. Economic Costs and the Price of Gas

In the absence of price controls, competition among producers should insure that the wellhead price of new gas reflected the economic costs incurred in making another decatherm available. Producers would expand supplies of gas as long as the price they received for an additional decatherm exceeded the costs they incurred in making it available. Conversely, they would contract their production, exploration, and development of new gas supplies when the price was less than the cost they incurred in making an additional decatherm available.

But a free competitive market does not exist at the wellhead. And although many pipelines purchase gas at higher than average prices, the combination of wellhead price controls and rolled-in pipeline pricing results, in nearly all instances, in a city gate price for gas which does not reflect its economic costs. . . .

In the absence of competition at the wellhead, the precise determination of the economic cost of gas is not possible. It can be approximated, however, by either of two approaches: (a) setting prices to reflect the cost of new gas supplies, or (b) setting prices to reflect the avoided costs of other fuels, such as oil, for which gas can substitute.

The cost to the nation of obtaining new supplies of gas can be measured in a number of ways. The price of imported gas (Canadian, Mexican, Algerian LNG) is one measure of these costs. Another is the cost of synthetic gas, while a third is the cost associated with exploring and developing new supplies. If the costs associated with each of these three types of gas are different, the price of the least costly source could be used as the measure of economic costs. It is this source that in a competitive environment would actually be used, in the absence of other considerations, to expand gas supplies. The two higher priced alternatives should, on strict economic or financial grounds, not be used when gas from the least costly source is available.

The price of alternative fuels can also be used to approximate the economic costs of gas, using an "avoided costs" concept. Currently, gas could substitute for or replace oil in many industrial applications and in some commercial and residential applications. As a consequence, the cost to the nation of a decision (by a firm or individual) to use gas is, in a real sense, the cost incurred in importing oil. For example, if residential consumers use gas instead of investing in conservation measures, less gas is available for industrial applications and oil must be imported as a replacement. . . .

Gas rates should reflect these avoided costs so that all consumers may knowledgeably make two decisions: (a) whether they wish to use gas or some alternative fuel such as coal, and (b) to what extent they wish to substitute conservation measures for the consumption of gas. When consumers evaluate conservation activities or the use of alternate fuels, they compare their consequent savings and costs. Because wellhead price controls and rolled-in pipeline pricing keep the price of gas below its economic costs, consumers receive smaller benefits from both conservation and conversion decisions than actually accrue to the nation. Consumers' benefits are measured by their avoided dollar expenditures of gas, which reflect Federal regulatory policies that depress the price of gas. On the other hand, the benefits to the nation are measured by the reduced expenditures for oil imports that occur because gas, made available through conservation or conversion, replaces or substitutes for imported oil.

The challenge in gas rate design is to reflect economic costs in rates. The decontrol provisions of the . . . [Natural Gas Policy Act of 1978 (NGPA)] are an important step in this direction. Ultimately they will lead to wellhead prices for gas which do reflect economic costs. Such prices, in turn, are more likely to lead to city gate and burner tip prices which reflect economic costs. However, as is discussed below, rolled-in or average cost pipeline pricing can thwart the achievement of economic cost rates. A major concern in the next decade will be to supplement the decontrol provisions of the NGPA in a manner which is most likely to lead to economic cost rates at the burner tip.

2. Achieving Economic Cost Rates

Rates reflecting the economic costs of gas can be achieved in a number of different ways. The essential feature of each is, however, that the price for use of an additional decatherm of gas would be set so as to reflect the costs to the nation that must be paid to expand gas supplies or the price that must be paid (in terms of increased exports) for additional oil imports. That is, the price would reflect the consequences to the nation of any decision to consume or conserve.

One method of achieving economic cost rates is for State regulatory commissions to order, as has been done in some cases, that distribution company rates reflect the price of alternate fuels or, if lower, the cost of new incremental supplies of gas which are not price regulated. Use of such rates for all customers may lead to revenue collection problems for a distribution company, however. In general, rates based on alternate fuel prices will exceed the city gate price a distribution company pays for gas. Depending on the size of the difference between economic cost rates and city gate prices, a distribution company might collect revenues in excess of those allowed (i.e., in excess of its revenue requirement), or fail to obtain from economic cost rates revenues sufficient to meet its revenue requirement.

Where excess revenues would result, one way to meet the revenue requirement would be to reduce or eliminate any customer charges. If customer charge reductions did not eliminate the excess revenues, the rate for initial blocks of usage could be reduced for some or all customer classes. In such an inverted rate structure, two different rates are charged for gas, a low rate for a base (and relatively inelastic) level of consumption and a high rate for all consumption above the base level. The low rate, called the initial block rate, is set at a level which will provide revenues consistent with the revenue requirement when the high tailblock rate reflects economic costs.

In the event that inadequate revenues would be obtained from economic cost rates, fixed charges can be employed. Such fixed charges might be in the form of a customer charge which would allow a distribution company to just meet its revenue requirement. Alternatively a demand charge reflecting the costs of expanding storage, or peaking supplies, or the capacity to deliver gas could be used for this purpose.

A second way to achieve rates which reflect economic costs is to alter the rate-setting procedures of pipelines. Instead of being based on rolled-in (average cost) pricing, pipeline rates could be required by the FERC to reflect the costs of the most expensive source of gas purchased that is not subject to price controls. To avoid over-collection of revenues, pipelines could use inverted block rates in which rates for the first block would reflect the costs of price-controlled gas plus the pipeline's fixed costs; tailblock rates would reflect the costs of the pipeline's most expensive source of gas plus variable transmission costs. For example, after deregulation of wellhead prices in 1985, the tailblock rate for many pipelines would reflect the price of deregulated gas, plus variable pipeline transmission costs.

If pipelines priced each unit of gas beyond some initial block at its actual cost, distributors would be induced to reflect this change in city gate prices in their own rates. Otherwise, they would be charging some customers prices for gas which were less than the city gate prices they were paying for that gas.

Burner tip rates which reflected the actual prices a pipeline paid for additional gas, not the average of all pipeline prices, would in turn affect the prices that pipelines were willing to pay for gas. Pipelines would only purchase gas at prices which the ultimate consumers of that gas would be willing to pay. Market interactions between pipelines and producers would then set wellhead prices at a level which reflected the economic costs of gas. Producers would expand their production of gas as long as the price pipelines were willing to pay for it exceeded the costs they incurred. It should also be noted that when burner tip rates reflect the actual prices a pipeline pays for gas, there may be little or no difference between the alternate approaches to calculating economic costs discussed above. If those individuals who were just willing to purchase gas at such burner tip prices used it to replace oil, the cost to the nation of additional gas would be equated with the avoided costs (i.e., cost savings) brought about by reduced oil imports.

Prices which reflect economic costs could also be obtained through decontrol not only of new gas (brought into production after 1977) but also of old gas. In this case, pipelines would have less ability to average high cost gas with low cost price-controlled volumes. Most of the gas sold by producers to pipelines would reflect the real resource cost of the most expensive source of supply. That price plus incremental distribution and transmission costs would determine the economic cost of gas at the burner tip. If this cost were used to establish the commodity charge for gas, the average rates to users (rather than just the tailblock rates) would reflect economic costs. Again, it might be observed that if the user who would just buy gas at such burner tip prices did so to replace oil, the two notions of economic cost rates would be very similar and reflected in rates.

Small Refiner Bias Analysis

Final Report January 1978
Prepared for U.S. Department of Energy, Economic Regulatory Administration
Office of Regulations

[An entitlement was a permit to refine a barrel of cheap domestic oil. They were issued in proportion to a refiner's output. Refiners with a lot of cheap oil had to buy entitlements from refiners who imported a lot of expensive foreign oil. As a result, billions of dollars changed hands each month during the mid-1970s. Under the small refiner bias program, extra entitlements were issued to small refiners.]

CHAPTER 1—SUMMARY

The small refiner bias program is part of the entitlements program operated by the Department of Energy (DOE) under the authority of the Emergency Petroleum Allocation Act (EPAA). The entitlements program was established to eliminate the substantial disparities in the cost of crude oil which resulted to refiners as a consequence of price controls imposed in 1973 on domestic crude oil and concurrent escalation in the price of foreign oil. The intended purpose of the small refiner bias program is to help maintain the competitive viability of small and independent refiners. It represents an extension and expansion of financial assistance previously provided under the Mandatory Oil Import Program (MOIP).

The bias program provides for issuance of additional entitlements to small refiners on a sliding scale basis as a function of company size. The highest number of additional entitlements per barrel of crude oil is obtained for crude runs of 10,000 barrels per day (B/D) or less. The highest number of additional entitlements per company occurs at a company size of 30,000 B/D. Above 175,000 B/D no bias entitlements are issuable.

The bias program has the effect of reducing the cost of crude for smaller companies. These savings are paid for by transfer payments under the entitlements program from larger companies and, ultimately, by their customers. The maximum per barrel subsidy level provided under the program at the present time is approximately $2/B. The annualized subsidy rate provided under the program, based on July, 1977 figures, is $659 million. If exceptions and appeals relief provided under the entitlements program to small refiners is taken into account as well, the annualized subsidy rate, based on July figures, is approximately $1.125 billion.

There is considerable controversy with regard to the appropriate level of small refiner assistance and the future course of the small refiner bias program. Authorization for the entitlements program, and, thus, the small refiner bias, presently expires at the end of 1979. This issue is made more pressing by the Administration's proposed National Energy Act which, if passed, would begin to replace the entitlements program with a crude oil equalization tax.

CHAPTER 2—REGULATORY BACKGROUND

As have other small businesses, small refiners have benefitted from a range of government programs designed to support their survival and growth with the intended purpose of contributing to a competitive and efficient market place. In the petroleum refining industry a number of these programs have been designed to facilitate access to raw material and product markets. These include:

1 Preference to small refiners in the sale of royalty oil produced on the outer continental shelf and of oil produced for sale from the Naval Petroleum Reserves.

2 The Buy/Sell program and "December 1 rule" initiated by the FEA (now DOE) under the Emergency Petroleum Allocation Act in response to the 1973 oil embargo and as an accompaniment to the resulting price controls instituted in the U.S.

3 Small business set asides in purchases by the Department of Defense Fuels Supply Center.

Other government programs, in addition to these, are designed to provide direct financial benefits to small refiners. These include:

1 Allocation of fee-free import licenses on a sliding scale basis in favor of small refiners.

2 Partial relief, at least through 1982, for some small refiners from EPA's gasoline lead phase-down regulations.

3 The small refiner bias and exceptions and appeals procedures developed as part of the petroleum price control and allocation programs under the Emergency Petroleum Allocation Act.

The small refiner bias program was implemented by FEA as one element in an express attempt to comply with the intent of Congress . . . that regulations adopted to allocate and price crude oil and refined products should to the maximum extent practicable provide for:

(D) preservation of an economically sound and competitive petroleum industry; including the priority needs to restore and foster competition in the producing, refining, distribution, marketing, and petrochemical sectors of such industry, and to preserve the competitive viability of independent refiners, small refiners, nonbranded marketers, and branded independent marketers

The small refiner bias is part of the entitlements program operated by DOE. The entitlements program was established to eliminate the substantial disparities in the cost of crude oil which resulted to refiners as a consequence of domestic price controls. As such, the basic program is not designed to favor one class of refiners over any other. . . .

Under . . . the small refiner bias, small refiners are issued additional entitlements on a sliding scale basis as a function of company size. The highest bias level per barrel of crude oil is obtained at crude runs of up to 10,000 B/D. The highest bias level in dollar per day occurs at a company size of 30,000 B/D. Above

175,000 B/D no bias entitlements are issuable. The general effect of the small refiner bias is to lower crude costs for small refiners by either permitting them to sell a greater number of entitlements or requiring them to purchase fewer entitlements. The exact amount of the benefits provided under the sliding scale formula depends upon the entitlement price determined for that month by DOE on the basis of domestic and imported crude purchases for the U.S. refining industry as a whole. Due to the nature of the entitlements program, small refiner bias benefits are funded by transfer payments from the larger companies rather than directly by the government.

DEVELOPMENT OF THE SMALL REFINER BIAS PROGRAM

The Mandatory Oil Import Program

The present small refiner bias program has its basis in the Mandatory Oil Import Program (MOIP) instituted in March of 1959. This program was adopted for reasons of national defense and protection of the domestic oil producing industry. The program contained provisions for historical allocations, to be phased out over time, to established importers. Allocations to all refiners not protected by the historical minimum were related to the level of the refiner's throughput. This was done on a sliding scale basis which granted a proportionately larger share of the total allocation to small refiners.

The reasoning for incorporating the sliding scale into the MOIP and for subsequent changes which increasingly favored small refiners was never officially stated. The original inclusion of the sliding scale has been attributed by others to at least two reasons. One was the Antitrust Division's desire to use the oil import programs to offset competitive advantages that integrated firms were believed to have over independent refiners. The other and, perhaps, initially more important reason was to provide for equitable allocations to two classes of large companies—the traditional importers and those who had begun significant international operations in the 1950's. For many companies in the latter group the historical minimums allowed under the program were low, and without the sliding scale their allocations based on refinery inputs would have very nearly equaled those of established importers of similar size.

DIRECTION OF THE SMALL REFINER BIAS PROGRAM

The basic price and allocation controls implemented under the authority of the EPAA were intended to be temporary emergency measures that would be phased out as market equilibrium was restored. Authorization of these measures and, thus, the entitlements program and the small refiner bias and related programs, presently expire in 1979. This raises the issue of the need for a continuation of a small refiner subsidy program in some manner beyond the limits of the present program. This issue is made more pressing by the Administration's present energy bill submitted to Congress which contains provisions for replacement of the entitlements program with a crude oil equalization tax.

Significant controversy surrounds the need for the appropriate level of any continuing subsidy program. This interest reflects in large part the very significant sums of money involved in the program. Concerns have been expressed by a number of the larger companies that present subsidy levels are excessive and are acting to stimulate the entry of relatively inefficient, inflexible refineries and to provide incentives for spin-off of individual small plants owned by larger companies unable to take full advantage of small refiner bias benefits. Somewhat similar concerns have been expressed at times by DOE (FEA) itself. DOE records indicate what appears to be an unusually large number of new small refiner entrants through the route of reactivating shut-down plants or spin-offs. Since March of 1976 there have been six spin-offs of operating plants and a total of fifteen shut-down plants reactivated as new businesses.

Some of the larger companies including some of the larger small refiners—who receive proportionately less bias benefits—have voiced the criticism that if there is to be a subsidy program that it should be related to refinery size rather than company size. Others have tried to make the point that it is not appropriate to compare refinery economies of scale alone as many of the smaller companies operate in areas distant from large refineries.

As with any segment of a diverse industry, small refiners do not speak with a single voice. Several individual companies have indicated to us in the course of this study that they would be willing to do without a subsidy program of any kind, if there were to be complete decontrol of both crude and product prices. Their position was that the present system of regulation (and the crude oil equalization tax program as proposed) restricted their ability to effectively compete against larger companies, and without decontrol, continuing subsidies would be required. We are not sure how widely or strongly this view is held.

Many small refiners, however, especially those receiving the greatest benefits under the bias sliding scale, view continuation of this program at its present level of benefits of vital importance to their survival and justified as an extension of historical government aid. One of the arguments made most strongly by supporters of a continued assistance program is the need to provide a competitive offset to compensate for what they view to be subsidization of refining operations of the large integrated companies by profits from their production operations.

CHAPTER 6—POSSIBLE CHANGES TO THE SMALL REFINER BIAS

Development of a bias program appropriate for the 1980's involves a number of aspects. These include assessment of likely changes in market conditions, specification of the sources of cost differences of concern and of the objectives of the program, as well as program formulation itself. The latter would desirably assess the benefits of the program as well as its costs.

Principal Market Changes

The principal market difference we expect in the 1980's relative to present conditions is equalization of foreign and domestic price differentials for sweet crude.

This will depend, of course, upon the nature of the particular legislation enacted to replace the entitlements program.

Environmental regulations will have the effect of slowly changing the mix of product sales on an industry level toward more emphasis on fuel oil sales, particularly, on low sulfur fuel oil. What EPA's long term position will be on gasoline pool lead limitations for small refiners is not clear. We have assumed no difference in this study in lead level.

Objectives of Continued Assistance

The basic rationale for the small refiner bias program has been the perceived need to "preserve the competitive viability" of this segment of the industry. This is a broad mandate from Congress which can be interpreted by DOE in a number of ways. For example:

1 Does this refer only to existing small refiners or to new entry as well?

2 If it refers primarily to existing small refiners does it mean that the viability of all existing small refiners is to be preserved? If not, what criteria are used in determining appropriate assistance levels?

3 If it refers to new entry, does it refer to entry at all size levels under all market conditions? In some cases, for example, a relatively small plant may provide an economic means for serving a specific market. In others, it would not be viable without significant outside assistance.

While important, these questions are in a sense secondary. The more primary questions are directed to the reasons motivating special concern for the viability of this segment of the industry. A number of possible reasons suggest themselves, with some more valid in an economic sense than others:

1 The existence of economies of scale in the industry. While this is not a comparative study across industries, we doubt that economies of scale in refining are that much greater than in a number of other industries. To adopt an explicit policy of equalizing such cost differences would seem to set a very significant precedent for this industry and inevitably other industries as well.

2 Concern that government imposed domestic price controls and associated regulations might limit the flexibility of small and independent refiners. This is a potentially valid concern. To the extent that present price control and allocation regulations will be phased out as planned and any replacement system such as a crude oil equalization tax program will be designed so as to not significantly limit the flexibility of this sector of the industry, it is a short term rather than a long term concern.

3 Concern that small and independent refiners are subject to unfair practices. The primary issue here seems to be the charge by small and independent refiners that they are at a disadvantage with regard to large integrated companies which many of them appear to view as subsidizing refining operations with profits from crude oil production. This is a very complex issue which has been the subject of

study by the FTC and others for a number of years without final resolution and is beyond the scope of this study. . . .

4 Concern with regard to the ability of small refiners to obtain crude and to market products on a competitive basis with larger companies. Such concerns presumably have been the impetus for the government sponsored royalty oil and DFSC set aside programs. The basic issue here is whether the crude and product supply markets are viewed to be so imperfect as to require greater assistance than these programs provide.

5 A possible tendency for regulation to perpetuate itself. The government has provided direct financial assistance to small refiners under the MOIP and now the small refiner bias program. This assistance has no doubt significantly contributed to the entry and survival of a number of small refiners. This raises questions of equity with regard to withdrawal of benefits from these companies. To be weighed against considerations such as these, of course, are questions of equity with regard to those who are asked to fund the program.

A clear consensus on which the above (or other) issues constitute the proper basis for the formulation of long term policy with regard to small and independent refiners would be a useful step toward the development of such a policy. Lack of clear definition of the issues involved will only prolong resolution of the present controversy.

More is needed, however, than just definition of the issues of concern. If the primary issue, for example, involves allegation of noncompetitive behavior, specifically, for example, the artificial subsidization of refining by production profits by the large integrated companies, analysis and judgments must be made with regard to the validity, extent, and significance of such alleged practices. From an economic point of view, the existence of noncompetitive practices would form a justifiable basis for government intervention in the industry.

Program Formulation

As with all government programs, development of any long term assistance program for small and independent refiners should be guided by considerations of cost effectiveness. From a strictly economic point of view, the costs for the program chosen should be more than balanced by resulting benefits. These would presumably be related to estimates of increased competition in the industry. . . .

Whether a continued subsidy program is or is not necessary or whether it would be the most cost effective approach if some form of government program were needed, we cannot say on the basis of this study. Two concluding points should be noted, however. First, the charge that integrated companies artificially subsidize refining operations implies a pattern of cost differences as a function of degree of crude supply self sufficiency rather than directly as a function of company or plant size. If true, this implies that a relatively large company should receive proportionately more assistance than a smaller company integrated to a greater degree. On an industry average basis it would also imply much less variation in the level of assistance provided to different size groupings of companies than provided by the present small refiner bias sliding scale. Second, the primary purpose of this analysis has been to provide perspective on certain important elements of the cost structure of the refining industry. Final resolution of the small refiner bias issue would seem to us to require analysis and judgments with regard to the extent, if any, of noncompetitive conditions (including any regulatory impediments to competition) in the industry. We do not mean to imply by this that such conditions do or do not exist, only that clarification of their extent and significance is a necessary step for resolution of the small refiner bias issue.

National Energy Plan II

U.S. Department of Energy (May 1978)

The oil embargo of 1973/74 signaled a fundamental change in the ability of the industrialized nations to chart their own economic destinies and to guarantee the economic security of their citizens. . . . In the U.S., the oil embargo led to nationwide shortages of petroleum, a $60 billion drop in GNP, more rapid inflation, and large balance-of-payments deficits that continue to plague the economy today.

The U.S. and other major world consumers can expect more disruptions in oil supplies, at other places and at other times, as a result of events such as wars and unrest abroad, politically-inspired embargoes, strikes, sabotage, and other emergencies. Over the long term, the supply of oil will be fundamentally limited by the capacities and production decisions of those few countries in which world oil resources are concentrated. When increases in production at current prices no longer can keep pace with rising world oil demand, prices will rise sharply to bring markets into balance. As world oil supplies tighten under fundamental long-term pressures, the instability of the basic supply sources threatens even more economic and political damage to the U.S. It will make even more difficult the transition to the coming era of scarcer, more expensive energy supplies.

THE NATURE OF THE SECURITY PROBLEM

It is all too easy to be distracted by the crisis of the moment, and to overreact or to lose sight of the fundamental problems that crisis reflects. It is also easy to reinterpret long-term trends on the basis of today's headlines. Even small swings in production and consumption can create a glut or shortfall in world oil markets almost overnight. The public sense of urgency about the energy problem may change. But the dangers posed to the nation's political and economic security have now become clear and present.

These dangers have arisen from America's rapid and massive shift to consumption of foreign oil. In 1971, the U.S. imported 3.9 million barrels per day

(MMBD), and paid only $4 billion for that oil to foreign producers. In 1979, the U.S. will likely import 8.5 to 9.0 MMBD and, with this year's surge in prices arising from the Iranian shortages, pay an import bill of over $50 billion.

The origin of this sudden vulnerability lies in the American economy's historic dependence on a flow of cheap energy. Energy prices in the U.S. fell in real terms through most of this century. Falling energy prices encouraged greater—even profligate—use of domestic oil and gas resources. Yet the country's resources of oil and gas are finite. These powerful forces did not collide until late in the 1960s. Domestic oil production peaked in 1970 and has declined since that time. U.S. production of natural gas peaked in 1973. Yet the Nation has clung to policies and habits that try to restore the past, keep prices low and continue wasteful patterns of use. Many have been slow to recognize that the true cost of each new barrel of oil being consumed is the cost of imported oil brought in to replace domestic supply.

In the past 5 years, the price of dependence on a few oil producer countries has been a series of unpleasant economic shocks. The first OPEC price increase of 1973/74 quadrupled the cost of oil, helped push the U.S. into a recession, and required painful adjustments from which it has only lately recovered. Oil imports have directly raised the cost of everything in the U.S. that uses oil or oil substitutes, and thus have been a direct and indirect source of U.S. inflation. They also have contributed to the large U.S. trade deficits in 1977 and 1978 which led to the recent depreciation of the dollar.

Finally, the rise in world oil prices has affected every American's standard of living. The U.S. economy has had to give up more and more goods and services to pay for the same amount of foreign oil. Americans are simply not as well off when the terms on which they buy a vital commodity such as oil change so adversely.

Over the next decade, the energy security problems facing the U.S. could worsen. The underlying supply and demand pressures for major world oil price increases in the 1980s are great. Any surplus production capacity that individual OPEC countries may have developed in recent years will almost certainly vanish by the mid-1980s, perhaps sooner. Producer governments with limited ability to absorb huge revenues have strong incentives to reduce the output below maximum technical limits and keep world oil markets tight.

The U.S. and the governments of the other consumer nations which are already linked in the International Energy Agency, are not powerless to influence the world energy situation, however. For their own security, they have no choice but to do so. They can limit the economic damage from higher world oil prices, and limit world oil price increases. Through policies that encourage conservation and use of alternative fuels, consuming nations can reduce the demand pressures that would lead to high world oil prices. They also can stimulate development of new, higher-cost energy technologies and resources, which can be introduced at the proper times to help limit further price increases. It will be essential, as world oil prices rise, to ensure that such higher-cost substitutes for oil are available quickly and in the quantities needed.

PLANNING FOR UNCERTAINTY

The first set of uncertainties concern supply. The world has vast oil and gas resources. The basic doubt is whether enough new oil sources can be discovered and produced at current prices to meet even a low growth in world oil demand. More and more of the world's oil has come recently from high-cost, hostile environments. Many geologists believe that most of the world's largest fields have already been discovered, and that future discoveries may be smaller in size than in the past. As production from existing fields declines, successful discoveries would have to occur at a rate never before experienced to prevent large jumps in world oil prices.

The second set of uncertainties concerns world energy demand. The world's appetite for oil in the next two decades will depend on economic growth, which is very difficult to predict. Conservation can hold down energy demand growth, but government policies, consumer behavior and the energy-efficiency of new capital goods and buildings are notoriously hard to predict, and their effects are hard to estimate. These factors will determine whether and how fast world oil demand reaches the limits of OPEC and non-OPEC production capacity.

Many other uncertainties also will affect future world oil price behavior. These include technological change, the policies of consumer-nation governments in developing substitutes for oil, and the role that communist governments will play in world oil markets as exporters, importers or both.

In short, the timing and size of price increases are clouded with uncertainty. However, under a broad variety of assumptions that span the range of responsible opinion, it is almost inevitable that demand at current prices will exceed supplies at those prices. . . .

TOWARD A U.S. ENERGY STRATEGY

Since the first OPEC price increase of 1973/74, the U.S. energy situation has continued to deteriorate. While there has been increased emphasis on conservation and demand growth has slowed, domestic production of energy has remained stationary for almost a decade.

The Nation stands at the threshold of a major transition in its sources of energy supply. Over the next two decades, the U.S. will meet its future demand growth not only with oil and gas, but increasingly with coal, nuclear power, renewables, and high-cost unconventional sources. No longer can it easily turn to imported oil to fill the supply gap, as it has in the past. Foreign oil will no longer be cheap and readily available. Moreover, the political costs of dependence will have become even more apparent and unacceptable.

THE NATIONAL ENERGY STRATEGY

An energy strategy must balance those measures that improve the Nation's long-run security and those that better prepare it to deal with sudden crises. It must recognize the different problems that can emerge in three time-frames: the near term (from now to 1985), the mid-term (from 1985 to 2000) and the long-term (2000 and beyond).

The Near Term (1979–85)

The challenge of the near term is to ensure that investments in new energy producing and consuming equipment are made in the degree and kind that reflect the new realities, and that existing stock and equipment are used in the most effective way.

Movement toward the pricing of oil and gas at their true replacement cost will prepare American consumers better for long-term price increases and stimulate greater production and conservation now. Removal of barriers to new production will eliminate excessive regulatory delays that now paralyze the construction of new refineries, pipelines, and other energy projects. Filling the Strategic Petroleum Reserve (SPR), diversification of world oil supplies, and other actions will cushion the economic impact of an interruption. All these measures can set the stage for actions that will buy even greater security in the mid-term.

The Mid-Term (1985–2000)

During the mid-term, the U.S. and the rest of the world will begin to shift from reliance on oil and gas to new and higher-cost forms of energy. Energy consumption growth should be far slower than once anticipated. Direct coal use, electricity and decentralized renewable sources will increase their share of the market. The uncertainties—especially those surrounding world oil supply and price—are much greater for the mid-term than for the near term. These uncertainties will give the U.S. a major opportunity to influence more directly its own energy future.

The Long-Term (2000 and beyond)

The U.S. faces two major transitions in energy markets between now and the middle of the 21st century. The first will occur during the mid-term when the U.S. moves from an energy system which has depended on traditional oil and gas sources (including imports) to one relying on unconventional supplies. These "transitional" energy supplies include some renewable technologies, enhanced oil recovery, oil shale, unconventional gas, and coal-derived products.

Since even those supplies are depletable, a second transition will begin after the year 2000. A set of "ultimate" technologies, including all the renewable and advanced nuclear technologies, would begin to displace traditional fuels and non-renewable conventional sources.

AN AGENDA FOR ACTION

The Federal government, State and local governments, and the private sector all have important responsibilities to advance conservation and specific fuel technologies in all three time periods. This section describes Federal policies and programs.

Conservation

Conservation continues to offer the greatest prospect of reducing dependence on unstable imports, reducing energy costs, and meeting environmental goals. The objectives of the Administration's conservation policies are two: to reduce the rate of growth in demand for energy and to improve the productivity of energy use—by increasing the energy efficiency of existing and future capital stocks of buildings, vehicles, homes, and industrial operations while sustaining economic growth. . . .

- Conservation will be encouraged by policies for replacement-cost pricing, as embodied in the Natural Gas Policy Act, the phased decontrol of crude oil prices, and the Public Utilities Regulatory Policy Act.

- Energy use in new buildings and appliances will be reduced by using the regulatory authorities in the Conservation Policy Act and other legislation. Energy use in automobiles will be regulated by fuel economy standards. The Administration will work to resolve promptly the issues surrounding future use of the diesel engine.

Oil

Financial incentives and the reduction of institutional barriers are the major tools to raise oil production.

- Domestic production will be increased by rapidly phasing out controls on crude oil and, until complete decontrol in 1981, by providing price incentives targeted for production from new discoveries, marginal wells, and the use of enhanced oil recovery techniques.

- To prevent excessive revenues from flowing to producers in the wake of decontrol, the President has requested that the Congress enact a Windfall Profits Tax.

- Oil shale technology will be developed and tested on a commercial scale through a production tax credit financed by the Windfall Profits Tax.

- To provide security in the event of a possible disruption, the Strategic Petroleum Reserve will be filled, ultimately to a level of one billion barrels.

Natural Gas

Natural gas policy has two high priority elements—use of the temporary domestic surplus to substitute gas for oil imports and incentives to increase conventional domestic production.

• Domestic production will be encouraged by financial incentives, including the higher prices stemming from the recently enacted Natural Gas Policy Act; through a more stable and predictable regulatory environment; the deregulation of high-cost gas, most notably that below 15 thousand feet; and, deregulation on a predictable basis.

• Surplus gas and reasonably-priced supplemental sources of gas will be used to displace foreign oil in existing industrial and utility facilities capable of burning both oil and gas; coal will continue to be the preferred fuel for existing coal-capable units and all new boiler facilities.

• Supplemental sources of gas will be used in the order of their cost-effectiveness and security. Under present circumstances, the order of attractiveness is: Alaskan production; pipeline gas from Canada and/or Mexico; short-haul liquefied natural gas (LNG); domestically produced synthetic gas, depending upon the resolution of certain technical problems and cost; and long-haul LNG.

Coal

Coal, the Nation's most abundant fossil energy resource, should be used in place of oil and gas wherever economically and environmentally feasible. Programs that increase the use of coal as a substitute for oil will receive the highest priority.

• Direct Use
—The Powerplant and Industrial Fuel Use Act (PIFUA) will be used to require coal use in all new electric utilities and major industrial fuel burning installations, and in existing coal capable facilities.
—Research, development, and demonstration (RD&D) programs will be used to develop environmental control technologies and environmentally acceptable means of direct coal use to enhance the overall market for coal and to increase the regulatory options available under the PIFUA.

• Coal Liquefication
—RD&D for direct coal liquefication processes will be used to develop the capability by the 1990s for commercial deployment of plants producing the most economic synthetic liquid fuel.

• Coal Gasification
—The Administration supports favorable rate treatment and loan guarantees for first-generation Lurgi technology.

Nuclear

The Presidential Commission will provide a complete accounting of the causes of the Three Mile Island accident and its handling by utility, State, and Federal officials. The Nation needs to develop safeguards that will allow light water reactors to continue to meet an increasing share of electrical energy needs.

• Light Water Reactor

—The Administration will work toward resolving nuclear waste management issues, including both away-from-reactor storage and permanent disposal. . . .

—Nuclear siting and licensing legislation will be proposed to streamline procedures without in any way sacrificing the safety of new power plants.

• Breeder Reactor

—R&D on breeder reactors will continue so that commercial development can be initiated, if justified by future market conditions and non-proliferation policies.

• Fusion

—Research on the magnetic and inertial confinement concepts will continue with the objective of demonstrating scientific feasibility in the mid-1980s.

Renewable Energy Sources

The Nation's capacity to use renewable resources should be enhanced. The maturity of these technologies varies greatly; some are economic now, others are in the early stages of R&D. Federal support must be tailored to each stage of development.

• Solar Energy

—Tax credits and other financial incentives will be used where necessary to accelerate market penetration of solar technologies that are economic or nearly economic now (solar hot water heating, certain industrial process heat systems, passive solar systems, direct wood burning, and low-head hydro).

—RD&D and/or product support will advance those technologies that have significant market potential and that replace oil and gas, but which are not yet competitive in the mass market (certain solar industrial process heat systems, active solar space heating, conversion of biomass to liquid and gaseous fuels, and wind systems).

—R&D and limited product support will develop those technologies with significant long-term potential, but which are far from economic application (solar cooling, photovoltaics, solar thermal, and ocean thermal energy conversion).

• Geothermal

—Tax incentives and loan guarantees are the primary tools to encourage the use of hydrothermal resources. RD&D will be used where the technology has not been demonstrated.

THE SIGNIFICANCE OF NEP-II

The actions already undertaken, and those currently proposed, will place the Nation's energy policy on a sound and long-lasting footing. Movement toward replacement cost pricing for crude oil, coupled with last year's action on natural gas pricing, will build a coherent economic framework for making more rational decisions about energy production and consumption—and thus about the Nation's energy future. These actions are coupled with a variety of measures, such as the Windfall Profits Tax, designed to assure equity for consumers.

By beginning to remove the roadblocks to timely and equitable decision-making on energy projects, the Nation can increase production of its domestic resources. By spurring the development of new technologies, the U.S. will lay the groundwork for their future use as world oil prices rise.

CHAPTER 18

REGULATION AND ANTITRUST

One might expect that antitrust enforcement would not really be relevant for regulated industries. In fact, antitrust issues have frequently arisen and played an important role in many of these industries. The cases in this chapter illustrate the possible areas of overlap between antitrust and regulation.

The first case, *Georgia v. Pennsylvania Railroad*, dealt with the rate bureaus maintained by the railroads. These bureaus were formed to facilitate the reaching of common and consistent railroad rates. In the early 1940s they were attacked under the federal antitrust laws. By coincidence, the first collusion case to reach the Supreme Court under the Sherman Act was against the Trans-Missouri Freight Association, a forerunner of the modern rate bureau. The revolution implicit in the Georgia v. Pennsylvania decision was short-lived, however. Congress repealed it with the passage of the Reed-Bulwinkle Act in 1948, thereby placing such restrictive arrangements under the jurisdiction of the Interstate Commerce Commission. Why is it necessary for the railroads to reach agreement on freight rates? Are such agreements conducive to the efficient functioning of the railroad industry?

The Noerr Motor Freight case focused on the political activities of the railroad industry. The railroads' public relations campaigns were unquestionably aimed at preventing competition via legislative interference, so they were attacked under the Sherman Act. The Supreme Court decided the case on a constitutional basis. To do otherwise would surely have changed the character of American democracy. On the other hand, the decision did mean that it is perfectly legal for firms to conspire to have the government rig the market for them, while it is unquestionably illegal for them to conspire to rig the market for themselves. Does this situation bother you? Should the efficiency of the marketplace be abandoned in favor of political goals? Would your decision be different if the industry in question was the dairy industry instead of the railroads?

The next two cases resulted from a jurisdictional dispute between the Federal Power Commission and the Antitrust Division of the Justice Department. The FPC approved the merger between El Paso Natural Gas and Pacific Northwest Pipeline, but their action was challenged by the state of California in *California v. FPC*. After that decision, the Justice Department sued in *U.S. v. El Paso Natural Gas*, seeking the divestiture of Pacific Northwest from El Paso. As a result of this decision, the role of antitrust in regulated industries was much broader than before. It is now possible to hold many of the transactions in regulated industries subject to the same antitrust criteria that firms in unregulated industries face. Does this injection of judicial review into regulatory proceedings seem redundant? Is regulation of economic activity inherently inconsistent with antitrust goals?

The fifth case is a straightforward antitrust case in the electric power industry. Again, the case began in a regulatory commission, the FPC. The defendant, Otter Tail Power Co., refused to supply cities with electricity and to "wheel" (transmit over its lines) power generated by others when those cities had established their own distribution companies instead of renewing their exclusive franchises with Otter Tail. After the FPC concluded that it could not act, the Antitrust Division initiated a case under the Sherman Act. The Supreme Court affirmed the District Court's decision under which Otter Tail was found to have violated the Sherman Antitrust Act by refusing to sell or wheel power.

Economists have had mixed reactions to the Otter Tail case. The main advantage of municipal power systems is that they don't pay corporate income tax and they can sell bonds at very low interest rates (interest on such bonds is exempt from the federal income tax). Those who criticize the decision feel that the formation of municipal systems based on these artificial advantages should not be encouraged by antitrust considerations. On the other hand, those who support the Supreme Court's decision believe that competition among companies that generate power is feasible if owners of transmission lines are required to wheel power and if distribution systems are independent of the generating companies. Try to decide whether the trend suggested by the Otter Tail decision would be in the consumers' interest.

The last case is the complaint filed in the government's massive antitrust suit against American Telephone and Telegraph Company (AT&T). The government alleges that AT&T has monopolized the telecommunications service and equipment markets in the United States. If the court rules that AT&T has violated the antitrust laws, it might be forced to divest some or all of Western Electric as well as its Long Lines Department. What would be the benefits of such a result? Do you think that it is necessary for AT&T to provide long-distance service as well as to manufacture telecommunications equipment? Without the Bell Long Lines Department, each local operating company would have to negotiate contracts with more than one common carrier. Would this be more or less efficient than the current system? What factors would you analyze in order to reach your decision?

Georgia v. Pennsylvania Railroad Co.

324 U.S. 439 (1945)

MR. JUSTICE DOUGLAS delivered the opinion of the Court.

The State of Georgia by this motion for leave to file a bill of complaint seeks to invoke the original jursidiction of this Court under Art. III, §2 of the Constitution. The defendents are some twenty railroad companies. . . .

The essence of the complaint is a charge of a conspiracy among the defendants in restraint of trade and commerce among the States. It alleges that they have fixed arbitrary and noncompetitive rates and charges for transportation of freight by railroad to and from Georgia so as to prefer the ports of other States over the ports of Georgia. It charges that some sixty rate bureaus, committees, conferences, associations and other private rate-fixing agencies have been utilized by defendants to fix these rates; that no road can change joint through rates without the approval of these private agencies; that this private rate-fixing machinery which is not sanctioned by the Interstate Commerce Act and which is prohibited by the anti-trust Acts has put the effective control of rates to and from Georgia in the hands of the defendants. The complaint alleges that these practices in purpose and effect give manufacturers, sellers and other shippers in the North an advantage over manufacturers, shippers and others in Georgia. It alleges that the rates so fixed are approximately 39 per cent higher than the rates and charges for transportation of like commodities for like distances between points in the North. It alleges that the defendants who have lines wholly or principally in the South are generally dominated and coerced by the defendants who have northern roads, and therefore that, even when the southern defendants desire, they cannot publish joint through rates between Georgia and the North when the northern carriers refuse to join in such rates.

The complaint alleges that the defendants are not citizens of Georgia; that Georgia is without remedy in her own courts, as the defendants are outside her jurisdiction; that she has no administrative remedy, the Interstate Commerce Commission having no power to afford relief against such a conspiracy; that the issues presented constitute a justiciable question.

The prayer is for damages and for injunctive relief. . . .

These carriers are subject to the anti-trust laws. Conspiracies among carriers to fix rates were included in the broad sweep of the Sherman Act. *United States v. Trans-Missouri Freight Assn.* [1897], *United States v. Joint Traffic Assn.* [1898]. Congress by §11 of the Clayton Act entrusted the [Interstate Commerce] Commission with authority to enforce compliance with certain of its provisions "where applicable to common carriers" under the Commission's jurisdiction. It has the power to lift the ban of the anti-trust laws in favor of carriers who merge or consolidate and the duty to give weight to the anti-trust policy of the nation before approving mergers and consolidations. But Congress has not given the Commission comparable authority to remove rate-fixing combinations from the prohibitions contained in the anti-trust laws. It has not placed these combinations under the control and supervision of the Commission. Nor has it empowered the Commission to proceed against such combinations and through cease and desist orders or otherwise to put an end to their activities. Regulated industries are not *per se* exempt from the Sherman Act. . . . None of the powers acquired by the Commission since the enactment of the Sherman Act relates to the regulation of rate-fixing combinations. Twice Congress has been tendered proposals to legalize rate-fixing combinations. But it has not adopted them. In view of this history we can only conclude that they have no immunity from the anti-trust laws.

It is pointed out, however, that under §1 (4) of the Interstate Commerce Act it is "the duty of every common carrier subject to this chapter to provide and furnish transportation upon reasonable request therefor, and to establish reasonable through routes with other such carriers, and just and reasonable rates, fares, charges, and classifications applicable thereto." And it is noted that agreement among carriers is provided in the establishment of joint rates. That is true. But it would be a perversion of those sections to hold that they legalize a rate-fixing combination of the character alleged to exist here. The collaboration contemplated in the fixing of through and joint rates is of a restrictive nature. We do not stop at this stage of the proceedings to delineate the legitimate area in which that collaboration may operate. . . . It is sufficient here to note that we find no warrant in the Interstate Commerce Act and the Sherman Act for saying that the authority to fix joint through rates clothes with legality a conspiracy to discriminate against a State or a region, to use coercion in the fixing of rates, or to put in the hands of a combination of carriers a veto power over rates proposed by a single carrier. The type of regulation which Congress chose did not eliminate the emphasis on competition and individual freedom of action in rate-making. The Act was designed to preserve private initiative in rate-making as indicated by the duty of each common carrier to initiate its own rates. If a combination of the character described in this bill of complaint is immune from suit, that freedom of action disappears. The coercive and collusive influences of group action take its place. A monopoly power is created under the aegis of private parties without Congressional sanction and without governmental supervision or control.

These considerations emphasize the irrelevancy to the present problem of the fact that the Commission has authority to remove discriminatory rates of the character alleged to exist here. Under §3 (1) of the Act rates are declared unlawful which give "any undue or unreasonable preference or advantage" to any port, region, district, territory, and the like. And the Commission has taken some action in that regard. The present bill does not seek to have the Court act in the place of the Commission. It seeks to remove from the field of rate-making the influences of a combination which exceed the limits of the collaboration authorized for the fixing of joint through rates. It seeks to put an end to discriminatory and coercive practices. The aim is to make it possible for individual carriers to perform their duty under the Act, so that whatever tariffs may be continued in effect or superseded by new ones may be tariffs which are free from the restrictive, discriminatory, and coercive influences of the combination. That is not to undercut or impair the primary jurisdiction of the Commission over rates. It is to free the rate-making function of the influences of a conspiracy over which the Commission has no authority but which if proven to exist can only hinder the Commission in the tasks with which it is confronted.

Moreover, the relief sought from this Court is not an uprooting of established rates. We are not asked for a decree which would be an idle gesture. We are not asked to enjoin what the Commission might later approve or condone. We are not asked to trench on the domain of the Commission; nor need any decree which may be ultimately entered in this cause have that effect. Georgia alleges, "No administrative proceedings directed against a particular schedule of rates would afford relief to the State of Georgia so long as the defendants remained free to promulgate rates by collusive agreement. Until the conspiracy is ended, the corrosion of new schedules, established by the collusive power of the defendant carriers acting in concert, would frustrate any action sought to be taken by administrative process to redress the grievances from which the State of Georgia suffers." Rate-making is a continuous process. Georgia is seeking a decree which will prevent in the future the kind of harmful conduct which has occurred in the past. . . . Dissolution of illegal combinations or a restriction of their conduct to lawful channels is a conventional form of relief accorded in anti-trust suits. No more is envisaged here. If the alleged combination is shown to exist, the decree which can be entered will be no idle or futile gesture. It will restore that degree of competition envisaged by Congress when it enacted the Interstate Commerce Act. It will eliminate from rate-making the collusive practices which the anti-trust laws condemn and which are not sanctioned by the Interstate Commerce Act. It will supply an effective remedy without which there can be only an endless effort to rectify the continuous injury inflicted by the unlawful combination. The threatened injury is clear. The damage alleged is sufficient to satisfy the preliminary requirements of this motion to file. There is no administrative control over the combination. And no adequate or effective remedy other than this suit is suggested which Georgia can employ to eliminate from rate-making the influences of the unlawful conspiracy alleged to exist here.

As we have said, we construe the bill to charge a conspiracy among defendants to use coercion in the fixing of rates and to discriminate against Georgia in the rates which are fixed. We hold that under that construction of the bill a cause of action under the anti-trust laws is alleged. We intimate no opinion whether the bill might be construed to charge more than that or whether a rate-fixing combination would be legal under the Interstate Commerce Act and the Sherman Act but for the features of discrimination and coercion charged here. We are dealing with the case only in a preliminary manner. . . .

[The Court proceeded to permit Georgia to file a bill of complaint alleging antitrust violations by the railroad rate bureaus.]

Eastern Railroad Presidents Conference v. Noerr Motor Freight, Inc.

365 U.S. 127 (1961)

Mr. JUSTICE BLACK delivered the opinion of the Court.

The case was commenced by a complaint filed in the United States District Court in Pennsylvania on behalf of 41 Pennsylvania truck operators and their trade association, the Pennsylvania Motor Truck Association. This complaint, which named as defendants 24 Eastern railroads, an association of the presidents of those railroads known as the Eastern Railroad Presidents Conference and a public relations firm, Carl Byoir & Associates, Inc., charged that the defendants had conspired to restrain trade in and monopolize the long-distance freight business in violation of §§ 1 and 2 of the Sherman Act. The gist of the conspiracy alleged was that the railroads had engaged Byoir to conduct a publicity campaign against the truckers designed to foster the adoption and retention of laws and law enforcement practices destructive of the trucking business, to create an atmosphere of distaste for the truckers among the general public, and to impair the relationships existing between the truckers and their customers. The campaign so conducted was described in the complaint as "vicious, corrupt, and fraudulent," first in that the sole motivation behind it was the desire on the part of the railroads to injure the truckers and eventually to destroy them as competitors in the long-distance freight business, and, secondly, in that the defendants utilized the so-called third-party technique, that is the publicity matter circulated in the campaign was made to appear as spontaneously expressed views of independent persons and civic groups when, in fact, it was largely prepared and produced by Byoir and paid for by the railroads. The complaint then went on to supplement these more or less general allegations with specific charges as to particular instances in which the railroads had attempted to influence legislation by means of their publicity campaign. One of several such charges was that the defendants had succeeded in persuading the Governor of Pennsylvania to veto a measure known as the "Fair Truck Bill," which would have permitted truckers to carry heavier loads over Pennsylvania roads.

In their answer to this complaint, the railroads admitted that they had conducted a publicity campaign designed to influence the passage of state laws relating to truck weight limits and tax rates on heavy trucks, and to encourage a more rigid enforcement of state laws penalizing trucks for overweight loads and other traffic violations, but they denied that their campaign was motivated either by a desire to destroy the trucking business as a competitor or to interfere with the relationships between the truckers and their customers. Rather, they insisted, the campaign was conducted in furtherance of their rights "to inform the public and the legislatures of the several states of the truth with regard to the enormous damage done to the roads by the operators of heavy and especially of overweight trucks, with regard to their repeated and deliberate violations of the law limiting the weight and speed of big trucks, with regard to their failure to pay their fair share of the cost of constructing, maintaining and repairing the roads, and with regard to the driving hazards they create. . . ." Such a campaign, the defendants maintained, did not constitute a violation of the Sherman Act, presumably because that Act could not properly be interpreted to apply either to restraints of trade or monopolizations that result from the passage or enforcement of laws or to the efforts of individuals to bring about the passage or enforcement of laws.

In this posture, the case went to trial. After hearings, the trial court entered a judgment, based upon extensive findings of fact and conclusions of law, that the railroads' publicity campaign had violated the Sherman Act while that of the truckers had not. In reaching this conclusion, the trial court expressly disclaimed any purpose to condemn as illegal mere efforts on the part of the railroads to influence the passage of new legislation or the enforcement of existing law. Instead, it rested its judgment upon findings, first, that the railroads' publicity campaign, insofar as it was actually directed at lawmaking and law enforcement authorities, was malicious and fraudulent—malicious in that its only purpose was to destroy the truckers as competitors, and fraudulent in that it was predicated upon the deceiving of those authorities through the use of the third-party technique; and, secondly, that the railroads' campaign also had as an important, if not overriding purpose, the destruction of the truckers' goodwill, among both the general public and the truckers' existing customers, and thus injured the truckers in ways unrelated to the passage or enforcement of law. . . .

* * *

We accept, as the starting point for our consideration of the case, the same basic construction of the Sherman Act adopted by the courts below—that no violation of the Act can be predicated upon mere attempts to influence the passage or enforcement of laws. It has been recognized, at least since the landmark decision of this Court in *Standard Oil Co. v. United States,* that the Sherman Act forbids only those trade restraints and monopolizations that are created, or attempted, by the acts of "individuals or combinations of individuals or corporations." Accordingly, it has been held that where a restraint upon trade or monopolization is the result of valid governmental action, as opposed to private action, no violation of the Act can be made out. . . .

We think it equally clear that the Sherman Act does not prohibit two or more persons from associating together in an attempt to persuade the legislature or the executive to take particular action with respect to a law that would produce a restraint or a monopoly. Although such associations could perhaps, through a process of expansive construction, be brought within the general proscription of "combination[s] . . . in restraint of trade," they bear very little if any resemblance to the combinations normally held violative of the Sherman Act, combinations ordinarily characterized by an express or implied agreement or understanding that the participants will jointly give up their trade freedom, or help one another to take away the trade freedom of others through the use of such devices as price-fixing agreements, boycotts, market-division agreements, and other similar arrangements. [Thus, there is an] essential dissimilarity between an agreement jointly to seek legislation or law enforcement, and the agreements traditionally condemned by §1 of the Act. . . . And we do think that the question is conclusively settled against the application of the Act, when this factor of essential dissimilarity is considered along with the other difficulties that would be presented by a holding that the Sherman Act forbids associations for the purpose of influencing the passage or enforcement of laws.

In the first place, such a holding would substantially impair the power of government to take actions through its legislature and executive that operate to restrain trade. In a representative democracy such as this, these branches of government act on behalf of the people and, to a very large extent, the whole concept of representation depends upon the ability of the people to make their wishes known to their representatives. . . . Secondly, and of at least equal significance, such a construction of the Sherman Act would raise important constitutional questions. The right of petition is one of the freedoms protected by the Bill of Rights, and we cannot, of course, lightly impute to Congress an intent to invade these freedoms. . . . For these reasons, we think it clear that the Sherman Act does not apply to the activities of the railroads at least insofar as those activities comprised mere solicitation of governmental action with respect to the passage and enforcement of laws. We are thus called upon to consider whether the courts below were correct in holding that, notwithstanding this principle, the Act was violated here because of the presence in the railroads' publicity campaign of additional factors sufficient to take the case out of the area in which the principle is controlling.

The first such factor relied upon was the fact, established by the finding of the District Court, that the railroads' sole purpose in seeking to influence the passage and enforcement of laws was to destroy the truckers as competitors for the long-distance freight business. But we do not see how this fact, even if adequately supported in the record, could transform conduct otherwise lawful into a violation of the Sherman Act. All of the considerations that have led us to the conclusion that the Act does not apply to mere group solicitation of governmental action are equally applicable in spite of the addition of this factor. The right of the people to inform their representatives in government of their desires with respect to the passage or enforcement of laws cannot properly be made to depend upon their intent in doing so. It is neither unusual nor illegal for people to seek action on laws in the hope that they may bring about an advantage to themselves and a disadvantage to their competitors. . . .

The second factor relied upon by the courts below to justify the application of the Sherman Act to the railroads' publicity campaign was the use in the campaign of the so-called third-party technique. The theory under which this factor was related to the proscriptions of the Sherman Act, though not entirely clear from any of the opinions below, was apparently that it involved unethical business conduct on the part of the railroads. . . . We can certainly agree with the courts below that this technique, though in widespread use among practitioners of the art of public relations, is one which falls far short of the ethical standards generally approved in this country. It does not follow, however, that the use of the technique in a publicity campaign designed to influence governmental action constitutes a violation of the Sherman Act. Insofar as that Act sets up a code of ethics at all, it is a code that condemns trade restraints, not political activity, and, as we have already pointed out, a publicity campaign to influence governmental action falls clearly into the category of political activity. The proscriptions of the Act, tailored as they are for the business world, are not at all appropriate for application in the political arena. . . .

There may be situations in which a publicity campaign, ostensibly directed toward influencing governmental action, is a mere sham to cover what is actually nothing more than an attempt to interfere directly with the business relationships of a competitor and the application of the Sherman Act would be justified. But this certainly is not the case here. No one denies that the railroads were making a genuine effort to influence legislation and law enforcement practices. Indeed, if the version of the facts set forth in the truckers' complaint is fully credited, as it was by the courts below, that effort was not only genuine but also highly successful. Under these circumstances, we conclude that no attempt to interfere with business relationships in a manner proscribed by the Sherman Act is involved in this case.

In rejecting each of the grounds relied upon by the courts below to justify application of the Sherman Act to the campaign of the railroads, we have rejected the very grounds upon which those courts relied to distinguish the campaign conducted by the truckers. In doing so, we have restored what appears to be the true nature of the case—a "no-holds-barred fight" between two industries both of which are seeking control of a profitable source of income. Inherent in such fights, which are commonplace in the halls of legislative bodies, is the possibility, and in many instances even the probability, that one group or the other will get hurt by the arguments that are made. In this particular instance, each group appears to have utilized all the political powers it could muster in an attempt to bring about the passage of laws that would help it or injure the other. But the contest itself appears to have been conducted along lines normally accepted in our political system, except to the extent that each group has deliberately deceived the public and public officials. And that deception, reprehensible as it is, can be of no consequence so far as the Sherman Act is concerned. That Act was not violated by either the railroads or the truckers in their respective campaigns to influence legislation and law enforcement. . . . And it follows from what we have said that those parts of the judgments below are wrong. They must be and are

Reversed.

California v. Federal Power Commission

369 U.S. 482 (1962)

Opinion of the Court by MR. JUSTICE DOUGLAS announced by MR. JUSTICE BRENNAN.

El Paso Natural Gas Company first acquired the stock of the Pacific Northwest Pipeline Corp. and then applied to the Federal Power Commission for authority to acquire the assets pursuant to §7 of the Natural Gas Act. This application was dated August 7, 1957. Prior thereto, on July 22, 1957, the Federal Government commenced an action against El Paso and Pacific Northwest, alleging that El Paso's acquisition of the stock of Pacific Northwest violated §7 of the Clayton Act. On September 30, 1957, El Paso and Pacific Northwest filed a motion to dismiss the antitrust suit or to stay it, pending completion of the proceedings before the Commission. On October 21, 1957, that motion was denied after hearing; and we denied certiorari.

In May and June 1958, the Department of Justice wrote four letters to the Commission, asking that the proceeding be stayed pending the outcome of the antitrust suit. On July 29, 1958, the Department of Justice was advised by the Commission that it would not stay its proceedings. The Commission invited the Antitrust Division of the Department to participate in the administrative proceedings; but it did not do so.

The hearings before the Commission started September 17, 1958. On October 2, 1958, El Paso and Pacific Northwest moved in the District Court for a continuance of the antitrust suit. On October 6, 1958, the Department of Justice asked the Commission to postpone its hearing, pending final outcome of the antitrust suit which had then been set for trial November 17, 1958. On October 7, 1958, the Commission wrote the District Court that if the court denied El Paso and Pacific Northwest's motion for a continuance and proceeded with the antitrust trial, the Commission would continue its merger hearings to a date that would not conflict with the trial date of the antitrust case, but that if the court granted the motion for continuance, the Commission would proceed with its hearing. On October 13, 1958, the District Court continued the antitrust suit until the final decision in the administrative proceedings. The latter proceedings were concluded, the Commission authorizing the merger on December 23, 1959. The merger was consummated December 31, 1959.

Petitioner intervened in the administrative proceedings August 27, 1957, and obtained review by the Court of Appeals, which affirmed the Commission, Judge Fahy dissenting. We granted certiorari.

Immunity from the antitrust laws is not lightly implied. . . . Under the Interstate Commerce Act, mergers of carriers that are approved have an antitrust immunity, as section 5 of that Act specifically provides that the carriers involved "shall be and they are hereby relieved from the operation of the antitrust laws. . . ."

There is no comparable provision under the Natural Gas Act. Section 7 of the

Clayton Act—which prohibits stock acquisitions "where in any line of commerce in any section of the country, the effect of such acquisition may be substantially to lessen competition, or to tend to create a monopoly"—contains a proviso that "Nothing contained in this section shall apply to transactions duly consummated pursuant to authority given by the . . . Federal Power Commission . . . under any statutory provision vesting such power in such Commission. . . ." The words "transactions duly consummated pursuant to authority" given the Commission "under any statutory provision vesting such power" in it are plainly not a grant of power to adjudicate antitrust issues. Congress made clear that by this proviso in §7 of the Clayton Act " . . . it is not intended that . . . any . . . agency" mentioned "shall be granted any authority or powers which it does not already possess." The Commission's standard, set forth in §7 of the Natural Gas Act, is that the acquisition, merger, etc., will serve the "public convenience and necessity." If existing natural gas companies violate the antitrust laws, the Commission is advised by §20 to "transmit such evidence" to the Attorney General "who, in his discretion, may institute the necessary criminal proceedings." Other administrative agencies are authorized to enforce §7 of the Clayton Act when it comes to certain classes of companies or persons; but the Federal Power Commission is not included in the list.

We do not decide whether in this case there were any violations of the antitrust laws. We rule only on one select issue and that is: should the Commission proceed to a decision on the merits of a merger application when there is pending in the courts a suit challenging the validity of that transaction under antitrust laws? We think not. We think the Commission in those circumstances should await the decision of the courts.

The Commission considered the interplay between §7 of the Clayton Act and §7 of the Natural Gas Act and said:

> Section 7 of the Clayton Act, under which the antitrust suit was brought, prohibits the acquisition by one corporation of the stock or assets of another corporation where 'the effect of such acquisition may be substantially to lessen competition, or to tend to create a monopoly.' Exempt, however, are transactions consummated pursuant to Commission authority. This shows, reasons the presiding examiner, that Congress placed reliance on the Commission not to approve an acquisition of assets in violation of the injunction of the Clayton Act, unless in the carefully exercised judgement of the Commission, the acquisition would nevertheless be in the public interest. What we are attempting to arrive at is the public convenience and necessity. In reaching our determination, we do not have authority to determine whether a given transaction is in violation of the Clayton Act, but we are required to consider the bearing of the policy on the antitrust laws on the public convenience and necessity. With the presiding examiner, we find that any lessening of competition whether in the consumer markets or the producing fields, does not prevent our approving the merger because there are other factors which outweigh the elimination of Pacific as a competitor. In any case, it appears that any lessening of competition is not substantial.

Apart from the fact that the Commission did undertake to make a finding reserved to the courts by §7 of the Clayton Act, there are practical reasons why it should have held its hand until the courts had acted.

One is that if the Commission approves the transaction and the courts in the antitrust suit later hold it to be illegal, an unscrambling is necessary. Thus a needless waste of time and money may be involved. . . .

Another practical reason is that a transaction consummated under the aegis of the Commission as being a matter of "public convenience and necessity" is bound to carry momentum into the antitrust suit. The very prospect of undoing what was done raises a powerful influence in the antitrust litigation.

The orderly procedure is for the Commission to await decision in the antitrust suit before taking action.

It is not for us to say that the complementary legislative policies reflected in §7 of the Clayton Act on the one hand and in §7 of the Natural Gas Act on the other should be better accommodated. Our function is to see that the policy entrusted to the courts is not frustrated by an administrative agency. Where the primary jurisdiction is in the agency, courts withhold action until the agency has acted. The converse should also be true, lest the antitrust policy whose enforcement Congress in this situation has entrusted to the courts is in practical effect taken over by the Federal Power Commission. Moreover, as noted, the Commission in holding that "any lessening of competition is not substantial" was in the domain of the Clayton Act, a domain which is entrusted to the court in which the antitrust suit was pending.

The judgment of the Court of Appeals is reversed and the case is remanded for proceedings in conformity with this opinion.

It is so ordered.

United States v. El Paso Natural Gas

376 U.S. 651 (1964)

Opinion of the Court by MR. JUSTICE DOUGLAS, announced by MR. JUSTICE CLARK.

This is a civil suit charging a violation of §7 of the Clayton Act, by reason of the acquisition of the stock and assets of Pacific Northwest Pipeline Corp. (Pacific Northwest) by El Paso Natural Gas Co. (El Paso). The District Court dismissed the complaint after trial, making findings of fact and conclusions of law, but not writing an opinion. The case is here on direct appeal.

The ultimate issue revolves around the question whether the acquisition substantially lessened competition in the sale of natural gas in California—a market of which El Paso was the sole out-of-state supplier at the time of the acquisition.

Pacific Northwest, though it had no pipeline into California, is shown by this record to have been a substantial factor in the California market at the time it was acquired by El Paso. At that time El Paso was the only actual supplier of out-of-state gas to the vast California market, *a market that expands at an estimated annual rate of 200 million cubic feet per day.* At that time Pacific Northwest was the only other important interstate pipeline west of the Rocky Mountains. Though young, it was prospering and appeared strong enough to warrant a "treaty" with El Paso that protected El Paso's California markets.

[Southern California] Edison's search for a firm supply of natural gas in California, when it had El Paso gas only on an "interruptible" basis, illustrates what effect Pacific Northwest had merely as a potential competitor in the California market. Edison took its problem to Pacific Northwest and, as we have seen, a tentative agreement was reached for Edison to obtain Pacific Northwest gas. El Paso responded, offering Edison a firm supply of gas and substantial price concessions. We would have to wear blinders not to see that the mere efforts of Pacific Northwest to get into the California market, though unsuccessful, had a powerful influence on El Paso's business attitudes within the State. We repeat that one purpose of §7 was "to arrest the trend toward concentration, the *tendency* to monopoly, before the consumer's alternatives disappeared through merger. . . ." *United States v. Philadelphia National Bank,* 374 U.S., at 367.

The effect on competition in a particular market through acquisition of another company is determined by the nature or extent of that market and by the nearness of the absorbed company to it, that company's eagerness to enter that market, its resourcefulness, and so on. Pacific Northwest's position as a competitive factor in California was not disproved by the fact that it had never sold gas there. Nor is it conclusive that Pacific Northwest's attempt to sell to Edison failed. . . .

Unsuccessful bidders are no less competitors than the successful one. The presence of two or more suppliers gives buyers a choice. Pacific Northwest was no feeble, failing company; nor was it inexperienced and lacking in resourcefulness. It was one of two major interstate pipelines serving the trans-Rocky Mountain States; it had raised $250 million for its pipeline that extended 2,500 miles through rugged terrain. It had adequate reserves and managerial skill. It was so strong and militant that it was viewed with concern, and coveted, by El Paso. If El Paso can absorb Pacific Northwest without violating §7 of the Clayton Act, that section has no meaning in the natural gas field. For normally there is no competition—once the lines are built and the long-term contracts negotiated—except as respects the incremental needs.

Since appellees have been on notice of the antitrust charge from almost the beginning—indeed before El Paso sought Commission approval of the merger—we not only reverse the judgment below but direct the District Court to order divestiture without delay.

Reversed.

[It may be of interest to know how this case came out. Divestiture was finally consummated in 1974, ten years after it was initially ordered. And, as soon as divestiture was complete, the newly independent Pacific Northwest Pipeline entered into a large contract to supply gas in southern California, thereby competing with El Paso Natural Gas.]

Otter Tail Power Co. v. United States

410 U.S. 366 (1973)

MR. JUSTICE DOUGLAS delivered the opinion of the Court.

In this civil antitrust suit brought by appellee against Otter Tail Power Co. (Otter Tail), an electric utility company, the District Court found that Otter Tail had attempted to monopolize and had monopolized the retail distribution of electric power in its service area in violation of §2 of the Sherman Act. The District Court found that Otter Tail had attempted to prevent communities in which its retail distribution franchise had expired from replacing it with a municipal distribution system. The principal means employed were (1) refusals to sell power at wholesale to proposed municipal systems in the communities where it had been retailing power; (2) refusals to "wheel" power to such systems, that is to say, to transfer by direct transmission or displacement electric power from one utility to another over the facilities of an intermediate utility; (3) the institution and support of litigation designed to prevent or delay establishment of those systems; and (4) the invocation of provisions in its transmission contracts with several other power suppliers for the purpose of denying the municipal systems access to other suppliers by means of Otter Tail's transmission systems.

Otter Tail sells electric power at retail in 465 towns in Minnesota, North Dakota, and South Dakota. The decree enjoins it from refusing to sell electric power at wholesale to existing or proposed municipal electric power systems in the areas serviced by Otter Tail, from refusing to wheel electric power over the lines from the electric power suppliers to existing or proposed municipal systems in the area, from entering into or enforcing any contract which prohibits use of Otter Tail's lines to wheel electric power to municipal electric power systems, or from entering into or enforcing any contract which limits the customers to whom and areas in which Otter Tail or any other electric power company may sell electric power.

The decree also enjoins Otter Tail from instituting, supporting, or engaging in litigation, directly or indirectly, against municipalities and their officials who have voted to establish municipal electric power systems for the purpose of delaying, preventing, or interfering with the establishment of a municipal electric power system. Otter Tail took a direct appeal to this Court under §2 of the Expediting Act; and we noted probable jurisdiction.

In towns where Otter Tail distributes at retail, it operates under municipally granted franchises which are limited from 10 to 20 years. Each town in Otter Tail's service area generally can accommodate only one distribution system, making each town a natural monopoly market for the distribution and sale of electric power at retail. The aggregate of towns in Otter Tail's service area is the geographic market in which Otter Tail competes for the right to serve the towns at retail. That competition is generally for the right to serve the entire retail market within the composite limits of a town and that competition is generally between

Otter Tail and a prospective or existing municipal system. These towns number 510 and of those Otter Tail serves 91%, or 465.

Otter Tail's policy is to acquire when it can existing municipal systems within its service areas. It has acquired six since 1947. Between 1945 and 1970, there were contests in 12 towns served by Otter Tail over proposals to replace it with municipal systems. In only three—Elbow Lake, Minnesota, Colman, South Dakota, and Aurora, South Dakota—were municipal systems actually established. Proposed municipal systems have great obstacles; they must purchase the electric power at wholesale. To do so they must have access to existing transmission lines. The only ones available belong to Otter Tail. While the Bureau of Reclamation has high-voltage bulk-power supply lines in the area, it does not operate a subtransmission network, but relies on wheeling contracts with Otter Tail and other utilities to deliver power for its bulk supply lines to its wholesale customers.

The antitrust charge against Otter Tail does not involve the lawfulness of its retail outlets, but only its methods of preventing the towns it served from establishing their own municipal systems when Otter Tail's franchises expired. The critical events centered largely in four cities—Elbow Lake, Minnesota, Hankinson, North Dakota, Colman, South Dakota, and Aurora, South Dakota. When Otter Tail's franchise in each of these towns terminated, the citizens voted to establish a municipal distribution system. Otter Tail refused to sell the new systems energy at wholesale and refused to agree to wheel power from other suppliers of wholesale energy.

Colman and Aurora had access to other transmission. Against them, Otter Tail used the weapon of litigation.

As respects Elbow Lake and Hankinson, Otter Tail simply refused to deal, although according to the findings it had the ability to do so. Elbow Lake, cut off from all sources of wholesale power, constructed its own generating plant. Both Elbow Lake and Hankinson requested the Bureau of Reclamation and various cooperatives to furnish them with wholesale power; they were willing to supply it if Otter Tail would wheel it. But Otter Tail refused, relying on provisions in its contracts which barred the use of its lines for wheeling power to towns which it served at retail. Elbow Lake after completing its plant asked the Federal Power Commission to require Otter Tail to interconnect with the town and sell it power at wholesale. The Federal Power Commission ordered first a temporary and then a permanent connection. Hankinson tried unsuccessfully to get relief from the North Dakota Commission and then filed a complaint with the federal commission seeking an order to compel Otter Tail to wheel. While the application was pending, the town council voted to withdraw it and subsequently renewed Otter Tail's franchise.

It was found that Otter Tail instituted or sponsored litigation involving four towns in its service area which had the effect of halting or delaying efforts to establish municipal systems. Municipal power systems are financed by the sale of electric revenue bonds. Before such bonds can be sold, the town's attorney must submit an opinion which includes a statement that there is no pending or threatened litigation which might impair the value or legality of the bonds. The record amply bears out the District Court's holding that Otter Tail's use of litigation halted or appreciably slowed the efforts for municipal ownership. "The delay thus occasioned and the large financial burden imposed on the towns' limited treasury dampened local enthusiasm for public ownership."

I

Otter Tail contends that by reason of the Federal Power Act it is not subject to antitrust regulation with respect to its refusal to deal. We disagree with that position.

"Repeals of the antitrust laws by implication from a regulatory statute are strongly disfavored, and have only been found in cases of plain repugnancy between the antitrust and regulatory provisions." *United States v. Philadelphia National Bank,* 374 U.S. 321. Activities which come under the jurisdiction of a regulatory agency nevertheless may be subject to scrutiny under the antitrust laws.

The District Court below determined that Otter Tail's consistent refusals to wholesale or wheel power to its municipal customers constituted illegal monopolization. Otter Tail maintains here that its refusals to deal should be immune from antitrust prosecution because the Federal Power Commission has the authority to compel involuntary interconnections of power pursuant to §202 (b) of the Federal Power Act. The essential thrust of §202, however, is to encourage voluntary interconnections of power. Only if a power company refuses to interconnect voluntarily may the Federal Power Commission subject to limitations unrelated to antitrust considerations, order the interconnection. The standard which governs its decision is whether such action is "necessary or appropriate in the public interest." Although antitrust considerations may be relevant, they are not determinative.

There is nothing in the legislative history which reveals a purpose to insulate electric power companies from the operation of the antitrust laws. To the contrary, the history of Part II of the Federal Power Act indicates an overriding policy of maintaining competition to the maximum extent possible consistent with the public interest. As originally conceived, Part II would have included a "common carrier" provision making it "the duty of every public utility to . . . transmit energy for any person upon reasonable request. . . ." In addition, it would have empowered the Federal Power Commission to order wheeling if it found such action to be "necessary or desirable in the public interest." These provisions were eliminated to preserve "the voluntary action of the utilities."

Thus, there is no basis for concluding that the limited authority of the Federal Power Commission to order interconnections was intended to be a substitute for or immunize Otter Tail from antitrust regulation for refusing to deal with municipal corporations.

II

The decree of the District Court enjoins Otter Tail from "[r]efusing to sell electric power at wholesale to existing or proposed municipal electric power systems in cities and towns located in [its service area]" and from refusing to wheel electric power over its transmission lines from other electric power lines to such cities and towns. But the decree goes on to provide:

> The defendant shall not be compelled by the Judgment in this case to furnish wholesale electric service or wheeling service to a municipality except at rates which are compensatory and under terms and conditions which are filed with and subject to approval by the Federal Power Commission.

So far as wheeling is concerned, there is no authority granted the Commission under Part II of the Federal Power Act to order it, for the bills originally introduced contained common carrier provisions which were deleted. . . . Insofar as the District Court ordered wheeling to correct anticompetitive and monopolistic practices of Otter Tail, there is no conflict with the authority of the Federal Power Commission.

As respects the ordering of interconnections, there is no conflict on the present record. Elbow Lake applied to the Federal Power Commission for an interconnection with Otter Tail and, as we have said, obtained it. . . . So the decree of the District Court, as far as the present record is concerned, presents no actual conflict between the federal judicial decree and an order of the Federal Power Commission. . . .

III

The record makes abundantly clear that Otter Tail used its monopoly power in the cities in its service area to foreclose competition or gain a competitive advantage, or to destroy a competitor, all in violation of the antitrust laws. The District Court determined that Otter Tail has "a strategic dominance in the transmission of power in most of its service area" and that it used this dominance to foreclose potential entrants into the retail area from obtaining electric power from outside sources of supply. Use of monopoly power "to destroy threatened competition" is a violation of the "attempt to monopolize" clause of §2 of the Sherman Act. . . .

When a community, serviced by Otter Tail, decides not to renew its retail franchise when it expires, it may generate, transmit, and distribute its own electric power. . . . There were no engineering factors that prevented Otter Tail from selling power at wholesale to those towns that wanted municipal plants or of wheeling the power. The District Court found—and its findings are supported— that Otter Tail's refusals to sell at wholesale or to wheel were solely to prevent municipal power systems from eroding its monopolistic position.

Otter Tail relies on its wheeling contracts with the Bureau of Reclamation and with cooperatives which it says relieve it of any duty to wheel power to municipalities served at retail by Otter Tail at the time the contracts were made. The District Court held that these restrictive provisions were "in reality, territorial allocation schemes," and were *per se* violations of the Sherman Act. . . . The fact that some of the restrictive provisions were contained in a contract with the Bureau of Reclamation is not material to our problem for, as the Solicitor General says, "government contracting officers do not have the power to grant immunity from the Sherman Act. . . ." The Solicitor General tells us that these restrictive provisions operate as a "hindrance" to the Bureau and were "agreed to by the Bureau only at Otter Tail's insistence," as the District Court found. The evidence supports that finding.

IV

The District Court found that the litigation sponsored by Otter Tail had the purpose of delaying and preventing the establishment of municipal electric systems "with the expectation that this would preserve its predominant position in the sale and transmission of electric power in the area." The District Court in discussing *Eastern Railroad Conference v. Noerr Motor Freight,* 365 U.S. 127, explained that it was applicable "only to efforts aimed at influencing the legislative and executive branches of the government." That was written before we decided *California Motor Transport Co. v. Trucking Unlimited,* 404 U.S. 508, where we held that the principle of *Noerr* may also apply to the use of administrative or judicial processes where the purpose is to suppress competition evidenced by repetitive lawsuits carrying the hallmark of insubstantial claims and thus within the "mere sham" exception announced in *Noerr.* On that phase of the order, we vacate and remand for consideration in light of our intervening decision in *California Motor Transport Co.*

V

Otter Tail argues that, without the weapons which It used, more and more municipalities will turn to public power and Otter Tail will go downhill. The argument is a familiar one. It was made in *United States v. Arnold, Schwinn & Co.,* 388 U.S. 365, a civil suit under §1 of the Sherman Act dealing with a restrictive distribution program and practices of a bicycle manufacturer. We said: "The promotion of self-interest alone does not invoke the rule of reason to immunize otherwise illegal conduct."

The fact that three municipalities which Otter Tail opposed finally got their municipal systems does not excuse Otter Tail's conduct. That fact does not condone the antitrust tactics which Otter Tail sought to impose. . . .

We do not suggest, however, that the District Court, concluding that Otter Tail violated the antitrust laws, should be impervious to Otter Tail's assertion that compulsory interconnection or wheeling will erode its integrated system and threaten its capacity to serve adequately the public. As the dissent properly notes, the Commission may not order interconnection if to do so "would impair [the utility's] ability to render adequate service to its customers." The District Court in this case found that the "pessimistic view" advanced in Otter Tail's "erosion study" is not supported by the record. Furthermore, it concluded that "it does not appear that Bureau of Reclamation power is a serious threat to the defendant nor that it will be in the foreseeable future." Since the District Court has made future connections subject to Commission approval and in any event has retained jurisdiction to enable the parties to apply for "necessary or appropriate" relief and presumably will give effect to the policies embodied in the Federal Power Act, we cannot say under these circumstances that it has abused its discretion.

Except for the provision of the order discussed in part IV of this opinion, the judgment is

Affirmed.

United States v. American Telephone and Telegraph Co.

U.S. District Court for the District of Columbia Civil Action No. 74-1698 (1974)

COMPLAINT

The United States of America, plaintiff, by its attorneys, acting under the direction of the Attorney General of the United States, brings this civil action to obtain equitable relief against the defendants named herein. . . .

THE DEFENDANTS

American Telephone and Telegraph Company (hereinafter referred to as "AT&T") is made a defendant herein . . . AT&T, directly and through subsidiaries, is engaged in providing telecommunications service and in the manufacture of telecommunications equipment.

Western Electric Company, Inc. (hereinafter referred to as "Western Electric"), is made a defendant herein . . . Western Electric is engaged . . . in the manufacture and supply of telecommunications equipment. Western Electric is a wholly-owned subsidiary of AT&T.

Bell Telephone Laboratories, Inc. (hereinafter referred to as "Bell Labs"), is made a defendant herein . . . Bell Labs is engaged in telecommunications research, development and design work. Bell Labs is owned jointly by AT&T and Western Electric.

TRADE AND COMMERCE

Telephone communications is the most common form of telecommunication between subscribers and includes among other services local exchange service for telephone calls between subscribers located within the same local telephone exchange area and long distance or "message toll service" for telephone calls between subscribers located in different exchange areas.

Local exchange service is provided by connecting all subscribers in the same local exchange area through one or more central offices. Typically, wire pairs connect each subscriber to telephone company central office switching facilities in that exchange area.

Message toll service is provided by connecting central offices in different local exchange areas. The connection of these local exchange areas, through trunk lines and toll switching offices, permits long distance telephone service throughout the United States. Message toll service typically involves the transmission of telecommunications via microwave radio or coaxial cable between local telephone exchanges, with central office switching equipment in each local exchange area providing each subscriber access to the long distance toll network. The long distance toll network is a nationwide web of trunk lines and toll offices linking all the telephone operating companies in the United States.

Telephone service in the United States is provided by the Bell System and by approximately 1,705 independent telephone companies. Telephone operating companies typically contract with subscribers for local exchange service, connecting the subscriber with the telephone company central office. Subscribers typically are charged installation fees and a monthly charge for service. The telephone companies retain title to the equipment installed and retain control over the equipment after service is terminated.

The Bell Companies provide local telephone service in the 48 contiguous states. As of December 31, 1973, the Bell Operating Companies served approximately 113.2 million telephones, or approximately 82 percent of the nation's telephones. Approximately 1,705 independent telephone companies account for the remaining 18 percent of the nation's telephones. The AT&T's Long Lines Department provides interstate telephone service. For the year ending December 31, 1973, more than 90 percent of all interstate telephone calls in the United States were routed in whole or in part over Bell System facilities. In 1973 the Bell System's total revenue from telephone service was approximately $22 billion. The Bell System is by far the largest supplier of telephone service in the United States.

In addition to telephone service, telecommunications includes the transmission of data, facsimile, audio and video programming, and other specialized forms of telecommunications. Transmission of these specialized telecommunications may be accomplished over the same nationwide switched network which accommodates telephone service or over private lines.

Private line service involves the leasing of telecommunications circuits to subscribers with a high volume of communications requirements between specific locations. Private lines may be used for the transmission of voice, data, audio and video programming, and other specialized forms of telecommunications. Private line service may simply connect two points or may be switched between and among multiple points. A private line may be connected with the switched telephone network.

The Bell System provides intercity private line service for the transmission of voice, data, facsimile, audio and video programming, and other telecommunications. Private line services are also provided by Specialized Common Carriers, Miscellaneous Common Carriers and Domestic Satellite Carriers. . . . Total revenue from private line service in 1973 was approximately $1.1 billion. In 1973 Bell System revenue from private line service was approximately $1 billion, or approximately 90 percent of total private line revenue. . . .

Telecommunications equipment is used to provide telephone service and other telecommunications and includes terminal equipment, switching equipment, and transmission equipment. Terminal equipment is equipment used principally in telecommunications and installed at the premises of the subscriber. Switching equipment is equipment in local exchange central offices and toll offices used to route and switch telecommunications between subscribers. Transmission equipment is used to transmit telecommunications.

Until about 1968, telephone operating companies typically prohibited the interconnection of customer provided terminal equipment with telephone company facilities and, with limited exception, provided all the terminal equipment located on subscribers' premises. Telephone operating companies were thus the only significant purchasers of telecommunications terminal equipment.

Telephone subscribers and other telecommunications customers may provide their own terminal equipment and need not rely solely on the offerings of telephone operating companies. Customers may obtain terminal equipment from numerous manufacturers and suppliers, known collectively as the "interconnect industry."

Western Electric manufactures and supplies telecommunications equipment for the Bell System and is the largest manufacturer of telecommunications equipment in the United States. . . . A substantial majority of the telecommunications transmission, switching and terminal equipment used by the Bell System is supplied by Western Electric. Although Western Electric also sells telecommunications equipment to government agencies, it typically does not sell equipment to independent telephone companies or other users of telecommunications equipment. In 1973, Western Electric's sales to the Bell System were $6.2 billion. Western Electric's total sales in 1973 were $7.0 billion. Western Electric is by far the largest supplier, and the Bell System is by far the largest purchaser, of telecommunications equipment in the United States.

AT&T provides services to each Bell Operating Company pursuant to agreements known as "License Contracts." Under these agreements AT&T undertakes to maintain arrangements whereby telephones and related equipment may be manufactured under patents owned or controlled by AT&T and may be purchased by each Operating Company for use within a specified territory; . . . and to furnish advice and assistance with respect to virtually all phases of the Operating Company's business. The License Contracts, or supplementary agreements in the case of four Operating Companies, provide for joint use of certain rights-of-way and facilities. Supplementary agreements cover the sharing of revenues derived by AT&T and the Bell Operating Companies from interstate and foreign services.

Western Electric manufactures and supplies equipment to AT&T and each Bell Operating Company pursuant to agreements known as "Standard Supply Contracts." Under these agreements as supplemented, Western Electric agrees, upon the order of each Operating Company and to the extent reasonably required for the latter's business, to manufacture materials or to purchase and inspect materials manufactured by others and to sell these materials to the Operating Company. Western Electric also agrees to maintain stocks at distribution points, to prepare equipment specifications, to perform installations of materials, and to repair, sell, or otherwise dispose of used materials. Under each agreement Western Electric's prices and terms are to be as low as to its most favored customers for like materials and services under comparable conditions.

Bell Labs conducts telecommunications research and development for Western Electric and the Bell System. Owned jointly by AT&T and Western Electric, Bell Labs' 1974 budget for telecommunications research and development exceeded $500 million. . . . Bell Labs is by far the largest telecommunications research and development facility in the United States.

VIOLATIONS ALLEGED

For many years past and continuing up to and including the date of the filing of this complaint, the defendants and co-conspirators have been engaged in an unlawful combination and conspiracy to monopolize, and the defendants have attempted to monopolize and have monopolized the aforesaid interstate trade and commerce in telecommunications service and submarkets thereof and telecommunications equipment and submarkets thereof in violation of Section 2 of the Sherman Act. Defendants are continuing and will continue these violations unless the relief hereinafter prayed for is granted.

The aforesaid combination and conspiracy to monopolize has consisted of a continuing agreement and concert of action among the defendants and co-conspirators, the substantial terms of which have been and are:

a That AT&T shall achieve and maintain control over the operations and policies of Western Electric, Bell Labs, and the Bell Operating Companies;

b That the defendants and co-conspirators shall attempt to prevent, restrict, and eliminate competition from other telecommunications common carriers;

c That the defendants and co-conspirators shall attempt to prevent, restrict, and eliminate competition from private telecommunications systems;

d That Western Electric shall supply the telecommunications equipment requirements of the Bell System;

e That defendants and co-conspirators shall attempt to prevent, restrict, and eliminate competition from other manufacturers and suppliers of telecommunications equipment.

EFFECTS

The aforesaid violations have had the following effects, among others:

a Defendants have achieved and maintained a monopoly of telecommunications service and submarkets thereof and telecommunications equipment and submarkets thereof in the United States.

b Actual and potential competition in telecommunications service and submarkets thereof and telecommunications equipment and submarkets thereof has been restrained and eliminated.

c Purchasers of telecommunications service and telecommunications equipment have been denied the benefits of a free and competitive market.

PRAYER

Wherefore, plaintiff prays:

That the Court adjudge and decree that defendants have combined and conspired to monopolize, have attempted to monopolize, and have monopolized interstate trade and commerce in telecommunications service and submarkets thereof and telecommunications equipment and submarkets thereof in violation of Section 2 of the Sherman Act.

That each of the defendants . . . be perpetually enjoined from continuing to carry out, directly or indirectly, the aforesaid combination and conspiracy to monopolize, attempt to monopolize, and monopolization of . . . telecommunications service and equipment and that they be perpetually enjoined from engaging in or participating in practices, contracts, agreements, or understandings, or claiming any rights thereunder, having the purpose or effect of continuing, reviving, or renewing any of the aforesaid violations or any violations similar thereto.

That defendant AT&T be required to divest all of its capital stock interest in Western Electric.

That defendant Western Electric be required to divest manufacturing and other assets sufficient to insure competition in the manufacture and sale of telecommunications equipment.

That defendant AT&T be required, through divestiture of capital stock interests or other assets, to separate some or all of the Long Lines Department of AT&T from some or all of the Bell Operating Companies, as may be necessary to insure competition in telecommunications service and telecommunications equipment.

PART FOUR

SOCIAL REGULATION

CHAPTER 19

THE "NEW" REGULATION

In spite of the widespread criticism of regulation in the 1960s and 1970s, its scope and impact were greatly expanded during these years. Some of this "new" regulation was of the old-fashioned economic variety. Our complex oil regulations started in 1971. However, most of the regulation was of a different sort. Such agencies as the Occupational Safety and Health Administration (OSHA), the Environmental Protection Agency (EPA), the Consumer Product Safety Commission (CPSC), the National Highway Traffic Safety Administration (NHTSA, pronounced "neetsa"), the Mine Enforcement Safety Administration (MESA) and its successor agency, the Mine Safety and Health Adminstration (MSHA), were not much concerned about the prices and profits of the firms they regulated. Their mandates were to make workplaces, consumer products, and automobiles safer, and in the case of the EPA, to make the environment both safer and more pleasant.

Actually, this sort of regulation is not entirely new. The Food and Drug Administration (FDA) dates back to 1906, though it acquired much of its clout in 1938 and its mandate was considerably expanded in 1962 when Congress directed it to require evidence of effectiveness as well as safety before it permitted a new drug to be marketed. The Department of Agriculture's Animal and Plant Health Inspection Service has been inspecting meat-packing plants since 1908. The Federal Trade Commission (FTC) has attempted to prevent false and misleading advertising from shortly after its establishment in 1914, though its power in that area was only clearly established with new legislation in 1938. And the Nuclear Regulatory Commission's (NRC) authority dates from 1947 when the Atomic Energy Commission was founded, though its regulatory functions were only separated from its promotional functions in 1972.

WHY REGULATE?—EXTERNALITIES

What is the point to this alphabet soup? Wouldn't the market perform just as well, if not better, without the bureaucrats?

In the case of the EPA, the answer is *definitely not.* The reason is "external costs"—costs that fall on someone other than the person or firm that causes them. Trucks on Los Angeles freeways cause such costs as the diesel fuel they consume, their drivers' work hours, and smog. The companies that own the trucks have to pay for the fuel and their drivers' time, and have a strong incentive to keep costs as low as possible. The same is distinctly not true of the smog. The cost of smog falls on you and me, not on the trucker. Moreover, anything a single trucking company does has no noticeable effect on the total amount of smog. The company has virtually no incentive to clean up the mess. The same story applies to a paper mill on the Wisconsin River that discharges waste products into the river and the bad smell it provides for residents in its neighborhood.

These external costs will be taken into account by the people who cause them only if the public intervenes. That is what the EPA is supposed to be doing. In general, it issues orders to car and truck manufacturers, paper mills, and members of many other industries requiring them to do specific acts to clean up their discharges into the surrounding environment.

Economists are in general agreement that external costs create a problem that the market will not solve by itself. They decidedly do *not* all agree that the EPA's orders are the best way to solve the problem.

SAFETY AND HEALTH REGULATION

But what about OSHA, MESA, FDA, NHTSA, CPSC, and the like? Are there external costs here, too? To some extent there are. As our medical system is set up, everyone pays for medical costs of at least the poor and the aged, and even those who have private health insurance pay for health costs of others covered by the same insurers. If a coal miner develops silicosis (black lung disease) or a cotton textile worker gets byssinosis (brown lung disease), there is a good chance that other people will pay a substantial part of the resulting medical expenses.

This is not the main point to such regulation, however. The assumption is that workers and consumers do not know enough to make wise decisions about where to work and what to consume. As a result, they are likely to work in jobs they wouldn't take or consume products they wouldn't buy if they really knew what was happening to them.

THE MARKET'S SOLUTIONS

If workers and consumers were wiser, the market *would* take care of the problem. Take a risky job such as underground coal mining. Coal miners are some of the best-paid blue collar workers in the country, but the majority of the population probably thinks "they can have it." If potential coal miners had clear ideas of the danger and working conditions, they would only take such jobs if they received a sufficiently high premium to compensate them for all their disadvantages. Moreover, the mine owners would have strong incentives to reduce the danger. Something like this does occur to some extent in the mines, but many people suspect that quite a lot of those working in the mines don't fully understand the risks they are taking, that they can't distinguish between safe and less-safe mines, and that they are not fully compensated for the risks they take.

The probability that workers and consumers don't know the risks they are taking with particular jobs or products is greater in other fields. Hardly any of us knows enough about drugs or food additives to avoid the dangerous products on our own. *Some* of us could learn enough to make intelligent decisions in that area *if* we were to take roughly seven years of university courses. But this is not a realistic alternative for most of us. Similarly, hardly anyone finds it worthwhile to inspect packing plants before eating the meat they sell or to test consumer products for hidden dangers. In the case of auto safety, in spite of strong statistical evidence, rules that require car makers to provide us with seat belts, and many years of propaganda, the majority of us still don't buckle up. And how is the market system to lead business to produce the right things if the seller systematically lies about his or her product—claiming that it cures athlete's foot or colds when it doesn't do either? Probably a majority of economists believe that some public intervention is appropriate in at least some of these respects, but again, they are often critical about what the regulators have actually done.

THE COSTS OF REGULATION

The new regulation is much more costly to the government than the old regulation has been. One reason is that agencies like EPA, OSHA, and CPSC regulate everyone, while the ICC, CAB, and FCC regulate only segments of the economy. But the Animal and Plant Health Inspection Service, NHSTA, and the NRC do have jurisdictions as narrow as the ICC's. A second reason is that effective regulation involves a great deal of inspection of individual plants. The Animal and Plant Health Inspection Service has a "live-in" inspector at every packing plant for each shift the plant is in operation! Other agencies are less thorough, but they all must provide much more inspection than agencies like the ICC, the CAB, and the FCC. At a more fundamental level, the "old" regulatory agencies set rates, decided who could produce, and the like, but within the rules, private firms were free to decide for themselves how much to produce and how to do it. The "new" regulatory agencies were trying to change many of those basic business decisions. This means much closer control of the firms involved than the "old" price-profit regulations ever required.

The EPA has a higher budget than any other regulatory agency (close to half a billion dollars), but its budget is small compared with the costs it imposes on business. The Council of Environmental Quality estimates that capital investments made to meet environmental requirements came to $5.6 billion in 1975, and this amount does not include the cost to auto owners of environmental controls on their cars—probably two or three hundred dollars per new car (including imports) or $1.6 to $2.4 billion per year. OSHA may be runner-up. No general estimate of its costs to industry are available, but a number of its orders affecting individual industries, such as the coke oven and cotton dust standards, were estimated to have involved business investments of more than a billion dollars each when they were issued. And the noise standard, which affected many industries, was expected to require $8 to $14 billion in business investment!

Some of the costs were even less direct than these. The FDA's requirement that new drugs be proven *effective* as well as *safe* coincided with a drastic decline in the number of "new chemical entities" (roughly, entirely new drugs) from about seventy-five per year to about fifteen per year. This may mean that many of the drugs introduced before the 1962 amendments were ineffective or that the well from which the spectacular pharmaceutical explosion after World War II was drawn was running dry. But it seems probable that the new rules played a part in the decline. The risks involved in developing a new drug were greater while the payoff was less. It took longer for a new drug to pass the test than before 1962, while the overall life of the patent (which included both the testing and commercial sale period) did not change. One aspect has changed. Before 1962 almost all new drugs were introduced in the United States. Today, about half are introduced abroad, though often by foreign subsidiaries of American firms.

Altogether, the costs of the new regulations are in the billions of dollars. They may account for part of the decline in the amount of real investment by business and the slowdown in productivity growth in the late 1970s. Orders by EPA, OSHA, and the like typically reduced the additional business income per dollar of new investment since much of the investment in a new power plant or paper mill added little, if anything, to the payoff to the firm making the investment.

Was it worth the costs? The results are not all in yet, but so far they are mixed. EPA has certainly accomplished something. Lake Erie and the Wisconsin River are noticeably cleaner. And Los Angeles smog is somewhat reduced, despite many additional cars. The CPSC points with pride to a sharp reduction in the number of child overdose cases, which it attributes to the new drug bottle caps that it required. The NHTSA apparently reduced auto deaths, if you believe that the lower death rate on newer model cars is the result of their rules, though the reduction of the speed limit from 70 to 55 did a great deal more. It is difficult to show any effect of OSHA on industrial accidents, partly because the statistics are collected on a different basis than before, but it has taken the first real action on byssinosis (brown lung disease in the cotton mills). This disease has been known to doctors for generations. Something was accomplished by some of the new regulations, but it still is not clear that the efforts involved were worth the costs involved.

WHAT TO DO ABOUT THE "NEW REGULATION"

Some people would say "a plague on all of them" and put the new regulators out of business. We've done this in a few cases. When the FDA was about to turn off the supply of diet drinks, a host of diet drink drinkers rose up and Congress extended the deadline for years. When NHTSA required that in 1973 interlock devices that wouldn't permit the car to start unless seat belts were fastened be provided on new cars, an even larger host of distressed drivers rose up, and the interlocks ended.

But the public is really concerned about the dangers involved in many of the areas where the new rules apply. That's why the legislation that led to the new agencies was passed. General or even selected deregulation does not seem to be in the cards although something like it was accomplished in some of the "old" regulation lines in the late 1970s.

Can anything be done to lessen the costs of the "new" regulation? There are several possibilities including the use of taxes or marketable rights either instead of, or as a supplement to, conventional regulation. An alternative calls for procedures that would make the regulators take the costs of their orders into account.

TAXES

The proposal of taxes that fall on those responsible for external costs is an old one. The logic is that if the polluter is charged so much per pound of sulphur dioxide put into the air or biodegradable junk put into the river (and if the tax rate correctly reflects the social costs of those emissions), then the polluter will include these taxes among his or her costs, take them into account along with other costs, and make decisions accordingly. The best method of production, therefore, will be that which minimizes the sum of capital, labor, materials, fuel, *and* environmental tax costs altogether and not just the sum of the first four expenses.

This approach has several advantages over simple rule making. First, it means that prices of pollution-creating goods will go up, either directly because of the tax or because of the pollution control devices and procedures installed to avoid the tax. This increase should lead consumers to buy fewer pollution-creating goods and more environmentally safer goods. The same will be true of EPA orders without a tax, if the orders are enforced and stick, which are big ifs.

Second, we will reduce pollution where it is easiest to reduce. When pollution controls are cheap, firms will adopt them and avoid the tax. Where controls are greater than the tax, the firm will pay the tax and go on polluting. As a result, we will get pollution control at the lowest cost.

Third, a pollution tax will provide the polluters, or their equipment suppliers, with a strong incentive to improve pollution control devices and reduce their costs. Again, an order by the EPA would have the same effect, *if it sticks.* But the EPA is unlikely to insist on impossible standards. If it appears that with current technology, compliance with its order is impossible, it probably won't close down the industry involved. With a tax, if cleanup is really impossible, costs and taxes will go up, but the firms involved will have plenty of incentive to get around those taxes. Such incentives to reduce costs have yielded huge returns in the past where the effort was to reduce labor, capital, materials and fuel costs, and there is every reason to expect the same in the environmental controls field. And cost reductions would keep the lobbyists away from the EPA. When the auto companies descend on Washington for the umpteenth time to argue for relief (because they can't meet the standards for three more years and will not be able to produce the 1983 models at all if the strict standards apply in 1983), the EPA could reply, "By all means postpone your improvements until they are feasible *and pay the tax for the interim.*" Such an answer impresses the mind.

Taxation has also been proposed as an alternative to OSHA. Why not simply impose a tax on industrial accidents and make the accident-prone employers pay for the mayhem for which they are responsible. Actually, we already have such a tax on large firms in the form of worker's compensation (the name was recently changed from "workman's compensation"). This program requires that the employers pay the officially designated losses to its employees according to schedules set by the state legislature—so much for an eye and so much for a thumb regardless of who is to blame for the accident. Employers are required to buy insurance to cover such losses. Most insurance companies base their rates to large employers on their accident records, so the more accidents they have, the higher their rate. This should give the big firms lots of incentive to keep accidents down. You may want to argue about what a thumb or an eye is worth, but given the valuations, the big employers pay them.

What about the small employers? A death in a foundry with thirty employees could put the firm out of business, if it were experience-rated like the big firms. Insurance companies put such firms in a more or less homogeneous group and base their charges on the whole group's experience. That doesn't give individual small firms much incentive to keep accidents down, but an accident tax would pose the same problem. Do we really want to put factories out of business every time there is an accidental death?

The accident tax does not deal with industrial diseases at all. They generally aren't covered by worker's compensation. The reason is straightforward. Who was to blame for the byssinosis that the worker developed if he or she had worked in more than one cotton mill? Most observers feel that this is where OSHA can accomplish something new. We've known about many industrial diseases since the nineteenth century, but we didn't do anything about them until OSHA came along.

Just what is the appropriate tax? In the case of the accident "tax" under worker's compensation, the tax is surely right if the state legislature has put the right values on a thumb or an eye, or a death. And those values have been determined by the right people if one believes in representative government. But what about the environment? In some cases we can estimate the right costs fairly accurately. In the case of containers we can ask the people who collect garbage and run garbage dumps what it costs to dispose of a can, a bottle, and plastic or paper containers and charge the manufacturers of those containers accordingly. Such a tax should be no harder to collect than a cigarette tax. If the consumers still buy disposable containers after the tax is imposed and the inevitable price increase of the affected products occurs, then it would be correct to keep producing containers. Consumers would be making a straightforward decision to buy and discard disposable containers even though returnable containers were available at lower net prices.

SALEABLE POLLUTION PERMITS

But what about sulfur dioxide? It undoubtedly increases the incidence of respiratory diseases, and, in the largest cities, kills people. What sort of tax is fitting here? Nobody knows. At least in some cases—such as paper mill effluents—we do have a good idea of what amount of pollution the environment can absorb. A tax may be a very crude approach to establishing the right level of pollution—we don't have any idea what a tax of 26¢ per pound will accomplish in reducing sulfur dioxide pollution in the atmosphere. Why not specify the amounts of SO_2 each of the plants in Chicago can emit and let them be bought and sold by the relevant firms. Those who could turn off their emissions of SO_2 easily could sell their permits to those who couldn't, and we would get the desired reduction in pollution at the lowest possible cost. And we would get precisely the level of pollution we wanted. Moreover, the price at which the permits sell would give us clear evidence of what our rules cost society.

There are obvious limits to this approach. It is difficult to imagine Congress specifying the number of accidental deaths in the steel industry and letting business buy and sell such permits at any price less than astronomical. And the optimal amount of pollution on a particular river is itself hard to guess. For instance, the river can probably "process" more paper mill waste in winter than in summer. Still, the approach may be worth an experiment. So far both EPA and OSHA have worked entirely through specific standards regardless of the costs.

COST BENEFIT ANALYSIS

The main criticism of the new regulators is that they do not consider the costs incurred by industry to comply with their regulations.

In an attempt to deal with this problem, the Ford administration required that all adminstrative agencies (answerable to the President rather than to Congress) submit "inflation impact statements" estimating the costs and benefits of any new orders they were contemplating before the orders were issued. The Carter administration continued this policy, though the statements were renamed "economic impact statements." This policy affected much of the "new regulation" because many of the agencies involved were administrative agencies. This was true of the EPA, OSHA, MESA, NHTSA, and FDA but not true of the independent agencies such as the FTC and CPSC.

The statements were often brief and cursory, sometimes only two mimeographed pages. Even the agencies that submitted thorough analyses, for instance, OSHA, were often vague about the expected benefits. And the statements were criticized because the costs were usually based on existing technology and on data from the affected industries, which had strong incentives to overstate prospective costs. The hope was that agencies would pay attention to these important variables, though few had done so previously.

In fact the issues involved are not at all easy to settle. They often involve decisions about health and life. The cotton dust standard was estimated to cost $200,000 per case of byssinosis prevented. About a fifth of the workers in cotton mills get the disease, and it leaves them with asthma for the rest of their lives, though they seldom die early as a result of byssinosis. Is prevention worth $200,000 per case? One of the authors took a poll in his classes. Undergraduate students voted yes, while graduate students voted decidedly no. OSHA did in fact issue the order. Most of the decisions are much less clear-cut than this one.

But there have been changes, perhaps as a result of cost benefit analysis. After half a decade of emphasis on accident standards, where an effect has been hard to discern and where worker's compensation already provided some employer incentive, OSHA has shifted its emphasis to where we had no real policy before, to industrial diseases such as byssinosis.

CONCLUSION

We are likely to have the "new regulation" with us for a long time. If costs are given short shrift, the effect can be enormously expensive, but the problems involved are very real. Getting the regulators to consider the costs, while continuing to deal with the important difficulties, should be one of the big issues of the 1980s. Not every environmental or health and safety problem is worth the social cost of "solving" it. If we continue to ignore the costs imposed on industry, we are likely to pay with low productivity and a stagnant economy. If we ignore the environmental, safety, and health effects of some aspects of modern industry, we will face a deteriorating and maybe dangerous environment and continuing human costs of industrial disease and danger to consumers. The problem is to find a way to attain a cleaner, safer environment without sacrificing the vitality of American industry.

Many similar problems have been solved in the past through technological improvements. We can't help but believe that a major element of the solution is to set up incentive systems that will induce business to search for solutions. We are still far from such incentives, however.

CHAPTER 20

ENVIRONMENT

Environmental problems are not new, although they are probably more wide-spread and more widely publicized than in earlier times. In the United States, the federal government has embarked on an ambitious and controversial program of environmental regulation. The Environmental Protection Agency (EPA) was es-tablished in 1970 to spearhead the federal effort to preserve and enhance the nation's environmental resources. The EPA regulates the discharge of pollutants into the nation's air, land, and water.

The first case illustrates the complex issues that frequently arise in environmen-tal protection. Reserve Mining Company discharged iron ore wastes into the air and water around its plant in Minnesota. It is believed, but not documented, that these discharges might cause forms of cancer. The appeals court judge, however, refused to shut down the plant, noting that the health effects were unpredictable while the economic and social costs of closing the plant were not. Do you agree with the judge's reasoning? How would you evaluate the costs of closing the plant versus the costs of keeping it open? Economists frequently value a person's life by the income that person would have earned had he or she lived and continued to work. What do you think of this approach? Can you think of any alternative approach? If you can, would it affect your decision regarding the operation of Reserve Mining's plant?

The second case addresses the issue of whether or not pollution can be in-creased in very clean areas without violating the nation's Clean Air Act. The focus is thus not on the reduction of pollution, but rather on its acceptable increase. The court interprets the act to say that it is not permissible to degrade the environ-ment, regardless of how clean it might still be. Do you agree with this decision? If this policy had been in effect thirty years ago, could California still have become industrialized and would it still be the most populous state in the country? Could millions of people have retired to Florida and Arizona? Can you reconcile this conflict between growth and degradation of the environment?

In order to reduce pollution, the EPA has, among other things, established emissions standards for individual pollution sources such as a vent or a smokestack. The third case presents the EPA's "bubble" policy, a substantial departure from source-by-source regulation. Instead of focusing on an individual pollution source, the EPA focuses on all the emissions from a single plant. In effect, the plant is viewed as being covered by a giant bubble. The EPA monitors the total emissions from that bubble, but not from each smokestack or vent inside it. The EPA believes that this policy will lead to a more efficient reduction of emissions. Do you see why? Do you see any problems that might arise in inplementing this policy? For example, would you treat all emissions the same? If not, can you still use the bubble policy?

One of the most controversial aspects of environmental protection is its cost. The fourth case presents excerpts from an EPA report that lists the costs of compliance with the nation's Clean Air and Water Acts. The EPA also estimates the benefits of reducing pollution. What can you conclude from the EPA's cost and benefit data? Has the EPA reduced pollution too much? Too little? Many people argue that it is not possible to compare the costs and benefits of reducing pollution. Do you see why? Does this mean that we should ignore the information we have on costs and benefits? What role, if any, should this information have in the formulation of government policy?

The existence of some species of wildlife is threatened by human pollution and elimination of these animals' natural habitats. In an effort to prevent the extinction of endangered species, Congress passed the Endangered Species Act of 1973. This act directs federal agencies to ensure that their activities do not jeopardize the continued survival of endangered species. Not surprisingly, there soon arose a conflict between economic development and an endangered species. The Supreme Court addressed this conflict in the last case in this chapter. It ruled that the completion of the Tellico Dam on the Little Tennessee River would violate the Endangered Species Act by threatening the only known habitat of the snail darter. Do you agree with the Court's decision? Would your decision be the same if the endangered species was a spider? The bald eagle? If the construction project was a synthetic fuel plant? A highway?

Reserve Mining Company v. Environmental Protection Agency

514 F. 2d 492 (1975)

BRIGHT, Circuit Judge.

The United States, the States of Michigan, Wisconsin, and Minnesota, and several environmental groups seek an injunction ordering Reserve Mining Company to cease discharging wastes from its iron ore processing plant in Silver Bay, Minnesota, into the ambient air of Silver Bay and the waters of Lake Superior. On April 20, 1974, the district court granted the requested relief and ordered that the discharges immediately cease, thus effectively closing the plant. Reserve Mining Company appealed that order and we stayed the injunction pending resolution of the merits of the appeal. . . .

I INTRODUCTION

In 1947, Reserve Mining Company (Reserve), then contemplating a venture in which it would mine low-grade ore ("taconite") present in Minnesota's Mesabi Iron Range and process the ore into iron-rich pellets at facilities bordering on Lake Superior, received a permit from the State of Minnesota to discharge the wastes (called "tailings") from its processing operations into the lake.

Reserve commenced the processing of taconite ore in Silver Bay, Minnesota, in 1955, and that operation continues today. Taconite mined near Babbitt, Minnesota, is shipped by rail some 47 miles to the Silver Bay "beneficiati[on]" plant where it is concentrated into pellets containing some 65 percent iron ore. The process involves crushing the taconite into fine granules, separating out the metallic iron with huge magnets, and flushing the residual tailings into Lake Superior. The tailings enter the lake as a slurry of approximately 1.5 percent solids. The slurry acts as a heavy density current bearing the bulk of the suspended particles to the lake bottom. In this manner, approximately 67,000 tons of tailings are discharged daily.

The states and the United States commenced efforts to procure abatement of these discharges as early as mid-1969. These efforts, however, produced only an unsuccessful series of administrative conferences and unsuccessful state court proceedings. The instant litigation commenced on February 2, 1972, when the United States—joined eventually by the States of Minnesota, Wisconsin, and Michigan and by various environmental groups—filed a complaint alleging that Reserve's discharge of tailings into Lake Superior violated the Rivers and Harbors Act of 1899, . . . the pre-1972 Federal Water Pollution Control Act and the federal common law of public nuisance.

Until June 8, 1973, the case was essentially a water pollution abatement case, but on that date the focus of the controversy shifted to the public health impact of the tailings discharge and Reserve's emissions into the ambient air. Arguing the health issue in the district court, plaintiffs maintained that the taconite ore mined by Reserve contained an asbestiform variety of the amphibole mineral cumming-tonite-grumerite, and that the processing of the ore resulted in the discharge into the air and water of mineral fibers substantially identical and in some instances identical to amosite asbestos. This contention raised an immediate health issue, since inhalation of asbestos at occupational levels of exposure is associated with an increased incidence of various forms of cancer.

On April 20, 1974, the district court entered an order closing Reserve's Silver Bay facility. In an abbreviated memorandum opinion, the court held that Reserve's water discharge violated federal water pollution laws and that its air emissions violated state air pollution regulations, and that both the air and water discharges constituted common law nuisances. . . .

II HEALTH ISSUE

The initial, crucial question for our evaluation and resolution focuses upon the alleged hazard to public health attributable to Reserve's discharges into the air and water.

As will be evident from the discussion that follows, we adhere to our preliminary assessment that evidence is insufficient to support the kind of demonstrable danger to the public health that would justify the immediate closing of Reserve's operations. We now address the basic question of whether the discharges pose any risk to public health and, if so, whether the risk is one which is legally cognizable. This inquiry demands separate attention to the discharge into the air of Silver Bay and the discharge into Lake Superior.

A The Discharge Into Air

As we noted in our stay opinion, much of the scientific knowledge regarding asbestos disease pathology derives from epidemiological studies of asbestos workers occupationally exposed to and inhaling high levels of asbestos dust. Studies of workers naturally exposed to asbestos dust have shown "excess" cancer deaths and a significant incidence of asbestosis. The principal excess cancers are cancer of the lung, the pleura (mesothelioma) and gastrointestinal tract ("gi" cancer).

Several principles of asbestos-related disease pathology emerge from these occupational studies. One principle relates to the so-called 20-year rule, meaning that there is a latent period of cancer development of at least 20 years. Another basic principle is the importance of initial exposure, demonstrated by significant increases in the incidence of cancer even among asbestos manufacturing workers employed for less than three months (although the incidence of disease does increase upon longer exposure). Finally, these studies indicate that threshold values and dose response relationships, although probably operative with respect to asbestos-induced cancer, are not quantifiable on the basis of existing data.

Additionally, some studies implicate asbestos as a possible pathogenic agent in circumstances of exposure less severe than occupational levels. For example, several studies indicate that mesothelioma, a rare but particularly lethal cancer frequently associated with asbestos exposure, has been found in persons experiencing a low level of asbestos exposure.

Plaintiffs' hypothesis that Reserve's air emissions represent a significant threat to the public health touches numerous scientific disciplines, and an overall evaluation demands broad scientific understanding. We think it significant that Dr. Brown, an impartial witness whose court-appointed task was to address the health issue in its entirety, joined with plaintiffs' witnesses in viewing as reasonable the hypothesis that Reserve's discharges present a threat to public health. Although, as we noted in our stay opinion, Dr. Brown found the evidence insufficient to make a scientific probability statement as to whether adverse health consequences would in fact ensue, he expressed a public health concern over the continued long-term emission of fibers into the air. . . .

B The Discharge Into Water

The claim that Reserve's discharge of tailings into Lake Superior causes a hazard to public health raises many of the same uncertainties present with respect to the discharge into air. . . . In two respects, however, the discharge into water raises added uncertainties: first, whether the ingestion of fibers, as compared with their inhalation, poses any danger whatsoever; and second, should ingestion pose a danger, whether the exposure resulting from Reserve's discharge may be said to present a legally cognizable risk to health.

* * *

. . . [T]he medical and scientific conclusions here in dispute clearly lie "on the frontiers of scientific knowledge." The trial court, not having any proof of actual harm, was faced with a consideration of 1) the probabilities of any health harm and 2) the consequences, if any, should the harm actually occur.

The District of Columbia Circuit was recently confronted with a problem analogous to the one now before us in *Ethyl Corporation v. Environmental Protection Agency,* Civil No. 73-2205 (D.C. Cir., Jan. 28, 1975). The court, faced with a regulation of the Environmental Protection Agency requiring the phased reduction of the lead content in motor vehicle gasoline promulgated pursuant to a statute authorizing a restriction only if the emission product of a fuel or fuel additive "will endanger the public health or welfare," rejected the EPA regulation stating that "the case against auto lead emissions is a speculative and inconclusive one at best." The majority reasoned that in the absence of past harm, no potential consequences can be considered.

These concepts of potential harm, whether they be assessed as "probabilities and consequences" or "risk and harm," necessarily must apply in a determination of whether any relief should be given in cases of this kind in which proof with certainty is impossible. The district court, although not following a precise probabilities-consequences analysis, did consider the medical and scientific evidence bearing on both the probability of harm and the consequences should the hypothesis advanced by the plaintiffs prove to be valid.

In assessing probabilities in this case, it cannot be said that the probability of harm is more likely than not. Moreover, the level of probability does not readily convert into a prediction of consequences. On this record it cannot be forecast that the rates of cancer will increase from drinking Lake Superior water or breathing Silver Bay air. The best that can be said is that the existence of this asbestos contaminant in air and water gives rise to a reasonable medical concern for the public health. The public's exposure to asbestos fibers in air and water creates some health risk. Such a contaminant should be removed.

VII REMEDY

As we have demonstrated, Reserve's air and water discharges pose a danger to the public health and justify judicial action of a preventive nature.

In fashioning relief in a case such as this involving a possibility of future harm, a court should strike a proper balance between the benefits conferred and the hazards created by Reserve's facility. In its pleadings Reserve directs our attention to the benefits arising from its operations, as found by a Minnesota state district court, as follows:

> In reliance upon the State and Federal permits as contemplated by [Reserve] and the agencies issuing the permits prior to such issuance [Reserve] constructed its plant at Silver Bay, Minnesota. [Reserve] also developed the Villages of Babbitt and Silver Bay and their schools and other necessary facilities where many of [Reserve's] employees live with their families as do the merchants, doctors, teachers, and so forth who serve them. [Reserve's] capital investment exceeds $350,000,000. As of June 30, 1970 [Reserve] had 3,367 employees. During the calendar year 1969, its total payroll was approximately $31,700,000; and it expended the sum of $27,400,000 for the purchase of supplies and paid state and local taxes amounting to $4,250,000. [Reserve's] annual production of 10,000,000 tons of taconite pellets represents approximately two-thirds of the required pellets used by Armco and Republic Steel, the sole owners of Reserve, 15% of the production of the Great Lakes [ore] and about 12% of the total production of the United States.

The district court justified its immediate closure of Reserve's facility by characterizing Reserve's discharges as "substantially" endangering the health of persons breathing air and drinking water containing the asbestos-like fibers contained in Reserve's discharges. The term "substantially" in no way measures the danger in terms of either probabilities or consequences. Yet such an assessment seems essential in fashioning a judicial remedy.

Concededly, the trial court considered many appropriate factors in arriving at a remedy, such as a) the nature of the anticipated harm, b) the burden on Reserve and its employees from the issuance of the injunction, c) the financial ability of Reserve to convert to other methods of waste disposal, and d) a margin of safety for the public.

An additional crucial element necessary for a proper assessment of the health hazard rests upon a proper analysis of the probabilities of harm. . . .

With respect to the water, these probabilities must be deemed low for they do not rest on a history of past health harm attributable to ingestion but on a medical theory implicating the ingestion of asbestos fibers as a causative factor in increasing the rates of gastrointestinal cancer among asbestos workers. With respect to air, the assessment of the risk of harm rests on a higher degree of proof, a correlation between inhalation of asbestos dust and subsequent illness. But here, too, the hazard cannot be measured in terms of predictability, but the assessment must be made without direct proof. But, the hazard in both the air and water can be measured in only the most general terms as a concern for the public health resting upon a reasonable medical theory. Serious consequences could result if the hypothesis on which it is based should ultimately prove true.

A court is not powerless to act in these circumstances. But an immediate injunction cannot be justified in striking a balance between unpredictable health effects and the clearly predictable social and economic consequences that would follow the plant closing.

In addition to the health risk posed by Reserve's discharges, the district court premised its immediate termination of the discharges upon Reserve's persistent refusal to implement a reasonable alternative plan for on-land disposal of tailings.

During these appeal proceedings, Reserve has indicated its willingness to deposit its tailings on land and to properly filter its air emissions. At oral argument, Reserve advised us of a willingness to spend 243 million dollars in plant alterations and construction to halt its pollution of air and water. Reserve's offer to continue operations and proceed to construction of land disposal facilities for its tailings, if permitted to do so by the State of Minnesota, when viewed in conjunction with the uncertain quality of the health risk created by Reserve's discharges, weighs heavily against a ruling which closes Reserve's plant immediately.

Indeed, the intervening union argues, with some persuasiveness, that ill health effects resulting from the prolonged unemployment of the head of the family on a closing of the Reserve facility may be more certain than the harm from drinking Lake Superior water or breathing Silver Bay air.

Furthermore, Congress has generally geared its national environmental policy to allowing polluting industries a reasonable period of time to make adjustments in their efforts to conform to federal standards. In the absence of an imminent hazard to health or welfare, any other program for abatement of pollution would be inherently unreasonable and invite great economic and social disruption. Some pollution and ensuing environmental damage, are, unfortunately, an inevitable concomitant of a heavily industrialized economy. In the absence of proof of a reasonable risk of imminent or actual harm, a legal standard requiring immediate cessation of industrial operations will cause unnecessary economic loss, including unemployment, and, in a case such as this, jeopardize a continuing domestic source of critical metals without conferring adequate countervailing benefits.

We believe that on this record the district court abused its discretion by immediately closing this major industrial plant. In this case, the risk of harm to the public is potential, not imminent or certain, and Reserve says it earnestly seeks a practical way to abate the pollution. A remedy should be fashioned which will serve the ultimate public weal by insuring clean air, clean water, and continued jobs in an industry vital to the nation's welfare.

Reserve must be given a reasonable opportunity and a reasonable time to construct facilities to accomplish an abatement of its pollution of air and water and the health risk created thereby. In this way, hardship to employees and great economic loss incident to an immediate plant closing may be avoided.

We cannot ignore, however, the potential for harm in Reserve's discharges. This potential imparts a degree of urgency to this case that would otherwise be absent from an environmental suit in which ecological pollution alone were proved. Thus, any authorization of Reserve to continue operations during conversion of its facilities to abate the pollution must be circumscribed by realistic time limitations. Accordingly, we direct that the injunction order be modified as follows.

A The Discharge Into Water

Reserve shall be given a reasonable time to stop discharging its wastes into Lake Superior. A reasonable time includes the time necessary for Minnesota to act on Reserve's present application to dispose of its tailings at Milepost 7, or to come to agreement on some other site acceptable to both Reserve and the state. Assuming agreement and designation of an appropriate land disposal site, Reserve is entitled to a reasonable turn-around time to construct the necessary facilities and accomplish a changeover in the means of disposing of its taconite wastes.

Should Minnesota and Reserve be unable to agree on an on-land disposal site within this reasonable time period, Reserve, Armco, and Republic Steel must be given a reasonable period of time thereafter to phase out the Silver Bay facility. In the interests of delineating the rights of the parties to the fullest extent possible, this additional period of time is set at one year after Minnesota's final administration determination that it will offer Reserve no site acceptable to Reserve for on-land disposal of tailings.

B Air Emissions

Pending final action by Minnesota on the present permit application, Reserve must promptly take all steps necessary to comply with Minnesota law applicable to its air emissions, as outlined in this opinion.

. . . Reserve must use such available technology as will reduce the asbestos fiber count in the ambient air at Silver Bay below a medically significant level. According to the record in this case, controls may be deemed adequate which will reduce the fiber count to the level ordinarily found in the ambient air of a control city such as St. Paul.

Sierra Club v. Ruckelshaus

344 F. Supp. 253 (1972), affirmed 412 U.S. 541 (1973)

JOHN H. PRATT, District Judge.

. . . this matter came before the Court on plaintiffs' motion for temporary restraining order wherein they sought to enjoin the Administrator of the Environmental Protection Agency from approving certain portions of state air pollution control plans—implementing the national primary and secondary standards—which had been submitted to the Administrator pursuant to the Clean Air Act of 1970. . . .

The Administrator, in recent testimony before Congress, indicated that he had declined to require state implementation plans to provide against significant deterioration of the existing clean air areas—i.e., areas with levels of pollution lower than the secondary standard—because he believed that he lacked the power to act otherwise.

Previously, the Administrator has promulgated a regulation permitting states to submit plans which would allow clean air areas to be degraded, so long as the plans were merely "adequate to prevent such ambient pollution levels from exceeding such secondary standard."

Plaintiffs' claim that the Administrator's interpretation of the extent of his authority is clearly erroneous and that his declination to assert his authority, evidenced in his remarks before Congress and his promulgation of a regulation that is contrary to the Clean Air Act, amounts to a failure to perform a nondiscretionary act or duty.

In discussing the merits of the present action—i.e., the extent of the Administrator's authority and the validity of the questioned regulation—we turn to the stated purpose of the Clean Air Act of 1970, the available legislative history of the Act and its predecessor, and the administrative interpretation of the Act.

PURPOSE OF THE ACT

In Section 101(b) of the Clean Air Act, Congress states four basic purposes of the Act, the first of which is "to protect and enhance the quality of the nation's air resources so as to promote the public health and welfare and the productive capacity of its population." On its face, this language would appear to declare Congress' intent to improve the quality of the nation's air and to prevent deterioration of that air quality, no matter how presently pure that quality in some sections of the country happens to be.

LEGISLATIVE HISTORY

The "protect and enhance" language of the Clean Air Act of 1970 stems directly from the predecessor Air Quality Act of 1967. The Senate Report underlying the

1967 Act makes it clear that all areas of the country were to come under the protection of the Act.

Turning now to the legislative history of the 1970 Act, we note at the outset that both Secretary Finch and Under Secretary Veneman of HEW testified before Congress that neither the 1967 Act nor the proposed Act would permit the quality of air to be degraded.

More important, of course, is the language of the Senate Report accompanying the bill which became the Clean Air Act of 1970. The Senate Report, in pertinent part, states: "In areas where current air pollution levels are already equal to or better than the air quality goals, the Secretary shall not approve any implementation plan which does not provide, to the maximum extent practicable, for the continued maintenance of such ambient air quality." The House Report, although not as clear, does not appear to contradict the Senate Report.

ADMINISTRATIVE INTERPRETATION

On the other hand, the present Administrator, in remarks made in January and February of 1972 before certain House and Senate Subcommittees, has taken the position that the 1970 Act allows degradation of clean air areas. Several Congressional leaders voiced their strong disagreement with the Administrator's interpretation.

The Administrator's interpretation of the 1970 Act, as disclosed in his current regulations, appears to be self-contradictory. On the one hand, 40 C.F.R. Section 50.2(c) (1970) provides: "The promulgation of national primary and secondary air quality standards shall not be considered in any manner to allow significant deterioration of existing air quality in any portion of any State." Yet, in 40 C.F.R. Section 51.12(b), he states: "In any region where measured or estimated ambient levels of a pollutant are below the levels specified by an applicable secondary standard, the State implementation plan shall set forth a control strategy which shall be adequate to prevent such ambient pollution levels from exceeding such secondary standard."

The former regulation appears to reflect a policy of non-degradation of clean air but the latter mirrors the Administrator's doubts as to his authority to impose such a policy upon the states in their implementation plans. In our view, these regulations are irreconcilable and they demonstrate the weakness of the Administrator's position in this case.

INITIAL CONCLUSIONS

Having considered the stated purpose of the Clean Air Act of 1970, the legislative history of the Act and its predecessor, and the past and present administrative interpretation of the Acts, it is our judgment that the Clean Air Act of 1970 is based in important part on a policy of non-degradation of existing clean air and that 40 C.F.R. Section 51.12(b), in permitting the states to submit plans which allow pollution levels of clean air to rise to the secondary standard level of pollution, is contrary to the legislative policy of the Act and is, therefore, invalid. Accordingly, we hold that plaintiffs have made out a claim for relief.

INJUNCTIVE RELIEF

Whether this Court may properly grant injunctive relief depends on whether the plaintiffs have met the four criteria set forth in *Virginia Petroleum Jobbers Ass'n v. Federal Power Commission,* 259 F.2d 921 (1958). . . .

First, have the plaintiffs made a strong showing that they are likely to prevail on the merits? It appears to us, from our foregoing discussion, that the plaintiffs have made such a showing in this case.

Second, have the plaintiffs shown that without such relief they would suffer irreparable injury? In view of the nature and extent of the air pollution problem, once degradation is permitted the range of resulting damages could well have irreversible effects. Thus, we hold that plaintiffs have made the requisite showing of irreparable injury.

Third, will the issuance of a stay cause any significant harm or inconvenience to the Administrator or other parties interested in the proceedings? We are persuaded that no substantial harm or inconvenience will result from our order granting the preliminary injunction. The order is a very limited one. It was submitted by the plaintiffs' counsel after consultation with counsel for the Administrator with sufficient time and flexibility so that he may exercise his expertise and carry out his duties under the Act with as little inconvenience as possible.

Fourth, and finally, where lies the public interest? It seems to us that the public interest in this case strongly supports the legislative policy of clean air and the non-degradation of areas in which clean air exists.

CONCLUSION

Having separately considered the four criteria for injunctive relief, and having found that plaintiffs have met each of these criteria, we conclude that we can and should grant the requested relief.

Air Pollution Control; Recommendation for Alternative Emission Reduction Options within State Implementation Plans

Environmental Protection Agency, 40 CFR Part 52 (1979)

The policy statement set forth below (1) outlines how states can revise their State Implementation Plans to permit sources to place a greater burden of control where the marginal cost of control is low and to reduce control requirements where the cost is high and (2) encourages states to be receptive to proposals from sources seeking to employ a more economically efficient mix of controls.

This policy statement, commonly referred to as the "bubble" concept, is one in a series of steps designed to produce a coherent, easy-to-use system, which we have sometimes called "controlled trading." Other steps have included the offset and banking policies. This system will reconcile improved air quality with economic growth at the least possible cost, encourage firms to develop new ways to control pollution, and enable government and industry to solve problems more flexibly.

INTRODUCTION

The Clean Air Act requires states to develop State Implementation Plans (SIPs) and source-specific compliance schedules to attain and maintain ambient air quality standards. In developing these plans, states establish emission limits which, when applied to emission points contributing to the ambient air problem, are calculated to ensure that the standards are met. In making these decisions, states regularly take into account the nature and amount of emissions from each emission point, the control technology available, and the time required for its installation.

SIPs, however, are not always as economically efficient as they could be, and current regulations and policies do not prompt companies to seek innovations in control technology. For these reasons, the Environmental Protection Agency is adopting this policy explaining how plants can reduce control where costs are high in exchange for a compensating increase in control where abatement is less expensive. We strongly recommend that the states (1) inform sources that the alternative emission reduction approach is available, (2) explain this policy's advantages and conditions of use, and (3) be receptive to proposals from sources that want to use a more cost-effective mix of controls. Properly applied, this policy should promote greater economic efficiency and increased innovation by providing plant managers with an economic incentive to develop new control strategies. This is a rare opportunity to provide such positive incentives.

It is important to note, however, that with one exception EPA can only approve alternative control strategies in areas where states have successfully demonstrated that they can meet air quality standards by the statutory deadlines. Therefore, EPA will not allow sources to use the alternative approach in a way that jeopardizes attaining requirements of the Clean Air Act by permitting degradation of air quality in excess of the SIP requirements or by weakening enforcement. To avoid these problems, EPA has carefully stipulated the use of the alternative approach. . . .

THE ALTERNATIVE EMISSION REDUCTION CONCEPT

The primary tests to which EPA subjects State Implementation Plans include:

• Do their provisions ensure the attainment and maintenance of ambient air quality standards as expeditiously as practicable?

- Do their provisions ensure reasonable further progress toward attainment?
- Are their provisions enforceable?

If the control method adopted meets these requirements, EPA generally does not stipulate the degree to which a source must control individual emission points.

Under the alternative emission reduction concept, a source with multiple emission points (stacks, vents, ports, etc.)—each of which is subject to specific emission limitation requirements under an approved SIP—may propose to meet the SIP's total emission control requirements for a given criteria pollutant with a mix of controls that is different from that mandated by the existing or proposed regulations. Sources will have the opportunity to come forward with alternative abatement strategies that would result in the same air quality impact but at less expense by placing relatively more control on emission points with a low marginal cost of control and less on emission points with a high cost.

The SO_2 regulation for the Cincinnati Gas and Electric Company's Beckjord Power Plant in Ohio provides one example of how a source can use the alternative emission reduction approach. This SIP regulation contains an alternative set of limits that the power plant may use in lieu of a uniform limit at each of its five boiler stacks. The plant still must meet specific limits at its individual stacks, but it can select these limits by using equations that make the air quality effects of the emissions under the emission reduction alternative equal to the air quality impact permitted under the uniform emissions limit. This flexibility allows the power plant to apply the lowest-cost mix of low sulfur coal, and/or stack gas cleaning controls among the plant's five boilers. In this case, a clear and conclusive demonstration has been made that differences in emissions from each of the stacks will not result in overall differences in ambient air quality attainment or maintenance.

Another situation where a source can apply this approach is in different stages of a plant's production process that emit the same kind of pollutant. For example, the surface coating and miscellaneous metal categories within an automotive assembly plant are both sources of hydrocarbons. A source may want to continue using lacquer in its repair operation within the assembly plant. By applying greater control to the miscellaneous metal category (such as switching to powder coating) the source could reduce the amount of control needed for the auto assembly category. This approach would allow the source to achieve the same overall emissions requirement at a lower cost.

* * *

EPA will insist on an adequate equivalency demonstration proving that the alternative emission reduction approach will result in attainment and maintenance of standards and will comply with Prevention of Significant Deterioration requirements. The greater the difference in the types of emissions to be traded, the more detailed the demonstration must be. Thus, a trade between a stack emission and a fugitive emission will require a more detailed demonstration of equivalence than would a trade between two emissions of a more similar nature, such as two closely located stacks of the same height.

This condition will apply with particular force to trades involving open dust emissions (such as emissions from roads and storage piles). It is especially difficult to ensure equivalent effects on air quality for such trades because of (1) the uncertainty in determining emission rates from open dust sources, (2) the difficulty of predicting the effectiveness of control technology, and (3) the shortcomings of air quality models for this type of source. In addition, the adequacy of modeling techniques has not been verified for certain situations. As a result, there is substantial uncertainty regarding the accuracy of some model projections, such as for the complex interaction between open dust sources and structures at industrial sites, although these techniques may be verified and improved in the future. In such situations, EPA believes that the economic benefits that might result from a reduced marginal cost of control are not sufficiently great to outweigh the risk of having trades approved that would not adequately protect air quality standards. Therefore, EPA generally will not approve any proposed alternative emission strategy based on a modeling demonstration that proposes to substitute controls on open dust emissions for reasonable controls on the more significant sources of process emissions.

A source that wishes to control one emission point less in exchange for controlling another emission point more must demonstrate that the trade will in fact be even. This can only be done if the emissions from both emission points (and increases and decreases in them) can be acceptably quantified and related to ambient air quality considerations. Direct measurement is preferred, although indirect quantification is acceptable. . . .

Clearly, sources cannot apply trade-offs across criteria pollutant categories, e.g., they cannot trade SO_2 against hydrocarbons. Further, even within a category, pollutants that pose significant health hazards cannot be traded against less harmful pollutants. For example . . . Coke oven particulate emissions, because of their carcinogenicity, should not be traded against particulate emissions from any other source.

EPA will closely examine the comparability of particle size distribution in particulate emission trades because fine particles disperse more widely in the air than coarse particles and stay in the air longer. Sources should also be aware that EPA is considering an inhalable particulate standard. If EPA promulgates such a standard, some alternative approaches that EPA has approved may no longer be adequate to meet new standards. Trades involving open dust sources are of particular concern in this regard.

* * *

Control agencies in routine situations frequently obtain court decrees to insure compliance. In these circumstances, it may be appropriate to modify court decrees if a source presents an approvable alternative approach.

Over the past few years, control agencies and EPA have devoted considerable time and effort to arrive at decrees with some important sources, often involving several plants. EPA considers such court decrees to be of critical importance in achieving air quality objectives. Therefore, alternative control strategies should not be used to change the requirements specified in these existing court decrees.

The only exception is the use of alternatives to remedy the failure of control strategies specified in the consent decrees to work as expected.

In the future, important sources may be involved in similar negotiations to which the states and EPA have devoted considerable resources. These sources may wish to use the alternative approach. Under these conditions, sources should be sure either to: (1) Come forward with their alternatives and obtain agreement from the control agencies that the proposal is acceptable before entering into the court decree or (2) include a provision in the decree that explicitly allows for consideration of alternatives. Otherwise they may well find that the states and EPA will be unwilling to modify the requirements of the court decree to allow the use of an alternative approach because of the amount of effort already invested to obtain a settlement. Consent decree negotiations now nearing completion should not be delayed for the formulation of alternative plans.

CONCLUSION

EPA believes that the alternative emission reduction approach, properly applied, will be of significant benefit to the states and to industry. We therefore encourage states to review the policy carefully, to inform sources of the options, to explain the policy's advantages and conditions of use, and to be receptive to industry proposals.

The Cost of Clean Air and Water—Report to Congress, August 1979

Environmental Protection Agency

This report to Congress is mandated by the Clean Air and Water Acts. In both Acts, the Administrator of the Environmental Protection Agency is directed to make and report detailed estimates of the costs of carrying out the respective Acts. . . .

The estimates reported here are limited to costs associated with Federal regulatory actions resulting from the Clean Air and Clean Water Acts, and do not account for costs voluntarily incurred by pollutors, required by State or local governments only, or mandated by other Federal laws. The estimates given here do not include costs incurred prior to the dates of the respective Acts (Air—1970, Water—1972), nor is any estimate given of the expenditures which would have taken place if the Acts had not been passed.

COST OF IMPLEMENTING THE ACTS

In the presentation of costs, 1977 is the base year; all costs are expressed in millions of 1977 dollars. Investment and annual costs are reported for two historical periods: 1970–77 (Air), 1972–77 (Water) and are projected for the period from 1977 through 1986.

The costs reported include:

- Capital costs of equipment and installation

- Capital recovery (depreciation) and interest on unrecovered capital

- Direct operating and maintenance costs.

The costs are the result of engineering estimates; they are not obtained from industry surveys. The estimates are based on the assumed application of existing technology, and are developed by various techniques such as the use of "model" plants, or actual data on an existing plant. Various other assumptions are used, such as the utilization of an "average" air-pollution regulation typical of all State Implementation Plans. The assumptions used are judged to result in an overstatement of costs, since no allowances are made for in-process changes or technological innovation, either of which might reduce the costs of pollution control.

COMPARISON OF COSTS

In terms of the combined costs . . . the highest levels of expenditures are associated with the Energy Industries (largely electric power plants and petroleum refining) and Mobile Sources. The balance of the industry groups fall into either an intermediate range of expenditures, e.g., Food Processing, Chemical Industries, Metals, Softgoods, Waste Disposal, and Industrial Heating, or into a lower range of expenditures, e.g., the Construction Materials, Manufacturing, and Service groups.

The estimates reported allow a broad comparison of past and future expenditures. One observation is that investment to meet air pollution control regulations over the entire 1970–1986 period will be about 20 percent greater than investment to meet water pollution control regulations. A further observation is that, although the investments for air pollution control over the entire period are higher, sunk investment costs (i.e., before 1977) are roughly equal for air and water pollution control. This overall observation is, of course, subject to qualification in instances of individual industries.

The 1977 annualized cost of pollution control due to Federal Regulations was estimated to be $23 billion, or about one percent of 1977 GNP. The cumulative cost from 1970 to 1977 was $84.8 billion, and the projected cost over the period of 1977 to 1986 is estimated at $360 billion.

. . . [With regard to Air Pollution Control Costs] the groups showing the largest portions of investment costs include the Energy Industries (specifically, power plants), and Mobile Sources. The Mobile Sources costs include costs for lead phase-down and lead-free gasoline production; these elements of cost may be associated with the Petroleum Refining Industry in other studies. The next largest range of expenditures are . . . for the Metals and Food Processing groups.

Some of the individual features which may be noted . . . include the singularly high levels of expenditures for the control of Mobile Sources; these costs reflect the projected automobile populations that contain pollution control, as well as increasing stringency of regulations. The costs reported for electric utilities do not include any control costs stemming from the 1977 Amendments. The cost estimate for the electric utilities industry reflects the application of a mix of control technologies and fuel switching to achieve compliance.

. . . [For Water Pollution Control Costs] the highest level of expenditure is . . . for the energy industry (largely for Petroleum Refining and, again, electric power plants) with the next highest levels of expenditures . . . for the Chemical Industries (principally the organic chemicals industry), and for the so-called "Softgoods" group; almost all the latter costs are associated with the pulp and paper industry.

The water pollution control costs . . . include Federal grants for construction of municipal treatment plants as an investment expenditure. The cost of water pollution control for the electric utilities . . . has, as a major component, the cost to meet thermal limits on discharge water and replacement of capacity lost to the operation of the required cooling towers.

BENEFITS

Historically, the benefits research program at the EPA has given primary attention to developing the capabilities to compute national estimates of the total damage from pollution, i.e., estimating the potential benefits of eliminating pollution entirely. Basically, the program has categorized the various types of economic damages from pollution (medical bills, property damage, etc.) by media and pollutant. Individual projects generally involved estimating the extent and value of the more important damages for which some data exist. At best, past studies have been used to defend overall EPA programs, though they may not have been all that useful for this purpose. There have been a few attempts to demonstrate the feasibility of evaluating the benefits of control of individual pollutants (e.g., EPA-sponsored analyses of nitrates, nonfluorinated halomethanes, chlorobenzilate, etc.) but these were not done in direct support of actual EPA regulatory decisions. The EPA has never applied comprehensive benefit estimation methodologies to a contemplated regulatory decision.

National Estimates

The national damage estimates have concentrated on air and water pollution control. Best EPA-generated estimates have been very crude, sometimes based on faulty or incomplete methodologies and always on inadequate data bases. The ranges defined by EPA and other estimates to date have been: air pollution damages from $2.0 billion to $35.4 billion and water pollution damages from $4.5 billion to $18.6 billion. These studies have been characterized as only providing crude, order-of-magnitude estimates of the damages.

The "Wyoming" Study

A recently completed EPA study done by a consortium of professors (primarily at the University of Wyoming) may provide significantly more reliable estimates of national morbidity and mortality damages from air pollution than the EPA has had before. The study also assesses potential benefits from air clean-up in the Los Angeles area. The results are:

- National mortality effects of $5 to $16 billion per year

- National morbidity effects of $36 billion per year

- Potential benefits of $0.95 billion per year from a 30 percent air clean-up of the South Coast Basin of Southern California.

New Perspective on Damages

Besides suggesting that previous studies may have substantially underestimated both the health and other economic damages from air pollution, and thus the benefits of control, the new study and other recent work by many of the same environmental economists suggest a new perspective on air pollution damages and their measurement.

The new work indicates that the major air pollution damages are from increased chronic illness and from aesthetic effects like reduced visibility. This contrasts with earlier views that increased deaths were the major source of damage.

The economic damages attributable to increased air pollution-related deaths are roughly comparable to earlier studies, but this is largely accidental: although the new estimates of mortality effects are lower than earlier studies have indicated, these lower estimates are offset by higher estimates of the value society places on increased risk of death.

The study also concludes that many benefits, such as aesthetic ones, which are "traditionally viewed as intangible and thereby nonmeasurable can, in fact, be measured" and can be made comparable to economic values expressed in the marketplace.

Derivation of New Health Estimates

The researchers derived their estimates of damage to health through two independent approaches. One approach examined data from the University of Michigan Survey Research Center on illnesses among a random selection of the U.S. population. This information was compared statistically with indicators of biological and social situation, life styles, income levels, physical environment, and air pollution levels in the county of residence. The analyses suggest the extent to which each indicator is associated with time lost from work because of illness.

The studies found statistically significant associations between lost work time because of chronic illness and ambient levels of both nitrogen dioxide and total suspended particulates. The researchers arrived at the $36 billion estimate for 60 percent control by projecting the relationship between lost time and particulate levels in their sample to the national urban population using the wage rates of the sample population to put a monetary value on the time lost from work. The authors emphasized, however, that their conclusions should be regarded as preliminary because of the short time they have worked with the data and the many combinations of explanatory hypotheses they will need to test.

In the second approach, the researchers concentrated on the death rates in 60 cities across the country, comparing them to air pollution levels and other factors that might influence those rates such as smoking, doctors per capita, and diet. The researchers found statistically significant associations between death from pneumonia and influenza and the level of sulfur dioxide. The study valued the benefits that would result from reduced mortality if there were a 60 percent improvement in air quality at $5 to $16 billion annually.

Los Angeles Benefits Also Large

In addition to studying health damages from air pollution, the same study also attempts to quantify air pollution damages in one air quality region—the Los Angeles Basin. It found that a 30 percent improvement in air quality would provide benefits of $650 to $950 million per year (or $350 to $500 per household) for this city alone.

This part of the study used interview surveys and analyses of property values to support its conclusions. In the interview survey people were first given a subjective understanding of the health effects and location of Los Angeles smog using maps of pollution levels (which varied from poor to quite good) throughout the Basin and later shown photographs of a view obscured by different levels of pollution. They were then asked how much they would be willing to pay for improved air quality. In the property value analyses, the researchers compared the selling prices of houses which were similar but which were located in areas experiencing different levels of pollution. The houses in the clean air areas had a substantially higher value than those in more polluted areas. The fact that the benefit estimates derived from the two approaches are similar lends credence to both.

In their interview survey, the researchers found that people living in the Los Angeles Basin believe aesthetic effects such as impairment of visibility account for 22 percent to 55 percent of the damages associated with air pollution. These findings are consistent with an earlier survey many of the same researchers undertook for the Electric Power Research Institute, which found that people living in the Four Corners area of the Southwest would pay an average of $90 a year to avoid having visibility reduced by 50 miles, i.e., from 75 to 25 miles.

THE ECONOMIC IMPACT OF EPA'S PROGRAM

This section is included to provide some perspective as to the economic effects of EPA programs. Widely disparate views on the economic impact of EPA's program have been expressed by some environmentalists—who say the program stimulates the economy and creates jobs—and by some businessmen—who say the program causes capital shortages and inflation in boom times and causes unemployment and stifles profitability in recessionary times.

The truth probably lies somewhere in between. While costs of pollution programs are high in absolute terms, the overall effects on prices, GNP, and employment are projected to be small and neither strongly positive nor negative in the long run.

Most concern about economic effects should be focused on a few heavily polluting industries which either are very capital-intensive materials producing industries or are characterized by many economically marginal operations. Of key importance for these industries are (a) concerns about limits on expansion due to capital shortfalls or siting constraints posed by environmental regulations and (2) the effects of these limits on growth in these and related industries.

This section does not discuss whether environmental programs (or various elements of them) have favorable benefit/cost ratios, since few credible benefits data have been generated which would allow such analysis. This section does briefly detail what is and is not known about the costs, macroeconomic and microeconomic impacts, energy impacts, and key economic impact issues associated with the environmental program.

Costs

The Federal pollution control program is projected to cost about *$360 billion in the period 1977–86* above expenditure levels which would have resulted without new Federal requirements since 1970. About $229 billion, or about 2/3 of these expenditures are the result of the Clean Air Act. Capital investment for Federally-required controls will be about $142 billion over the same period. About $81 billion of this total (57%) is as a result of the Clean Air Act.

The 1977 annualized cost of pollution control due to Federal Regulations was estimated to be $23.2 billion, or about one percent of 1977 GNP. Air pollution control costs were $14.3 billion in 1977, or about 62% of the combined air and water costs.

Total (air and water) pollution abatement investment by industry (excluding Mobile Sources and Cost to Governments) was $10.8 billion in 1977. This represents about 5.8% of 1977 fixed nonresidential private investment. Consumer investment for Mobile Source pollution control was slightly under $3 billion in vehicles and parts.

Macroeconomic Impacts

These costs can be put in perspective by looking at their macroeconomic effect on the economy. The magnitudes of these effects depend upon the general state of the economy. In a slack economy pollution control investment can stimulate growth and employment with little real effect on prices, while in a tight economy such investment can increase prices and tend to replace other capital spending plans with a relatively small effect on employment. Macroeconomic forecasts can project these effects, but only with a wide band of uncertainty.

Price and Growth Effects—A Data Resources, Inc. (DRI) forecast prepared for EPA and CEQ in January 1979 shows that *the Consumer Price Index is currently about 2.7% higher* than it would have been without Federal pollution requirements and that by 1986 this difference will be about 3.6%, meaning that *consumer prices will increase between 0.2% and 0.3% per year more* than they would without these requirements over the period 1970–1986.

DRI estimates that GNP is currently very marginally higher than it would have been because Federal pollution requirements have caused use of capital and other resources that would not otherwise have been used. As the economy improves, environmental investment will increasingly be made instead of, rather than in addition to, other expenditures. DRI estimates that by 1986 *GNP will be almost 1.0% lower* than it would have been without Federal pollution requirements.

These estimated effects on prices and GNP use conventional measures for these variables. Since these measures do not take into account the benefits of *the environmental programs in terms of improved public health and welfare, these forecasts exaggerate the negative impacts on inflation and economic growth.*

Employment Effects—Employment is affected in a number of ways by environmental requirements. The program directly creates jobs in the construction (46,000 on-site jobs on EPA-funded sewage treatment projects in July 1976, with an equivalent number of off-site jobs) and the pollution control manufacturing industry (Arthur D. Little, Inc., estimates current employment to be nearly 36,000 and projects employment to grow to nearly 44,000 in this industry by 1983 as a result of the 1970 and 1972 air and water legislation), with many more indirect jobs stimulated by these expenditures.

On the other hand, when pollution control costs result in higher prices, lower demand and hence lower production and lower employment result. Furthermore, some transitional unemployment results from closing of marginal plants which cannot afford to comply with environmental requirements. Since January 1971, 132 closures involving nearly 24,500 jobs have occurred for which the firm has said that pollution requirements were a significant factor; 40 closures involved Federal action.

The combination of these factors according to the DRI macroeconomic projection will result in *increased employment through 1986 due to the stimulative effect of pollution control investment.* The jobs created in manufacturing, installing, and operating/maintaining pollution control equipment outweigh the dampening effect of higher prices on economic growth. DRI estimates the unemployment rate to be about 0.2% lower in 1979, 0.4% lower in both 1980 and 1981, and 0.2% lower in 1986 due to Federal pollution requirements.

Tennessee Valley Authority v. Hill

437 U.S. 153 (1978)

MR. CHIEF JUSTICE BURGER delivered the opinion of the Court.

I

The Little Tennessee River originates in the mountains of northern Georgia and flows through the national forest lands of North Carolina into Tennessee, where it converges with the Big Tennessee River near Knoxile. The lower 33 miles of the Little Tennessee takes the river's clear, free-flowing waters through an area of great natural beauty. . . .

In this area of the Little Tennessee River the Tennessee Valley Authority, a wholly owned public corporation of the United States, began constructing the Tellico Dam and Reservoir Project in 1967, shortly after Congress appropriated initial funds for its development. Tellico is a multipurpose regional development project designed principally to stimulate shoreline development, generate sufficient electric current to heat 20,000 homes, and provide flatwater recreation and flood control, as well as improve economic conditions in "an area characterized by underutilization of human resources and outmigration of young people." Of particular relevance to this case is one aspect of the project, a dam which TVA determined to place on the Little Tennessee, a short distance from where the river's waters meet with the Big Tennessee. When fully operational, the dam would impound water covering some 16,500 acres—much of which represents valuable and productive farmland—thereby converting the river's shallow, fast-flowing waters into a deep reservoir over 30 miles in length.

The Tellico Dam has never opened, however, despite the fact that construction has been virtually completed and the dam is essentially ready for operation. . . .

. . . Exploring the area around Coytee Springs, which is about seven miles from the mouth of the river, a University of Tennessee ichthyologist, Dr. David A. Etnier, found a previously unknown species of perch, the snail darter, or Percina (Imostoma) tanasi . . . [a] three-inch, tannish-colored fish, whose numbers are estimated to be in the range of 10,000 to 15,000. . . .

Until recently the finding of a new species of animal life would hardly generate a cause celebre. This is particularly so in the case of darters, of which there are approximately 130 known species, 8 to 10 of these having been identified only in the last five years. The moving force behind the snail darter's sudden fame came some four months after its discovery, when the Congress passed the Endangered Species Act of 1973. This legislation, among other things, authorizes the Secretary of the Interior to declare species of animal life "endangered" and to identify the "critical habitat" of these creatures. When a species or its habitat is so listed, the following portion of the Act—relevant here—becomes effective:

The Secretary [of the Interior] shall review other programs administered by him and utilize such programs in furtherance of the purposes of this chapter. All other Federal departments and agencies shall, in consultation with and with the assistance of the Secretary, utilize their authorities in furtherance of the purpose of this chapter by carrying out programs for the conservation of endangered species and threatened species listed pursuant to section 1533 of this title and by taking such action necessary to insure that actions authorized, funded, or carried out by them do not jeopardize the continued existence of such endangered species and threatened species or result in the destruction or modification of habitat of such species.

In January 1975, the respondents in this case and others petitioned the Secretary of the Interior to list the snail darter as an endangered species. After receiving comments from various interested parties, including TVA and the State of Tennessee, the Secretary formally listed the snail darter as an endangered species on October 8, 1975. In so acting, it was noted that "the snail darter is a living entity which is genetically distinct and reproductively isolated from other fishes." More important for the purpose of this case, the Secretary determined that the snail darter apparently lives only in that portion of the Little Tennessee River which would be completely inundated by the reservoir created as a consequence of Tellico Dam's completion.

II

We begin with the premise that operation of the Tellico Dam will either eradicate the known population of snail darters or destroy their critical habitat. Petitioner does not now seriously dispute this fact. In any event, under the Act, the Secretary of the Interior is vested with exclusive authority to determine whether a species such as the snail darter is "endangered" or "threatened" and to ascertain the factors which have led to such a precarious existence. . . . As we have seen, the Secretary promulgated regulations which declared the snail darter an endangered species whose critical habitat would be destroyed by creation of the Tellico Reservoir. Doubtless petitioner would prefer not to have these regulations on the books, but there is no suggestion that the Secretary exceeded his authority or abused his discretion in issuing the regulations. Indeed, no judicial review of the Secretary's determinations has ever been sought and hence the validity of his actions are not open to review in this Court.

Starting from the above premise, two questions are presented: (a) would TVA be in violation of the Act if it completed and operated the Tellico Dam as planned? (b) if TVA's actions would offend the Act, is an injunction the appropriate remedy for the violation? For the reasons stated hereinafter, we hold that both questions must be answered in the affirmative.

(A)

It may seem curious to some that the survival of a relatively small number of three-inch fish among all the countless millions of species extant would require the permanent halting of a virtually completed dam for which Congress has expended more than $100 million. The paradox is not minimized by the fact that Congress continued to appropriate large sums of public money for the project, even after congressional Appropriations Committees were apprised of its apparent impact upon the survival of the snail darter. We conclude, however, that the explicit provisions of the Endangered Species Act require precisely that result.

One would be hard pressed to find a statutory provision whose terms were any plainer than those in §7 of the Endangered Species Act. Its very words affirmatively command all federal agencies "to insure that actions authorized, funded or carried out by them do not jeopardize the continued existence" of an endangered species or "result in the destruction or modification of habitat of such species. . . ." This language admits of no exception. Nonetheless, petitioner urges, as do the dissenters, that the Act cannot reasonably be interpreted as applying to a federal project which was well under way when Congress passed the Endangered Species Act of 1973. To sustain that position, however, we would be forced to ignore the ordinary meaning of plain language. . . .

Concededly, this view of the Act will produce results requiring the sacrifice of the anticipated benefits of the project and of many millions of dollars in public funds. But examination of the language, history, and structure of the legislation under review here indicates beyond doubt that Congress intended endangered species to be afforded the highest of priorities.

It is against this legislative background that we must measure TVA's claim that the Act was not intended to stop operation of a project which, like Tellico Dam, was near completion when an endangered species was discovered in its path. While there is no discussion in the legislative history of precisely this problem, the totality of congressional action makes it abundantly clear that the result we reach today is wholly in accord with both the words of the statute and the intent of Congress. The plain intent of Congress in enacting this statute was to halt and reverse the trend toward species extinction, whatever the cost. This is reflected not only in the stated policies of the Act, but in literally every section of the statute. All persons, including federal agencies, are specifically instructed not to "take" endangered species, meaning that no one is "to harass, harm, pursue, hunt, shoot, wound, kill, trap, capture, or collect" such life forms. Agencies in particular are directed to "use . . . all methods and procedures which are necessary" to preserve endangered species. In addition, the legislative history undergirding §7 reveals an explicit congressional decision to require agencies to afford first priority to the declared national policy of saving endangered species. The pointed omission of the type of qualifying language previously included in endangered species legislation reveals a conscious decision by Congress to give endangered species priority over the "primary missions" of federal agencies.

Furthermore, it is clear Congress foresaw that §7 would, on occasion, require agencies to alter ongoing projects in order to fulfill the goals of the Act. . . .

One might dispute (this) . . . by saying that in this case the burden on the public through the loss of millions of unrecoverable dollars would greatly outweigh the loss of the snail darter. But neither the Endangered Species Act nor Art. III of the

Constitution provides federal courts with authority to make such fine utilitarian calculations. On the contrary, the plain language of the Act, buttressed by its legislative history, shows clearly that Congress viewed the value of endangered species as "incalculable". . . .

(B)

Having determined that there is an irreconcilable conflict between operation of the Tellico Dam and the explicit provisions of §7 of the Endangered Species Act, we must now consider what remedy, if any, is appropriate. . . .

Here we are urged to view the Endangered Species Act "reasonably," and hence shape a remedy "that accords with some modicum of common sense and the public weal." But is that our function? We have no expert knowledge on the subject of endangered species, much less do we have a mandate from the people to strike a balance of equities on the side of the Tellico Dam. Congress has spoken in the plainest of words, making it abundantly clear that the balance has been struck in favor of affording endangered species the highest of priorities, thereby adopting a policy which it described as "institutionalized caution."

Our individual appraisal of the wisdom or unwisdom of a particular course consciously selected by the Congress is to be put aside in the process of interpreting a statue. Once the meaning of an enactment is discerned and its constitutionality determined, the judicial process comes to an end. We do not sit as a committee of review, nor are we vested with the power of veto. . . .

We agree with the Court of Appeals that in our constitutional system the commitment to the separation of powers is too fundamental for us to pre-empt congressional action by judicially decreeing what accords with "common sense and the public weal." Our Constitution vests such responsibilities in the political branches.

Affirmed

CHAPTER 21

CONSUMER AND WORKER PROTECTION

Throughout the 1970s, there was an acceleration in regulatory activities that were designed to "protect" people. People may need to be protected from dangers of which they are aware as well as from dangers of which they are unaware. This section presents cases that illustrate some of the activities of four federal agencies that have responsibility for protecting consumers: (1) Federal Trade Commission (FTC); (2) Food and Drug Administration (FDA); (3) National Highway Traffic Safety Administration (NHTSA); and (4) Consumer Product Safety Commission (CPSC). In addition, one case is included from the agency empowered to protect workers—Occupational Safety and Health Administration (OSHA).

The most important marketing tool for manufacturers of consumer products is advertising. In addition to antitrust enforcement, the FTC is actively involved in the area of consumer protection. It has, for example, adopted numerous policies to reduce deceptive advertising and to increase the informational content of advertisements. In the first case, the FTC ordered Warner-Lambert to stop making claims that its oral antiseptic Listerine could prevent or cure colds. In addition, Warner-Lambert was required to run corrective advertising stating that Listerine cannot prevent or cure colds. Do you believe that consumers could not tell whether or not Listerine was effective? Could you? Are there some products where you can evaluate claims and do not need the FTC's help?

The second case presents a situation where it is very difficult for consumers to evaluate the effectiveness of a product—terminally ill cancer patients using Laetrile, a possible anticancer drug. Do you support the FDA's position? If someone believes that Laetrile helps him or her, should the government prevent that person from taking the drug? What if that person then stops seeking additional medical treatment?

The NHTSA has the authority to establish safety standards for automobiles. Throughout the 1960s and 1970s, it issued a variety of regulations regarding the interior and exterior design of cars, including the installation of seat and shoulder belts. The third case concerns a regulation that will require cars, beginning with the 1982 model year, to be equipped with a "passive restraint system" such as the air bag. This device will inflate as the car collides with another car, thereby preventing passengers from hitting the car's dashboard. Do you favor this regulation? Is it cost-effective? Many people argue that this mandatory standard is not appropriate, that it should be voluntary instead. Do you agree? Do you use seat belts now when you are in a car? Why might it be in society's interest to have a mandatory standard instead of a voluntary standard?

The CPSC has broad jurisdiction over products that Americans purchase for home or recreational use. It has the authority to establish safety standards to ensure that these products are safe for consumer use. The fourth case is a legal challenge to the first such standard issued by the commission, a standard for swimming pool slides. What do you think of the standard? Will it substantially reduce the number of injuries that result from using swimming pool slides? Will it increase the number of drownings? Do you believe that the risk of injury is sufficient to warrant regulation of swimming pool slides? Are there other products where you believe regulation is more urgently required?

The last case addresses the issue of occupational injuries. OSHA was established in an effort to reduce job-related injuries and illnesses. It was thus authorized to establish safety standards that would reduce workers' exposure to job hazards, including hazardous substances. A concern in the last case is that workers' exposure to benzene may cause, among other things, leukemia. In 1977, OSHA adopted a stringent standard limiting exposure to benzene. Industry fought this standard claiming that it would prevent only a few leukemia cases while imposing substantial costs on industry. Do you agree with OSHA's position? Industry's position? Should workers ever be exposed to a suspected carcinogen? On the other hand, the world is not riskless. People do, for example, choose to continue smoking cigarettes. Does it make sense to make all workplaces riskless?

Warner-Lambert Co. v. Federal Trade Commission

562 F. 2d 749 (1977), cert. denied 435 U.S. 950 (1978)

J. SKELLY WRIGHT, Circuit Judge:

The Warner-Lambert Company petitions for review of an order of the Federal Trade Commission requiring it to cease and desist from advertising that its product, Listerine Antiseptic mouthwash, prevents, cures, or alleviates the common cold. The FTC order further requires Warner-Lambert to disclose in future Listerine advertisements that: "Contrary to prior advertising, Listerine will not help prevent colds or sore throats or lessen their severity."[1] We affirm but modify the order to delete from the required disclosure the phrase "Contrary to prior advertising."

I BACKGROUND

The order under review represents the culmination of a proceeding begun in 1972, when the FTC issued a complaint charging petitioner with violation of Section 5(a)(1) of the Federal Trade Commission Act by misrepresenting the efficacy of Listerine against the common cold.

Listerine has been on the market since 1879. Its formula has never changed. Ever since its introduction it has been represented as being beneficial in certain respects for colds, cold symptoms, and sore throats. Direct advertising to the consumer, including the cold claims as well as others, began in 1921.

Following the 1972 complaint, hearings were held before an administrative law judge (ALJ). In 1974 the ALJ issued an initial decision sustaining the allegations of the complaint. Petitioner appealed this decision to the Commission. On December 9, 1975 the Commission issued its decision essentially affirming the ALJ's findings. It concluded that petitioner had made the challenged representations that Listerine will ameliorate, prevent, and cure colds and sore throats, and that these representations were false.

II SUBSTANTIAL EVIDENCE

The first issue on appeal is whether the Commission's conclusion that Listerine is not beneficial for colds or sore throats is supported by the evidence. The Commission's findings must be sustained if they are supported by substantial evidence on the record viewed as a whole. We conclude that they are.

. . . [T]he Commission found that Listerine has no significant beneficial effect on the symptoms of sore throat. The Commission recognized that gargling with Listerine could provide temporary relief from a sore throat by removing accumu-

---

[1] This requirement terminates when petitioner has expended on Listerine advertising a sum equal to the average annual Listerine advertising budget for the period of April 1962 to March 1972, approximately ten million dollars.

lated debris irritating the throat. But this type of relief can also be obtained by gargling with salt water or even warm water. The Commission found that this is not the significant relief promised by petitioner's advertisements. It was reasonable to conclude that "such temporary relief does not 'lessen the severity' of a sore throat any more than expectorating or blowing one's nose 'lessens the severity' of a cold."

III THE COMMISSION'S POWER

Petitioner contends that even if its advertising claims in the past were false, the portion of the Commission's order requiring "corrective advertising" exceeds the Commission's statutory power. The argument is based upon a literal reading of Section 5 of the Federal Trade Commission Act, which authorizes the Commission to issue "cease and desist" orders against violators and does not expressly mention any other remedies. The Commission's position, on the other hand, is that the affirmative disclosure that Listerine will not prevent colds or lessen their severity is absolutely necessary to give effect to the prospective cease and desist order; a hundred years of false cold claims have built up a large reservoir of erroneous consumer belief which would persist, unless corrected, long after petitioner ceased making the claims.

. . . [T]he threshold question is whether the Commission has the authority to issue such an order. We hold that it does.

IV THE REMEDY

Having established that the Commission does have the power to order corrective advertising in appropriate cases, it remains to consider whether use of the remedy against Listerine is warranted and equitable.

Our role in reviewing the remedy is limited. The Supreme Court has set forth the standard:

> The Commission is the expert body to determine what remedy is necessary to eliminate the unfair or deceptive trade practices which have been disclosed. It has wide latitude for judgment and the courts will not interfere except where the remedy selected has no reasonable relation to the unlawful practices found to exist.

The Commission has adopted the following standard for the imposition of corrective advertising:

> (I)f a deceptive advertisement has played a substantial role in creating or reinforcing in the public's mind a false and material belief which lives on after the false advertising ceases, there is clear and continuing injury to competition and to the consuming public as consumers continue to make purchasing decisions based on the false belief. Since this injury cannot be averted by merely requiring respondent to cease disseminating the advertisement, we may appropriately order respondent to take affirmative action designed to terminate the otherwise continuing ill effects of the advertisement.

We think this standard is entirely reasonable. It dictates two factual inquiries: (1) did Listerine's advertisements play a substantial role in creating or reinforcing in the public's mind a false belief about the product? and (2) would this belief linger on after the false advertising ceases? It strikes us that if the answer to both questions is not yes, companies everywhere may be wasting their massive advertising budgets. Indeed, it is more than a little peculiar to hear petitioner assert that its commercials really have no effect on consumer belief.

We turn next to the specific disclosure required: "Contrary to prior advertising, Listerine will not help prevent colds or sore throats or lessen their severity." Petitioner is ordered to include this statement in every future advertisement for Listerine for a defined period. In printed advertisements it must be displayed in type size at least as large as that in which the principal portion of the text of the advertisement appears and it must be separated from the text so that it can be readily noticed. In television commercials the disclosure must be presented simultaneously in both audio and visual portions. During the audio portion of the disclosure in television and radio advertisements, no other sounds, including music, may occur.

These specifications are well calculated to assure that the disclosure will reach the public. It will necessarily attract the notice of readers, viewers, and listeners, and be plainly conveyed. Given these safeguards, we believe the preamble "Contrary to prior advertising" is not necessary. . . .

Finally petitioner challenges the duration of the disclosure requirement. By its terms it continues until respondent has expended on Listerine advertising a sum equal to the average annual Listerine advertising budget for the period April 1962 to March 1972. That is approximately ten million dollars. Thus if petitioner continues to advertise normally the corrective advertising will be required for about one year. We cannot say that is an unreasonably long time in which to correct a hundred years of cold claims. But, to petitioner's distress, the requirement will not expire by mere passage of time. If petitioner cuts back its Listerine advertising, or ceases it altogether, it can only postpone the duty to disclose. The Commission concluded that correction was required and that a duration of a fixed period of time might not accomplish that task, since petitioner could evade the order by choosing not to advertise at all. The formula settled upon by the Commission is reasonably related to the violation it found.

Accordingly, the order, as modified, is Affirmed.

United States v. Rutherford

442 U.S. 544 (1979)

MR. JUSTICE MARSHALL delivered the opinion of the Court.

The question presented in this case is whether the Federal Food, Drug, and Cosmetic Act precludes terminally ill cancer patients from obtaining Laetrile, a drug not recognized as "safe and effective" within the meaning of the Act.

I

Section 505 of the Federal Food, Drug and Cosmetic Act prohibits interstate distribution of any "new drug" unless the Secretary of Health, Education and Welfare approves an application supported by substantial evidence of the drug's safety and effectiveness. . . .

In 1975, terminally ill cancer patients and their spouses brought this action to enjoin the Government from interfering with the interstate shipment and sale of Laetrile, a drug not approved for distribution under the Act. Finding that Laetrile, in proper dosages, was nontoxic and effective, the District Court ordered the Government to permit limited purchases of the drug by one of the named plaintiffs. On appeal by the Government, the Court of Appeals for the Tenth Circuit did not disturb the injunction. However, it instructed the District Court to remand the case to the Food and Drug Administration for determination whether Laetrile was a "new drug" and if so, whether it was exempt from premarketing approval under either of the Act's grandfather clauses.

After completion of administrative hearings, the Commissioner issued his opinion on July 29, 1977. He determined first that no uniform definition of Laetrile exists; rather, the term has been used generically for chemical compounds similar to, or consisting at least in part of, amygdalin, a glucoside present in the kernels or seeds of most fruits. The Commissioner further found that Laetrile in its various forms constituted a "new drug" as defined in §201 (p)(1) of the Act because it was not generally recognized among experts as safe and effective for its prescribed use. . . .

Having determined that Laetrile was a new drug, the Commissioner proceeded to consider whether it was exempt from premarketing approval under the 1938 or 1962 grandfather provisions. On the facts presented, the Commissioner found that Laetrile qualified under neither clause. First, there was no showing that the drug currently known as Laetrile was identical in composition or labeling to any drug distributed before 1938. Nor could the Commissioner conclude from the evidence submitted that, as of October 9, 1962, Laetrile in its present chemical compositions was commercially used or sold in the United States, was generally recognized by experts as safe, and was labeled for the same recommended uses as the currently marketed drug.

On review of the Commissioner's decision, the District Court sustained his determination that Laetrile, because not generally regarded as safe or effective constituted a new drug. . . . The court also approved the Commissioner's denial of an exemption under the 1938 grandfather clause. However, concluding that the record did not support the Commissioner's findings as to the 1962 grandfather provision, the District Court ruled that Laetrile was entitled to an exemption from premarketing approval requirements. Alternatively, the court held that, by denying cancer patients the right to use a nontoxic substance in connection with their personal health, the Commissioner had infringed constitutionally protected privacy interests.

The Court of Appeals addressed neither the statutory nor the constitutional rulings of the District Court. Rather, the Tenth Circuit held that "the 'safety' and 'effectiveness' terms used in the statute have no reasonable application to terminally ill cancer patients." Since those patients, by definition, would "die of cancer regardless of what may be done," the court concluded that there were no realistic standards against which to measure the safety and effectiveness of a drug for that class of individuals. The Court of Appeals therefore approved the District Court's injunction permitting use of Laetrile by cancer patients certified as terminally ill. However, presumably because the Commissioner had found some evidence that Laetrile was toxic when orally administered, the Court of Appeals limited relief to intravenous injections for patients under a doctor's supervision. In addition, the court directed the FDA to promulgate regulations "as if" the drug had been found " 'safe' and 'effective' " for terminally ill cancer patients.

II

The Federal Food, Drug and Cosmetic Act makes no special provision for drugs used to treat terminally ill patients. . . . the Act requires premarketing approval for "any new drug" unless it is intended solely for investigative use or is exempt under one of the Act's grandfather provisions. . . .

In the Court of Appeals' view, an implied exemption from the Act was justified because the safety and effectiveness standards set forth in §201 (p)(1) could have "no reasonable application" to terminally ill patients. We disagree. Under our constitutional framework, federal courts do not sit as councils of revision, empowered to rewrite legislation in accord with their own conceptions of prudent public policy. Only when a literal construction of a statute yields results as manifestly unreasonable that they could not fairly be attributed to congressional design will an exception to statutory language be judicially implied. Here, however, we have no license to depart from the plain language of the Act, for Congress could reasonably have intended to shield terminal patients from ineffectual or unsafe drugs.

A drug is effective within the meaning of §201(p)(1) if there is general recognition among experts, founded on substantial evidence, that the drug in fact produces the results claimed for it under prescribed conditions. Contrary to the Court of Appeals' apparent assumption, effectiveness does not necessarily denote capacity to cure. In the treatment of any illness, terminal or otherwise, a drug is effective if it fulfills, by objective indices, its sponsor's claims of prolonged life, improved physical condition, or reduced pain.

So too, the concept of safety under §201(p)(1) is not without meaning for terminal patients. Few if any drugs are completely safe in the sense that they may be taken by all persons in all circumstances without risk. Thus, the Commissioner generally considers a drug safe when the expected therapeutic gain justifies the risk entailed by its use. For the terminally ill, as for anyone else, a drug is unsafe if its potential for inflicting death or physical injury is not offset by the possibility of therapeutic benefit. Indeed, the Court of Appeals implicitly acknowledged that safety considerations have relevance for terminal cancer patients by restricting authorized use of Laetrile to intravenous injections for persons under a doctor's supervision.

Moreover, there is a special sense in which the relationship between drug effectiveness and safety has meaning in the context of incurable illnesses. An otherwise harmless drug can be dangerous to any patient if it does not produce its purported therapeutic effect. But if an individual suffering from a potentially fatal disease rejects conventional therapy in favor of a drug with no demonstrable curative properties, the consequences can be irreversible. . . . The FDA's practice also reflects the recognition, amply supported by expert medical testimony in this case, that with diseases such as cancer it is often impossible to identify a patient as terminally ill except in retrospect. Cancers vary considerably in behavior and in responsiveness to different forms of therapy. Even critically ill individuals may have unexpected remissions and may respond to conventional treatment. Thus, as the Commissioner concluded, to exempt from the Act drugs with no proven effectiveness in the treatment of cancer "could lead to needless death and suffering among . . . patients characterized as terminal who could actually be helped by legitimate therapy."

It bears emphasis that although the Court of Appeals' ruling was limited to Laetrile, its reasoning cannot be so readily confined. To accept the proposition that the safety and efficacy standards of the Act have no relevance for terminal patients is to deny the Commissioner's authority over all drugs, however toxic or ineffectual, for such individuals. If history is any guide, this new market would not be long overlooked. Since the turn of the century, resourceful entrepreneurs have advertised a wide variety of purportedly simple and painless cures for cancer, including linaments of turpentine, mustard, oil, eggs and ammonia; peatmoss; arrangements of colored floodlamps; pastes made from glycerin and limburger cheese; mineral tablets; and "Fountain of Youth" mixtures of spices, oil and suet. In citing these examples, we do not, of course, intend to deprecate the sincerity of Laetrile's current proponents, or to imply any opinion on whether that drug may ultimately prove safe and effective for cancer treatment. But this historical experience does suggest why Congress could reasonably have determined to protect the terminally ill, no less than other patients, from the vast range of self-styled panaceas that inventive minds can devise.

We note finally that construing §201(p)(1) to encompass treatments for terminal diseases does not foreclose all resort to experimental cancer drugs by patients for whom conventional therapy is unavailing. The Act exempts from premarketing approval drugs intended solely for investigative use if they satisfy certain preclinical testing and other criteria. An application for clinical testing of Laetrile by the National Cancer Institute is now pending before the Commissioner. That the Act makes explicit provision for carefully regulated use of certain drugs not yet demonstrated safe and effective reinforces our conclusion that no exception for terminal patients may be judicially implied. Whether, as a policy matter, an exemption should be created is a question for legislative judgment, not judicial inference.

The judgment of the Court of Appeals is reversed and the case remanded for further proceedings consistent with this opinion.

So ordered.

Federal Motor Vehicle Safety Standards: Occupant Restraint Systems

Department of Transportation
Federal Register, July 5, 1977

Under the National Traffic and Motor Vehicle Safety Act . . . the Department of Transportation is responsible for issuing motor vehicle safety standards that, among other things, protect the public against unreasonable risk of death or injury to persons in the event accidents occur. . . .

The total number of fatalities annually in motor vehicle accidents is approximately 46,000 (estimate for 1976), of which approximately 25,000 are estimated to be automobile front seat occupants. Two major hazards to which front seat occupants are exposed are ejection from the vehicle, which increases the probability of fatality greatly, and impact with the vehicle interior during the crash. Restraint of occupants to protect against these hazards has long been recognized as a means to substantially reduce the fatalities and serious injuries experienced at the front seating positions.

One of the Department's first actions in implementing the Act was promulgation in 1967 of Standard No. 208, Occupant Crash Protection, to make it possible for vehicle occupants to help protect themselves against the hazards of a crash by engaging seat belts. The standard requires the installation of lap and shoulder seat belt assemblies (Type 2) at front outboard designated seating positions (except in convertibles) and lap belt assemblies (Type 1) at all other designed seating positions. The standard became effective January 1, 1968.

While it is generally agreed that when they are worn, seat belt assemblies are highly effective in preventing occupant impact with the vehicle interior or ejection from the vehicle, only a minority of motorists in the United States use seat belts. For all types of belt systems, National Highway Traffic Safety Administration (NHTSA) studies show that about 20 percent of belt systems are used. The agency's calculations show that only about 2,600 deaths (and corresponding numbers of injuries) of front seat occupants were averted during 1976 by the restraints required by Standard No. 208 as it is presently written.

Two basic approaches have been developed to increase the savings of life and mitigation of injury afforded by occupant restraint systems. More than 20 nations and two provinces of Canada have enacted mandatory seat belt laws to increase usage and thereby the effective lifesaving potential of existing seat belt systems. The other approach is to install automatic passive restraints in passenger cars in place of, or in conjunction with, active belt systems. These systems are passive in the sense that no action by the occupant is required to benefit from the restraint. Passive restraint systems automatically provide a high level of occupant crash protection to virtually 100 percent of front seat occupants.

The two forms of passive restraint that have been commercially produced are inflatable occupant restraints (commonly known as air bags) and passive belts. Air bags are fabric cushions that are rapidly filled with gas to cushion the occupant against colliding with the vehicle interior when a crash occurs that is strong enough to register on a sensor device in the vehicle. The deployment is accomplished by the rapid generation or release of a gas to inflate the bag. Passive belt systems are comparable to active belt systems in many respects, but are distinguished by automatic deployment around the occupant as the occupant enters the vehicle and closes the door.

. . . [T]he Department has considered each available means to increase crash protection in arriving at the most rational approach. As proposed the possibility of "driver-side only" passive protection was considered, but was rejected because of the unsatisfactory result of having one front seat passenger offered protection superior to that offered other front seat passengers in the same vehicle. On balance, there was found to be little cost or lead-time advantage to this approach. The possibility of reinstituting a type of safety belt interlock was rejected because the agency's authority was definitively removed by the Congress less than three years ago and there is no reason to believe that Congress has changed its position on the issue since that time.

Mandatory Belt Use Laws.   One of the means proposed . . . to achieve a large reduction in highway deaths and injuries is Federal legislation to induce State enactment of mandatory seat belt use laws, either by issuance of a highway safety program standard or by making State passage of such laws a condition for the receipt of Federal highway construction money.

The prospects for passage of mandatory seat belt use laws by more than a few States appear to be poor. None of the commenters suggested that passage of such laws was likely. A public opinion survey sponsored by the Motor Vehicle Manufacturers Association and conducted by Yankelovich, Skelly, and White, Inc., indicated that a 2-to-1 majority nationwide opposes belt use laws. Many such bills have been presented, no State has enacted one up to now. Also, Congress denied funding for a program to encourage State belt use laws in 1974, suggesting that it does not look favorably upon Federal assistance in the enactment of these laws.

More recently, Congress removed the Department's authority to withdraw Federal safety funding in the case of States that do not mandate the use of motorcycle helmets on their highways. The close parallel between requiring helmet use and requiring seat belt use argues against the likelihood of enactment of belt use laws.

These strong indications that Congress would not enact a belt use program in the foreseeable future demonstrate, in large measure, why the success of other nations in enacting laws is not parallel to the situation in the United States. In the belt use jurisdictions most often compared to the United States (Australia and the Provinces of Canada), the laws were enacted at the State or Province level in the first instance, and not at the Federal level. In the Department's judgment, the most reasonable course of action to obtain effective belt use laws in the United States will be to actively encourage their enactment in one or more States. An attempt to impose belt use laws on citizens by the Federal government would create difficulties in Federal-State relations, and could damage rather than further the interests of highway safety.

Effectiveness of Passive Restraints. . . . the best estimates of effectiveness in preventing deaths and injuries of the various types of restraint systems under consideration . . . (are) summarized in Table II. Several comments concerning the effectiveness of passive restraint systems were submitted. . . .

The Insurance Institute for Highway Safety submitted another estimate of air bag effectiveness based on the experience with the GM cars in highway use. A selection was made of accidents in which the air bag was designed to operate, based on frontal damage, direction of impact, and age of occupant. In these accidents, air bags were determined to have reduced fatalities by 66 percent, as compared to 55 percent for three-point belts. . . .

Cost of Passive Restraints. Passive belts have been estimated in the past by the Department to add $25 to the price of an automobile, relative to the price of

TABLE II
EFFECTIVENESS OF OCCUPANT CRASH PROTECTION SYSTEMS[1]

	Fatalities prevented per year	Injuries prevented per year
Lap and shoulder (15%) and lap (5%) belts (nominal projection)[2]	3,000	39,000
Lap and shoulder (35%) and lap (5%) belts (optimistic projection)	6,300	86,000
Lap and shoulder belt (70% usage)	11,500	162,000
Lap and shoulder belt (100% usage)	16,300	231,000
Lap belt (100% usage)	10,900	96,000
Driver-only air cushion[3]		
Nominal projection	9,600	86,000
Optimistic projection	11,500	107,000
Full-front air cushion		
Nominal projection[4]	12,100	104,000
Optimistic projection[5]	13,500	115,000
Passive Belts		
Nominal projection[6]	9,800	117,000
Optimistic projection[7]	10,700	129,000

[1] These estimates assume the car population and occupant fatality rates to be that of 1975 (approximately 100 million cars and 27,200 people, respectively), 10 million cars to be manufactured annually, and the distribution of injuries by severity to be the same as in 1975. . . .
[2] [The percentage figures indicate the percentage of car occupants using a given restraint system.]
[3] . . . These estimates assume 72.56% of front seat occupants are drivers.
[4] Assumes 20% lap belt usage by all front seat occupants.
[5] Assumes 40% lap belt usage by all front seat occupants.
[6] Assumes 60% passive belt usage, i.e., 40% of people defeat the system.
[7] Assumes 70% passive belt usage, i.e., 30% of people defeat the system.

cars with present active belt systems. The increased operating costs over the life of a vehicle with passive belts is estimated to be $5. These figures are assumed valid for purposes of this review, and were not contested in the comments received.

If as projected passive restraints are effective in saving lives and reducing injuries, as compared to existing belt systems at present use rate, the insurance savings that will result will offset a major portion, and possibly all, of the cost to the consumer of the systems. . . .

In its comments to the docket, Nationwide Mutual Insurance Companies estimated that savings in insurance premiums should average $32.50 per insured car per year if all cars were equipped with air bags. Of this amount, 75 percent is the result of an assumed savings of 24.6 percent in the bodily injury portion of automobile insurance premiums, 21 percent from a 1.5 percent reduction in health insurance premiums (30 percent of the 5 percent of the premiums that pay for auto-related injuries), and the remainder from savings in life insurance premiums. The American Mutual Insurance Alliance and Allstate referred to existing 30 percent discounts in first-party coverage and concluded that comparable reductions would be expected to follow a mandate of passive restraints.

It has been argued that these savings would be largely offset by the increased cost of collision and property damage insurance due to the increased cost of repairing a car with a deployed air bag. This claim appears to be largely unfounded. Using figures based on field tests, it is estimated that each year 300,000 automobiles will be in accidents of sufficient severity to deploy the air bag. . . . Accepting vehicle manufacturer estimates, it is further assumed that the cost of replacing an air bag will be 2.5 times the original equipment cost. . . . Combining these assumptions with the estimated $112 cost of installing a full front air cushion in a new vehicle gives a total annual cost of replacement of $50.4 million, or a per car cost of less than 51 cents per year. Increases in collision premiums should, therefore, not exceed $1 per car per year. It is noted that deployment in non-crash cases would be covered by "comprehensive" insurance policies.

The $32.50 annual insurance savings estimated by Nationwide would be sufficient to pay for the added operating cost (around $4 per year) of an air-bag-equipped car with enough left over to more than pay for the initial cost of the system. Discounting at the average interest rate on new car loans measured in real terms (6 percent), the air bag would almost recover the initial cost in 4 years, with a savings over operating cost of $107.

Side Effects of Air Bag Installation. Some concerns were expressed in the comments about air bags that might be grouped as possible undesirable side effects. One of these was injuries that might be caused by design deployment. There is no question that any restraint system that must decelerate a human body from 30 mph or more to rest within approximately 2 feet can cause injury. Belt systems often cause bruises and abrasions in protecting occupants from more serious injuries. The main question is whether any injuries caused by air bags are generally within acceptable limits, and are significantly less severe than those that would have been suffered had the occupants in question not been restrained by the air bags. The evidence from the vehicles on the road indicates that this is indeed the case. The injuries cited by GM as possibly caused or aggravated by air bag deployment are in the minor to moderate category. From this it can be concluded that injuries caused by design deployment, though worthy of careful monitoring with a view to design improvements by manufacturers, do not provide a serious argument against a passive restraint requirement.

A closely related question that has caused concern in the past is whether air bags pose an unreasonable danger to occupants who are not in a normal seating position, such as children standing in front of a dashboard or persons who have been moved forward by panic braking. Much development work has been devoted to this problem in the past, to design systems that minimize the danger to persons who are close to the inflation source. The most important change in this area has probably been the general shift away from inflation systems that depend on stored high-pressure gas, in favor of pyrotechnic gas generators. With these systems the flow of gas can be adjusted to make the rate slower at the beginning of inflation, so that an out-of-position occupant is pushed more gently out of the way before the maximum inflation rate occurs.

Inadvertent actuation of an air bag may be a particular concern to the public, as noted by both General Motors and Ford. The sudden deployment of an air bag in a non-crash situation would generally be a disconcerting experience. The experience with vehicles on the road, and tests that have been performed on 40 subjects who were not aware that there were air bags in their vehicles, indicate that loss of control in such situations should be rare: none has occurred in the incidents up to now. There is little question, however, that inadvertent actuation could cause loss of control by some segments (aged, inexperienced, distracted) of the driving population, and it must be viewed as a small but real cost of air bag protection.

Some private individuals expressed in their comments, concern over possible ear damage, or injuries that might be caused to persons with smoking materials in their mouths, or wearing eyeglasses. Although some early tests with oversized cushions of prototype design produced some temporary hearing losses, later designs have reduced the sound pressures to the point where ear damage is no longer a significant possibility. With respect to eyeglasses and smoking materials, the results from the vehicles on the road have been favorable. Of the occupants that had been involved in air cushion deployments as of a recent date, 71 had been smoking pipes or wearing eyeglasses or other facial accessories. None of these received injuries beyond the minor level. From this it can be concluded that these circumstances do not create particular hazards to occupants of air-bag-equipped vehicles.

General Motors and the National Automobile Dealers commented that product liability arising from air bag performance would be a major expense. The insurance company commenters, on the other hand, suggested that the presence of air bags in vehicles could reduce auto companies' product liability.

There is little evidence that the mandating of passive restraints will lead to increases in product liability insurance premiums. Although the advent of new technology has often been accompanied by an increase in products liability insurance, it is unclear how much of the increase is attributable to increased risk and how much to inflation. Officials of the Department of Commerce and at least two major insurance companies doubt that Federal passive restraint requirements will lead to increased risk and insurance premiums. They point out that Federal requirements are imposed to make products safer, and safe products are less likely to cause injury.

Small Cars.   An important consideration in the decision concerning passive restraints is their suitability and availability for small cars which because of the energy shortage will comprise an increasing segment of the vehicle population in future years. Passive belts have been sold as standard equipment in over 65,000 Volkswagen cars, and must be viewed as a proven means of meeting a passive restraint requirement. Some vehicle body designs may require some modification for their installation, but passive belts could be used as restraints for most bucket-seat arrangements at moderate cost with present technology.

Some manufacturers have expressed doubt that a large proportion of their customers would find passive belts acceptable, because of their relatively obtrusive nature and the resistance shown by the U.S. public to wearing seat belt systems, i.e., belts that occupants must buckle and unbuckle. These manufacturers submitted no supporting market surveys. Further, there is reason to believe that the experience with active belt systems is not an accurate indicator of the experience to be expected with passive belts. The Department anticipates that some manufacturers will install passive belts in the front seats of small cars having only two front seats. Passive belts would not confront the occupants of those seats with the current inconvenience of having to buckle a belt system to gain its protection or of having to unbuckle that system to get out of their cars. Unlike the interlock active belt system of several years ago, the passive belt systems will have no effect on the ability of drivers to start their cars.

The "packaging" problems of installing air bag systems are greater for small cars than for larger ones. They occupy space in the instrument panel area that might otherwise be utilized by other items such as air conditioning ducts, glove compartment, or controls and displays. Toyo Kogyo (Mazda) and Honda indicated that their instument panels might have to be displaced 4 inches rearward, that some engine compartment and wheel-base changes might be needed, and that some dash-mounted accessories might have to be deleted or mounted elsewhere. This type of problem is expected to be important to the existing choice between air bag and passive belt systems.

Lead Time and Production Readiness.   There was considerable discussion in the comments to the docket about the ability of the automobile industry to develop the production readiness to provide passive restraint systems for all passenger cars. The installation of passive restraint systems requires the addition of new hardware and modification of vehicle structures in such a way that the system provides performance adequate to meet the standard and a high level of safety and reliability on the road. A new industrial capacity will have to be generated to supply components for air bag systems. Major capital expenditures will have to be made by the vehicle industry to incorporate air bag systems into production models. The Department estimates that the total capital required for tooling and equipment for the production of passive restraint systems in new cars is approximately $500 million.

Based on its evaluation, the Department has determined that a lead time of four full years should precede the requirement for the production of the first passive-equipped passenger cars. This lead time accords with General Motors' requested lead time to accomplish the change for all model lines. . . .

In addition to a long lead time, the Department considers that the mandate should be accomplished in three stages, with new standard- and luxury-sized cars (a wheelbase of more than 114 inches) meeting the requirement on and after September 1, 1981, new intermediate- and compact-size cars (a wheelbase of more than 100 inches) also meeting the requirements on and after September 1, 1982, and all new passenger cars meeting the requirement on and after September 1, 1983.

The determination of which car sizes to include in each year of the phased implementation was made in consideration of the effect on each manufacturer and the difficulty involved in engineering passive restraints into each size class of automobile. Because of the extensive experience with passive restraints in full size cars, and the space available in the instrument panels of these cars to receive air bag systems, this size car was deemed to be most susceptible to early implementation.

The gradual phase-in schedule is intended to permit manufacturers to absorb the impact of introducing passive restraining systems without undue technological or economic risk at the same time they undertake efforts to meet the challenging requirements imposed by emissions and fuel economy standards for automobiles in the early 1980's.

* * *

The amendment is therefore issued, to become effective beginning September 1, 1981, for those passenger cars first subject to the new requirements. The reasons underlying the effective dates set forth in the standard have been discussed above. The establishment of the effective dates is accomplished at this time to provide the maximum time available for preparations to meet the requirements. The Congressional review period will be completed prior to the commitment of significant new resources by manufacturers to meet the upcoming requirements of the standard.

Issued on June 30, 1977.

Brock Adams, Secretary of Transportation.

Aqua Slide 'N' Dive Corporation v. The Consumer Product Safety Commission

569 F. 2nd 831 (1978)

RONEY, Circuit Judge:

In this proceeding for review authorized by the Consumer Product Safety Act, Aqua Slide 'N' Dive Corporation, an interested manufacturer, challenges the legality of a "Safety Standard for Swimming Pool Slides" adopted by the Consumer Product Safety Commission.

I INTRODUCTION

Congress created the Consumer Product Safety Commission, an independent regulatory agency, in 1972. Among the purposes of the Commission are protection of the public "against unreasonable risks of injury associated with consumer products" and assistance to consumers "in evaluating the comparative safety" of such products.

This case involves the Commission's first exercise of its power under the Act to promulgate standards to ensure that manufactured products are safe for consumer use. . . .

The statute specifies the kinds of requirements a standard may impose, and provides that they must be "reasonably necessary to prevent or reduce an unreasonable risk of injury associated with [a consumer] product."

The Act took effect in late 1972. In mid-1973 both a trade association known as the National Swimming Pool Institute and the plaintiff in this action, Aqua Slide, petitioned the Commission . . . seeking promulgation of a safety standard for swimming pool slides. Aqua Slide's admitted motive was to prevent a product ban or forced repurchase threatened by the Bureau of Product Safety, a predecessor of the Commission, acting under either the Federal Hazardous Substance Act or the Child Protection and Toy Safety Act. . . . As the manufacturer of 95% of the 350,000 swimming pool slides presently in use in the United States, Aqua Slide had a substantial interest at stake in the proposed regulatory action.

The Commission granted the petition and sought offers to develop the requested standard. When no suitable offers were forthcoming, it published a second solicitation, and, in January 1975, accepted an offer made by NSPI. . . . The Institute submitted the result of their efforts to the Commission in May 1975. The NSPI proposal sought to prevent slide injuries by specifying that slides must impart a low angle of attack into the water, by requiring manufacturers to include warning signs on new slides, and by limiting installation of large slides to water more than four feet deep. Because of a perceived danger of drowning in deep water, the Institute recommended a ladder chain device to warn children to stay off large slides.

The Commission modified the Institute's proposal in several respects. It rewrote the warning signs, and included a specific mention of the danger of paralysis. The Commission decided it did not have jurisdiction to regulate slide installation, and so it substituted required instructions which recommended appropriate installation depths. The ladder chain provision, however, remained mandatory. . . .

Aqua Slide brought a timely petition for review to this Court. The Court denied Aqua Slide's motion to stay enforcement and the standard became effective on July 17, 1976.

II STANDARD OF REVIEW

The standard of review—substantial evidence on the record taken as a whole—is easily stated, but its application to the informal record allowed by this Act poses novel questions for which existing case law provides no clear answer. Congress put the substantial evidence test in the statute because it wanted the courts to scrutinize the Commission's actions more closely than an "arbitrary and capricious" standard would allow. The substantial evidence test is used to assess the weight of a factual finding. As a general rule, substantial evidence review is applied in connection with a formal hearing, at which an unbiased officer presides, rules of evidence apply, and parties may both subpoena and cross-examine witnesses. . . .

In this context, the duty of the Court to discern "substantial evidence on the record as a whole" requires a look at both substance and procedure. While the ultimate question is whether the record contains "such relevant evidence as a reasonable mind might accept as adequate to support a conclusion," the inability of any court to weigh diverse technical data also demands an inquiry to determine whether the Commission "carried out [its] essentially legislative task in a manner reasonable under the state of the record before [it]."

The task of review first requires a look to the statute and legislative intent to determine the criteria necessary to establish the required findings. Then the relevant portions of the record must be ascertained, primarily by reference to pages cited by the parties. Both the facts which detract from the agency position as well as those which support it are to be considered. . . . After taking procedure into account and weighing the evidence, the Court must determine whether the established facts reasonably satisfy the criteria necessary to support the ultimate statutory finding. If they do, then the Commission has sustained its burden of adducing "substantial evidence on the record as a whole" for its finding.

III "REASONABLE NECESSITY"

The Act requires a finding that the standard is "reasonably necessary to eliminate or reduce an unreasonable risk of injury." Aqua Slide argues that substantial evidence does not support the Commission's conclusion, that this standard is "reasonably necessary," in two particulars: (i) the warning signs have not been tested, may not work, and may be so explicit as to deter slide use unnecessarily, (ii) the ladder chain has not been shown effective.

The Act does not define the term "reasonably necessary," and apparently Congress intended the Commission and the courts to work out a definition on a case-by-case basis. The legislative history, and the holdings of other cases decided under similar statutes, do discuss the meaning of "unreasonable risk," and indicate that term is interrelated with the "reasonably necessary" requirement. The necessity for the standard depends upon the nature of the risk, and the reasonableness of the risk is a function of the burden a standard would impose on a user of the product.

In *Forester v. Consumer Product Safety Commission,* 559 F. 2d 774 (1977), the D.C. Circuit defined "unreasonable risk" in the Federal Hazardous Substances Act, as involving

> a balancing test like that familiar in tort law: The regulation may issue if the severity of the injury that may result from the product, factored by the likelihood of the injury, offsets the harm the regulation itself imposes upon manufacturers and consumers.

In this case, the legislative history specifies the costs to consumers that are to be considered: increases in price, decreased availability of a product, and also reductions in product usefulness. Implicit in this analysis is an understanding that the regulation is a feasible method of reducing the risk. . . . Also, an important predicate to Commission action is that consumers be unaware of either the severity, frequency, or ways of avoiding the risk. If consumers have accurate information, and still choose to incur the risk, then their judgment may well be reasonable. . . .

The Senate Report provides an example of the kind of analysis Congress had in mind. It said a sharp knife might pose a reasonable risk of injury, because dulling the blade to make it safe would also make it useless. A sharp knife in a child's silverware set, however, might be unreasonable. In the Forester case, the D.C. Circuit found the Commission failed to show the risk of protrusions on a bicycle frame was unreasonable because it had not considered the extent to which a regulation which banned the protrusions would impair the bicycle's utility. . . . The Commission does not have to conduct an elaborate cost-benefit analysis. It does, however, have to shoulder the burden of examining the relevant factors and producing substantial evidence to support its conclusion that they weigh in favor of the standard.

In this case, the severity of the risk is so terrible that virtually any standard which actually promised to reduce it would seem to be "reasonably necessary." Both the Commission and the Institute concentrated their fact-gathering efforts on an attempt to identify the precise nature of the risk. After surveying slide accidents, and considering the result of scientific studies of slide dynamics, the Commission identified a risk of "quadriplegia and paraplegia resulting from users (primarily adults using the swimming pool slide for the first time) sliding down the slide in a head first position and striking the bottom of the pool." The risk is greater than an inexperienced "belly-slider" would anticipate, because improper head first entry can cause an uncontrollable "snap rotation of the body" that "allows the arms to clear the bottom prior to head impact." Also, a curved slide can disorient persons who are using it for the first time. Without question, paraplegia is a horrible injury.

The risk of paraplegia from swimming pool slides, however, is extremely remote. More than 350,000 slides are in use, yet the Commission could find no more than 11 instances of paraplegia over a six-year period. According to Institute figures, the risk, for slide users, is about one in 10 million, less than the risk an average person has of being killed by lightning. The standard faces an initial difficulty because it is not easy to predict where paraplegia will next occur, and to burden all slide manufacturers, users, and owners with requirements that will only benefit a very few, is questionable. Remote risks have been found "unreasonable," but the context was one in which the safety standard promised to eliminate the danger entirely. . . . Aqua Slide argues that because of the low frequency, this Court should hold the risk to be "reasonable" and set aside the entire standard. . . . Given the severity of the injury, however, and the precedent of other cases, it seems likely that a standard which actually promised to reduce the risk without unduly hampering the availability of the slides or decreasing their utility could render this risk "unreasonable." The question then is whether the specific provisions of the standard which Aqua Slide challenges have been shown to accomplish that task.

A   Warning Signs

Given the infrequency of the risk, it was incumbent upon the Institute and the Commission to produce evidence that the standard actually promised to reduce the risk. Instead, both the Institute and the Commission gave the matter short shrift. To begin with, the standard only applies to new slides. It does not affect slides now in use, despite an Institute finding that "[t]here are many more slides in use than produced per year by a factor of ten to one." It is odd that the Commission chose this limited method of addressing the risk rather than deciding to use its power to conduct a public education campaign, which could reach far more slide users. A Red Cross representative told the Institute that its safety courses could inform 3,000,000 people a year of the risk of slide injury.

Furthermore, the record contains only the most ambiguous of indications that the warning signs would actually be heeded by slide users. The Commission did not test the signs. The only testing was done at the last minute by one Institute committee member, who conducted experiments for two days. The letter describing the tests, although it concluded that the signs "would seem capable of effecting significant risk reduction," also indicated that the test subjects "claimed they understood the belly slide message, but this seemed questionable," the message was "long," few readers "did more than glance" at it, and "[i]t should be cautioned that the signs will not be a strong countermeasure to unsafe acts, but of limited effectiveness."

The Commission rewrote the signs because of "a concern that the offeror's warning is not sufficiently strong to motivate safe use of the slides." Even after it had rewritten the signs to make them more explicit, it considered the possibility that users would ignore the signs to be so strong as to justify encouraging placement of slides in deep water, despite increased risk of drowning. In the preamble to the proposed standard, it could do no more than say the signs "may achieve" a reduction in dangerous belly slides. Certainly the evidence of actual injuries bespeaks the kind of foolhardiness for which proper instructions would provide no cure. One accident victim had been drinking, and a jury apparently concluded he had hit a chair floating in a pool. Another dove through a hoop. Still a third went down a slide improperly installed in only three feet of water. Another went down on his knees, a position about which the proposed warning sign is silent. While Congress intended for injuries resulting from foreseeable misuse of a product to be counted in assessing risk, that does not warrant adoption of a standard which has not been shown to prevent misuse.

To rebut this evidence, which raises serious questions about the efficacy of the warning signs, the Government cites only Institute discussions at which the Committee expressed their feelings that the signs would be a "positive step." . . . The issue here is not whether there is evidence to show that the Institute signs would be reasonable, but whether there is evidence to show the Commission's signs are reasonably necessary. While it is no doubt rational to assume the warning signs would be heeded, mere rationality is not enough. The statute requires substantial evidence to support the Commission's ultimate conclusion that the signs are a reasonably necessary means of reducing an unreasonable risk. . . .

In short, the Commission provided little evidence that the warning signs would benefit consumers. The risk is remote. The evidence that the signs would reduce the risk rests more on inference than it does on proof. In weighing the "reasonable necessity" for the signs, the crucial question then, is whether the benefit has a reasonable relationship to the disadvantages the sign requirement imposes.

In this case, the prime disadvantage to which Aqua Slide points is the warning's effect on the availability of the slides. Because the Commission did not test the signs, it provided little evidence of whether the signs were so explicit and shocking in their portrayal of the risk of paralysis as to constitute an unwarranted deterrent to the marketing of slides, and, hence, their availability to users. The record provides only scant assurance that purchasers would not be so alarmed by the warning signs that they would unnecessarily abstain. The signs do not indicate paralysis is a one in 10 million risk. The only evidence concerning the marketing impact the Commission's signs would have is a Commission staff report, based on the Battelle study. . . .

The Commission report indicated 20 percent of total sales would be lost over six years. Perhaps as much as half of the 42 percent drop in slide sales from 1973 to 1974 could be attributed just to uncertainty about what the standard would say. The Commission apparently thought that, because, absent the standard, the industry was expected to grow each year by 51 percent, the net effect would be merely to slow the industry's rate of growth and harm investment. That conclusion, if supported by reliable evidence, would be beyond the power of this Court to disturb. In this case, however, the evidence on which the Commission relies was only made public after the period for public comment on the standard had closed. Consequently, critics had no realistic chance to rebut it. . . . In fact, Aqua Slide alleges the report is unreliable and has petitioned this Court for remand so it would have an opportunity to make its views known. The Commission's economic report constitutes the only record evidence concerning the economic impact of the standard. As such it is the "basic data" upon which the Commission relied. . . . The statute requires that the Commission's findings be supported by substantial evidence, and that requirement is not met when the only evidence on a crucial finding is alleged to be unreliable and the Commission has not exposed it to the full public scrutiny which would encourage confidence in its accuracy. . . .

Certainly, on this record, the economic finding is crucial. The only way to tell whether the relationship between the advantages and disadvantages of the signs is reasonable is to know exactly what those disadvantages are. Yet the Commission's study of the standard's economic impact lacks the indicia of reliability. At the same time, the proof that signs will significantly reduce the risk is weak. We consequently hold that the Commission has failed to provide substantial evidence to demonstrate the reasonable necessity of the warning sign requirement and the mandatory intended use instructions which repeat the warning.

B Ladder Chain

The one aspect of the standard which does promise to reduce the risk of paraplegia is the placement of large slides in deep water. The Commission concluded it did not have jurisdiction over slide placement, so it included placement "recommendations" in the standard, and made them a part of the required intended use instructions. Deep water placement, however, presented the Commission with an increased risk of child drownings.

The Commission thought the risk of drownings was so great that it "must be considered" in the standard. The record supports that view. One commercial pool owner reported a number of near-drownings when his slide was located in five feet of water, which stopped when he relocated the slide in shallower depths.

A member of the National Safety Council staff wrote a letter to the Institute urging it to take the risks of drowning into account. Members of the committee reasoned that deep water slides, because of their playground analogies, would be an "attractive nuisance" to children. A standard that increased drownings would reduce slide utility, not enhance it, and would call into serious question the reasonable necessity for adopting the standard.

The Commission took two steps to reduce the risk of drowning associated with deep water slides. It redrew the warning sign to include a drowning figure and it required all such slides to have a ladder chain. That warning sign, however, was never tested for effectiveness. The only tests performed on the ladder chain were done by Institute consultant Robert Weiner, who tried one out on his neighbors' children at a pool in his own back yard. The scant five pages of Institute committee discussion, which provides the only support for the chain cited by the Government, does not provide persuasive evidence that the chain would prevent a child from climbing the ladder. One Institute committee member, who had observed chains in use, said the chains would "create some difficulty." The Commission concluded the chain's presence "should, on balance, create a safer product."

This is not the stuff of which substantial evidence is made. While expert opinion deserves to be heeded, it must be based on more than casual observation and speculation, particularly where a risk of fatal injury is being evaluated. If the chain were impossible to test, perhaps reliance on expert opinion alone would be sufficient. Here, however, the Commission conducted elaborate tests to show that deep water requirement would prevent paralysis, but it made no similar effort to prove the ladder chain would stop drownings. . . .

In this case the need is apparent but the assurance that the standard will work is not. The installation instructions create a risk of drowning. The Commission balanced that risk against a reduced likelihood of paraplegia if slides were placed in deep water. That balance, however, relied on the ability of the ladder chain and warning sign to mitigate the drowning risk. Because the Commission failed to produce substantial evidence to show the ladder chain and warning sign would work, its balance collapses and [the standard] must be set aside.

C Conclusion

In evaluating the "reasonable necessity" for a standard, the Commission has a duty to take a hard look, not only at the nature and severity of the risk, but also at the potential the standard would have on the utility, cost or availability of the product. In this case, the Commission neglected that duty. Aqua Slide has raised serious doubts about the warning sign and ladder chain requirements, their effectiveness, and their impact on the availability and utility of the slides. The Commission did not test its warning signs. It did not establish that users would heed them and "belly slide" in the proper manner. It deprived the public of any meaningful chance to challenge its investigation into the possibility that the signs were so explicit in their mention of "paralysis" that they might unnecessarily frighten away those who would be willing to buy them if they knew how remote the risk actually was. The Commission has not adequately demonstrated the ability of the ladder chain to avert the serious danger of drowning that placing slides in deeper water would create. The Commission has failed to produce substantial evidence to support the warning sign and ladder chain requirements, and because those requirements are integral parts of the standard's scheme for preventing paralytic injury, [the standard] must be set aside. . . .

Industrial Union Department, AFL-CIO v. American Petroleum Institute

440 U.S. 906 (1980)

MR. JUSTICE STEVENS announced the judgment of the Court. . . .

The Occupational Safety and Health Act of 1970 (the Act) was enacted for the purpose of ensuring safe and healthful working conditions for every working man and woman in the Nation. This case concerns a standard promulgated by the Secretary of Labor to regulate occupational exposure to benzene, a substance which has been shown to cause cancer at high exposure levels. The principal question is whether such a showing is a sufficient basis for a standard that places the most stringent limitation on exposure to benzene that is technologically and economically possible.

Wherever the toxic material to be regulated is a carcinogen, the Secretary has taken the position that no safe exposure level can be determined and that [the Act] requires him to set an exposure limit at the lowest technologically feasible level that will not impair the viability of the industries regulated. In this case, after having determined that there is a causal connection between benzene and leukemia (a cancer of the white blood cells), the Secretary set an exposure limit on airborne concentrations of benzene of one part benzene per million parts of air (1 ppm), regulated dermal and eye contact with solutions containing benzene, and imposed complex monitoring and medical testing requirements on employers whose workplaces contain 0.5 ppm or more of benzene.

On pre-enforcement review, the United States Court of Appeals for the Fifth Circuit held the regulation invalid. 581 F. 2d 493 (1978). The court concluded that OSHA had exceeded its standard-setting authority because it had not shown that the new benzene exposure limit was "reasonably necessary or appropriate to provide safe or healthful employment" . . . and because [the Act] does "not give OSHA the unbridled discretion to adopt standards designed to create absolutely risk-free workplaces regardless of costs." Reading the two provisions together, the Fifth Circuit held that the Secretary was under a duty to determine whether the benefits expected from the new standard bore a reasonable relationship to the costs that it imposed. The court noted that OSHA had made an estimate of the costs of compliance, but that the record lacked substantial evidence of any discernible benefits.

I

Benzene is a familiar and important commodity. It is a colorless, aromatic liquid that evaporates rapidly under ordinary atmospheric conditions. Approximately 11 billion pounds of benzene were produced in the United States in 1976. Ninety-four percent of that total was produced by the petroleum and petrochemical industries, with the remainder produced by the steel industry as a byproduct of coking operations. Benzene is used in manufacturing a variety of products including motor fuels (which may contain as much as 2% benzene), solvents, detergents, pesticides, and other organic chemicals.

The entire population of the United States is exposed to small quantities of benzene, ranging from a few parts per billion to 0.5 ppm, in the ambient air. Over one million workers are subject to additional low-level exposures as a consequence of their employment. The majority of these employees work in gasoline service stations, benzene production (petroleum refineries and coking operations), chemical processing, benzene transportation, rubber manufacturing and laboratory operations.

Benzene is a toxic substance. Although it could conceivably cause harm to a person who swallowed or touched it, the principal risk of harm comes from inhalation of benzene vapors. When these vapors are inhaled, the benzene diffuses through the lungs and is quickly absorbed into the blood. Exposure to high concentrations produces an almost immediate effect on the central nervous system. Inhalation of concentrations of 20,000 ppm can be fatal within minutes; exposures in the range of 250 to 500 ppm can cause vertigo, nausea, and other symptoms of mild poisoning. Persistent exposures at levels above 25-40 ppm may lead to blood deficiencies and diseases of the blood-forming organs, including aplastic anemia, which is generally fatal.

As early as 1928, some health experts theorized that there might also be a connection between benzene in the workplace and leukemia. In the late 1960's and early 1970's a number of epidemiological studies were published indicating that workers exposed to high concentrations of benzene were subject to a significantly increased risk of leukemia. . . .

* * *

Whenever initial monitoring indicates that employees are subject to airborne concentrations of benzene above 1 ppm averaged over an eight-hour workday, with a ceiling of 5 ppm for any 15-minute period, employers are required to modify their plants or institute work practice controls to reduce exposures within permissible limits. Consistent with OSHA's general policy, the regulation does not allow respirators to be used if engineering modifications are technologically feasible. Employers in this category are also required to perform monthly monitoring so long as their workplaces remain above 1 ppm, provide semiannual medical examinations to exposed workers, post signs in and restrict access to "regulated areas" where the permissible exposure limit is exceeded, and conduct employee training programs where necessary.

The permanent standard is expressly inapplicable to the storage, transportation, distribution, sale or use of gasoline or other fuels subsequent to discharge from bulk terminals. This exception is particularly significant in light of the fact that over 795,000 gas station employees, who are exposed to an average of 102,700 gallons of gasoline (containing up to 2% benzene) annually, are thus excluded from the protection of the standard.

As presently formulated, the benzene standard is an expensive way of providing some additional protection for a relatively small number of employees. According to OSHA's figures, the standard will require capital investments in engineering controls of approximately $266 million, first-year operating costs (for monitoring, medical testing, employee training and respirators) of $187 million to $205 million and recurring annual costs of approximately $34 million. The figures outlined in OSHA's explanation of the costs of compliance to various industries indicate that only 35,000 employees would gain any benefit from the regulation in terms of a reduction in their exposure to benzene. Over two-thirds of these workers (24,450) are employed in the rubber manufacturing industry. Compliance costs in that industry are estimated to be rather low, with no capital costs and initial operating expenses estimated at only $34 million ($1390 per employee); recurring annual costs would also be rather low, totalling less than $1 million. By contrast, the segment of the petroleum refining industry that produces benzene would be required to incur $24 million in capital costs and $600,000 in first-year operating expenses to provide additional protection for 300 workers ($82,000 per employee), while the petrochemical industry would be required to incur $20.9 million in capital costs and $1 million in initial operating expenses for the benefit of 552 employees ($39,675 per employee).

Although OSHA did not quantify the benefits to each category of worker in terms of decreased exposure to benzene, it appears from the economic impact study done at OSHA's direction that those benefits may be relatively small. Thus, although the current exposure limit is 10 ppm, the actual exposures outlined in that study are often considerably lower. For example, for the period 1970–1975 the petrochemical industry reported that, out of a total of 496 employees exposed to benzene, only 53 were exposed to levels between 1 and 5 ppm and only seven (all at the same plant) were exposed to between 5 and 10 ppm.

II

Any discussion of the 1 ppm exposure limit must, of course, begin with the Agency's rationale for imposing that limit. The written explanation of the standard fills 184 pages of the printed appendix. Much of it is devoted to a discussion of the voluminous evidence of the adverse effects of exposure to benzene at levels of concentration well above 10 ppm. This discussion demonstrates that there is ample justification for regulating occupational exposure to benzene and that the prior limit of 10 ppm, with a ceiling of 25 ppm (or a peak of 50 ppm) was reasonable. It does not, however, provide direct support for the Agency's conclusion that the limit should be reduced from 10 ppm to 1 ppm.

The evidence in the administrative record of adverse effects of benzene exposure at 10 ppm is sketchy at best. OSHA noted that there was "no dispute" that certain nonmalignant blood disorders, evidenced by a reduction in the level of red or white cells or platelets in the blood, could result from exposures of 25-40 ppm. It then stated that several studies had indicated that relatively slight changes in normal blood values could result from exposures below 25 ppm and perhaps below 10 ppm. OSHA did not attempt to make any estimate based on these studies of how significant the risk of nonmalignant disease would be at exposures of 10 ppm or less. Rather, it stated that because of the lack of data concerning the linkage between low-level exposures and blood abnormalities, it was impossible to construct a dose-response curve at this time. OSHA did conclude, however, that the studies demonstrated that the current 10 ppm exposure limit was inadequate to ensure that no single worker would suffer a nonmalignant blood disorder as a result of benzene exposure. . . .

With respect to leukemia, evidence of an increased risk (i.e., a risk greater than that borne by the general population) due to benzene exposures at or below 10 ppm was even sketchier. . . .

In the end OSHA's rationale for lowering the permissible exposure limit to 1 ppm was based, not on any finding that leukemia has ever been caused by exposure to 10 ppm of benzene and that it will *not* be caused by exposure to 1 ppm, but rather on a series of assumptions indicating that some leukemias might result from exposure to 10 ppm and that the number of cases might be reduced by reducing the exposure level to 1 ppm. In reaching that result, the Agency first unequivocally concluded that benzene is a human carcinogen. Second, it concluded that industry had failed to prove that there is a safe threshold level of exposure to benzene below which no excess leukemia cases would occur. In reaching this conclusion OSHA rejected industry contentions that certain epidemiological studies indicating no excess risk of leukemia among workers exposed at levels below 10 ppm were sufficient to establish that the threshold level of safe exposure was at or above 10 ppm. It also rejected an industry witness' testimony that a dose-response curve could be constructed on the basis of the reported epidemiological studies and that this curve indicated that reducing the permissible exposure limit from 10 to 1 ppm would prevent at most one leukemia and one other cancer death every six years.

Third, the Agency applied its standard policy with respect to carcinogens, concluding that, in the absence of definitive proof of a safe level, it must be assumed that any level above zero presents some increased risk of cancer. As the Government points out in its brief, there are a number of scientists and public health specialists who subscribe to this view, theorizing that a susceptible person may contract cancer from the absorption of even one molecule of a carcinogen like benzene.

Fourth, the Agency reiterated its view of the Act, stating that it was required . . . to set the standard either at the level that has been demonstrated to be safe or at the lowest level feasible, whichever is higher. If no safe level is established, as in this case, the Secretary's interpretation of the statute automatically leads to the selection of an exposure limit that is the lowest feasible. Because of benzene's importance to the economy, no one has ever suggested that it would be feasible to eliminate its use entirely, or to try to limit exposures to the small amounts that are omnipresent. Rather, the Agency selected 1 ppm as a workable exposure level and then determined that compliance with that level was technologically feasible and that "the economic impact of . . . [compliance] will not be such as to threaten the financial welfare of the affected firms or the general economy." It therefore held that 1 ppm was the minimum feasible exposure level. . . .

Finally, although the Agency did not refer in its discussion of the pertinent legal authority to any duty to identify the anticipated benefits of the new standard, it did conclude that some benefits were likely to result from reducing the exposure limit from 10 ppm to 1 ppm. This conclusion was based, again, not on evidence, but rather on the assumption that the risk of leukemia will decrease as exposure levels decrease. Although the Agency had found it impossible to construct a dose-response curve that would predict with any accuracy the number of leukemias that could be expected to result from exposures at 10 ppm, at 1 ppm, or at any intermediate level it nevertheless "determined that the benefits of the proposed standard are likely to be appreciable. . . ."

III

Our resolution of the issues in this case turns, to a large extent, on the meaning of and the relationship between . . . [what] is "reasonably necessary and appropriate to provide safe or healthful employment," and "the standard which most adequately assures, to the extent feasible, on the basis of the best available evidence, that no employee will suffer material impairment of health or functional capacity. . . ."

In the Government's view . . . the term "standard" has no legal significance or at best merely requires that a standard not be totally irrational. It takes the position . . . that [the Act] requires OSHA to promulgate a standard that either gives an absolute assurance of safety for each and every worker or that reduces exposures to the lowest level feasible. . . . The respondent industry representatives, on the other hand, argue that the Court of Appeals was correct in holding that the "reasonably necessary and appropriate" language . . . along with the feasibility requirement . . . requires the Agency to quantify both the costs and the benefits of a proposed rule and to conclude that they are roughly commensurate.

In our view, it is not necessary to decide whether either the Government or industry is entirely correct. For we think it is clear that . . . the Act . . . requires the Secretary, before issuing any standard, to determine that it is reasonably necessary and appropriate to remedy a significant risk of material health impairment. Only after the Secretary has made the threshold determination that such a risk exists with respect to a toxic substance, would it be necessary to decide whether [it] requires him to select the most protective standard he can consistent with economic and technological feasibility, or whether, as respondents argue, the benefits of the regulation must be commensurate with the costs of its implementation. Because the Secretary did not make the required threshold finding in this case, we have no occasion to determine whether costs must be weighed against benefits in an appropriate case.

* * *

Given the conclusion that the Act empowers the Secretary to promulgate health and safety standards only where a significant risk of harm exists, the critical issue becomes how to define and allocate the burden of proving the significance of the risk in a case such as this, where scientific knowledge is imperfect and the precise quantification of risks is therefore impossible. The Agency's position is that there is substantial evidence in the record to support its conclusion that there is no absolutely safe level for a carcinogen and that, therefore, the burden is properly on industry to prove, apparently beyond a shadow of a doubt, that there is a safe level for benzene exposure. The Agency argues that, because of the uncertainties in this area, any other approach would render it helpless, forcing it to wait for the leukemia deaths that it believes are likely to occur before taking any regulatory action.

We disagree. As we read the statute, the burden was on the Agency to show, on the basis of substantial evidence, that it is at least more likely than not that long-term exposure to 10 ppm of benzene presents a significant risk of material health impairment. Ordinarily, it is the proponent of a rule or order who has the burden of proof in administrative proceedings. . . .

In this case OSHA did not even attempt to carry its burden of proof. The closest it came to making a finding that benzene presented a significant risk of harm in the workplace was its statement that the benefits to be derived from lowering the permissible exposure level from 10 to 1 ppm were "likely" to be "appreciable." The Court of Appeals held that this finding was not supported by substantial evidence. Of greater importance, even if it were supported by substantial evidence, such a finding would not be sufficient to satisfy the Agency's obligations under the Act.

Contrary to the Government's contentions, imposing a burden on the Agency of demonstrating a significant risk of harm will not strip it of its ability to regulate carcinogens, nor will it require the Agency to wait for deaths to occur before taking any action. First, the requirement that a "significant" risk be identified is not a mathematical straitjacket. It is the Agency's responsibility to determine, in the first instance, what it considers to be a "significant" risk. Some risks are plainly acceptable and others are plainly unacceptable. If, for example, the odds are one in a billion that a person will die from cancer by taking a drink of chlorinated water, the risk clearly could not be considered significant. On the other hand, if the odds are one in a thousand that regular inhalation of gasoline vapors that are two percent benzene will be fatal, a reasonable person might well consider the risk significant and take appropriate steps to decrease or eliminate it. Although the Agency has no duty to calculate the exact probability of harm, it does have an obligation to find that a significant risk is present before it can characterize a place of employment as "unsafe."

Second, OSHA is not required to support its finding that a significant risk exists with anything approaching scientific certainty. Although the Agency's findings must be supported by substantial evidence, . . . the Secretary . . . [can] regulate on the basis of the "best available evidence." As several courts of appeals have held, this provision requires a reviewing court to give OSHA some leeway where its findings must be made on the frontiers of scientific knowledge. Thus, so long as they are supported by a body of reputable scientific thought, the Agency is free to use conservative assumptions in interpreting the data with respect to carcinogens, risking error on the side of over-protection rather than under-protection.

Finally, the record in this case and OSHA's own rulings on other carcinogens indicate that there are a number of ways in which the Agency can make a rational judgment about the relative significance of the risks associated with exposure to a particular carcinogen.

It should also be noted that, in setting a permissible exposure level in reliance on less-than-perfect methods, OSHA would have the benefit of a backstop in the form of monitoring and medical testing. Thus, if OSHA properly determined that the permissible exposure limit should be set at 5 ppm, it could still require monitoring and medical testing for employees exposed to lower levels. By doing so, it could keep a constant check on the validity of the assumptions made in developing the permissible exposure limit, giving it a sound evidentiary basis for decreasing the limit if it was initially set too high. . . .

* * *

In this case the record makes it perfectly clear that the Secretary relied squarely on a special policy for carcinogens that imposed the burden on industry of proving the existence of a safe level of exposure, thereby avoiding the Secretary's threshold responsibility of establishing the need for more stringent standards. In so interpreting his statutory authority, the Secretary exceeded his power.

[In a case involving the textile industry, the Supreme Court subsequently ruled that OSHA is not required by the Occupational Safety and Health Act to conduct benefit-cost analysis before promulgating a standard, *American Textile Manufacturers Institute v. Donovan,* U.S. Supreme Court Slip Opinion, No. 79–1429 (1981).]

LIST OF CASES

LIST OF CASES